TR6

REPAIR OPERATION MANUAL

PUBLICATION PART NUMBER 545277/E2

Issued by the

SERVICE DIVISION

**** TRIUMPH MOTORS BRITISH LEYLAND UK LIMITED ****

ISBN 1 869826 132

A MEMBER OF THE BRITISH LEYLAND MOTOR CORPORATION

Purchasers are advised that the specification details set out in this Manual apply to a range of vehicles and not to any one. For the specification of a particular vehicle, purchasers should consult their Distributor or Dealer.

The Manufacturers reserve the right to vary their specifications with or without notice, and at such times and in such manner as they think fit. Major as well as minor changes may be involved in accordance with the manufacturer's policy of constant product improvement.

Whilst every effort is made to ensure the accuracy of the particulars contained in this Manual, neither the Manufacturer nor the Distributor or Dealer, by whom this Manual is supplied, shall in any circumstances be held liable for any inaccuracy or the consequences thereof.

CONTENTS

INTRODUCTION

The purpose of this manual is to assist skilled mechanics in the efficient repair and maintenance of British Leyland vehicles. Using the appropriate service tools and carrying out the procedures as detailed will enable the operations to be completed in the time stated in the 'Repair Operation Times'.

Indexing

For convenience, the manual is divided into a number of divisions. Page 01–3 lists the titles and reference number of the various divisions.

A list of the operations within each division appears in alphabetical order on the page preceding each division.

Operation Numbering

A master index of numbered operations has been compiled for universal application to all vehicles manufactured by the British Leyland Motor Corporation and, therefore, because of the different specifications of various models, continuity of the numbering sequence cannot be maintained throughout this manual.

Each operation described in the manual is allocated a number from the master index and cross-refers with an identical number in the 'Repair Operation Times'. The number consists of six digits arranged in three pairs.

Each instruction within an operation has a sequence number and, to complete the operation in the minimum time, it is essential that the instructions are performed in numerical sequence commencing at 1 unless otherwise stated. Where applicable, the sequence numbers identify the relevant components in the appropriate illustration.

Emission Control Equipment

With the exception of Section 17, all remaining sections of this manual relate to basic vehicles not fitted with *anti-pollution* equipment. Where an operation is affected by the presence of this equipment, refer also to Anti-pollution (Section 17).

Service Tools

Where performance of an operation requires the use of a service tool, the tool number is quoted under the operation heading and is repeated in, or following, the instruction involving its use. An illustrated list of all necessary tools is included in section 99.

References

References to the left- or right-hand side in the manual are made when viewing from the rear. With the engine and gearbox assembly removed, the 'timing cover' end of the engine is referred to as the front. A key to abbreviations and symbols is given on page 01–5.

Amendments

Revised and additional procedures resulting from changes in the vehicle specifications will be issued as revised or additional pages.

The circulation of amendments will be confined to Distributors and Dealers of British Leyland Motor Corporation Limited.

REPAIRS AND REPLACEMENTS

When service parts are required it is essential that only genuine British Leyland Stanpart or Unipart replacements are used.

Attention is particularly drawn to the following points concerning repairs and the fitting of replacement parts and accessories.

Safety features embodied in the car may be impaired if other than genuine parts are fitted. In certain territories, legislation prohibits the fitting of parts not to the vehicle manufacturer's specification. Torque wrench setting figures given in the Repair Operation Manual must be strictly adhered to. Locking devices, where specified, must be fitted. If the efficiency of a locking device is impaired during removal it must be renewed. Owners purchasing accessories while travelling abroad should ensure that the accessory and its fitted location on the car conform to mandatory requirements in their country of origin.

The car warranty may be invalidated by the fitting of other than genuine British Leyland parts. All British Leyland Stanpart or Unipart replacements have the full backing of the factory warranty.

British Leyland Distributors and Dealers are obliged to supply only genuine service parts.

ABBREVIATIONS AND SYMBOLS

Across flats (bolt size)	A.F.
After bottom dead centre	A.B.D.C.
After top dead centre	A.T.D.C.
Alternating current	a.c.
Amperes	amp
Ampere-hour	Ah
**Atmospheres	Atm**
Before bottom dead centre	B.B.D.C.
Before top dead centre	B.T.D.C.
Bottom dead centre	B.D.C.
Brake horse-power	b.h.p.
Brake mean effective pressure	b.m.e.p.
British Standards	B.S.
Carbon monoxide	CO
Centigrade (Celsius)	C
Centimetres	cm
Cubic centimetres	cm^3
Cubic inches	in^3
Cycles per minute	c/min
Degree (angle)	deg. or °
Degree (temperature)	deg. or °
Diameter	dia.
Direct current	d.c.
Fahrenheit	F
Feet	ft
Feet per minute	ft/min
Fifth	5th
Figure (illustration)	Fig.
First	1st
Fourth	4th
Gallons (Imperial)	gal
Gallons (U.S.)	U.S. gal
**Grammes (force)	gf
Grammes (mass)	g**
High compression	h.c.
High tension (electrical)	h.t.
Horse-power	hp
Hundredweight	cwt
Inches	in
Inches of mercury	inHg
Independent front suspension	i.f.s.
Internal diameter	i.dia.
Kilogrammes (force)	kgf
Kilogrammes (mass)	kg
Kilogramme centimetre	kgf cm
Kilogramme metres	kgf m
Kilogrammes per square centimetre	kg/cm^2
Kilometres	km
Kilometres per hour	km/h
Kilovolts	kV
King pin inclination	k.p.i.
Left-hand	L.H.
Left-hand steering	L.H.Stg.
Left-hand thread	L.H.Thd.
Low compression	l.c.
Low tension	l.t.
Maximum	max.
Metres	m
Microfarad	mfd
Midget Edison Screw	MES
Miles per gallon	m.p.g.
Miles per hour	m.p.h.
Millimetres	mm
Millimetres of mercury	mmHg
Minimum	min.
Minus (of tolerance)	
Minute (of angle)	
Negative (electrical)	–
**Newton metres	Nm**
Number	No.
Ohms	ohm
Ounces (force)	ozf
Ounces (mass)	oz
Ounce inch (torque)	ozf in
Outside diameter	o.dia.
Overdrive	O/D
Paragraphs	para.
Part Number	Part No.
Percentage	%
Petrol Injection	P.I.
Pints (Imperial)	pt
Pints (U.S.)	U.S. pt
Plus or minus	±
Plus (tolerance)	+
Positive (electrical)	+
Pounds (force)	lbf
Pounds (mass)	lb
Pounds feet (torque)	lbf ft
Pounds inches (torque)	lbf in
Pounds per square inch	lb/in^2
Radius	r
Ratio	:
Reference	ref.
Revolutions per minute	rev/min
Right-hand	R.H.
Right-hand steering	R.H.Stg.
Second (angle)	''
Second (numerical order)	2nd
Single carburetter	SC
Society of Automobile Engineers	S.A.E.
Specific gravity	sp. gr.
Square centimetres	cm^2
Square inches	in^2
Standard	std
Standard wire gauge	s.w.g.
Synchronizer/synchromesh	synchro.
Third	3rd
Top dead centre	T.D.C.
Twin carburetters	TC
United Kingdom	UK
Volts	V
Watts	W

Screw threads

American Standard Taper Pipe	N.P.T.F.
British Association	B.A.
British Standard Fine	B.S.F.
British Standard Pipe	B.S.P.
British Standard Whitworth	B.S.W.
Unified Coarse	U.N.C.
Unified Fine	U.N.F.

LOCATION OF COMMISSION AND UNIT NUMBERS

THE COMMISSION NUMBER is the identification number which is required for registration and other purposes. It is stamped on a plate attached to the left hand front wheel arch (not U.S.A.) and is visible when the bonnet is raised. On vehicles for the U.S.A. type markets this plate is attached to the body adjacent to the left hand door striker plate and the Commission Number is also stamped on a small plate visible through the left hand side of the windscreen.

The significance of the Commission Numbers and suffix is as follows:

CP/CR this prefix denotes 'TR6' model range *AND* that a Petrol Injection engine unit is fitted.
CC/CF is an alternative prefix denoting model range *AND* that a Carburetter engine unit is fitted.
1234 – is the accumulated total build of this model.
L – denotes left hand steering
(No letter is given to right hand steering models).
U – denotes U.S.A. type markets 1972 condition.

The Commission Number plate also bears code symbols for identification of the vehicle's exterior colour, trim material and trim colour. Refer to page 04-6.

THE ENGINE NUMBER is stamped on a machined flange on the left hand side of the cylinder block. The significance of the Engine Numbers and suffix is as follows:

CP/CR this prefix denotes model range *AND* that the engine unit is fitted with Petrol Injection.
CC/CF is an alternative prefix denoting model range *AND* that the engine unit is fitted with Carburetters.
1234 – is the accumulated total build of the type.
H – denotes High Compression. Alternatively.
L – denotes Low Compression. Alternatively.
U – denotes U.S.A. type markets 1972 condition.
E – denotes engine unit.

THE GEARBOX NUMBER is stamped on the left hand side of the gearbox casing. The significance of the Gearbox Numbers is as follows:

CD – this prefix denotes model range.
1234 – is the accumulated build of this type.
There are no suffix letters.

THE REAR AXLE NUMBER is stamped on the bottom flange of the axle housing. The significance of the Axle Numbers is as follows:

CP/CR this prefix denotes model range *AND* that the axle unit is for use with Petrol Injection engines.
CD – is an alternative prefix denoting model range *AND* that the axle unit is for use with Carburetter engines.
1234 – is the accumulated build of the type.
There are no suffix numbers.

IMPORTANT: In all communications relating to Service and Spares it is essential to quote Commission Number, paint and trim codes and unit numbers (if applicable).

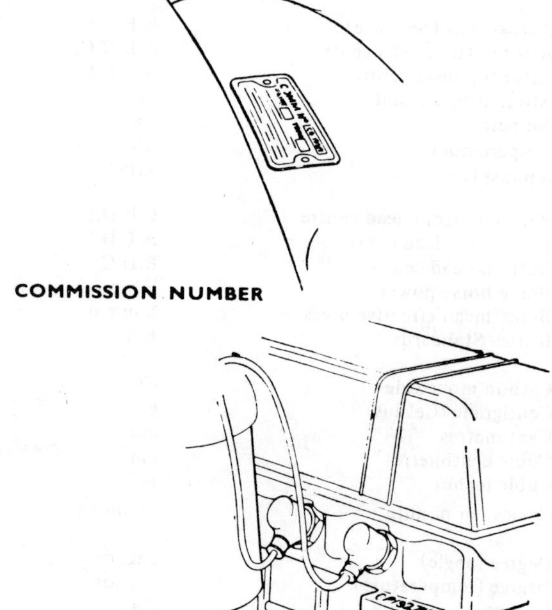

COMMISSION NUMBER

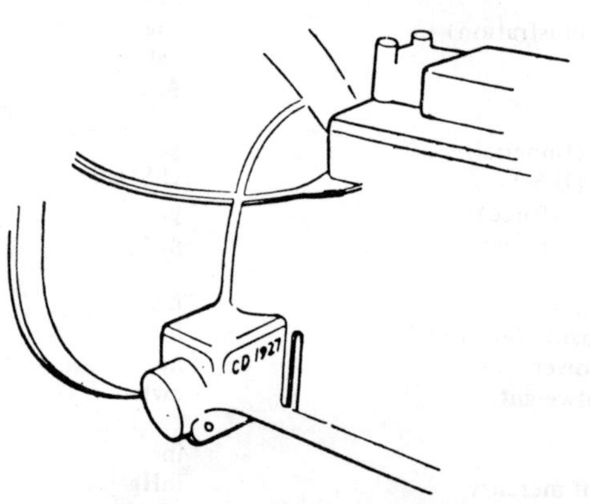

ENGINE NUMBER

GEARBOX SERIAL NUMBER

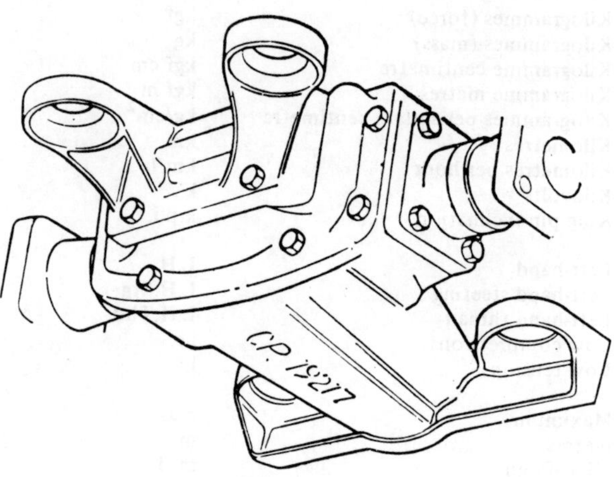

REAR AXLE NUMBER

AMENDMENTS

To assist in identifying amendments on revised pages two stars (**) will be inserted at the beginning and end of the amended paragraph, section, instruction or illustration.

To ensure that a record of amendments to this manual is available, this page will be re-issued with each set of revised pages. The amendment number, date of issue, appropriate instructions and revised page numbers will be quoted.

Revised pages must be inserted in place of existing pages carrying the same number, and the old pages discarded.

Additional pages or complete major assembly groups may be issued. In such cases the new pages must be inserted immediately following the existing pages carrying the next lowest number

Date	Filing Instructions			
	Discard	Issue	Insert	Issue
3/73	01.2	1	01.2	2
	01.3	1	01.3	2
	01.5	1	01.5	2
	01.7	1	01.7	2
	04.1	1	04.1	2
	04.3	1	04.3	2
	04.6	1	04.6	2
	05.1	1	05.1	2
	06.2	1	06.2	2
	09.1	1	09.1	2
	12.17.13 Sheet 3	1	12.17.13 Sheet 3	2
	12.17.13 Sheet 4	1	12.17.13 Sheet 4	2
	12.21.26	1	12.21.26	2
	12.29.18 Sheet 4	1	12.29.18 Sheet 4	2
	19.1 PI	1	19.1 PI	2
	19.20.05 PI Sheet 1	1	19.20.05 PI Sheet 1	2
	–	–	19.20.05 PI Sheet 5	1
	19.20.07 PI	1	19.20.07 PI Sheet 1	2
	–	–	19.20.07 PI Sheet 2	1
	19.20.26 PI	1	19.20.27 PI	1
	19.35.01 PI	1	19.35.01 PI Sheet 1	2
	–	–	19.35.01 PI Sheet 2	1
	19.40.00 PI	1	19.40.00 PI	2
	19.1 C	1	19.1 C	2
	26.30.31	1	26.30.31	2
	30.1	1	30.1	2
	30.10.01	1	30.10.01	2
	30.15.01	1	30.15.01	2
	30.15.02 Sheet 2	1	30.15.02 Sheet 2	2
	–	–	30.15.15	2
	37.12.19 Sheet 3	1	37.12.19 Sheet 3	2
	37.16.01	1	37.16.01	2
	37.20.04 Sheet 6	1	37.20.04 Sheet 6	2
	40.10.01 A	1	40.10.01 A	2
	40.16.10 A	1	40.16.10 A	2
	–	–	Section 40J	1
	51,25.19 Sheet 6	1	51.25.19 Sheet 6	2
	57.60.01	1	57.60.01	2
	76.3	1	76.3	2

Date	Filing Instructions			
	Discard	Issue	Insert	Issue
	76.10.05	1	76.10.05	2
	99.1	1	99.1	2
	99.00.06	1	99.00.06	2
9/73	01.7	2	01.7	3
	04.1	2	04.1	3
	04.3	2	04.3	3
	04.5	1	04.5	2
	06.1	2	06.1	3
	06.2	2	06.2	3
	06.4	1	06.4	2
	09.1	2	09.1	3
	12.41.05 Sheet 1	1	12.41.05 Sheet 1	2
	12.45.05 Sheet 7	1	12.41.05 Sheet 7	1
	12.60.44	1	12.60.44	2
	17.1	1	17.1	2
	17.20.31	1	17.20.31	2
	–	–	17.45.01	1
	19.20.02C	1	19.20.02C	2
	30.15.02 Sheet 2	2	30.15.02 Sheet 2	3
	33.25.12	1	33.25.12	2
	–	–	40.00.06 J	1
	–	–	40.00.08 J	1
	–	–	40.00.10 J	1
	–	–	40.00.12 J	1
	51.25.19 Sheet 2	1	51.25.19 Sheet 2	2
	76.1	1	76.1	2
	76.10.02 Sheet 2	1	76.10.02 Sheet 2	2
	76.22.15	1	76.22.15	2
** 3/74	01-5	2	01-5	3
	01-7	3	01-7	4
	04-1	3	04-1	4
	05-1	2	05-1	3
	06-4	2	06-4	3
	09-1	3	09-1	4
	12.29.18 Sheet 3	1	12.29.18 Sheet 3	2
	12.29.18 Sheet 4	2	12.29.18 Sheet 4	3
	12.53.03	1	12.53.03	2
	37.12.01	1	37.12.01	2
	37.12.04	1	37.12.04	2**

Date	Filing Instructions				Date	Filing Instructions			
	Discard	Issue	Insert	Issue		Discard	Issue	Insert	Issue
** 3/74	37.20.01 Sheet 1 37.20.01 Sheet 2 64.15.14 Sheet 1 74.10.00 Sheet 1 76.10.05 76.22.08 86.35.15 Sheet 2	1 1 1 1 2 1 1	37.20.01 Sheet 1 37.20.01 Sheet 1 64.15.14 Sheet 74.10.00 Sheet 1 76.10.05 76.22.08 86.35.15 Sheet 2	2 2 2 2 3 2 2 **					

ENGINE

Number of cylinders	6 in line	
Bore of cylinders	2·94 in (74·7 mm)	
Stroke of crankshaft	3.74 in (95 mm)	
Capacity	152 in² (2498 cm²)	
	PETROL INJECTION	**CARBURETTER/U.S.A. MARKET**
Compression ratio	9·5:1	**7·5:1 – 1974 Models 7·75:1 – 1972/73 Models** 8·50:1 – Pre 1972 Models

LUBRICATION

Oil pump	High capacity eccentric lobe type
Oil filter	Full flow type, replaceable element
Oil warning light	Extinguishes at 3 to 5 lbf/in² (0·21 to 0·35 kgf/cm²) oil pressure

COOLING SYSTEM

Type	Water, "No Loss" system
Circulation	By impellor type pump. Vee belt drive
Pressure	13 lbf/in² (0·91 kgf/cm²)
Thermostat	Opens at 82°C (180°F) normal climate 88°C (190°F) cold climate

FAN

1974/1973 models (all)	13 blades 14½ in (368 mm) dia.
1972 models P.I.	7 blade 12½ in (318 mm) dia.
Carb.	13 blade 14½ in (368 mm) dia.
1971 models (all)	7 blade 12½ in (318 mm) dia.
Pre 1971 models (all)	8 blade 12½ in (318 mm) dia.

FUEL SYSTEM

Tank	Tank at rear	Tank at rear 1971 only – with separate overflow tank
Pump	Electric lift pump in luggage compartment	Mechanically operated diaphragm type on engine
Metering Distributor	Lucas	
Carburetter 1974/1973 Model		2 Stromberg 175 CDSEV sidedraught (Exhaust Emissions Controlled)
1972 Model		2 Stromberg 175 CDSE sidedraught (Exhaust Emissions Controlled)
1971 Model		2 Stromberg 175 CD-2-SE sidedraught (Exhaust Emissions Controlled)
Pre 1971 Model		2 Stromberg 175 CDSE sidedraught (Exhaust Emissions Controlled)
Air cleaner	Combined air cleaner and silencer with replaceable element	
Crankcase ventilation 1974/73/72/71 Models	Closed circuit breathing from rocker cover to air collector manifold	Valveless closed circuit breathing from rocker cover to constant depression side of carburetters.
Pre 1971 Models		Closed circuit breathing through one-way valve to inlet manifold
Evaporative emission control. From 1971 Models		Sealed tank filler cap. Vapour emissions from the tank are vented, – 1974/73/72 Models: via a seperator canister – 1971 Model: via the overflow tank to a charcoal canister located in the engine compartment. Canister is purged by carburetter depression.
Pre 1971 Models		Not applicable

GENERAL SPECIFICATION DATA

CLUTCH

Make/type	Laycock
Release mechanism	Hydraulically operated
Plate diameter	8½ in. (216 mm)

GEARBOX

Manual

Synchromesh . . . . . . On forward gears

		O/D Top 'J'	O/D Top 'A'	Top	O/D 3rd 'J'	O/D 3rd 'A'	3rd	O/D 2nd 'A' only	2nd	1st	Rev.
Gear Ratios		—	—	1·00	—	—	1·39	—	2·10	2·99	3·37
Overall ratios	Petrol Injection	2·75	2·83	3·45	3·83	3·76	4·78	5·69	7·25	10·33	11·62
	Carb/U.S.A. Market	2·95	3·03	3·70	4·11	4·03	5·13	6·10	7·77	11·08	12·47

Overdrive (where fitted)

	From Comm. No. CR567/CF1U	Up to Comm. No. CR567/CF1U
Make/type	Laycock Type J	Laycock Type A
Operative on	Top and 3rd gears	Top, 3rd and 2nd gears
Overall ratios	0·797:1	0·82:1

FINAL DRIVE

Type	Hypoid bevel gears in rear axle
Ratio Petrol Injection	3·45:1
Carb/U.S.A. Market	3·70:1

EFFECTIVE GEARING

Engine speeds (rev/min) at road speeds of:

		O/D Top 'J'	O/D Top 'A'	Top	O/D 3rd 'J'	O/D 3rd 'A'	3rd	O/D 2nd 'A' only	2nd	1st	Rev.
10 m.p.h.	Petrol Injection	376	386	471	523	514	654	777	990	1412	1516
	Carb/U.S.A. Market	383	395	482	532	526	667	795	1009	1438	1552
10 km/h	Petrol Injection	235	240	292	325	319	406	482	621	878	952
	Carb/U.S.A. Market	240	245	300	331	327	414	494	627	893	975

ROAD SPEED DATA

Road speed at 1,000 rev/min engine speed:

		'J' type	'A' type
O/D Top	Petrol Injection	26·6 m.p.h. (42·8 km/h)	26.9 m.p.h. (43·3 km/h)
	Carb/U.S.A. Market	26·1 m.p.h. (42 km/h)	25·1 m.p.h. (40·4 km/h)
Top Gear	Petrol Injection	21·2 m.p.h. (34·2 km/h)	
	Carb/U.S.A. Market	20·7 m.p.h. (33·4 km/h)	

Road speed at 2,500 ft/min piston speed

Top gear	Petrol Injection	85 m.p.h. (137 km/h)
	Carb/U.S.A. Market	83 m.p.h. (134 km/h)

STEERING

Make/type		Alford and Alder, Rack and pinion
Turning Circle	1974/73/72/71 Models	34 feet (10·4 metres)
	Pre 1971 Models	33 feet (10·1 metres)
Steering wheel diameter	1974/1973 Models**	14½ in. (368 mm)
	Pre 1973 Models	15 in. (381 mm)

Turns lock to lock 3¼

BRAKE SYSTEM

Operation:

Foot pedal	Hydraulic on all four wheels Tandem master cylinder operates on front and rear brakes independently
Handbrake	Mechanical on rear wheels only.

Front

Type	Caliper disc
Dimensions	Disc diameter 10·875 in. (276 mm)
Lining area	20·7 in² (133·6 cm²)
Swept area	233·0 in² (1500 cm²)

Rear

Type	Drum with leading and trailing shoes
Dimensions	9 in x 1¾ in (228 x 44·5 mm)
Lining area	60·5 in² (390 cm²)
Swept area	99·0 in² (639 cm²)
Servo	Direct acting servo providing 2·2:1 nominal boost ratio

WHEELS AND TYRES

Wheels . . . . **Steel disc type 5½J rims. Wire wheels optional (earlier models) with 5½K rims **

		PETROL INJECTION	CARBURETTER/U.S.A. MARKET
Tyres		165HR – 15SP or XAS	185SR – 15X (red band) or G.800
Tyre pressures: front	All conditions	22lb/in² (1·547kg/cm²)	20 lbs/in² (1·406 kg/cm²)
	High speed	28lb/in² (1·969kg/cm²)	
rear	All conditions	26lb/in² (1·828kg/cm²)	24lb/in² (1·687kg/cm²)
	High speed	32lb/in² (2·250kg/cm²)	

CHASSIS DATA

Wheelbase	7 ft 4 in (2240 mm)	
Track: front	4 ft 2¼ in (1276 mm)	
rear	4 ft 1¾ in (1264 mm)	
Wheel alignment: (2 up condition) front	0 to 1/16 in toe in (0 to 1·5875 mm)	
rear	0 to 1/16 in toe in (0 to 1·5875 mm)	
Ground clearance: (2 up condition)	6 in (152 mm)	
Camber: (2 up condition) front	0° ± ½°	¼° negative ± ½°
rear	1° negative ± ½°	1° negative ± ½°
Caster: (2 up condition)	2¾° ± ½°	2¾° ± ½°
King pin inclination (2 up condition)	9° ± ¾°	9¼° ± ¾°

ELECTRICAL EQUIPMENT (see electrical section for full details)

Electrical system	12 volt negative earth	
Battery capacity	57 amp hour at 20 hour rate	
Alternator: type	Lucas 15 ACR	USA Market 1974/73 18 ACR 1972 17 ACR
output	28 amps	USA Market 1974/73 43 amps 1972 36 amps
Starter motor	Lucas M 100 pre engaged type	

OVERALL DIMENSIONS

Length	12 ft 11 in (3937 mm)	**1973 USA 13ft 6⅛ in. (4118 mm)**
Width	4 ft 10 in (1470 mm)	
Height (unladen) to top of windscreen	3 ft 10 in (1170 mm)	
Soft top, hood errect	4 ft 2 in (1270 mm)	

WEIGHTS (approx)

Dry (excluding extra equipment)	** Petrol Injection	1971/72/73/74 model 20½ cwt (1035 kg)– pre 1971 model 20¾ cwt (1053 kg)
	Carb/U.S.A. market	1971/72/73/74 model 20½ cwt (1035 kg)– 1970 model 21 cwt (1067 kg) pre 1970 model 19¼ cwt (983 kg)
Basic kerb (including water, oil, fuel & tools)	Petrol Injection	21½ cwt (1085 kg)
	Carb/U.S.A. Market	1971/72/73/74 model 21½ cwt (1085 kg) 1970 model 22 cwt (1118 kg) – pre 1970 model 20¼ cwt (1034 kg)
Kerb (including optional extras, water, oil etc)	Petrol Injection	22½ cwt (1145 kg)
	Carb/U.S.A. Market	1971/72/73/74 model 22½ cwt (1145 kg) –1970 model 23 cwt (1168 kg) – pre 1970 model 21¼ cwt (1079 kg)
Maximum gross vehicle weight	Petrol Injection	1970/71/72/73/74 model 26¾ cwt (1360kg) – pre 1970 model 25¾ cwt (1308 kg)
	Carb/U.S.A. Market	1971/72/73/74 model 26½ cwt (1345 kg – 1970 model 25½ cwt (1295 kg) – pre 1970 model 24·6 cwt (1257 kg) **

TOWING INFORMATION

Maximum recommended trailer weight

20 cwt (1016 kg) when the trailer being towed is equipped with brakes.
3·94 cwt (200 kg) when the trailer being towed is not equipped with brakes – providing that the total car and trailer laden weights do not exceed the maximum gross vehicle weight.

Maximum starting gradient (fully laden car and trailer)	5·1	with car engine in peak condition
Maximum climbable gradient (fully laden and trailer)	3·8	

GENERAL SPECIFICATION DATA

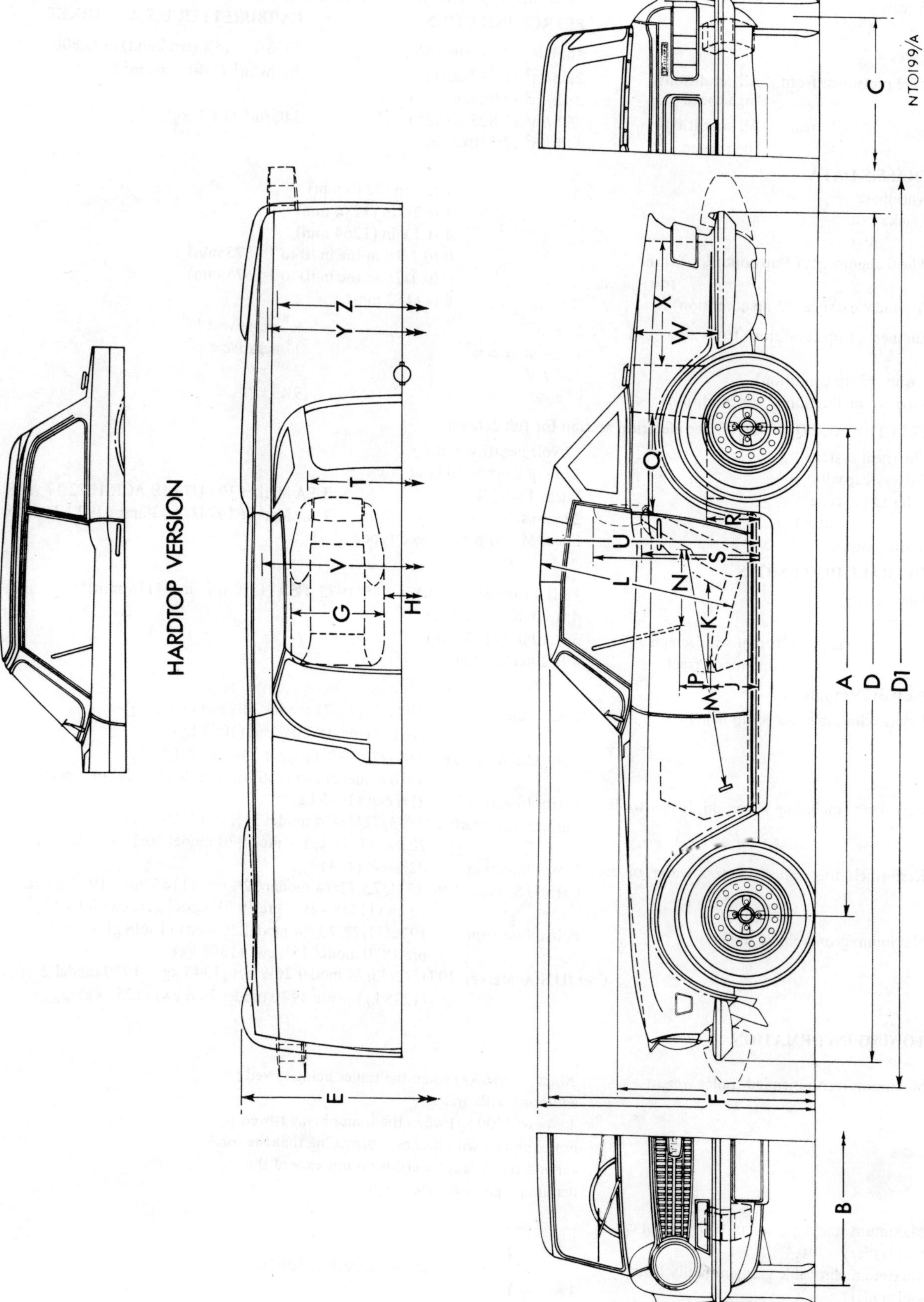

VEHICLE DIMENSIONS

Dim.	Description	inches	mm
A	Wheelbase	88·00	2240
B	Front track:		
	Disc or Wire wheels	50·25	1276
C	Rear track:		
	Disc or Wire wheels	49.75	1264
D	Overall length	155·00	3937
D1	Overall length (1974 USA Market)	162·13	4118
E	Overall width	58·00	1470
F	Height (unladen)		
	Soft top – hood erect	50·00	1270
	to top of windscreen	46·00	1170
	Hood folded and windscreen removed	40·00	1020
G	Seat width	19·00	483
H	Width between seats	6·00	152
J	Seat height – floor to cushion	7·50	190
K	Seat depth	16·50	419
L	Headroom from seat cushion	36·00	915
M	Seat squab to clutch pedal:		
	Max.	40·50	1030
	Min.	36·00	915
N	Seat squab to steering wheel:		
	Max.	18·50	470
	Min.	14·00	355
P	Seat cushion to steering wheel	6·50	165
Q	Length of luggage space behind seats:		
	Max.	21·50	546
	Min.	17·00	432
R	Floor to luggage platform	9·00	229
S	Height – floor to top of seat squab	22·50	572
	U.S.A. only		
	floor to top of seat restraint	30·00	762
T	Width between wheel arches	33·50	850
U	Maximum interior height	40·50	1030
V	Maximum interior width	50·50	1282
W	Luggage compartment height:		
	Max.	13·50	343
	Min.	9·50	242
X	Luggage compartment depth	20·00	508
Y	Luggage compartment width:		
	Max.	46·00	1170
	Min.	44·00	1117
Z	Luggage compartment effective opening width	43·00	1091

PAINT AND TRIM CODING SYSTEM

The commission number plate affixed to the scuttle side panel bears code symbols for identification of the vehicle's exterior colour, trim material and trim colour.

Colour Code

Nine basic colours are allocated a number as shown in the table. Shades of these colours are classified as 1st shade, 2nd shade, 3rd shade, etc. The number of each shade change prefixes the basic colour to indicate the shade colour. Dual colours are identified by two code numbers separated by a stroke, e.g. 19/26 denotes 'White' and 'Wedgwood', the predominant colour being White, this symbol being quoted first.

The main trim material is identified by prefixing the colour code number with a letter, e.g.:

Leathercloth – No prefix letter
Leather – Prefix letter H
Cloth – Prefix letter C

Basic colour	Basic colour number	1st shade	2nd shade	3rd shade	4th shade	5th shade	6th shade	7th shade	8th shade	9th shade	10th shade	11th shade	12th shade
Black	01	11											
Red	02	12 Matador	22 Cherry	32 Signal	42 Burgundy	52 Scarlet	62 Inca Red	72 Pimiento	** 82 Carmine	92 Magenta **			
Brown	03	13 Light Tan	23 Sienna	33 New Tan	43 Saddle Tan	53 Dark Brown	** 63 Chestnut **						
Yellow	04	14 Jonquil	24 Wimpey	34 Jasmine	** 44 Beige **	54 Saffron	** 64 Mimosa **						
Green	05	15 Cactus	25 Confer	35 Olive	45 Lichfield	55 Laurel	65 Emerald						
Blue	06	16 Midnight	26 Wedg-wood	36 Dark Blue	46 Renoir	56 Royal	66 Valencia	76 Print Blue	86 Navy Blue	96 Sapphire	106 Mallard	** 116 Ice	126 French **
Purple	07	17 Damson	27 Shadow Blue										
Grey	08	18 Gunmetal	28 Dark Grey	38 Phantom	48 Dolphin	58 Shadow Blue	68 Slate	78 Grey					
White	09	19 White	29 Sebring White	** 39 Honey-suckle **									

ENGINE

Firing order	1–5–3–6–2–4			
No. 1 cylinder	at front			
Idle speed Petrol Injection	**700 to 850 rev/min**			
Carb/U.S.A. market	800 to 850 rev/min			
Fast idle speed Petrol Injection	**1300 to 1500 rev/min**			
Carb/U.S.A. market	1100 to 1300 rev/min			
Valve clearance (cold)	0·010 in (0·25 mm)			
Valve clearance adjustment	Screw and locking nut on rocker			
Location of timing marks	Scale on pulley, pointer on timing cover			

Valve timing	Petrol Injection		Carburetter/U.S.A. Market	
	1974/73	Pre 1973	**1974/73/72 Models**	Pre 1972 Models
Inlet opens	18° B.T.D.C.	35° B.T.D.C.	18° B.T.D.C.	10° B.T.D.C.
closes	58° A.B.D.C.	65° A.B.D.C.	58° A.T.D.C.	50° A.T.D.C.
Exhaust opens	58° B.B.D.C.	65° B.B.D.C.	58° B.B.D.C.	50° B.B.D.C.
closes	18° A.T.D.C.	35° A.T.D.C.	18° A.T.D.C.	10° A.T.D.C.

Ignition timing:
static }
dynamic } See 86.35.00

FUEL INJECTION

Pressure from pump	104 to 110 lbf/in² (7·31 to 7·73 kgf/cm²)
Pressure at injector	50 lbf/in² (3·52 kgf/cm²)
Manifold depression at idling speed	12½ in (3·81 cm) of mercury

CARBURETTER

Make/type	**Stromberg 175 C.D.S.E.V.**	Carburetters are matched to camshaft and distributor See 86.35.00
Main jet	0·100 in (0·254 cm)	
Needle	B.I.A.F.	
Float height	0·629 to 0·669 in (16 to 17 mm)	

IGNITION COIL

	1974/73 Models	Pre 1973 Models
Make/type	Lucas 15 C6	Lucas H.A.12
Primary winding resistance	1·30 to 1·45 ohms	3·) to 3·5 ohms

BALLAST RESISTOR

Make/type	**Fitted into harness – 1974/73 Models**	Not fitted to pre 1973 Models
Resistance	1.30 to 1·45 ohms	

IGNITION DISTRIBUTOR

Make/type	Lucas 22D6 – see 86.35.00
Rotation viewed on rotor	Anticlockwise
Dwell angle	See 86.35.00
Capacitor capacitance	0·20 Microfarads
Contact breaker gap	0·014 to 0·016 in (0·35 to 0·40 mm)
Centrifugal advance	See 86.35.00
Vacuum advance	See 86.35.00

SPARKING PLUGS

Make/type Petrol injection	Champion N9Y
Carb/U.S.A. Market	**1974/73 Models – Champion N9Y** Pre 1973 Models – Champion UN 12Y
Gap	0·025 in (0·63 mm)

TORQUE WRENCH SETTINGS

Operation	Description		Specified Torque (lbf.ft.)	(kgf.m.)
ENGINE				
Alternator mounting bracket to cylinder block	5/16" UNF		22	3·0
Alternator to mounting bracket	5/16" UNF		22	3·0
Alternator to adjusting link	5/16" UNC		20	2·8
Camshaft chainwheel attachment	5/16" UNF		24	3·3
Clutch attachment	5/16" UNF		20	2·8
Connecting rod bolt	3/8" UNF	Phosphated	46	6·4
		colour dyed	50	6·9
Crankshaft cover to block	5/16" UNF		20	2·8
Crankshaft sealing block attachment	5/16" UNF		14	2·0
Cylinder head attachment	7/16" UNF		80	11·1
Distributor and P.I. pump pedestal attachment	5/16" UNF		14	2·0
Distributor to pedestal	5/16" UNF		20	2·8
Distributor pedestal end plug	1/4" UNF		9	1·2
Fan attachment	5/16" UNF		14	2·0
Flywheel attachment	7/16" UNF		**95	13·1**
Front engine plate attachment	5/16" UNF		22	3·0
Front engine plate and cam locating plate attachment	5/16" UNF		22	3·0
Main bearing bolts	7/16" UNF		65	9·0
Mounting rubber bracket to engine	3/8" UNF		32	4·4
Mounting rubber to engine bracket	3/8" UNF		32	4·4
Mounting rubber to frame	3/8" UNF		32	4·4
Manifold attachment	3/8" UNF		25	3·5
Manifold to exhaust pipe	3/8" x 16 N.C.		25	3·5
Oil gallery seal	1/8" N.P.S.I.		8	1·1
Oil gallery plug	3/4" UNF		35	4·8
Oil gallery plug	1/4" N.P.S.I.		14	2·0
Oil filter attachment	7/16" UNC		20	2·8
Oil pressure relief valve	5/8" UNF		35	4·8
Petrol injection nozzle attachment	1/4"UNC		7	1·0
Petrol pump attachment	1/4" UNF		9	1·2
Petrol pump attachment	5/16" UNF		14	2·0
Rear engine plate attachment	5/16" UNF		22	3·0
Rear engine plate and gearbox to block	5/16" UNF		22	3·0
Rocker pedestal attachment	3/8" UNF		34	4·7
Rocker cover attachment	5/16" UNF		2	0·3
Rocker shaft locating screw	No. 12 x 28 UNF		5	0·7
Rocker oil feed plug	5/16" UNF		20	2·8
Spark plug attachment	14 mm		20	2·8
Starter motor attachment	3/8" UNF		34	4·7
Sump attachment	5/16" UNF		20	2·8
Sump drain plug	3/8" x18		25	3·5
Timing cover attachment	5/16" UNF Stud		16	2·2
Timing cover attachment	5/16" UNF x 7/8"		20	2·8
Timing cover attachment	5/16" UNF x 3/8		10	1·4
Water valve adaptor to cylinder head	3/8" B.S.P.		20	2·8
Water pump pulley attachment	5/16" UNF		14	2·0
Water pump attachment	5/16" UNF		14	2·0
Water pump to cylinder head	5/16" UNF		20	2·8
Water pump plug	3/8" UNF		25	3·5
Water pump plug	5/8" UNF		35	4·8

ENGINE

Firing order	1 5 3 6 2 4
No. 1 cylinder	at front
Idle speed Petrol Injection	750 to 800/850 rev/min
Carb/U.S.A. market	800 to 850 rev/min
Fast idle speed Petrol Injection	1100 to 1300/1500 rev/min
Carb/U.S.A. market	1100 to 1300 rev/min
Valve clearance (cold)	0·010 in (0·25 mm)
Valve clearance adjustment	Screw and locking nut on rocker
Location of timing marks	Scale on pulley, pointer on timing cover

Valve timing

	Petrol Injection		Carburetter/U.S.A. Market	
	** 1973	Pre 1973 **	1973/1972 Model	Pre 1972 Model
Inlet opens	** 18° B.T.D.C.	35° B.T.D.C.	18° B.T.D.C.	10° B.T.D.C.
closes	58° A.B.D.C.	65° A.B.D.C.	58° A.T.D.C.	50° A.T.D.C.
Exhaust opens	58° B.B.D.C.	65° B.B.D.C.	58° B.B.D.C.	50° B.B.D.C.
closes	18° A.T.D.C.	35° A.T.D.C.	18° A.T.D.C. **	10° A.T.D.C.

Ignition timing:
static
dynamic } See 86.35.00

FUEL INJECTION

Pressure from pump	104 to 110 lbf/in² (7·31 to 7·73 kgf/cm²)
Pressure at injector	50 lbf/in² (3·52 kgf/cm²)
Manifold depression at idling speed	12½ in (3·81 cm) of mercury

CARBURETTER

Make/type	**Stromberg 175 C.D.S.E. (V)	Carburetters are matched to camshaft and distributor See 86.35.00
Main jet	0·100 in (0·254 cm) **	
Needle	B.I.A.F.	
Float height	0·629 to 0·669 in (16 to 17 mm)	

IGNITION COIL

	** 1973 Model	** Pre 1973 Model **
Make/type	Lucas 15 C6	Lucas H.A.12
Primary winding resistance	1·30 to 1·45 ohms **	3·0 to 3·5 ohms

BALLAST RESISTOR

Make/type	** Fitted into harness – 1973 Models	** Not fitted to pre 1973 Models **
Resistance	1.30 to 1·45 ohms **	

IGNITION DISTRIBUTOR

Make/type	Lucas 22D6 – see 86.35.00
Rotation viewed on rotor	Anticlockwise
Dwell angle	See 86.35.00
Capacitor capacitance	0·20 Microfarads
Contact breaker gap	0·014 to 0·016 in (0·35 to 0·40 mm)
Centrifugal advance	See 86.35.00
Vacuum advance	See 86.35.00

SPARKING PLUGS

Make/type Petrol injection	Champion N9Y	
Carb/U.S.A. Market	** 1973 Model – Champion N9Y	Pre 1973 Model – ** Champion UN 12Y
Gap	0·025 in (0·63 mm)	

TORQUE WRENCH SETTINGS

Operation	Description		Specified Torque (lbf.ft.)	(kgf.m.)
ENGINE				
Alternator mounting bracket to cylinder block	5/16" UNF		22	3·0
Alternator to mounting bracket	5/16" UNF		22	3·0
Alternator to adjusting link	5/16" UNC		20	2·8
Camshaft chainwheel attachment	5/16" UNF		24	3·3
Clutch attachment	5/16" UNF		20	2·8
** Connecting rod bolt	3/8" UNF	Phosphated	46	6·4
		colour dyed	50	6·9
Crankshaft cover to block	5/16" UNF		20	2·8
Crankshaft sealing block attachment	5/16" UNF		14	2·0
Cylinder head attachment	7/16" UNF		80	11·1
Distributor and P.I. pump pedestal attachment	5/16" UNF		14	2·0
Distributor to pedestal	5/16" UNF		20	2·8
Distributor pedestal end plug	1/4" UNF		9	1·2
Fan attachment	5/16" UNF		14	2·0
Flywheel attachment	7/16" UNF		75	10·4
Front engine plate attachment	5/16" UNF		22	3·0
Front engine plate and cam locating plate attachment	5/16" UNF		22	3·0
Main bearing bolts	7/16" UNF		65	9·0
Mounting rubber bracket to engine	3/8" UNF		32	4·4
Mounting rubber to engine bracket	3/8" UNF		32	4·4
Mounting rubber to frame	3/8" UNF		32	4·4
Manifold attachment	3/8" UNF		25	3·5
Manifold to exhaust pipe	3/8" x 16 N.C.		25	3·5
Oil gallery seal	1/8" N.P.S.I.		8	1·1
Oil gallery plug	3/4" UNF		35	4·8
Oil gallery plug	1/4" N.P.S.I.		14	2·0
Oil filter attachment	7/16" UNC		20	2·8
Oil pressure relief valve	5/8" UNF		35	4·8
Petrol injection nozzle attachment	1/4"UNC		7	1·0
Petrol pump attachment	1/4" UNF		9	1·2
Petrol pump attachment	5/16" UNF		14	2·0
Rear engine plate attachment	5/16" UNF		22	3·0
Rear engine plate and gearbox to block	5/16" UNF		22	3·0
Rocker pedestal attachment	3/8" UNF		34	4·7
Rocker cover attachment	5/16" UNF		2	0·3
Rocker shaft locating screw	No. 12 x 28 UNF		5	0·7
Rocker oil feed plug	5/16" UNF		20	2·8
Spark plug attachment	14 mm		20	2·8
Starter motor attachment	3/8" UNF		34	4·7
Sump attachment	5/16" UNF		20	2·8
Sump drain plug	3/8" x18		25	3·5
Timing cover attachment	5/16" UNF Stud		16	2·2
Timing cover attachment	5/16" UNF x 7/8"		20	2·8
Timing cover attachment	5/16" UNF x 3/8		10	1·4
Water valve adaptor to cylinder head	3/8" B.S.P		20	2·8
Water pump pulley attachment	5/16" UNF		14	2·0
Water pump attachment	5/16" UNF		14	2·0
Water pump to cylinder head	5/16" UNF		20	2·8
Water pump plug	3/8" UNF		25	3·5
Water pump plug	5/8" UNF		35	4·8

Operation	Description	Specified Torque (lbf.ft)	(kgf.m)
FUEL INJECTION PIPE SYSTEM			
Flexible pipe to filter	1/2" UNF	9	1·2
Flexible pipe to metering unit	3/8" B.S.P.	20	2·8
Flexible pipe to motor pump	3/8" B.S.P.	20	2·8
Flexible pipe to relief valve	3/8" B.S.P.	20	2·8
Flexible pipe to relief valve	1/4" B.S.P.	20	2·8
In line relief valve assembly relief valve to strainer housing	3/8" B.S.P.	40	5·5
Pipe to motor pump	3/8" B.S.P.	20	2·8
Pipe to filter	1/2" UNF	9	1·2
Relief valve assembly to Tee-piece	3/8" B.S.P.	40	5·5
ENGINE (CARBURETTER VERSION ONLY)			
Carburetter attachment	5/16" UNF	14	2·0
Distributor pedestal attachment	5/16" UNF	14	2·0
Distributor to pedestal	1/4" UNF	9	1·2
Inlet manifold plug	3/4" S.A.E.	35	4·8
Manifold attachment	5/16" UNF	20	2·8
Manifold hose adaptor	1/2" P.T.F.	32	4·4
Manifold to front pipe	3/8" x 16 N.C.	25	3·5
Servo adaptor to manifold	5/8" UNF	32	4·4
GEARBOX			
Change speed lever to top cover	1/4" UNF	9	1·2
Clutch housing cover attachment	5/16" UNF	20	2·8
Clutch slave cylinder attachment	5/16" UNF	20	2·8
Countershaft end cover to gearbox	5/16" UNC	20	2·8
Countershaft and Reverse shaft to gearbox	5/16" UNC	14	2·0
Extension to gearbox	5/16" UNC	20	2·8
Front cover to gearbox	5/16" UNC	20	2·8
Gearbox to engine	5/16" UNF	20	2·8
Mounting rubber to gearbox extension	1/2" UNF	65	9·0
Mounting rubber to frame crossmember	7/16" UNF	46	6·4
Overdrive adaptor plate	5/16" UNC	20	2·8
Propshaft flange to mainshaft	3/4" UNF	120	16.6
Propshaft attachment	3/8" UNF	34	4.7
Sealing ring cover plate attachment	1/4" UNF	9	1·2
Selectors and forks to shaft	5/16" UNF	9	1·2
Speedo bearing locking screw	5/16" UNC	9	1·2
Top cover to gearbox	5/16" UNC	20	2·8
Top up and drain plugs	3/8" UNF	25	3·5
OVERDRIVE ** -- 'A' TYPE			
Cap to top cover and overdrive switch bracket	1/4" UNF	9	1·2
Overdrive unit retaining	5/16" UNC	20	2·8
Speedo driven gear to rear cover	5/16"UNC	9	1·2

TORQUE WRENCH SETTINGS

Operation	Description	Specified Torque (lbf.ft)	(kgf.m)
OVERDRIVE – 'J' TYPE			
Adaptor to gearbox	¼" U.N.F. setscrew	9	1·2
Overdrive to adaptor	¾" stud	7	1·0
Overdrive to rear engine mounting	⅜" U.N.F./U.N.C. stud	25	3·5
Rear engine mounting attachment	7/16" U.N.F. bolt	38	5·2
Steady strap to overdrive unit	5/16" U.N.F. stud	20	2·8
REAR AXLE			
Bearing caps to housing	⅜" UNF	38	5·2
Crown wheel to housing	⅜" UNF	46	6·4
Cover and rear mounting plate attachment	⅜" UNF	32	4·4
Controlled rebound mounting to bracket	5/16" UNF	20	2·8
Hypoid housing to rear cover	5/16" UNF	20	2·8
Inner driving flange to inner axle	⅝" UNF	120	16·6
Nose plate to axle	⅜" UNF	38	5·2
Oil seal housing to hypoid housing	5/16" UNF	20	2·8
Oil level plug	⅜" UNF	25	3·5
Prop shaft flange to pinion	⅝" UNF	120	16·6
Rear mounting plate to frame	⅜" UNF	25	3·5
FRONT SUSPENSION			
Anti-roll bar mounting bracket to lower wishbone	⅜" UNF	32	4·4
Anti-roll bar fixing	5/16" UNF	4	0·6
Anti-roll bar link to lower wishbone	7/16" UNF	38	5·2
Anti-roll bar to link	⅜" UNF	16	2·2
Brake disc attachment	⅜" UNF	34	4·7
Brake caliper and shield attachment	7/16" UNF	65	9·0
Brake caliper mounting bracket and tie rod lever attachment	⅜" UNF	34	4·7
Damper to spring pan mounting	7/16" UNF	65	9·0
Lockstop bolts to trunnion	5/16" UNF	20	2·8
Lower wishbone mounting bracket to frame	⅜" UNF	25	3·5
Lower wishbone to mounting bracket	½" UNF	46	6·4
Lower wishbone to vertical link	9/16" UNF	65	9·0
Lower wishbone to spring pan	⅜" UNF	32	4·4
Shock absorber mounting to spring pan	⅜" UNF	25	3·5
Stub axle to front hub	½" UNF	Tighten to 5 lbf.ft. Unscrew one flat and insert split pin to give ·003in to ·005in (0·076 to 0.127 mm) end float.	
Stub axle to vertical link	½" UNF	65	9·0
Top ball joint to upper wishbone	⅜" UNF	32	4·4
Top ball joint to vertical link	½" UNF	50	6·9
Upper wishbone to fulcrum pin	7/16" UNF	40	5·5
Upper wishbone fulcrum to chassis frame	⅜" UNF	32	4·4
Wheel stud	7/16" UNF	80	11·1

Operation		Specified Torque (lbf.ft)	(kgf.m)
REAR SUSPENSION			
Bump rubber attachment	3/8" UNF	20	2·8
Damper mounting to bracket	7/16" UNF	65	9·0
Damper link attachment	3/8" UNF	20	2·8
Damper arm to link	7/16" UNF	46	6·4
Inner driven flange to outer axle	3/8" UNF	34	4·7
Outer driven flange to axle and hub	1 3/8" UNF	To be tightened to give ·002 in to ·005 in. (0·051 to 0·127 mm) End float.	
Rear hub assembly	5/8" UNF	120	16·6
	Nylok Nut Castellated Nut	120	16·6†**
Trailing arm to mounting bracket	7/16" UNF	46	6·4
Trailing arm mounting bracket to frame	3/8" UNF	34	4·7
Trailing arm to brake plate	5/16" UNF	16	2·2
Wire wheel extension attachment	7/16" UNF	65	9·0
Wheel attachment	7/16" UNF	80	11·1

** †Tighten to 90lb.f.ft. (12·5 Kgf.m.) Then continue tightening until split pin can be inserted**.

Operation		(lbf.ft)	(kgf.m)
STEERING			
Adaptor to upper and lower column	5/16" UNF	20	2·8
Adaptor to rubber coupling	5/16" UNF	20	2·8
Ball joint to tie rod lock nut	1/2" UNF	38	5·2
Ball joint tie rod to steering lever	7/16" UNF	38	5·2
Lower clamp to outer column and body	1/4" UNF	10	1·4
Outer column tie rod to body	1/4" UNF	10	1·4
Rack to chassis	5/16" UNF	16	2·2
Safety clamp to column	1/4" UNF	9	1·2
Safety clamp grub screw	7/16" UNF	20	2·8
Steering wheel attachment	9/16" UNS	34	4·7
Top clamp to outer column	5/16" UNF	20	2·8
Top clamp to body	1/4" UNF Setscrew	10	1·4
Top clamp to body	1/4" UNF Weld bolt	8	1·1
Universal joint attachment	5/16" UNF	20	2·8

Operation		(lbf.ft)	(kgf.m)
CHASSIS			
Cross tube to front suspension turrets	3/8" UNF	34	
Chassis to axle nose plate front of rear suspension . .	3/8" UNF	25	3·5
Chassis to axle back plate back of rear suspension . .	3/8" UNF	25	3·5
Gearbox mounting crossmember to chassis	3/8" UNF	34	4·7
Radiator shield attachment	3/8" UNF	32	4·4
Radiator to chassis	3/8" UNF	14	2·0
Radiator drain tap	1/4" P.T.F.	9	1·2

TORQUE WRENCH SETTINGS

Operation	Description	Specified Torque (lbf.ft)	Specified Torque (kgf.m)
BODY			
Brake servo attachment	5/16" UNF	14	2·0
Brake limiting valve to body	1/4" UNF	9	1·2
Brake master cylinder to servo	3/8" UNF	24	3·3
Body mounting to rear suspension crossmember	3/8" UNF	14	2·0
Door hinge attachment	5/16" UNF	20	2·8
Door lock striker attachment	1/4" UNF	9	1·2
Door lock to door	1/4" UNF	9	1·2
Front bumper side fixing	5/16" UNF	20	2·8
Front bumper centre to support bracket	3/8" UNF	25	3·5
Front bumper support bracket to chassis	3/8" UNF	32	4·4
Fuel tank drain plug	5/8" UNF	32	4·4
Handbrake fulcrum pin	3/8" UNF	24	3·3
Hard top to screen attachment	5/16" UNF	9	1·2
Hard top bracket to tie bar	5/16" UNF	9	1·2
Hard top to rear deck	1/4" UNF	9	1·2
Rear bumper outrigger brackets to shackles	3/8" UNF	32	4·4
Rear bumper support bracket to chassis	3/8" UNF	32	4·4
Rear bumper front and side to bracket fixing	3/8" UNF	32	4.4
Safety harness pivot bolt	7/16" UNF	32	4.4
Safety harness eye bolt	7/16" UNF	32	4.4
Seat slides to floor	1/4" UNF	9	1.2
Seat to slide	5/16"UNF	7	1.0

RECOMMENDED LUBRICANTS – BRITISH ISLES

(The products recommended are not listed in order of preference)

COMPONENT	BP	CASTROL	DUCKHAMS	ESSO	MOBIL	PETROFINA	REGENT	SHELL
ENGINE AND OIL CAN	Super Visco-static 20-50	Castrol GTX	Duckhams Q20-50	Uniflo	Mobiloil Super 10W/50 or Mobiloil Special 20W/50	Fina Super Grade Motor Oil SAE 20W/50	Havoline Motor Oil 20W-50	Shell Super Multigrade
GEARBOX AND OVERDRIVE REAR AXLE AND LOWER STEERING SWIVELS	BP Gear Oil SAE 90 EP	Castrol Hypoy	Duckhams Hypoid 90	Esso Gear Oil GX 90/140	Mobilube HD 90	Fina Pontonic XP 90-140	Multigear Lubricant EP 90	Shell Spirax 90 EP
FRONT & REAR HUBS BRAKE CABLES GREASE GUN	Energrease L2	Castrol LM Grease	Duckhams LB 10	Esso Multi-purpose Grease H	Mobilgrease MP	Fina Marson HTL 2	Marfak All purpose	Shell Retinex A

RECOMMENDED LUBRICANTS – OVERSEAS

(The products recommended are not listed in order of preference)

COMPONENT	Air temp. °C	Air temp. °F	API Designation	BP	CASTROL	DUCKHAMS	ESSO	MOBIL	PETROFINA	SHELL	TEXACO
ENGINE	over 30	over 80	SD or SE	*BP Super Visco-Static	Castrol GTX Castrol Super 20W/50 or XLR (USA only)	Q20/50 (Q10-50)	Esso Extra Motor Oil 20W/50 (Uniflow)	Mobiloil Super 10W/50 Mobiloil Special 20W/50	Fina Supergrade Motor Oil 20W/50	Shell Super Motor Oil	Havoline 20W/50
CARB. DASHPOTS (USA Markets)	30 to 0	80 to 30	SD or SE								
OIL CAN	0 to −20	30 to −4	SD or SE		Castrolite or Castrol GTZ	Q10-40	Esso Extra Motor Oil 10W/30	Mobiloil Super 10W/50	Fina Supergrade Motor Oil 10W/40		Havoline 10W/30
	below −20	below −4	SD or SE		Castrol 5W/20	Q5-30	Esso Extra Motor Oil 5W/20	Mobiloil 5W/20	Fina Supergrade 5W/30		Havoline 5W/20
GEARBOX AND OVERDRIVE REAR AXLE	over 0	over 30	GL4	BP Gear Oil SAE 90 EP	Castrol Hypoy	Duckhams Hypoid 90	Esso Gear Oil GX 90	Mobilube HD 90	Fina PONTONIC MP SAE 90	Shell Spriax 90 EP	Multigear Lubricant EP 90
LOWER STEERING SWIVELS	below 0	below 30	GL4	BP Gear Oil SAE 80 EP	Castrol Hypoy 80	Duckhams Hypoid 80	Esso Gear Oil GX 80	Mobilube HD 80	Fina PONTONIC MP SAE 80	Shell Spirax 80 EP	Multigear Lubricant EP 80
FRONT AND REAR HUBS BRAKE CABLES GREASE GUN				BP Energrease L2 or Energrease MP (USA only)	Castrol LM Grease or MP Grease (USA only)	Duckhams LB 10	Esso Multi-purpose Grease H	Mobilgrease MP	Fina Marson HTL 2	Shell Retinax A or Darina AX (USA only)	Marfak All-purpose

* OILS MARKED THUS ARE AVAILABLE IN MULTIGRADE FORMS WITH VISCOSITY CHARACTERISTICS APPROPRIATE TO THE AMBIENT TEMPERATURE RANGE IN INDIVIDUAL MARKETS.

** WHERE CIRCUIT RACING OR OTHER SEVERE COMPETITIVE EVENTS ARE CONTEMPLATED IT IS ADVISABLE, IN VIEW OF THE INCREASED OIL TEMPERATURE ENCOUNTERED, TO USE OILS OF HIGH VISCOSITY.

** RECOMMENDED LUBRICANTS AND ANTI-FREEZE SOLUTIONS – U.S.A. MARKET

COMPONENT	SERVICE CLASSIFICATION	AMBIENT TEMPERATURE RANGE	SAE VISCOSITY CLASSIFICATION
Engine	API - SE	Above 14°F (-10°C)	10W/50 10W/40 20W/50 20W/40
		-5°F to 50°F (-20°C to +10°C)	10W/50 10W/40 10W/30
		Below 14°F (-10°C)	5W/30 5W/20
Gearbox and Overdrive Final Drive	API - GL4	Above 32°F (0°C)	Hypoid 90
		Below 32°F (0°C)	Hypoid 80
Steering Rack, Hubs & Chassis Grease Points	NLGI 2 multi-purpose grease		
Brake & Clutch Fluid	DOT 3 Type Brake Fluid (FMVSS No. 116) also meeting SAE J1703d		
Anti-Freeze	Permanent type ethylene glycol base with suitable inhibitor for mixed metal systems		
Windshield Washer	Windshield Washer Anti freeze fluid (Proprietary Brands) **		

** **RECOMMENDED HYDRAULIC FLUIDS**

Clutch and Brake Reservoirs: Castrol Girling Brake and Clutch Fluid – Crimson or Unipart 550 Brake Fluid.
Where these proprietary brands are not available, other fluids which meet the S.A.E. J.1703 specification may be used.

RECOMMENDED FUEL

The Triumph TR6 engine is designed to operate on fuel having a minimum octane rating of 97 (High compression engines) OR 91 (Lower compression engines): this is equivalent to the British 4 star and 2 star rating respectively.
Where such fuels are not available and it is necessary to use fuels of lower or unknown rating, the ignition timing must be retarded from the specified setting, just sufficiently to prevent audible detonation (pinking) under all operating conditions, otherwise damage to the engine may occur.

IMPORTANT: When cars for the U.S.A. market enter the "United States" the ignition timing must be set to suit the use of the recommended grade of fuel AND TO COMPLY WITH REGULATIONS ON EMISSIONS FROM THE CRANKCASE AND EXHAUST.

ANTI-FREEZE SOLUTIONS

Only solutions which meet B.S.I. 3151 or 3152 specifications may be used.

			25%	30%	35%	50%
ANTI-FREEZE CONCENTRATION			25%	30%	35%	50%
SPECIFIC GRAVITY OF COOLANT AT 15·5° (60°F)			1·039	1·048	1·054	1·076
ANTI-FREEZE QUANTITY		PINTS IMP.	2·8	3·3	3·9	5·5
		PINTS U.S.A.	3·3	4·0	4·7	6·6
		LITRES	1·6	1·9	2·2	3·2
DEGREE OF PROTECTION	**Complete** Car may be driven away immediately from cold		−12°C 10°F	−16°C 3°F	−20°C −4°F	−36°C −33°F
	Safe Limit Coolant in mushy state. Engine may be started and driven away after short warm-up period		−18°C 0°F	−22°C −8°F	−28°C −18°F	−41°C −42°F
	Lower Protection Prevents frost damage to cylinder head, block and radiator. Thaw out before starting engine		−26°C −15°F	−32°C −26°F	−37°C −35°F	−47°C −53°F

CAPACITIES

Fuel tank	USA 1974/1973 condition	9½ gal (11·4 US gal)	(43 Litres)
. . . .	1974/1973 other markets PI	10¾ gal (12·9 US gal)	(48·6 Litres)
. . . .	Pre 1973 other Markets PI and Pre 1972 USA condition	11¼ gal (13·5 US gal)	(51 Litres)
. . . .	U.S.A. 1972 condition	10¼ gal (12·3 US gal)	(46·5 Litres)
Engine sump and oil filter	. . . .	9 pints (10·8 US pints)	(5·10 Litres)
Engine sump (drain and refill)	. . . .	8 pints (9·6 US pints)	(4·25 Litres)
Gearbox (from dry)	. . . .	2 pints (2·4 US pints)	(1·13 Litres)
Gearbox and overdrive (from dry)	'A' type . . .	3½ pints (4·2 US pints)	(2·0 Litres)
	'J' type . . .	2·66 pints (3·2 US pints)	(1·5 Litres)
Rear axle (from dry)	. . . .	2¼ pints (2·7 US pints)	(1·27 Litres)
. . . .	U.S.A. pre 1970 condition	2½ pints (3·0 US pints)	(1·42 Litres)
Cooling system (including heater)	. . . . . .	11 pints (13·2 US pints)	(6·21 Litres)
Heater	. . . .	1 pint (1·2 US pints)	(0·57 Litres) **

MAINTENANCE OPERATIONS

LUBRICATION CHART

Weekly or before a long journey

1. Check/top up cooling system level.
2. Check/top up engine oil level.

Every 3,000 miles (5,000 km)

1. Check/top up cooling system level.
2. Check/top up engine oil level.
3. Check/top up brake and clutch fluid reservoirs.

Every 6,000 miles (10,000 km)

1. Check/top up cooling system level.
2. Change engine oil.
3. Lubricate steering rack and pinion.
4. Using OIL lubricate lower steering swivels. Grease suspension upper ball joints.
5. Check/top up carburetter piston damper(s) and lubricate throttle linkage.
6. Check/top up brake and clutch fluid reservoirs.
7. Lubricate accelerator, brake and clutch pedal pivots.
8. Check/top up gearbox oil level.
9. Check/top up rear axle oil level.
10. Lubricate inner drive shaft universal joints.
11. Lubricate handbrake linkage and cable.
12. Lubricate all door, bonnet and boot locks and hinges.
13. Lubricate battery terminals (petroleum jelly).
15. Lubricate distributor.

Every 12,000 miles (20,000 km)

1. Check/top up cooling system level.
2. Change engine oil.
3. Lubricate steering rack and pinion.
4. Using OIL lubricate lower steering swivels. Grease suspension upper ball joints.
5. Check/top up carburetter piston damper(s) and lubricate throttle linkage.
6. Check/top up brake and clutch fluid reservoirs.
7. Lubricate accelerator, brake and clutch pedal pivots.
8. Check/top up gearbox oil level.
9. Check/top up rear axle oil.
10. Lubricate inner drive shaft universal joints.
11. Lubricate handbrake linkage and cable.
12. Lubricate all door, bonnet and boot locks and hinges.
13. Lubricate battery terminals (petroleum jelly).
14. Renew oil filter element.
15. Lubricate distributor.
16. Lubricate water pump.

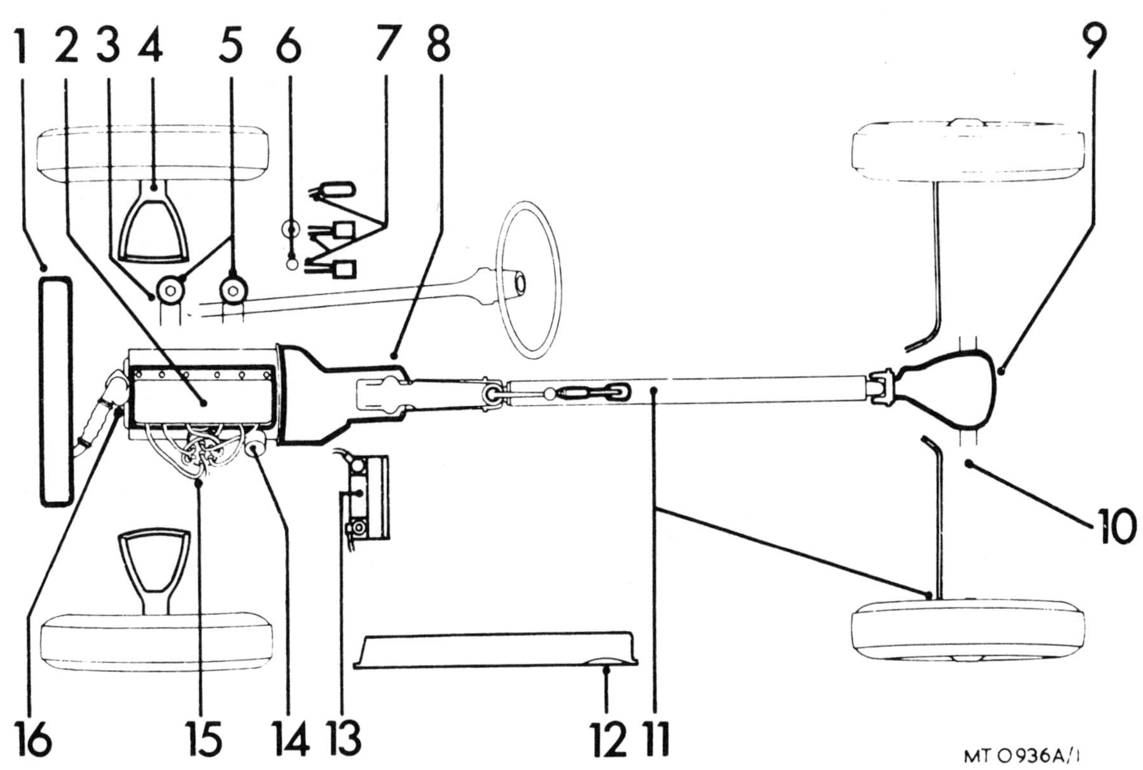

SUMMARY CHART

The Summary Chart below lists general recommendations for Service Operations and Intervals. Overseas Service Engineers are advised to consult the 'Passport to Service' booklet supplied with the car for amendments to these recommendations that may be specially applicable to their local operating conditions OR that may be obligtory to meet Regulations for a specific Country.

Operation Number	10.10.03	10.10.06	10.10.12	10.10.24
Interval in miles x 1,000	1	3	6	12
Interval in Kilometres x 1,000	1·6	5	10	20
Operation Description				
ENGINE COMPARTMENT				
1. Check/top up engine oil level (E)		X		
2. Check/top up cooling system (E)	X	X	X	X
3. Check/top up brake fluid reservoir	X	X	X	X
4. Check/top up clutch fluid reservoir	X	X	X	X
5. Check/top up windscreen washer fluid reservoir	X	X	X	X
6. Check/top up battery	X	X	X	X
7. Check/top up carburetter piston(s) damper(s)(E)	X		X	X
8. Drain engine oil and refill (E)	X		X	X
9. Renew oil filter element (E)				X
10. Clean fuel pump sediment bowl	X			X
11. Lubricate distributor and check automatic advance (E)	X		X	X
12. Check/adjust/report condition of distributor points (E)	X		X	
13. Distributor points – renew (E)				X
14. Check/adjust ignition timing using electronic equipment (E)	X		X	X
15. Check/report ignition wiring for fraying, chafing and deterioration (E)	X		X	X
16. Condensor and coil check for breakdown on oscilascope tune (E)			X	X
17. Clean/adjust sparking plugs (E)			X	
18. Renew sparking plugs (E)				X
19. Check/adjust torque of cylinder head nuts/bolts (E)	X			
20. Check/report cylinder compression (E)			X	X
21. Check/adjust valve rocker clearances (E)	X			X
22. Clean engine oil filler cap (E)				X
23. Clean carburetter air cleaner elements (E)			X	
24. Renew carburetter air cleaner elements (E)				X
25. Check/adjust/report condition of all driving belts (E)	X	X	X	X
26. Check security of starter motor and alternator retaining bolts	X			
27. Check security of engine mountings	X			
28. Check/adjust carburetter settings (E)	X		X	X
29. Carburetter – overhaul – at 24,000 miles (E)				
30. Fuel filter – change (E)				X
31. Fuel system – check for leaks (E)	X			X
32. Lubricate accelerator linkage/pedal fulcrum and check operation	X		X	X
33. Check battery condition: clean and grease connections			X	X
34. Check/report for oil/fuel/fluid leaks (general) (E)	X	X	X	X
35. Check/report leaks from cooling and heater systems (E)	X		X	X
36. Evaporative and crankcase ventilations systems – check hoses and restrictors for blockage, security and deterioration (E)			X	X
37. Carbon canister – renew filter (E)				X
38. Carbon canister – renew 48,000 miles (E)				
39. Lubricate water pump				X

Operation Number Interval in miles x 1,000 Interval in Kilometres x 1,000	10.10.03 1 1·6	10.10.06 3 5	10.10.12 6 10	10.10.24 12 20
Operation Description				
UNDERBODY				
40. Check/top up level of gearbox and overdrive oil	X		X	X
41. Check/top up level of final drive unit oil	X		X	X
42. Lubricate lower steering swivel	X		X	X
43. Lubricate all grease points except hubs	X		X	X
44. Lubricate steering rack and pinion			X	X
45. Lubricate handbrake linkage and cable guides			X	X
46. Check transmission, engine, final drive, suspension and steering unit for oil leaks and report	X	X	X	X
47. Check visually brake, fuel and clutch pipes, hoses and unions for chafing, leaks and corrosion and report	X	X	X	X
48. Check/report exhaust system for leakage and security (E)		X	X	X
49. Check security of suspension fixings, tie-rod levers, steering unit attachments and steering universal joint coupling bolts	X			X
50. Check security of propeller shaft and drive shaft universal coupling bolts				X
51. Check security of sub-frame or body mountings	X			X
52. Check/report condition of steering unit/joints for security, backlash and gaiter condition	X	X	X	X
EXTERIOR				
53. Adjust front hubs				X
54. Check/adjust front and rear wheel alignment with tracking equipment	X			
55. Check/report front and rear wheel alignment with tracking equipment			X	X
56. Inspect brake pads for wear, and discs for condition		X	X	X
57. Inspect and report brake linings for wear and drums for condition				X
58. Check security of road wheel fastenings	X	X	X	X
59. *Check that tyres are in accordance with manufacturers specification		X	X	X
60. *Check visually and report depth of tread, cuts in tyre fabric, exposure of ply or cord structure, lumps or bulges	X	X	X	X
61. Check/adjust tyre pressures (including spare wheel)	X	X	X	X
62. Check/adjust headlamp alignment	X			
63. Check/report headlamp alignment		X	X	X
64. Check, if necessary replace windscreen wiper blades		X	X	X
65. Fuel tank filler cap – check seal for security (E)	X		X	X
INTERIOR				
66. Check brake pedal travel and hand brake operation adjust if necessary	X			
67. Check/report brake pedal travel and handbrake operation		X	X	X
68. Check operation of window controls, locks and bonnet release	X			
69. Check function of all electrical systems and windscreen washer	X	X	X	X
70. Lubricate clutch and brake pedal pivots			X	X
71. Lubricate all locks, door hinges, strikers and bonnet release	X		X	X
72. Check/report condition and security of seats and seat belts		X	X	X
73. Check/report rear view mirrors for looseness, cracks and crazing		X	X	X
ROAD TEST				
74. Road/roller test and report additional work required	X		X	X
75. Ensure cleanliness of controls, door handles, steering wheels etc	X	X	X	X

***Important** – If the tyres do not conform with legal requirements report to the owner.

Items marked (E) are particularly relevant to the emmission and evaporative control systems and must receive attention at the recommended intervals to keep these systems in good order.

The maintenance summary list on pages 10.00.02 and 10.00.03 gives details of mile and kilometer intervals for the following operations. The figure in parenthesis to the left of each heading refers to the item number on the summary list.

(1) Check/top up engine oil level

NOTE: Allow time for oil to drain back into sump after running engine.

Stand vehicle on level ground.

1. Withdraw dipstick, wipe it clean and replace in position.
2. Withdraw dipstick again and note oil level.
3. Wipe dipstick clean and replace in position.

If topping up is necessary:-

4. Remove oil filler cap.
5. Add recommended grade of oil, via filler cap, to bring level just below high mark on dipstick. **DO NOT OVERFILL**
6. Replace filler cap.
7. Allow time for added oil to drain into sump, then check final oil level using the procudure in 1 to 3 above.

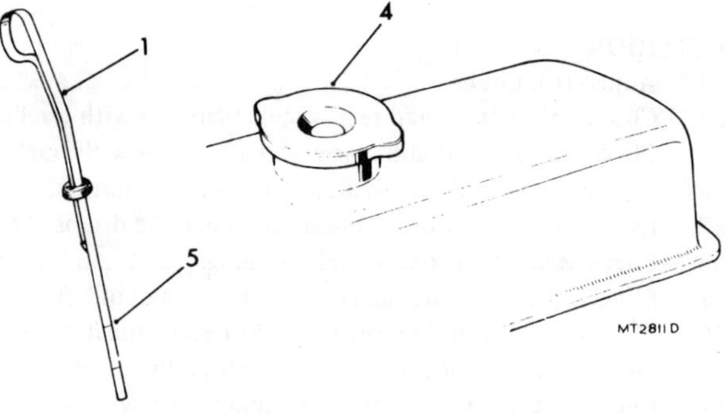

(2) Check/top up cooling system

WARNING: Do NOT remove cooling system filler caps or plugs when engine is hot.

1. Remove radiator expansion tank cap.
2. If necessary, top up expansion tank with soft water to maintain level at approximately half full.
3. Replace cap.

If the expansion tank is empty:-

4. Remove the cooling system filler cap.
5. Add soft water, via filler cap, until the system is full.
6. Replace filler cap.
7. Half fill expansion tank with soft water using the procedure in 1 to 3 above.
8. Run the engine until normal operating temperature is reached, allow engine to cool and re-check cooling system level.

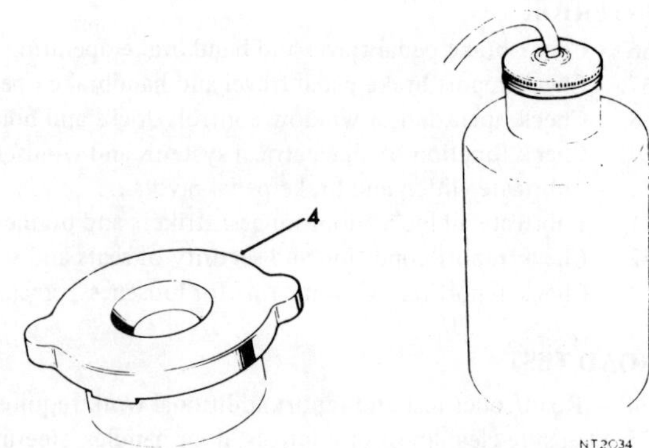

(3) Check/top up brake fluid reservoir

1. Check fluid level against mark on side of reservoir.

   If topping up is necessary:-

2. Wipe clean the reservoir cap and surrounding area.
3. Remove the reservoir cap.
4. Add fluid to bring level above danger mark on side of reservoir.

WARNING: **Use only new fluid of the correct specification. Do NOT use fluid of unknown origin, or fluid that has been exposed to the atmosphere, or fluid that has been discharged during bleeding operations.**

5. Replace reservoir cap.
6. Remove any spilled fluid with a clean cloth.

CAUTION: Paintwork can be damaged by direct contact with brake fluid.

(4) Check/top up clutch fluid reservoir

1. Wipe clean the reservoir cap and surrounding area.
2. Remove the reservoir cap.
3. Check fluid level against mark on side of reservoir.
4. If necessary, add fluid to bring level up to mark on side of reservoir.

WARNING: **Use only new fluid of the correct specification. Do NOT use fluid of unknown origin, or fluid that has been exposed to the atmosphere, or fluid that has been discharged during bleeding operations.**

5. Replace reservoir cap.
6. Remove any spilled fluid with a clean cloth.

CAUTION: Paintwork can be damaged by direct contact with clutch fluid.

(5) Check/top up windscreen washer fluid level

1. Check fluid level in translucent reservoir.

   If topping up is necessary:-

2. Wipe clean the reservoir cap and surrounding area.
3. Remove the reservoir cap.
4. Add soft water to bring level up to approximately 1 in (25·4 mm) from top of reservoir.
5. Replace reservoir cap.

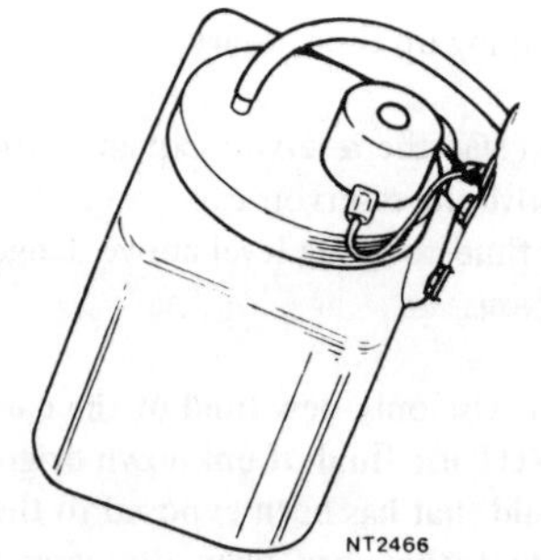

CAUTION: As a precaution against freezing conditions, fill the reservoir with a mixture of one part methylated spirits and two parts water.
Do NOT use glycol anti-freeze solutions in the washer reservoir, as these may discolour paintwork and damage wiper blades and sealing rubbers.

(6) Check/top up battery

NOTE: Alternative procedures are given for each of the two battery types that may be fitted.

1. Lift and tilt battery cover.
2. Check electrolyte level, which if correct should just cover the separators.

   If topping up is necessary:-

3. Add DISTILLED WATER until the filler tubes are full and the trough is just covered.
4. Replace battery cover.

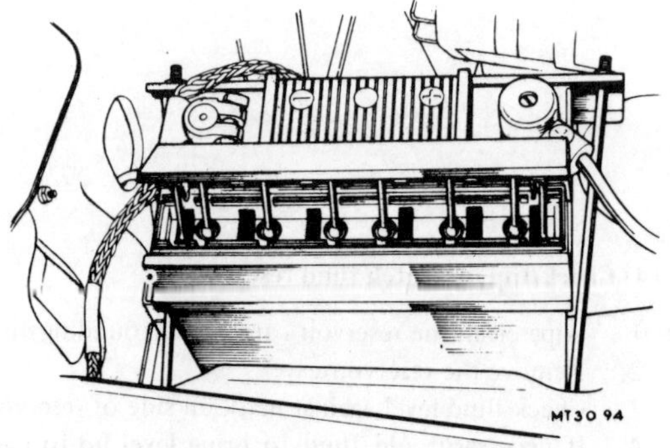

Alternatively:-

1. Remove battery filler plugs.
2. Check electrolyte level, which if correct should just cover the separators.

   If topping up is necessary:-

3. Add DISTILLED WATER until the separators are just covered. DO NOT OVERFILL.
4. Replace filler plugs.

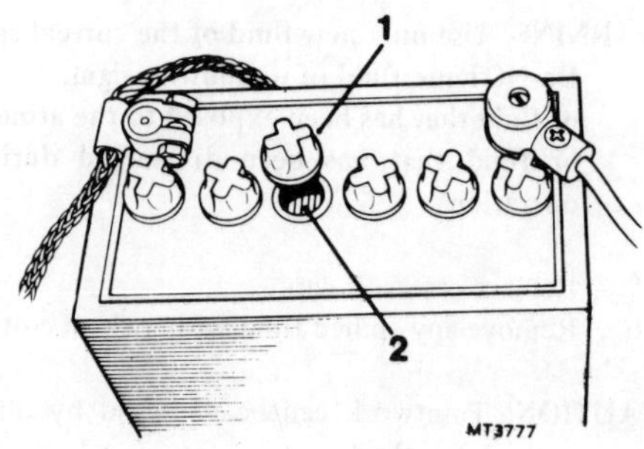

CAUTION: Paintwork can be damaged by direct contact with the base of filler plugs.

(7) **Check/top up carburetter piston(s) damper(s)**

1. Unscrew hexagon plug from top of carburetter.
2. Withdraw plug and damper assembly from carburetter.
3. Replace plug and damper assembly to check oil level, which if correct will offer resistance to the assembly when the bottom of the plug threads are ¼ in (6 mm) above the rim of the dashpot.
4. If necessary, again withdraw plug and damper assembly and add a recommended engine oil, using an oil can, until the oil level is correct.
5. Replace plug and damper assembly.
6. Screw hexagon plug firmly in position.

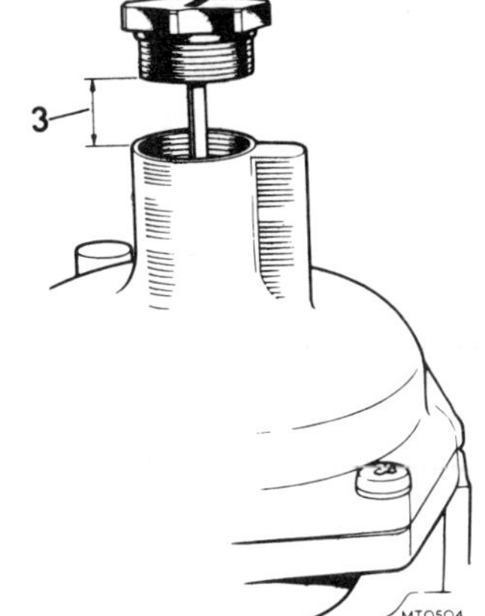

(8) **Drain engine oil and refill**

NOTE: This operation is best carried out when the engine is warm and with the vehicle standing level on a ramp or over a pit.

1. Wipe clean the engine drain plug and surrounding area.
2. Place a suitable receptical under the drain plug.
3. Unscrew the drain plug slowly until oil begins to escape.
4. When the rate of oil flow lessens, remove drain plug from sump and allow oil to drain completely.
5. Wipe clean the drain plug and replace it in sump.
6. Tighten drain plug to 20 to 25 lbf ft. (2·8 to 3·5 kgf m).
7. Remove oil filler cap.
8. Add a recommended engine oil, via filler cap, to bring level just below high mark on dipstick. **DO NOT OVERFILL.**
9. Replace oil filler cap.
10. Allow time for added oil to drain into sump, then check final oil level on dipstick.

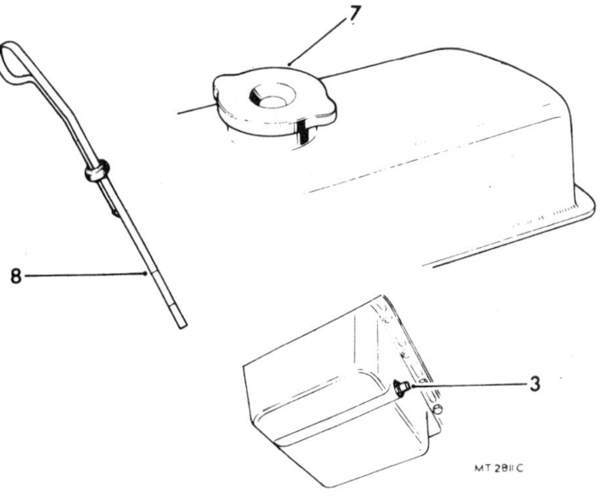

(9) Renew oil filter element

See 12.60.01 and 12.60.08.

(10) Clean fuel pump sediment bowl

See 19.45.05

(11) Lubricate distributor and check automatic advance

Lubricate distributor – See 86.35.18

Check automatic advance

1. Fit a strobe Timing Light in accordance with the Timing Light manufacturers instructions.
2. Disconnect vacuum pipe between distributor and induction side of engine.
3. Start engine.

Check centrifugal advance.

4. Using a second operator to vary engine speed, check apparent movement of timing marks under strobe light.
5. Reconnect vacuum pipe.

Check vacuum advance

6. Repeat the procedure in 4 above, comparing engine timing with and without vacuum pipe connected.
7. Stop engine.

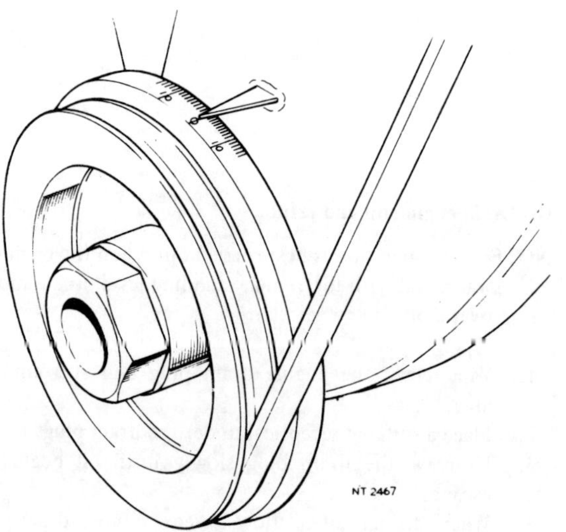

NOTE: If more accurate results are required electronic tuning equipment may be used in conjunction with the data on page 86.35.00. This is extra to normal service requirements.

(12) Check/adjust/report condition of distributor points

See 86.35.14.

(13) Renew distributor points

See 86.35.13

(14) Check/adjust ignition timing

See 86.35.16

(15) Check/report ignition wiring for fraying, chaffing and deterioration

Low tension circuit.

1. Check exposed wiring between coil and ignition switch.
2. Check ignition coil connections.
3. Check wiring between coil and distributor.
4. Check distributor external connections.
5. Remove distributor cap and check internal wiring.
6. Check internal distributor connections.
7. Replace distributor cap.

High tension circuit.

8. Check lead between coil and distributor.
9. For each sparking plug in turn:–
   Check lead between plug and distributor.
10. Check high tension lead connections.
11. Report wiring condition.

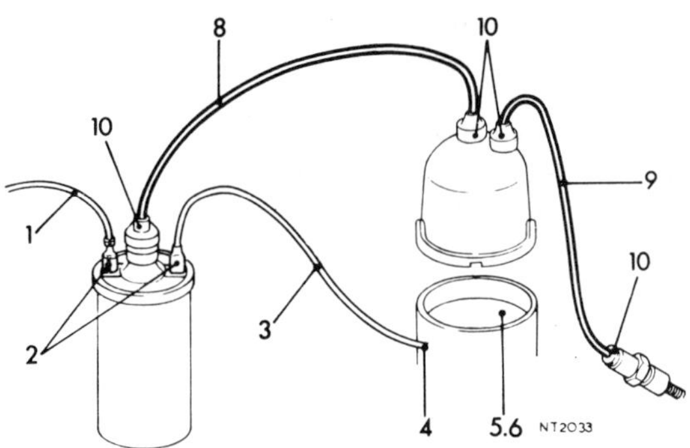

(16) Check condensor and coil for breakdown on oscilascope tune

Using proprietory electronic testing equipment

1. Check distributor condensor performance.
2. Check ignition coil performance.

(17) **Clean/adjust sparking plugs**

For each sparking plug in turn

1. Remove ignition high tension lead from plug.
2. Unscrew plug from engine using a special plug spanner or a box type spanner.
3. Wipe clean ceramic body of plug.
4. Visually check plug body for cracks, and renew plug if cracks are present.
5. Unscrew end terminal cap from plug.
6. Clean plug terminal threads with a wire brush.
7. Clean cap threads using a low pressure air line.
8. Screw end terminal cap firmly into position on plug.
9. Clean electrode area and plug threads with a wire brush or sand blasting machine.
10. Visually check electrode surfaces for damage, and renew plug if damage is present.
11. Check electrode gap, which if correct will just allow a 0·025 in (0·64 mm) feeler gauge to slide slowly between the electrodes under light pressure.

If adjustment is necessary.

12. *(a)* Using a suitable tool, carefully move the side electrode.
    (b) Recheck the gap and repeat this procedure until the gap is correct.
13. Check sealing washer for cracks and distortion, and renew washer if necessary.
14. Refit sparking plug to engine.
15. Tighten plug to 14 to 20 lbf ft (1·9 to 2·8 kgf m).
16. Refit high tension lead to plug.

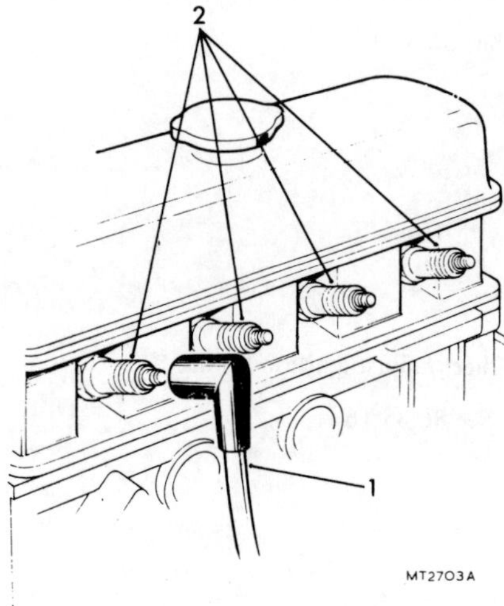

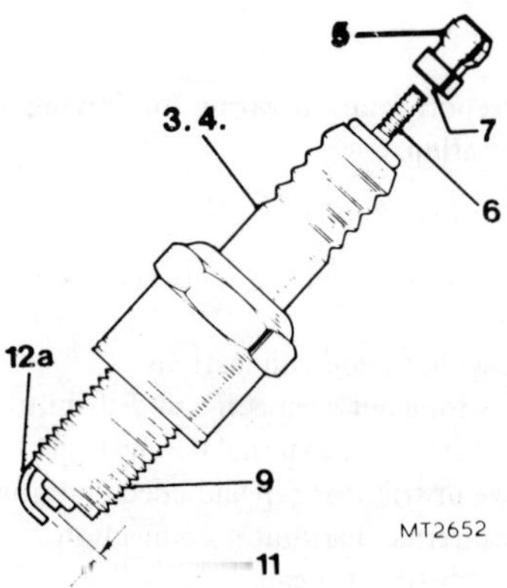

(18) **Renew sparking plugs**

For each sparking plug in turn

1. Remove ignition high tension lead from plug.
2. Unscrew plug from engine using a special plug spanner or a box type spanner.
3. Discard plug.
4. Visually check new plug for damage to body and electrodes, discard plug if damage is present.
5. Check electrode gap on new plug, which if correct will just allow a 0·025 in (0·64 mm) feeler gauge to slide slowly between the electrodes under light pressure.

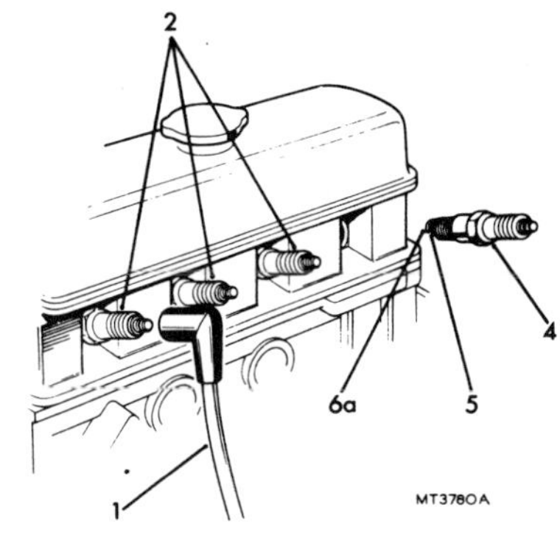

If adjustment is necessary.

6. *(a)* Using a suitable tool, carefully move the side electrode.
   (b) Recheck the gap and repeat this procedure until the gap is correct.
7. Check sealing washer for cracks and distortion, and renew washer if necessary.
8. Fit new sparking plug to engine.
9. Tighten plug to 14 to 20 lbf ft (1·9 to 2·8 kgf m).
10. Refit high tension lead to plug.

(19) **Check/adjust torque of cylinder head nuts/bolts**

1. Remove rocker cover – See 12.29.42.
2. Using the sequence shown, tighten cylinder head nuts to 60 to 80 lbf ft (8·3 to 11·1 kgf m).
3. Check/adjust valve rocker clearances – See 12.29.48.
4. Check rocker cover gasket for damage, and renew if necessary.
5. Refit rocker cover – See 12.29.42.
6. With gears in neutral, handbrake on, start engine and check for leaks from rocker cover gasket.

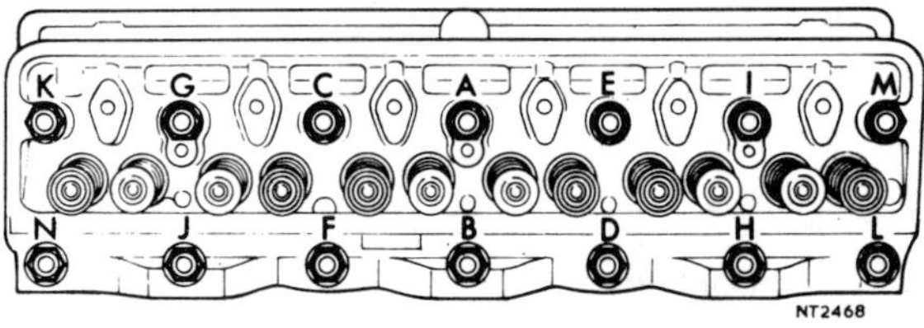

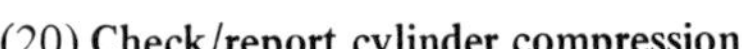

(20) **Check/report cylinder compression**

See 12.25.01

(21) **Check/adjust valve rocker clearances**

See 12.29.48

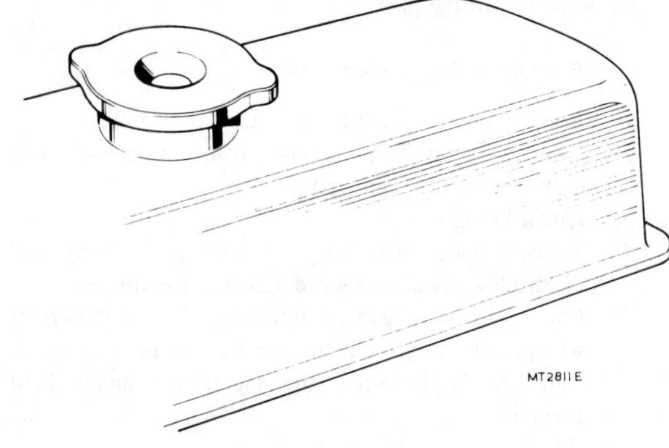

(22) Clean engine oil filler cap

1. Remove filler cap.
2. Clean cap with clean petrol.
3. Allow to dry.
4. Refit filler cap.

(23) Clean carburetter air cleaner elements

See 19.10.08

(24) Renew carburetter air cleaner elements

See 19.10.08

(25) Check/adjust/report condition of driving belts

1. Check and adjust – See 26.20.01
2. Report condition where belt is visibly
   (a) worn or
   (b) damaged.

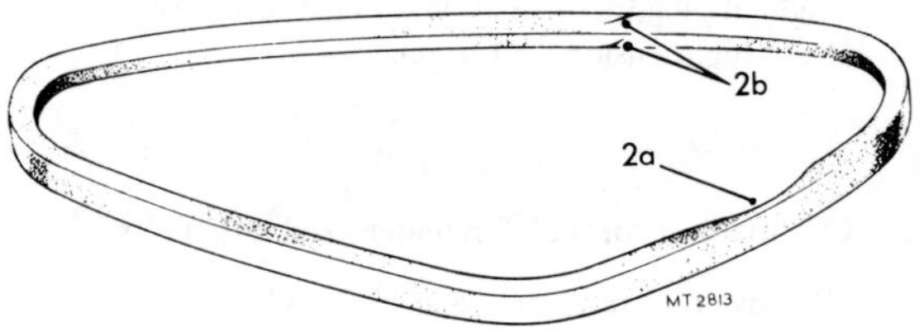

(26) Check security of starter motor and alternator retaining bolts

1. Check security of starter motor retaining bolts, which if correct should be tightened to 26 to 34 lbf ft (3·6 to 4·7 kgf m).
2. Check security of alternator to adjusting link bolt, which if correct should be tightened to 15 to 20 lbf ft (2·1 to 2·8 kgf m).
3. Check security of alternator mounting bracket bolt, which if correct should be tightened to 16 to 22 lbf ft (2·2 to 3·0 kgf m).

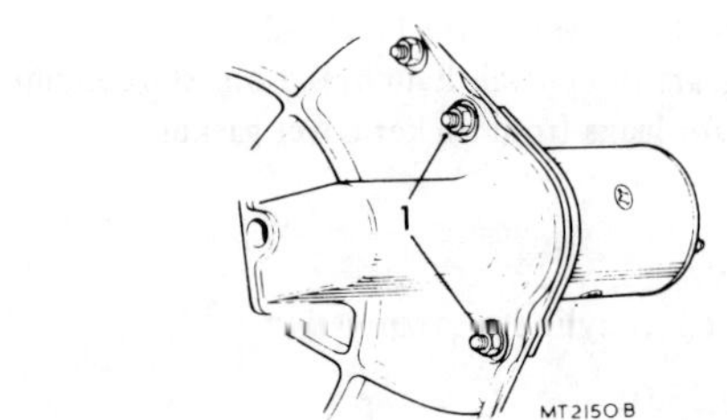

(27) Check security of engine mountings

1. Check security of front engine mountings, which if correct should be tightened to 24 to 32 lbf ft (3·3 to 4·4 kgf m).
2. Check security of rear engine mountings, which if correct should be tightened to 50 to 60 lbf ft (6·9 to 9·0 kgf m). Mounting rubber to gearbox AND 38 to 46 lbf ft (5·2 to 6·4 kgf m) mounting rubber to cross member.

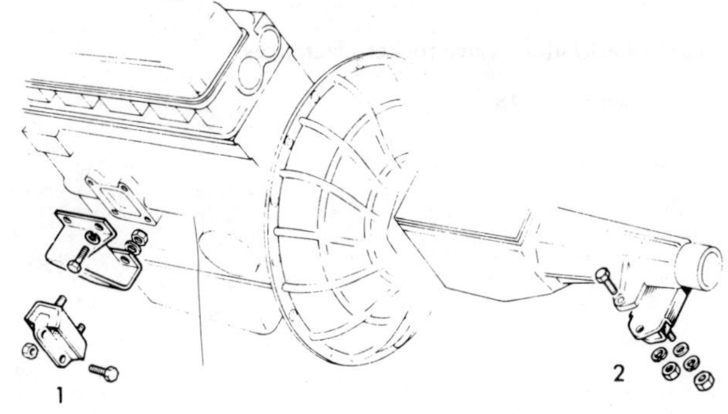

(28) **Check/adjust carburetter settings**

See 19.15.02

(29) **Overhaul carburetter**

See 19.15.18.

(30) **Change fuel filter**

See 19.25.01

(31) **Check fuel system for leaks**

1. Check for leaks from fuel system connections.
2. Check fuel pipes for fractures and damage.
3. Check for leaks from fuel tank(s), pump and carburetter(s)/metering distributor.
   On vehicles fitted with an evaporative control system, additional checks are given under 17.15.01.

(32) **Lubricate accelerator linkage/pedal fulcrum and check operation**

1. Lubricate accelerator linkage on carburetter(s)/metering distributor, using an oil can.
2. Wipe away surplus oil from linkage.
3. Check for roughness in linkage operation.
4. Lubricate accelerator pedal fulcrum, using an oil can.
5. Wipe away surplus oil from pedal fulcrum.

CAUTION: Surplus oil on the pedal fulcrum can cause staining of the carpet.

6. Check carburetter/metering distributor throttle response to initial movement of the accelerator pedal.

   If adjustment is necessary – see 19.20.05

7. Check carburetter/metering distributor throttle position with accelerator pedal fully depressed.

   If adjustment is necessary – See 19.20.05.

(33) **Check battery condition: clean and grease connections**

With battery in location

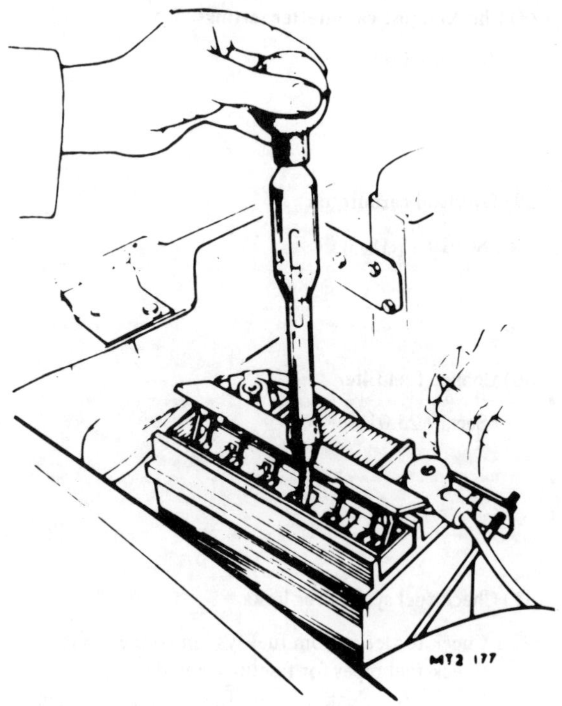

1. Check battery and surrounding area for corrosion from battery chemicals.
2. Clean off any corrosion found.
3. Check visually for cracks in battery case.
4. Report any case cracks found.
5. Check security of terminal connections.
6. Coat terminals with petroleum jelly.

For each cell in turn:-

7. Check electrolyte specific gravity, using an hydrometer, which if correct will approximate to the tabled readings below.

NOTE *(a)* Do NOT check S.G. immediately after adding distilled water as a false reading may be obtained.
(b) S.G. readings approximately equal for each cell indicate a battery in good condition. Conversely, if one or more cells show a reading lower than the others the battery is approaching the end of its useful life.

Charge condition of cell – temperate climate

Ambient Temperature °C	Specific Gravity of Electrolyte		
	Charged	**Half-Charged**	**Discharged**
5	1·287	1·207	1·117
15	1·280	1·200	1·110
25	1·273	1·193	1·103
35	1·226	1·186	1·096

Charge condition of cell – tropical climate

Ambient Temperature °C	Charged	Half-Charged	Discharged
15	1·250	1·180	1·100
25	1·243	1·173	1·093
35	1·236	1·166	1·086
52	1·224	1·154	1·074

8. Check voltage, using a heavy discharge tester, which if correct will give approximately equal readings for each cell.
CAUTION: This check should **NOT** be made on a battery in a low state of charge as shown by procedure 7 as damage to the battery can result.

NOTE*(a)*Before making this check on a battery that has just completed an operational journey, the headlamps should be switched on for 2 or 3 minutes to remove any surface charge.*(b)* Voltage readings approximately equal for each cell indicate a battery in good condition. Conversely, if one or more cells show a reading lower than the others, or a reading that falls during the test, the battery is approaching the end of its useful life.

(34) **Check/report oil/fuel/fluid leaks**

1. Check for oil leaks from engine and transmission.
2. Check for fuel leaks from pump, carburetter/metering distributor, pipes, joints and unions.
3. Check for fluid leaks from brake master cylinder, pipes, joints and unions.
4. Check for fluid leaks from clutch master cylinder, pipes, joints and unions.
5. Report any leaks found.

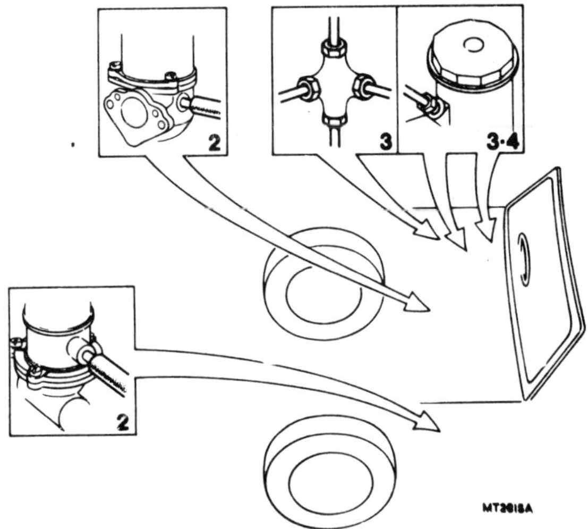

(35) **Check/report leaks from cooling and heater systems.**

1. Check for leaks from engine and radiator drain taps/plugs, (where fitted).
2. Check for leaks from water hose joints.
3. Check for leaks from water hoses through damage or porosity.
4. Check for leaks from water pump, thermostat housing, radiator and heater unit.
5. Report any leaks found.

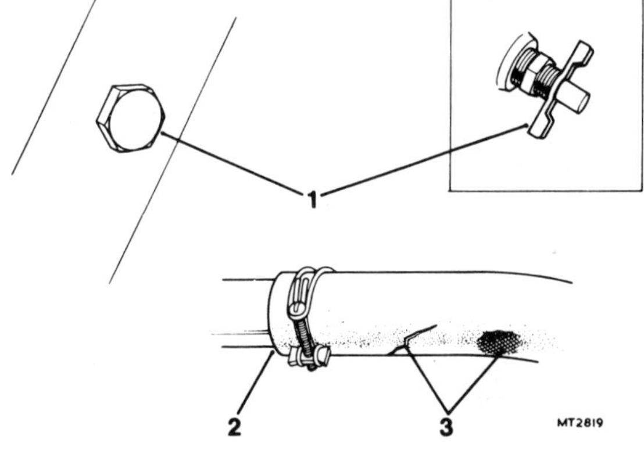

(36) **Evaporative and crankcase ventilation systems-check hoses and restrictors for blockage, security and deterioration.**

See 17.15.01 and 17.15.36

(37) **Carbon canister –renew filter**

See 17.15.07

(38) **Carbon canister – renew at 48,000 miles**

See 17.15.13.

(39) **Lubricate water pump**

1. Wipe clean sealing plug and surrounding area.
2. Remove plug and fit a suitable grease nipple
3. Apply a grease gun until grease exudes from the pressure release hole in the side of the pump.
4. Remove grease nipple and replace blanking plug.
5. Wipe away surplus grease.

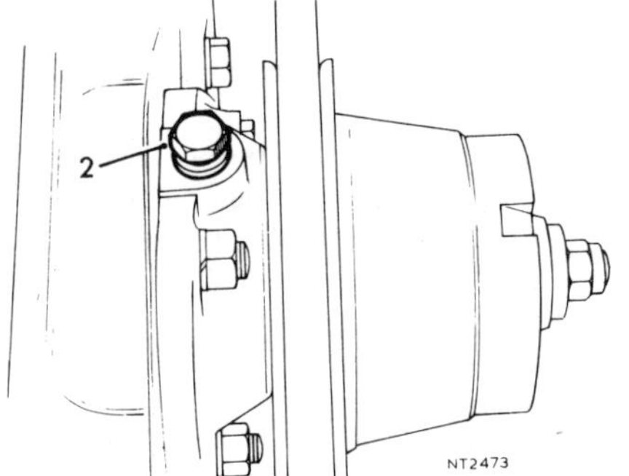

NOTE: OPERATIONS 40 to 52 ARE BEST CARRIED OUT WITH THE CAR ON A RAMP OR OVER A PIT.

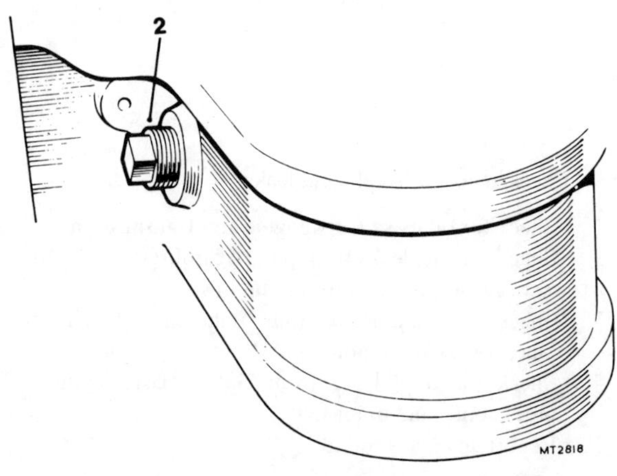

(40) Check/top up level of gearbox and overdrive oil

With vehicle standing level

1. Wipe clean gearbox filler plug and surrounding area.
2. Remove filler plug.
3. Add new oil of the recommended grade, via the filler plug hole, until the oil level reaches the bottom of the hole.
4. Allow surplus oil to drain.
5. Replace filler plug.
6. Tighten plug to 20 to 25 lbf ft (2·8 to 3·5 kgf m).
7. Wipe away surplus oil.

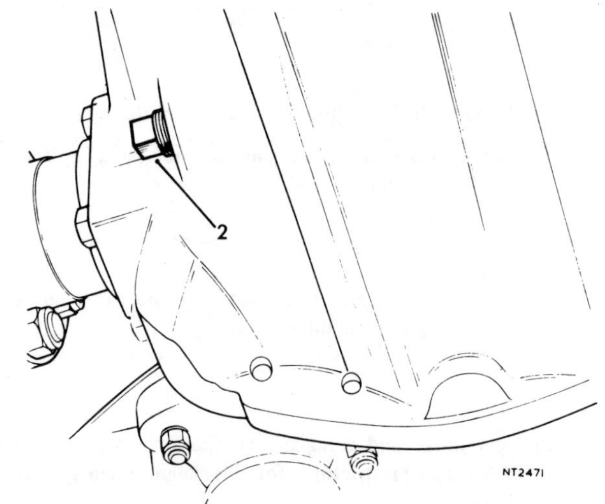

(41) Check/top up level of final drive unit oil

With vehicle standing level

1. Wipe clean final drive unit filler plug and surrounding area.
2. Remove filler plug.
3. Add new oil of the recommended grade, via the filler plug hole, until the oil level reaches the bottom of the hole.
4. Allow surplus oil to drain.
5. Replace filler plug.
6. Tighten plug to 20 to 25 lbf ft (2·8 to 3·5 kgf m).
7. Wipe away surplus oil.

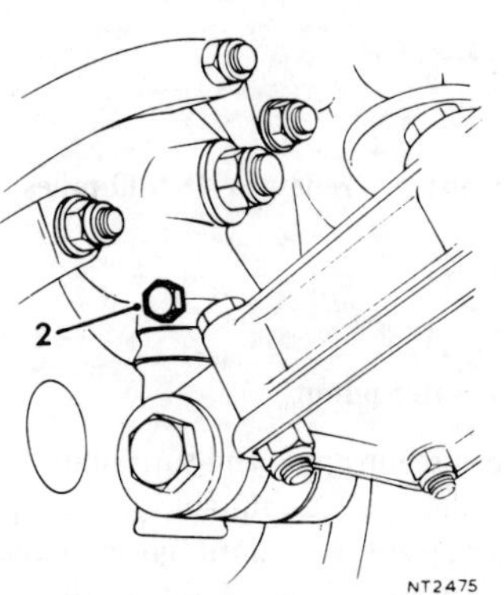

(42) Lubricate lower steering swivel

WARNING: OIL must be used for the operation. Do NOT use grease.

1. Wipe clean the plug and surrounding area.
2. Remove the plug.
3. Fit a suitable grease nipple to the plug hole.
4. Using a grease gun, **CHARGED WITH A RECOMMENDED OIL,** lubricate the lower steering swivel, via the grease nipple, until oil exudes from the bearing.
5. Remove grease nipple
6. Refit plug.
7. Wipe away surplus oil.

(43) Lubricate all grease points except hubs

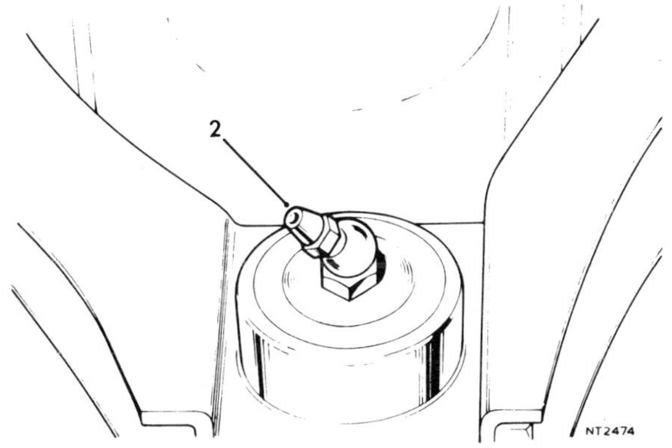

Suspension upper ball joint

1. Wipe clean the sealing plug and surrounding area
2. Remove plug and fit a suitable grease nipple.
3. Apply a grease gun until grease exudes from the joint.
4. Remove grease nipple and replace sealing plug.
5. Wipe away surplus grease.

Inner drive shaft universal joint

1. Wipe clean the grease nipple and surrounding area.
2. Apply a grease gun and give **5 STROKES ONLY**.
3. Wipe away surplus grease.

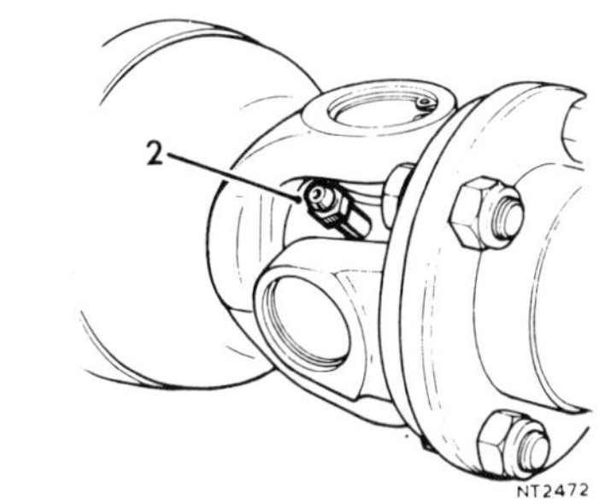

(44) Lubricate steering rack and pinion

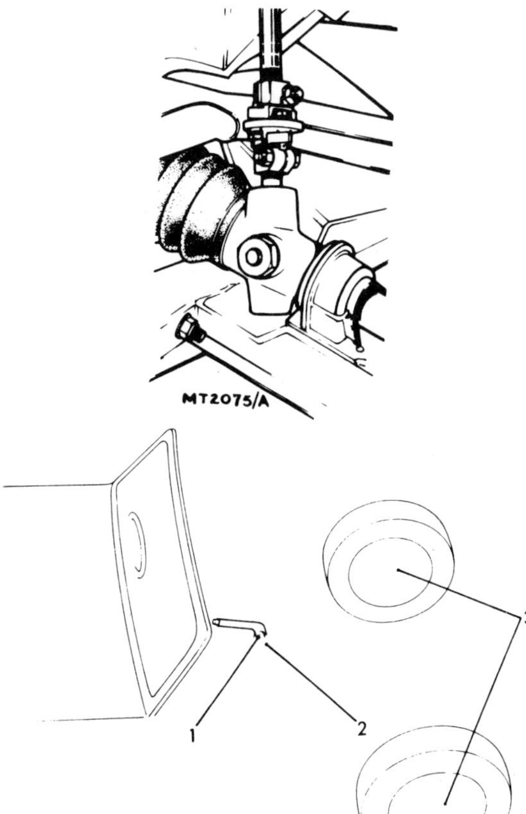

1. Wipe clean the plug and surrounding area.
2. Remove the plug.
3. Fit a suitable grease nipple to the plug hole.
4. Apply a grease gun to nipple and stroke for 5 times only.

   CAUTION: Over greasing can cause damage to the rubber bellows.

5. Remove grease nipple.
6. Refit plug.
7. Wipe away surplus grease.

(45) Lubricate handbrake linkage and cables

1. Lubricate handbrake pivot.
2. Smear grease around handbrake lever cable connections, working it well into the clevis pin.
3. Smear grease around brake drum cable connections, working it well into the clevis pin.
4. Grease exposed sections of inner cable to resist corrosion.

(46) Check engine, transmission, final drive, suspension and steering unit for oil leaks and report.

(47) Check visually brake, fuel and clutch pipes, hoses and unions for chaffing leaks and corrosion and report.

Check visually

1. Brake and clutch pipes.
2. Brake and clutch hoses.
3. Brake and clutch pipe and hose unions.
4. Fuel pipes.
5. Fuel pipe unions.

for chaffing leaks and corrosion.

6. Report any defects found.

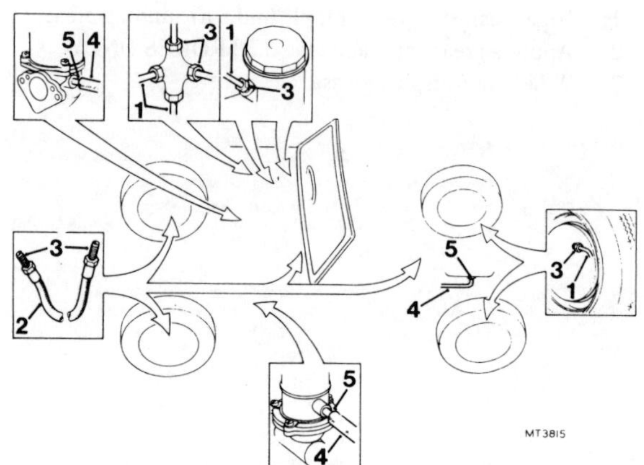

(48) Check/report exhaust system for leakage and security

1. Place car on ramp or over a pit.
2. Check security of exhaust pipe to manifold nuts, which if correct should be tightened to 20 to 25 lbf ft (2·8 to 3·5 kgf m).
3. Check security of exhaust pipe joint clips.
4. Check security of exhaust system mounting bolts.
5. Using a second operator, run engine at fast idle speed.
6. Check exhaust system joints for leaks.
7. Check exhaust pipes for leaks arising from damage or deterioration.
8. Check exhaust silencers for leaks arising from damage or deterioration.
9. Stop engine.
10. Report any defects found.

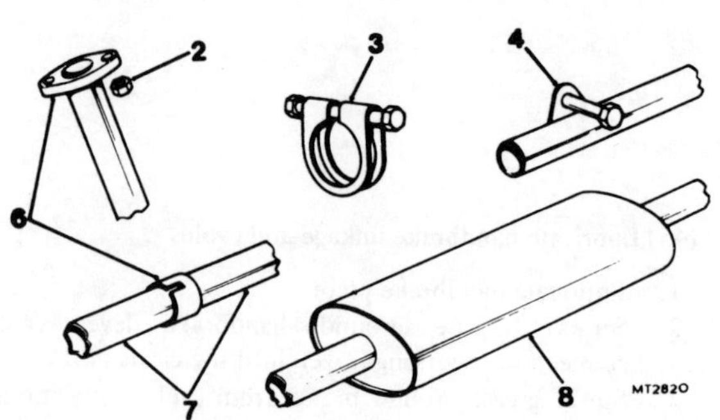

(49) Check security of suspension fixings, tie-rod levers, steering unit attachment and steering universal joint coupling bolts.

Check security of

1. Suspension fixings,
2. Tie-rod levers,
3. Steering unit attachment,
4. Steering universal joint coupling bolts.

(50) Check security of propeller shaft and drive shaft universal coupling bolts

1. Check security of propeller shaft coupling bolts, which if correct should be tightened to 26 to 34 lbf ft (3·6 to 4·7 kgf m).
2. Check security of half shaft to final drive unit coupling bolts, which if correct should be tightened to 26 to 34 lbf ft (3·6 to 4·7 kgf m).

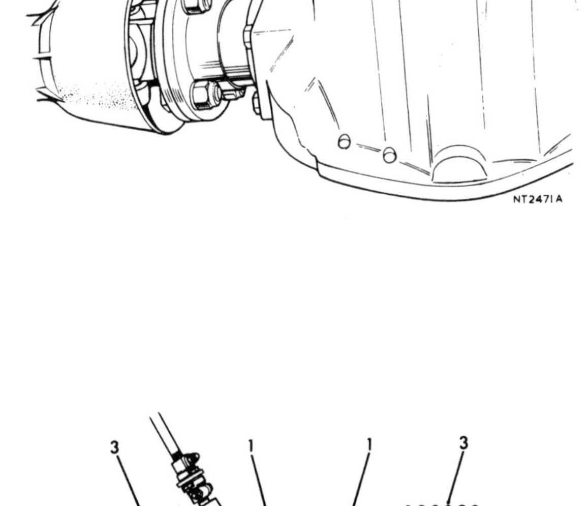

(51) Check security of sub-frame or body mountings

Using page 06 as a guide

1. Check security of sub-frame mounting bolts/nuts.

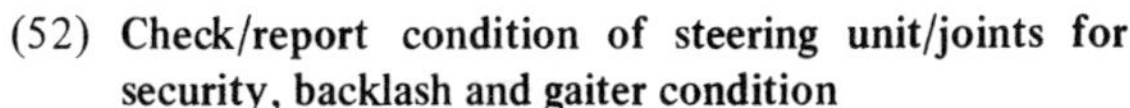

(52) Check/report condition of steering unit/joints for security, backlash and gaiter condition

1. Check security of steering unit mounting and steering joints, using page 06 as a guide.
2. Check steering for backlash.
3. Check condition of steering gaiters.
4. Report any defects found.

(53) Adjust front hubs

See 60.25.13

(54)(55) Check/adjust/report front and rear wheel alignment with tracking equipment.

Front wheel alignment – See 57.65.01

Rear wheel alignment See 64.25.17

(56) Inspect brake pads for wear and discs for condition

Front brakes

1. Jack up front of car and place safely on stands.
2. Remove front brake pads – See 70.40.02

   CAUTION: Do NOT depress the brake pedal while pads are removed.
3. Report pad condition if the friction lining has been reduced to 0·125 inch (3 mm) or if there is not sufficient material to provide a thickness of 0·125 in (3 mm) at the completion of a further 3,000 miles (5,000 km) motoring.
4. Check brake discs for excessive scoring and report this if present.
5. Check brake discs for run out and report this if it exceeds 0·007 in (0·178 mm).
6. Refit front brake pads – See 70.40.02
7. Lower car off stands.

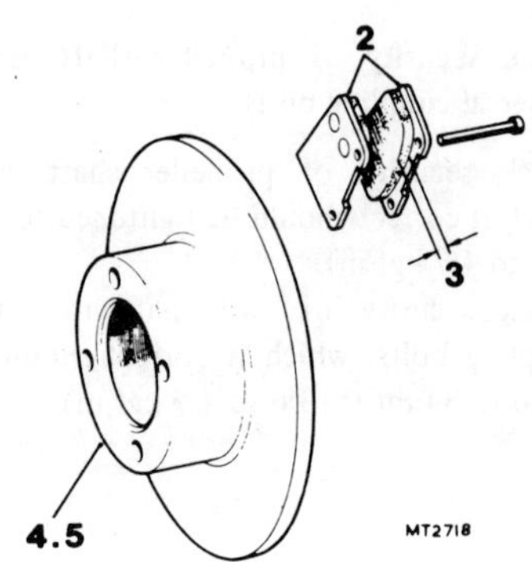

(57) Inspect and report brake linings for wear and drums for condition

1. Jack up car and place safely on stands.
2. Remove road wheel – See 74.20.01.
3. Remove brake drum – See 70.10.02 (front) or 70.10.03 (rear).
4. Check brake linings for wear and report if linings are excessively worn.
5. Check brake linings for damage and contamination by oil or grease and report if linings are damaged or contaminated.
6. Check brake drums for wear, scoring or other damage and report if drums are excessively worn, scored or damaged.
7. Remove dust, oil and grease from brake drum and backplate.
8. Refit brake drum – See 70.10.02 (front) or 70.10.03 (rear).
9. Refit road wheel – See 74.20.01.
10. Lower car off stands.

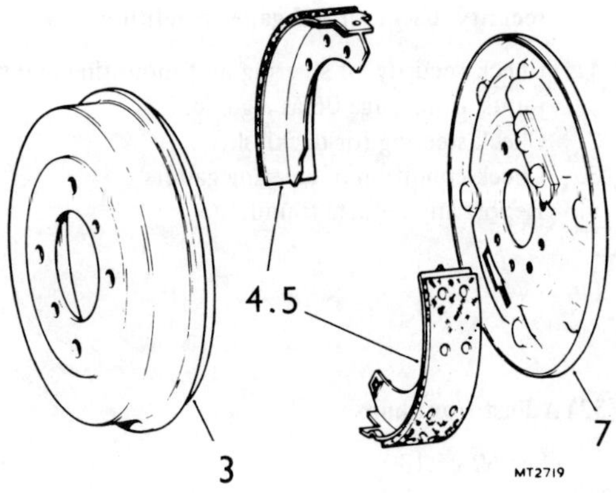

(58) Check security of road wheel fastenings.

Disc Wheels

For each wheel in turn:-

1. Check tightness of road wheel securing nuts, which if correct should be tightened to 60 to 80 lbf ft (8·3 to 11·1 kgf m).

Wire Wheels

For each wheel in turn

1. Visually check that adaptor is fitted on the correct side.
2. Remove road wheel – See 74.20.01.
3. Check tightness of the adaptor securing nuts, which if correct should be tightened to 55 to 65 lbf ft (7·6 to 9·0 kgf m).
4. Replace road wheel – See 74.20.01 ensuring that the centre nut is correctly secured.

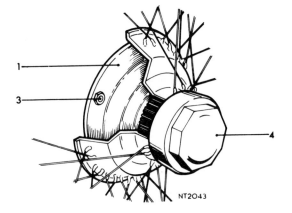

(59) Check that tyres are in accordance with manufacturers specification

For each road wheel and spare wheel:-

1. Check that tyres are in accordance with vehicle manufacturers recommendations for type and size and report any deviation.
2. Check for mixing of cross ply and radial ply tyres and report if both types are present on the vehicle (including spare wheel).

WARNING: **It is illegal in the U.K. and highly dangerous to mix cross ply and radial ply tyres on the same axle or to fit radial ply tyres to the front wheels only.**

(60) Check visually and report depth of tread, cuts in tyre fabric, exposure of ply or cord structure, lumps or bulges

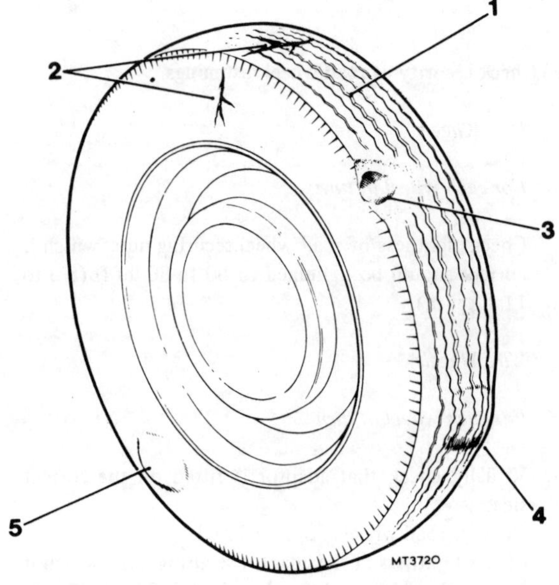

For each road wheel and spare wheel:-

1. Check tread depth, which if correct should show 1 mm (0·039 in) of tread (excluding wear bars) over three quarters of the breadth for the entire circumference of the tyre.

WARNING: It is illegal in the U.K. to use a car of this type fitted with tyres that have a tread depth below this minimum or tyres on which the tread is worn level with the wear indicator bars.

Check for

2. Cuts in the tyre fabric.
3. Exposure of ply or cord structure.
4. Lumps or bulges on tyre circumference.
5. Lumps, bulges or other damage on tyre walls.

WARNING: It is illegal in the U.K. to use a car fitted with tyres in a damaged condition.

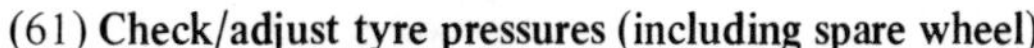

(61) Check/adjust tyre pressures (including spare wheel)

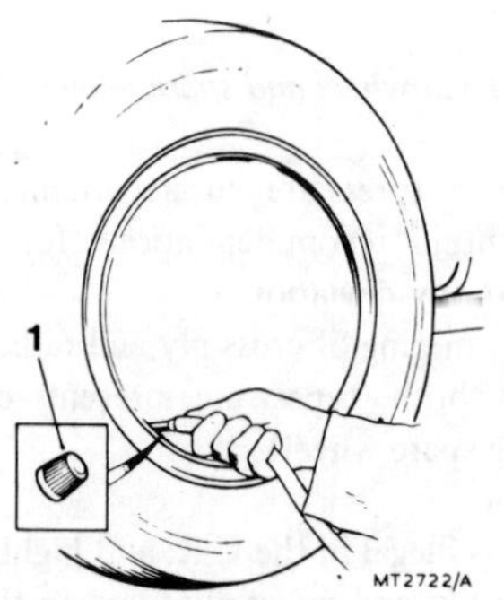

With all tyres at ambient temperature:-

1. Remove protective dust cap.
2. Using a tyre pressure gauge, tested for accuracy, check tyre pressure.

   Recommended tyre pressures for the different tyre types that may be fitted are shown on page 04-3

3. Adjust tyre pressure as necessary.
4. Replace dust cap or renew if missing.

WARNING: It is illegal in the U.K. to use a car with the tyres inflated to a pressure that is not suitable for the use to which the vehicle is put.

(62)(63) Check/adjust/report headlamp alignment

See 86.40.18

(64) Check, if necessary replace windscreen wiper blades

1. Examine each wiper blade in turn for damage.
2. With wiper blades in position and windscreen wet, operate wiper motor.
3. Check wiper blade operation for smearing and adequate removal of dirt.
4. Stop wiper motor.
5. If the checks in procedures 1 and 3 are not satisfactory, replace one or both wiper blades as necessary – See 84.15.05.

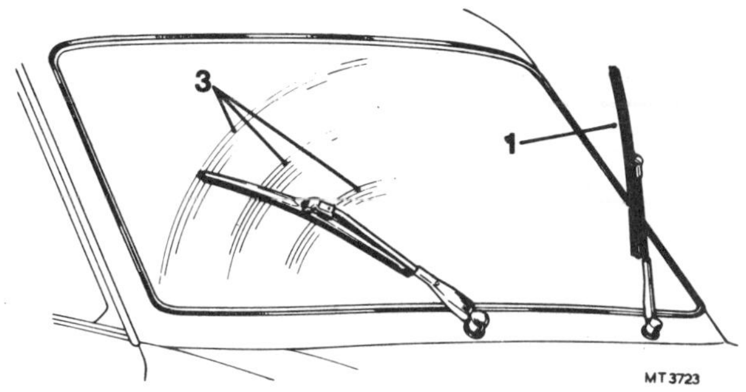

(65) Fuel tank filler cap – check seal for security

See 17.15.01

(66) Check brake pedal travel and handbrake operation, adjust if necessary.

1. With handbrake in 'off' position, check brake pedal for sponginess and excessive travel.
2. If brake pedal has spongy operation, bleed and adjust brakes – See 70.25.01.
3. If brake pedal travel is excessive, adjust brakes – See 70.25.03.
4. With foot clear of brake pedal, check handbrake for excessive travel.
5. If handbrake travel is excessive, adjust handbrake – See 70.35.10.

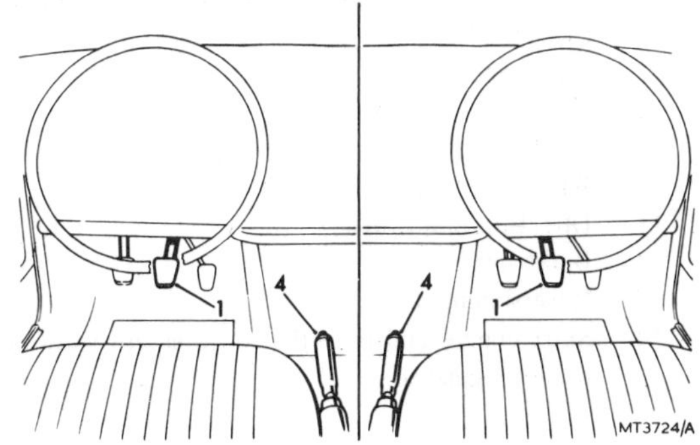

(67) Check/report brake pedal travel and handbrake operation.

1. With handbrake in 'off' position, check brake pedal for spongy operation and excessive travel.
2. Report brake pedal condition.
3. With foot clear of brake pedal, check handbrake for excessive travel.
4. Report handbrake operation.

(68) Check operation of window controls, locks and bonnet release.

Check operation of:-

1. Window raising and lowering controls.
2. Internal door locks.
3. External door locks.
4. Luggage compartment lock.
5. Bonnet release controls.
6. Report any defects found.

(69) Check function of all electrical systems and windscreen washer.

In sequence, check operation of:-

1. Side, tail and headlamps (including headlamp dip/main beam and 'flash' controls).
2. Instrument panel illumination.
3. Interior light.
4. Horn(s).
5. Auxiliary lights.

With ignition circuits energised, check operation of:

6. All warning lights (including 'hazard' warning lights if fitted).
7. Fuel level indicator.
8. Heater blower motor.
9. Windscreen washers.
10. Windscreen wipers.
11. Direction indicators.
12. Brake lights.
13. Reversing lights.
14. Start engine and note that oil pressure warning light has extinguished.

Check operation of:-

15. Charging system warning light in relation to engine speed.
16. Temperature indicator.
17. Radio (if fitted),
18. Switch off engine and return ignition switch to the auxiliary position, then recheck the function of any fitted accessories e.g. a radio, that are supplied with power from this switch position.
19. Report any defects found.

(70) Lubricate clutch and brake pedal pivots.

Using an oil can, lubricate

1. Clutch pedal pivot.
2. Brake pedal pivot.
3. Wipe away surplus oil to prevent staining the carpet.

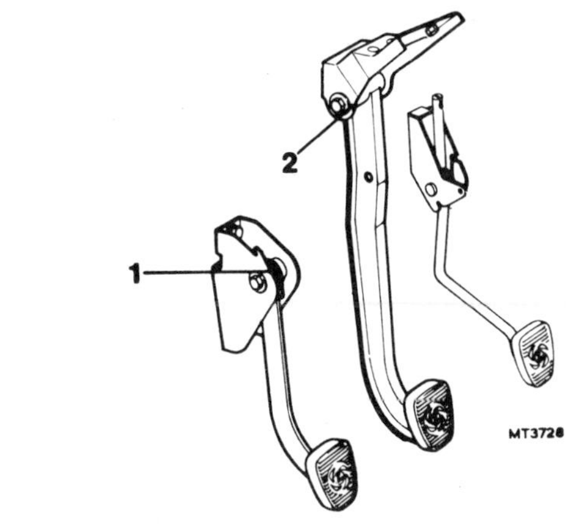

(71) Lubricate all locks, door hinges, strikers and bonnet release.

Using an oil can, lubricate

1. Door locks.
2. Door hinges.
3. Door strikers.
4. Luggage compartment lock.
5. Bonnet release mechanism.
6. Wipe away surplus oil.

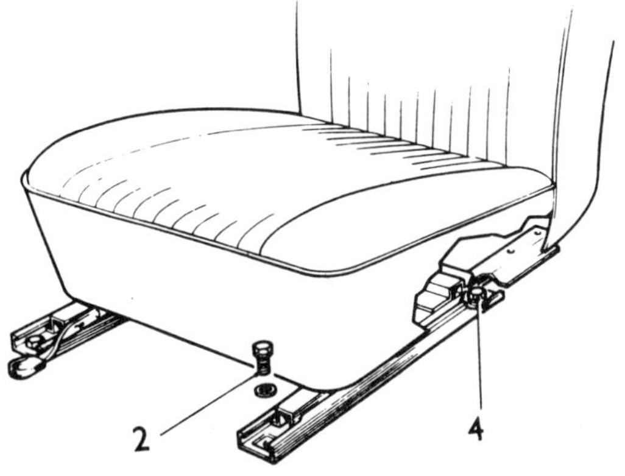

MT2053

(72) Check/report condition and security of seats and seat belts.

1. Move driver's seat back to its fullest extent.
2. Check security of front bolts holding seat runner to floor.
3. Move driver's seat forward to its fullest extent.
4. Check security of rear bolts holding seat runner to floor.
5. With seat in middle position, check security of seat in runner.
6. Repeat the procedure in 1 to 5 for passenger seat.
7. Check seat tipping and lock mechanisms.
8. Check seat belts for wear and damage.
9. Check seat belt connections for wear and damage.
10. Check security of seat belt anchorage bolts, which if correct should be tightened to 24 to 32 lbf ft (3·3 to 4·4 kgf m).
11. Report any defects found.

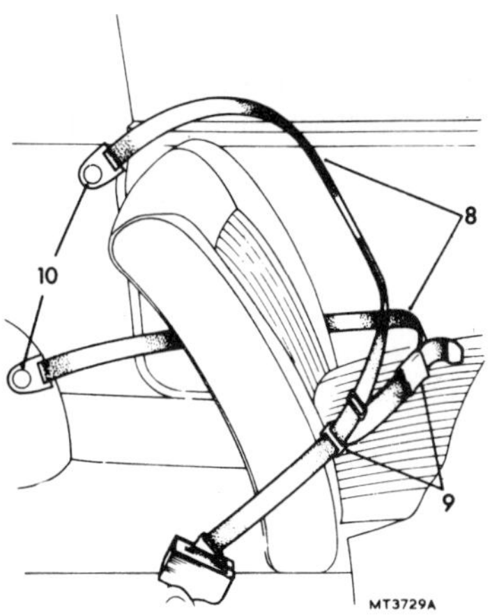

(73) Check/report rear view mirrors for looseness, cracks and crazing.

1. Check interior mirror for looseness, cracks and crazing.
2. Check external mirrors (when fitted) for looseness, cracks and crazing.
3. Report on condition of mirrors.

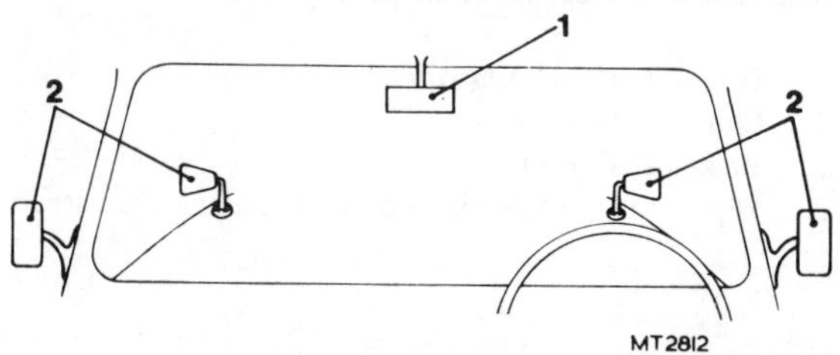

(74) Road/Roller test and report additional work required

In addition to the general road test, pay particular attention to:-

1. The efficiency and function of the footbrake and handbrake.
2. The function of the steering mechanism.
3. The function of the speedometer.

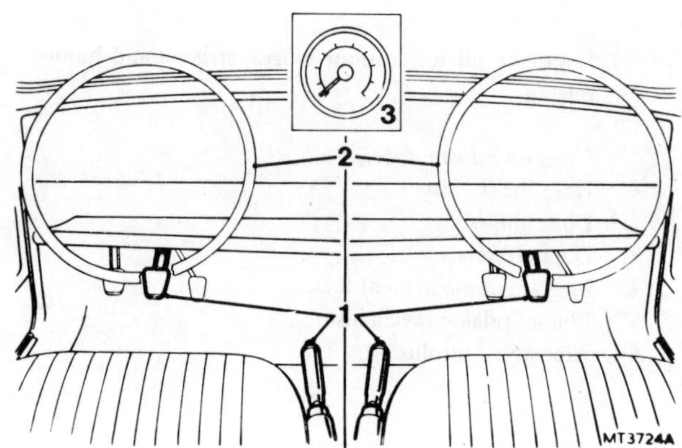

(75) Ensure cleanliness of controls, door handles, steering wheel etc.

1. Check steering wheel, gear lever, bonnet release control and fascia controls etc. for dirt and damage attributable to the service just completed.
2. Check door trims, locks and window controls for dirt and damage attributable to the service just completed.
3. Check seats, carpets and pedal rubbers for dirt and damage attributable to the service just completed.

ENGINE OPERATIONS

Continued

Continued

DISTRIBUTOR DRIVE SHAFT – CARBURETTER ENGINE

– Remove and refit **12.10.22**

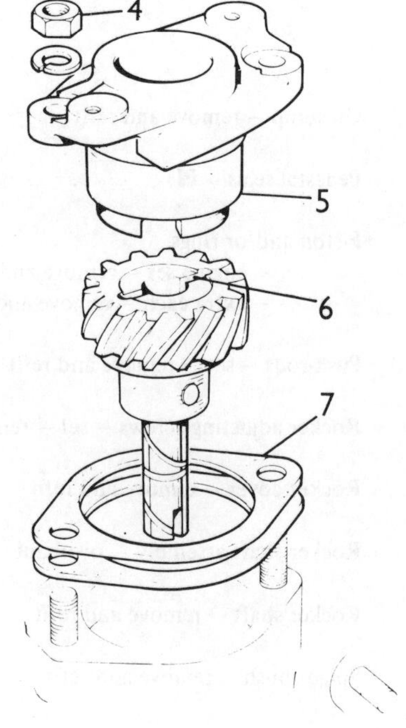

Removing

1. Isolate the battery.
2. Turn the engine over until the pointer on the timing cover coincides with the 4° A.T.D.C. mark on the crankshaft pulley, number one cylinder firing.
3. Remove the distributor 86.35.20.
4. Remove the two nuts and spring washers securing the pedestal to the cylinder block.
5. Remove the pedestal.
6. Check that the position of the distributor drive slot is correct (see instruction 13) and lift out the distributor drive shaft and gear.
7. Remove the gaskets.

Establishing the distributor drive shaft end-float

8. Place a flat washer on top of the oil pump shaft bush.
9. Fit the distributor drive shaft and gear in position over the washer ensuring that the oil pump drive dog is engaged.
10. Fit the pedestal without gaskets and using a feeler gauge measure and note the gap A between the pedestal and cylinder block flange.
11. Remove the pedestal and distributor drive shaft and measure the thickness of the washer with a micrometer.
12. Allowing 0·005 in (0·127 mm) end-float assess the required number and thickness of gaskets needed as in the following examples a and b.

a.

Washer thickness B	0·075 in (1·905 mm)
Measured gap A	0·074 in (1·880 mm)
End float	0·001 in (0·025 mm)
Gaskets required to the value of	0·004 in (0·102 mm)

b.

Washer thickness B	0·075 in (1·905 mm)
Measured gap A	0·080 in (2·032 mm)
Pre-load	– 0·005 in (– 0·127 mm)
Gasket required to the value of	0·010 in (0·254 mm)

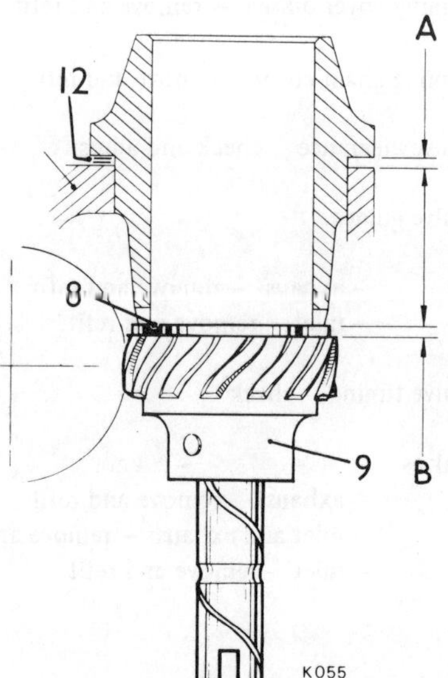

Continued

Refitting

13. Fit the distributor drive shaft and gear ensuring that the oil pump drive dog engages correctly and the distributor drive off-set slot is towards the engine.
14. Fit the gaskets as calculated and assemble the pedestal to the cylinder block and secure with the two nuts and spring washers.
15. Refit the distributor and check the ignition timing.

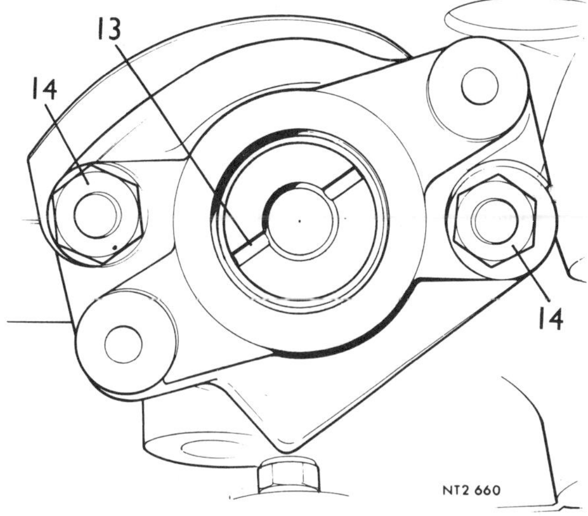

DISTRIBUTOR DRIVE SHAFT – P.I.

– Remove and refit **12.10.22**

Removing

1. Isolate the battery.
2. Disconnect the main fuel feed union to the fuel metering distributor.
3. Disconnect the tachometer drive from the ignition distributor.
4. Disconnect the fuel distributor unit lubricate return pipe.
5. Turn the crankshaft to bring numbers one and six pistons to T.D.C. number one firing.
6. Note the position of the rotor arm and remove the distributor complete with the cap and leads.
7. Remove the two nuts and washers securing the pedestal to the cylinder block.
8. Remove the pedestal complete with the fuel metering distributor whilst preventing the ignition distributor drive shaft from being removed as well.

NOTE: Take care not to allow the fuel metering distributor drive pinion to rotate so that the necessity to retime will be prevented.

9. Check that the position of the ignition distributor gear drive slot is correct for reassembly purposes.
10. Remove the distributor drive shaft and gear complete and note the position of the oil pump drive dog.

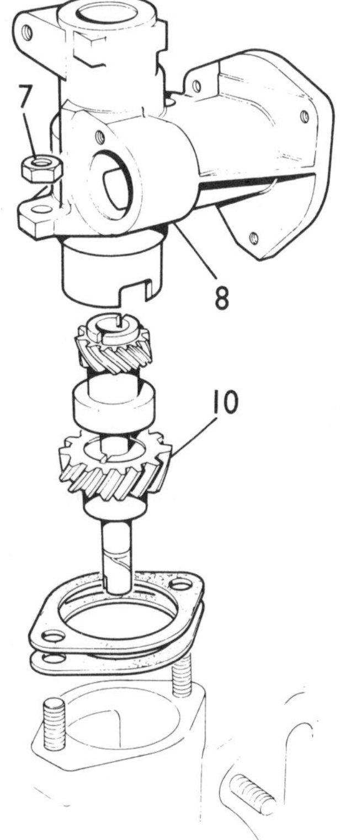

Continued

Establishing distributor drive shaft end-float

11. Place a flat washer on top of the oil pump shaft bush.
12. Fit the distributor drive shaft and gear in position over the washer ensuring that the oil pump drive dog is engaged.
13. Fit the pedestal without gaskets and using a feeler gauge measure and note the gap 'B' between the pedestal and the cylinder block flange.
14. Remove the pedestal and the distributor drive shaft. Remove the measure the thickness of the washer with a micrometer.
15. Allowing 0·005 in (0·127 mm) end float assess the required number and thickness of gaskets needed as in the following examples a and b:–

a.	Washer thickness A	0·075 in (1:905 mm)
	Measured gap B	0·074 in (1·880 mm)
	End-float	0·001 in (0·025 mm)
	Gaskets required to the value of	0·004 in (0·102 mm)
b.	Washer thickness A	0·075 in (1·905 mm)
	Measured gap B	0·080 in (2·032 mm)
	Pre-load	–0·005 in (– 0.127 mm)
	Gaskets required to the value of	0.010 in (0·254 mm)

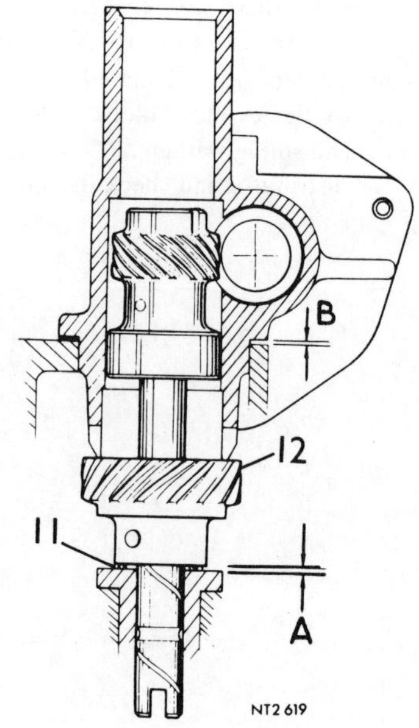

NT2 619

Refitting

16. Fit the distributor drive shaft and gear ensuring that the shaft engages properly with the oil pump drive shaft and the distributor drive off-set slot is towards the engine.
17. Fit the gaskets as calculated and assemble the pedestal and metering unit to the cylinder block and secure with the two nuts and washers.
18. Check the fuel metering distributor timing instructions 3 to 6 19.35.01 and adjust instructions 7 to 11 19.35.01 if necessary.
19. Reverse instructions 1 to 4 and run the engine.

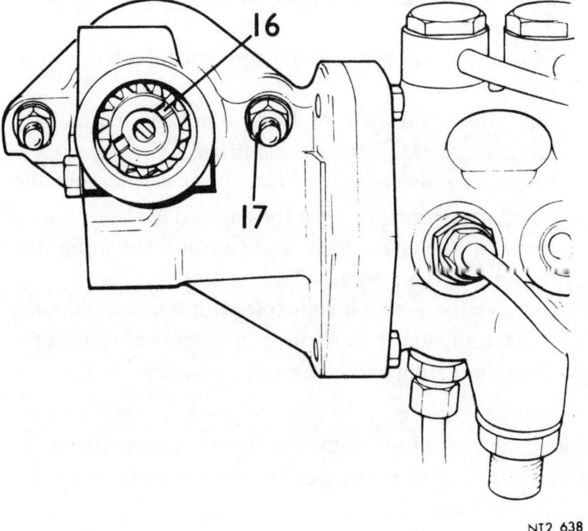

NT2 638

DATA

Distributor drive shaft end-float 0·003 to 0·007 in (0·076 to 0·177 mm).

PEDESTAL OIL SEALS – P.I. ONLY

– Remove and refit .12.10.24

Removing

1. Isolate the battery.
2. Turn the engine over until number one piston is at T.D.C. on the firing stroke and the ignition distributor rotor arm is pointing to number one cylinder electrode in the distributor cap. Do not turn the engine again until completion of the operation.
3. Remove the ignition distributor.
4. Remove the three bolts securing the fuel metering distributor to the pedestal flange and move the unit away from the pedestal. Instruction 8 19.35.07.
5. Remove the plastic drive dog and rubber 'O' ring.
6. Check that the position of the distributor drive shaft off-set slot is correct for the purposes of reassembly.
7. Remove the two nuts securing the pedestal to the cylinder block.
8. Withdraw the pedestal complete with the drive shaft ensuring that the gaskets between the pedestal and the cylinder block are left in position since they are necessary to maintain the correct end-float on the distributor drive shaft. See operation 12.10.22.

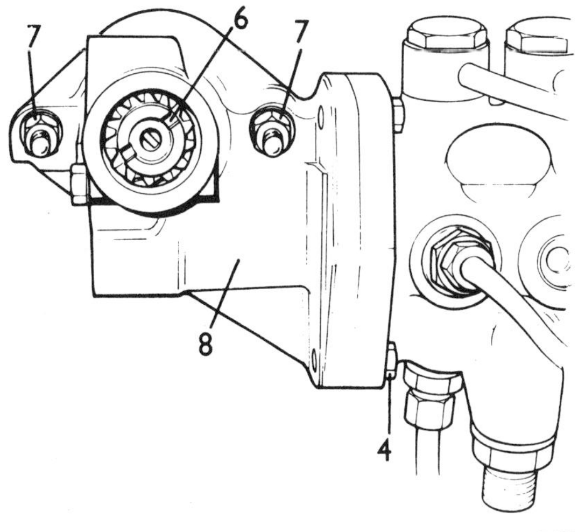

9. Remove the plug retaining bolt from the pinion housing.
10. Using a soft drift gently tap the drive end of the pinion shaft to release the plug and 'O' ring.
11. Continue tapping the pinion to remove it from the pedestal.
12. Using a suitable hooked tool remove the two seals taking care not to damage the pedestal bore.

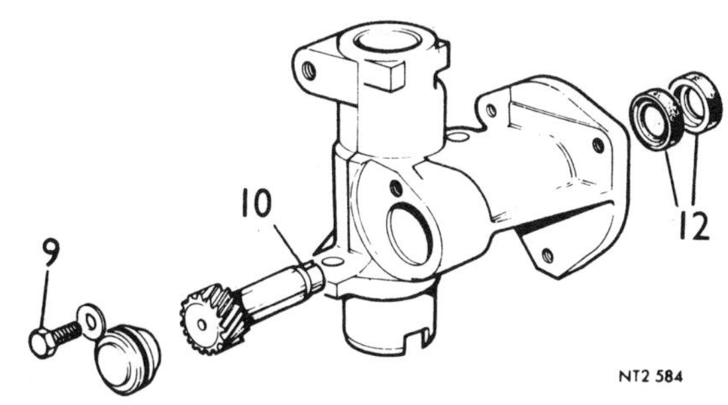

Continued

Refitting

13. Degrease and clean all components to be refitted.

NOTE: The two lip type seals are fitted 'back to back' i.e. the lips facing away from each other. The function of the seals is to prevent cross pollution of the engine oil and the fuel from the metering distributor. A leak bleed hole A is provided between the seals to enable a leak from either seal to be noticed. It is therefore important that the seals are correctly located there-by preventing the hole from being covered by the seals.

14. Lubricate the first oil seal and with the lip face leading press-in the seal squarely, using a 29/32 in (22·9 mm) drift, to the end of the bore leaving the bleed hole uncovered.
15. Lubricate the second seal and with the lip face trailing press in the seal until flush with the end of the inner bore and 0·71 in (18 mm) from the flange boss – dimension B
16. Check that the bleed hole is clear since rubber flashings from the seals may cause an obstruction.

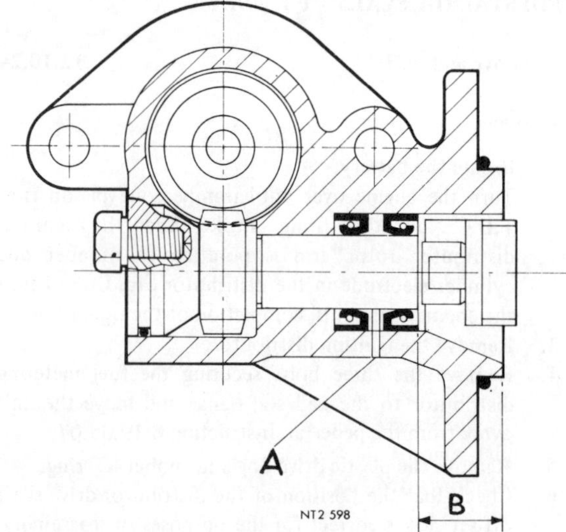

17. To prevent damage being caused to the seals when fitting the pinion, make up a protective cover to the dimensions shown.
18. With the protective cover in position press the pinion through the oil seals.

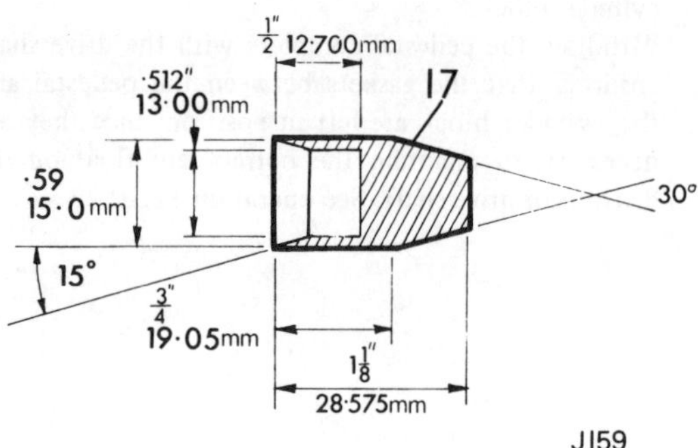

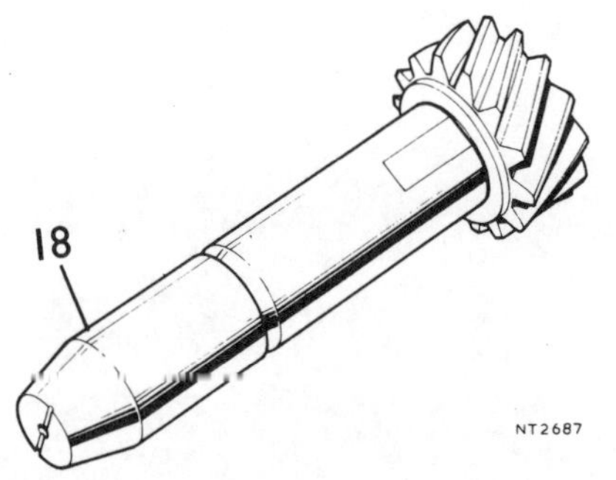

19. Fit a new 'O' ring to the plug and lubricate before fitting to the pedestal.
20. Secure the plug with the retaining bolt and washer and remove the protective cover from the pinion.
21. Refit the distributor drive shaft ensuring that the off-set slot in the drive member is correct – instruction 6.
22. Check that the gaskets between the pedestal and cylinder block mating faces are in position.

CAUTION: Should the gaskets be damaged or lost the drive shaft end-float must be re-established. See operation 12.10.22.

23. Refit the pedestal to the cylinder block ensuring that the pinion drive slot is in the vertical position. Secure with the nuts and washers. See instruction 13 – 19.35.07.

NOTE: It may be necessary to remove and refit the pedestal several times in order to turn the pinion to achieve the correct position of the slot.

24. Refit the metering distributor – instructions 14 to 18. 19.35.07.
25. Refit the ignition distributor checking that the conditions are the same as in instructions 2.
26. Reconnect the battery.

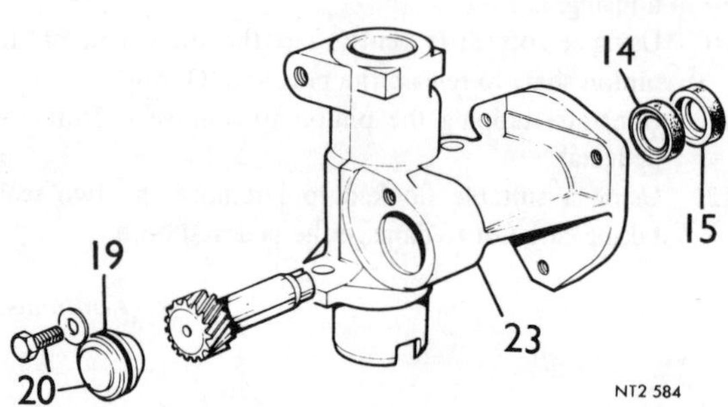

CAMSHAFT

– Remove and refit **12.13.01**

Special tool S341

Removing

1. Remove the radiator grille 76.55.03.
2. Remove the cylinder head 12.29.10.
3. Withdraw the camfollowers, identifying them for reassembly.

NOTE: Instructions 4 to 6 – Carburetter engines and Instructions 7 to 11 for P.I. engines.

4. Remove the mechanical fuel pump 19.45.08.
5. Disconnect the tachometer drive and remove the two nuts securing the pedestal to the cylinder block and withdraw the ignition distributor and pedestal complete.
6. Check that the position of the distributor drive slot is correct for reassembly purposes and remove the drive gear.
7. Disconnect the tachometer drive.
8. Slacken the ignition distributor clamp bolt and remove the distributor.
9. Disconnect the main fuel feed to the metering distributor.
10. Remove the two nuts and withdraw the pedestal complete with the metering distributor.
11. Check that the position of the ignition distributor drive slot is correct for reassembly purposes and remove the drive gear shaft.
12. Remove the timing chain and sprockets 12.65.12.
13. Remove the two bolts and withdraw the camshaft keeper plate.

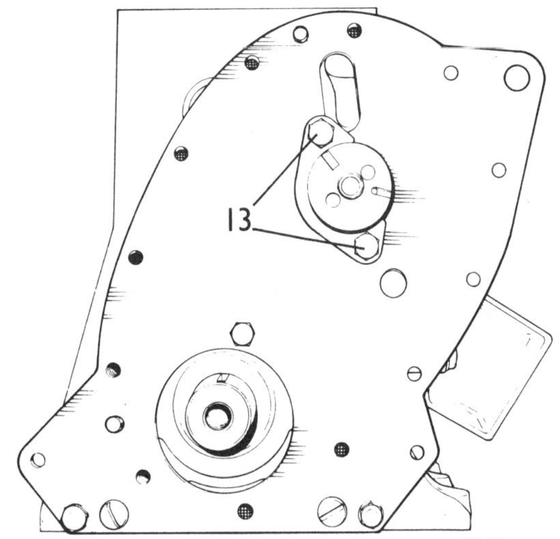

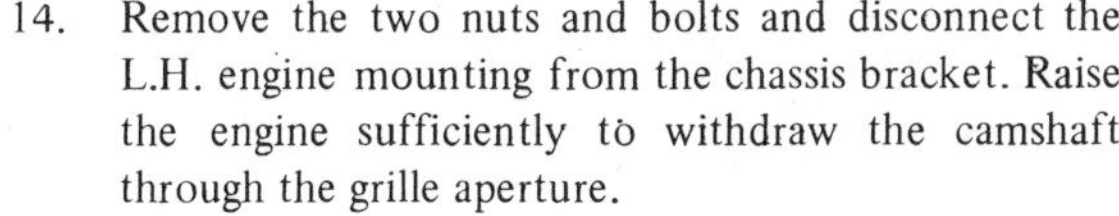

14. Remove the two nuts and bolts and disconnect the L.H. engine mounting from the chassis bracket. Raise the engine sufficiently to withdraw the camshaft through the grille aperture.

CAUTION: Ensure that before raising the engine the speedometer cable is repositioned so that it will not become trapped between the bell housing and the bulkhead.

Continued

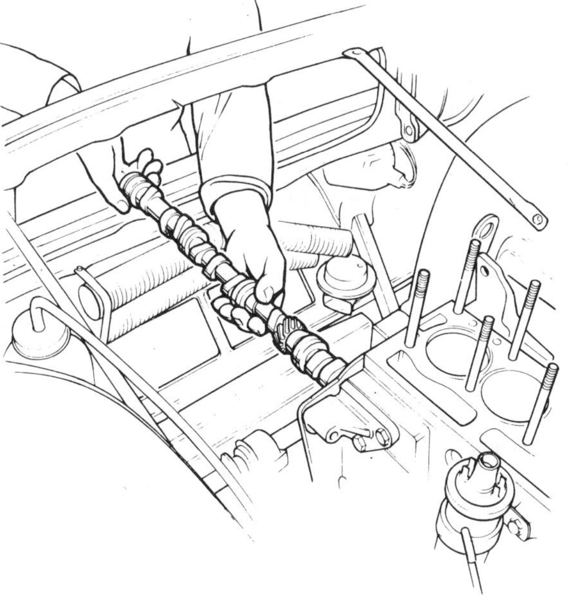

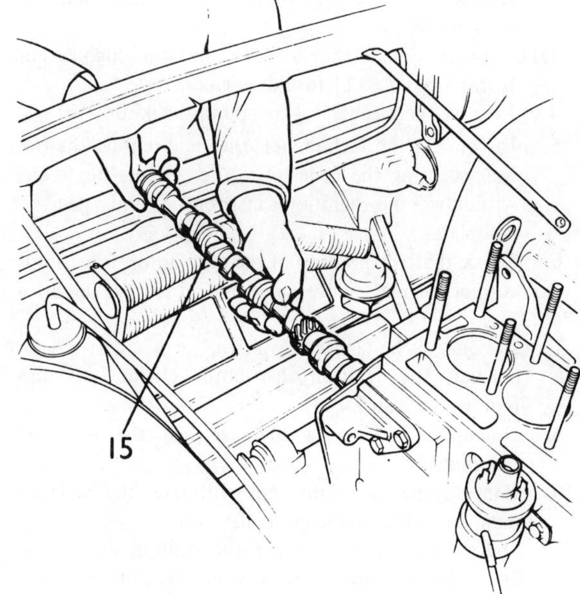

Refitting

15. With the flat end leading and the spigot end trailing pass the camshaft through the radiator grille and insert it into the cylinder block taking care not to damage the camshaft bearing surfaces in the block.
16. Secure the camshaft in position with the keeper plate and tighten the retaining bolts.
17. Lower the engine and reconnect the L.H. engine mounting.
18. Check the camshaft end float by pulling the camshaft out against the keeper plate and measuring the gap between the camshaft and the keeper plate with a feeler gauge – See Data. Renew the keeper plate if the gap is outside the limits.
19. Check the camshaft and crankshaft sprocket alignment – instructions 8 and 9 12.65.12.
20. Check that numbers one and six pistons are at T.D.C. number one firing.
21. Fit the camfollowers.
22. Fit the cylinder head, push rods and rocker shaft assembly.
23. Time the valves and refit the timing chain and sprockets – instructions 79 to 87, 12.41.05.
24. Reverse instructions 4 to 6 or 7 to 11.
25. Reverse instructions 1 to 4, 12.65.12.
26. Refit the radiator grille.

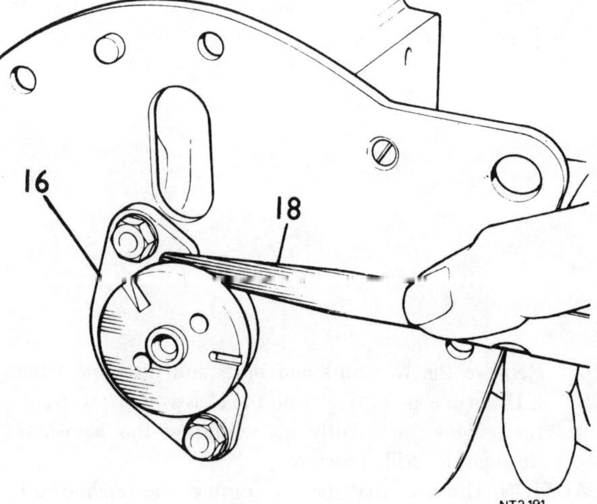

DATA

End float	0·004 – 0·008 in (0·102 – 0·20 mm)
Journal diameter	1·8402 – 1·8407 in (46·7411 – 46·7538 mm)

CONNECTING RODS AND PISTONS

– Remove and refit **12.17.01**

Removing

1. Isolate the battery.
2. Remove the cylinder head 12.29.10.
3. Drain and remove the sump 12.60.44.
4. Remove the connecting rod bearings – instructions 3 to 8, 12.17.16.
5. Push the connecting rods and pistons up the cylinder bores and extract the assemblies from the cylinder block.

Refitting

6. Dealing with each piston and connecting rod in turn, lubricate the bores and carefully insert the assembly into the respective cylinder ensuring:-
   a. that the open face of the connecting rod big-end bearing is towards the non-thrust side of the engine i.e. facing the camshaft.
   b. the arrow ▲ on top of the piston is pointing to the front of the engine.
7. Stagger the piston ring gaps avoiding a gap on the thrust side of the piston.
8. Using a piston ring compressor gently push the piston into the bore.
9. Repeat instructions 6 to 8 on the remaining pistons.
10. Fit the upper bearing shells to the connecting rods, pull the connecting rods on to the crankpins and fit the bearing caps and lower shells – instructions 9 – 13, 12.17.16.
11. Refit the sump.
12. Refit the cylinder head.
13. Ensure that the sump is refilled with the correct grade of new oil to the high mark on the dipstick before reconnecting the battery.

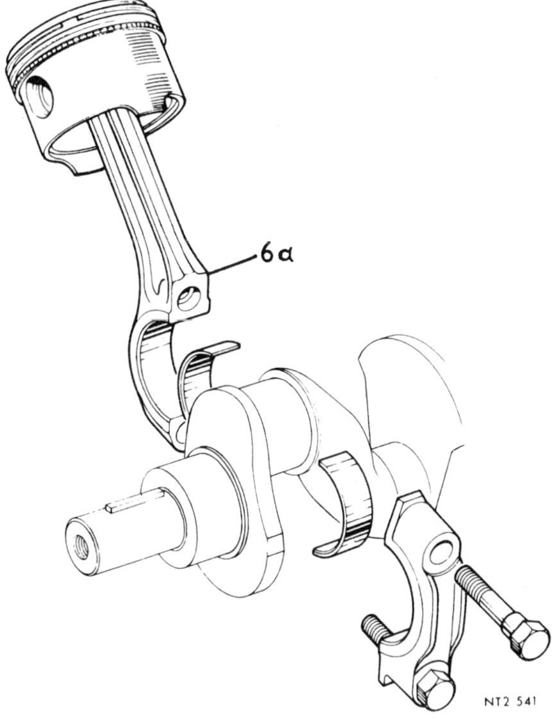

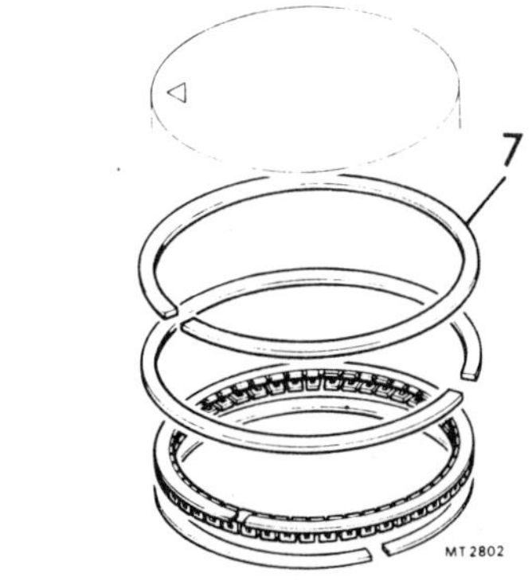

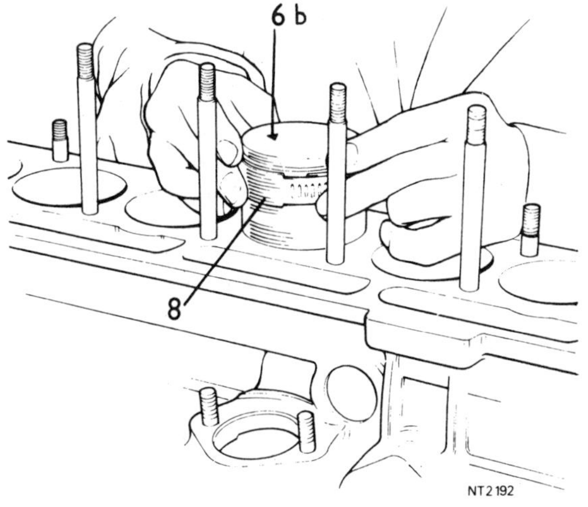

PISTONS AND/OR RINGS – ENGINE SET

– Remove and refit **12.17.03**

Pistons and/or rings – extra each **12.17.06**

See operation 12.17.10.

CONNECTING RODS AND PISTONS

– Overhaul **12.17.10.**

Gudgeon pin bush – each – remove and refit **12.17.13**

Special tools: S335, S336-4

NOTE: Do not mix any of the components during this operation.

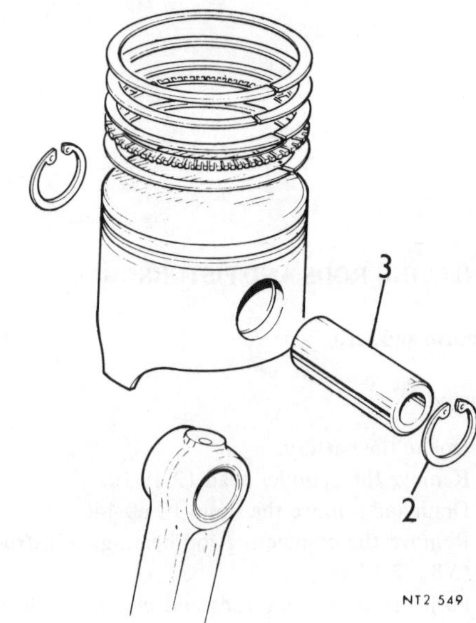

Removing

1. Remove the connecting rods and pistons 12.17.01.

Dismantling

2. Remove the two circlips retaining the gudgeon pin in the piston.
3. Push out the gudgeon pin and separate the piston from the connecting rod but mark for reassembly.
4. Remove from the piston the two compression rings and the oil control ring.
5. Repeat operations 2 to 4 on the remaining pistons and connecting rod assemblies.
6. Degrease all components and remove carbon deposits from the pistons.

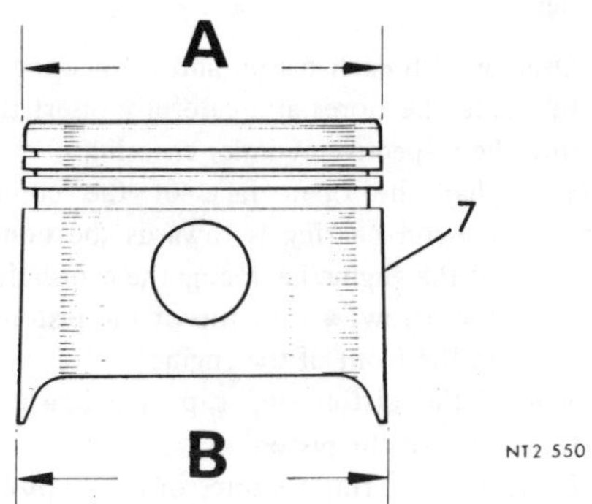

Examination and checking

7. Check the top dimension (A) of the pistons across the ring lands at right angles to the gudgeon pin – see Data.
8. Check the dimension (B) of the pistons across the skirt at right angles to the gudgeon pin – see Data.

NOTE: The grade of each bore i.e. (A) or (B) is stamped on the cylinder block. The piston grade (A) or (B) is stamped on the piston crown, as illustrated.

9. Check the dimensions of the piston ring grooves and the gap between the piston ring and piston groove – see Data.
10. Examine the gudgeon pin for scores and pitting. Check for wear – see data, and note that the gudgeon pin should be a light finger push fit in the piston at a temperature of 68°F.

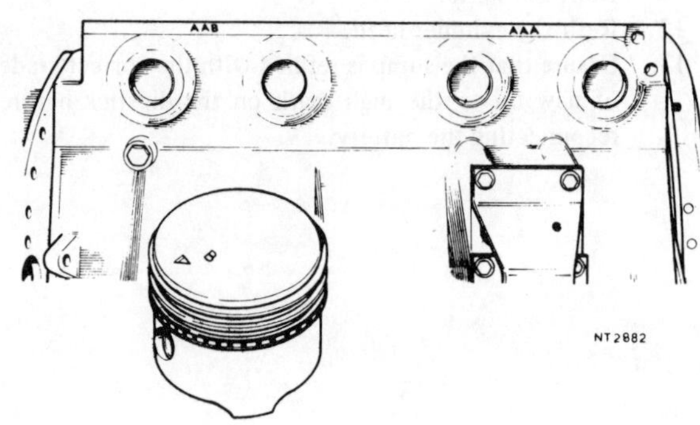

Continued

11. Check the piston ring gaps when inserted squarely into the bores – see data.

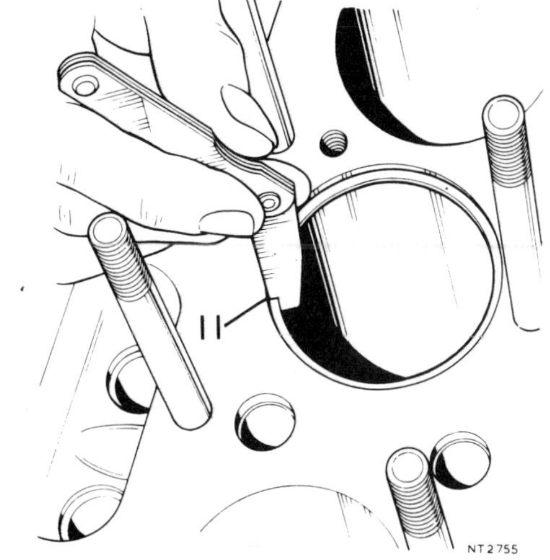

12. Using special tool S335 and adaptor arbor S336–4, check the connecting rods for
   a) bend and
   b) twist –

   see data. Rods that exceed the tolerances in both conditions should be re-aligned or renewed.

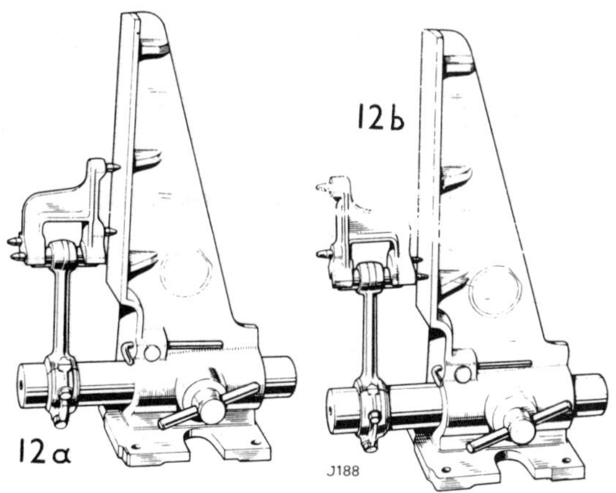

13. Check the gudgeon pin bush in the connecting rods for wear and if necessary remove the old bush and fit a new one using a suitable hand press. Ensure that the oil hole in the bush corresponds with the hole in the connecting rod. Ream the new bush to size – see Data.

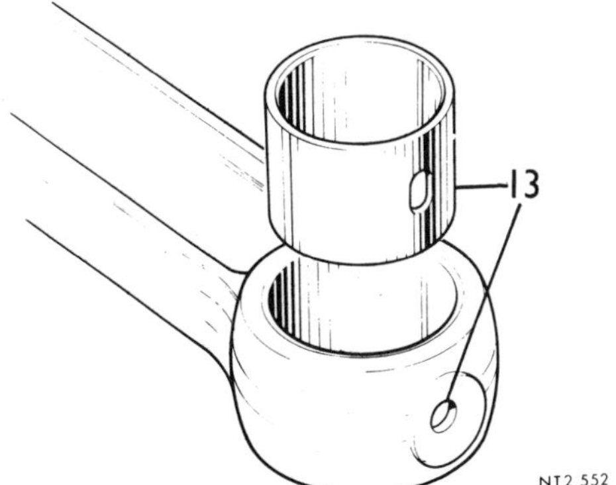

Continued

Reassembling

14. Fit the piston rings in the following order

NOTE: The oil control ring comprises three parts (A), (B) and (C) namely the centre expander rail flanked by two identical chrome rails.

- A Fit the expander rail into the bottom groove ensuring that the ends butt, not overlap.
- B Fit the bottom chrome rail to bottom groove.
- C Fit the top chrome rail to bottom groove.
- ** D Fit the second compression ring to the centre groove in the piston, with the words 'TOP' uppermost. **
- E Fit the top compression chrome ring with the groove downwards.

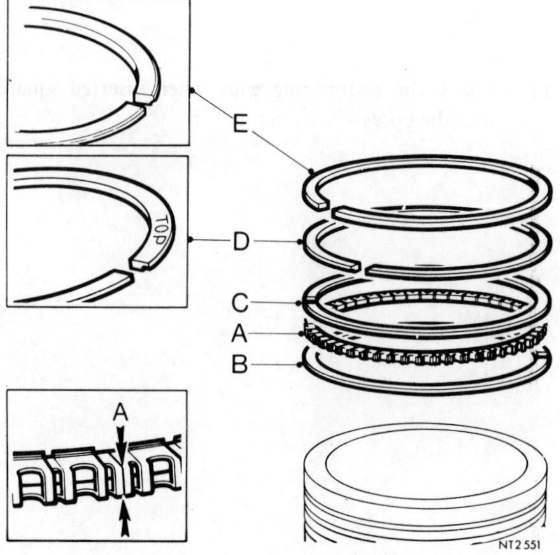

15. Refit the pistons to the connecting rods ensuring that:
    - *a.* When assembled the relationship is as described and illustrated in instruction 6, 12.17.01.
    - *b.* The gudgeon pins are properly located by the circlips.
    - *c.* The oil holes in the piston gudgeon pin bosses are clear.
16. Refit the connecting rods and pistons to the engine, instructions 6 to 14, 12.17.01 ensuring that the sump is refilled with new oil to the high mark on the dipstick before the battery is reconnected.

Continued

DATA

Piston grades and dimensions

Bore size:	Grade A	2·9405 – 2·9410 in (74·689 – 74·701 mm)
	Grade B	2·9411 – 2·9416 in (74·704 – 74·717 mm)
Piston top dia.	Grade A	2·9363 – 2·9368 in (74·582 – 74·595 mm)
	Grade B	2·9369 – 2·9374 in (74·597 – 74·610 mm)
Piston bottom dia.	Grade A	2·9380 – 2·9385 in (74·625 – 74·638 mm)
	Grade B	2·9386 – 2·9391 in (74·640 – 74·653 mm)
Pistons available – oversize		+0·020 in (+0·508 mm)
Groove width:	top compression	0·064 – 0·065 in (1·625 – 1·650 mm)
	2nd compression	0·064 – 0·065 in (1·625 – 1·650 mm)
	Oil control	0·157 – 0·158 in (4· – 4· mm)

Piston rings

Top compression	
– width	0·130 – 0·123 in (3·302 – 3·124 mm)
– thickness	0·0615 – 0·0625 in (1·562 – 1·588 mm)
– diameter	2·9405 in (74·689 mm)
– gap when fitted to above dia. bore	0·012 – 0·017 in (0·304 – 0·431 mm)
– free gap	0·390 – 0·516 in (9·9 – 13·1 mm)
2nd compression	
– width	0·123 – 0·130 in (3·124 – 3·302 mm)
– thickness	0·0615 – 0·0625 in (1·562 – 1·588 mm)
– diameter	2·9405 in (74·7 mm)
– gap when fitted to above dia. bore	0·008 – 0·013 in (0·203 – 0·254 mm)
– free gap	0·460 in (11·68 mm)
Oil control – chrome rail	
– width	0·135 – 0·141 in (3·43 – 3·58 mm)
– thickness	0·0230 – 0·0250 in (0·584 – 0·635 mm)
– diameter	2·9405 in (74·7 mm)
– gap when fitted to above dia. bore	0·015 – 0·055 in (0·381 – 1·397 mm)
Oil control – expander **rail**	
– width	0·125 in (3·17 mm)
– thickness	0·1415 – 0·1515 in (3.594 – 3.838 mm)
– gap when fitted	NIL – ends to butt
Oversize rings	+0·010 in (0·254 mm) +0·020 in (+0·508 mm) +0.030 in (+0·762)
Gudgeon pin	
– length	2·447 – 2·451 in (62·153 – 62·774 mm)
– diameter	0·8123 – 0·8125 in (20·632 – 20.645 mm)
Connecting rod	
– small end bush fitted internal dia.	0·8122 – 0·8126 in (20·624 – 20·640 mm)
– external diameter	0·937 – 0·938 in (23·79 – 23 ·82 mm)
– bend and twist in length of gudgeon pin	0·0015 in Max. (0·038 mm Max.)

CONNECTING ROD BEARINGS – SET

– Remove and refit 12.17.16

Connecting rod bearings – one 12.17.17

Connecting rod bearings – extra each 12.17.18

Removing

1. Isolate the battery.
2. Drain and remove the sump 12.60.44.
3. Dealing with each connecting rod bearing in turn and starting with number one, turn the crankshaft until the bearing is in an accessible position.

NOTE: So that the connecting rods and caps may be identified with their respective cylinder bores, each rod and cap is numbered from one to six starting at the front of the engine. Furthermore the number on the cap and rod are adjacent and must always be refitted this way round.

4. Check that the connecting rods and caps are numbered in accordance with the above note.
5. Remove the bolts securing the cap to the connecting rod.
6. Withdraw the cap complete with the bearing shell and extract the shell.
7. Push the connecting rod and piston up the bore just sufficiently to enable the upper bearing shell to be removed.
8. Repeat operations 3 to 7 on the remaining bearings, keeping the bearing shells identified with their respective connecting rods and caps if the original shells are to be refitted.

Refitting

9. Lubricate and fit the upper bearing shell to the connecting rod ensuring that the tag locates properly in the recess.
10. Fit the lower bearing shell to the connecting rod cap locating the tag in the recess.
11. Clean the connecting rod and cap mating faces and check that the dowels are in position.
12. Lubricate the bearing and crank pin and fit the cap, ensuring that it is positioned the correct way round – see note preceeding instruction 4. A further check to ensure correct assembly is that the two shell bearing recesses are on the same side.
13. Pull the connecting rod on to the crankpin and using NEW BOLTS secure the bearing cap to the connecting rod tightening evenly to 38 to 46 lbf ft (5·2 to 6·4 kgf m).
14. Repeat instructions 9 to 13 on the remaining bearings.
15. Refit the sump and fill with new oil to the high mark on the dipstick.
16. Reconnect the battery.

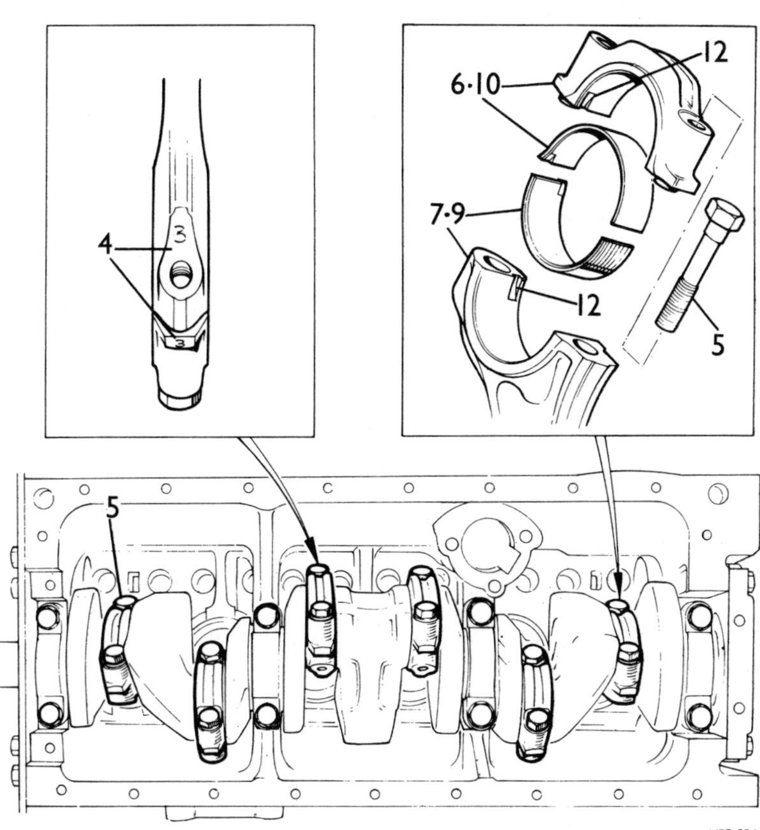

CRANKSHAFT PULLEY

– Remove and refit **12.21.01**

Special tool S341

Removing

1. Isolate the battery.
2. Remove the radiator 26.40.01.
3. Remove the fan blades.
4. Remove the fan adaptor – Carburetter engines only 26.25.06.
5. Remove the chassis cross tube, 76.10.05.
6. Remove the fan belt.
7. Remove the special bolt securing the fan extension.
8. Remove the fan extension by tapping it with a hammer to free it from its locating dowels.
9. Remove the steering rack 'U' bolts and ease the rack forward sufficiently to withdraw the pulley without fouling, 57.25.01 instructions 5 and 6.
10. Withdraw the crankshaft pulley.

Refitting

11. Check that the crankshaft key is in position and the key-way in the pulley is free from burrs. Drift the pulley on to the crankshaft squarely until it butts against the oil seal sleeve in the timing cover.
12. Check that the two fan extension location dowels are in position and their locating holes are free from burrs. Fit the extension and secure with the special bolt.
13. Refit the steering rack using special tool S341, 57.25.01 instructions 11 to 16.
14. Refit and adjust the fan belt 26.20.07.
15. Reverse instructions 1 to 5.

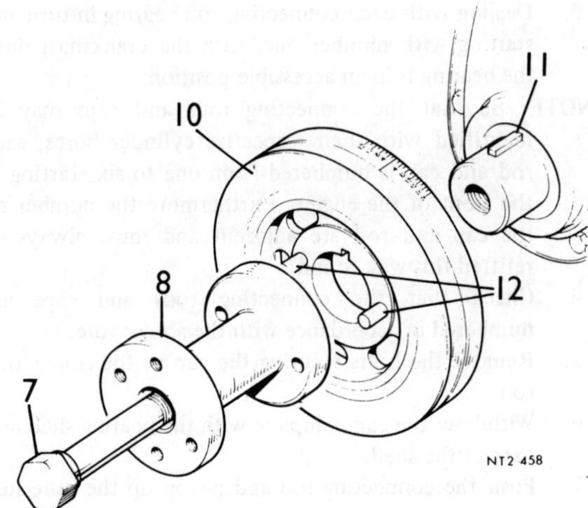

CRANKSHAFT REAR OIL SEAL

– Remove and refit **12.21.20**

Removing

1. Remove the gearbox assembly, 37.20.01.
2. Remove the rear adaptor plate instructions 2 and 3, 12.53.03.
3. Remove the two rear centre sump bolts.

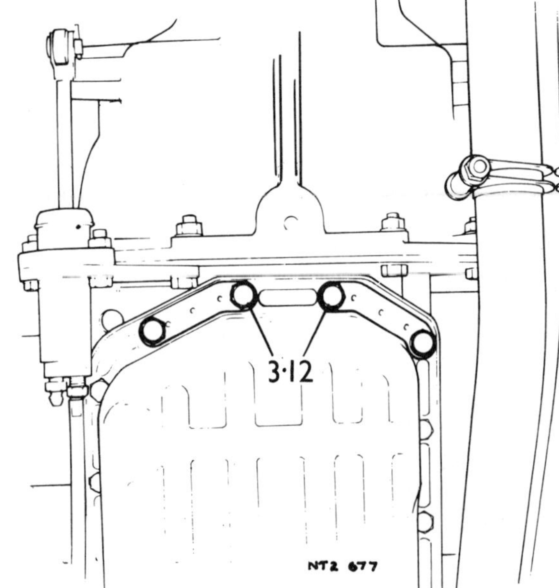

4. Remove the seven bolts and spring washers securing the oil seal housing to the crankcase and remove the housing complete with the seal, taking care not to damage the sump gasket.
5. Press out the oil seal taking care not to damage or distort the housing.

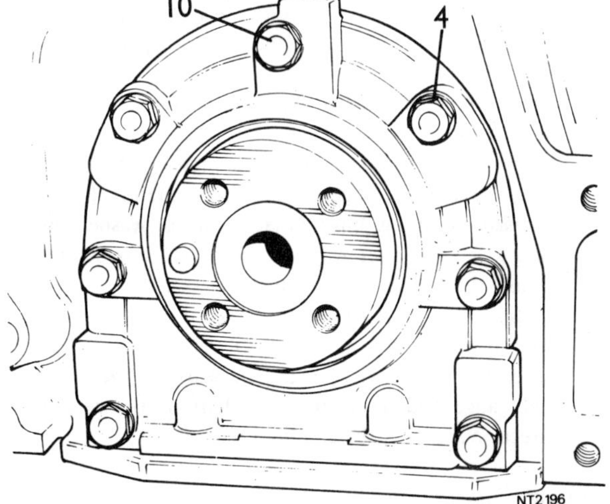

Refitting

6. Clean the oil seal housing and crankcase mating faces ensuring all traces of old gasket and jointing are removed.
7. Place the oil seal housing on a flat surface with the machined face uppermost. Smear the outside diameter of a new oil seal with grease and with the lip side trailing press in the seal. Remove surplus grease from the housing.
8. Apply sealing compound to the crankcase and oil seal housing mating faces and fit a new gasket.
9. Lubricate the oil seal inner diameter and the crankshaft with clean engine oil and carefully ease the oil seal and housing over the crankshaft and locate it on the crankcase face.

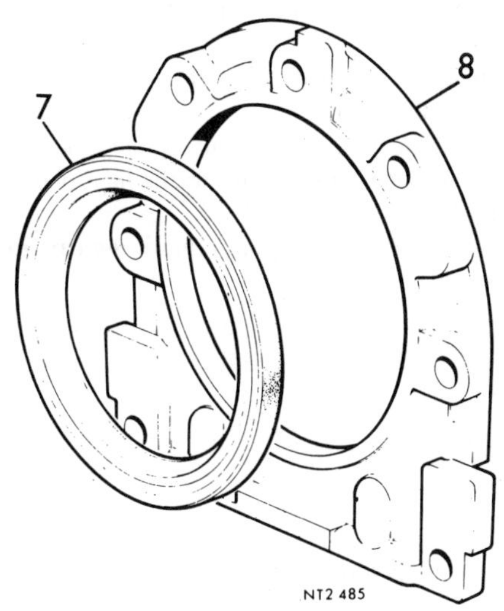

10. Secure the housing to the crankcase noting that the top bolt has a copper washer under the head to prevent oil seepage due to the bolt protruding into the crankcase.
11. Use spring washers under the remaining bolt heads and tighten evenly. Ensure that any surplus sealing compound is removed.
12. Refit the two sump bolts.
13. Refit the adaptor plate instructions 4 and 5, 12.53.03.
14. Refit the gearbox assembly, 37.20.01.

CRANKSHAFT END-FLOAT

– Check and adjust **12.21.26**

Check

1. Isolate the battery.
2. Attach a magnetic type dial gauge stand to a convenient place on the cylinder block, place a dial in position so that the stylus rests squarely against the crankshaft pulley.
3. Raise the car on a ramp and lever the crankshaft back towards the rear of the engine.
4. Zero the dial gauge and lever the crankshaft forward and note the reading on the gauge. See data.
5. Repeat instructions 3 and 4 two or three times to ensure a constant reading.
6. Remove the dial gauge and stand, lower the ramp and reconnect the battery.

Adjusting

7. Isolate the battery.
8. Drain and remove the sump 12.60.44.
9. Remove the two bolts securing the rear main bearing cap to the crankcase, and withdraw the cap and lower shell.
10. Rotate the crankshaft to facilitate the removal of the thrust washers.
11. Fit new thrust washers feeding them into the recesses in the crankcase. If necessary, rotate the crankshaft to assist the fitting. Ensure that the thrust washers are installed the correct way i.e. the oil grooves bearing against the crankshaft journal sides.
12. Attach a dial gauge to the crankcase so that the stylus rests squarely against a crankshaft web.
13. Lever the crankshaft forward or rearward, zero the dial gauge and lever the crankshaft in the reverse direction and note the end-float reading.

Refitting

14. Fit the rear main bearing cap and lower shell ensuring that the cap and shell are fitted correctly. Secure with the main bearing bolts and tighten to 50 to 65 lbf ft (6·9 to 9·0 kgf m).
15. Refit the sump 12.60.44 ensuring that it is filled with a recommended grade of oil to the high mark on the dipstick.
16. Reconnect the battery, and remove the car from the ramp.

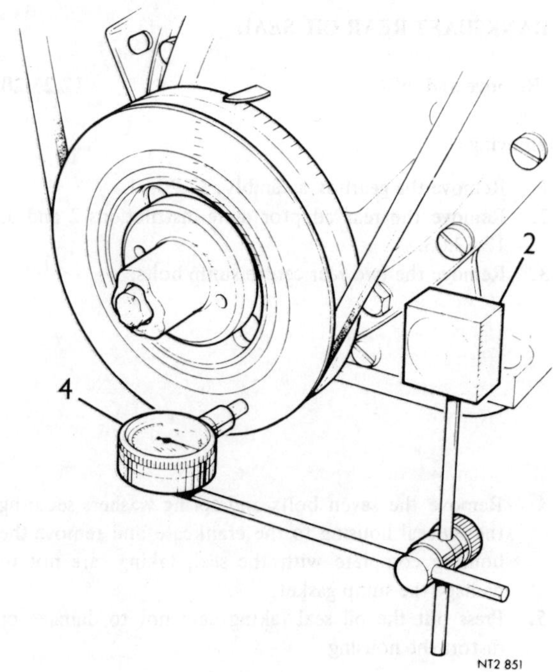

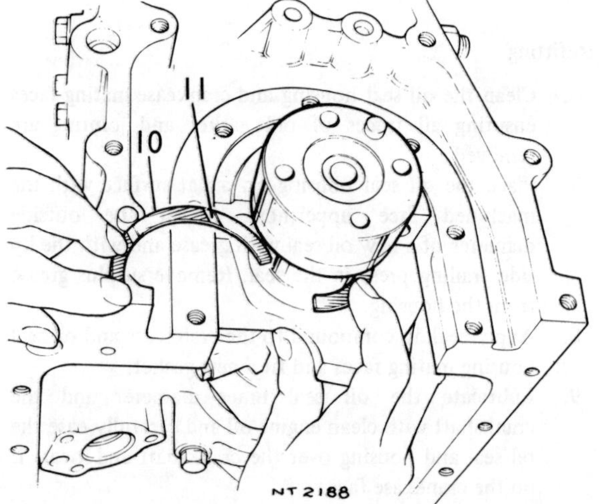

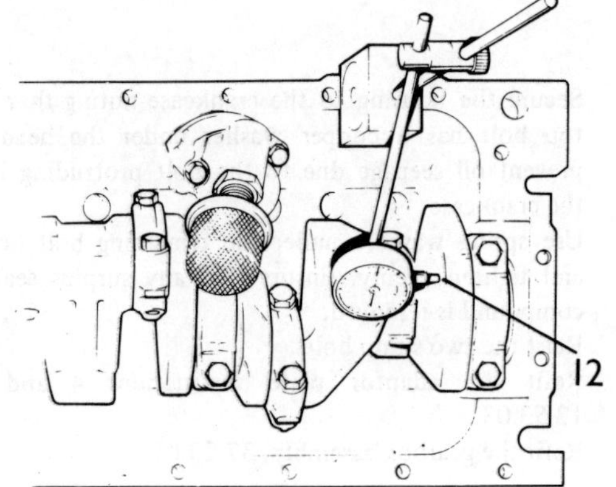

NT 2761

DATA

Crankshaft end-float 0·006 – 0·008 in (0·1524 – 0·2032 mm)

** Oversize thrust washers are available – 0·005 in (0·127 mm)**

CRANKSHAFT

– Remove and refit 12.21.33

Removing

1. Remove the engine and gearbox assembly, 12.37.01.
2. Remove the gearbox from the engine.
3. Remove the clutch assembly.
4. Remove the flywheel.
5. Remove the engine rear adaptor plate.
6. Remove the crankshaft pulley – instructions 5 to 7 and instruction 9, 12.21.01.
7. Remove the timing chain and sprockets – instructions 5 to 7, 12.65.12.
8. Remove the alternator.
9. Remove the engine front mounting plate.
10. Remove the sump – insturction 4, 12.60.44.
11. Remove the front sealing block.
12. Remove the rear main oil seal and housing – instruction 4, 12.21.20.
13. Remove the six connecting rod caps complete with lower shells. Instructions 3 to 8, 12.17.16.
14. Remove the oil pump.
15. Remove the four main bearing caps complete with lower shells – instructions 9 to 10, 12.21.39.
16. Withdraw the crankshaft, leaving the thrust bearing and upper shells in position.

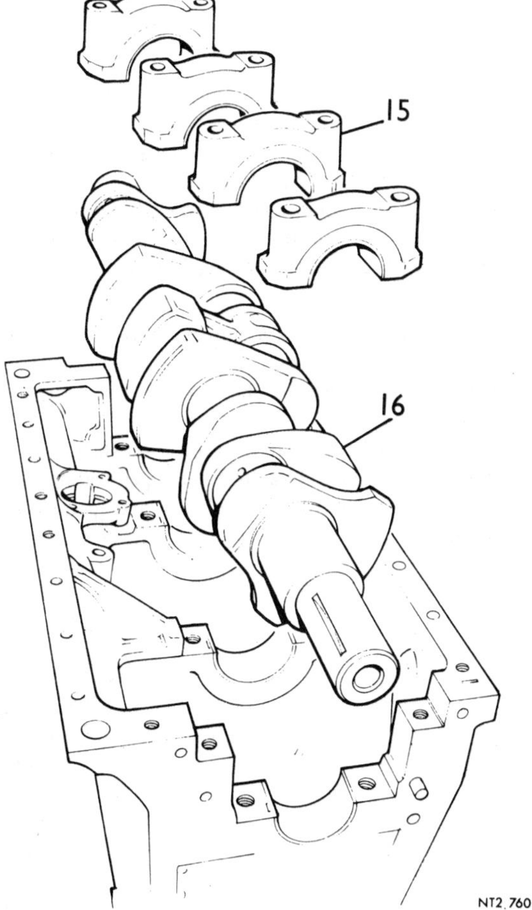

Refitting

17. Reverse instructions 15 and 16.
18. Check the crankshaft end-float and if necessary adjust – instruction 54 12.41.05.
19. Refit the six connecting rods to the crankpins – instructions 9 to 14, 12.17.16.
20. Refit the oil pump.
21. Refit the rear main oil seal and housing – instructions 5 to 10, 12.21.20.
22. Refit the front sealing block – instructions 5, 12.41.05.
23. Refit the sump.
24. Refit the engine front mounting plate and gasket.
25. Refit the timing chain and sprockets – instructions 8 to 11, 12.65.12 – ensuring that the crankshaft is first turned so that numbers one and six pistons are at T.D.C. with number one firing.
26. Refit the timing cover – instructions 16 to 18. 12.65.01.
27. Refit the alternator.
28. Refit the crankshaft pulley and fan extension.
29. Reverse instructions 1 to 5.

MAIN BEARINGS – SET

– Remove and refit **12.21.39**

Main bearing – each **12.21.40**

Main bearing – front – instructions 1 to 4, 6 to 14 and 16 **12.21.41**

Main bearings centre and rear – instructions 1 to 3, 5 to 13, 15 and 16 **12.21.42**

Removing

1. Isolate the battery.
2. Drain the oil and remove the sump 12.60.44.
3. Release the drive belt tension.
4. Remove the crankcase front sealing block, instructions 4 to 8, 12.25.11
5. Remove the oil pump to enable access to be gained to the rear centre main bearing, instruction 4, 12.60.26.
6. Dealing with each main bearing in turn, slacken the two bearing cap bolts.

NOTE: The bearing caps are numbered from 1 to 4, beginning at the front of the engine and it is important that these are checked before the caps are removed and mixed.

7. Withdraw the bearing cap with the lower shell.
8. With the tag end leading, slide the upper bearing shell out from between the crankcase and crankshaft journal.

CAUTION Do not permit the crankshaft to remain unsupported for longer than is necessary since compression of the timing cover and rear main oil seals may cause subsequent leakage.

Refitting

9. Dealing with each main bearing in turn, lubricate and feed the upper bearing shell – tag end trailing – between the crankcase bearing bore and the crankshaft journal. Ensure that the tag locates properly into the corresponding recess in the crankcase bore.
10. Select the correct bearing cap – see note following instruction 6 – and fit the bearing shell ensuring that the tag locates in the corresponding recess in the cap.
11. Fit the cap to its corresponding journal noting that the side of the cap containing the shell location recess is fitted adjacent to the recess in the crankcase bearing bore i.e. opposite side to the camshaft.
12. Using NEW BOLTS tighten evenly to 50 to 65 lbf ft (6·9 to 9·0 kgf m).
13. Check and if necessary adjust crankshaft end float 12.21.26.
14. Refit the crankcase front sealing block – instructions 9 to 16, 12.25.11
15. Refit the oil pump.
16. Reverse instructions 1 to 3, ensuring that the sump is filled with new oil to the high mark on the dipstick.

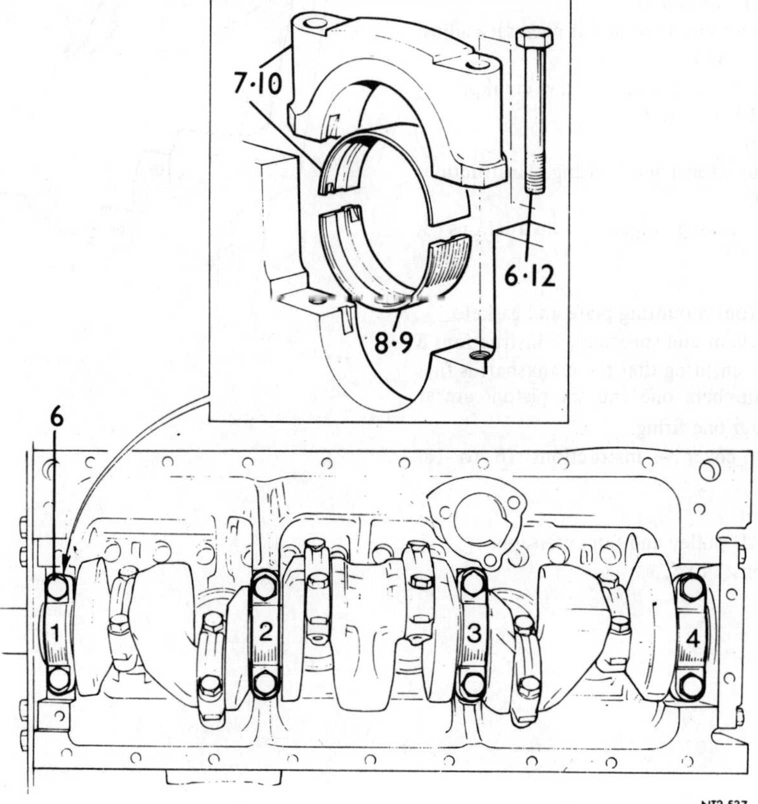

SPIGOT BUSH

– Remove and refit **12.21.45**

Removing

1. Remove the flywheel 12.53.07.
2. From the back of the flywheel remove the spigot bush.

Refitting

3. Fit the spigot bush into the back of the flywheel ensuring that it is a loose fit.
4. Refit the flywheel – instruction 8 to 14, 12.53.07.

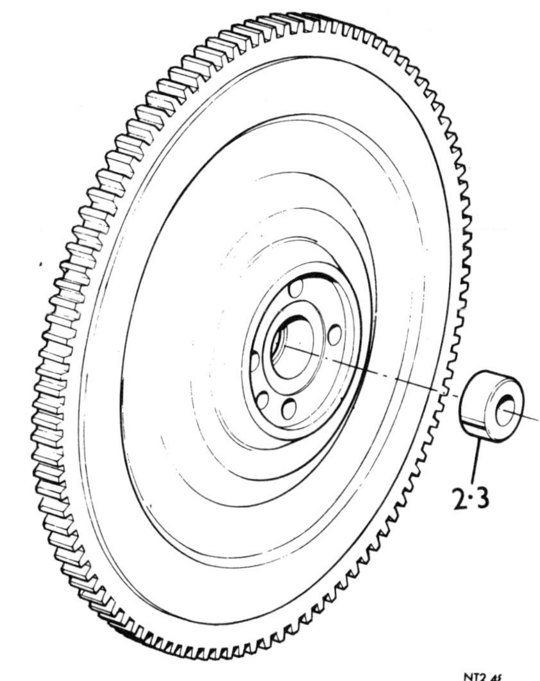

CYLINDER PRESSURES

– Check **12.25.01**

1. Start and run the engine until the normal operating temperature is attained as indicated by the temperature gauge on the control panel.
2. Stop the engine and remove the spark plugs.
3. Fit a compression gauge to number one cylinder.
4. Turn the engine over with the starter motor only with the throttles wide open.
5. Record the gauge reading – See DATA.
6. Repeat instructions 3 to 5 on the remaining cylinders.
7. Remove the gauge and refit the spark plugs.

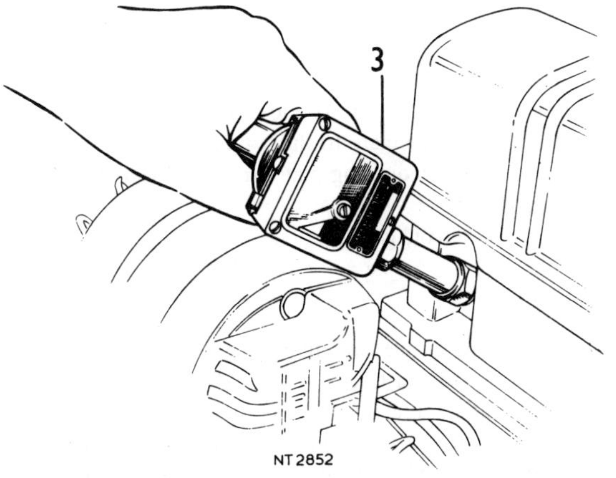

DATA

All cylinders should have pressures within 10 lb/in^2 (0·70 kg/cm^2) of each other.

CYLINDER BLOCK DRAIN PLUG

– Remove and refit **12.25.07**

Removing

1. Isolate the battery.
2. Place a resceptacle under the drain plug to catch the coolant.
3. Remove the plug from the cylinder block with the sealing washer.

Refitting

4. Clean the plug and cylinder block threads, fit a new sealing washer and refit the plug.
5. Refil the cooling system 26.10.01.
6. Reconnect the battery, start the engine and check for coolant leaks from the plug.

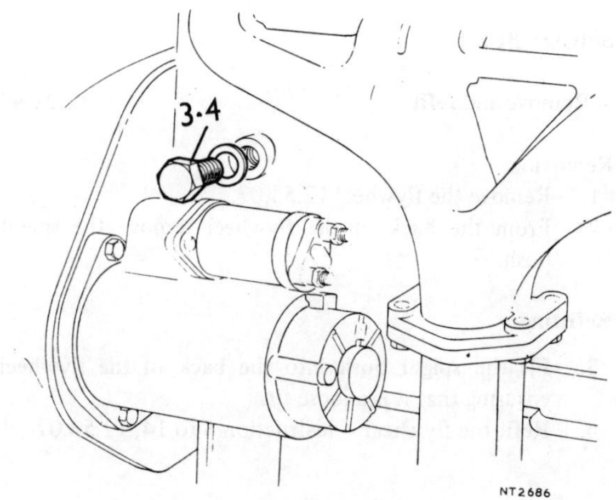

CYLINDER BLOCK FRONT MOUNTING PLATE GASKET

– Remove and refit **12.25.10**

Special tool S341

Removing

1. Remove the timing chain and sprockets 12.65.12.
2. Remove the alternator 86.10.02.
3. Remove the camshaft keeper plate.
4. Remove the three bolts and two screws securing the front mounting plate to the cylinder block.
5. Remove the mounting plate from the locating dowels and studs.
6. Remove the old gasket.

Refitting

7. Clean the engine and mounting plate mating faces, ensuring that all traces of the old gasket and jointing compound are removed.
8. Coat both sides of the new gasket with jointing compound and place it in position. Ensure that the gasket locates properly over the dowels and lies perfectly flat on the engine face.
9. Locate the mounting plate in position over the dowels and studs.
10. Secure the mounting plate with the three bolts and two screws.
11. Refit the camshaft keeper plate.
12. Reverse instructions 1 and 2.

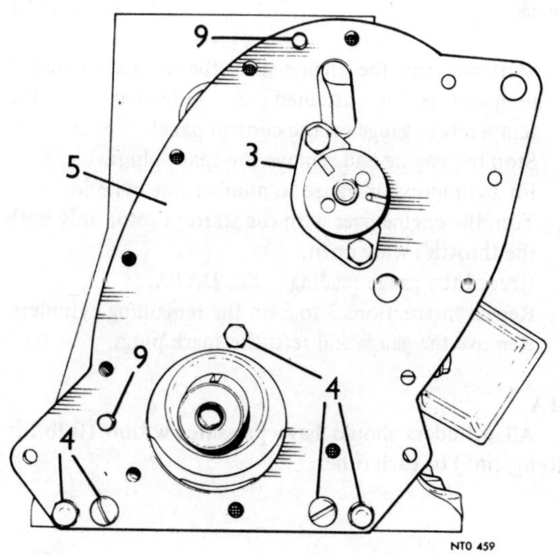

CRANKCASE FRONT SEALING BLOCK

– Remove and refit **12.25.11**

Removing

1. Place the car on a ramp and isolate the battery.
2. Drain the sump oil.
3. Remove the sump 12.60.44.
4. Remove the two screws from the front mounting plate.
5. Remove the lowest bolt from the timing chain cover.
6. Remove the two retaining screws from the sealing block.
7. Using a thin blade knife, carefully ease the front mounting plate gasket away from the sealing block.
8. Carefully withdraw the sealing block.

Refitting

9. Clean the sealing block and crankcase mating faces.
10. Coat the sealing block gaskets and the exposed part of the front mounting plate gasket with sealing compound.
11. Fit the gaskets to the crankcase.
12. Fit the sealing block and loosely secure with the retaining screws.
13. Fit and tighten the timing cover bolt.
14. Fit and tighten the front mounting plate to sealing block screws.
15. Finally tighten the sealing block retaining screws.
16. Smear the wedges with sealing compound and drive them into the slots. Trim the protruding ends of the wedges flush with the sealing block but do not undercut.
17. Refit the sump.
18. Refil the sump with oil to the high mark on the dipstick.
19. Reconnect the battery and remove the car from the ramp.

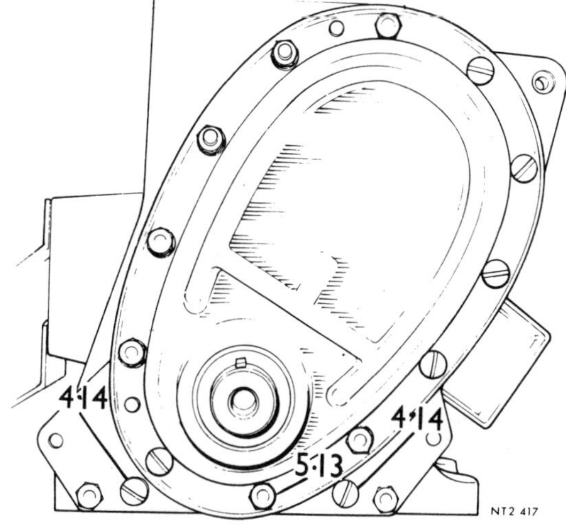

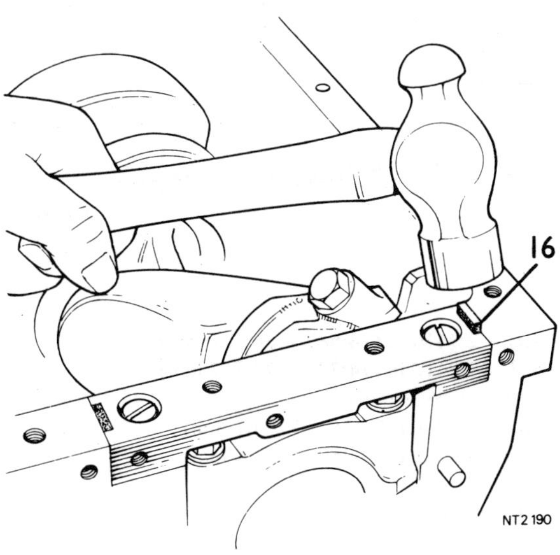

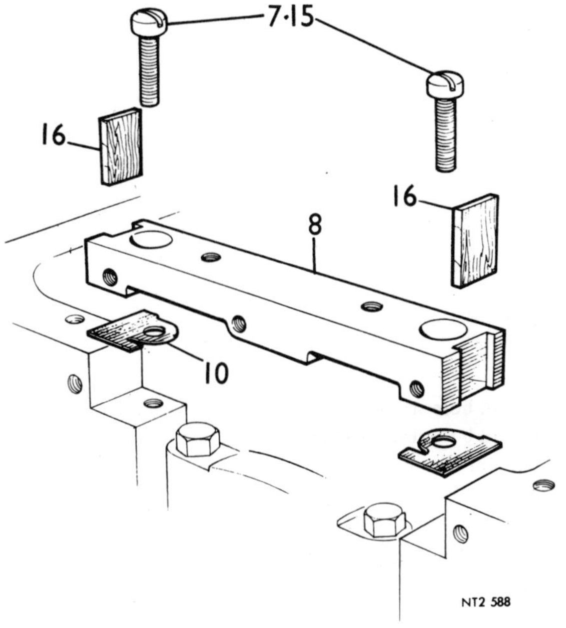

CYLINDER BLOCK

– Rebore 12.25.23

1. Strip the engine 12.41. 05.
2. Measure the cylinder bores for taper, ovality and maximum wear.
3. Rebore and hone to dimensions in data.

NOTE: Maximum rebore oversize from standard is +0·020 in. Cylinders that cannot be satisfactorily rebored within this limit may be sleeved to restore them to the original size as follows:

a. Bore out the cylinders to 3·059 to 3·062 in (77·699 – 77·775 mm).

b. Remove sharp edges from top of cylinders.

c. Lightly oil the outside diameter of the sleeve – DO NOT GREASE.

d. Insert the sleeve into the cylinder so that the cut-a-ways in the sleeve line up with the corresponding slots in the bottom of the cylinder bore.

e. Press the sleeve into the bore squarely with a minimum pressure of 2 ton f. until it is flush with the top of the cylinder block.

NOTE: Whilst the sleeve is flush with the top face of the cylinder block the sleeve will never-the-less be proud of the recess surrounding each bore. Therefore it will be necessary to machine the top of the sleeve down flush with the bottom of the recess. This note relates to later engines.

f. True-up the cut-aways with a file so that no overlap of the cylinder block slots remain.

g. Bore and hone the sleeve bores to size – see data.

4. Rebuild the engine 12.41.05 fitting:

a. new oversize pistons to rebored dimensions or

b. standard graded pistons to sleeved bores

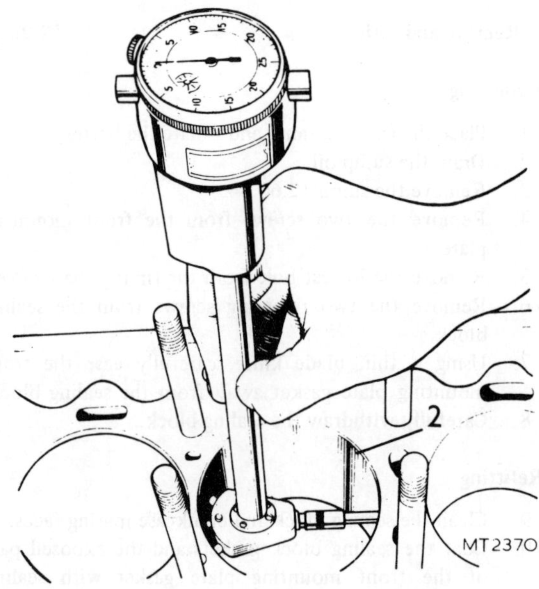

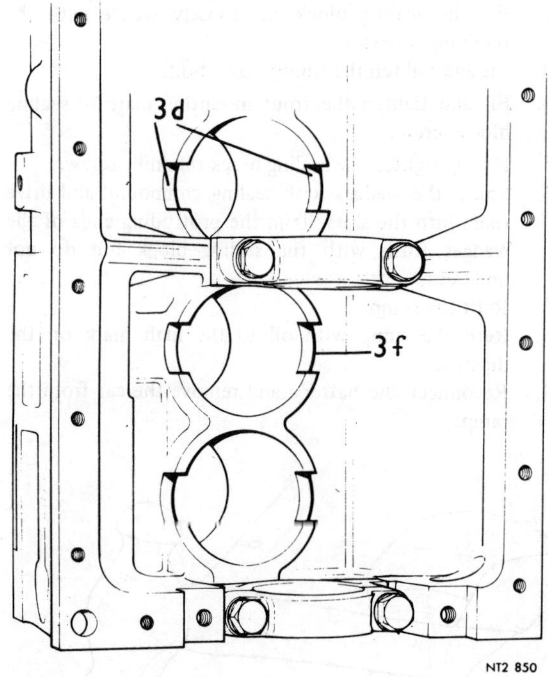

DATA

Standard bore size – Grade A	2·9405 – 2·9410 in (74·689 – 74·701 mm)
Standard bore size – Grade B	2·9411 – 2·9416 in (74·704 – 74·717 mm)
Maximum rebore size –	+0·020 in (+0·508 mm)
Diameter of sleeve –	3·066 – 3·067 in (77·876 – 77·901 mm)
Bore-out cylinder to accept sleeve	3·059 – 3·062 in (77·698 – 77·774 mm)
Minimum sleeve fitting pressure	2 ton f.
Length of sleeve	5·770 in (136·558 mm)

CYLINDER HEAD GASKET

– Remove and refit **12.29.01**

See 12.29.10.

CYLINDER HEAD

– Remove and refit **12.29.10**

which includes – Cylinder head gasket – remove and refit **12.29.01**

Removing

1. Isolate the battery.
2. Drain the cooling system 26.10.01.
3. Disconnect the following:–
   a. The servo hose at the induction manifold.
   b. The breather pipe at the rocker cover.
   c. H.T. leads to spark plugs.
   d. The water temperature sensor connection
   e. Fuel pipes at the injectors (Petrol injection engines only) 19.60.14.
   f. The water hoses at the thermostat housing and water pump housing.
   g. The air intake hose (P.I. engines only).
   h. The heater hose to the heater control valve.
   i. The throttle linkage at the bulkhead cross shaft (carburetter engines only) and the cable at the induction manifold (P.I. only).
   j. The mixture control or cold start cable and spring.
   k. The heater control cable at heater valve.
   l. The metering unit vacuum hose at the manifold (P.I. engines).
4. Remove the fan belt and disconnect the alternator adjustment link at the cylinder head, slacken the pivot bolt nut and swing the alternator away from the engine.
5. Remove the water pump complete with water pump housing 26.50.03.
6. Remove the rocker cover 12.29.42.
7. Remove the rocker shaft 12.29.54.
8. Withdraw the push rods and identify for reassembly.
9. Disconnect the exhaust manifold from the cylinder head leaving the exhaust pipe attached.
10. Remove the P.I. induction manifold or the inlet manifold complete with carburetters and air cleaner.
11. Pull and fasten the exhaust manifold away from the cylinder head studs.
12. Release the cylinder head nuts in the reverse rotation as shown in operations 12.29.27.
13. Lift off the cylinder head.
14. Remove and discard the cylinder head gasket.

Refitting

15. Clean the cylinder block and cylinder head mating faces removing all traces of carbon deposit and old gasket.
16. Fit a new cylinder head gasket.
17. Fit the cylinder head and tighten the cylinder head retaining nuts in the sequence shown in operation 12.29.27, and tighten progressively to 60 – 80 lbf ft (8·3 – 11·1 kgf m).
18. Reverse instructions 1 to 11.

NOTE: Later engines that have a recess round the top of each bore must have the correct cylinder head gasket fitted. These gaskets have a tag at the rear end marked 'TOP' which protrudes from the cylinder head.

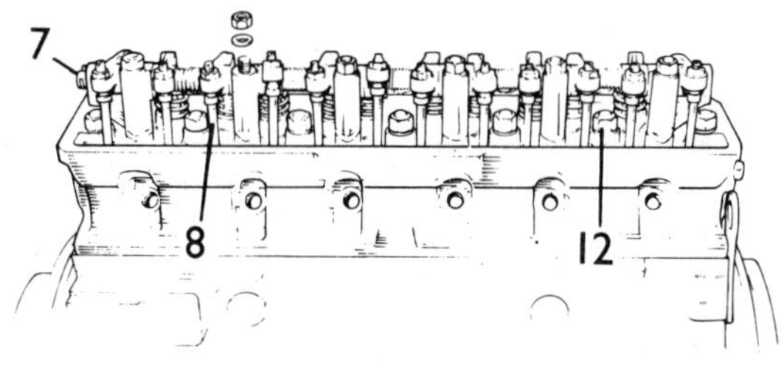

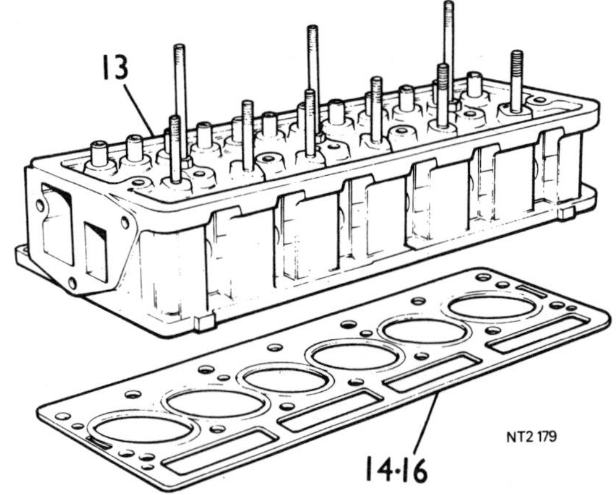

CYLINDER HEAD

– Overhaul **12.29.18**

Which includes

Valves – exhaust – remove and refit **12.29.60**

Valves inlet and exhaust – remove and refit **12.29.62**

Valves – inlet – remove and refit **12.29.63**

Valve guide – inlet – remove and refit **12.29.70**

Valve guide – exhaust – remove and refit **12.29.71**

Inlet valve seat – remove and refit **12.29.76**

Exhaust valve seat – remove and refit **12.29.77.**

Special tools: S60A-2, 6118B

Removing

1. Remove the cylinder head 12.29.10.
2. Remove the spark plugs.
3. Remove the water valve adaptor complete with water valve.
4. Using valve spring compressor 6118B, remove the inlet and exhaust valves, and springs, and identify for reassembly.

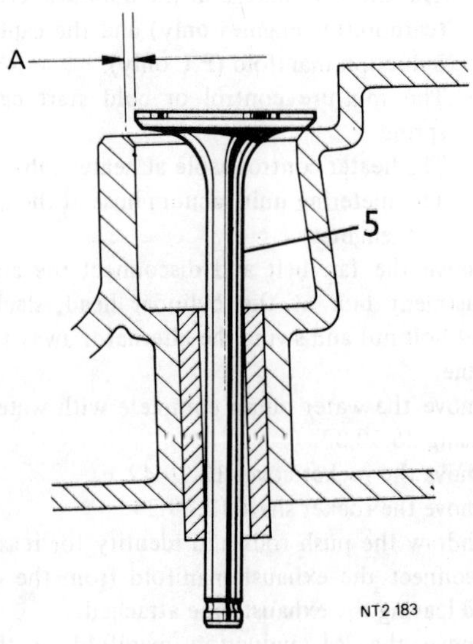

Valve guides

5. Check the inlet and exhaust valve guides for wear. Insert a new valve in each guide in turn and tilt the valve diametrically. If movement across the valve seat – dimention (A) – exceeds 0·20 in (0·508 mm), the valve guide should be replaced.

continued

6. The replacement of valve guides is best carried out using special tool 60A with the appropriate adaptor, to ensure the correct height of the guide above the cylinder head – see Data. Assemble the new valve guide in the tool with the chamfered end leading. Position the tool on the combustion chamber face and draw the new guide into position whilst withdrawing the old one.

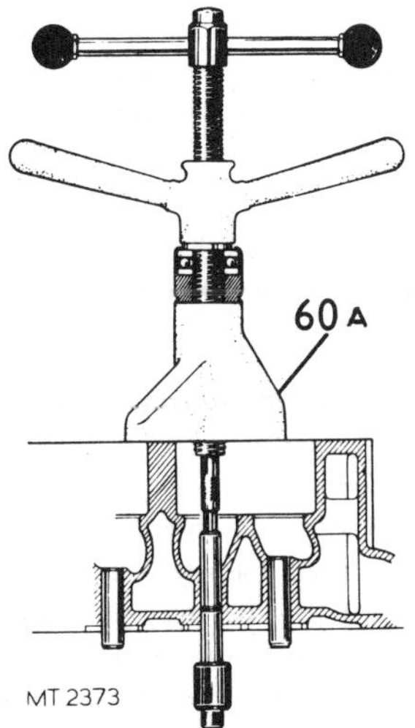

Valves

7. Examine the valves and discard any with worn or bent stems and badly pitted or burnt heads. Valves that have the head thickness reduced to 1/32 in (0·8 mm) dimension (A), should also be discarded. Valves in an otherwise satisfactory condition may be refaced.

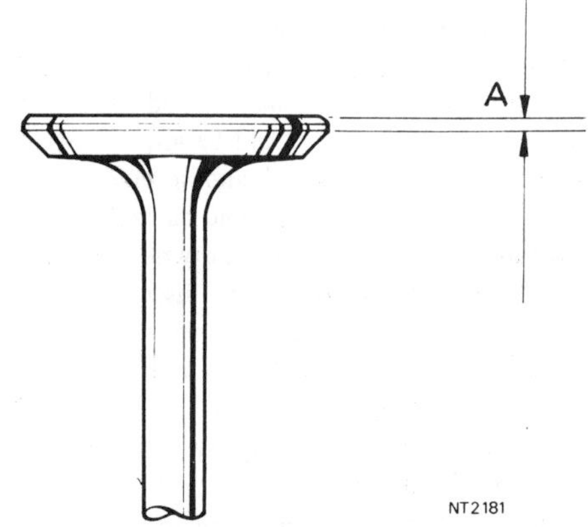

Valve springs

8. Examine valve springs (inner and outer – see Data) for cracks and distortion. Check the springs for free and load length against the information in Data. Discard any springs that do not meet the required standard.

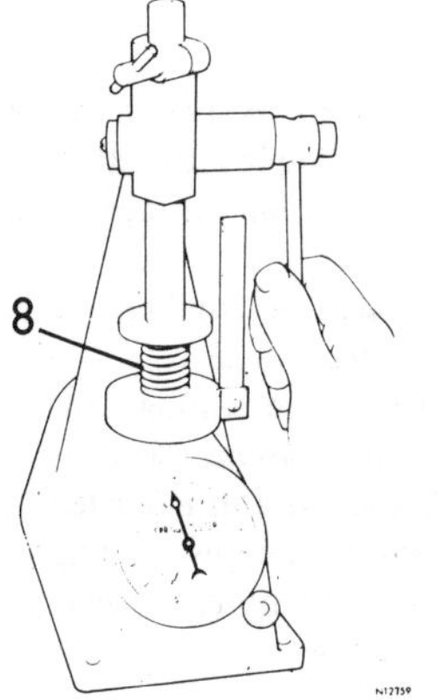

continued

Valve seats

9. Check valve seats for wear, pits, scores and pocketing. Reface where necessary removing only the minimum of material, to avoid a gas tight seal and a correctly seating valve.

   a. Correctly seating valve
   b. Incorrectly seating valve

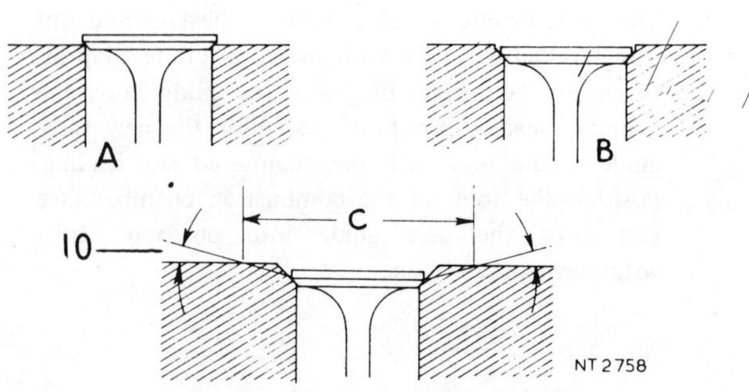

10. If it has been necessary to remove more material than desirable, a 15° cutter may be used to reduce the width of the seating.

CAUTION: It is important to observe that when using this cutter the machined diameter C must not exceed 1·43 in (36·21 mm) for the inlet port seat and 1·26 in (31·23 mm) for the exhaust. Failure to heed this precaution may render the cylinder head useless for the fitting of valve seat inserts at a later date.

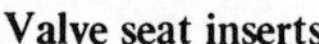

Valve seat inserts

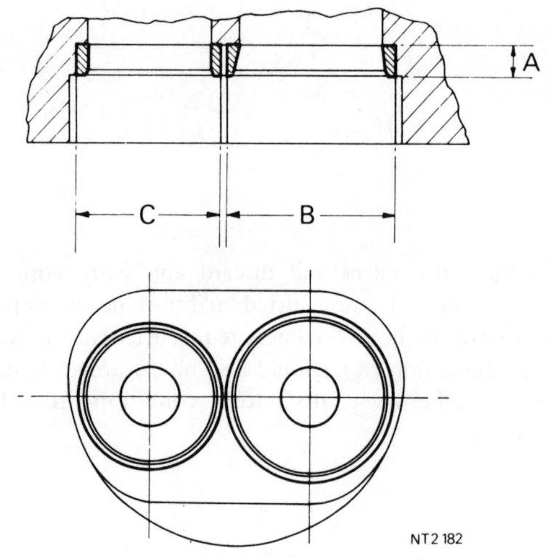

11. Where valve seats cannot be restored by machining. Valve seat inserts may be fitted. In instances where a valve seat insert is already fitted and requires renewing the old insert should be ground away until thin enough to be cracked and levered out. Care, however, should be used to avoid damaging the insert pocket during this operation otherwise difficulty may be encountered in fitting the new insert.
12. Machine the cylinder head to dimensions A, B and C given in Data. Remove burrs and swarf and carefully press the insert squarely into the cylinder head. Secure the insert by peening over the surrounding cylinder head material.
13. Cut the insert seat faces at an inclusive angle of 89° providing a chamfer of 0·040 – 0·045 in (1.016 - 1·14 mm) dimension D.

See data page 12.29.18 Sheet 5.

Grinding in valves

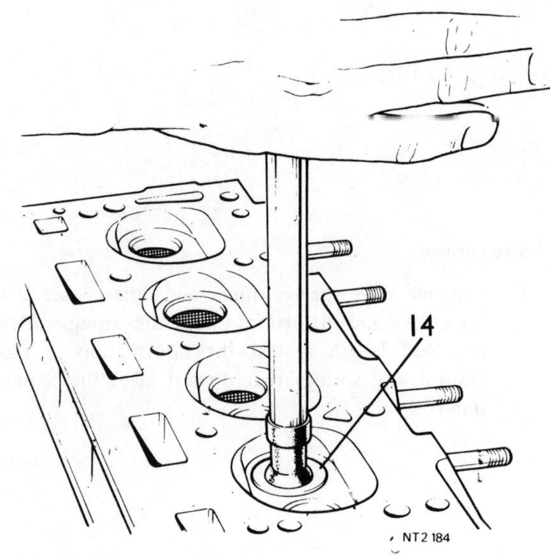

14. Use coarse followed by fine carborundum paste to lap-in the valves. Employ the diabalo action until a continuous narrow line is obtained on the valve seating.
15. Clean off all traces of grinding compound from the valve and seating. Smear a small quantity of engineers' blue on the seating and revolve the valve against its seating about ¼ in (6 mm) in both directions. A good seal in indicated by a continuous band of marking on the valve and its seat.
16. After lapping-in identify each valve for reassembly to its respective seating.

continued

Reassembly

17. Lubricate the valve stems with clean engine oil and assemble them to the cylinder head.
18. Fit the valve spring seats over the valve stems.
19. Place the valve springs over the valve stems ensuring that they locate correctly in the seats. (See Data for engines fitted with double valve springs.)

NOTE: On later P.I. models the valve collar arrangement on both inlet and exhaust valves is as shown on valve (A).

20. Place the valve spring collar(s) over the valve (A) and using valve spring compressor 6118B fit the split valve cotters to secure the valve. *and/or*
21 Place the top outer collar in position on the valve spring. – Valve B.
22. Place the top inner valve collar in position and using the valve spring compressor secure the valve with the split valve cotters.

NOTE: Repeat operation 20, 21 and 22 on the remaining valves.

23. Reverse instructions 1 to 3.

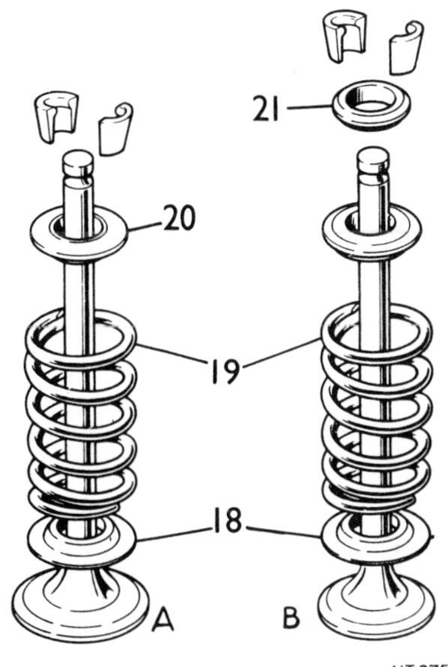

**

VALVES	INLET	EXHAUST	
Petrol Injection Engine		Up to Eng. No. CR 2844 Intermittent from Eng. No. CR 2845 to CR 2935	Intermittent from Eng. No. CR 2845 to CR 2851 Complete from Eng. No. CR 2936
Carburetter Engine		Up to Eng. No. CF 12500	From Eng. No. CF 12501
Head diameter	1·443 – 1·447in (36·65 – 36·75mm)	1·256 – 1·260in (31·90 – 32·00mm)	1·193 – 1·197in (30·30 – 30·40mm)
Stem diameter	0·3107 – 0·3113in (7·87 – 7·90mm)	0·3100 – 0·3105in (7·87 – 7·88mm)	0·3100 – 0·3106in (7·87 – 7·89mm)
Length	4·598 – 4·606in (116·79–116·99mm)	4·590 – 4·613in (116·58 – 117·17mm)	4·597 – 4·607in (116·76 – 117·01mm)
Seat angle	90° inclusive $\pm^{30'}_{00}$	90° inclusive $\pm^{30'}_{00}$	90° inclusive $\pm^{30'}_{00}$ **

Valve guides

Length	2·06in (52·386 mm)	2·25 in (57·15 mm)
External diameter	0·5015 – 0·5020 in (12·725 – 12·751 mm)	0·5015 – 0·5020 in (12·725 – 12·751 mm)
Bore diameter	0·312 – 0·313 in (7·925 – 7·95 mm)	0·312 – 0·313 in (7·925 – 7·95 mm)
Height above head	0·63 in (16·0 mm)	0·63 in (16·0 mm)

Continued

VALVE SPRINGS

Engine No.	Petrol Injection Engine	Carburetter Engine	Engine No.
	Double springs	Single spring	
From Eng. No. CP 25001 to Eng. No. CP 75000	**Inner** – Free length . . . 1·56 in (39·624 mm) – Solid length (compressed) 0·730 in (18·542 mm) – Outer diameter . . 0·730 in (18·542 mm) – Wire diameter . . 0·076 in (1·930 mm) – Rate when fitted . 28·5 lb/in – Working coils . . 6 **Outer** – Free length . . . 1·57 in (39·878 mm) – Solid length (compressed) 0·918 in (23·32 mm) – Inner diameter . . 0·795 in (20·193 mm) – Wire diameter . . 0·136 in (3·454 mm) – Rate when fitted . 150 lb/in – Working coils . . 4	– Free length . . . 1·59 in (40·386 mm) – Solid length (compressed) 0·96 in (24·384 mm) – Inner diameter . 0·795 in (20·193 mm) – Wire diameter . . 0·148 in (3·759 mm) – Rate when fitted . 235 lb/in – Working coils . . 3½	From Eng. No. CC 25001 to Eng. No. CC 75000
	Single spring		
From Eng. No. CP75001	– Free length . . . 1·52 in (38·60 mm) – Solid length (compressed) . . . 0·875 in (22·22 mm) – Inner diameter . . . 0·795 in (20·19 mm) – Wire diameter . . . 0·152 in (3·86 mm) – Rate when fitted . . . 240 lb/in – Working coils . . . 3¾		From Eng. No. CC75001
	Double springs		
From Eng. No. CR 1 and future	**Inner** – Free length . . . 1·14 in (28·96 mm) – Solid length (compressed) . . . 0·552 in (14·021 mm) – Inner diameter . . . 0·578 in (14·68 mm) – Wire diameter . . . 0·92 in (23·68 mm) – Rate when fitted . . . 85·6 lb/in – Working coils . . . 4 **Outer** As single spring fitted from Engines No. CP 75001/CC 75001		From Eng. No. CF 1 and future

Valve seat inserts

Inlet

Outside diameter	1·4875 – 1·4885 in (37·783 – 37·808 mm)
Height	0·247 – 0·250 in (6·274 – 6·35 mm)

Exhaust

Outside diameter	1·2845 – 1·2855 in (32·626 – 32·652 mm)
Height	0·247 – 0·250 in (6·274 – 6·35 mm)

Cylinder head maching dimensions

Depth of bore into head – Dimension (A)	0·250 – 0·255 in (6·35 – 6·45 mm)
Inlet – dimension (B)	1·484 – 1·485 in dia. (37.69 – 37·72 mm)
Exhaust – dimension (C)	1·281 – 1·282 in. dia. (32·54 – 32·56 mm)
Radius at base of pocket	0·03 in (0·76 mm)
Valve seat angle	89° inclusive
Valve seat chamfer – dimension (D)	0·040 – 0·045 in (1·016 – 1·143 mm)

DECARBONIZE, REFACE ALL VALVES AND SEATS GRIND IN VALVES, TUNE ENGINE

– 12.29.21

Dismantling

1. Remove the cylinder head 12.29.10.
2. Remove the inlet and exhaust valves and identify for reassembly 12.29.62
3. Remove carbon deposits from the cylinder head combustion chambers and ports.
4. Clean the face of the cylinder head, removing all traces of carbon and high spots. Clean out the water ways.
5. Reface the valve seats removing only the minimum of material – instructions 9 and 10, 12.29.18.
6. Degrease the valves and remove all traces of carbon. Reface the valves to the correct seat angle – see Data.
7. Grind-in the valves to their respective seats in the cylinder head – instructions 14 to 16, 12.29.18.
8. Turn the crankshaft until numbers one and six pistons are at T.D.C. Fill the remaining cylinder bores with rag and blank off the water passages and camfollower apertures. Using a wooden spatular remove carbon from the piston crowns leaving a band of carbon round the periphery of the piston crown.
9. Repeat instruction 8 on numbers two to five pistons.
10. Remove the blanking material from the cylinder bores, water passages and camfollower apertures and clean the cylinder block face removing carbon and high spots.

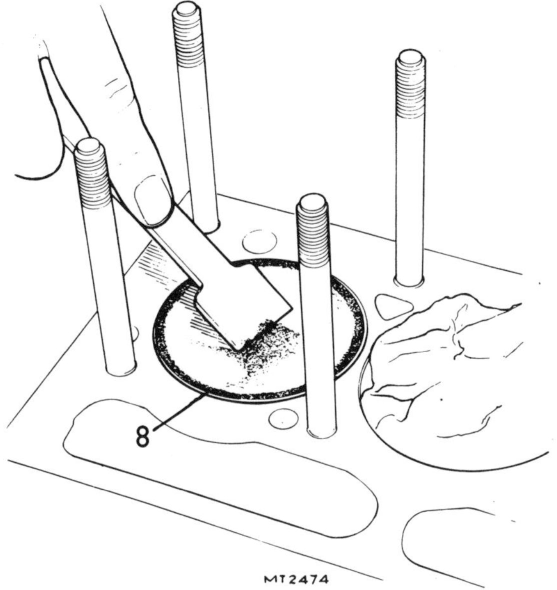

Reassembling

11. Lubricate and refit the valves to their respective guides – instructions 17 to 22, 12.29.18.
12. Refit the cylinder head 12.29.10.
13. Tune the engine 12.49.02.

CYLINDER HEAD NUTS

– Tighten 12.29.27

1. Remove the rocker cover 12.29.42.
2. Remove the rocker shaft 12.29.54.
3. To avoid distortion tighten the cylinder head nuts progressively to 60 to 80 lbf ft (8·3 to 11·1 kgf m) in the following sequence: A, B, C, D, E, F, G, H, I, J, K, L, M, N.
4. Refit the rocker shaft 12.29.54.
5. Refit the rocker cover 12.29.42.

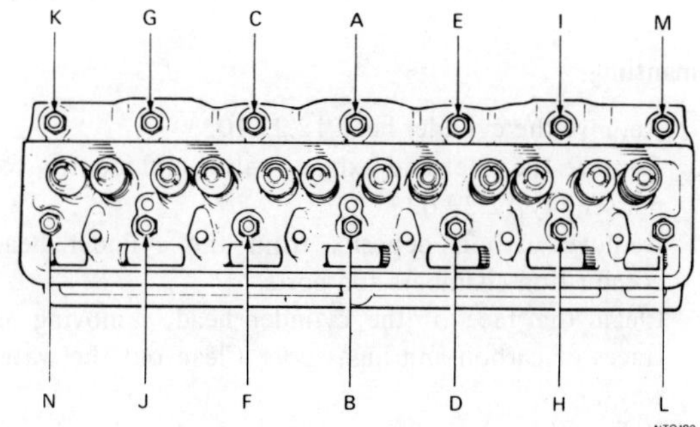

ROCKER COVER

– Remove and refit 12.29.42

Removing

1. Remove the three nuts complete with plain and fibre washers securing the rocker cover to the cylinder head.
2. Disconnect the breather pipe from the rocker cover.
3. Lift off the rocker cover.
4. Remove the gasket.

Refitting

5. Clean the cylinder head and rocker cover mating faces.
6. Fit a new rocker cover gasket.
7. Fit the rocker cover and secure with the washers and nuts, ensuring that the fibre washer is fitted first – next to the rocker cover. Tighten the nuts to 1 to 2 lbf ft (0·15 to 0·3 kgf m). To avoid distortion do not over tighten.
8. Reconnect the breather pipe to the rocker cover.

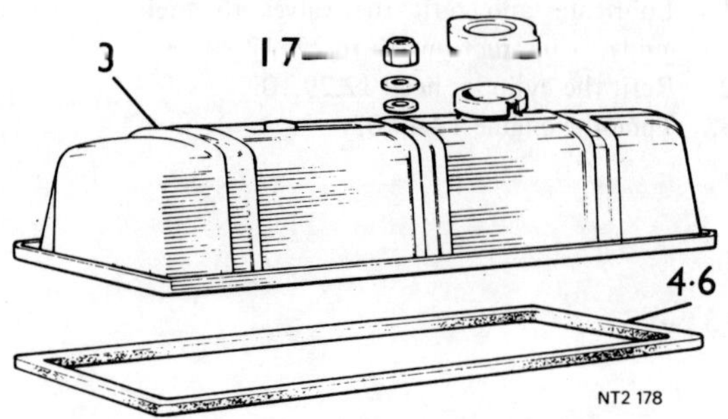

VALVE CLEARANCE

– Check and adjust 12.29.48

1. Isolate the battery and remove the spark plugs.
2. Remove the rocker cover 12.29.42.
3. Counting from the front of the engine, turn the crankshaft until 10 and 12 valves are open, i.e. valve springs fully compressed.
4. Using a feeler gauge, check the gap between the rocker pad and valve tip of numbers 1 and 3 valves.
5. If adjustment is required insert a screwdriver blade in the slot in the adjustment pin and slacken the locknut. Turn the adjustment pin to increase or decrease the gap and tighten the locknut.
6. Check and if necessary adjust the remaining valve clearances in the following sequence.
   Check or adjust No. 8 and 11 valves with Nos. 2 and 5 valves open
   Check or adjust No. 4 and 6 valves with Nos. 7 and 9 valves open
   Check or adjust No. 10 and 12 valves with Nos. 1 and 3 valves open
   Check or adjust No. 2 and 5 valves with Nos. 8 and 11 valves open
   Check or adjust No. 7 and 9 valves with Nos. 4 and 6 valves open
7. Reverse instructions 1 and 2.

DATA

Valve clearance 0·010 in (0·25 mm)

ROCKER SHAFT

– Remove and refit 12.29.54

Removing

1. Remove the rocker cover 12.29.42.
2. Remove the six nuts and washers securing the rocker shaft pedestals to the cylinder head.
3. Lift off the rocker shaft.

Refitting

4. Reverse instructions 1 to 3 ensuring:–
   a. The rocker adjustment screw ball ends locate properly in the push rod cups.
   b. The pedestal securing nuts are tightened evenly to 26 to 34 lbf ft (3·6 to 4·7 kgf m).
5. Adjust the valve clearances 12.29.48.

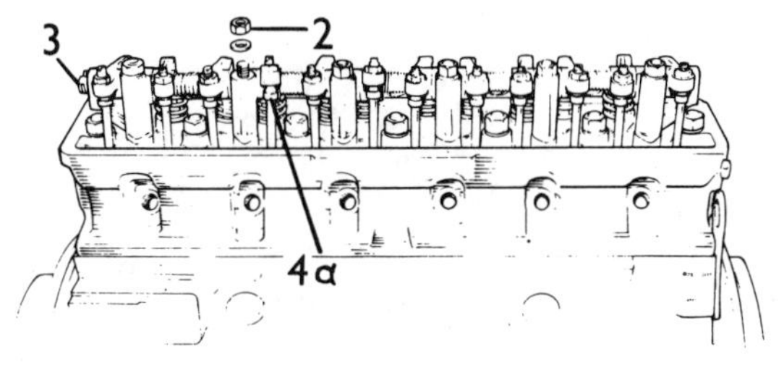

ROCKER SHAFT ASSEMBLY

– Overhaul **12.29.55**

Dismantling

1. Remove the rocker shaft assembly 12.29.42.
2. Withdraw the split pin from the front end of the rocker shaft.
3. Remove the rockers, pedestals, springs and spacers from the front end of the shaft noting the order for reassembly.
4. Remove the screw locating the shaft to number six pedestal.
5. Remove number six pedestal with number twelve rocker and flat spring.

Examination

6. Check the rocker shaft for wear on the rocker running areas using the unworn parts of the shaft as a guide. Examine the shaft for scores and pitting. Renew the shaft if unsatisfactory.
7. Examine the rocker pads for wear and pitting and renew if unservicable. Regrinding the pads as a method of restoration is not recommended. Check the rocker bores for wear against an unworn part of the rocker shaft. Excessively worn rockers should be discarded. Ensure the oil way holes are clear.
8. Examine the rocker spacing springs and renew any that are broken or have lost their tension.

Reassembling

9. Assemble number twelve rocker and number six pedestal to the rocker shaft ensuring that the flat spring is correctly positioned between the rocker and pedestal.
10. Fit the remaining rockers, spacers, and spacer springs as illustrated. Ensure that the flat spring is positioned correctly between number one rocker and pedestal. Secure with a new split pin.
11. Refit the rocker shaft and lubricate with clean engine oil before fitting the rocker cover.

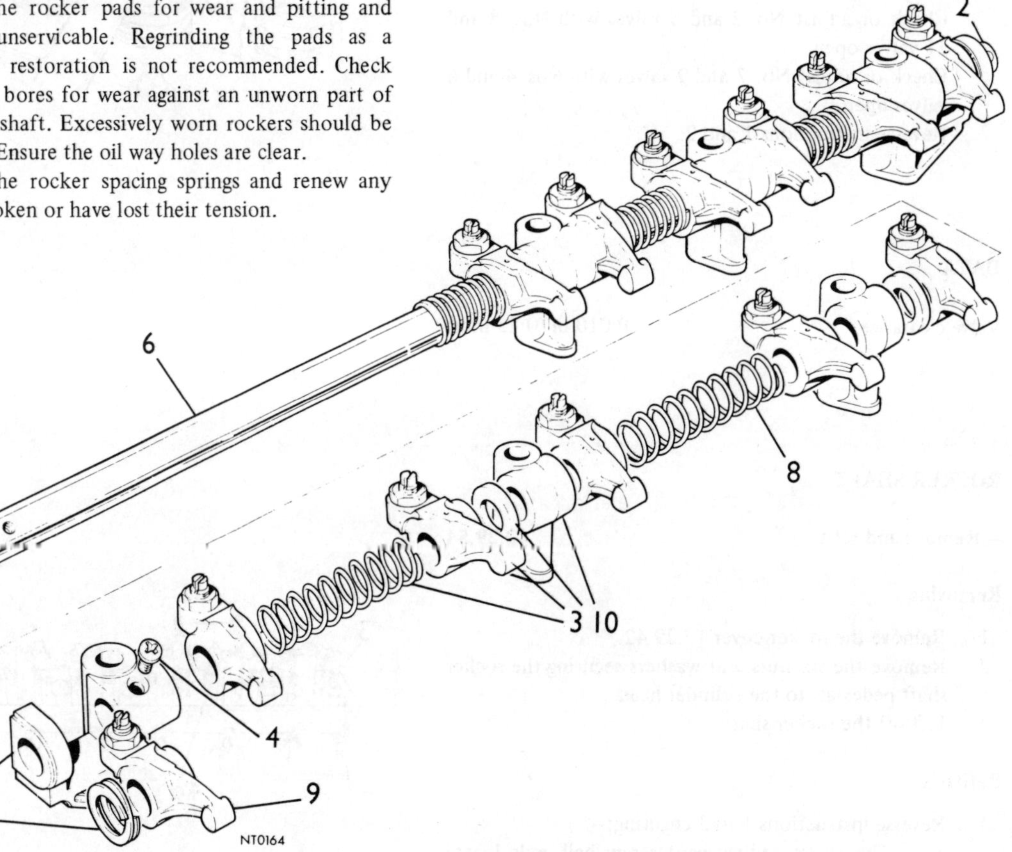

DATA

Diameter of shaft	·5607 – ·5612 in (14·242 – 14·254 mm)
Bore size of rockers	·563 – ·564 in (14·300 – 14·325 mm)
Bore size of pedestals	·563 – ·564 in (14·300 – 14·325 mm)
Spring free length	2·71 in (68·8 mm)

ROCKER ADJUSTING SCREWS

– Remove and refit **12.29.56**

Removing

1. Remove the rocker shaft assembly 12.29.54.
2. Remove the rocker adjusting screw locknuts.
3. Remove the rocker adjusting screws.

Refitting

4. Reverse instructions 1 to 3.
5. Adjust the valve clearances 12.29.48.

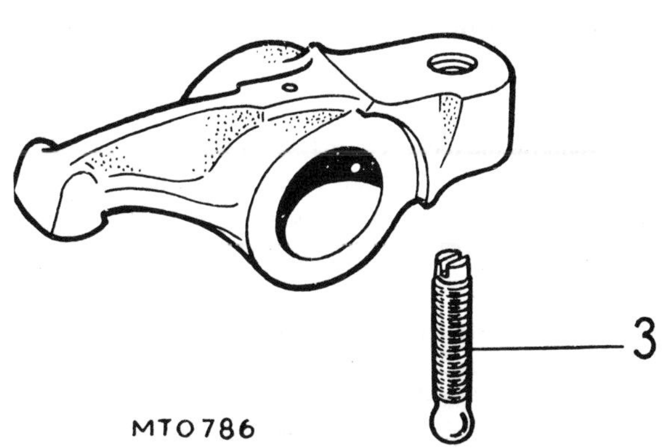

CAM FOLLOWERS

– Remove and refit **12.29.57**

Removing

1. Remove the cylinder head 12.29.10.
2. Lift out the eight cam followers and identify for reassembly.

Refitting

3. Reverse instructions 1 and 2 ensuring:–
   a. Worn or pitted cam followers are renewed.
   b. Each follower is free to slide and rotate in its respective bore.

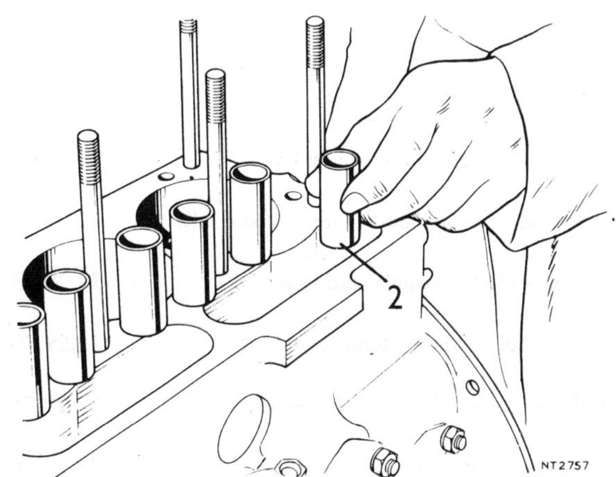

DATA

Cam follower dia.	0·799 in – 0·80 in (20·31 – 20·12 mm)
Bore in cylinder block	0·8002 in – 0·8009 (20·325 – 20·343 mm)

PUSH RODS

– Remove and refit **12.29.59**

Removing

1. Remove the rocker cover 12.29.42.
2. Remove the rocker shaft assembly 12.29.54.
3. Lift out the push rods and identify for reassembly.

Refitting

4. Reverse instructions 1 to 3 ensuring:–
   a. Push rods with worn or pitted cup and ball ends and bent shaft are renewed.
   b. The cup ends are located correctly in the rocker adjusting screw ball and the ball end of the push rods seat properly in their respective cam followers.
5. Adjust the valve clearances 12.29.48

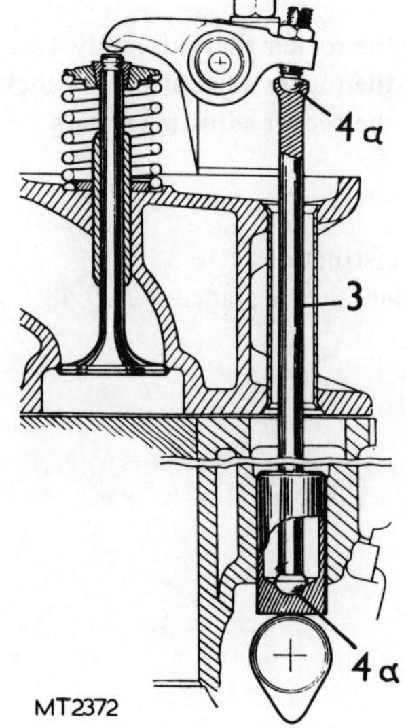

Valves – exhaust – remove and refit	**12.29.60**
Valves inlet and exhaust – remove and refit	**12.29.62**
Valves – inlet – remove and refit	**12.29.63**
Valve guide – inlet – remove and refit	**12.29.70**
Valve guide – exhaust – remove and refit	**12.29.71**
Inlet valve seat – remove and refit	**12.29.76**
Exhaust valve seat – remove and refit	**12.29.77**

See 12.29.18.

ENGINE AND GEARBOX ASSEMBLY

– Remove and refit **12.37.01**

Removing

1. Isolate the battery.
2. Remove the bonnet 76.16.01.
3. Drain the radiator.
4. Remove the air cleaner to air intake manifold hose – P.I. only.
5. Remove the radiator cowling.
6. Remove the radiator.
7. Remove the bottom hose from the water pump.
8. Remove the air intake manifold 19.70.01 – P.I. engine.
9. Remove the air cleaner – carburetter engine.
10. Drain the engine coolant.
11. Remove the chassis cross tube 76.10.05.
12. Disconnect the alternator.
13. Disconnect the coil.
14. Disconnect the alternator multi-socket connector
15. Disconnect the oil warning light.
16. Disconnect the oil gauge pipe.
17. Disconnect the fuel main feed pipe.
18. Disconnect the metering unit spill-off pipe – P.I.
19. Disconnect the excess fuel lever – P.I.
20. Disconnect the earth strap from the rear lifting eye end, refit the bolt.
21. Disconnect the water temperature transmitter lead.
22. Disconnect the tachometer drive.
23. Disconnect the throttle cable.
24. Disconnect the fast idle cable – P.I.
25. Disconnect the mixture control cable – carburetter model.
26. Disconnect the fast idle return spring – P.I.
27. Disconnect the brake servo pipe.
28. Disconnect the two heater hoses.
29. Disconnect the heater control cable.
30. Disconnect the starter motor leads.
31. Jack-up the car and support it on chassis stands and disconnect the clutch slave cylinder and bracket from the bell housing.
32. Disconnect the exhaust pipe from the manifold.
33. Remove the chassis stands and lower the car.
34. Remove the gearbox tunnel cover 76.25.07.
35. Remove the gear lever 37.16.04.
36. Disconnect the leads from the transmission switches.
37. Disconnect the propeller shaft from the transmission.
38. Remove the engine and gearbox rear mounting bolts.
39. Disconnect the speedometer cable from the gearbox.
40. Attach a lifting sling to a hoist and attach the sling to the engine lifting eyes and ease the weight of the engine off the front mountings.
41. Disconnect the engine mounting from the engine bracket on the drivers' side.
42. Remove the engine mounting from the chassis frame on the passengers' side.
43. Raise the engine, pull forward to clear the bulkhead, raise the front of the engine and hoist clear of the car.
44. Drain the engine oil.
45. Remove the sling.

Refitting

46. Attach a sling to the engine lifting eyes and attach the sling to the hoist.
47. Raise the engine and gearbox assembly and move it towards the engine compartment. Lift the front of the engine so as to enable the transmission end to enter the bulkhead aperture and lower the assembly vertically into position.
48. Loosely connect the R.H. and L.H. engine mountings.
49. Place the rear mounting bolts in position and lower the engine and remove the sling.
50. Secure the L.H. and R.H. front mountings.
51. Raise the car on a jack and support the car on chassis stands.
52. Fit the exhaust pipe to the manifold using a new gasket.
53. Fit the clutch slave cylinder and bracket to the bell housing and lower the car.
54. Secure the R.H. rear mounting bolt to the exhaust pipe bracket captive nut.
55. Tighten the L.H. rear mounting bolt with the nut and spring washer.
56. Connect the propeller shaft to the transmission drive flange.
57. Connect the speedometer drive.
58. Connect the leads to the transmission switches.
59. Fit and adjust the gear lever 37.16.04.
60. Fit the gearbox tunnel cover.
61. Reverse instructions 2 to 31.
62. Refit the engine sump with new oil to the high mark on the dipstick.
63. Check the gearbox oil level.
64. Reconnect the battery.

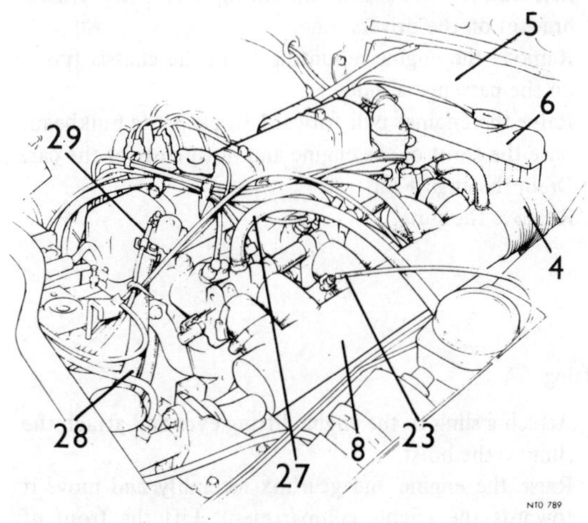

5
6
29
4
28
27
8
23
NTO 789

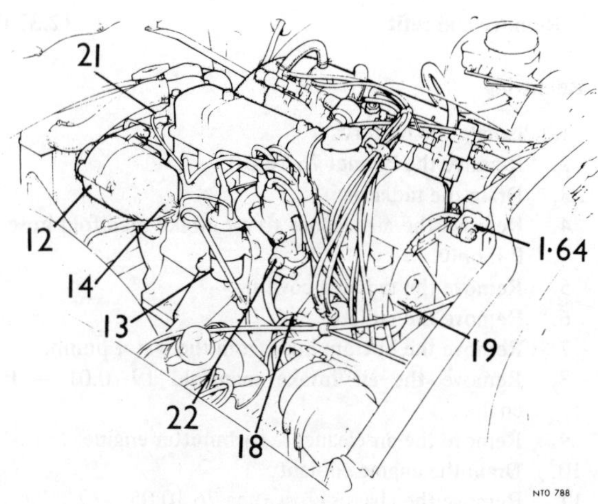

21
12
1·64
14
13
19
22
18
NTO 788

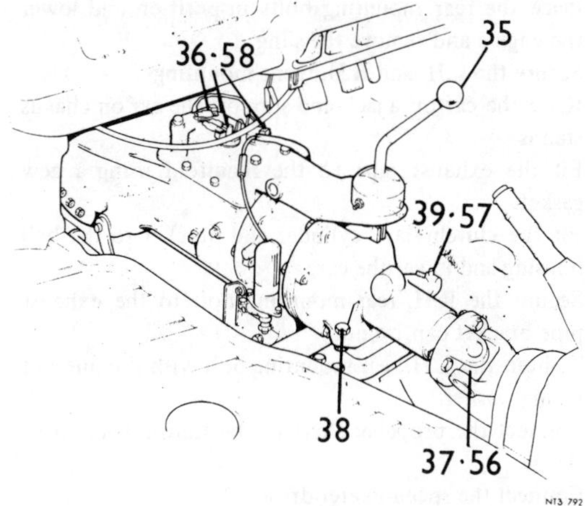

36·58
35
39·57
38
37·56
NTS 792

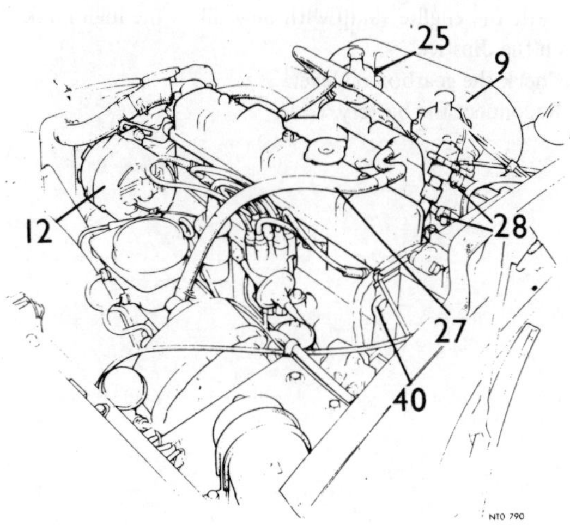

25
9
12
28
27
40
NTO 790

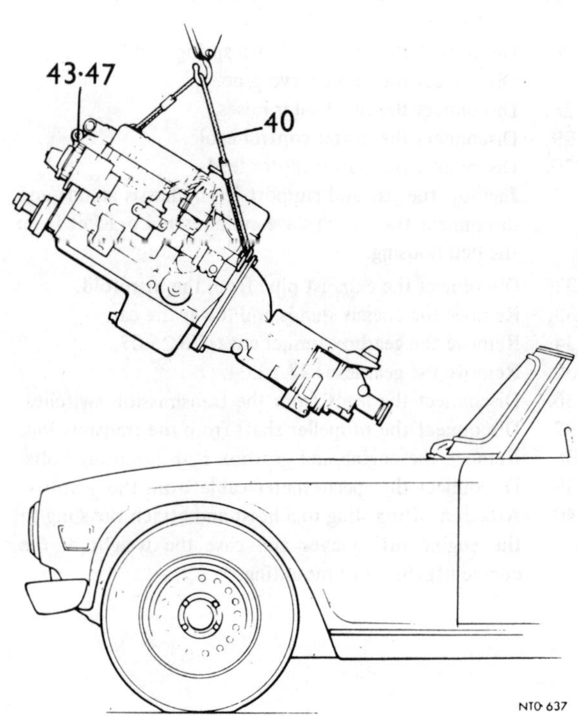

43·47
40
NTO 637

BRITISH
LEYLAND

1. Engine backplate
2. Crankshaft rear oil seal housing.
3. Gasket–crankshaft rear oil seal housing.
4. Bush–oil pump spindle and distributor drive.
5. Oil switch.
6. Engine mounting.
7. Bracket–engine mounting.
8. Relief valve–oil pressure.
9. Body–oil pump.
10. Sump.
11. Cylinder block.
12. Packing–front sealing block.
13. Main bearing cap.
14. Front sealing block.
15. Gasket–sump.
16. Oil seal– timing cover.
17. Timing cover.
18. Gasket–timing cover.
19. Tensioner–timing chain.
20. Engine front plate.
21. Gasket–engine front plate.
22. Main bearing shells.

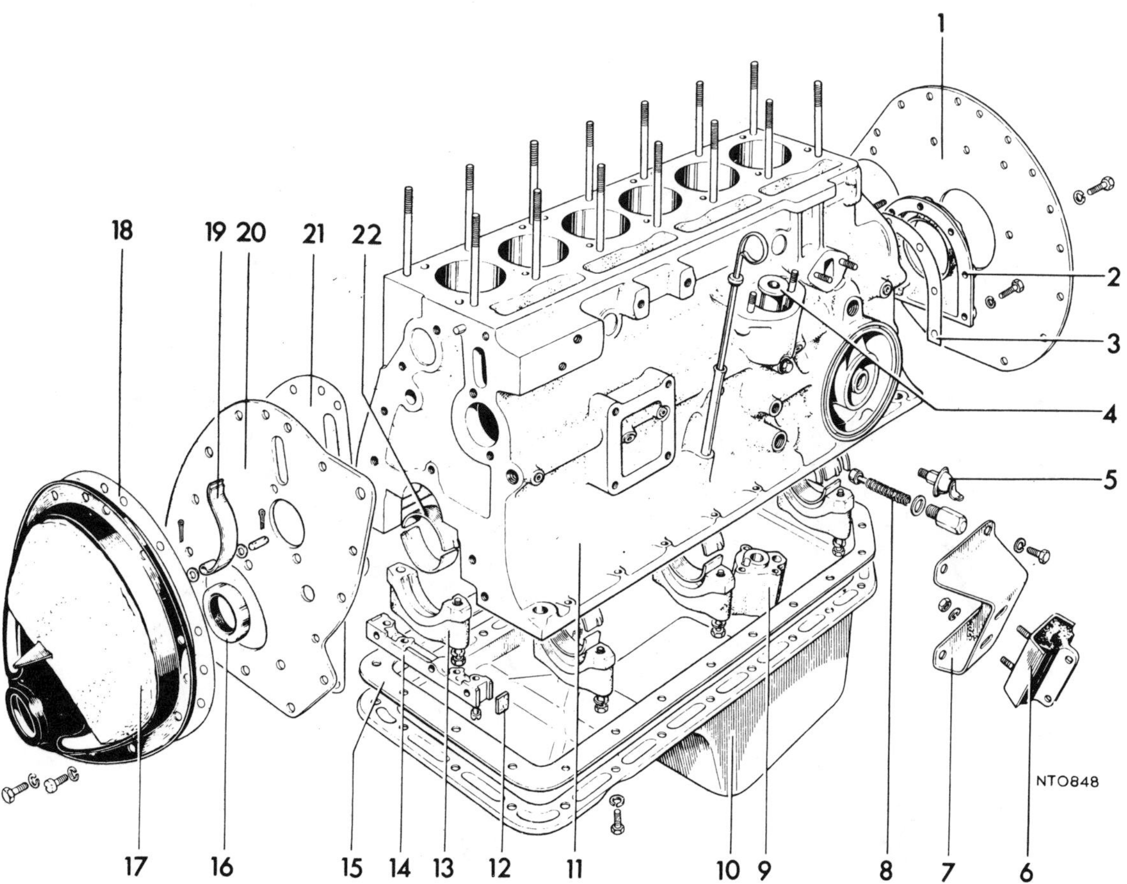

23 Camshaft
24 Distributor drive gear
25 Flywheel
26 Bush – crankshaft
27 Crankshaft
28 Inner rotor and spindle – oil pump
29 Outer rotor – oil pump
30 Shims – sprocket alignment
31 Sprocket – crankshaft
32 Oil Thrower
33 Spacer
34 Pulley – crankshaft
35 Timing chain
36 Lockplate – camshaft sprocket
37 Sprocket – camshaft
38 Keeper plate – camshaft
39 Bearing cap – connecting rod
40 Bearing shells – connecting rod
41 Connecting rod
42 Circlip
43 Gudgeon pin
44 Bush – connecting rod
45 Piston
46 Piston rings

NTO 849

ENGINE ASSEMBLY

– Strip and rebuild **12.41.05**

Stripping

1. Remove the engine and gearbox assembly from the car 12.37.01.
2. Remove the gearbox from the engine.
3. Remove the following – carburetter engine
   a. the inlet manifold complete with carburetters.
   b. the fuel pump and outlet pipe.
   c. the ignition distributor 86.35.20.
   d. the pedestal and distributor drive shaft
4. Remove the following – P.I. engine
   a. the injector pipes from the injectors.
   b. the metering unit vacuum pipe.
   c. the ignition distributor complete with the pedestal distributor drive shaft and fuel metering distributor.
   d. the inlet manifold complete.
   e. the air intake manifold support bracket.
5. Remove the alternator and drive belt.
6. Remove the water pump complete with the housing.
7. Remove the exhaust manifold and gasket.
8. Remove the oil filter assembly and dipstick.
9. Remove the oil pressure relief valve.
10. Remove the ignition coil and earth strap. Noting the location of the suppressor on latter USA market engines.**
11. Remove the starter motor.
12. Remove the engine mounting brackets.
13. Remove the oil pressure switch.
14. Remove the fan blades.
15. Remove the crankshaft pulley and fan extension, instructions 6, 7 and 9, 12.21.01.
16. Remove the clutch assembly.
17. Remove the rocker cover.
18. Remove the six pedestal nuts and lift off the rocker shaft assembly.
19. Slacken the cylinder head securing nuts in the reverse order as in operation 12.29.27.
20. Lift off the cylinder head.
21. Remove and discard the cylinder head gasket.
22. Remove the twelve push rods and cam followers and identify for reassembly.
23. Remove the five bolts, two nuts and five set screws securing the timing cover and carefully ease the cover off the two dowels and two studs.
24. Withdraw the crankshaft collar and oil thrower.
25. Straighten the lock tabs and remove the two bolts securing the camshaft sprocket and remove the crankshaft and camshaft sprocket complete with the timing chain.
26. Remove the two bolts securing the camshaft keeper plate to the cylinder block and remove the plate.
27. Carefully withdraw the camshaft from the cylinder block.
28. Remove the three bolts and two set screws from the engine front mounting plate and withdraw the plate and gasket.
29. Remove the four bolts holding the flywheel assembly to the crankshaft and lift-off the flywheel.
30. Remove the spigot bush from the back of the flywheel.
31. Remove the seven bolts and remove the engine rear mounting plate.
32. Remove the twenty three bolts and withdraw the sump and gasket.
33. Remove the three bolts and withdraw the oil pump.
34. Remove the two screws securing the front sealing block to the crankcase and withdraw the block.
35. Remove the seven bolts securing the rear main oil seal housing to the crankcase and remove the housing and seal.

CAUTION: It is vital that during the following operations, 36 to 39, that no intermixing of components is allowed to occur. The Connecting rod big-ends and the main bearings are numbered for identification purposes and their respective bolts, caps and bearings must not loose their identity.

36. Remove the connecting rod bolts and withdraw the caps and lower shells.
37. Push the pistons and connecting rods up the bores and withdraw from the top of the cylinder block.
38. Assemble the caps and bearings to their respective connecting rods.
39. Remove the main bearing bolts and withdraw the caps and lower bearing shells.
40. Lift out the crankshaft.
41. Remove the thrust bearings from the rear main bearing.
42. Remove the main bearing upper shells.
43. If necessary, drive the oil pump shaft bush out from the underside of the cylinder block using a suitable drift with a pilot.
44. If necessary, remove the cylinder head holding down studs from the block.
45. Remove: *a.* the rear sling eye, *b.* the front sling eye, and *c.* the alternator bracket.
46. Overhaul the cylinder head 12.29.18.
47. Overhaul the connecting rods and pistons 12.17.10 instructions 2 to 15.
48. Overhaul the oil pump instructions 4 to 11. 12.60.32.

Continued

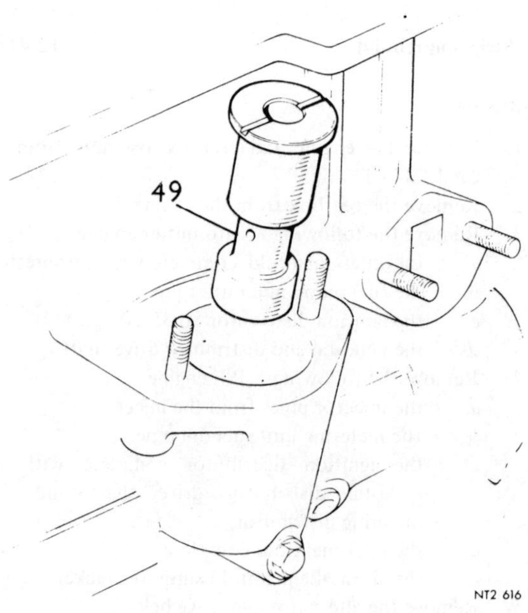

Rebuilding

NOTE: The following rebuilding instructions assume that all the individual components and assemblies have been examined, worn parts renewed and assemblies reconditioned.

49. Drive the oil pump shaft bush into the cylinder block using a drift with a pilot.

50. Fit the upper main bearing shells to the cylinder block ensuring that the tags locate in the recesses.
51. Fit the lower bearing shells to the bearing caps ensuring that the tags locate in the recesses.
52. Lubricate and lower the crankshaft into the crankcase.
53. Insert the thrust bearings into the grooves in the cylinder block ensuring that the oil grooves face towards the sides of the crankshaft journal.
54. Fit the bearing caps to their respective bearings as indicated by the numbers stamped on the caps and ensure that they are fitted the correct way round i.e. the shell bearing recesses in the block and cap adjacent. Tighten the retaining bolts evenly to 50 to 65 lbf ft (6·9 to 9·0 kgf m).

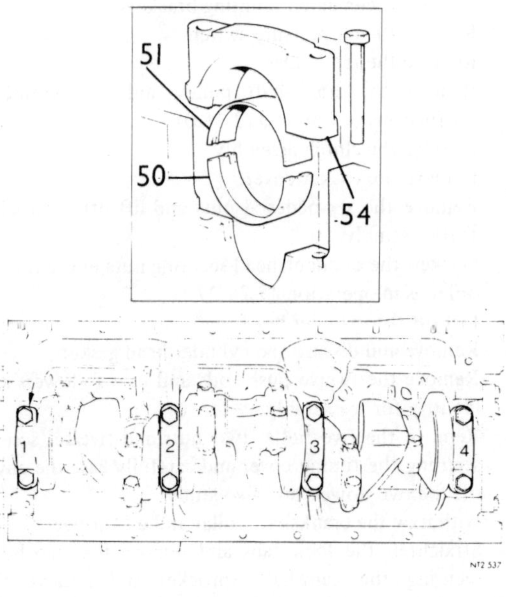

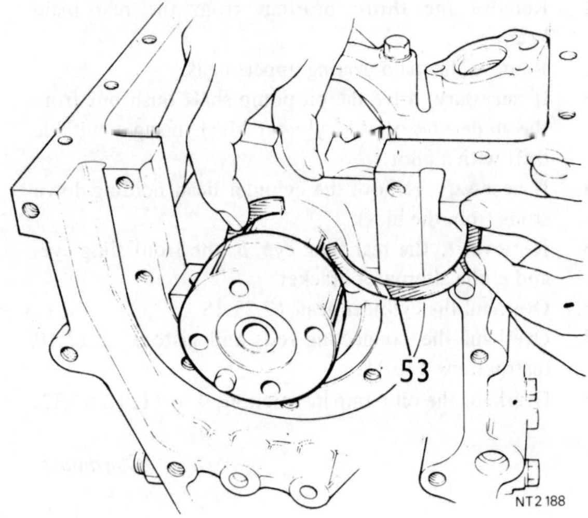

Continued

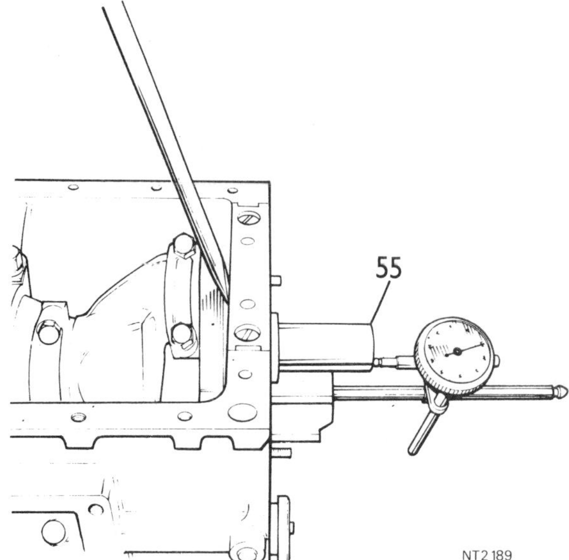

55. Check the crankshaft end float by attaching a dial gauge to the cylinder block so that the stylus rests in a loaded condition squarely on the end of the crankshaft. Lever the crankshaft forward or rearward and zero the gauge. Lever the crankshaft in the opposite direction and note the reading. See data for correct end float.

56. Assemble the front sealing block to the crankcase as follows:
   - *a.* Fit a gasket to both sides of the cylinder block mating face using jounting compound.
   - *b.* Fit the sealing block with the three tapped holes facing outwards and loosely secure with the two set screws.
   - *c.* Drive wedges into the slots having first coated them with jointing compound.
   - *d.* Line up the front face of the sealing block with the crankcase using a straight edge.
   - *e.* Finally tighten the set screws and trim the protruding ends of the wedges flush with the crankcase taking care not to undercut them, thereby causing a passage for oil leakage.

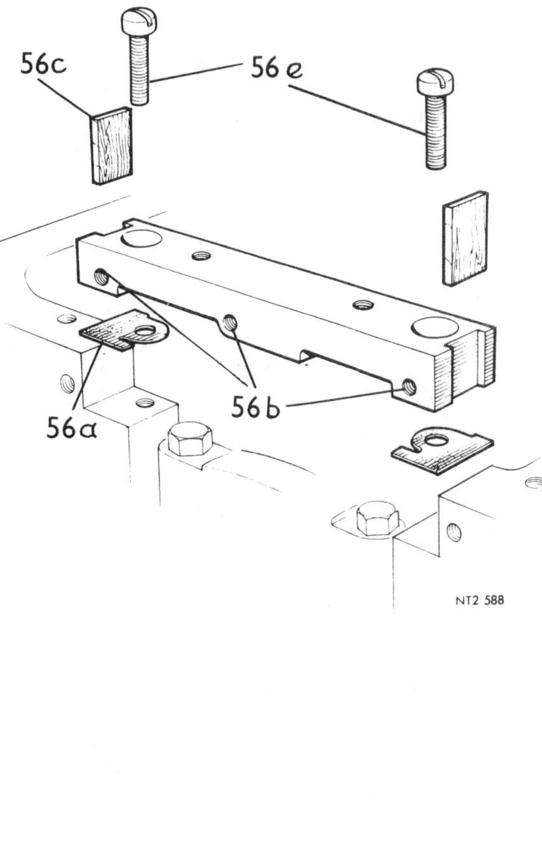

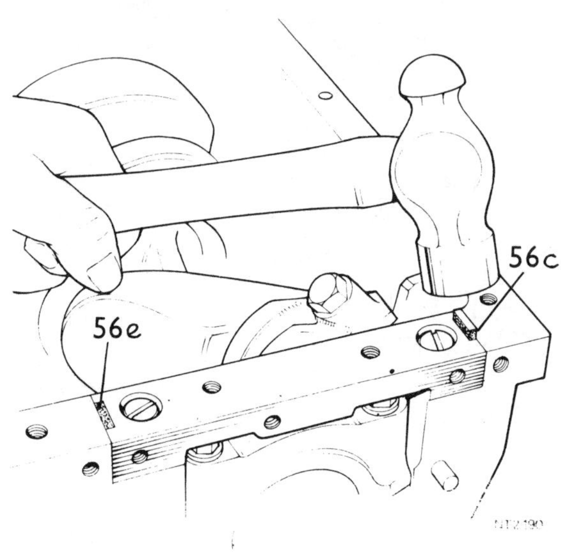

Continued

57. Coat a new oil seal with grease and press it into the rear main oil seal housing with the lip face towards the crankshaft. Remove surplus grease.
58. Fit a gasket to the cylinder block mating face using jointing compound and carefully slide the seal and housing over the crankshaft and secure in position with the seven bolts and six spring washers.

NOTE: The top bolt A has a copper washer under the head to prevent oil seepage since the bolt protrudes into the crankcase

59. Fit the connecting rods and pistons, instructions 6 to 10, 12.17.01.
60. Fit the oil pump complete with the strainer.
61. Place a sump gasket into position on the crankcase and fit the sump noting that the four longer bolts are fitted to the rear reinforcement plates.
62. Fit the engine rear adaptor plate ensuring that it locates over the dowel.
63. Secure the plate with the seven bolts and spring washers.
64. Insert the spigot bush into the back of the flywheel.
65. Fit the flywheel to the crankshaft locating it over the dowel. Secure with the four bolts tightening evenly to 50 – 75 lbf ft (6·9 – 10·4 kgf m).
66. Attach a dial gauge stand to the cylinder block and position a dial gauge so that the stylus rests 4·0 in (102 mm) from the centre of the flywheel. Check the flywheel run-out which must not exceed 0·004 in (0·1016 mm) – See 12.53.07.

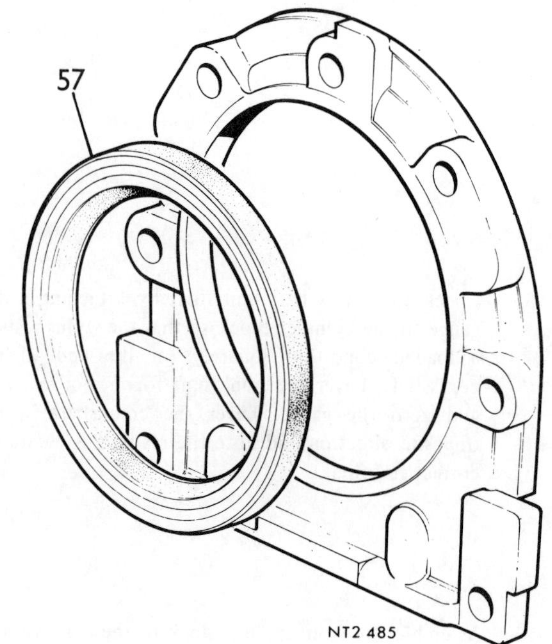

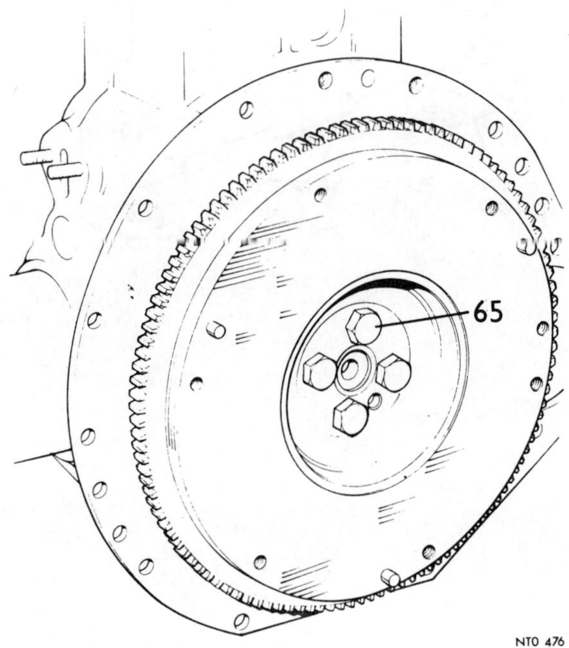

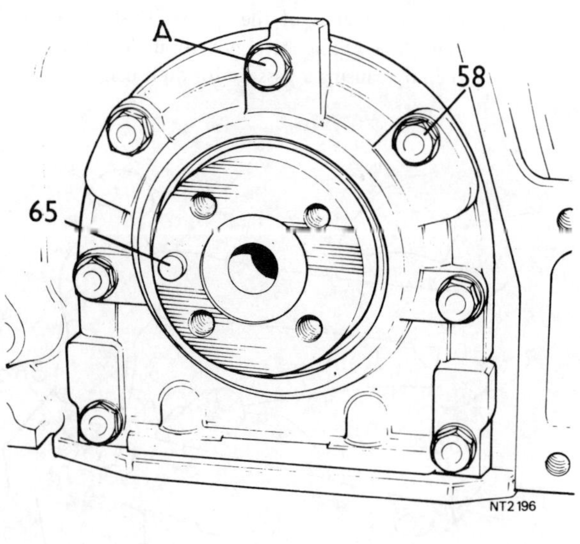

Continued

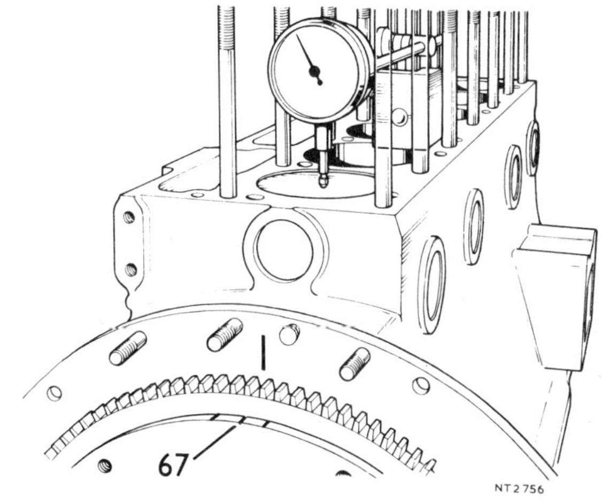

67. To obtain the true T.D.C. mark on the flywheel, attach a dial gauge stand to the cylinder block top face and position a dial gauge so that the stylus rests on top of number one piston. Turn the crankshaft in a clockwise direction until the piston reaches the highes point as indicated by the dial gauge. Make a scribe mark on the flywheel outer edge opposite the line on the engine rear adaptor plate. Turn the crankshaft in an anti-clockwise direction until the piston again reaches its highest point and make a further mark on the flywheel opposite the line on the adaptor plate. To obtain the true T.D.C. mark bisect the gap between the two scribe lines with a chisel.
68. Fit the engine front mounting plate gasket using jointing compound and fit the mounting plate locating it over the two dowels.
69. Secure the plate with the three bolts and two screws.
70. With the flat end leading and the spigot end trailing, insert the camshaft into the cylinder block.
71. Secure the camshaft with the keeper plate and two bolts.
72. Check the camshaft end-float.
73. Turn the crankshaft so that number one and six pistons are at true T.D.C.
74. Turn the camshaft so that the milled cut-a-way is positioned at twenty – past – four which is approximately the correct position for timing.
75. Fit the camfollowers.
76. Re-stud the block and fit the cylinder head, ensuring:–
    a. A new gasket is fitted.
    b. The retaining nuts are tightened to the correct torque and in the correct sequence 12.29.27.
77. Fit the push rods ensuring that the ball ends locate properly in the camfollowers.
78. Fit the rocker shaft assembly and secure with the six nuts and spring washers.
79. Adjust all valve clearances 12.29.48.
80. Adjust numbers eleven and twelve valve clearances to 0·120 in.

NOTE: This clearance may vary according to the lift of the camshaft employed. The clearance should be sufficient to enable feeler gauges of reasonable thickness to be inserted when the valves are on the 'rock'.

81. Oscillate the camshaft a few degrees so that numbers eleven and twelve valves are on the 'rock' whilst checking both valve clearances with two feeler gauges of the same value. When the clearances are the same the camshaft and crankshaft are in their correct relationship.

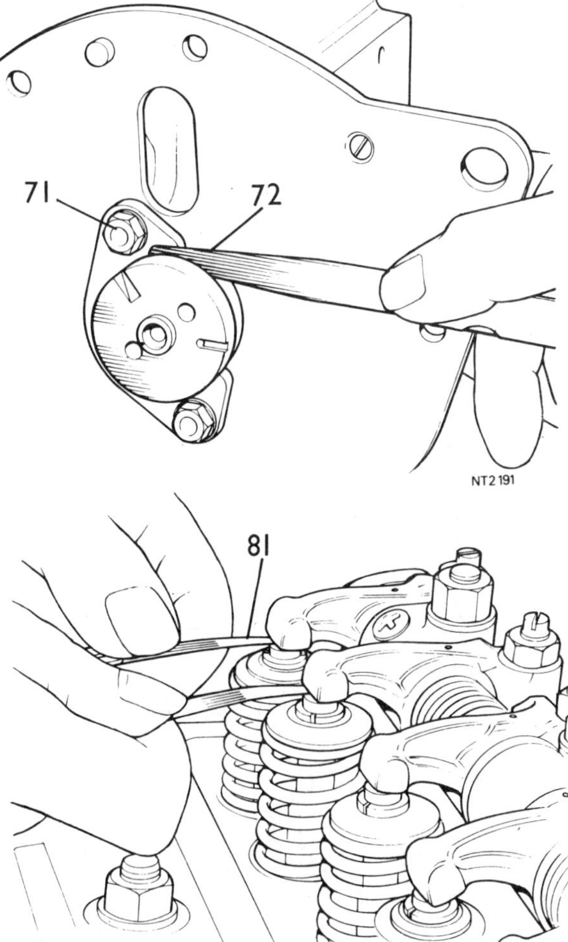

Continued

82. Temporarily fit the camshaft and crankshaft sprockets and check their alignment with a straight edge.
83. Adjust the alignment by fitting shims behind the crankshaft sprocket.
84. Encircle the sprockets with the timing chain and fit the sprockets to the engine.
85. If the original sprockets and camshaft are being fitted check that punch marks A and B coincide and punch marks C line up.
86. If new sprockets and camshaft are being fitted make the appropriate punch marks.
87. Secure the camshaft sprocket with the two bolts and lock with the tab washer.

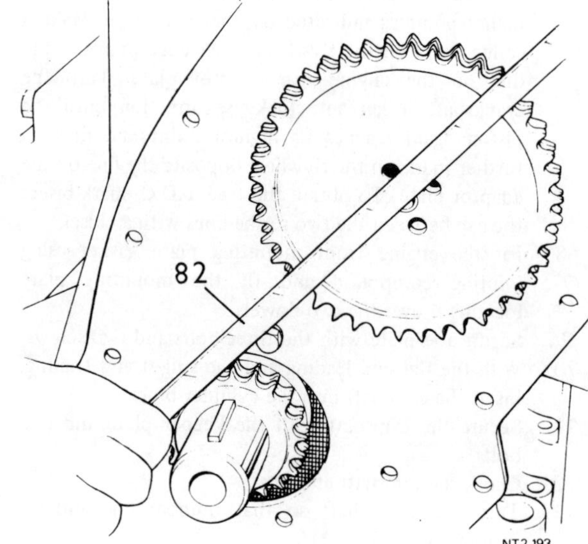

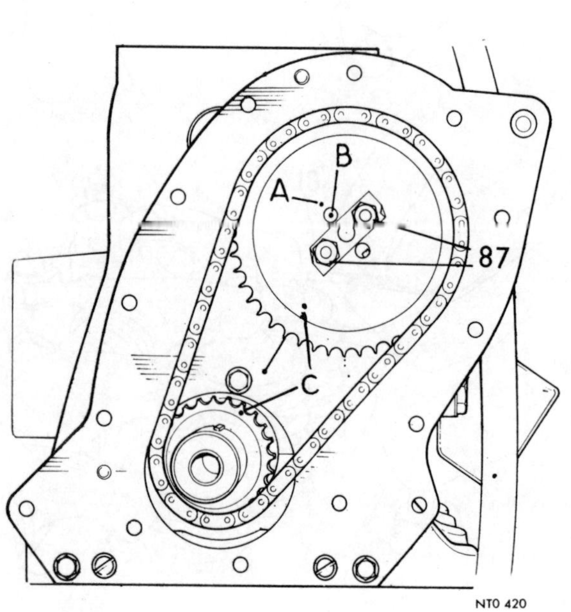

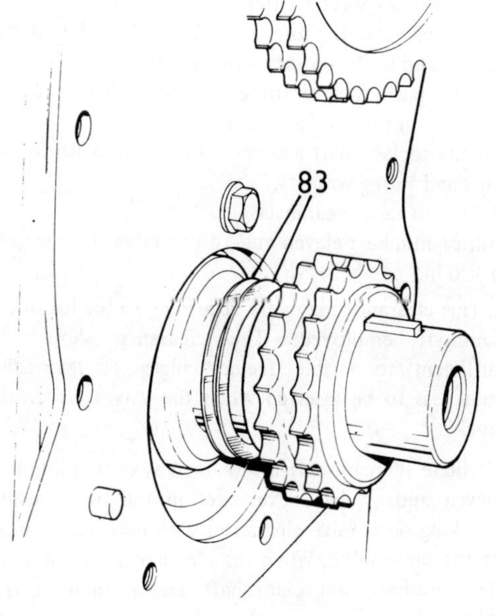

Continued

88. Fit the oil thrower ensuring that the dished surface faces away from the crankshaft sprocket.
89. Using a new gasket and jointing compound, fit the timing chain cover – instructions 15 to 18, 12.65.01.

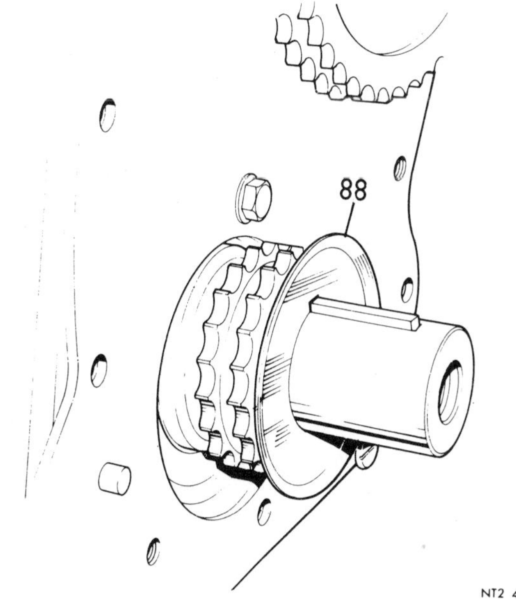

90. Fit the oil pressure relief valve assembly.
91. Fit the oil filter assembly and dipstick.
92. Fit the crankshaft pulley and fan extension, instructions 10 and 11, 12.21.01.
93. Fit the rocker cover using a new gasket and ensuring that fibre washers are fitted first and plain washers under the retaining nuts.

NOTE: The following instructions, 94 to 97, relate to P.I. engine.

94. Establish the distributor drive shaft end-float – instructions 11 to 15, 12.10.22.
95. Turn the crankshaft until number one and six pistons are at T.D.C. with number one firing.
96. Fit the distributor drive shaft so that the off-set slot is positioned as illustrated. Ensure however that the slot at the bottom end of the shaft engages properly in the oil pump drive dog.
97. Fit the pedestal complete with the fuel metering distributor and time the metering distributor to the engine – instructions 7 to 10, 19.35.01

Continued

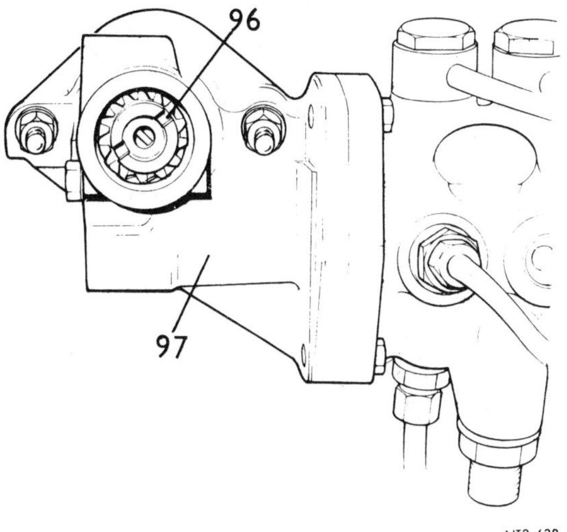

NOTE: The following instructions, 96 to 99, relate to the carburetter engine.

98. Establish the distributor drive shaft end-float – instructions 8 to 12, 12.20.22. (Carburetter engine).
99. Turn the crankshaft until number one and six pistons are at T.D.C. with number one firing.
100. Fit the distributor drive gear with the offset slot in the position illustrated.
101. Fit and secure the pedestal with the two nuts and washers.
102. Fit the ignition distributor leaving the clamp bolt slack until the ignition is timed when the engine is refitted to the car.
103. Fit the front and rear lifting eyes.
104. Fit the exhaust manifold and gasket.
105. Fit the inlet manifold complete with carburetters or

106. Fit the P.I. inlet manifold.
107. Connect the injector pipes to their respective injectors – P.I. only.
108. Connect the vacuum hose from the metering unit to the inlet manifold – P.I. only.
109. Fit the air intake manifold support bracket – P.I. only.
110. Fit the mechanical fuel pump and delivering pipe to the carburetters.
111. Fit the water pump complete with its housing instructions 11 to 14, 26.50.63.
112. Fit the clutch assembly, instructions 4 to 7, 33.10.01.
113. Fit the starter motor.
114. **Fit the ignition coil and earth strap and (later USA market engines only) the ignition suppressor.**
115. Fit the alternator and drive belt and adjust the belt tension.
116. Fit the engine mounting brackets.
117. Fit the fan blades.
118. Fit the gearbox to the engine.
119. Re-fit the engine and gearbox assembly to the car ensuring:–
    - *a.* The engine sump is replenished with new oil of the correct grade to the high mark on the dipstick.
    - *b.* The gear box oil level is checked.
    - *c.* The cooling system is re-filled.
120. Time the ignition 86.35.15.
121. Tune and adjust the carburetters 19.15.02, or check and adjust the butterflies – P.I. engines 19.20.05.
122. Check the engine and cooling system for oil and water leaks.

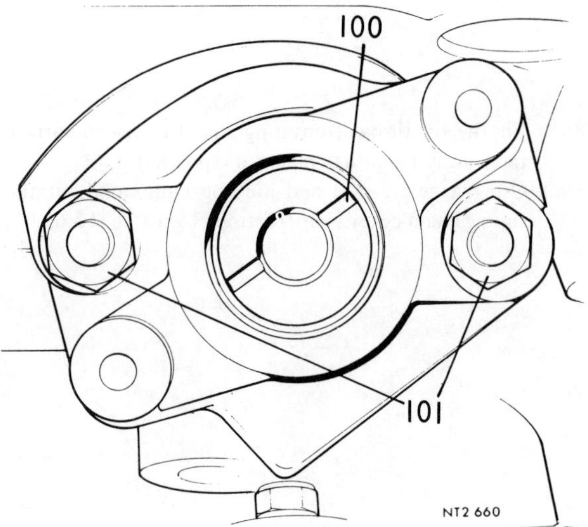

ENGINE MOUNTING – FRONT – L.H.

– Remove and refit	**12.45.01**
– Front – R.H.	**12.45.03**
– Front – Set	**12.45.04**

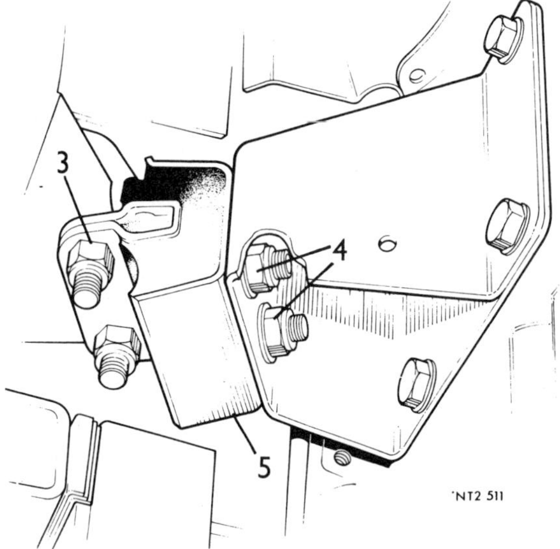

Removing

1. Isolate the battery.
2. Support the weight of the engine under the sump.
3. Remove the two nuts and bolts securing the mounting to the chassis bracket.
4. Remove the two nuts and spring washers securing the mounting to the engine bracket.
5. Remove the engine mounting from the car.

Refitting

6. Reverse instructions 1 to 5.

ENGINE MOUNTING – REAR CENTRE – WITH OVERDRIVE FITTED

– Remove and refit **12.45.08**

Removing

1. Isolate the battery.
2. Remove the fascia support bracket 76.46.09.
3. Turn back the carpets on the transmission cover, remove the speedometer drive access cover and disconnect the speedometer cable from the angle drive.
4. Remove the speedometer angle drive from the overdrive.
5. Slacken off all the bolts securing the transmission cover to the floor and ease the cover off the floor in order to provide sufficient space between the transmission and the cover when the overdrive or gearbox extension is raised as in instruction 9.
6. Raise the car on a ramp and remove the front exhaust pipe together with the inner and outer intermediate exhaust pipe assembly.
7. Remove the four nuts, bolts, plain and spring washers securing the chassis plate to the chassis brackets

NOTE: The rear R.H. bolt can be removed after instruction 9.

8. Remove the two nuts complete with plain and spring washers securing the mounting rubber to the mounting plate.
9. Place a jack under the overdrive, and raise it sufficiently to allow the chassis plate to be removed from the studs in the rubber mounting.

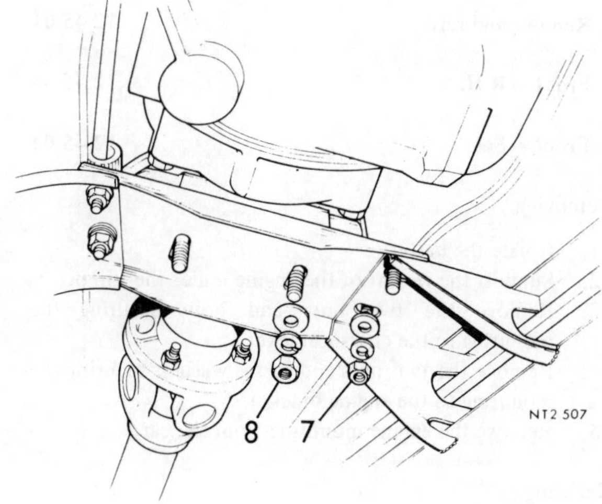

10. Working within the car, release the R.H. bolt from the captive nut welded to the exhaust pipe hanger bracket and remove the bracket. Leave the bolt complete with spring washer in position.

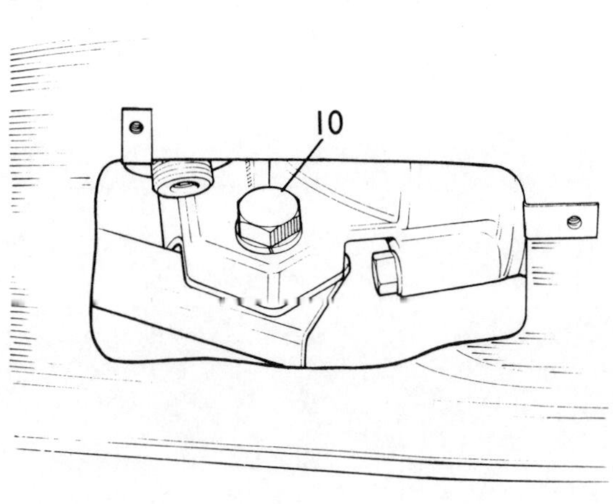

Continued

11. Working under the car, remove the L.H. nut and spring washer from the bolt securing the rubber mounting to the overdrive. Leave the bolt in position.
12. Remove the mounting from the chassis.

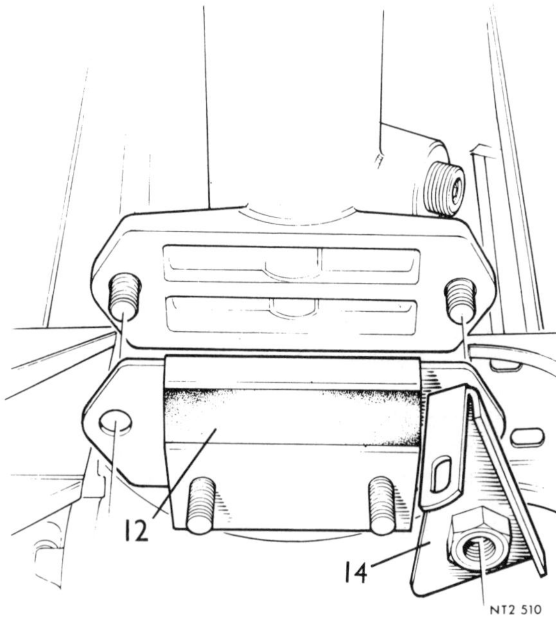

Refitting

13.- Clean the overdrive and the mounting mating faces and offer-up the mounting to the securing bolts. Fit and loosely tighten the L.H. nut and spring washer.
14. Fit the exhaust pipe hanger bracket with the captive nut to the R.H. side and secure with the bolt and spring washer.
15. Finally tighten the L.H. and R.H. bolts evenly.
16. Place the chassis plate in position with the narrowest width towards the rear of the car and attach it to the chassis brackets with the four bolts, but do not fit the nuts at this stage.
17. Lower the overdrive unit so that the mounting studs pass through the two elongated holes. To achieve this, movement of the mounting plate is possible within the limits of the four elongated holes.
18. Secure the chassis plate to the chassis brackets with the four nuts, bolts, spring and plain washers.
19. Fit and tighten the two nuts with plain and spring washers to the mounting studs.
20. Reverse instructions 1 to 6.

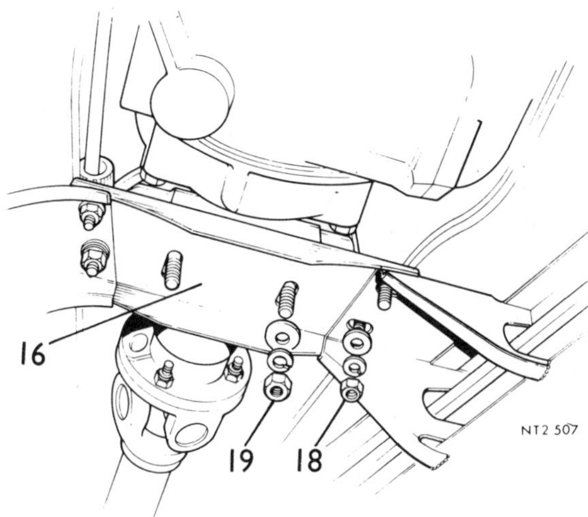

continued

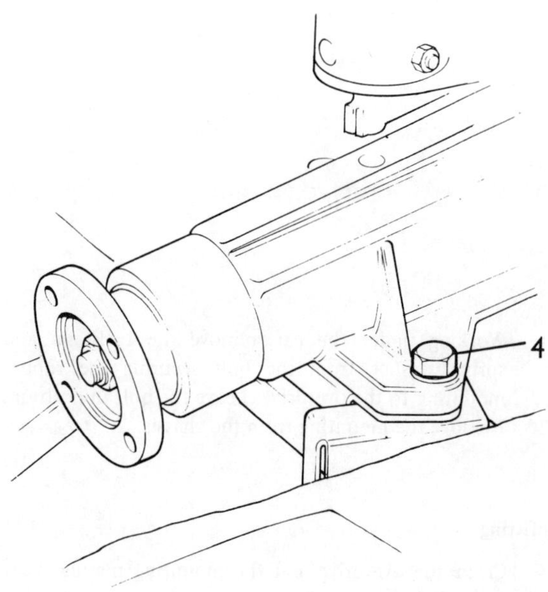

ENGINE MOUNTING – REAR CENTRE – WITHOUT OVERDRIVE

– Remove and refit **12.45.08**

Removing

1. Isolate the battery.
2. Remove the transmission cover 76.25.07.
3. Place the car on a ramp and disconnect the exhaust assembly from the centre hanger bracket.
4. Working within the car, remove the R.H. mounting bolt and withdraw the hanger bracket and captive nut.
5. Remove the L.H. mounting bolt and nut.
6. Working beneath the car, remove the two nuts securing the mounting to the gearbox extension.
7. Raise the gearbox extension with a jack sufficiently to withdraw the mounting from the chassis.

Refitting

8. With gearbox extension still in the raised position fit the mounting and secure to the extension with:–
   a. The captive nut and hanger bracket on the R.H. side and
   b. The nut, bolt and spring washer on the L.H. side.
9. Lower the gearbox extension allowing the mounting fixing studs to pass through the holes in the chassis cross-member.
10. Secure the mounting to the cross-member with the two nuts and spring washers.
11. Reconnect the exhaust pipe assembly to the hanger bracket.
12. Refit the transmission cover 76.25.07.
13. Reconnect the battery.
14. Remove the car from the ramp.

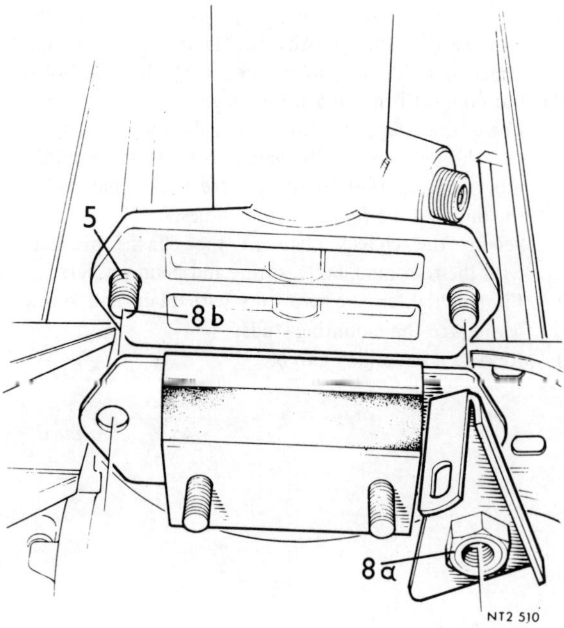

ENGINE TUNE

– check and adjust distributor points

– check and adjust spark plugs

– check and adjust ignition timing

– check and adjust valve clearances

– tune carburetters

– check and adjust throttle butterflies – P.I.

– clean fuel pump filter – carburetter engine 12.49.02

– spray check fuel injectors – P.I.

– check fuel metering distributor timing – P.I.

– clean fuel metering distributor inlet filter – P.I.

– check the manifold depression – P.I.

– road test

1. Examine and measure the gap of the distributor points and adjust or renew as necessary 86.35.13.
2. Remove the spark plugs, examine their condition and renew if necessary. Otherwise clean and adjust the gaps 86.35.01.
3. Check the ignition timing and adjust if required 86.35.16.
4. Check and if necessary adjust the valve clearances in the correct sequence 12.29.48.
5. Tune the carburetters 19.15.02.
6. Carburetter Cars – clean the fuel pump filter 19.45.05.
7. Petrol Injection Cars: check and adjust the throttle butterflies 19.20.05.
8. Petrol Injection Cars: check the spray pattern of all six injectors and clean and renew as necessary 19.60.02.
9. Petrol Injection Cars: check the timing of the fuel metering distributor and re-time if required.
10. Petrol Injection Cars: remove and clean or renew the fuel metering distributor inlet filter 19.35.15.
11. Petrol Injection Cars – check the manifold depression 12.00.00.
12. Road test the car.

MANIFOLD DEPRESSION – P.I.

– Check 12.49.03

1. Connect a T piece between the inlet manifold and metering distributor control unit vacuum hose.
2. Connect a vacuum gauge to the T piece.
3. Start the engine and set it to idle at 800 to 850 r.p.m. and note and compare the reading on the gauge with the figure in data.
4. Stop the engine, remove the gauge and T piece and connect the vacuum hose to the manifold.

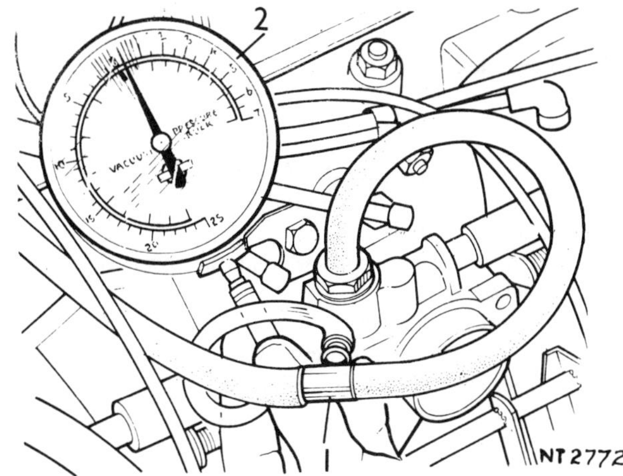

DATA

Manifold depression . . . . 7 to 8 in. Hg. (237 – 271 m bar) at 800 r.p.m.

ENGINE REAR GEARBOX ADAPTOR PLATE

– Remove and refit **12.53.03**

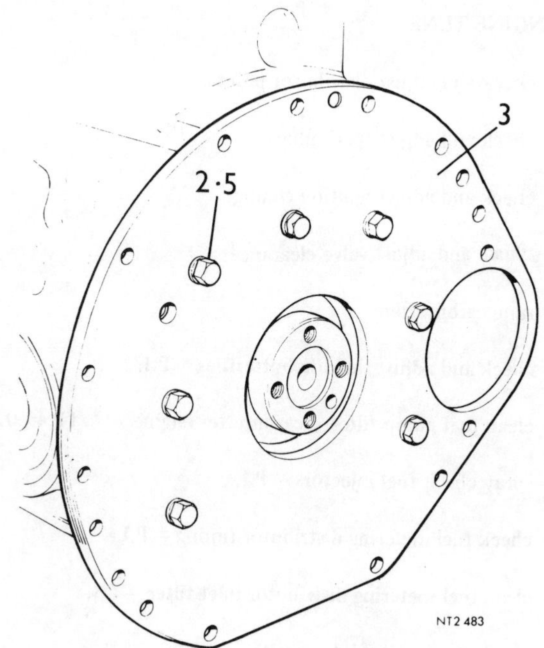

Removing

1. Remove the starter motor 86.60.01.
2. Remove the flywheel 12.53,07.
3. Remove the seven bolts and spring washers securing the adaptor plate to the cylinder block.
4. Remove the plate carefully easing it off the two locating dowels.

Refitting

5. Clean the cylinder block and adaptor mating faces and fit the plate to the cylinder block ensuring that it locates squarely over the two dowels.
6. Secure the plate to the cylinder block with the seven bolts and spring washers.
7. Refit the flywheel – instructions 7 to 14, 12.53.07.
8. Refit the starter motor 86.60.01.

FLYWHEEL

– Remove and refit **12.53.07**

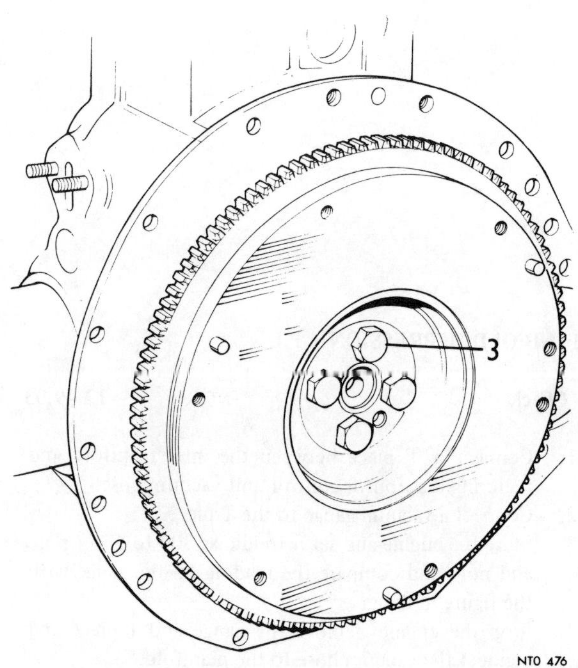

Removing

1. Remove the gearbox assembly from the car 37.20.01.
2. Remove the clutch from the flywheel – instructions 2 and 3, 33.10.01
3. Remove the four bolts securing the flywheel to the crankshaft.
4. Lift off the flywheel.
5. Remove the spigot bush from the back of the flywheel – instruction 2, 12.21.45.

Continued

Refitting

6. Fit the spigot bush – instruction 3, 12.21.45.
7. Clean the crankshaft and flywheel mating faces and fit the flywheel to the crankshaft ensuring that the dowel in the crankshaft locates properly in the flywheel.
8. Secure the flywheel with the four bolts and tighten evenly to 50 – 75 lbf ft (6·9 to 10·4 kgf m).

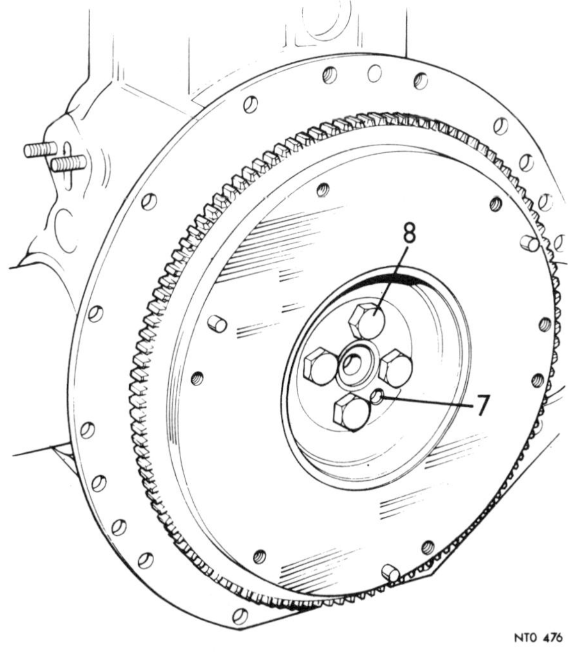

9. Using a dial gauge at dimension A from centre, check the flywheel for run-out, see Data.
10. Refit the clutch – instructions 4 to 7, 33.10.01.
11. Refit the gearbox. 37.20.01.

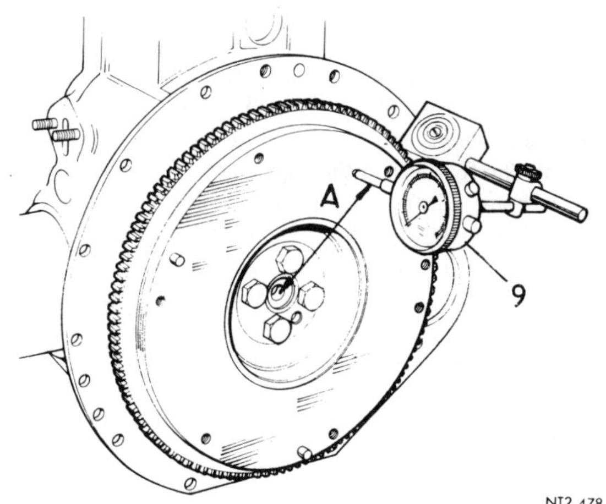

DATA

Flywheel run out not to exceed . . . . 0·004 in (0·101 mm) at a radius of 4·0 in (101 mm) from the centre dimension A.

STARTER RING GEAR

– Remove and refit **12.53.19**

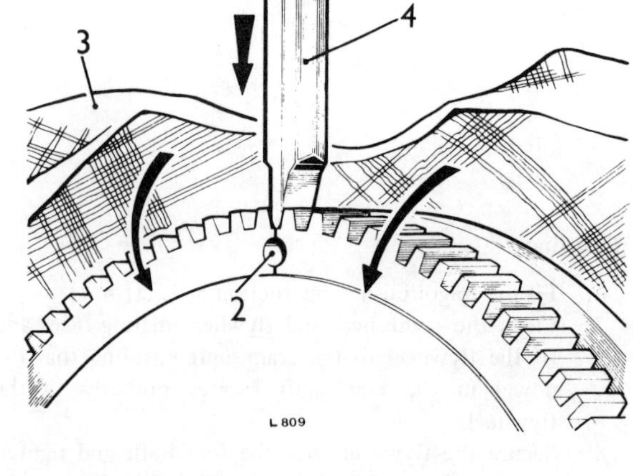

Removing

1. Remove the flywheel 12.53.07.
2. Place the flywheel assembly on a bench and drill a ¼ in (6·35 mm) hole midway between the root diameter of any two teeth and the inside diameter of the ring gear.
3. Hold the flywheel assembly in a soft jawed vice and place a heavy cloth over the ring gear for protection against flying fragments.

WARNING: ENSURE ADEQUATE PROTECTION, PARTICULARLY FOR THE EYES, TO PREVENT INJURY FROM FLYING FRAGMENTS WHEN THE RING GEAR IS SPLIT

4. Place a cold chisel above the drilled hole between the two teeth and strike the chisel sharply to split the ring gear.

Refitting

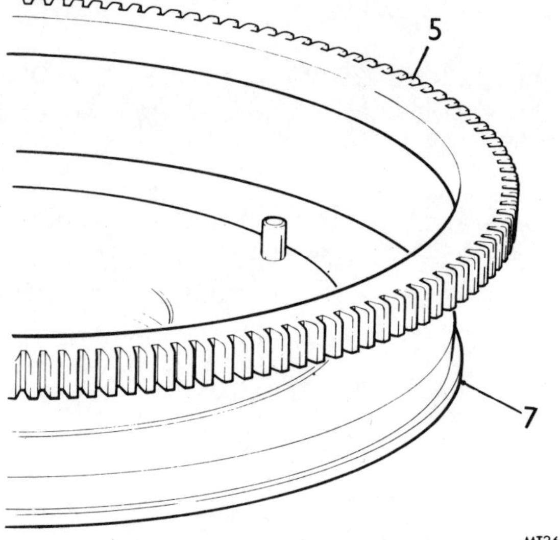

5. Heat the replacement ring gear uniformally to a maximum temperature of 200°C.
6. Place the flywheel on a flat surface, clutch face side uppermost and clean the ring location.
7. Fit the ring gear to the flywheel ensuring that it locates against the shoulder on the flywheel round the entire circumference.
8. Hold the ring gear in position until it contracts sufficiently to grip the flywheel and allow it to cool gradually to avoid distortion.
9. Check, with a feeler gauge, the gap that may exist between the ring gear and the flywheel shoulder and ensure that it does not exceed 0·025 in (·635 mm) in any one area of 6 in (15 cm) around the circumference.
10. Refit the flywheel to the engine and secure with the four bolts – instructions 7 and 8, 12.53.07.
11. Check the flywheel for run-out and eccentricity – insturctions 10 and 11, 12.53.07.
12. Check the ring gear for eccentricity using a dial gauge – see Data.
13. Refit the gearbox and if fitted the overdrive to the engine.
14. Refit the gearbox and overdrive assembly to the car.

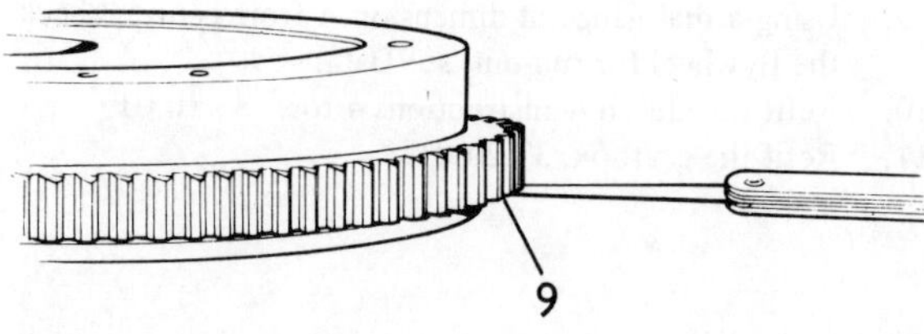

DATA

Maximum fitting temperature for ring gear	200°C
Maximum gap between flywheel shoulder and ring gear in any one area of 6 in (15 cm) around the circumference	0·025 in (·635 mm)
Maximum ring gear excentricity when attached to flywheel	0·010 in (·254 mm)
Flywheel and ring gear assembly balance to be within	0·20 oz. in

ENGINE LUBRICATION

– Description 12.60.00

Oil circulation

Oil drawn from the engine sump by a rotor type pump, is delivered via a non-adjustable pressure relief valve to a full flow type oil filter. Oil, by-passed from the relief valve, is returned to the engine sump, and the filtered oil passes to the engine main oil gallery. From the gallery, oil is distributed to the camshaft and crankshaft journals. Drillings, in the crankshaft allow oil to pass to the crankpins and surplus oil from the crankpins lubricates the cylinder walls by splash action thrown-up by the crankshaft.

The camshaft rear bearing supplies a reduced flow of oil to the hollow rocker shaft and valve assembly. Reduction of the flow is achieved by means of two machined flats on the camshaft rear journal. The flats present an increased volume to the oil supply to the camshaft rear bearing thus reducing the overall flow to the cylinder head. Oil spillage from the valve assembly lubricates the camfollowers, cams and the distributor drive shaft and gears before returning to the sump.

The timing chain and sprockets are lubricated via a scroll on the camshaft front journal and by oil mist from the crankcase. Oil leakage from the crankcase is prevented by lip type seals fitted to the front and rear of the crankshaft.

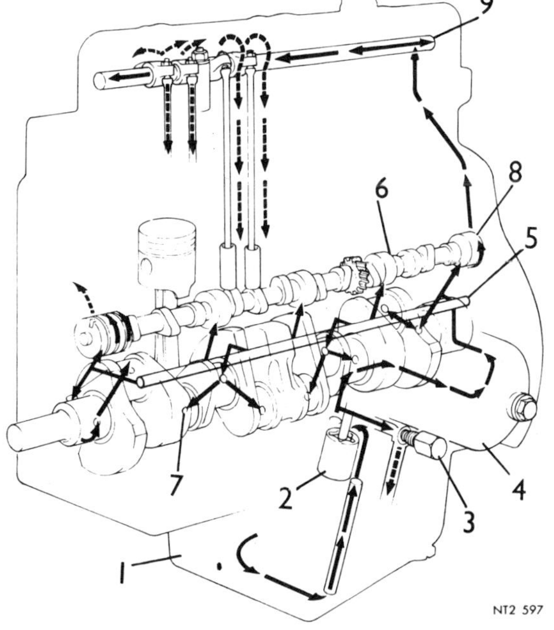

1. Sump
2. Oil pump
3. Pressure relief valve
4. Oil filter
5. Engine main oil gallery
6. Camshaft
7. Crankcase oil drilling
8. Camshaft rear bearing
9. Rocker shaft

Oil filtration

A full flow replaceable element type oil filter is fitted to the crankcase and secured by a single bolt. Sealing of the unit is achieved by a rubber ring between the filter body and crankcase and a rubber washer under bolt head.

Oil delivered from the pressure relief valve to the filter body passes through and out of the centre of the filter element into the engine main oil gallery – A.

In the event of the filter element becoming blocked, due to neglect, lubrication of the engine is never-the-less assured by a by-pass valve which allows unfiltered oil to flow through the filter body direct to the main oil gallery – B.

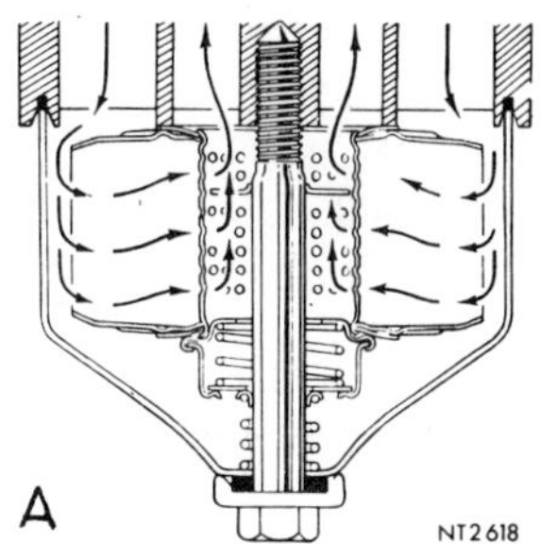

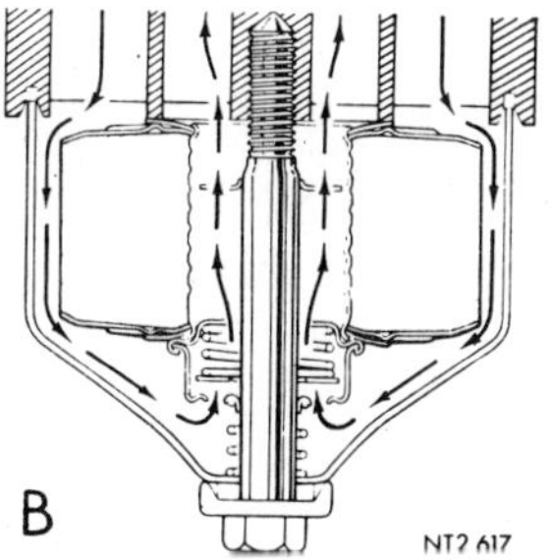

OIL FILTER ELEMENT

– Remove and refit **12.60.02**

Removing

1. Isolate the battery.
2. Place a suitable receptacle under the oil filter to prevent oil leakage onto the floor.
3. Unscrew the central securing bolt and withdraw the filter assembly from the engine.
4. Remove and discard the filter element.
5. Remove the crankcase sealing ring.

Refitting

6. Clean the filter body and renew the seals if necessary.
7. Clean the crankcase and fit a new sealing ring.
8. Insert a new filter element in the filter body and secure the assembly to the crankcase, tightening the central bolt to 15 – 20 lbf ft (2·1 to 2·8 kgf m).
9. Reconnect the battery, start the engine and check:
   a. for oil leaks from the filter
   b. the low oil pressure warning light on the control panel goes out
   c. that the oil pressure gauge registers the normal pressure.

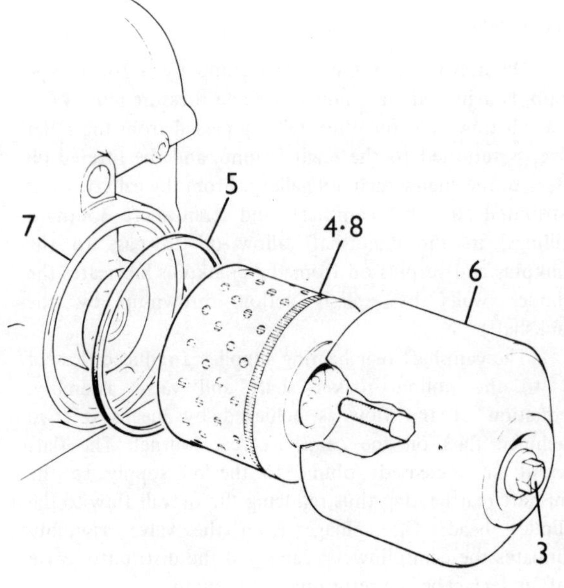

OIL PICK-UP STRAINER

– Remove and refit **12.60.20**

Removing

1. Remove the sump 12.60.44.
2. Slacken the lock nut.
3. Unscrew the strainer from the pump cover plate.

Continued

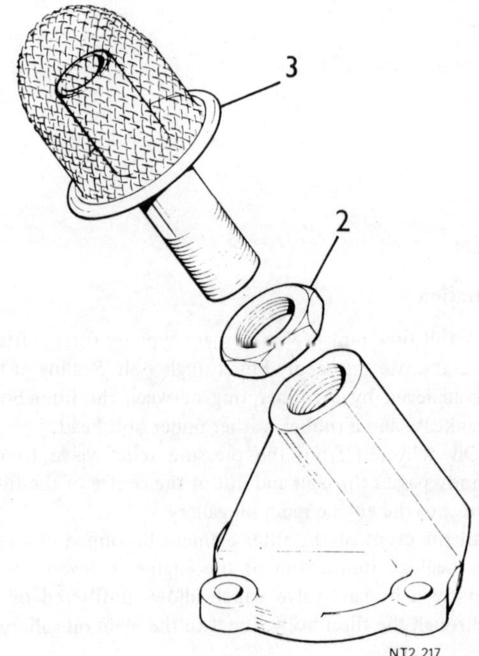

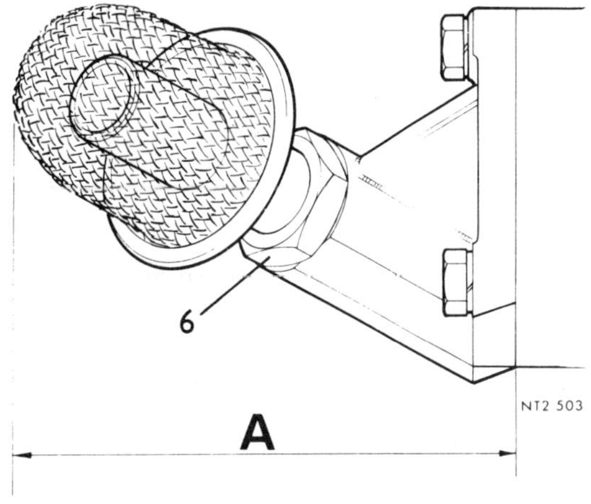

Refitting

4. Wash the strainer gauze in petrol and allow to dry.
5. Screw the strainer into the pump cover plate until the measurement A between the pump body face and the end of the strainer gauze is 4·25 in (180 mm).
6. Tighten the locknut to 20 – 24 lbf ft (2·8 – 3·3 kgf m).
7. Refit the sump 12.60.44.

OIL PUMP

– Remove and refit **12.60.26**

Removing

1. Isolate the battery.
2. Drain the oil sump.
3. Remove the sump 12.60.44.
4. Slacken the three bolts retaining the pump to the crankcase and whilst holding the pump cover in position slacken the bolts completely and remove the pump.

NOTE: If the pump is not to receive attention use 'slave' nuts on the bolts to keep the pump cover in position to prevent the ingress of foreign matter.

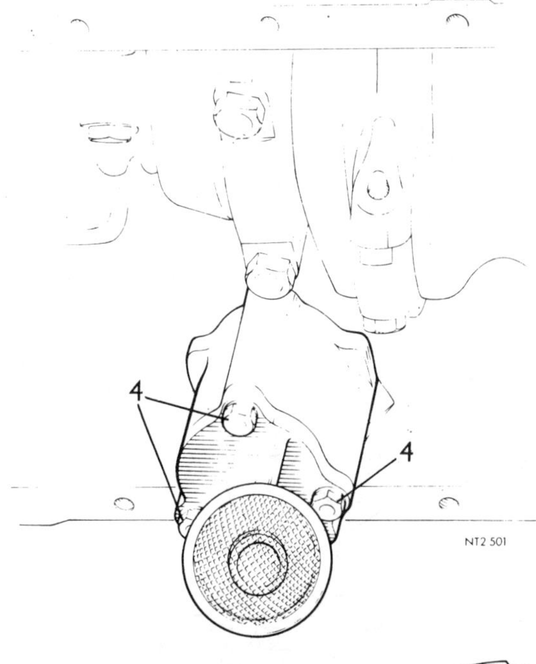

Refitting

5. Clean the crankcase and oil pump mating faces and offer up the pump to the crankcase ensuring that the oil pump spindle engages positively into the distributor drive gear shaft before evenly tightening the bolts and spring washers to 7 – 9 lbf ft (1·0 – 1·2 kgf m).
6. Reverse instructions 1 to 3.

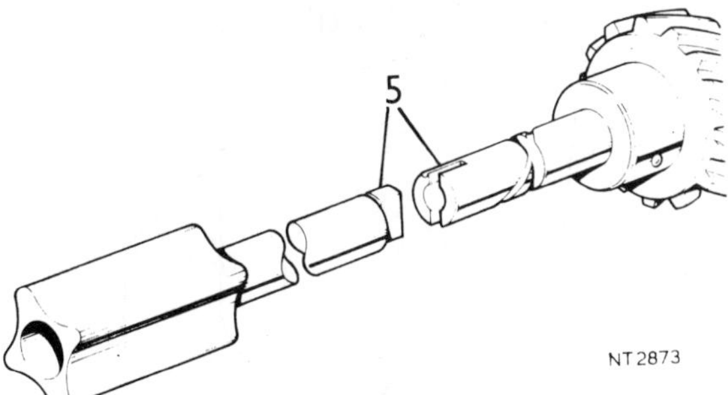

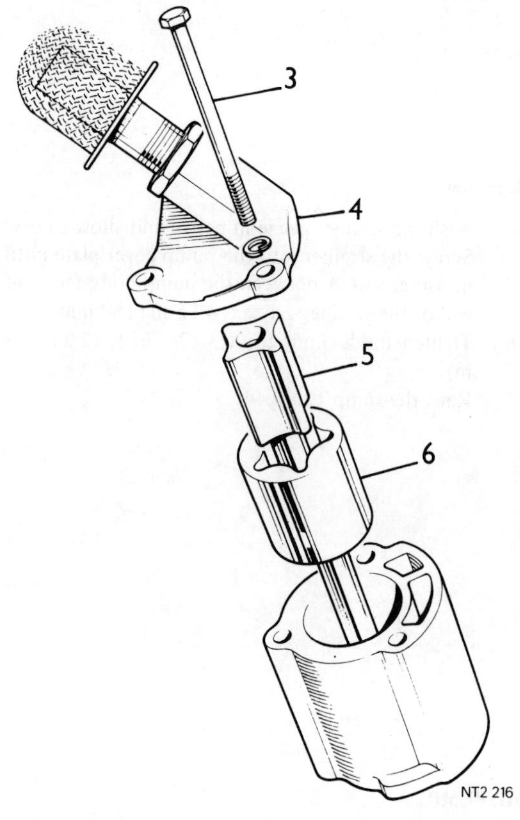

OIL PUMP

– Overhaul **12.60.32**

1. Remove the oil pump 12.60.26.
2. Remove the pick-up strainer 12.60.20.
3. Remove the three securing bolts and washers.
4. Lift off the pump cover.
5. Remove the inner rotor and shaft assembly.
6. Remove the outer rotor.

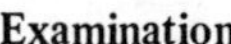

Examination

7. Clean oil from the body and rotors, examine the components for wear, pitting and corrosion.
8. Place the pump in a vice and using a feeler gauge check as follows:
   a. With a straight edge across the pump body face check the clearance between the rotors and the straight edge. See Data.
   b. Check the clearance between the inner and outer rotors. See Data.

Continued

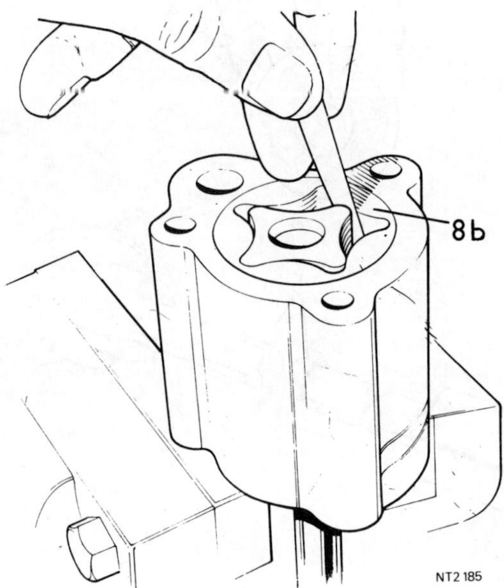

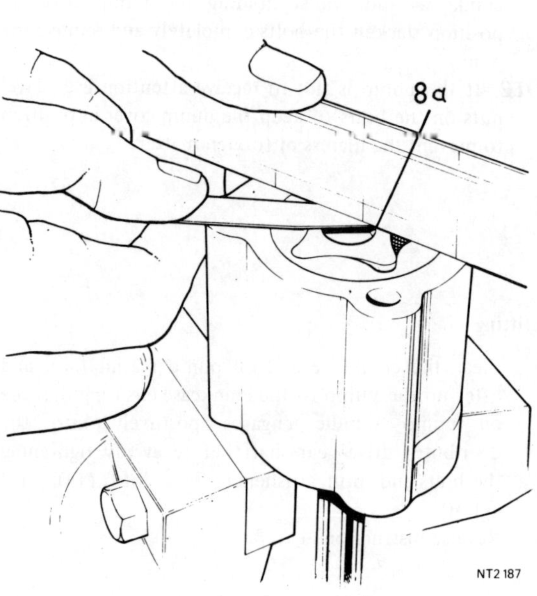

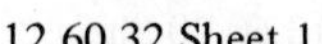

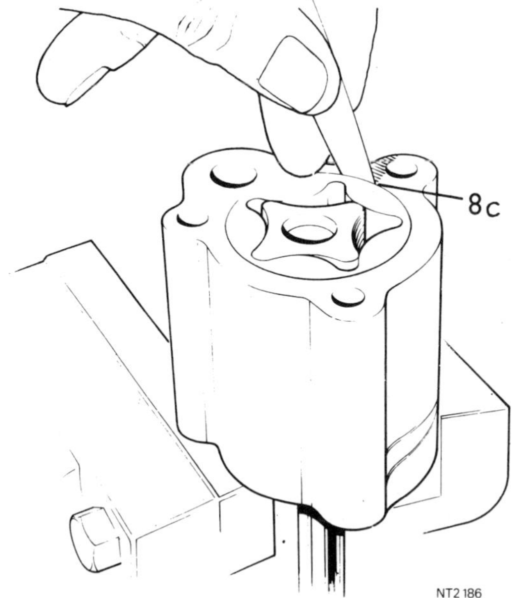

c. Check the clearance between the outer rotor and the body. See Data.

9. Examine the cover plate for scoring and test on a surface plate for distortion.

10. Reassemble the pump fitting any new parts necessary to satisfy the above quoted tolerances. Renew any components that are unsatisfactory due to pitting, scoring or corrosion.

CAUTION: The inner rotor and spindle and the outer rotor are supplied only as an assembly and under no circumstances must they be separated and fitted as individual replacements to a worn pump.

11. Refit the oil pick-up strainer 12.60.20.

12. Refit the pump to the crankcase instructions 5 and 6, 12.60.26.

DATA

Pump capacity (approx.)	3·00 GP/min at 1000 r.p.m. using SAE 30 oil at 80°C
Maximum clearance between outer rotor and pump body	0·010 (0·254 mm)
Maximum clearance between outer and inner rotors	0·001 – 0·004 (0·0254 – 0·102 mm)
Maximum clearance between the cover plate and rotors (end clearance)	0·004 (0·102 mm)

OIL SUMP

– Remove and refit 12.60.44

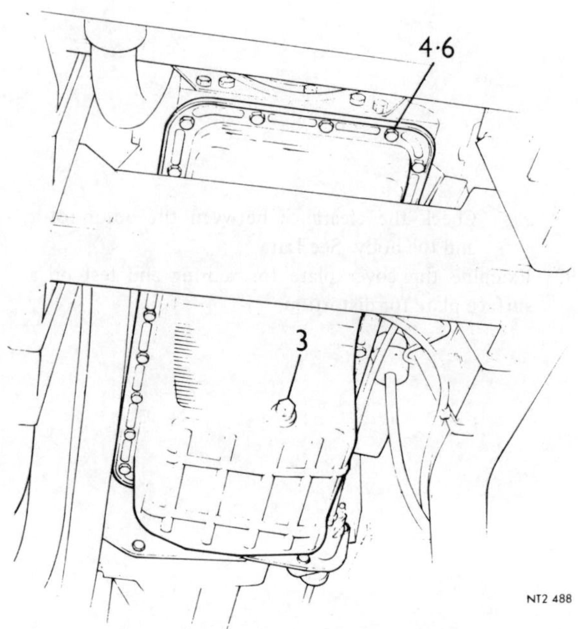

Removing

1. Place the car on a ramp.
2. Isolate the battery.
3. Remove the drain plug and drain the oil.

NOTE: The illustration shows the position of the drain plug on earlier engines.
On later engines the plug is situated to the rear left hand side of the sump.

4. Remove the twenty three bolts and spring washers and withdraw the sump.

Refitting

5. Clean the sump inside and out and remove all traces of old gasket from the sump and crankcase mating faces.
6. Place a new gasket in position and offer up the sump to the crankcase and secure it with the bolts and washers, noting that the four longest bolts fit at the rear through the reinforced plates.
7. Refit the drain plug and refill the sump with a recommended grade of oil and check for leaks.

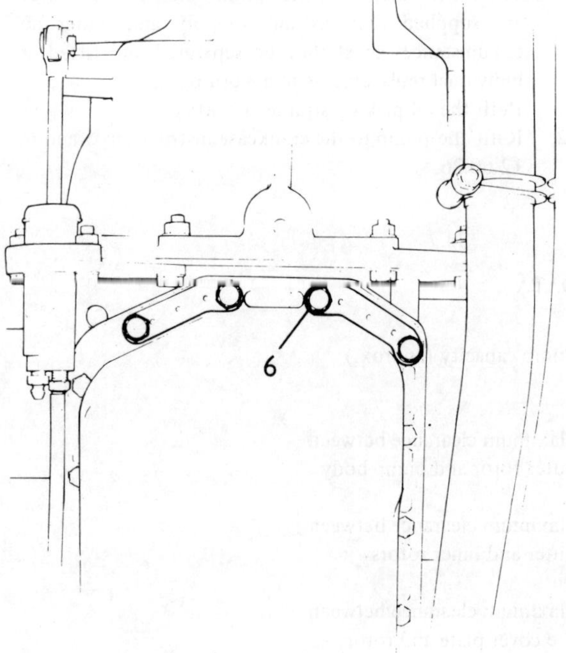

OIL PRESSURE RELIEF VALVE

– Remove and refit 12.60.56

Removing

1. Isolate the battery.
2. Unscrew the pressure relief valve body from the cylinder block.
3. Remove the washer.
4. Take out the plunger.
5. Remove the spring.

Refitting

6. Examine all components for pitting and corrosion and renew if necessary.
7. Check the free length of the spring and renew if not in accordance with data.
8. Clean the components and reverse instructions 1 to 5.

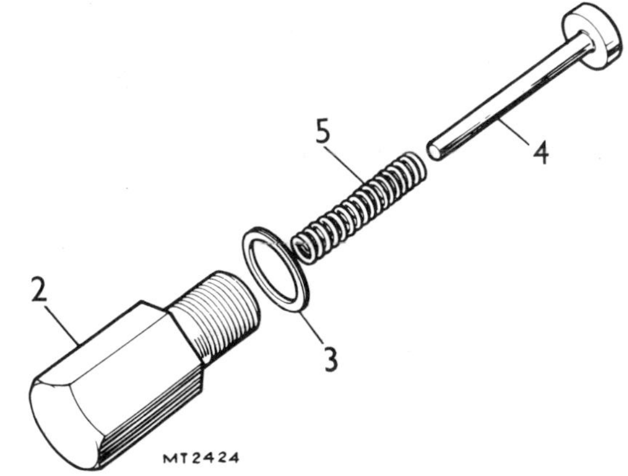

DATA

Spring rate	53 lb/ins
Free length	1·53 in approx. (40 mm)

TIMING CHAIN COVER

– Remove and refit 12.65.01

Special tool S341

Removing

1. Isolate the battery.
2. Drain the cooling system 26.10.01.
3. Remove the radiator cowling.
4. Remove the radiator 26.40.01.
5. Remove the fan blades.
6. Remove the chassis cross tube 76.10.05.
7. Remove the fan belt 26.20.07.
8. Remove the steering rack 'U' bolts and ease the rack forward 57.25.01, instructions 5 and 6.
9. Remove the centre bolt securing the fan extension and crankshaft pulley and remove the extension by tapping it with a hammer to free it from its locating dowels.
10. Withdraw the crankshaft pulley 12.21.01.

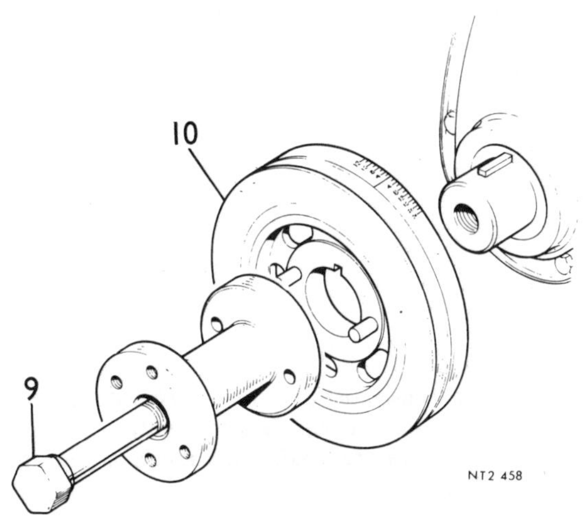

Continued

11. Remove the set screws, bolts and nuts and spring washers securing the timing chain cover to the cylinder block and engine front plate.

NOTE: The timing chain cover is located by two dowels and two studs.

12. Prise the timing chain cover from the engine taking care not to damage or distort the cover.
13. Remove the oil seal sleeve.
14. Remove the gasket.

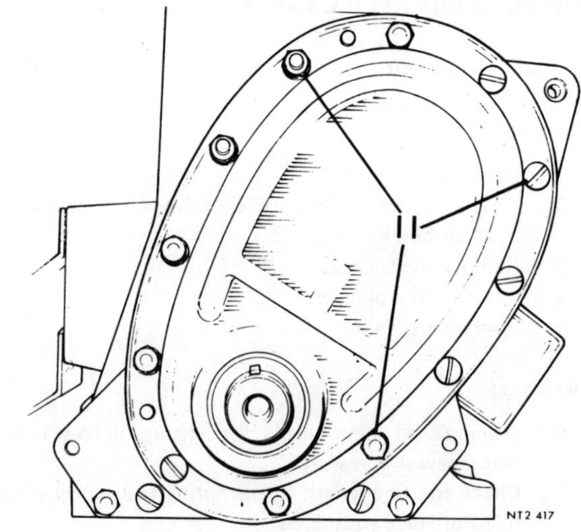

Refitting

15. Clean the timing chain cover and engine mating faces and fit a new gasket.
16. Fit the timing cover locating it over the studs and dowels. Fit the screws and bolts on their correct positions as ilustrated and tighten evenly.

NOTE: To facilitate the fitting of the timing chain cover, compress the timing chain tensioner with a suitable length of wire. Care however, should be taken when withdrawing the rod not to tear the gasket.

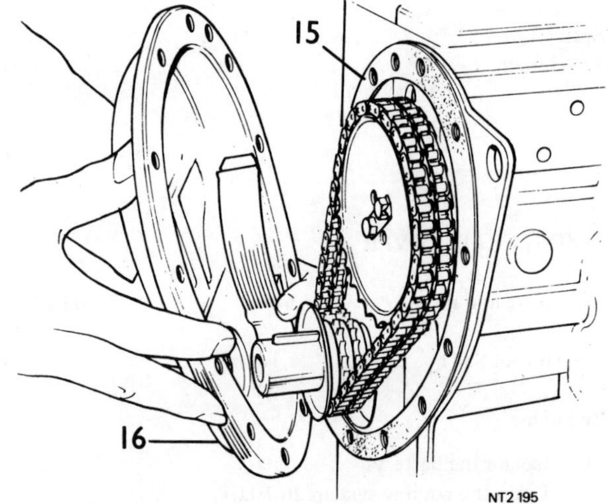

18. Smear the timing cover oil seal and sleeve with oil and with the chamfered end leading, gently press the sleeve on to the crankshaft and through the timing cover oil seal.
19. Reverse instructions 9 and 10.
20. Reposition the steering rack and fit and tighten the 'U' bolts 57.25.01 instructions 11 to 16, using special tool S341.
21. Reverse instructions 1 to 7.

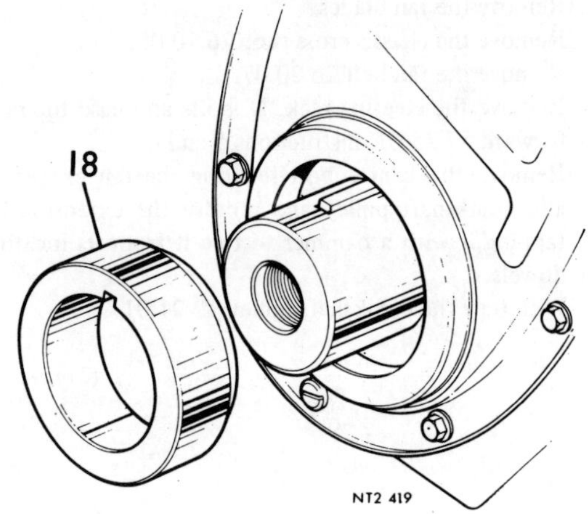

TIMING COVER OIL SEAL

– Remove and refit **12.65.05**

Special tool S341

Removing

1. Remove the timing chain cover 12.65.01.
2. Carefully prise out the seal, avoiding damage to the timing cover seal location.

Refitting

3. Clean the timing cover, smear the oil seal with oil.
4. With the lip face trailing press the seal squarely into the timing cover.
5. Refit the timing chain cover 12.65.01.

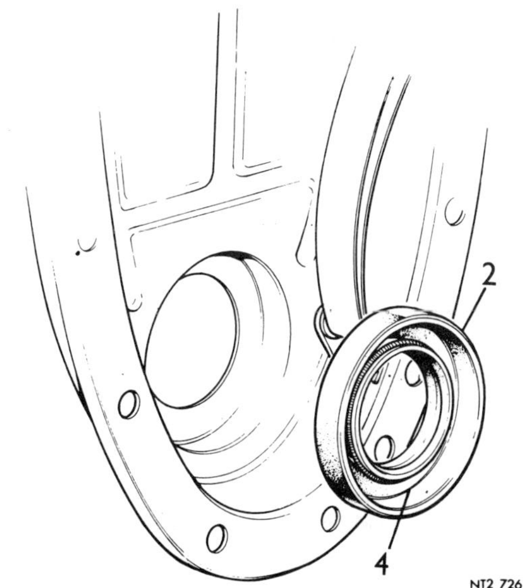

VALVE TIMING

– Check **12.65.08**

1. Remove the rocker cover 12.29.47.
2. Adjust the rocker clearances of numbers eleven and twelve valves to 0·120 in (3·04 mm) to give a working clearance.

NOTE: This clearance may vary according to the lift of the camshaft employed. The clearance should be sufficient to enable feeler gauges of reasonable thickness to be inserted when the valves are on the 'rock'.

3. Turn the crankshaft in the normal running direction until number one piston is at T.D.C. on the compression stroke, indicated by the mark on the crankshaft pulley coinciding with the pointer on the timing cover.
4. Check that numbers one and two valves are fully closed by ascertaining with a feeler gauge that clearance exists between the valve tips and rocker pads.
5. Using two feeler gauges of the same thickness check that the rocker clearances of numbers eleven and twelve are the same. Oscillate the crankshaft to achieve this condition. Ensure however that when the rocker clearances are the same the conditions in instructions 3 and 4 are maintained.

NOTE: The actual rocker clearance is not important providing the clearances are the same.

6. Should the valve timing prove to be incorrect retiming will be necessary – 12.65.12 instructions 1 to 7 and 12.41.05 instructions 79 to 85.
7. Reset the rocker clearances of numbers eleven and twelve valves. See Data operation 12.29.48.
8. Refit the rocker cover 12.29.42.

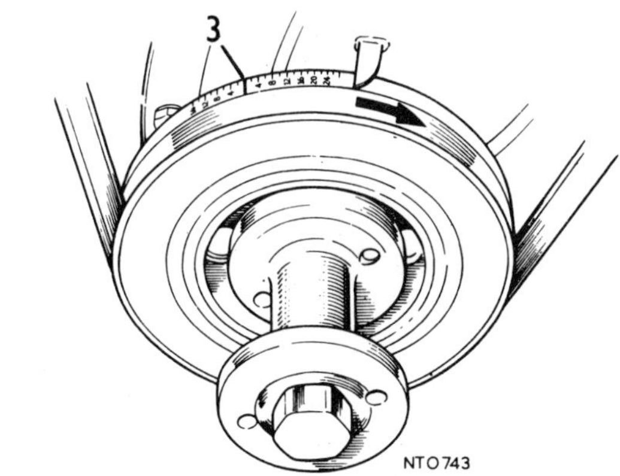

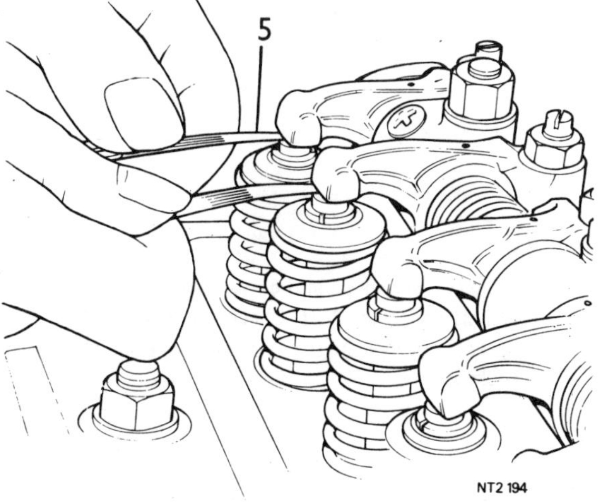

TIMING CHAIN AND SPROCKETS

– Remove and refit **12.65.12**

Special tool S341

Timing chain – remove and refit **12.65.14**

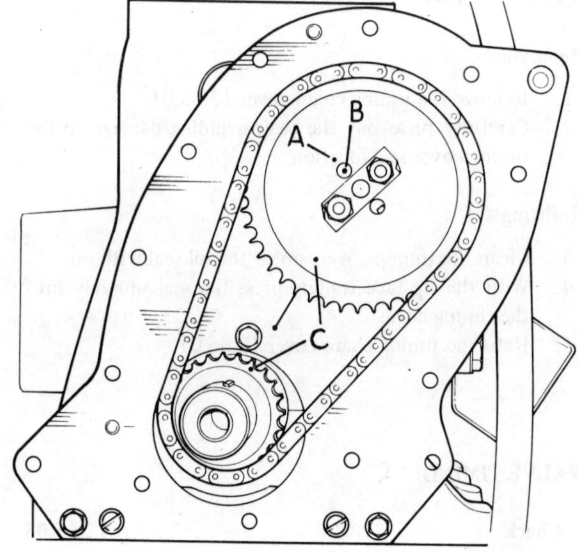

Removing

1. Isolate the battery.
2. Remove the timing chain cover 12.65.14.
3. Remove the oil seal sleeve.
4. Remove the oil thrower.
5. Turn the engine over until numbers one and six pistons are at T.D.C. number one firing, check that the timing marks A and B are in evidence and marks C on the camshaft and crankshaft sprockets line-up.
6. Straighten the lock tabs on the camshaft sprocket and remove the bolts.
7. Remove the timing chain complete with the camshaft and crankshaft sprockets.

NOTE: Ensure that the crankshaft and camshaft are not turned whilst the chain and sprockets are removed.

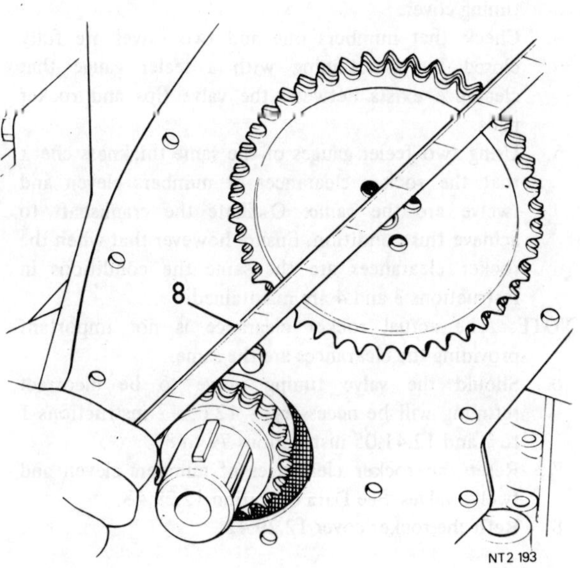

Refitting

8. Fit the two sprockets in their normal positions on the camshaft and crankshaft. Check the alignment of the sprockets by placing a straight edge across the sprocket.

Continued

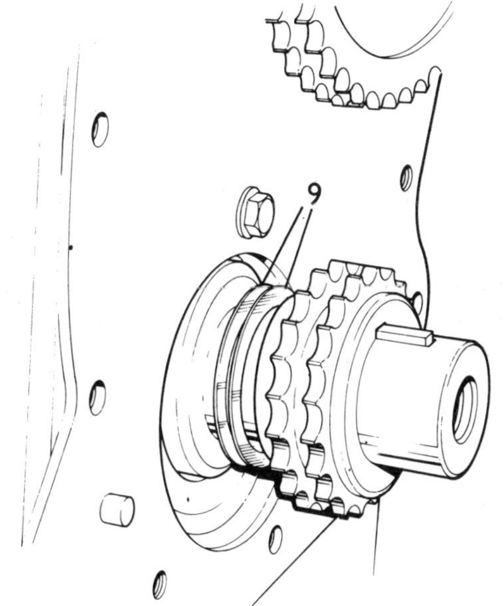

9. If the sprockets are out of alignment, adjust by removing the drive key and fitting shims behind the crankshaft sprocket. Refit the key.

NOTE: Two shim thicknesses are available 0·004 in (0·10 mm) and 0·006 (0·52 mm).

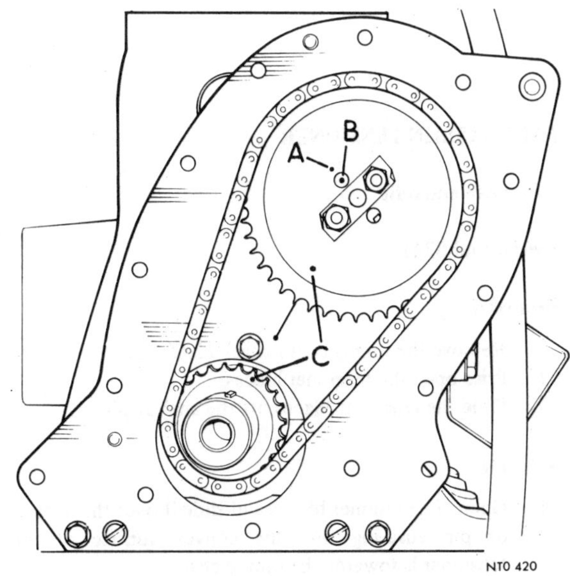

10. Remove the sprockets and encircle them with the timing chain and refit to their respective positions keeping the chain taut on the drive side. If the original sprockets are being refitted, make sure that punch marks A on the sprocket and B on the end of the camshaft correspond, and Punch marks C on the crankshaft and camshaft sprockets line-up.
11. If new sprockets are being fitted, check their alignment as in instructions 8 and 9, and fit them in position and secure and make the appropriate punch marks A, B, and C.

continued

12. Reverse instructions 1 to 4, ensuring that the oil thrower is fitted with the dished face towards the timing cover.

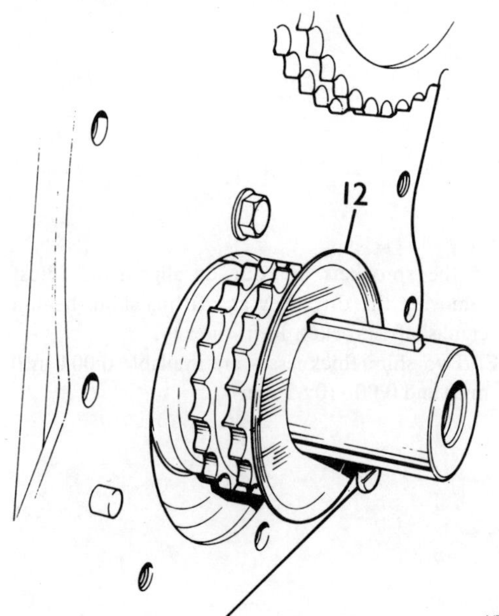

TIMING CHAIN TENSIONER

– Remove and refit **12.65.28**

Special tool S341.

Removing

1. Remove the timing chain cover 12.65.01.
2. Prise open the tensioner blades.
3. Slide the tensioner blades off the anchor pin.

Refitting

4. Open the tensioner blades and slide it over the anchor or pin ensuring that the convex surface of the tensioner is towards the timing chain.
5. Refit the timing chain cover 12.65.01.

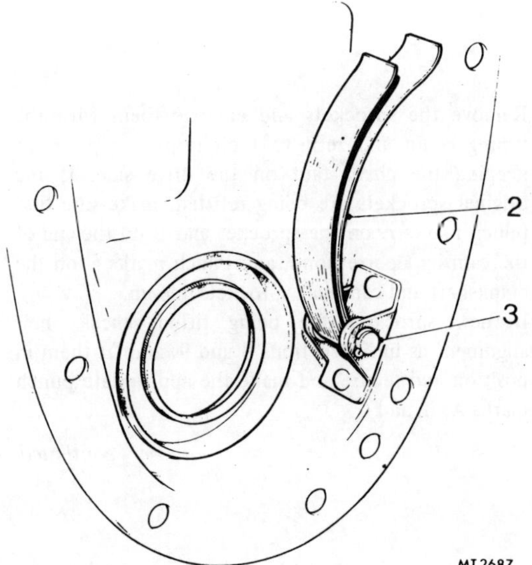

EMISSION CONTROL OPERATIONS

POOR/ROUGH IDLE	LOSS OF POWER/POOR DRIVE AWAY	MISFIRING (under load conditions)	HIGH FUEL CONSUMPTION	HIGH IDLING SPEED	OVERHEATING (at idle speed)	LEAN RUNNING	ARCING AT PLUGS	SMELL OF FUEL	RICH MIXTURE	STALLING	ENGINE RUN ON	CAUSE	ACTION
SYMPTOM													
X	X	X										DISTRIBUTOR C. B. POINTS	CHECK DWELL ANGLE/CHECK GAP & RESET/RENEW POINTS
X	X	X										SPARKING PLUGS	CHECK GAP AND RESET/RENEW DEFECTIVE PLUG
X	X	X					X					IGNITION WIRING	INSPECT FOR FRAYING CHAFFING & DETERIORATION/RENEW
X	X		X									CHOKE MECHANISM	CHECK FAST IDLE ADJUSTMENT/CAM AND CABLE/ADJUST
X	X		X									CHOKE MECHANISM	REMOVE STARTER BOX AND CLEAN INTERFACE
X	X			X						X		VACUUM FITTINGS, HOSES AND CONNECTIONS	CHECK PIPING CONDITION AND SECURITY/RENEW AS NECESSARY
X	X					X						OIL FILLER CAP	CHECK FOR SECURITY/TIGHTEN CAP
X	X					X						VENTILATION HOSES	CHECK HOSES FOR SECURITY, BLOCKAGE & DETERIORATION
X			X									CARBURETTER	SEE CARBURETTER FAULT FINDING CHART
	X											DISTRIBUTOR	LUBRICATE/CHECK OPERATION BY REMOVING PIPE & NOTING R.P.M.
	X		X									CARBURETTER AIR CLEANER	CLEAN OR RENEW ELEMENT
	X			X	X							IGNITION TIMING AND ADVANCE SYSTEMS	CHECK AND RESET DYNAMIC TIMING
		(X)										CONDENSOR AND COIL	CHECK FOR BREAKDOWN ON OSCILLASCOPE TUNE
			X					X				HOSE CONNECTIONS	CHECK FOR HOSE DAMAGE AND DETERIORATION
									X			CARBON STORAGE CANISTER	RENEW CANISTER
					(X)							THERMOSTATIC SWITCH	CHECK SWITCH OPERATION AND RENEW IF NECESSARY
											X	RUNNING ON CONTROL VALVE	CHECK VALVE OPERATION AND RENEW IF NECESSARY
X												E.G.R. VALVE	CHECK VALVE OPERATION AND RENEW IF NECESSARY

EVAPORATIVE LOSS CONTROL SYSTEM

– Leak testing **17.15.01**

Test apparatus: Water manometer, pressure regulating valve, pressure sealing valve and pressurised air supply. An alternative to the manometer is an accurate pressure gauge reading 0 to 30 in of water with which a pressure relief valve or weak rubber connection will be necessary to protect against over-pressurising the system.

WARNING: **During the test, pressure will be applied to the fuel tank breather system. The pressure, albeit very low, may displace pipe connections or cause an emission of fuel vapour. It is, therefore , important to avoid naked lights or actions likely to cause sparks during this test. It is also dangerous to exceed the pressure quoted.**

Test Procedure

1. At the carbon canister detach the tube from the seperator tank and insert the pressurising tube of the test apparatus.
2. Apply 20 in of water pressure to the system and close the sealing valve. DO NOT EXCEED 25 in OF WATER PRESSURE.
3. After two minutes, check the pressure in the system. If the pressure has fallen more than 2 in of water, investigation and rectification is necessary.

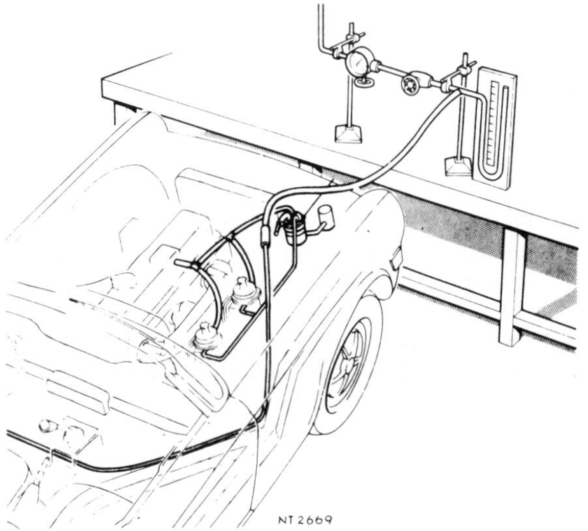

ADSORPTION CANISTER AIR FILTER

– Pre 1973 Cars only

– Remove and refit 17.15.07

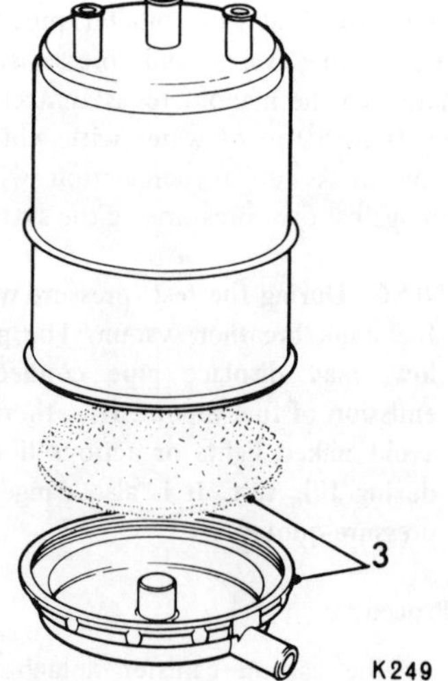

Removing

1. Remove the nut and screw on the canister securing strap.
2. Lift the canister clear of the bracket.
3. Unscrew the base of the canister and lift out the filter.
4. Clean any carbon particles from the base of the canister.

Refitting

5. Fit the new filter into body of canister.
6. Reverse 1 to 3 ensuring that the canister pipes are still in position and that they present leak free joints.

WARNING: Because of the possible presence of fuel fumes, avoid naked lights or actions likely to cause sparks.

ADSORPTION CANISTER

– Remove and refit 17.15.13

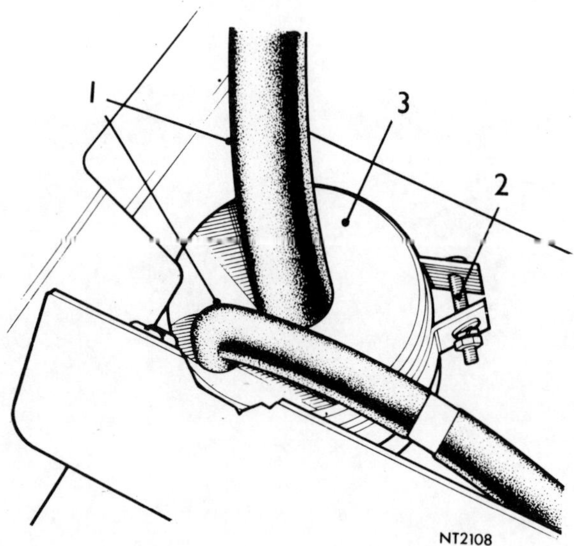

Removing

1. Disconnect the two pipes into the top of the canister.

1a. 1973 vehicles – disconnect the three pipes into the top and one pipe from the bottom.

2. Remove the nut and screw on the canister securing strap.
3. Remove the canister.

Refitting

4. Reverse instructions 1 to 3 ensuring that all connections are leak free.

WARNING: Because of the posible presence of fuel fumes, avoid naked lights or action likely to cause sparks.

EXPANSION TANK

– Remove and refit 17.15.19

Removing

1. Drain the fuel.
2. Remove the spare wheel and cover.
3. Remove the luggage compartment rear trim cover (8 screws plus two connectors for lamp).
4. Slacken the hose clip – filler pipe to tank.
5. Disconnect the two connectors at the fuel gauge transmitter.
6. Remove the six bolts securing the fuel tank to the body and lower the fuel tank to spare wheel well.
7. Disconnect the two pipes at the tank.
8. Slacken the clips securing the tank to the fuel tank.
9. Remove the tank.

Refitting

10. Reverse instructions 1 to 9, ensure that all pipe connections are leak free.

WARNING: **Because of the pressence of fuel fumes avoid naked lights or actions likely to cause sparks.**

NOTE: On earlier models a larger tank is bolted to a bracket at the rear of the luggage compartment right trim pad and is connected by seperate pipes to each corner of the main fuel tank.

CONTROL PIPE – CANISTER TO TANK

– Remove and refit **17.15.24**

Purge pipe – canister to crankcase breather **17.15.36**

1. All piping in the evaporative control and engine breather systems is push fitted. Access to the tank end, of the control pipe is via the luggage compartment trim pad. When refitting pipes ensure that all restrictors are replaced in the line and that all connections are leak free.

CARBURETTER EMISSION PACK – RED

– Remove and refit **17.20.07**

1. Fit the gaskets and sealing washers of this pack in accordance with the overhaul procedure detailed in 19.15.17.

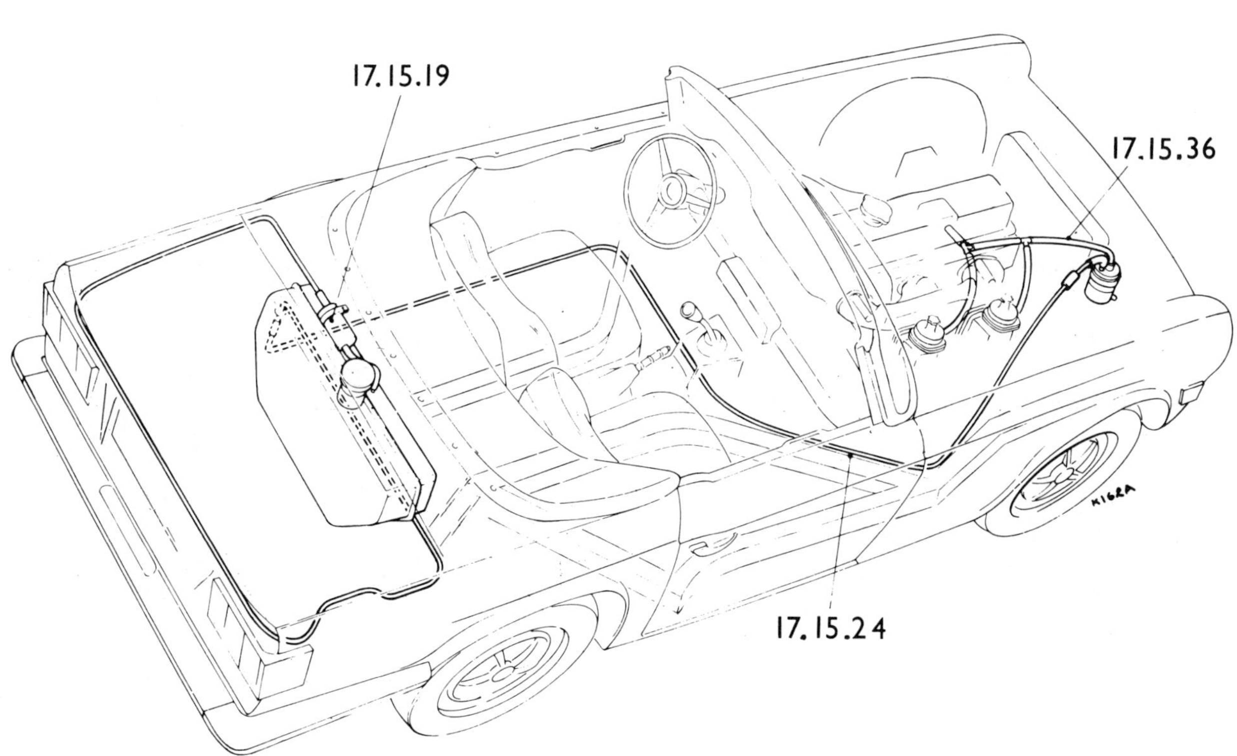

THERMOSTATIC SWITCH (FITTED TO LATER CARS ONLY)

– Remove and refit **17.20.31**

Removing

1. Drain part of the coolant.
2. ** Disconnect the vacuum pipes at the switch. **
3. Slacken the two hose clips.
4. Remove the switch complete with mounting tube.
5. Secure the tube in a vice and unscrew the switch.

Refitting

6. Reverse instructions 1 to 5, apply sealing compound to the thread of the switch.

C. O. LEVELS AT IDLE

– Check **17.35.01**

Special tools: Approved infra-red gas analyser

1. Attain normal engine running temperature.
2. Set the idle speed to that quoted on the emission control label 19.15.01.
3. Check ignition timing, reset if necessary 86.35.16.
4. Re-check idle speed – adjust if necessary.
5. Insert the gas analyser probe as far as possible into the exhaust pipe.
6. Check the C. O. reading (compare with emission control label).

7a. Adjust mixture if necessary 19.15.01.
 b. Check idle speed – adjust if necessary.

8. Withdraw the analyser probe.
9. Switch off the ignition.

NOTE: Do not allow the engine to idle for longer than 3 minutes without a 'clear out' burst of 1 minute at 2000 rev/min.

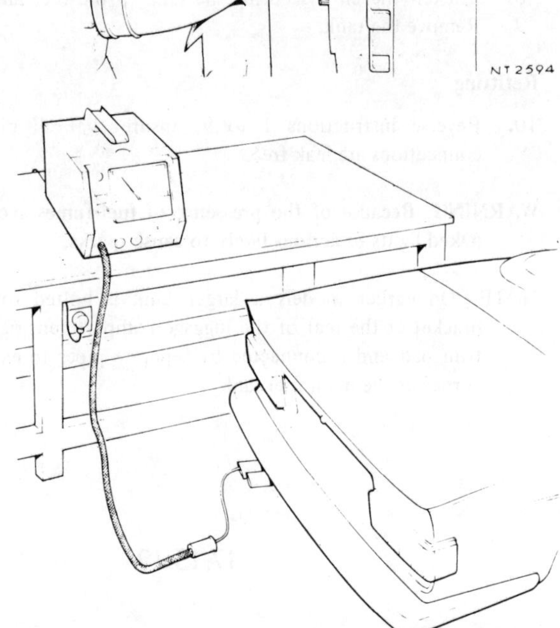

RUNNING ON CONTROL VALVE

(Not fitted to pre 1973 cars)

– Remove and refit **17.40.01**

Removing

1. Remove the carbon canister 17.15.07.
2. Disconnect the two electrical leads to the solenoid at the top of the valve.
3. Disconnect the vacuum signal pipe.
4. Remove the securing bolts and lift off the valve complete with mounting bracket.

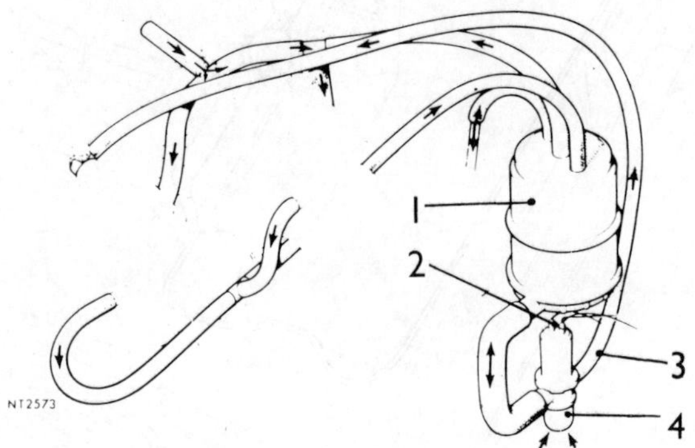

Refitting

5. Reverse instructions 1 to 4.

E.G.R. CONTROL VALVE

(Not fitted to pre 1974 cars)

– Remove and refit 17.45.01

Removing

1. Disconnect the throttle control cable.
2. Disconnect the vacuum control tube.
3. Unscrew the cam retaining nut.
4. Lift off the cam complete with valve.

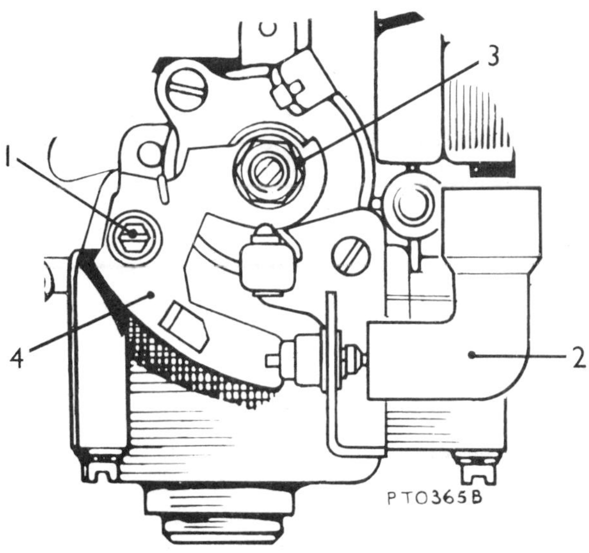

Refitting

5. Reverse instructions 1 to 4 ensuring the security of the vacuum tube connections and the setting of the throttle cable i.e. no tightness, no play.

EXHAUST GAS RECIRCULATION (E.G.R.) VALVE

(Not fitted to pre 1974 cars)

Remove and refit 17.45.05
E.G.R. Valve to manifold pipe 17.45.10

Removing

1. Disconnect the vacuum control valve pipe from the top of the valve.
2. Slacken the unions securing the steel pipe to the inlet manifold and the valve.

NOTE: As the steel pipe is longer on one side of the bend than the other it should be marked to ensure correct refitting.

3. Remove the steel pipe.
4. Slacken the locknut at the base of the valve.
5. Unscrew the valve and remove from the head.

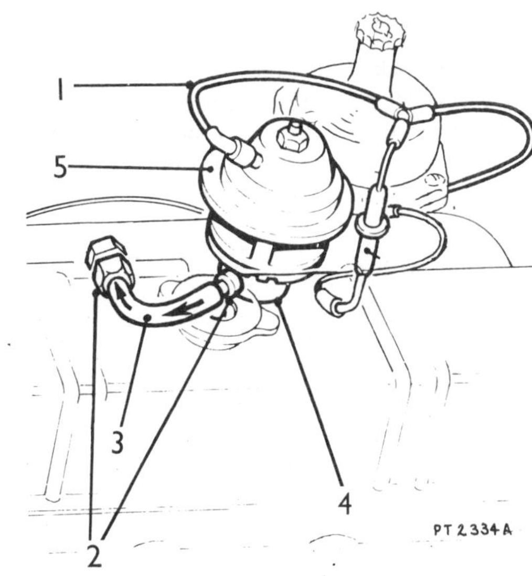

Cleaning

6. Clean the assembly area of the valve with a wire brush. Use a standard spark plug machine to clean the valve and seat. Insert the valve opening into the machine and lift the diaphragm evenly by using two fingers, one each side of the support strut. Blast the valve for approx. 30 seconds, remove and inspect, if necessary repeat until all carbon deposits are removed. Use compressed air to remove all traces of carbon grit from the valve. Use a flexiwire brush to clean the steel pipe – blow clear of carbon grit.

Refitting

7. Refit by reversing the instructions 1 to 6 – check the position of the steel pipe before attempting to tighten it.

E.G.R. SYSTEM VACUUM CONTROL TUBING

(Not fitted to pre 1974 cars)

Remove and refit **17.45.15**

All tubing in the system is push fit. Check the condition of tubing and connectors before refitting and test the operation of the valve to ensure leak free fitting.

E.G.R. SYSTEM

(Not fitted to pre 1974 cars)

Check **17.45.20**

A system check of the valve carried out with the unit in situ is by "blipping" the throttle and observing the valve unit, which must be actuated by the sudden shift of engine speed. The valve will settle back and it is not possible to perform a total check to find small leaks by this method. For a complete check on the operation of the valve connect the vacuum pipe of a distributor vacuum test unit to the valve and ensure that the valve is actuated, held, and that there is no leak in vacuum.

To check the sealing of the control valve, apply vacuum to the tubing from the three way connector to the valve, it will be readily apparent if the valve is not sealing.

PETROL INJECTION

FUEL SYSTEM OPERATIONS

Continued

FUEL SYSTEM – P.I. OPERATIONS – *Continued*

PETROL INJECTION FAULT DIAGNOSIS

Primary Checks

Experience has shown that very often faults attributed to the Petrol Injection System are in fact caused by the engine being in poor state of tune. It is therefore essential that before attempting any fault diagnosis of the P.I. System the Primary Checks, detailed below, must be carried out first.

1. Check fuel supply is clean and adequate.
2. Ensure the battery is charged and in good condition.
3. Clean, check and set spark plug gaps.
4. Check and adjust valve clearances. 12.25.48.
5. Check compression pressures. 12.25.61.
6. Check ignition timing. 86.35.15.
7. Renew faulty rubber balance pipe connectors linking the three manifolds, and check the tightness of the vacuum adaptors.
8. Check and adjust throttle butterflies. 19.20.05.
9. Check manifold depression. 12.49.03.

Special Equipment.

1. Pressure gauge 0 to 120 lb f/in^2 (0 to 8·4 kg/cm^2)
2. Ammeter 0 to 10 amps
3. Voltmeter 0 to 20 volts.
4. Pressure test adaptor.
5. 15ft. (4·6 m) of twin cable 28/·012 in. Two nipples soldered on one end of cable. Cable Connector for connection in series to pump.
6. Air-flow meter.
7. Vacuum gauge.
8. Metering unit outlet union seal removal and renewal tools. – see 19.35.14.

SYMPTOM	CAUSE	ACTION
Engine will not start.	*a.* Inertia cut-out switch has operated.	Push switch down to complete pump circuit – 86.65.59
	b. Blocked fuel filter.	Check fuel filter and renew element – 19.25.07
	c. Pump inoperative	Check pump end-float. Check brushes. Check for gear seizure – 19.45.15.
	d, No spray from injectors.	Remove each injector in turn and test – 19.60.02
	e. Incorrect or no line pressure.	Check line pressure and adjust pressure relief valve – 19.65.01
	f. Incorrect injection order.	Check that the pipes are fitted to the injectors in correct order.
Engine cutting out.	*a.* Slipping drive belt.	Check drive belt tension.
	b. Incorrect line pressure.	Check line pressure statically and during road test with pressure gauge and ammeter. 19.45.01.
	c. Fuel tank breather pipe blocked.	Clear or renew pipe.
	d. Blocked fuel filter.	Renew filter. 19.25.07

Continued

SYMPTOM	CAUSE	ACTION
Erratic Idling or lack of response.	*a.* Incorrect injection order.	Check that the injector pipes are fitted to the injectors in correct order.
	b. Incorrect idling speed.	Check and adjust idling. 19.20.05
	c. Excess fuel lever incorrectly adjusted.	Check and if necessary adjust clearance. 19.35.02
	d. Incorrect line pressure.	Check and if necessary adjust line pressure at the pressure relief valve. 19.65.01
	e. Metering Unit incorrectly timed to the engine.	Check and if necessary adjust timing. 19.35.01
	f. Continuous injection.	Check each injector in turn 19.35.14. Check outlet union seals and renew if necessary.
	g. Fuel leaks.	Check for leaks from metering unit.
Engine Mis-firing.	*a.* Lack of fuel in tank or blockage.	Replenish with fuel of the correct octane rating and check tank outlet to line.
	b. Excess fuel lever incorrectly set.	Check lever is returning to the off position. Check clearance – 19.35.02
	c. Faulty injection.	Remove each injector in turn and test – 19.60.02
	d. Faulty non-return valve in one of the metering unit unions.	Renew the union concerned 19.35.14
	e. Incorrect line pressure.	Check line pressure and adjust pressure relief valve. 19.65.01
	f. Faulty pressure relief valve.	Check by substitution.
	g. Constantly fouled spark plugs on Nos. 2 and 5 cylinders.	Check banjo seals on Nos. 2 and 5 injector pipes at metering unit connection.
Excessive fuel consumption.	*a.* Fuel leakage.	Check for fuel leakage from all connections and pedestal seals.
	b. Excess fuel lever out of adjustment.	Check excess fuel lever is returning to the off position. Check clearance – 19.35.02
	c. Loose Calibration Cover Securing Screws letting in air.	Check tightness and sealing of cover.
	d. Incorrect line pressure.	Check line pressure statically and during road test. Adjust if necessary – 19.65.00

AIR CLEANER – P.I.

– Remove and refit **19.10.01**

Removing

1. Remove the radiator cowling 76.79.04
2. Remove the hose connecting the air cleaner outlet to the air intake manifold.
3. Disconnect the inlet hoses to the air cleaner, running forward of the radiator.
4. Remove the nut and bolt and single nut securing the air cleaner bracket to the radiator stay.
5. Remove the air cleaner and bracket from the car.

Refitting

6. Reverse instructions 1 to 5.

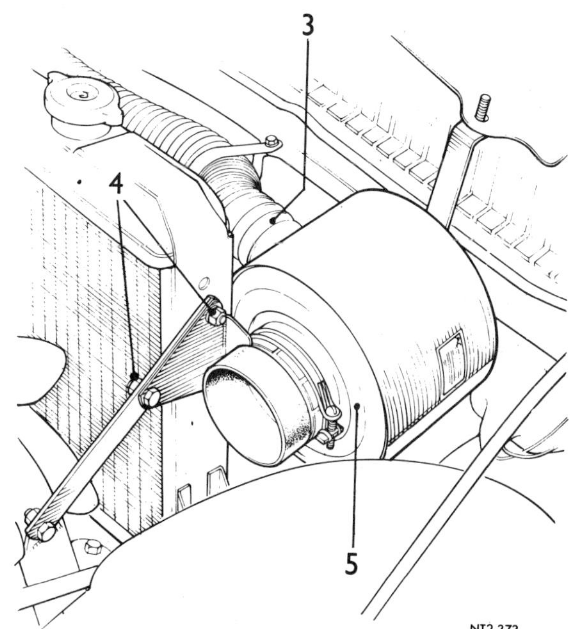

AIR CLEANER – P.I.

– Renew element **19.10.08**

Dismantling

1. Remove air cleaner from the car 19.10.01.
2. Remove the cover plate retaining nut and steady bracket.
3. Withdraw the cover plate and discard the element.
4. Remove and if necessary discard the sealing rings.
5. Clean the container and cover plate.

Reassembling

6. Place the sealing rings in position at both ends of the element.
7. Insert the new paper element into the container.
8. Refit the cover and steady bracket and secure with the nut.
9. Refit the air cleaner assembly to the car 19.10.01.

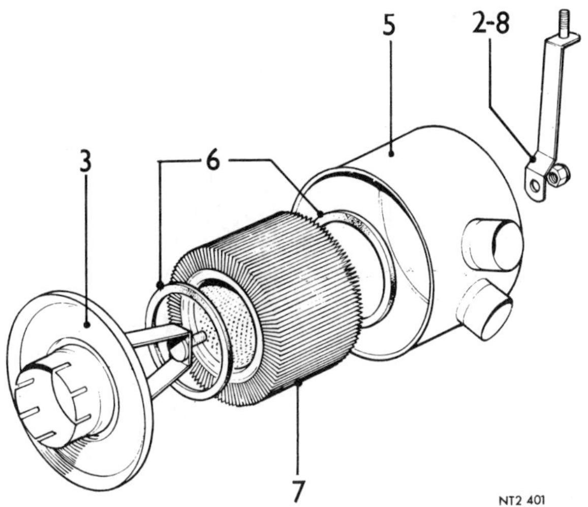

THROTTLE PEDAL

– Remove and refit **19.20.01**

Removing

1. Disconnect the throttle cable from the pedal bracket.
2. Disconnect the pedal return spring.
3. Remove the two bolts and nuts securing the pedal assembly and pivot bracket to the body.
4. Withdraw the pedal and shaft assembly from the bulkhead bush and remove from the car.

Refitting

5. Reverse instructions 1 to 4.
6. Adjust pedal stop bolt so that the head touches the floor with the throttle butterflies in the fully open position.

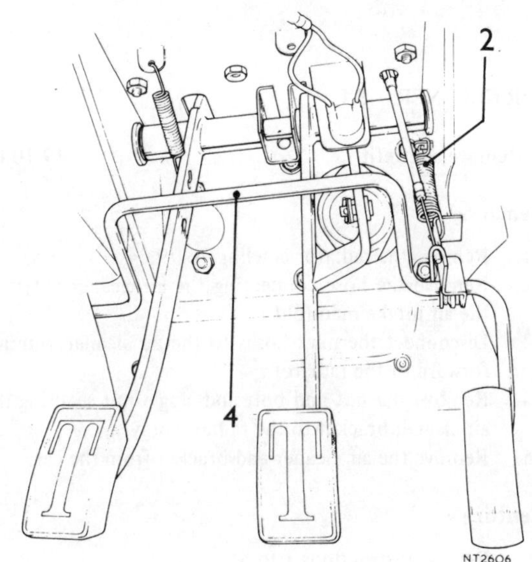

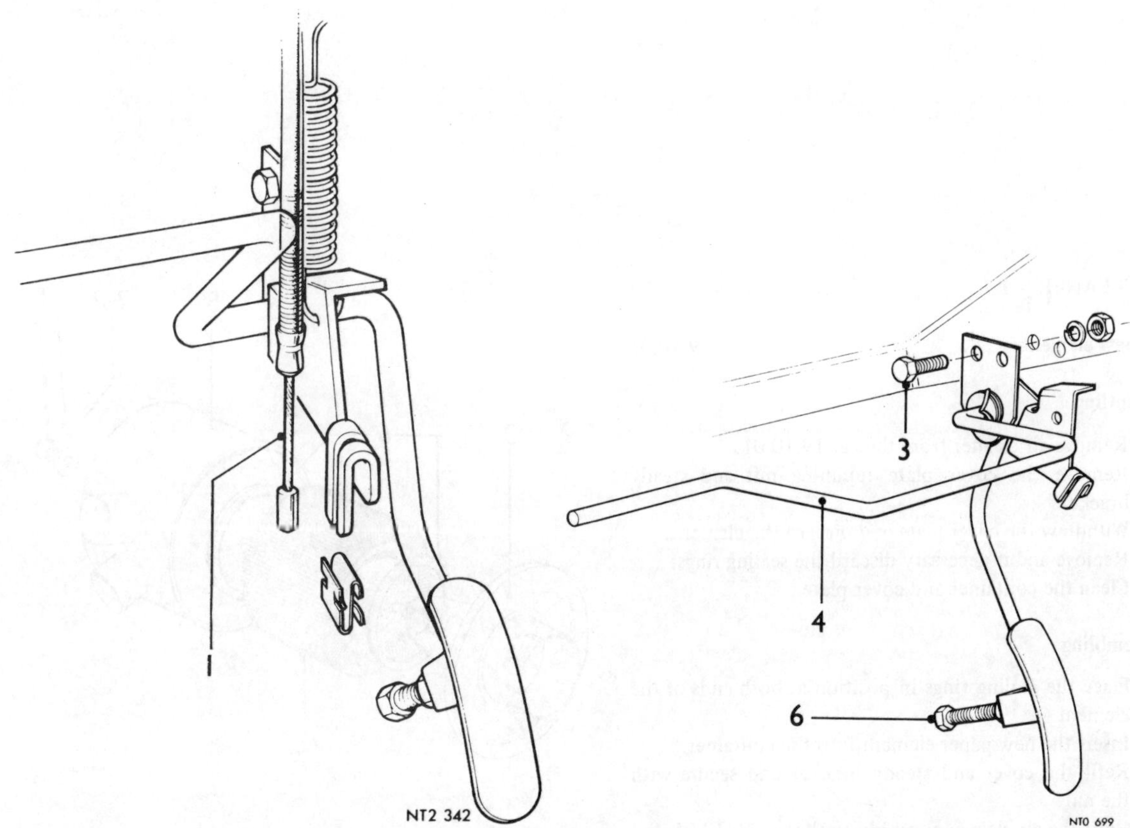

THROTTLE BUTTERFLIES
****(Up to Engine No. CP 77609E)****
– Check and adjust **19.20.05**

Check

1. Start the engine and warm to normal operating temperature.
2. Remove the air intake manifold 19.70.01.
3. Ensure that the cold start lever on the metering unit is back against its stop and that there is clearance between the cam and adjusting screw on the manifold linkage.

4. Hold a Crypton synchro check meter against number six intake and open the butterflies by turning the throttle adjusting screw clockwise sufficiently for a
** reading to register on the meter scale (eg 3).**

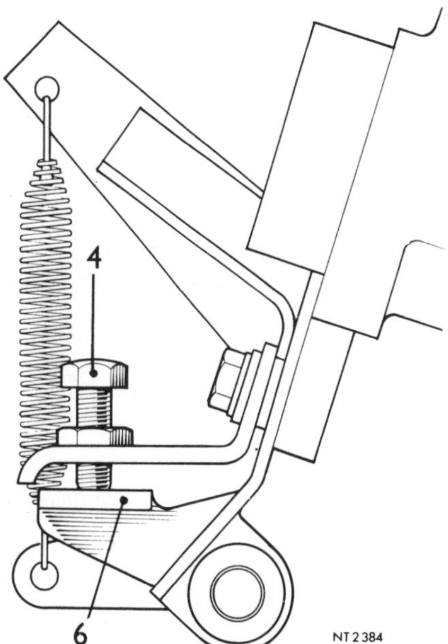

5. With the engine revolutions maintained compare the readings from number three and one intakes with that of number six.
6. If the readings are all the same no adjustment is required and the throttle adjusting screw should be reset and locked so that it just touches the countershaft operating lever.

Continued

Adjustment

7. Should adjustment of the butterflies be necessary, maintain the engine at normal operating temperature, check as in instruction 3 and with the air intake manifold removed proceed as follows:-

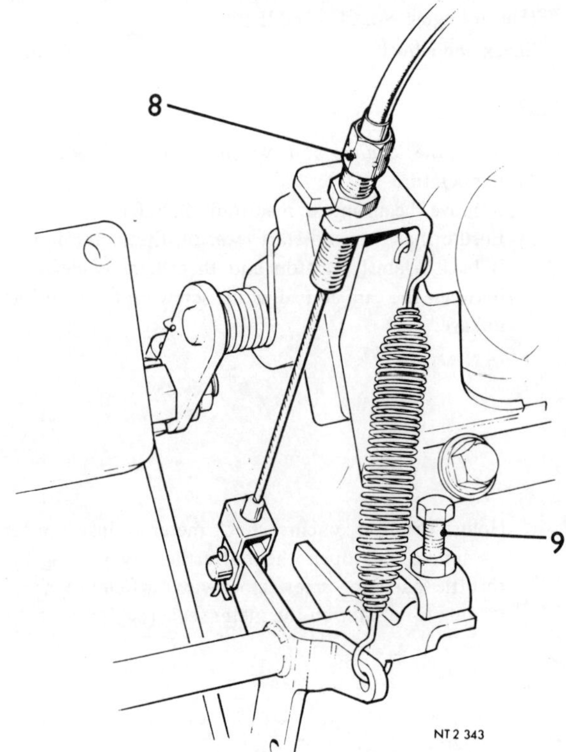

8. Slacken the throttle cable adjuster so that there is no tension in the cable.

9. Turn the throttle adjusting screw anti-clockwise so that it is well clear of the countershaft operating lever.

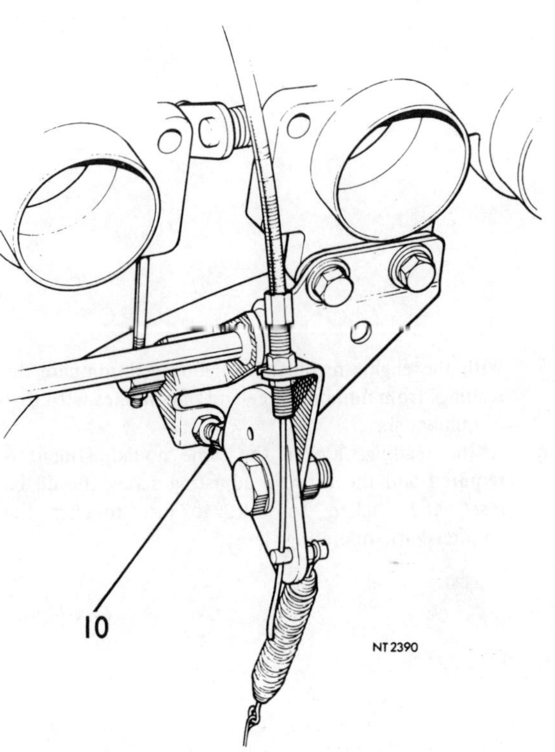

10. Slacken the cold start adjusting screw clockwise so that the screw head is well clear of the cam.

Continued

11. Release the lock nut of the rear vertical link and

    a. adjust the link so that the brazed-on washer just touches the butterfly shaft trunnion.
    b. Lock the nut against the lower trunnion.

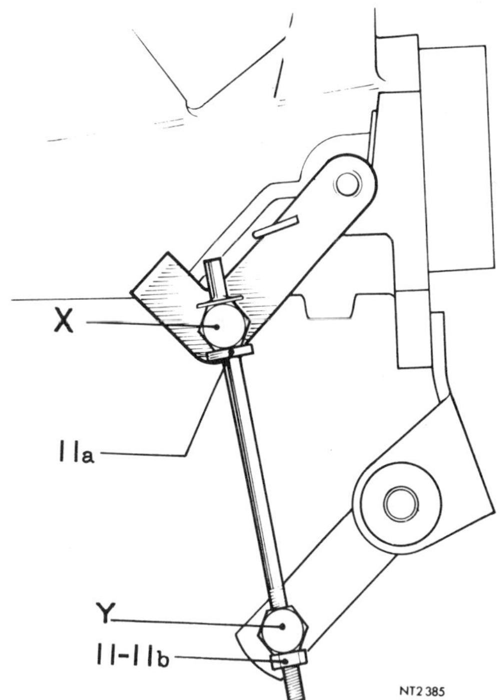

12. Start the engine and again hold the crypton synchro check meter against number six intake and by means of the throttle adjusting screw (turning clockwise) open the intake butterflies thereby increasing the engine revolutions until a convenient reading (say 3), registers on the meter scale.
13. Slacken the centre vertical link lock-nut and hold the meter against number three intake and by means of the centre vertical link adjust the butterflies of numbers three and four intakes so that the same reading as in instruction 12 is recorded. Lock the nut against the lower trunnion.

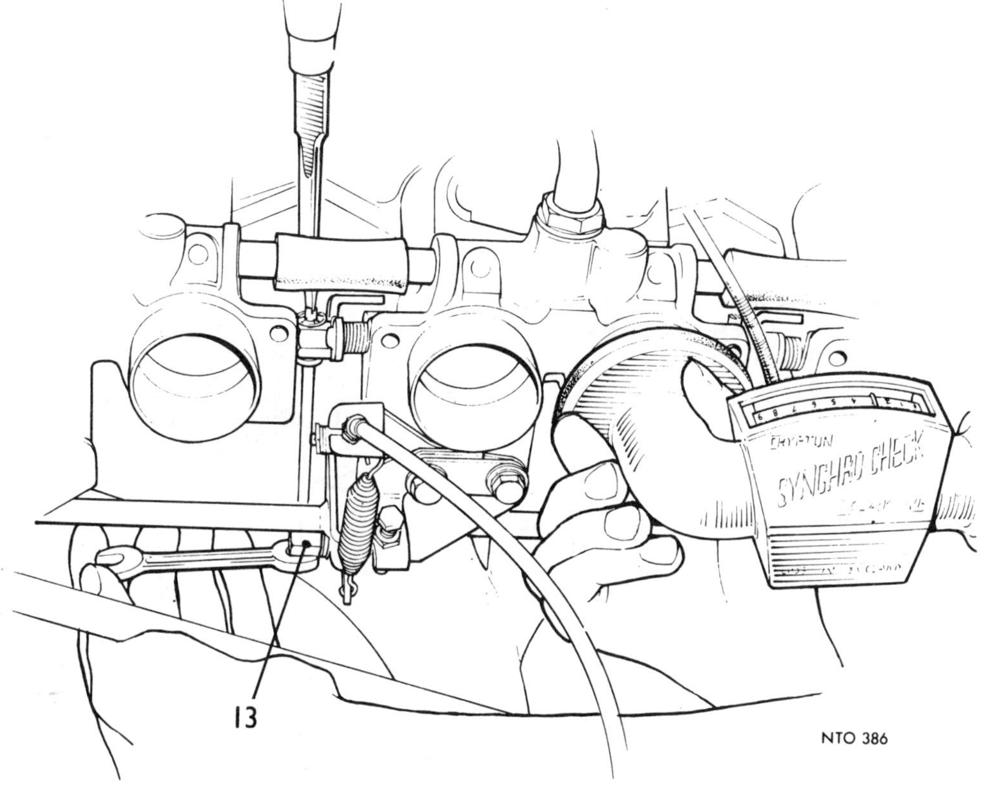

14. Release the locknut on the front vertical link and hold the meter against number one intake and adjust the link until the meter reading registers the same as in instructions 12 and 13. Lock the nut against the lower trunnion.

Continued

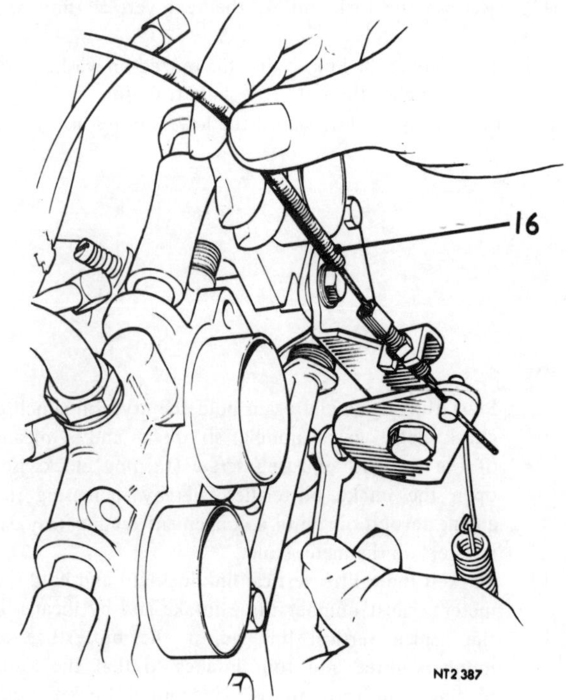

15. Re-check the metering readings on numbers three and six intakes and re-adjust if necessary.
16. Adjust the fast idle speed by pulling the cold start cable out of the adjuster with the cam turned to its maximum lift position. Turn the adjusting screw against the cam until the engine revolutions maintain a steady 1500 to 1800 r.p.m.

NOTE: Do not pull the cold start cable with the control knob on the control panel since it will also operate the excess fuel lever on the metering unit thereby increasing the quantity of fuel delivered to the injectors.

17. Turn the throttle adjusting screw so that it just touches the countershaft operating lever and secure with the lock nut. See instruction 6.

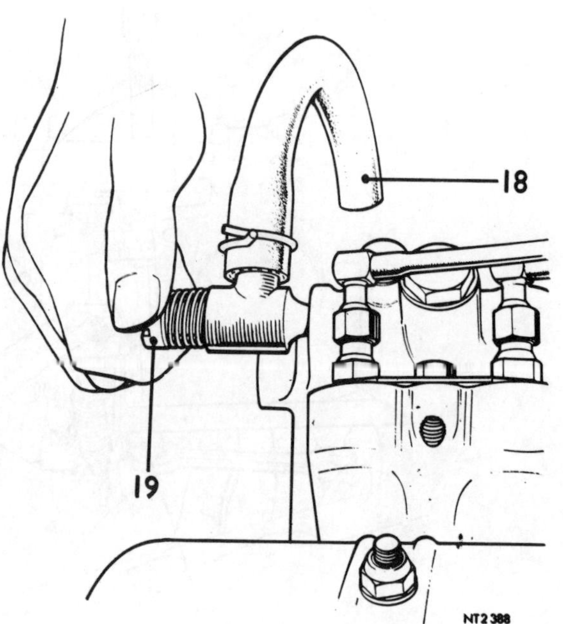

18. As a check to ensure that all the butterflies are fully closed hold a finger over the end of the air valve pipe so that the engine stalls.
19. Start the engine and by means of the air valve adjusting screw regulate the air bleed to give an idling speed of 750 to 800 r.p.m.

20. Adjust the throttle and cold start cables to remove excessive slack and secure with the locknuts.
21. Stop the engine and refit the air intake manifold. 19.70.01.

Data

Idling speed . . . . 750 to 800 r.p.m.

Fast idling speed . . . . . .1500 to 1800 r.p.m.

THROTTLE BUTTERFLIES
(From Engine No. CR 1E)

– Check and adjust 19.20.05

1. Start the engine and warm to the normal operating temperature.
2. Remove the air intake manifold 19.70.01.
3. Check that the throttle cable is correctly adjusted.
4. Ensure that the cold start lever on the metering unit is back against its stop and that there is clearance between the cam and adjusting screw on the manifold linkage.
5. Screw in the front adjuster until the centre pair of butterflies are just opening and the front pair are just closing. Back off the adjuster until the centre butterflies just close.
6. Screw in the rear adjuster until the rear pair of butterflies are just opening and the centre pair are just closing. Back off the adjuster until the rear butterflies just close.

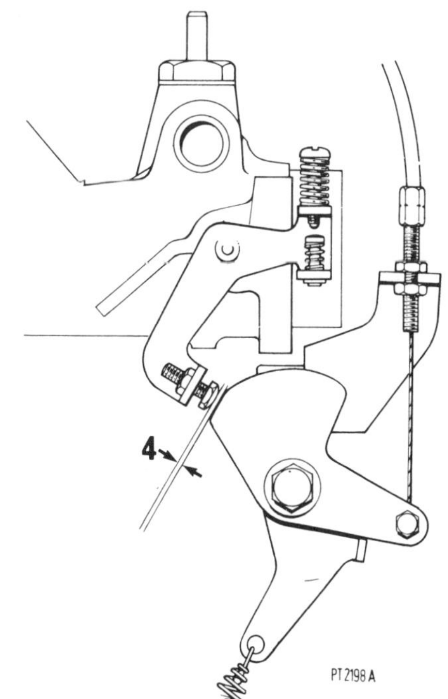

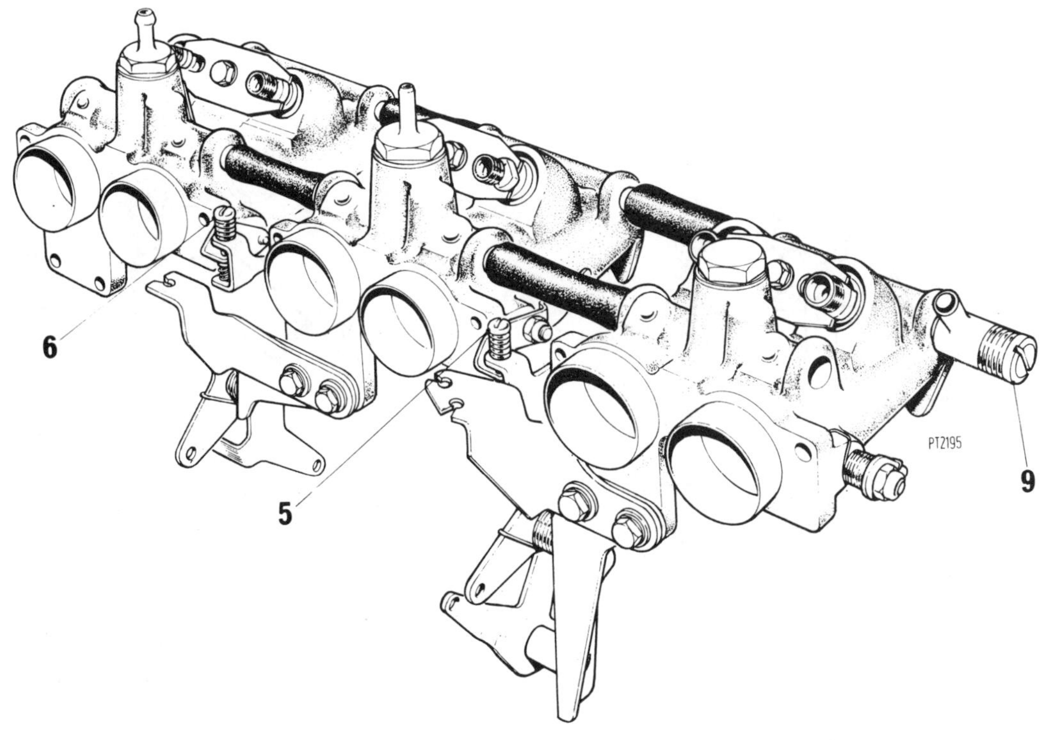

7. Check the closure of all the butterflies with a 0·002 in. (0·05 mm) feeler gauge. The feeler gauge should not pass between the butterfly plate and the bore.
8. Adjust the link rod to obtain a clearance of 0·020 – 0·030 in. (0·5 – 0·75 mm) between the nylon roller on the primary lever and the link rod lever.
9. Start the engine and adjust the air bleed valve to achieve an idling speed of 750 – 800 r.p.m. Screwing in the valve increase the speed.
10. Open the fast idle cam and check the engine speed. If necessary slacken the locknut and adjust the contact screw to achieve a fast idle speed of 1500 – 1800 r.p.m.
11. Refit the air intake manifold 19.70.01

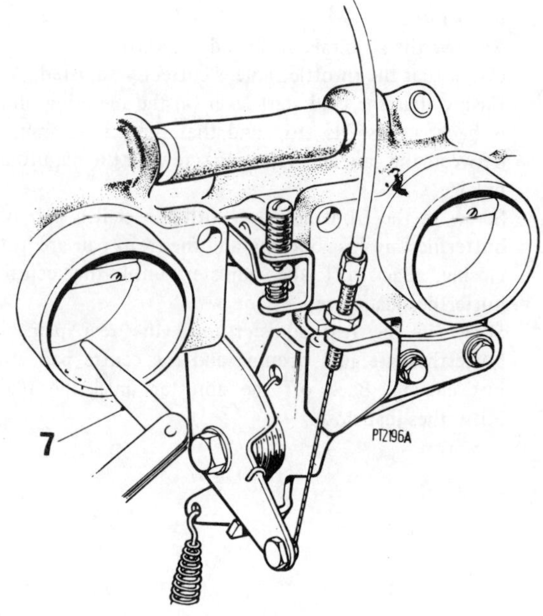

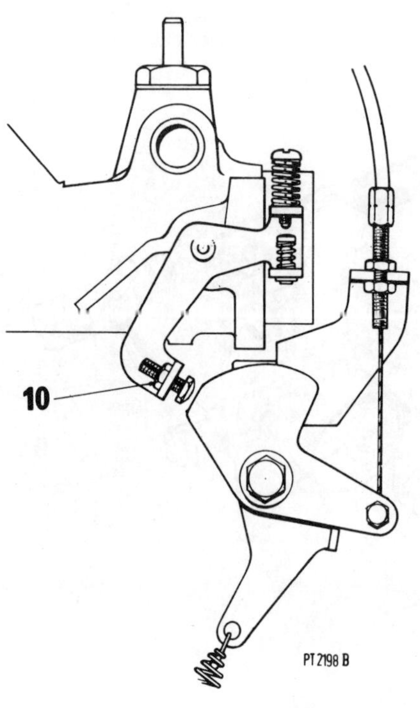

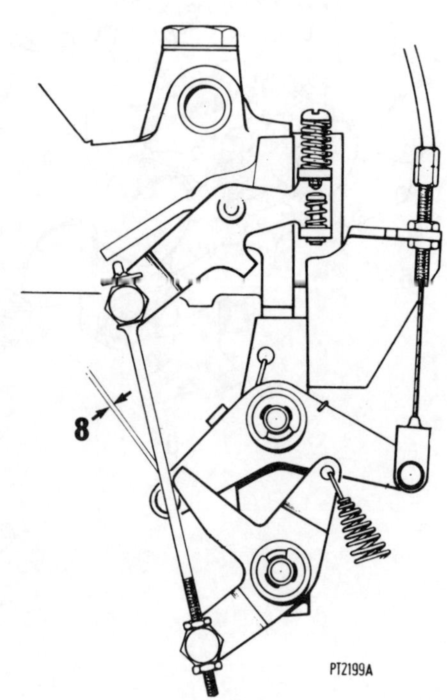

THROTTLE CABLE

– Remove and refit 19.20.06

Removing

1. Remove the spring clip retaining the inner cable to the throttle pedal.
2. Disconnect the inner cable from the pedal.
3. Remove the rubber sealing washer from the brass ferrule on the bulkhead.
4. Pull the outer cable complete through the bulkhead hole sufficiently to enable the cable gripper to be removed.

NOTE: The spring steel cable gripper in the bulkhead cable clearance hole must be removed before the complete cable is withdrawn from the bulkhead, otherwise the ferrule at the end of the outer cable will be pulled off.

5. Remove the cable from the bulkhead.
6. Remove the split pin from the clevis pin securing the inner cable fork to the countershaft lever.
7. Remove the lower locknut from the cable adjuster and remove the cable complete from the bracket.

Refitting

8. Thread the rubber sealing washer on to the pedal end of the cable.
9. Thread the cable gripper over the cable and insert the cable into the bulkhead.
10. Position the cable gripper into the bulkhead hole and push the brass ferrule into the hole so that it is held firm by the gripper and the shoulder is flush with the bulkhead.
11. Reverse instructions 1 to 3 and 6 and 7.
12. Adjust the cable tension by means of the cable adjuster.

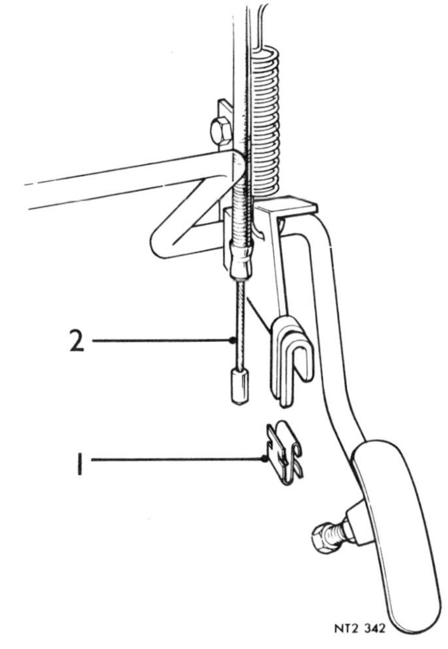

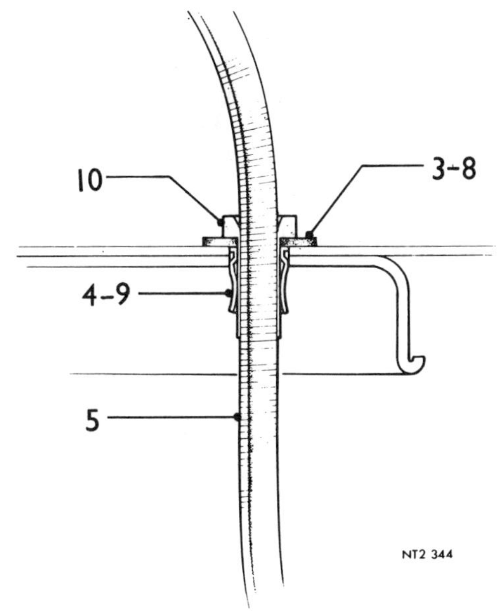

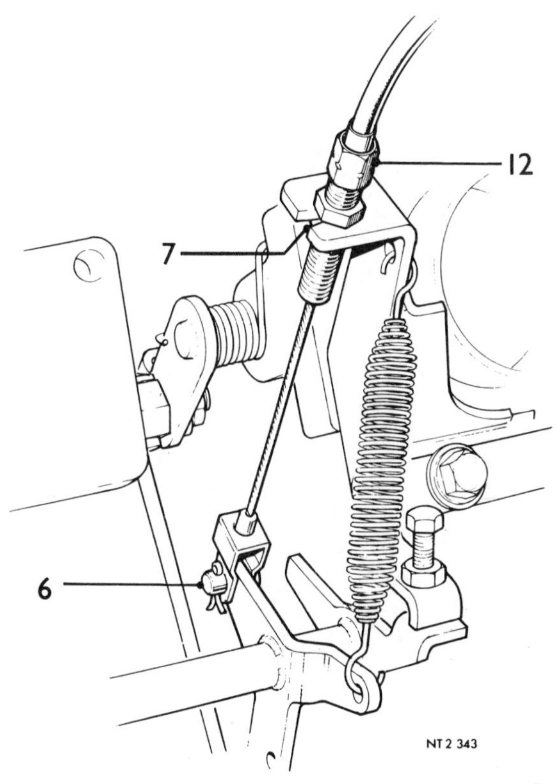

THROTTLE LINKAGE – P.I.
****(Up to Engine No. CP 77609E)****
– Remove and refit **19.20.07**

Removing

1. Remove the air intake manifold 19.70.01
2. Disconnect the throttle cable and the return spring from the linkage 19.20.06.
3. Disconnect the cold start control cable and return spring 19.20.26.
4. Remove the spring clips from three vertical links.
5. Remove the six bolts complete with washers securing the linkage to the induction manifold.
6. Remove the linkage complete from the engine.

Refitting

7. Offer-up the linkage to the manifold passing each of the three vertical links through the throttle spindle trunnions. Secure the linkage by the centre throttle bracket only using two bolts, plain and spring washers.
8. Loosely secure the two endbrackets to the manifold so that the brackets may be moved laterally within the limits of the elongated holes.
9. Adjust the countershaft by means of the elongated holes in the two end brackets so that no end-float exists in the shaft. Ensure, however that the vertical links are at right angles to the countershaft. Tighten the four securing bolts.
10. Check and if necessary adjust the position of the cold start cam in relation to its adjusting screw, ensuring that the cam is central on the screw head.
11. Fit the spring clips to the trunnion end of the vertical links.
12. Reconnect the throttle cable and spring.
13. Reconnect the cold start cable and spring.
14. Adjust the linkage 19.20.05.
15. Refit the air intake manifold 19.70.01.

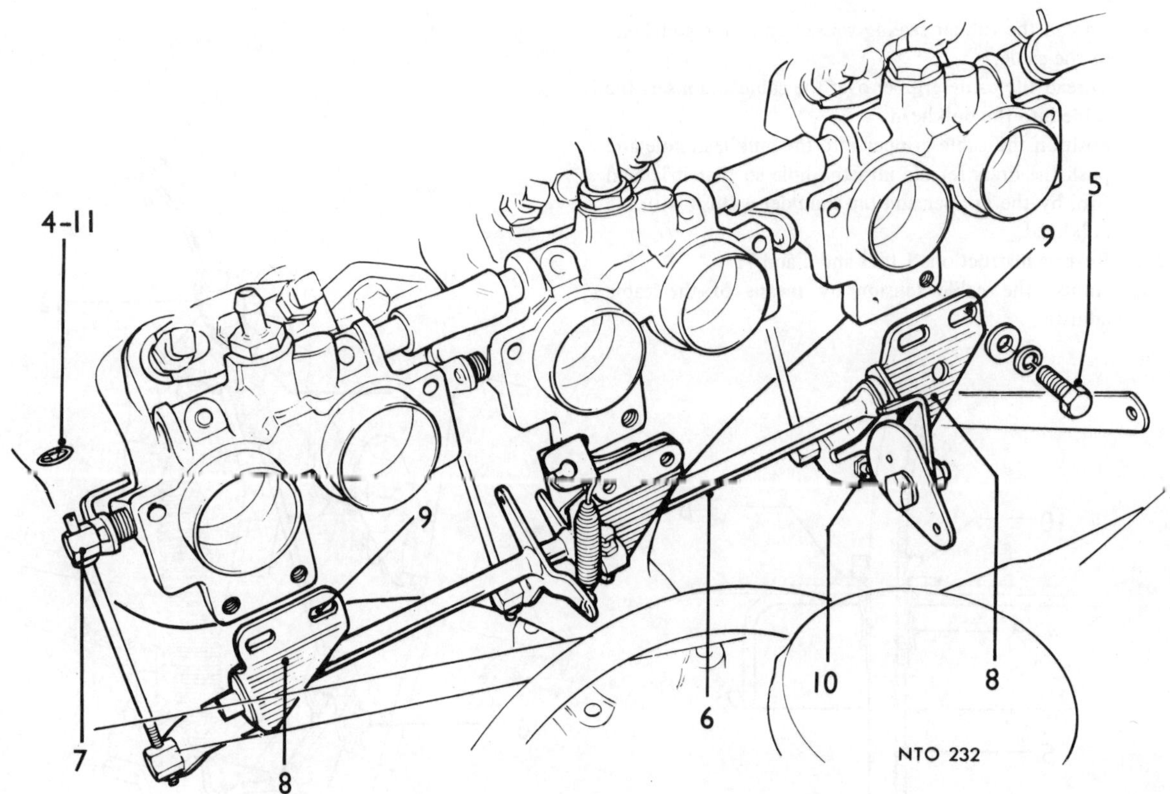

THROTTLE LINKAGE
(From Engine No. CR1E)

– Remove and refit **19.20.07**

Removing

1. Remove the air intake manifold 19.70.01.
2. Disconnect the throttle cable from the linkage.
3. Remove the retaining clip from the vertical link rod.
4. Remove two bolts, plain and spring washers securing the linkage to the induction manifold.
5. Withdraw the linkage.

Refitting

6. Reverse instructions 4 and 5.
7. *a.* Adjust the vertical link rod so that the brazed-on washer just touches the butterfly spindle trunnion.
   b. The cam lever is in contact with the roller on the throttle lever.
   c. The throttle lever is against its stop.
8. Tighten the vertical link locknuts and refit the retaining clip.
9. Refit and adjust the throttle cable.
10. Refit the air intake manifold.

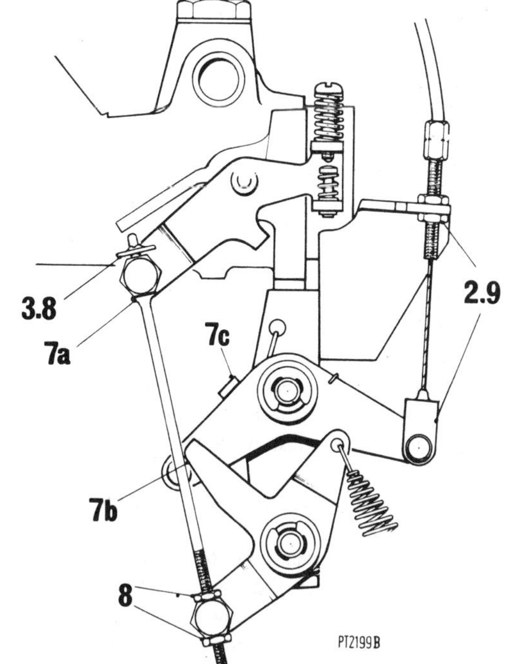

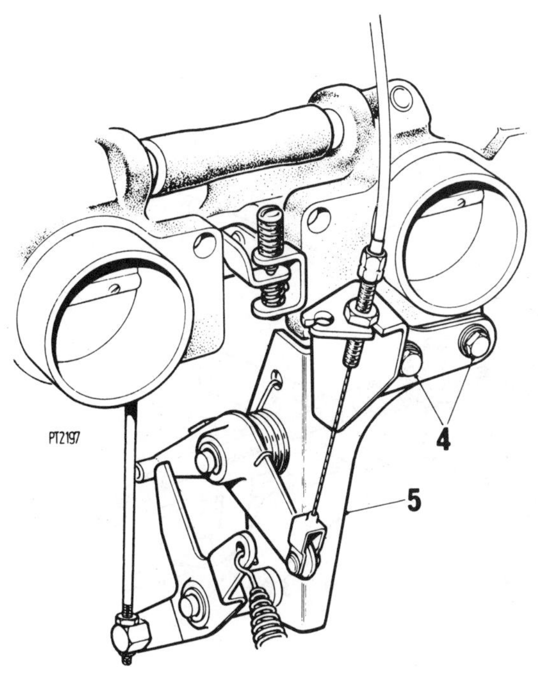

COLD START CABLE

– Remove and refit **19.20.26**

Removing

1. Disconnect the inner cable from the metering distributor excess fuel lever.
2. Disconnect the inner cable from the cold start cam on the throttle linkage and release the spring.
3. Unscrew the locknut behind the control panel and withdraw the cable complete through the control panel, locknut and bulkhead.

Refitting

4. Feed the cable complete through the control panel hole and pass the locknut over the cables.
5. Secure the outer cable to the control panel with the locknut so that the end of the threaded part of the outer cable is flush with the plated ferrule on the control panel.
6. Feed the engine end of the cable through the bulkhead.
7. Connect the inner cable to the metering distributor excess fuel lever and ensure that there is sufficient slack in the cable to allow the lever to rest against its stop when the control knob is pushed fully home.
8. Connect the inner cable to the cam on the throttle linkage and adjust the cable by means of the adjuster. Ensure that there is clearance between the cam and adjusting screw.

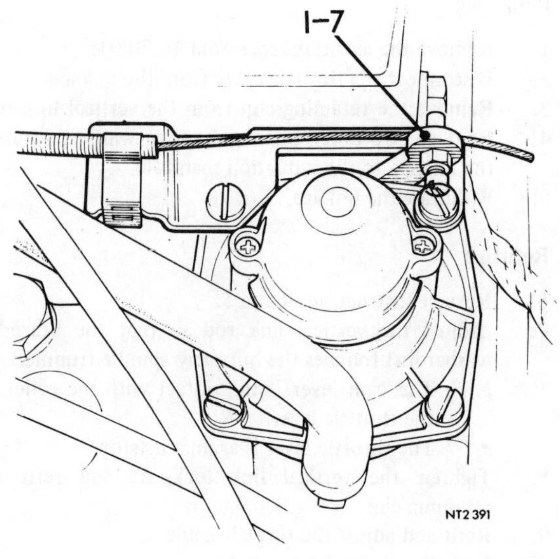

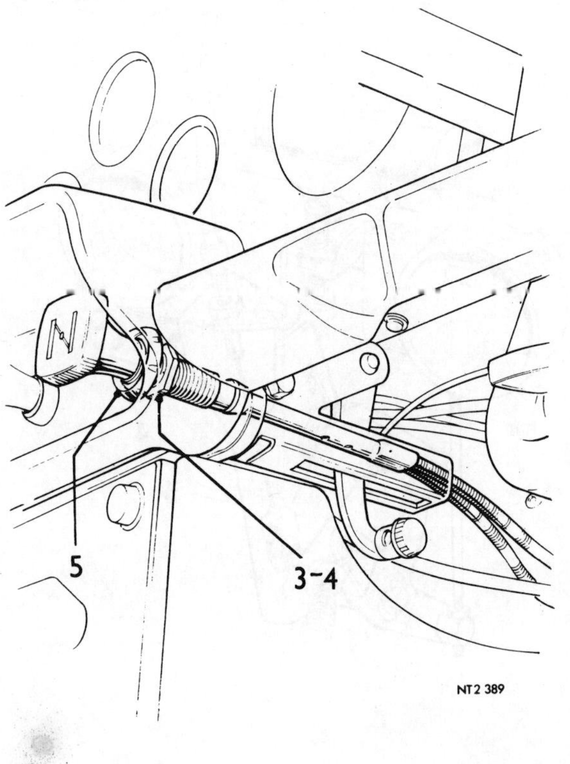

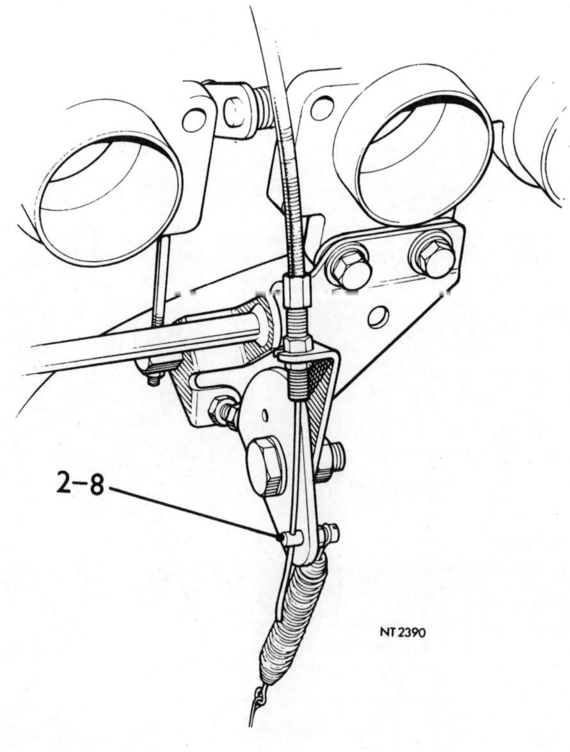

COLD START CABLE

– Remove and refit **19.20.26**

Removing

1. Disconnect the inner cable from the metering distributor excess fuel lever.
2. Disconnect the inner cable from the cold start cam on the throttle linkage and release the spring.
3. Unscrew the locknut behind the control panel and withdraw the cable complete through the control panel, locknut and bulkhead.

Refitting

4. Feed the cable complete through the control panel hole and pass the locknut over the cables.
5. Secure the outer cable to the control panel with the locknut so that the end of the threaded part of the outer cable is flush with the plated ferrule on the control panel.
6. Feed the engine end of the cable through the bulkhead.
7. Connect the inner cable to the metering distributor excess fuel lever and ensure that there is sufficient slack in the cable to allow the lever to rest against its stop when the control knob is pushed fully home.
8. Connect the inner cable to the cam on the throttle linkage and adjust the cable by means of the adjuster. Ensure that there is clearance between the cam and adjusting screw.

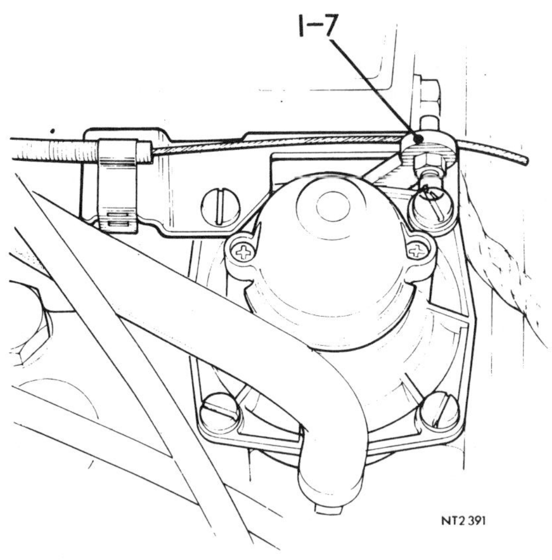

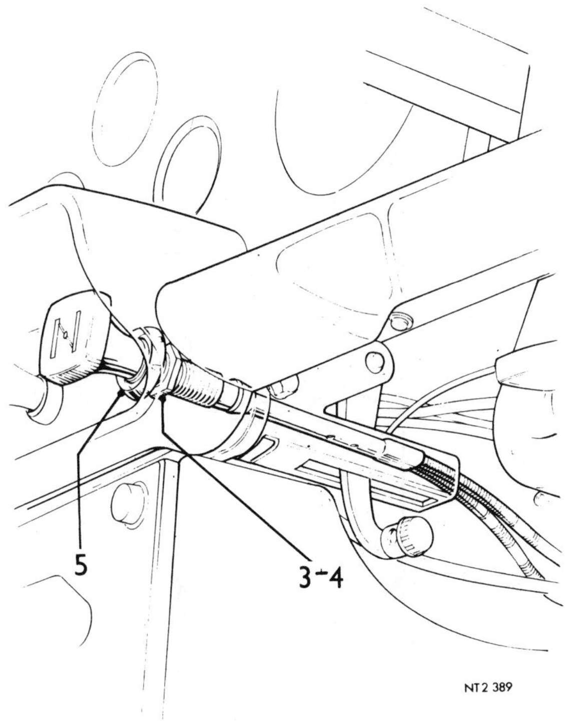

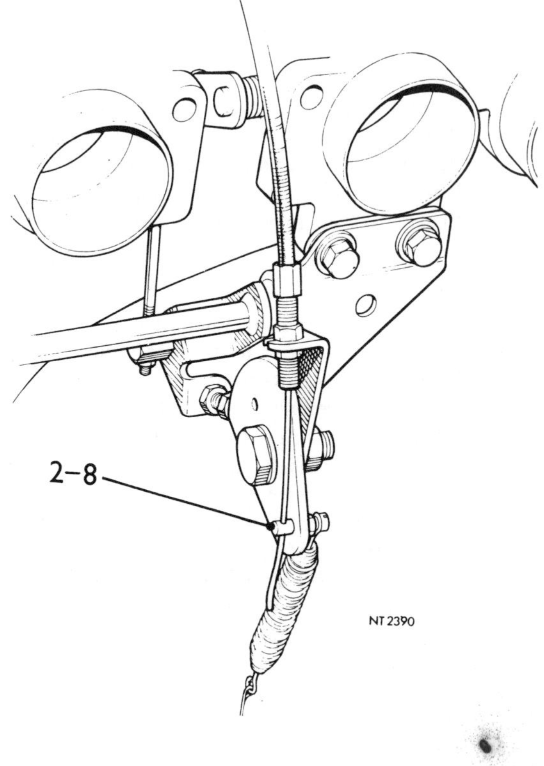

FUEL MAIN FILTER

– Remove and refit **19.25.02**

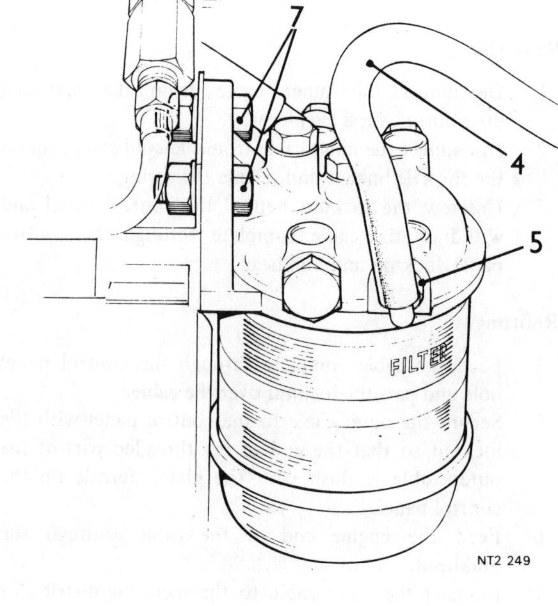

Removing

1. Isolate the battery.
2. Remove the spare wheel.
3. Remove the luggage compartment forward trim panel 76.13.17.
4. Clamp the gravity feed hose from the fuel tank to the filter inlet union.
5. Disconnnect the gravity feed supply to the filter at the inlet union.
6. Disconnect the outlet feed from the filter at the pump inlet union.

NOTE: As an alternative, the outlet feed hose may be detached from the extension pipe at the filter outlet, providing damage is not caused by using undue force to remove a tightly gripped hose.

7. Remove the two nuts and bolts securing the filter assembly to the car body and remove the filter from the car.

Refitting

8. Reverse instructions 1 to 7.

FUEL MAIN FILTER ELEMENT

– Remove and refit **19.25.07**

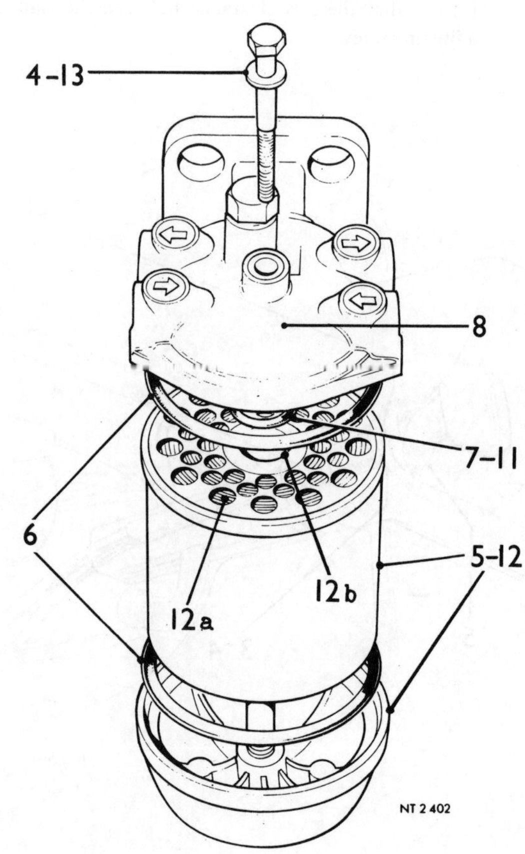

Removing

1. Isolate the battery.
2. Remove the spare wheel.
3. Clamp the gravity supply hose to the filter.
4. Remove the centre retaining bolt and sealing washer.
5. Remove the filter element and lower casing.
6. Remove the upper and lower sealing rings.
7. Remove the 'O' ring on the element location spigot.

Refitting

8. Clean the filter head and lower body.
9. Fit a new sealing ring to the filter head, ensuring that it seats properly in its groove.
10. Locate a new sealing ring to the filter lower body.
11. Fit a new 'O' ring to the filter element spigot, ensuring that it locates in its groove.
12. Fit a new filter element to the filter body ensuring:–
    a. The element is fitted so that the circular holes in the end of the element are uppermost.
    b. The large hole in the centre of the element locates correctly over the spigot and 'O' ring.
13. Secure the assembly with the central retaining bolt and sealing washer.
14. Remove the hose clamp, reconnect the battery and run the engine whilst checking for fuel leaks from the filter.
15. Refit the spare wheel.

COLD START LINKAGE **(From Engine No. CR1E)**

– Remove and refit **19.20.07**

Remove

1. Remove the air intake manifold. 19.70.01
2. Disconnect the cold start cable from the manifold linkage.
3. Disconnect the cold start cam return spring.
4. Remove the two bolts, plain and spring washers securing the linkage to the manifold.
5. Lift off the linkage.

Refitting

6. Reverse instructions 3 to 5.
7. Ensure that the cold start cam is against its stop.
8. Start the engine and warm to the normal operating temperature.
9. Slacken the locknut and turn the cam to the fully open position.
10. Adjust the screw until a fast idle speed of 1500 – 1800 r.p.m. is attained.
11. Reconnect and adjust the cold start cable.
12. Refit the air intake manifold.

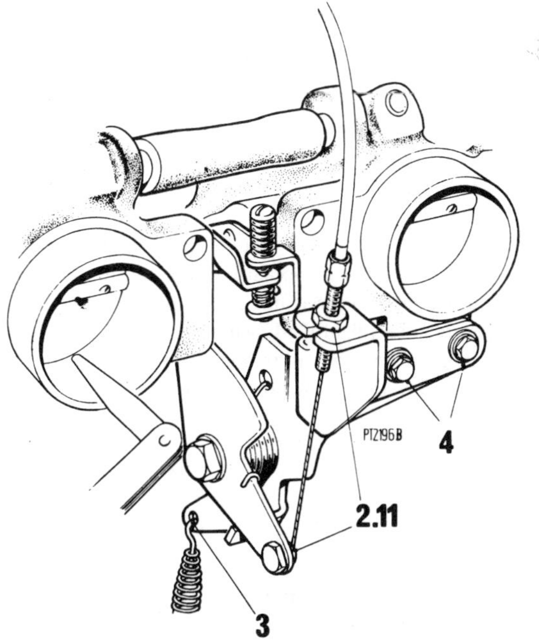

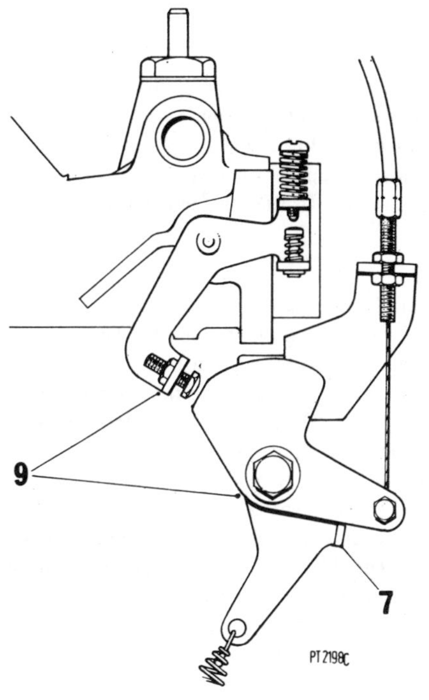

FUEL MAIN FILTER

– Remove and refit **19.25.02**

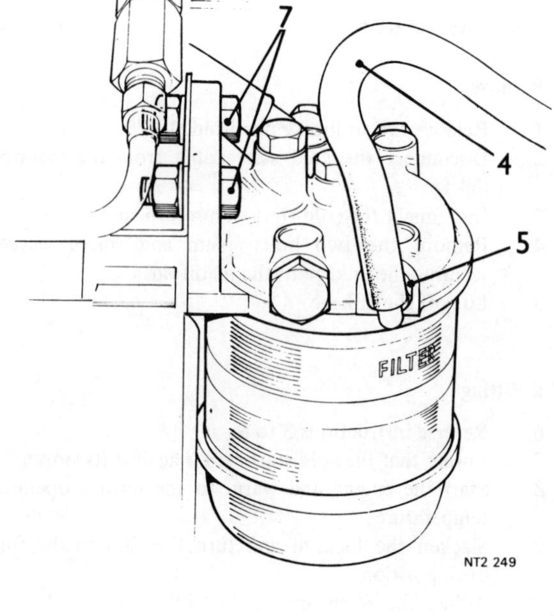

Removing

1. Isolate the battery.
2. Remove the spare wheel.
3. Remove the luggage compartment forward trim panel 76.13.17.
4. Clamp the gravity feed hose from the fuel tank to the filter inlet union.
5. Disconnnect the gravity feed supply to the filter at the inlet union.
6. Disconnect the outlet feed from the filter at the pump inlet union.

NOTE: As an alternative, the outlet feed hose may be detached from the extension pipe at the filter outlet, providing damage is not caused by using undue force to remove a tightly gripped hose.

7. Remove the two nuts and bolts securing the filter assembly to the car body and remove the filter from the car.

Refitting

8. Reverse instructions 1 to 7.

FUEL MAIN FILTER ELEMENT

– Remove and refit **19.25.07**

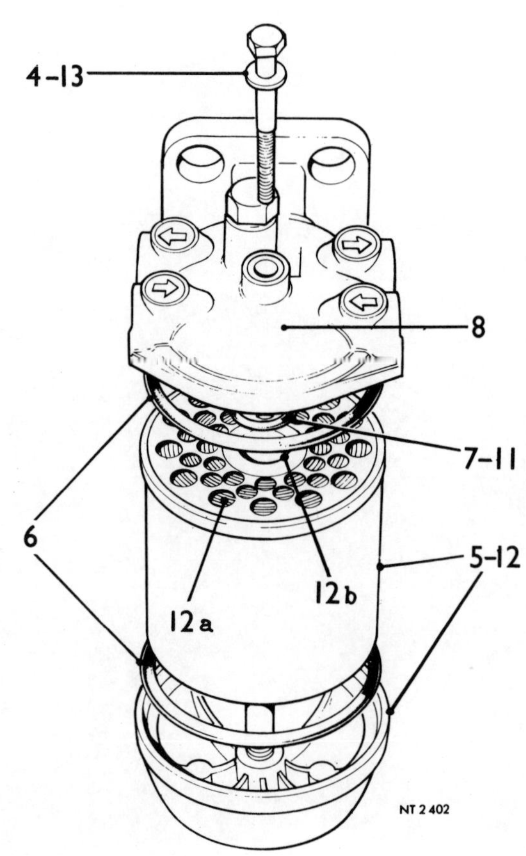

Removing

1. Isolate the battery.
2. Remove the spare wheel.
3. Clamp the gravity supply hose to the filter.
4. Remove the centre retaining bolt and sealing washer.
5. Remove the filter element and lower casing.
6. Remove the upper and lower sealing rings.
7. Remove the 'O' ring on the element location spigot.

Refitting

8. Clean the filter head and lower body.
9. Fit a new sealing ring to the filter head, ensuring that it seats properly in its groove.
10. Locate a new sealing ring to the filter lower body.
11. Fit a new 'O' ring to the filter element spigot, ensuring that it locates in its groove.
12. Fit a new filter element to the filter body ensuring:–
    a. The element is fitted so that the circular holes in the end of the element are uppermost.
    b. The large hole in the centre of the element locates correctly over the spigot and 'O' ring.
13. Secure the assembly with the central retaining bolt and sealing washer.
14. Remove the hose clamp, reconnect the battery and run the engine whilst checking for fuel leaks from the filter.
15. Refit the spare wheel.

PETROL INJECTION SYSTEM

General Description 19.35.00

The Lucas Mk. II petrol injection equipment used on the Triumph TR6 engine replaces carburetters as a means of inducing a combustible petrol-air mixture into the cylinders.

Essentially, the system consists of a pump, a pressure relief valve and a metering distributor, the latter delivering precisely timed and measured quantities of fuel to six injectors housed in an induction manifold. A normal petrol-air mixture is then induced, and compressed and ignited by a conventional ignition system.

Description of the Petrol Injection Circuit and Components Petrol Injection Circuit.

Fuel, gravity fed from the tank to a paper element filter is drawn into an electrically driven pump which delivers pressurised fuel to a metering distributor via a pressure relief valve. The valve, which is adjustable, maintains a constant pressure of fuel to the metering distributor and releases excess fuel pressure back to the tank via a return pipe. The metering distributor, controlled by vacuum from a pipe to the induction manifold measures, subject to engine requirements and delivers a charge of fuel to each of the six injectors at the commencement of the induction stroke of each piston. The injectors, housed in the induction manifold, contain a poppet valve which is set to open at 50 p.s.i. (3·52 kgf cm^2) and allows a charge of fuel in the form of a hollow cone spray into the induction manifold. Fuel which also lubricates the metering distributor is returned to the tank via the lubricating fuel return pipe.

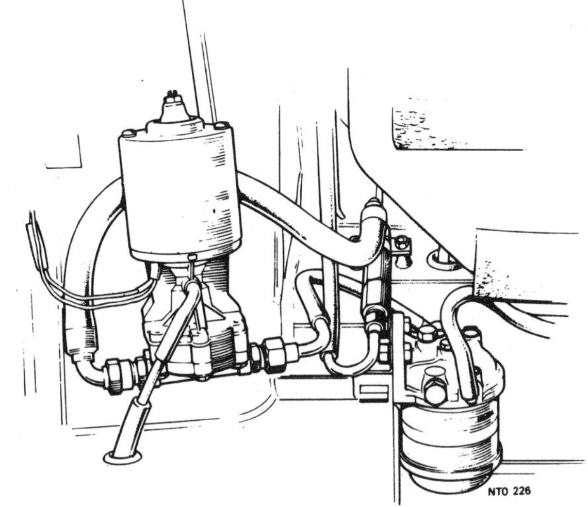

1. Filter
2. Pump
3. Pressure relief valve
4. Lubricating fuel return
5. Metering distributor
6. Vacuum control pipe
7. Injector pipes
8. Fuel tank

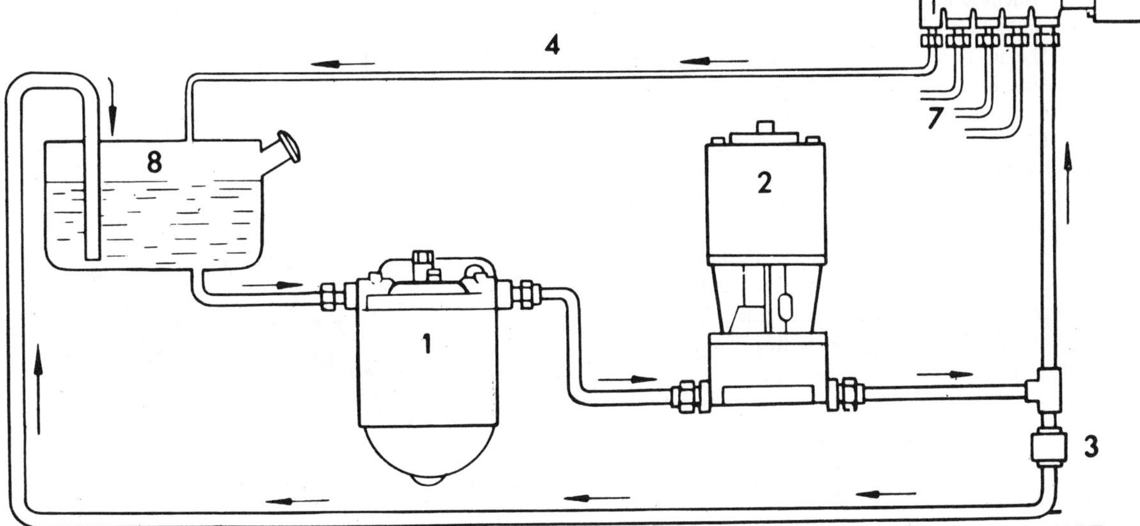

Fuel Filter

The fuel filter, which is gravity fed, is situated in the luggage compartment below the level of the fuel tank. The filter comprises a top assembly which is fixed to the luggage compartment floor and has inlet and outlet connections. A paper element housed in a metal canister is secured in position between the top assembly and a bottom sediment bowl by a single bolt.

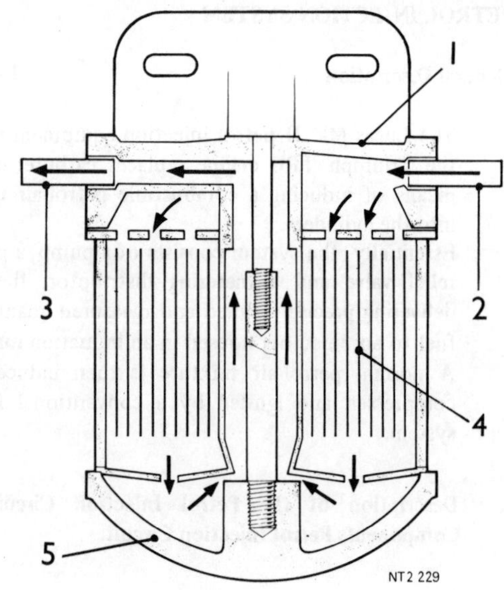

1. Top assembly
2. Inlet
3. Outlet
4. Paper element
5. Bottom bowl

Fuel Pump Unit

The fuel pump unit mounted in the luggage compartment consists of two main parts, an electric motor and a twin-gear pump.

The electric motor which drives the fuel pump by means of a nylon coupling, is a 12 volt high performance permanent magnet unit.

The motor is protected against the entry of fuel from the pump by a shaft seal. A 'Tell-tale' pipe in the motor base casting indicates whether the fuel has passed this seal.

Filtered fuel enters the pump through the inlet union and is expelled through the pump outlet by the rotating action of the spur-type gears. The pump pressure is dependent upon the setting of the pressure relief valve.

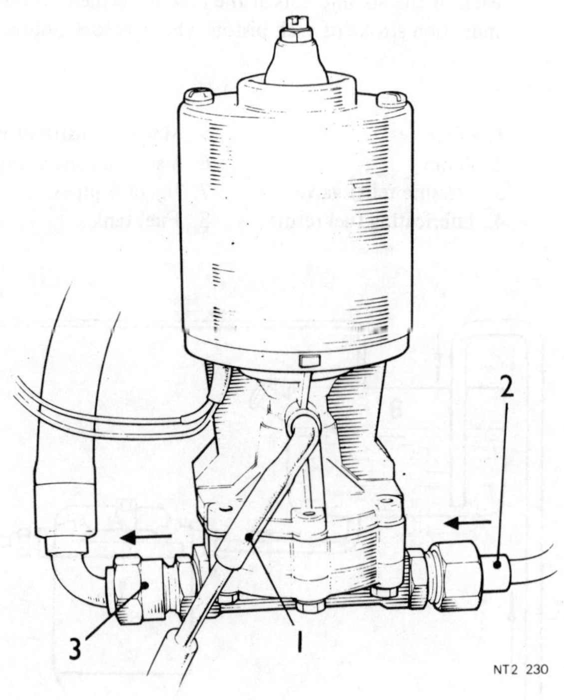

1 "Tell-tale" pipe
2 Pump inlet
3 Pump outlet

Metering Distributor Assembly

The metering distributor assembly is mounted on the engine and is driven by a pinion shaft gear off the ignition distributor driving gear. The assembly comprises two main units namely the metering unit and the control unit.

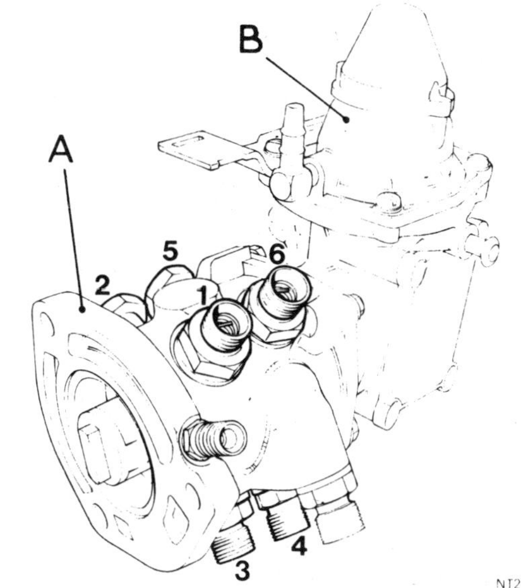

A Metering Unit
B Control Unit

Metering Unit

The metering unit consists of an outer casing with one inlet and six outlet ports. Located and seated inside the casing so that it cannot revolve or move axially is a sleeve with six inlet and six outlet ports arranged in spaced pairs 60° apart, inlet and outlet alternating. A space between the body and the sleeve forms a reservoir for pressurised fuel. The six outlet ports are coincident with the outlet ports in the outer casing and sealed unions containing non-return valves connect the sleeve and body ports to injector delivering pipes. A rotor which has two radial ports to a central bore and is driven by the pinion shaft gear, revolves within the sleeve. The central bore of the rotor contains a shuttle with a fixed stop at one end and a variable stop at the other.

When the engine is started and the rotor turns within the sleeve, the rotor port at the variable stop end becomes coincident with the port in the sleeve leading to the fuel reservoir in the outer casing. Fuel at high pressure enters the rotor bore and drives the shuttle to the fixed stop end of the rotor. This movement of the shuttle displaces fuel in the rotor bore through the ports in the rotor and sleeve and out through the non-return valve in the union serving number one cylinder.

A further 120° rotation of the rotor causes the rotor ports at the fixed stop end to align with the sleeve port leading to the pressurised fuel reservoir. Fuel now enters at the fixed stop end of the rotor and drives the shuttle back towards the variable stop end. The displaced fuel from the rotor bore ports passes to number five cylinder via the sleeve port and non-return valve union.

The shuttle continually moves between the two stops displacing an accurate amount of fuel to each cylinder in turn. The quantity of fuel delivered at each injection is dependent upon the distance the shuttle travels which is determined by the control unit.

1. Fixed stop
2. Rotor drive
3. Outlet to No. 1 injector
4. Outlet to No. 2 injector
5. Variable control stop
6. Rotor
7. Sleeve
8. Body
9. Fuel inlet from pump
10. Shuttle

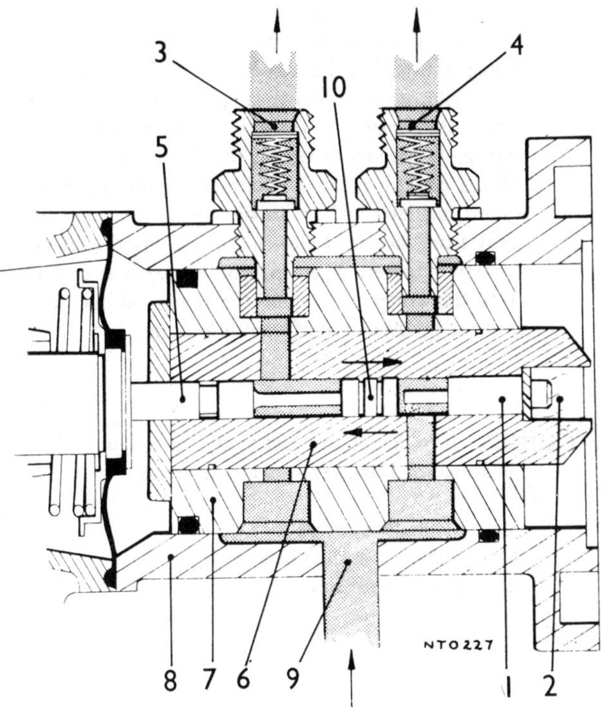

Control Unit

The control unit is attached to the metering unit by four bolts. A cam follower with a diaphragm seal set in an annular groove around its periphery projects through the leading face of the unit. The rear end of the cam follower bears against the outer two of three rollers carried on the control links, whilst the third roller of smaller diameter runs against the fuel cam or datum track.

The control links are pivoted at the top where they are attached to the centre of a spring controlled rubber diaphragm – the lower part of the control links are free.

Two springs are positioned between the diaphragm and three concentric calibration screws. The top of the diaphragm and the calibration screws are in a chamber connected by a pipe to the manifold.

The fuel cam or datum track is secured by two screws to a carrier which is in contact with an external control screw. The carrier is pivoted at point X and the pivot extends through the rear face of the unit. The excess fuel lever is pivoted at the rear face of the unit and has a cam face at the lower end which contacts the cam carrier pivot.

Engine fuel demands, according to throttle openings and load, are reflected in changes in inlet manifold depression. The change is sensed by the spring loaded diaphragm which takes up a position balancing the loading of the springs against the depression in the chamber. The central links are thus raised or lowered along the cam track allowing the follower in or out of the forward face of the unit and so regulate the metering unit variable stop. To prevent the full hydraulic force of the variable stop from impinging on the control linkage a balancing spring is fitted on the cam follower which results in only light pressure between the follower and the rollers. Movement of the excess fuel lever for cold starting is effected by pulling the choke control knob on the control panel. This alters the position of the excess fuel lever and the carrier for the cam is drawn away from the cam follower thus causing the shuttle to travel further. When the control knob is pushed back the carrier is returned to the normal operating position by the action of a tension spring.

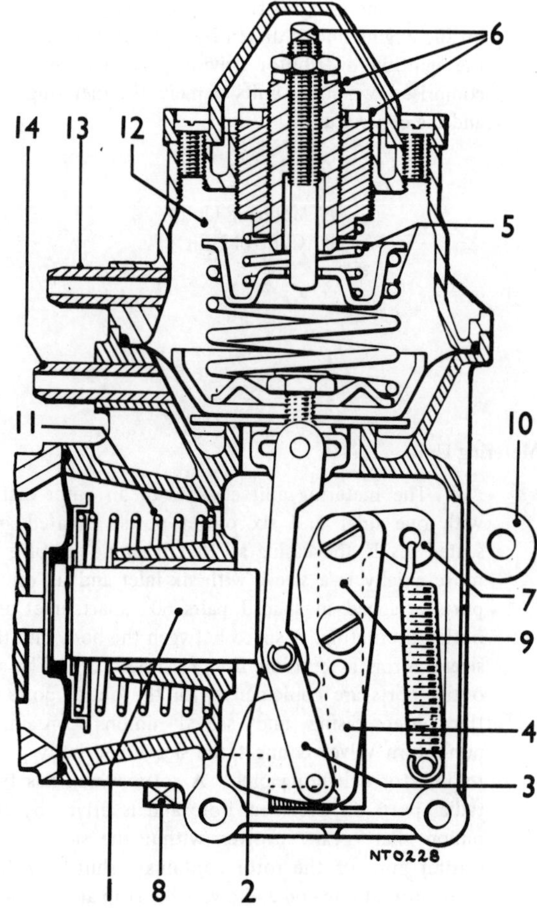

1. Cam follower
2. Rollers
3. Control links
4. Fuel cam (datum tank)
5. Calibration springs
6. Calibration screws
7. Fuel cam carrier
8. Full load setting screw
9. Point X
10. Excess fuel lever
11. Balance spring
12. Depression chamber
13. To manifold
14. To atmosphere

CAUTION: It is important that under no circumstances must the following adjustments be altered:-

a) Calibration screws
b) Full load setting screw
d) Datum track screws

Pressure relief valve assembly

The pressure relief valve is mounted in the luggage compartment between the pump and the filter. The unit consists of three parts, namely an adjustable valve, a strainer housing and a brass 'T' piece.

Fuel from the pump enters and leaves the assembly through the 'T' piece. The valve is set to provide a constant pressure of 106 – 110 p.s.i. (7·45 – 7·70 kgf/cm^2) to the metering distributor and fuel in excess of this pressure is fed back to the tank through the strainer housing and valve.

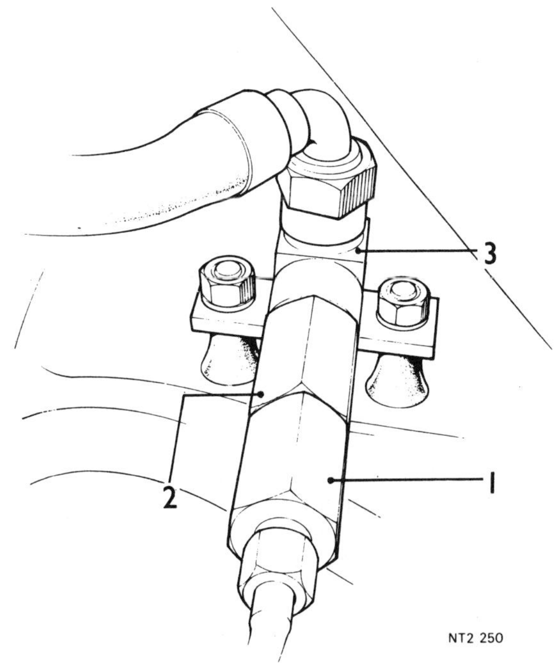

1. Adjustable Valve
2. Strainer housing
3. T piece

Injectors

The injectors are fitted into the inlet manifold and secured in pairs by a clamping plate. Fuel pipes from the metering unit are secured to the injectors by union nuts. The unions are numbered one to six for identification purposes. A poppet valve in the injector is set to open at 50 p.s.i. (3·52 kgf m^2) to provide a 60° hollow cone spray of atomised fuel.

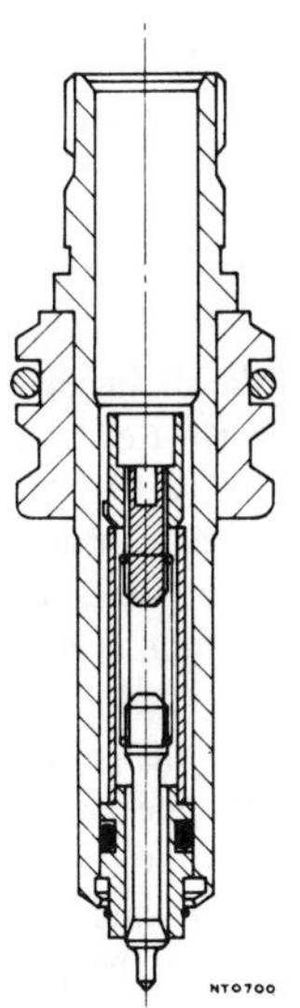

FUEL METERING DISTRIBUTOR TIMING
**** (Up to Engine No. CP 77609E)****
– Check and adjust **19.35.01**

Check

1. Isolate the battery.
2. Turn the engine until the T.D.C. mark on the crankshaft pulley is in line with the pointer and number one piston is on its firing stroke.
3. Disconnect number six injector pipe from the metering distributor.
4. Remove number six outlet union from the metering distributor body and observe the relationship of the sleeve port to the rotor port.
5. Illustration A shows the ACCEPTABLE range of rotor port positions in relation to the rotor sleeve port. The direction of rotation of the rotor is clockwise looking at the drive end of the rotor.

NOTE: Black shading represents the rotor.
The arrow indicates direction of rotor rotation.

AA shows the sleeve port almost covered by the rotor.

AB shows the sleeve port half covered by the rotor.

AC shows the sleeve port and the rotor port almost in line moving towards a full hole.

6. Illustration B represents an UNACCEPTABLE range of rotor and sleeve port positions.

BA shows the rotor and sleeve port almost in line.

BB shows the rotor covering half of the sleeve port.

BC shows the rotor almost covering the sleeve port and moving towards total closure of the sleeve port.

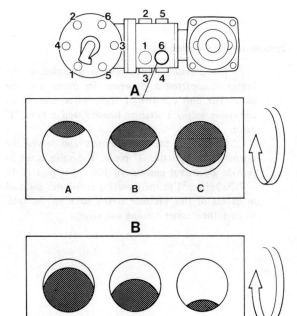

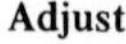

Adjust

7. In the event of the timing being incorrect, remove the metering distributor and pedestal complete instructions 1 to 8 12.10.22.
8. Insert a finger in the distributor shaft bore and turn the pinion gear anti-clockwise (towards the engine) until a full rotor hole is visible through number six outlet.
9. Continue to turn the gear anti-clockwise until the rotor hole just disappears from view, and then rotate the gear one extra tooth.
10. Lower the pedestal and metering distributor into position and recheck the position of the rotor hole.

NOTE: If the position of the hole is still not correct the gear may not have been turned sufficiently, therefore repeat instructions 8 to 10.

11. Secure the pedestal to the cylinder block, refit the ignition distributor and distributor cap and H.T. leads.
12. Reverse instructions 1 to 4, 12.10.22.

NT2 231

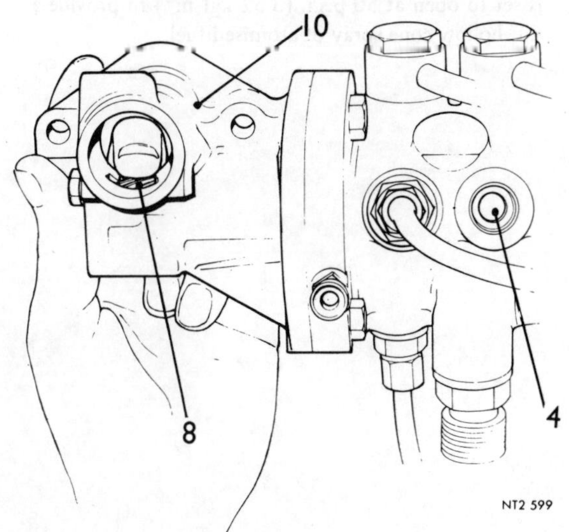

NT2 599

FUEL METERING DISTRIBUTOR TIMING
(From Engine No. CR1E)

– Check and adjust 19.35.01

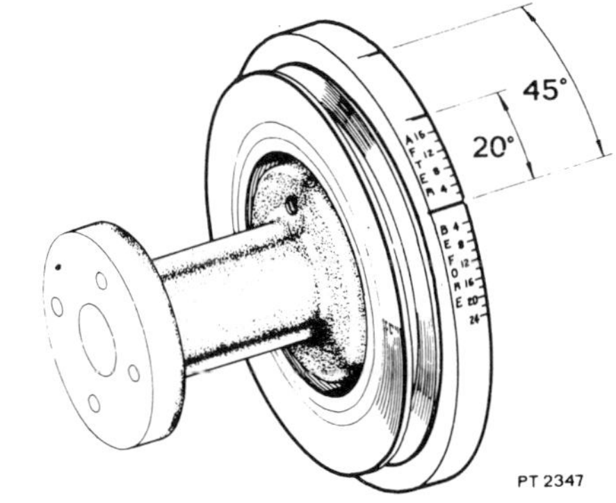

Check

1. Isolate the battery.
2. Remove the spark plugs and rocker cover.
3. Turn the engine in a running direction until No. 6 piston is at T.D.C. induction stroke, i.e. No. 6 inlet and exhaust valves on the rock.
4. Using a thin steel rule, mark off lines from the T.D.C. line on the crankshaft pulley 1 1/8 in. and 2 5/8 in. (29 mm and 67 mm) on the A.T.D.C. side of the pulley. The mark off lines should be sufficiently clear to be observed as timing marks and represent 20° and 45° A.T.D.C. respectively.
5. Remove number six outlet union from the metering distributor body. (No portion of the rotor hole should be visible in the outlet port).
6. Turn the crankshaft in a running direction until the leading edge of the hole in the rotor just appears on the upper side of the outlet port hole (the 'cracking' point); note the crankshaft angle at which this occurs. If this 'cracking' point occurs between the lines marked in 4, i.e. 20° – 45° A.T.D.C. the injection timing is satisfactory; if not, proceed as follows:
7. Remove the metering distributor and pedestal complete, 12.10.22 (instructions 1 to 8).
8. Insert a finger in the distributor shaft bore and turn the pinion gear anti-clockwise (towards the engine) until a full rotor hole is visible through number six outlet.
9. Continue to turn the gear anti-clockwise until the rotor hole just disappears from view, and then rotate the gear one extra tooth.
10. Lower the pedestal and metering distributor into position and recheck the position of the rotor hole.

NOTE: If the position of the hole is still not correct the gear may not have been turned sufficiently, therefore repeat instructions 8 to 10.

11. Secure the pedestal to the cylinder block, refit the ignition distributor cap and H.T. leads.
12. Reverse instructions 1 to 4, 12.10.22.

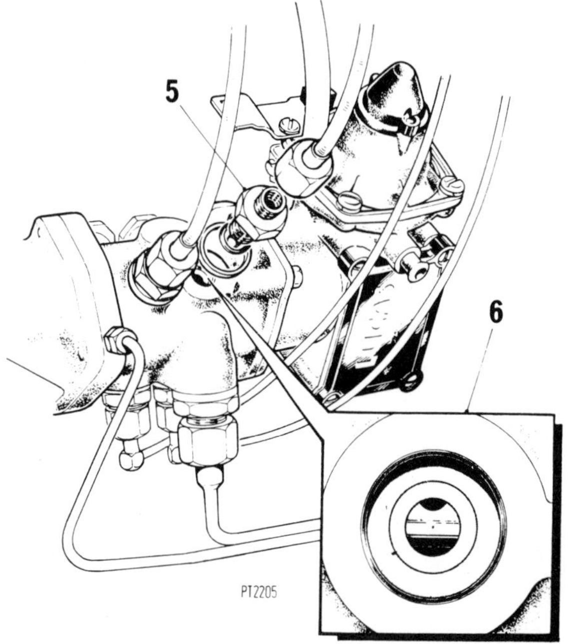

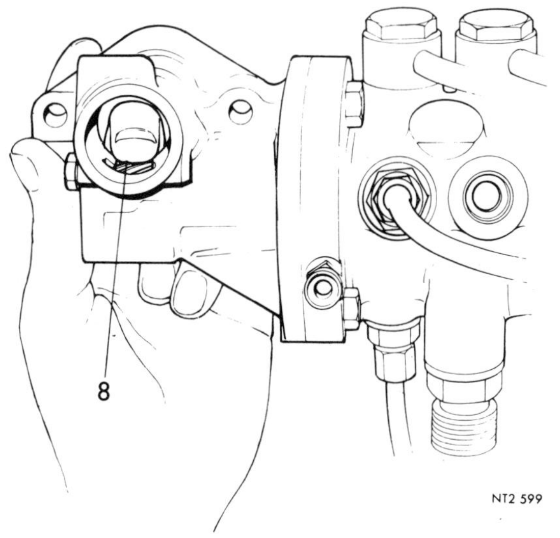

EXCESS FUEL LEVER

– Check and adjust **19.35.02**

1. Isolate the battery.
2. Remove the metering distributor 19.35.07.
3. Hold the excess fuel lever back against its stop and with a feeler gauge check the clearance A which should be 0·006 – 0·008 in (0·15 – 0·2 mm).
4. If adjustment is required slacken the locknut and turn the screw clockwise to increase and anti-clockwise to decrease the clearance. Tighten the locknut.
5. Reverse instructions 1 and 2.

NOTE: Clearance adjustment of the excess fuel lever should not be necessary during normal service. Should the adjustment be suspect, establish first, whether free play exists at the cable end of the lever. Providing that there is approximately ¼ in (6 mm) free play it is unlikely that the excess fuel lever is causing any malfunction and therefore the removal of the metering distributor would be unnecessary.

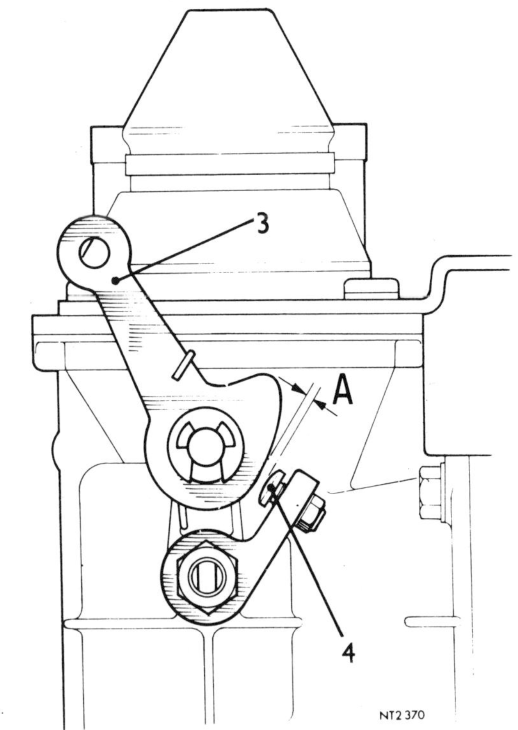

FUEL METERING DISTRIBUTOR

– Remove and refit **19.35.07**

Removing

1. Isolate the battery.
2. Disconnect the injector pipes at the injector.
3. Disconnect the vacuum pipe at the metering distributor.
4. Disconnect the cold start cable at the metering distributor.
5. Disconnect and blank off the main fuel feed pipe to the metering distributor.
6. Disconnect the metering distributor bleed off pipe.
7. Turn the engine over until numbers one and six pistons are at T.D.C. with number one cylinder firing. Do not turn the engine over again until completion of the operation.

Continued

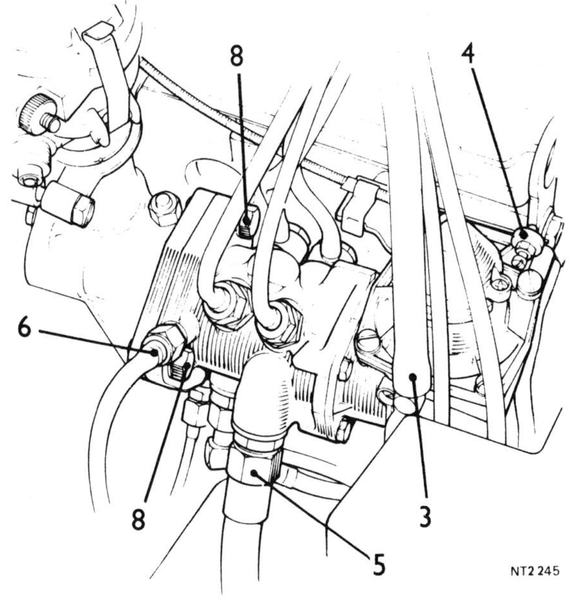

8. Remove the three bolts and washers securing the metering distributor to the pedestal flange and remove the unit from the engine.
9. Remove the plastic drive dog and the 'O' ring from the pedestal flange.
10. If necessary, remove the injector pipes.

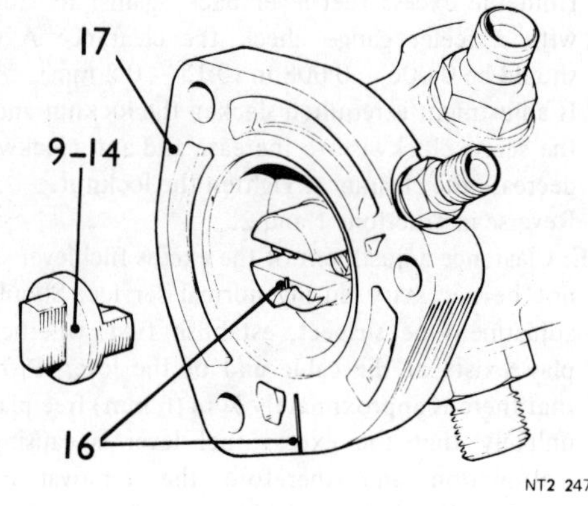

Refitting

11. Fit the injector pipes (if removed) to the metering distributor.
12. Check and if necessary adjust the cold start lever clearance 19.20.26.
13. Ensure that the engine has not been turned over and the drive gear pinion slot is in a vertical position with numbers one and six pistons at T.D.C. – number one firing and the ignition distributor rotor arm electrode pointing to number one cylinder electrode in the distributor cap.
14. Fit the plastic drive dog into the pinion gear drive slot using, if necessary a little grease to retain it in position. Ensure that it is fitted the correct way round i.e. the small driving member locating in the pinion drive slot.
15. Fit a new 'O' ring to the pedestal flange and ensure that the face is clean.
16. Turn the drive member of the metering distributor so that the scribed lines on the drive member and flange face coincide.
17. Clean the flange face and fit the metering distributor to the pedestal flange ensuring that the driving dog member locates properly in the drive member of the metering distributor.
18. Secure the metering distributor with the three bolts and washers and tighten evenly.
19. Reverse instructions 1 to 7.

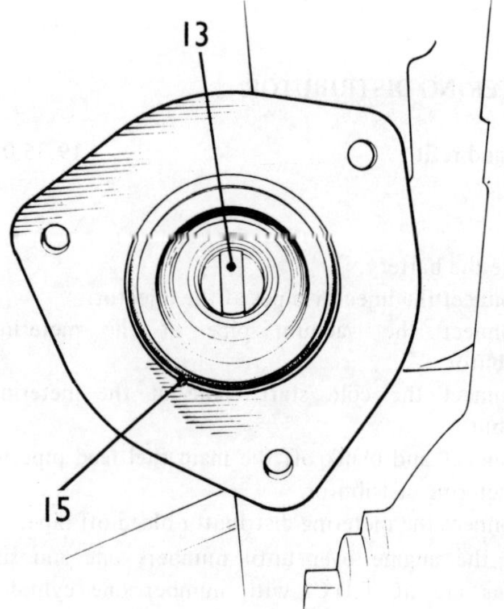

FUEL METERING DISTRIBUTOR OUTLET UNION AND ADAPTOR SEALS

– Remove and refit 19.35.14

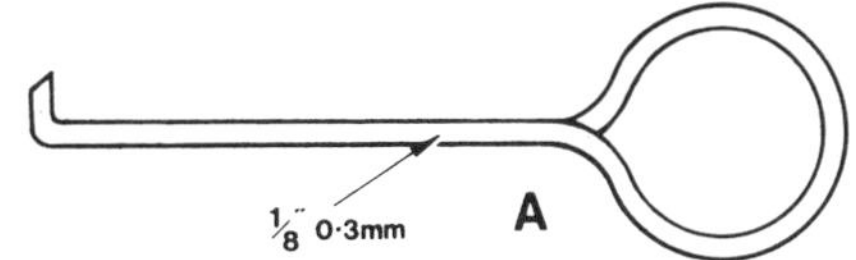

Special tools to make in the workshop.

A – Hook for removing sleeve sealing rings.
B – Sleeve alignment tool.
C – Tool for fitting sealing rings to the sleeve.

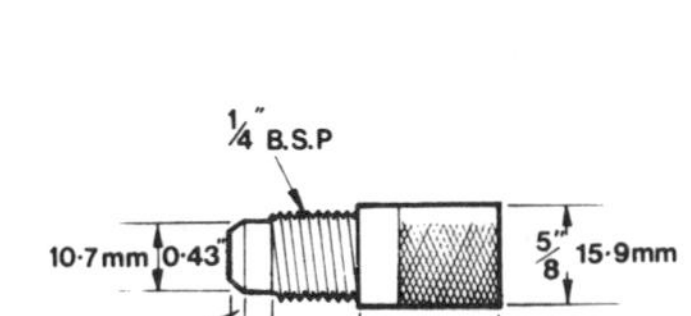

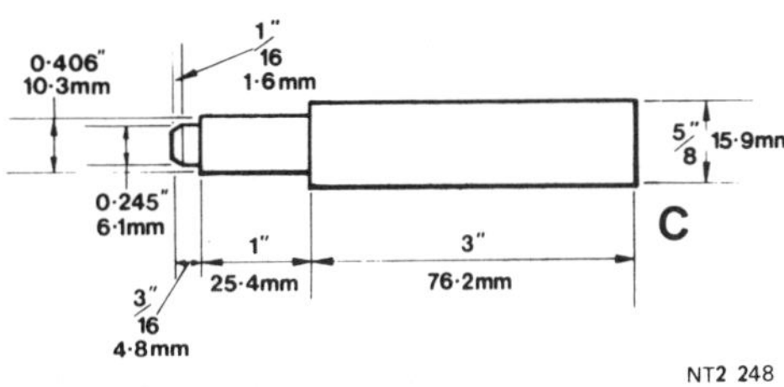

Removing

1. Isolate the battery.
2. Remove the metering distributor 19.35.07.
3. Remove the injector pipes from the metering distributor.
4. Hold the metering distributor in a vice and remove numbers one, six, three and four outlet unions complete with 'O' rings and sealing washers.

NOTE: The seals for numbers two and five outlets are removed when their respective injector pipes are removed.

5. Using special tool A, remove the six adaptor seals from the outlet ports.

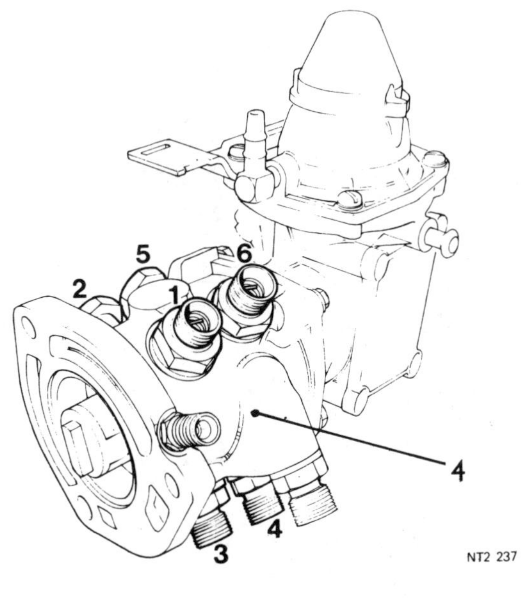

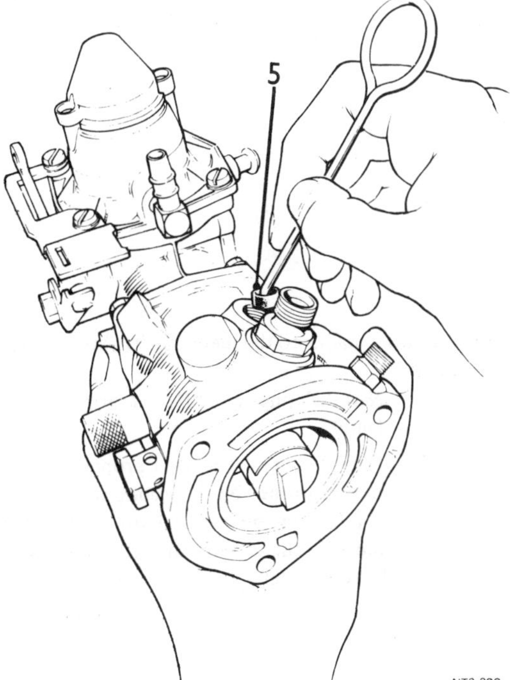

Continued

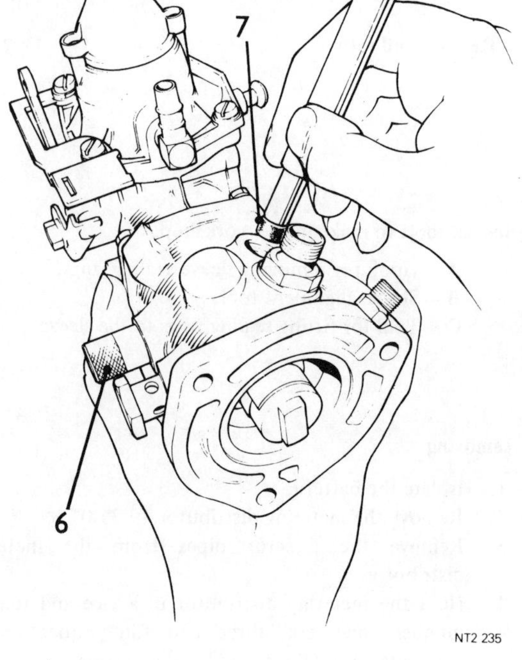

Refitting

6. Fit the alignment tool B to one of the outlet ports in the metering unit body so that it locates in the sleeve port.
7. Fit a new adaptor seal to each outlet port using the special seal location tool C, ensuring that the seals are pushed firmly into the sleeve locations.
8. Remove the alignment tool B and fit a seal in its place.

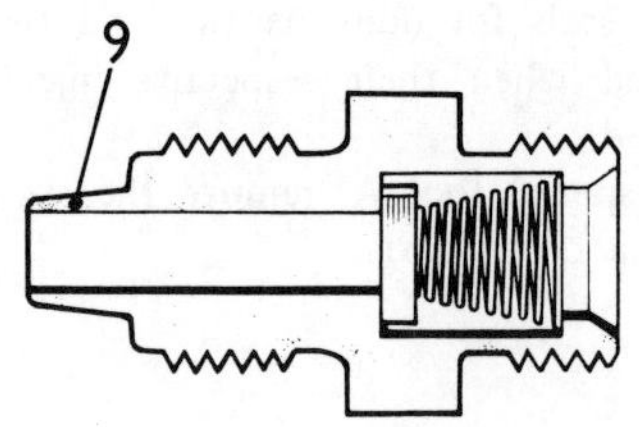

9. Check the non-return valves in the outlet unions – and banjo bolts as follows. Place the tapered end of the union in Kerosene and blow through the opposite end to see if the valve is leaking. **Caution**: Do not use an air line since the valve seat may be damaged due to the high pressure. If the valve proves to be leaking, even very slightly, renew the union complete.

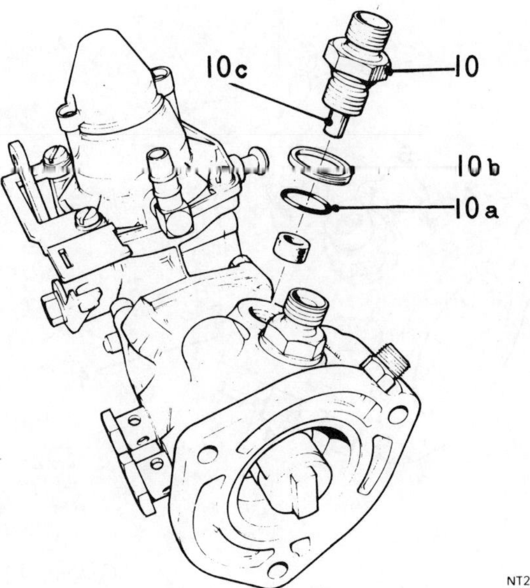

10. Fit the outlet unions to the metering distributor body ensuring:-
    a) New 'O' rings are fitted if origonals are faulty.
    b) The 'O' rings are located properly in the grooves formed by the sealing washers.
    c) The 'O' ring groove and the unthreaded end of the union are smeared with Petroleum Jelly.

Continued

11. Refit the injector pipes to the distributor.
12. Refit the banjo connectors ensuring new seals are fitted. Tighten the banjo bolts to 150 – 200 lb ins.
13. Check the excess fuel lever clearance 19.35.02.
14. Refit the metering distributor 19.35.07.
15. Reconnect the battery, start the engine and check for fuel leaks from the system.

NOTE: Later distributor units A employ 'O' rings to seal the outlet unions and these may be refitted providing they are in good condition. Earlier units B however, used 'Dowty' type seals and these *must* be renewed each time a union is removed.

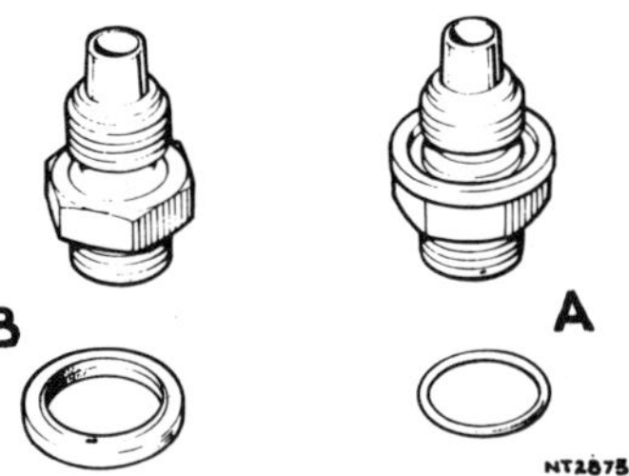

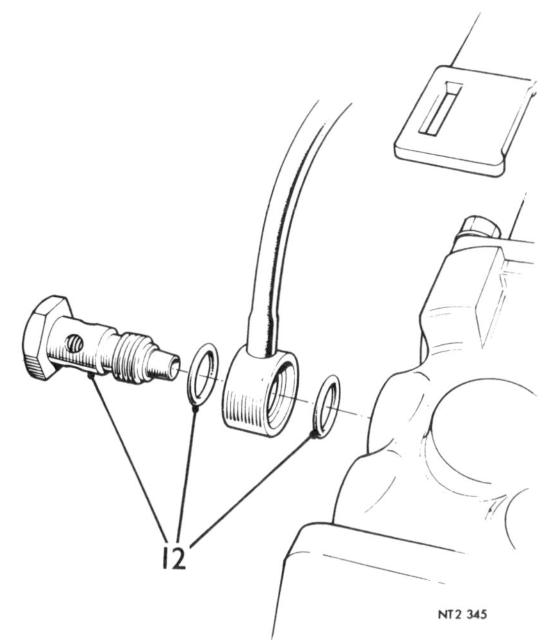

FUEL METERING DISTRIBUTOR INLET UNION AND FILTER

– Remove and refit 19.35.15

Removing

1. Isolate the battery.
2. Hold the union steady with an open ended spanner and disconnect the inlet pipe union nut.
3. Plug the inlet pipe to prevent fuel loss.
4. Remove the union complete with the 'O' ring, sealing washer and filter.
5. Remove the filter from the union.

Refitting

6. Wash the filter in petrol or renew if damaged.
7. Insert the filter into the union.
8. Refit the union ensuring that a new 'O' ring is fitted and that it locates properly in the groove formed by the sealing washer.

NOTE: To ensure that the 'O' ring is retained in the groove whilst fitting smear a little petroleum jelly into the groove.

9. Reconnect the inlet supply pipe, reconnect the battery. Start the engine and check for fuel leaks.

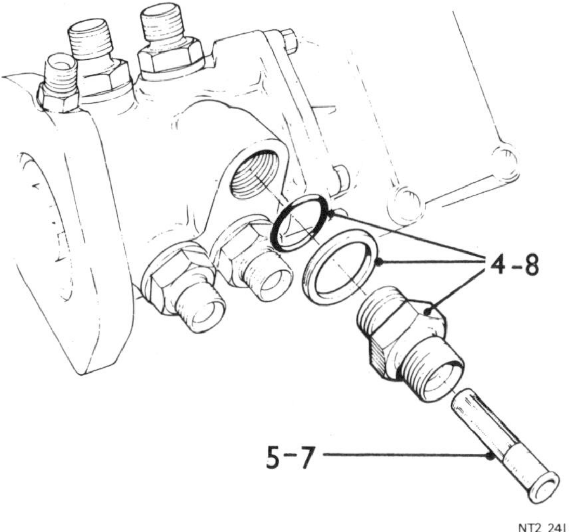

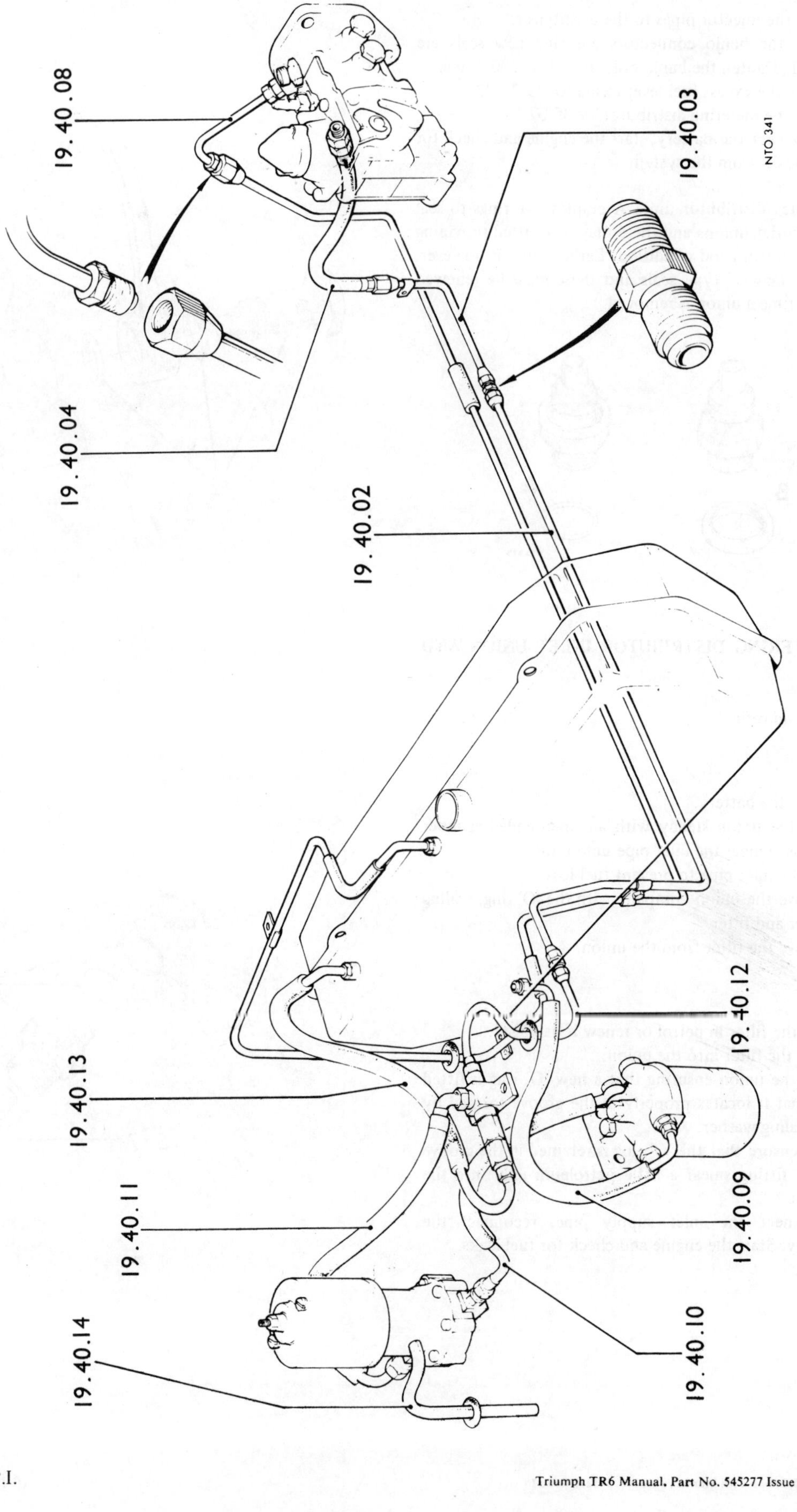

19.40.08
19.40.03
NTO 341
19.40.04
19.40.02
19.40.12
19.40.13
19.40.11
19.40.09
19.40.14
19.40.10

FUEL PIPES 19.40.00

NOTE: The pipes and hoses of the Petrol injection fuel system are illustrated with annotations giving operation numbers for removing and refitting. Detailed instructions for these operations are omitted since they are self explanatory. Access to the pipes within the luggage compartment is gained by removing the spare wheel cover, spare wheel and removing the forward trim panel 76.13.17.

PETROL PIPE MAIN LINE 19.40.02

PETROL PIPE MAIN LINE – CENTRE SECTION 19.40.03

PETROL PIPE MAIN LINE – ENGINE SECTION 19.40.04

PETROL PIPE METER TO TANK RETURN 19.40.08

PIPE – TANK TO FILTER INLET 19.40.09

PIPE – FILTER OUTLET TO PUMP 19.40.10

PIPE – PUMP OUTLET TO P.R.V. 19.40.11

PIPE –P.R.V. TO MAIN LINE 19.40.12

PIPE – P.R.V. RETURN TO TANK 19.40.13

PIPE – PUMP LEAK – DRAIN 19.40.14

HOSE – FILLER TO TANK – P.I.

– Remove and refit 19.40.19

Removing

1. Remove the luggage compartment forward trim panel. 76.13.17
2. Remove the rear compartment trim panel 76.13.20.
3. Working from the rear compartment, slacken the top hose clip securing the filler cap assembly to the filler hose.
4. From the luggage compartment slacken the hose clip securing the hose to the fuel tank.
5. Withdraw the filler cap assembly and the rubber sealing grommet.
6. Remove the filler hose complete with clips.

Refitting

* 7. Fit the hose to the fuel tank (using a sealant as necessary) and secure with a hose clip. **
8. Fit the filler cap securing clip to the hose, assemble the sealing grommet to the filler cap and fit the assembly to the tank filler hose. Secure with the hose clip.
9. Reverse instructions 1 and 2.

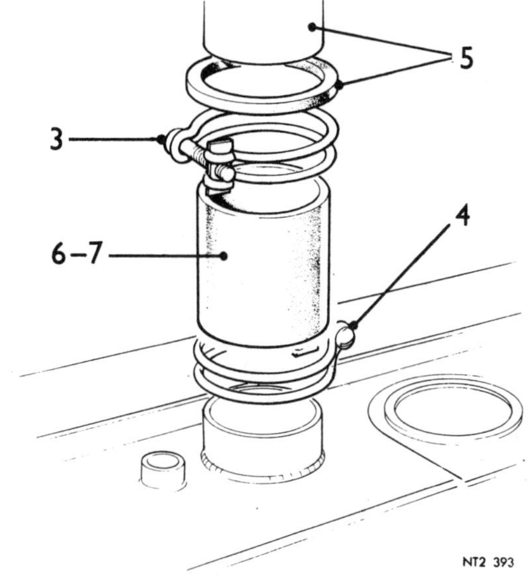

FUEL PUMP

Data and description 19.45.00

CAUTION: The fuel pump is controlled directly by the ignition/starter switch. The motor will therefore run continually while the ignition is on. If, during servicing, the ignition has to remain on for a long period with the engine not running isolate the unit as follows:

Early vehicles not fitted with fuel pump inertia cut out switch only–
Open the luggage boot lid. Remove the floor carpet. Remove the spare wheel cover panel. Remove two screws and washers and turn back the trim panel. Disconnect the white wire snap connector to isolate the unit.

Later vehicles fitted with fuel pump inertia cut out switch only –
Open the bonnet. Locate the switch mounted in a clip attached to the bulkhead. Pull up the button to trip the switch and isolate the fuel pump.

Data

Manufacturer	Lucas
Lucas part No.	54073012
Stanpart No.	214347
Running current	4 amp approximately
Light running – speed	2200 rev/min
current	1·4 amp
volts	13·5 volt
Armature winding resistance – adjacent commutator bars	0·16 to 0·24 ohm at 15 degrees C
Armature end float	0·004 to 0·010 in (0·10 to 0·25 mm)
Brush length – new	0·375 in (9·53 mm)
renew if less than	0·188 in (4·76 mm)
Brush spring pressure – when compressed to 0·158 in (4 mm)	5 to 7 oz (140 to 200 g)
Maximum delivery	16 gal (73 litres) per hour
Delivery pressure – controlled by pressure relief valve unit	100 to 110 lbf/in² (690 to 760 kN/m²)

The fuel pump consists of a permanent magnet electric motor driving a precision built twin gear pump. The drive is transmitted by a drive coupling which features a spiral formed on its upper surface to throw fuel up to lubricate the shaft seal. Failure of the shaft seal would be indicated by fuel leakage from the 'tell tail' pipe projecting from the base casting which is fitted with a drain pipe.

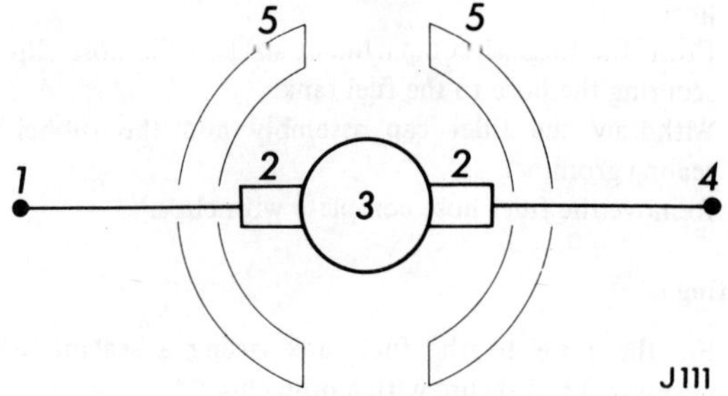

1. Supply connection
2. Brushes
3. Commutator
4. Earth connection
5. Permanent magnets

Component wiring diagram

FUEL PUMP

– Test on vehicle **19.45.01**

Service tools: S351, CBW 1B

1. Later vehicles fitted with fuel pump inertia cut out switch only –
   Open the bonnet. Locate the switch mounted in a clip attached to the bulkhead. Ensure that the button is depressed so that the switch is in its normal operating condition, with the contacts closed.
2. Obtain access to the fuel pump as follows:
   Open the luggage boot lid. Remove the floor carpet. Remove the spare wheel cover panel. Remove two screws and washers and turn back the trim panel as shown.
3. Check that the fuel pump runs as follows:
   Switch on the ignition. Check that the pump is running audibly or by touch.
4. Check electrical supply and earth as follows:
   Disconnect two snap connectors. Switch on the ignition. Use a voltmeter to check that a supply of 12 volts exists between the white wire and a good electrical earth. Use a suitable test circuit to check that the black wire is providing a good electrical earth. Connect two snap connectors observing polarity to ensure that the pump motor runs in the correct direction.
5. Check the running current as follows:
   Disconnect the white wire snap connector. Restore the circuit with an ammeter included in the white supply wire. Switch on the ignition. Check that the pump is running with the ammeter reading 3·5 to 5·0 amp. If the ammeter reading is not within this range the indication is that the pump requires overhaul or replacement.
6. Check the pressure output as follows:
   Open the bonnet. Prepare for fuel spillage. Insert a PI pressure test adaptor Churchill tool No. S351 in the fuel line as shown. Connect a pressure gauge Churchill tool No. CBW IB to the adaptor. Switch on the ignition. The pressure gauge reading should now be 100 to 110 lb/in^2 (690 to 760 kN/m^2). If the pressure gauge reading is low the indication is that the pump requires overhaul or replacement or a fault exists in the fuel line – refer to 19.00.01. If the pressure gauge reading is high the indication is that the pump is serviceable but a fault exists in the fuel line – refer to 19.00.01.

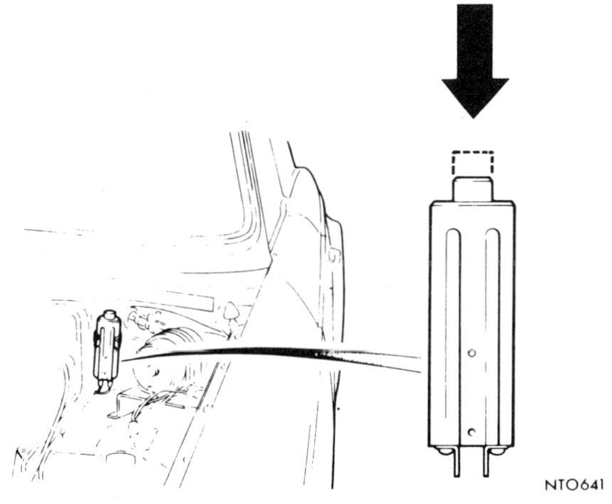

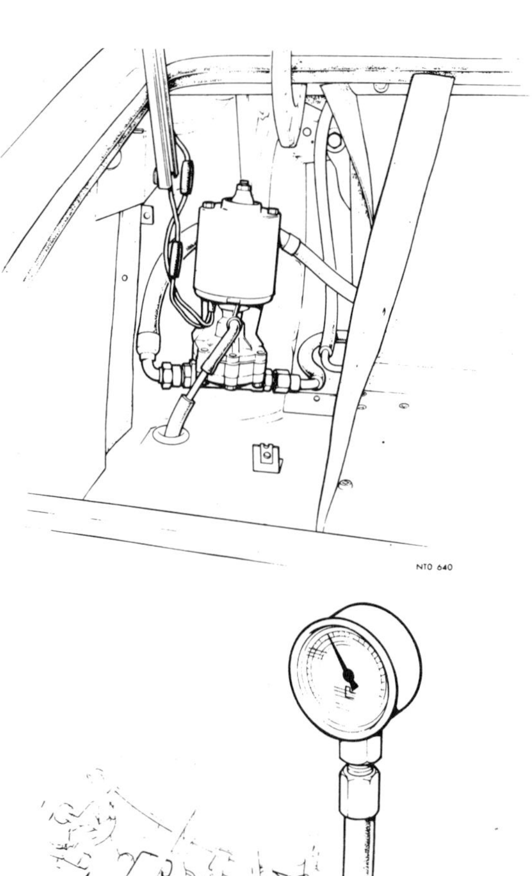

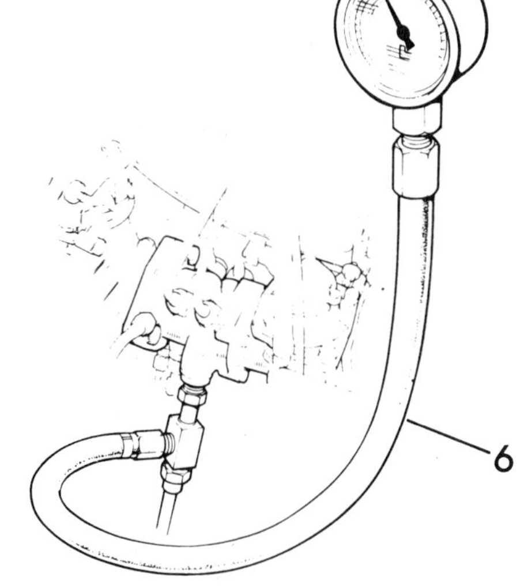

FUEL PUMP

– Remove and refit 19.45.08

Removing

1. Open the luggage boot lid.
2. Remove the floor carpet.
3. Remove the spare wheel cover panel.
4. Remove two screws securing the luggage boot lamp.
5. Withdraw the lamp assembly from the petrol tank trim panel.
6. Disconnect two Lucar connectors.
7. Remove eight screws and washers and withdraw the petrol tank trim panel.
8. Isolate the battery.
9. Disconnect two snap connectors.
10. Pull the drain pipe upwards from the body aperture grommet and then pull from fuel pump pipe.
11. Prepare for fuel spillage. Disconnect the inlet pipe coupling and the outlet pipe coupling.
12. Under wheel arch, remove three nuts and spring washers. Three plain washers may remain stuck to the body underseal.
13. Withdraw the fuel pump from its mounting.
14. Unscrew three special rubber mounting studs.

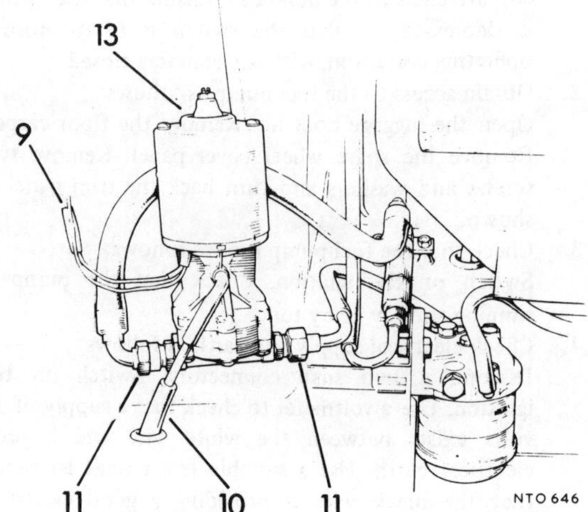

Refitting

15. Reverse instructions 10 to 14.
16. Connect two snap connectors observing polarity to ensure that the pump motor runs in the correct direction.
17. Connect the battery.
18. Turn on ignition to energise the fuel pump. Check the disturbed fuel pipe couplings to ensure no fuel leakage.
19. Reverse instructions 1 to 7.

FUEL PUMP

– Overhaul 19.45.15

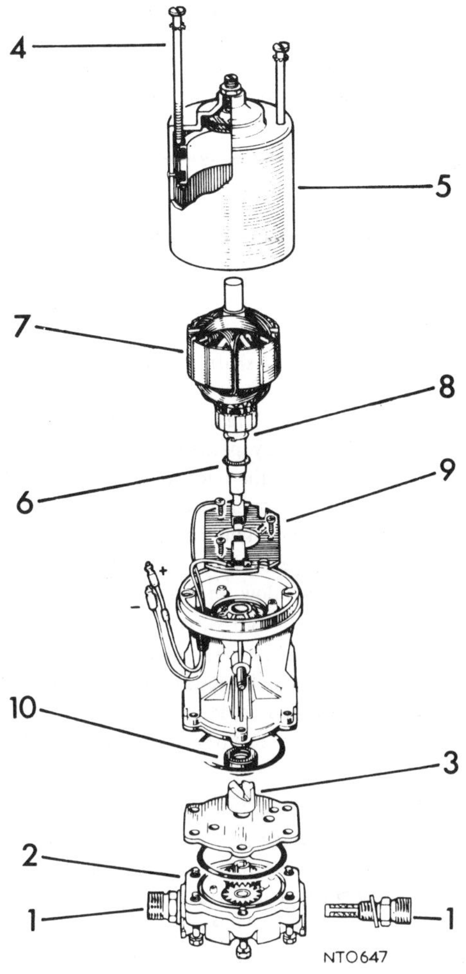

Dismantling

1. Remove the inlet connection and the outlet connection. Withdraw the strainer from the inlet connection.
2. Slacken six bolts equally and remove the gear pump assembly.
3. Remove the drive coupling.
4. Remove two through bolts.
5. Carefully withdraw the cover and armature about 0·5 in (12 mm). The brushes will drop clear of the commutator. Push each brush back to clear the circlip and thrust washer. Complete the withdrawal of the cover and armature.
6. Remove the thrust washer.
7. Pull the armature from the cover against the action of the permanent magnet.
8. If necessary remove the circlip.
9. Remove the brush assembly. Release the wires by carefully manoeuvring the rubber grommet upwards through the hole.
10. If necessary force the shaft seal from the base casting. Do not perform this operation unless a new shaft seal is available.

Bearings

11. The two self aligning motor bearings are not replaceable.

Brushes

12. Clean the brushes with a petrol moistened cloth. Ensure that the brushes move freely in the brushplate.
13. Check the brush length. Renew the brushplate assembly if less than 0·188 in (4·76 mm).
14. Using a suitable push type spring scale check the brush spring pressure. The pressure should be 5 to 7 oz (140 to 200 g) when compressed to 0·158 in (4 mm). If the pressure is low renew the brushplate assembly.

Commutator

15. Clean the commutator with a petrol moistened cloth. If the unit is in good condition it will be smooth and free from pits or burned spots. If necessary polish with fine glass paper. If excessively worn replace the armature.

Continued

Gear pump

16. If necessary an indication of the gear pump condition may be obtained by performing a flow test. With a motor terminal voltage of 13·5 volt approximately 1 gallon (4·5 litres) should be delivered in 3 minutes 45 seconds at 100 lbf/in^2 (700 kN/m^2).
17. Examine the interior of the gear pump. If there are indications of wear or damage replace the gear pump assembly.
18. Do not replace the gears or the housing individually. The components are mated and replacement must be by a complete gear pump assembly only.

Shaft seal

19. Failure of the shaft seal would be indicated by fuel leakage from the drain pipe.
20. If necessary an indication of the seal condition may be obtained by performing a bubble test. Connect a short pipe to the inlet connection and a short pipe to the outlet connection. Position the petrol pump above an open tank of paraffin. Immerse the free end of each pipe in the paraffin. Run the petrol pump. A continuous flow of bubbles from the outlet pipe indicates a defective seal.
21. If seal failure is suspected petrol may have contaminated the motor. The unit should therefore be dismantled as detailed above and all components inspected before a new shaft seal is fitted.

Spares

22. The motor and gear pump may be considered as two units. On the majority of vehicles replacement of either may be undertaken.
23. A few early vehicles were fitted with a gear pump with a narrow top plate as shown. On these units the top plates were matched to the motor base castings during production to prevent the possibility of top plate distortion causing gear binding. A 'narrow top plate' gear pump should not be fitted with a replacement motor. If a new motor is required it should be obtained by replacement of the complete fuel pump.

Strainer

24. Remove the inlet connection. Withdraw the strainer from the connection. Inspect and wash in clean petrol.

Continued

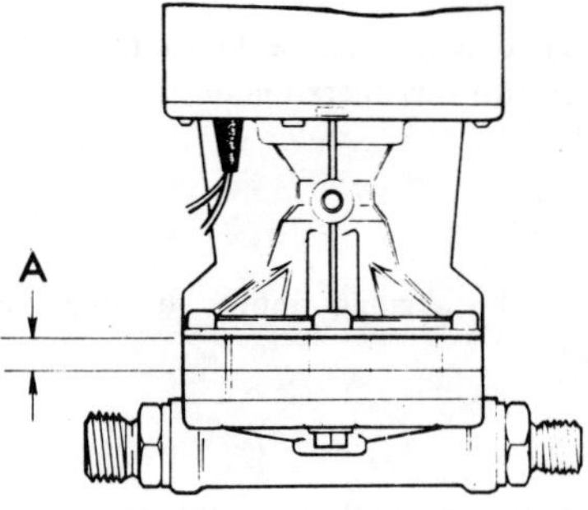

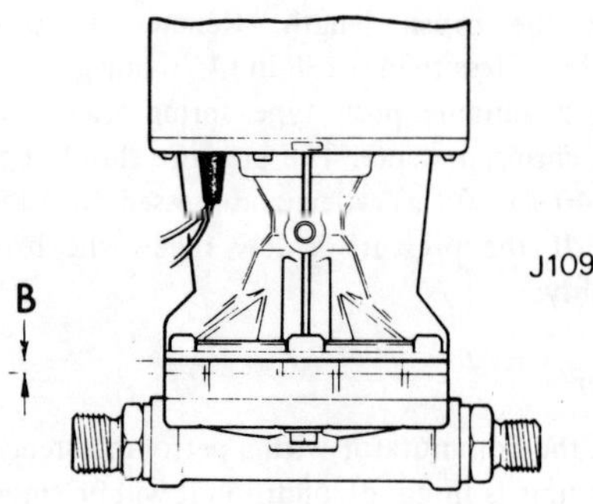

A Normal top plate
B Narrow top plate

Assemble

25. Fit the brush assembly.
26. If necessary fit the circlip.
27. Position the armature to the cover against the action of the permanent magnet.
28. Fit the thrust washer.
29. If the shaft seal is fitted only –
Provide a protective bullet as shown. Position the protective bullet over the shaft key. Lightly grease the bullet. Carefully insert the armature shaft through the base casting. Align the bullet to the shaft seal. Push each brush back to clear the thrust washer, circlip and commutator.
30. If the shaft seal is not fitted only –
Carefully insert the armature shaft through the base casting. Push each brush back to clear the thrust washer, circlip and commutator.
31. Seat the cover against the base casting flange. Turn the cover to align the marks shown. Fit the through bolts.
32. If the shaft seal is not fitted only –
Provide a protective bullet as shown. Position the protective bullet over the shaft key. Lightly grease the bullet. Carefully insert the shaft seal into the base casting.
33. Position the drive coupling to the motor.
34. Renew all disturbed rubber 'O' rings. Note that effective seals cannot be assured if new rubber 'O' rings are not fitted to the disturbed joints. Fit the gear pump assembly. Tighten six bolts equally.
35. Insert the strainer through the inlet connection. Fit the inlet connection and the outlet connection.
36. Adjust the armature end float as follows:
Hold the fuel pump vertical with the adjuster uppermost. Slacken the locknut. Screw the adjuster in until resistance is felt. Screw the adjuster out a quarter of a turn – maintain in this position and tighten the locknut.

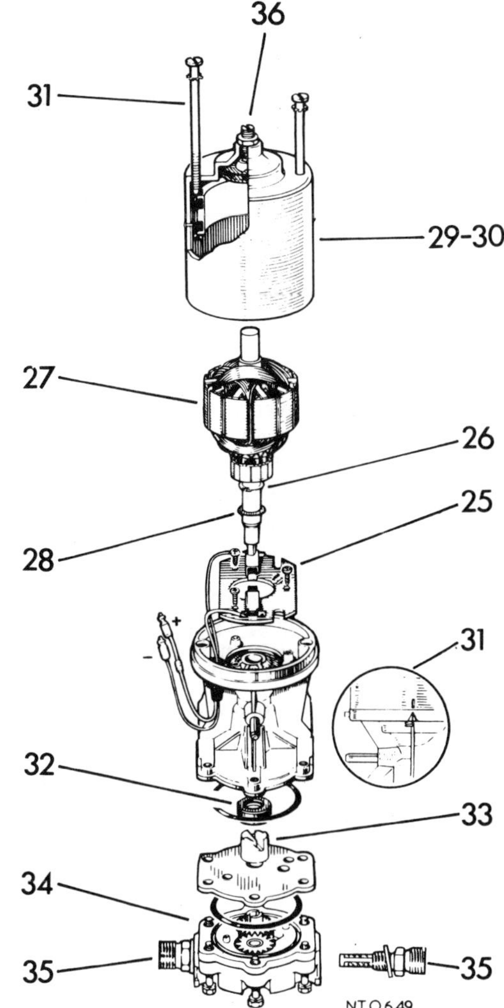

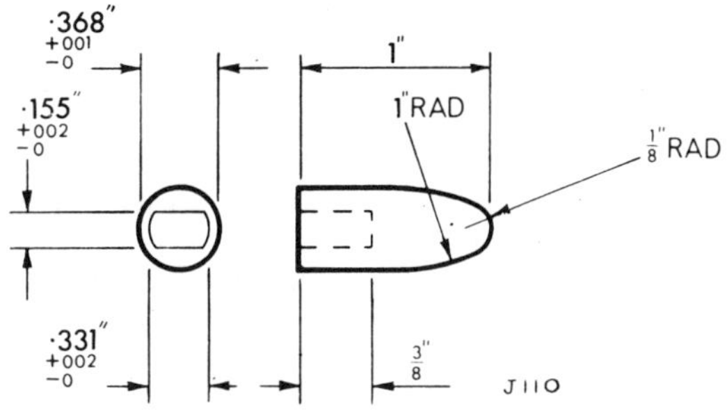

FUEL TANK – P.I.

– Remove and refit **19.55.01**

Removing

1. Isolate the battery.
2. Remove the luggage compartment forward trim panel 76.13.17.
3. Drain the fuel tank 19.55.02.
4. Disconnect the pipe-tank to filter inlet 19.40.09.
5. Disconnect the pipe-PRV return to the fueltank 19.40.13.
6. Disconnect the metering distributor lubrication fuel return to the tank, pipe 19.40.08.
7. Remove the fuel filler to tank hose 19.40.19.
8. Disconnect the tank gauge unit leads.
9. Remove the six bolts complete with plain and spring washers securing the fuel tank to the body.
10. Remove the fuel tank.

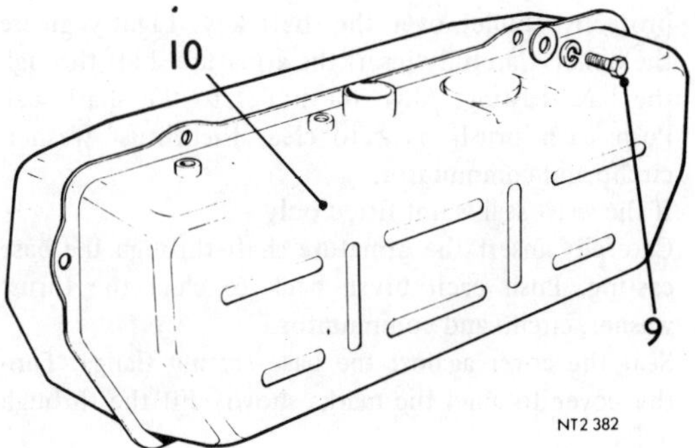

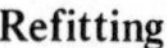

Refitting

11. Reverse instructions 3 to 10 inclusive.
12. Reconnect the battery, start the engine and examine for fuel leaks.
13. Refit the luggage compartment forward trim panel 76.13.17.

FUEL TANK – P.I.

– Drain **19.55.02**

WARNING: Extinguish all naked lights before commencing this operation.

1. Remove the spare wheel cover and spare wheel.
2. Place a suitable clean receptacle under the fuel tank gravity outlet point.
3. Disconnect the hose from the filter inlet and allow the fuel to drain.
4. Reconnect the hose to the filter inlet when the tank is empty.
5. Refit the spare wheel and cover.

CAUTION: If the fuel is to be returned to the tank ensure absolute cleanliness whilst draining and during storage, otherwise foreign matter and fluids may cause serious damage to the P.I. fuel system.

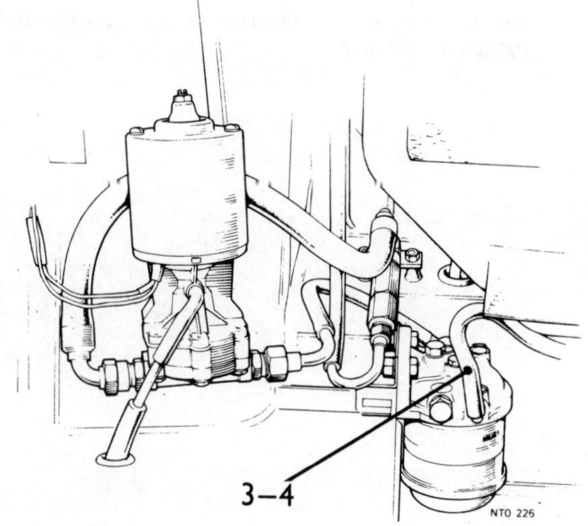

FUEL FILLER CAP – P.I.

– Remove and refit **19.55.08**

Removing

1. Remove the rear compartment trim panel 76.13.20.
2. Working from the rear compartment slacken the hose clip securing the filler hose to the filler cap extension.
3. Withdraw the filler cap complete assembly.
4. Remove the rubber sealing grommet.

Refitting

5. Assemble the rubber sealing grommet to the filler cap extension.
6. Fit the assemby to the body ensuring that the filler cap extension locates properly in the filler hose.
7. Secure the hose to the filler cap with the hose clip.
8. Refit the rear compartment trim panel 76.13.20.

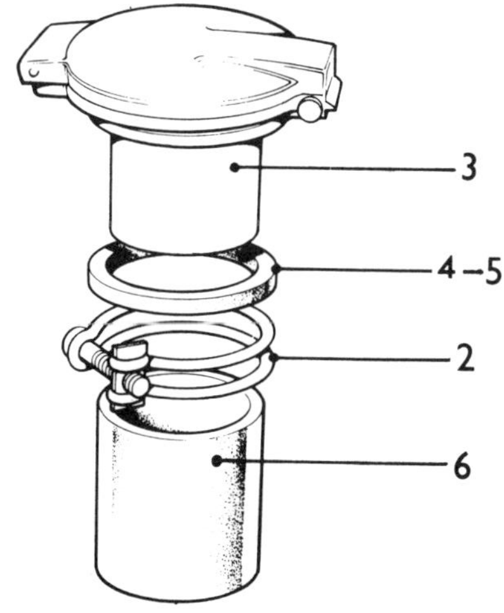

INJECTORS – SET

– Remove and refit **19.60.01**

Removing

1. Isolate the battery.
2. Disconnect the fuel pipe at the injector and check identification of the pipe for reassembly.

Note: The pipes are numbered 1 to 6 starting at the front of the engine.

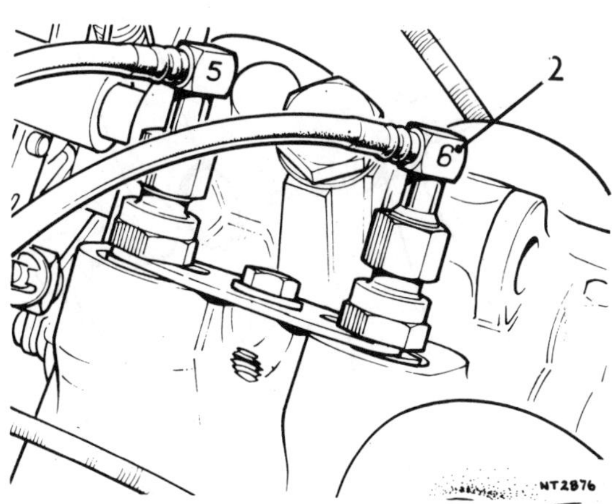

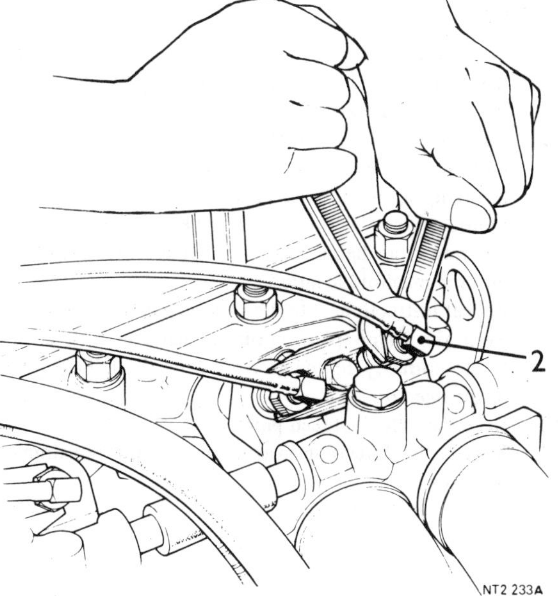

Continued

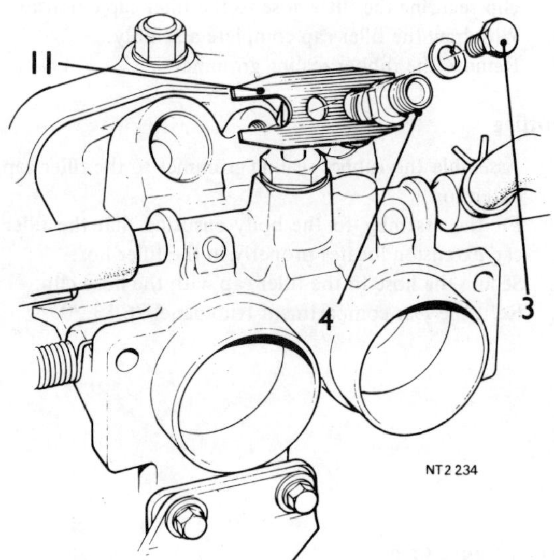

3. Remove the bolt securing the injector clamp plate to the injector manifold and remove the plate.

4. Grip the injector firmly and pull the injector from the manifold.

NOTE: Whilst the injector should come out of the manifold complete with the insulating block, it may in some instances leave the insulating block behind in the manifold.

5. If necessary – see above note – remove the insulating block from the manifold using a suitable tool taking care not to damage the manifold.
6. Remove the 'O' ring from the insulating block.

Refitting

7. Fit a new 'O' ring to the insulating block, ensuring that it is located in the top groove of the block i.e. the chamfered end of the block.
8. Insert the injector into the insulating block ensuring that the chamfered end of the block is uppermost and firmly up against the shoulder of the injector.
9. Lubricate the 'O' ring with engine oil – to prevent the ring from being torn – and push the assembly into the manifold location.
10. Repeat instructions 3 to 9 on the adjacent injector.
11. Refit the clamp plate ensuring that the fork ends locate correctly in the groove below the milled flats of the injector.
12. Reconnect the fuel feed pipes.
13. Repeat the foregoing instructions on the remaining injectors.
14. Reconnect the battery.

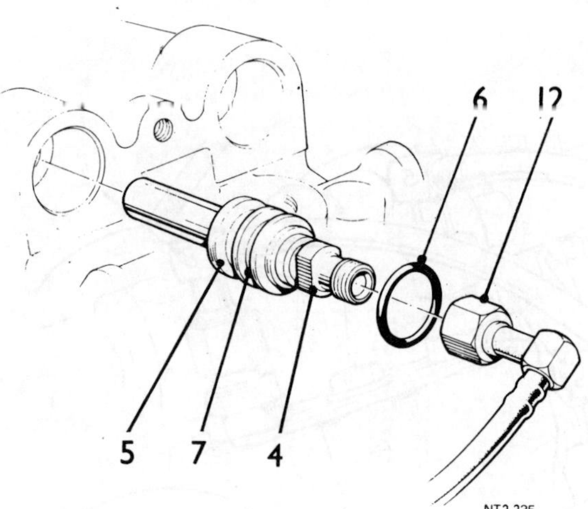

FUEL INJECTORS

– Spray check **19.60.02**

Testing without a rig

1. Remove the bolt securing the injector clamp plate to the manifold and remove the plate.
2. Start the engine and pull number one injector out of the manifold and observe the emission of fuel. The check should show a 60° hollow cone spray in regular pulsations. If there is any sign of dribbling or irregular cone formation the injector should be disconnected from its injection pipe – instruction 3, 19.60.01 and cleaned by passing dry filtered air through the injector in the direction of the fuel flow at a pressure of approximately 80 lb/in^2 (5·624 kg/cm^2)
3. Reconnect the injector to its injection pipe – test again and if satisfactory refit to the manifold. If unsatisfactory, renew the injector.
4. Repeat instructions 2 and 3 on number two injector.
5. Refit the clamp plate and secure with the bolt.
6. Repeat instructions 1 to 5 on the remaining injectors and stop the engine.

CAUTION: When checking fuel emission, direct spray into a glass jar to prevent atomized fuel being sprayed over the engine.

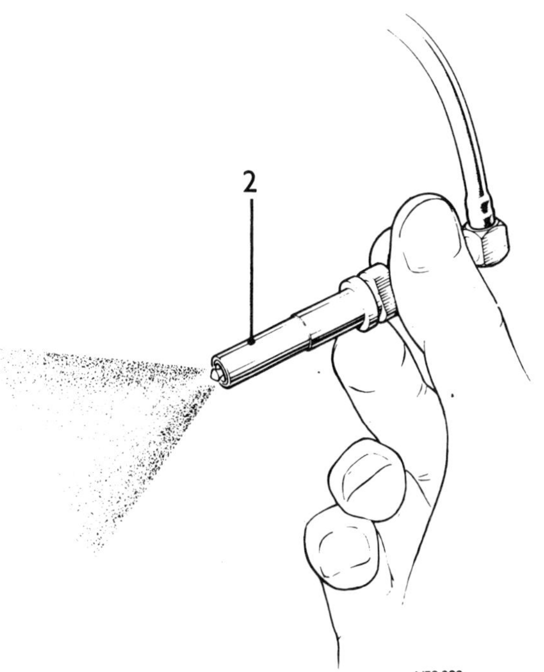

NOTE: A possible faulty injector may be identified without the necessity of removing each injector in turn as described in instruction 1 to 6 by following instructions 7 to 9.

7. Remove the cleats holding injection pipes together, and separate them to prevent the transmission of pulsations from one pipe to another.
8. Start the engine and hold each injector pipe in turn between the thumb and forefinger. A regular pulsation should be felt but a weak or missing pulsation suggests a possible faulty injector. No pulsation on two consecutive pipes, in the firing order, indicates that the first injector of the two is blocked.
9. Stop the engine and remove the suspect injector and clean as described in instruction 2. Refit or renew the injector and refit the cleats.

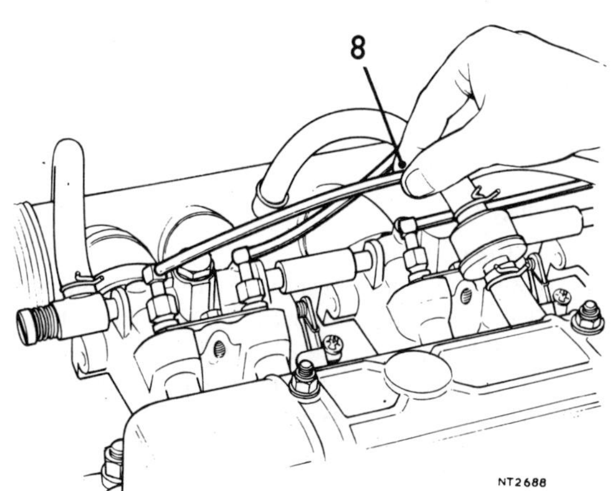

Continued

Testing – with a test rig on which the line pressure can be varied from 0 to 100 lbf/in^2 (0 to 689;50 Kn/m^2

10. Remove each injector in turn 19.60.01.
11. Use Fawley white spirit '100' plus 50 parts per million Santolene 'C' or Shell calibrating fluid 'C' for testing purposes.
12. Flow test the injector at 50 to 60 g.p.h. (227·298 to 272·758 litres per hour) at 100 lb/in^2 (689·50 Kn/m^2) pressure. During this test the cone or needle must freely vibrate off its seat and the injector must produce an evenly distributed cone of fuel at an angle of 55° to 60°.
13. Flow the injector with an applied pressure of 100 lbf/in^2 (689·50 Kn/m^2) and gradually reduce the pressure to zero. Use compressed air to remove fuel from the nozzle tip. Increase applied pressure to 40 lbf/in^2 (275·80 Kn/m^2) and check the time taken for a droplet of fuel to appear at the injector tip. This should not be less than 60 seconds.
14. Flow the injector with an applied pressure of 100 lbf/in^2 (689·50 Kn/m^2) and gradually reduce the pressure to zero and remove fuel from the nozzle tip with compressed air. Increase the applied pressure gradually and observe the pressure at which the injector sprays an evenly distributed cone of fuel. This should be between 45 and 55 lbf/in^2 (310·26 to 379·21 Kn/m^2).
15. Renew any injectors that fail the above test.

INJECTOR PIPE NUMBER ONE

– Remove and refit **19.60.15**

Removing

1. Isolate the battery.
2. Using a suitable open ended spanner across the milled flats, hold the injector steady and disconnect the pipe from the injector at the elbow union nut.
3. Check that the pipe is marked for re-assembly, if more than one pipe is to be removed.
4. Disconnect the pipe from the metering unit.

Refitting

5. Reverse instructions 1 to 4 ensuring:-
   a) A kinked pipe is renewed 19.60.24.
   b) Absolute cleanliness is observed.

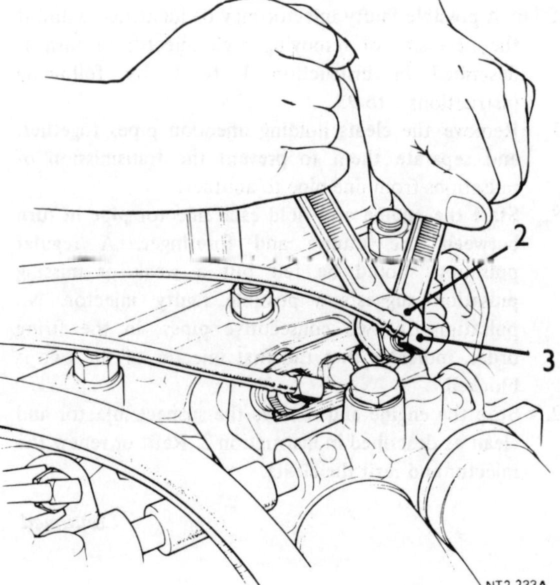

INJECTOR PIPE NUMBER TWO

– Remove and refit **19.60.16**

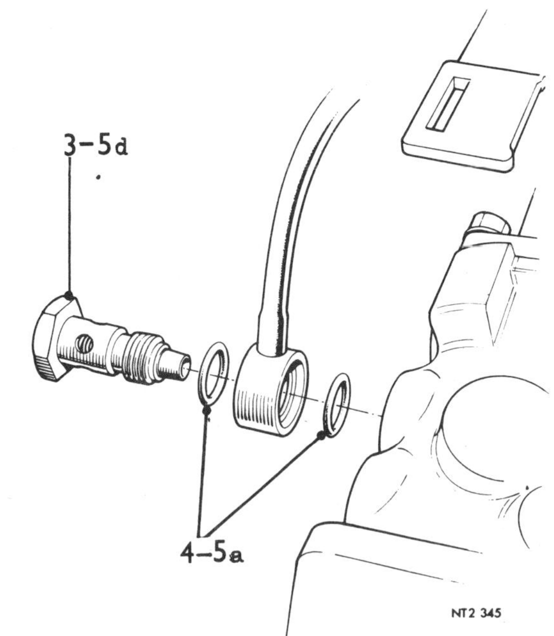

Removing

1. Isolate the battery.
2. Remove the fuel metering distributor 19.35.07.
3. Remove the banjo bolt.
4. Remove the two 'O' rings from the banjo connector.

Refitting

5. Reverse instructions 1 to 4 ensuring:-
   a) New 'O' rings are fitted if origonals are faulty.
   b) Absolute cleanliness is observed.
   c) A kinked pipe is renewed 19.60.24
   d) The banjo bolts are tightened to 150 to 200 lb ins.

INJECTOR PIPE NUMBER THREE

– Remove and refit **19.60.17**

Same as 19.60.15.

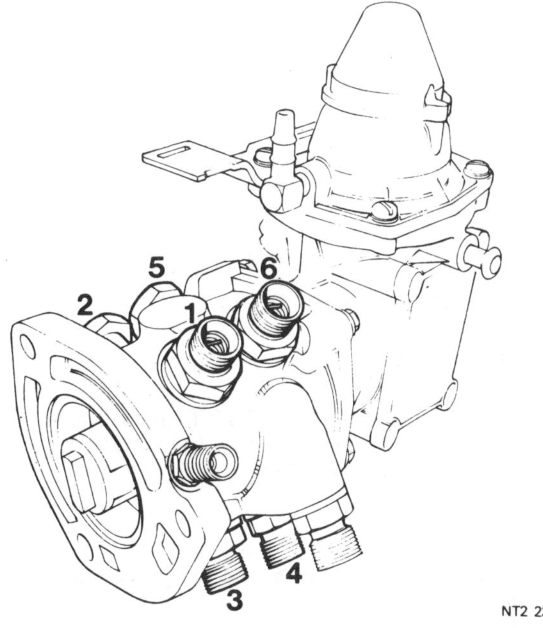

INJECTOR PIPE NUMBER FOUR

– Remove and refit **19.60.18**

Same as 19.60.15 except that for access to the union on the metering distributor number three pipe union on the distributor must be disconnected.

INJECTOR PIPE NUMBER FIVE

– Remove and refit **19.60.19**

Same as 19.60.16

INJECTOR PIPE NUMBER SIX

– Remove and refit **19.60.20**

Same as 19.60.15

INJECTOR PIPES

– Overhaul **19.60.24**

1. Isolate the battery.
2. Remove the metering distributor 19.35.07.
3. Remove the injector pipes from the metering distributor.
4. Cut the old pipes from the union connections.
5. Manufacture a clamp from a Tufnol block 2 in x 1 in x 1 in (50·8 mm x 25·4 mm x 25·4 mm). Drill a hole 0·250 in dia (6·35 mm) through the centre of the block and cut the block in half along the centre line of the hole.
6. Cut the new piping to the required length and clamp it in the block in a vice. Allow approximately 1/8 in (3 mm) protrusion of pipe above the clamp in addition to the length of pipe required to fit to the union conection. If a straight union connection is being fitted to the pipe, place the union nut over the pipe before it is clamped.
7. Locate the union connection into the pipe and gently tap it into position with a soft hammer.
8. Reverse instructions 1 to 3.

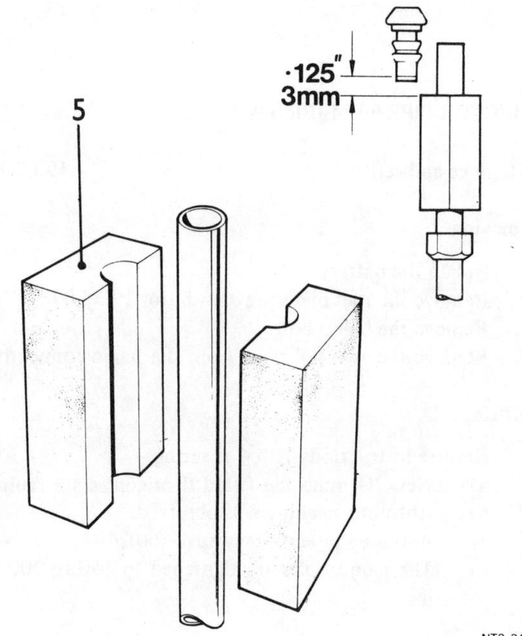

NT2 242

PRESSURE RELIEF VALVE

– Pressure test and adjust **19.65.01**

Special equipment – 0 to 120 p.s.i. (0 to 850 g/cm^2) pressure gauges and hose from the CBW 1A kit, connected to a S351 auaptor.

Test

1. Connect the pressure gauge and adaptor into the fuel line.
2. Switch on the ignition but do not start the engine. Check and note the gauge pressure which should be 106 to 110 p.s.i. (7453 to 7734 g/m^2).
3. Switch off the ignition.

Continued

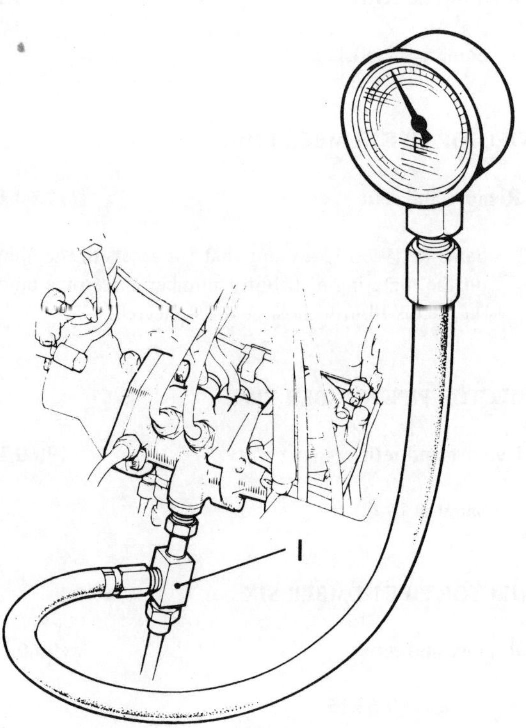

NTO 645

Adjust

4. Remove the luggage compartment forward trim panel and spare wheel.
5. Clamp the return hose from the pressure relief valve to the fuel tank and disconnect the hose from the pressure relief valve.
6. With a cross recessed screw driver adjust the relief valve by turning the nylon tensioner clockwise to increase the pressure and anti-clockwise to reduce the pressure.
7. Reconnect the hose to the pressure relief valve and release the clamp. Switch on the ignition and observe the pressure.
8. Repeat instructions 5 and 6 until a constant pressure within the limits in instruction 2 is achieved.
9. If a satisfactory pressure cannot be obtained and the pump is known to be working correctly, overhaul the valve 19.65.13 or renew it 19.65.07.
10. Disconnect the pressure gauge and reconnect the fuel line to the metering unit.
11. Refit the luggage compartment trim panel and spare wheel.

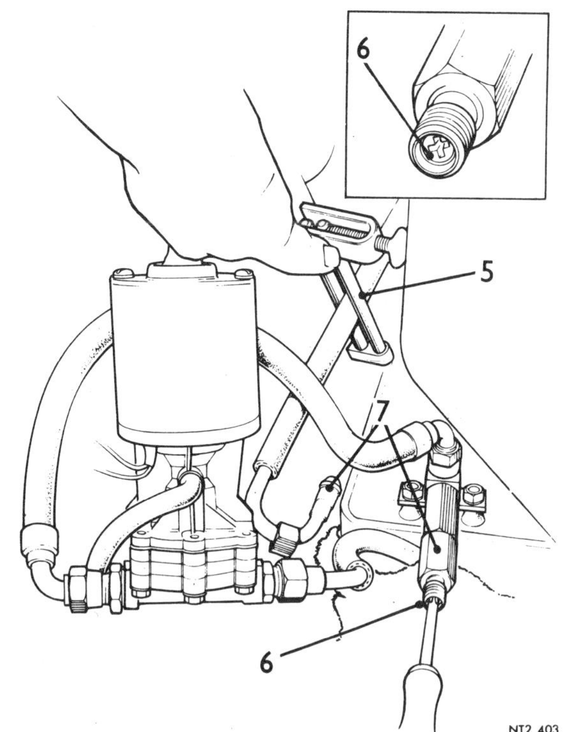

PRESSURE RELIEF VALVE

– Remove and refit **19.65.07**

Removing

1. Isolate the battery.
2. Remove the luggage compartment forward trim panel 76.13.17.
3. Disconnect the hose from the pump to the pressure relief valve.
4. Disconnect the pressure relief valve to fuel tank hose.
5. Disconnect from the rear of the 'T' piece the main fuel feed from the pressure relief valve to the fuel metering distributor.

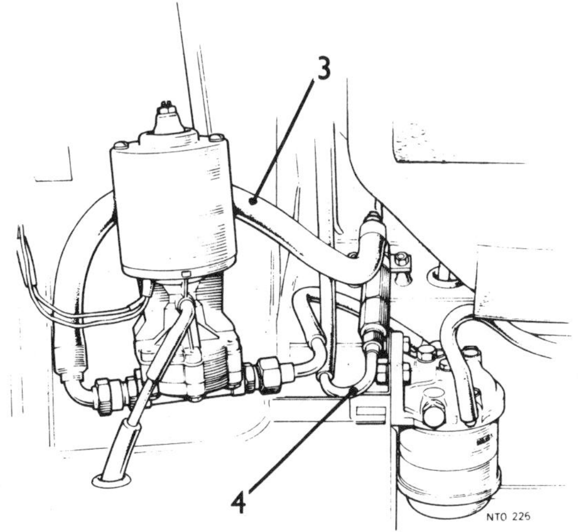

Continued

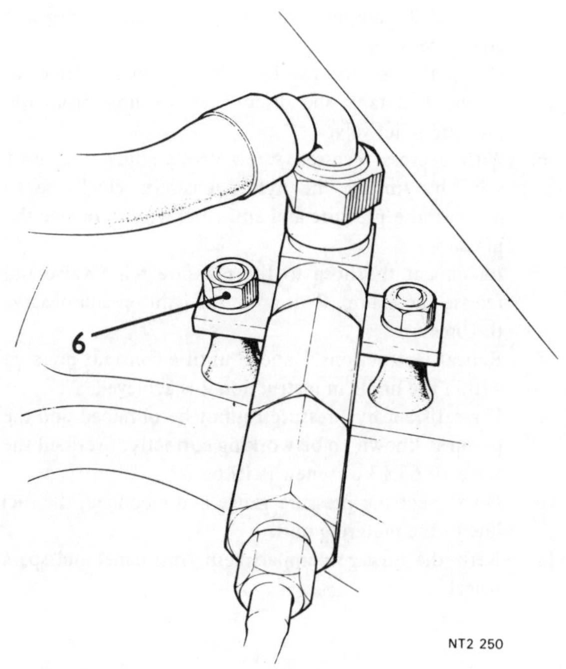

6. Remove two nuts complete with spring washers securing the 'T' piece and pressure relief valve assembly to the body and remove the assembly from the car.

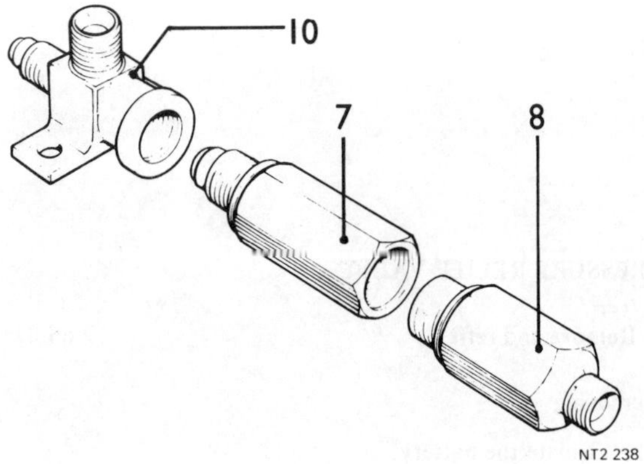

7. Disconnect the strainer housing complete with the pressure relief from the 'T' piece.
8. Remove the pressure relief valve from the strainer housing.

Refitting

9. Assemble the pressure relief valve to the strainer housing using a new washer and tightening to 30 – 40 lbf ft (4·1 to 5·5 kgf m).
10. Reconnect the strainer housing and pressure relief valve to the 'T' piece using a new washer and tighten to 30 to 40 lbf ft (4·1 to 5·5 kgf m).
11. Reverse instructions 1 to 6.

PRESSURE RELIEF VALVE

– Overhaul **19.65.13**

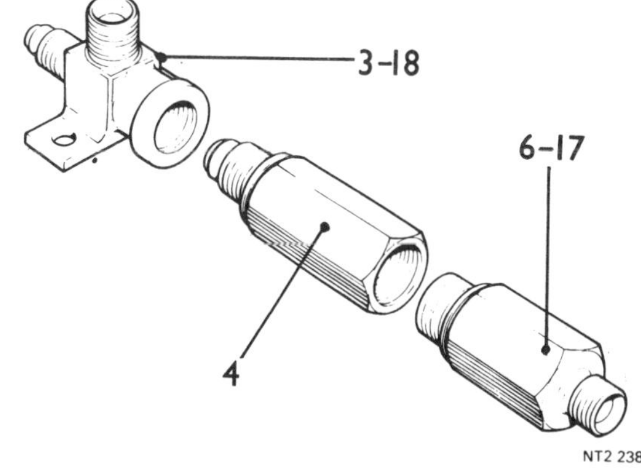

Dismantling

1. Isolate the battery.
2. Remove the pressure relief valve assembly from the car 19.65.07.
3. Disconnect the 'T' piece from the strainer housing.
4. Remove the strainer housing from the pressure relief valve.
5. From the inside of the strainer housing carefully press out the strainer.
6. Frm the pressure relief valve body remove:-
   a. The circlip
   b. The distance sleeve
   c. The valve and plunger
   d. The spring
   e. Plain washer
7. Using a cross recessed screw driver remove from the back of the valve body the nylon spring tensioner.

Examination

8. Examine carefully each part of the valve and body and check for wear, pitting and corrosion.
9. Ensure that the plunger moves freely in its housing and the housing is free to move in the valve body.
10. Examine the spring and check for cracks.
11. Examine the strainer and housing and renew the strainer if damaged.

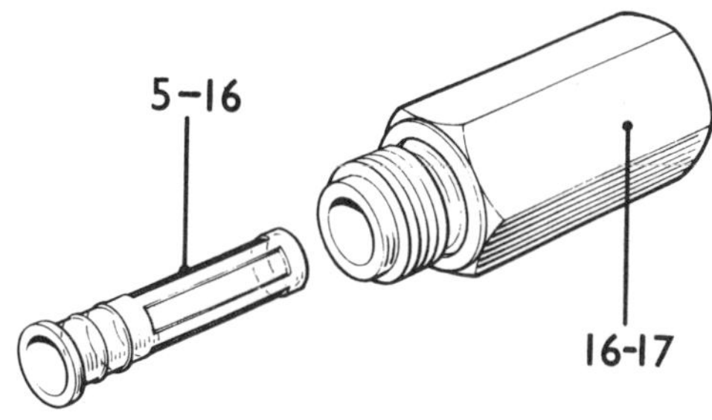

Reassembling

12. Wash all the parts in petrol and dry with an air line. DO NOT USE CLOTH.
13. Screw the nylon spring tensioner into the back of the valve body.
14. Insert the valve plunger in its housing.
15. Assembly the remaining components in the reverse order in instruction 6..
16. Insert the strainer into the strainer housing.
17. Assemble the valve body to the strainer housing using a new washer and tighten to 30 to 40 lbf ft (4·1 to 5·5 kgf m).
18. Fit the 'T' piece using a new washer and tighten as in instruction 17.
19. Reverse instructions 1 and 2.
20. Pressure test and adjust the pressure relief valve – 19.65.01

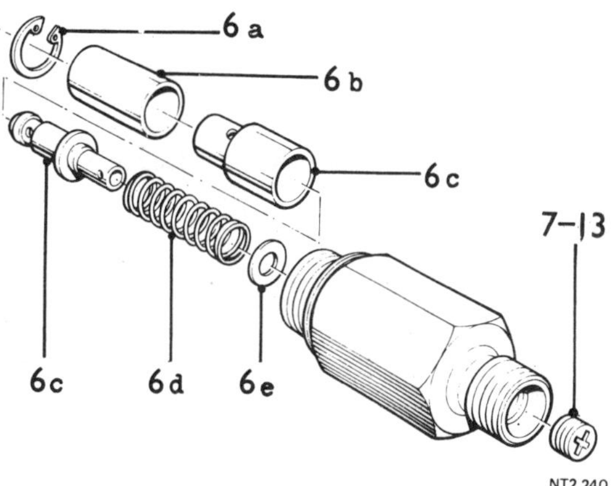

AIR INTAKE MANIFOLD

– Remove and refit **19.70.01**

Removing

1. Remove the hose connecting the air intake manifold to the air cleaner.
2. Disconnect the engine breather hose.
3. Disconnect the air valve hose.
4. Slacken the hose clips on numbers one and six intakes.

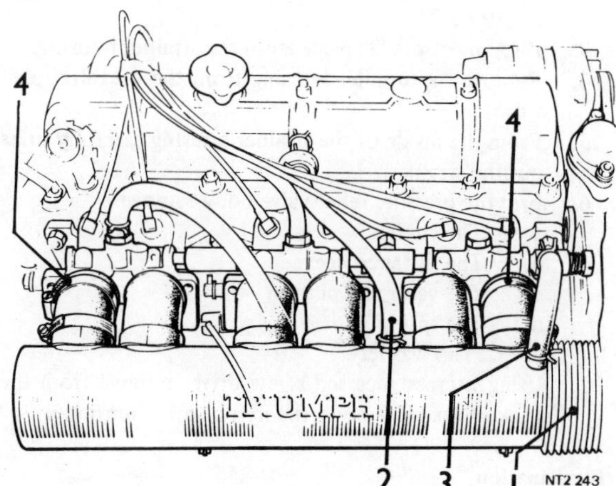

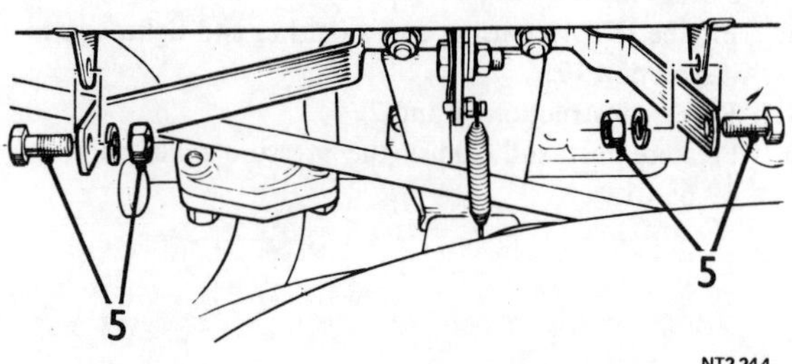

5. Remove two nuts and bolts securing the air intake manifold to the engine brackets.
6. Remove the air intake from the induction manifold.

Refitting

7. Reverse instructions 1 to 6.

FUEL SYSTEM OPERATIONS (TWIN CARBURETTER)

EMISSION CARBURETTER – FAULT DIAGNOSIS

NOTE: Before undertaking extensive carburetter servicing it is recommended that other engine factors and components such as cylinder compressions, valve clearance, distributor, sparking plugs, air intake temperature control system, etc., are checked for correctness of operation.

SYMPTOM	CAUSE	ACTION
1. Poor idle quality	*a.* Air leakage on induction manifold joints.	Remake joints as necessary. Check idle carbon monoxide level with CO meter.
	b. Throttles not synchronized.	Re-balance carburetters and re-set linkage.
	c. Air valve or valves sticking in piston guide-rods.	Clean air valve rods and guides and reassemble. Check piston free movement by hand· unit should move freely and retun to carburetter bridge with an audible click.
	d. Partially or fully obstructed float-chamber or diaphragm ventilation holes.	Check that gasket(s) are not causing obstruction or piping obstructed.
	e. Incorrect fuel level caused by maladjusted float assemblies or worn or dirty needle valve.	Reset float heights and clean or replace needle valves worn.
	f. Metering needle incorrectly fitted or wrong type of needle fitted.	Ensure shoulder of needle is flush with face of air valve and that needle bias is correct.
	g. Diaphragm incorrectly located or damaged.	Check location with air valve cover removed, piston depression holes should be in line with and face towards the throttle spindle. Renew diaphragm with correct type if damage is in evidence.
	h. Leakage from ignition retard unit pipe connections.	Re-make connections and re-check ignition settings.
	i. Temperature compensator faulty.	With engine and carburetter cold, check that compensator cone is seated, and free to move off seat, If any doubt exists, replace unit with new assembly.
	j. After considerable service leakage may occur at throttle spindle or secondary throttle spindles	Replace spindle seals or spindles as required.

continued

SYMPTOM	CAUSE	ACTION
	Piston damper inoperative	Check damper oil level and top up with specified oil· re-check damper operation by raising piston by hand whereupon resistance should be felt.
2. Hesitation or 'flat spot' *a, b, c, d, e, f, g* and *h* plus:	Air valve spring missing or wrong part fitted	Check correct grade of spring and refit as required.
	Ignition timing incorrect	Check and reset as required.
	Throttle linkage operation incorect	Check operation of linkage between carburetters and operation of secondary throttle links· reset or repalce parts as required.
3. Heavy fuel consumption 1 and 2 plus:	Leakage from the fuel connections, float-chamber joints or sealing plug 'O' rings	Replace gaskets and 'O' rings as required.
4. Lack of engine braking	Faulty by-pass valve	Replace by-pass valve with new unit.
	Sticking throttles	Check throttle operation and reset as required.
	Ignition retard unit inoperative	Check ignition setting at idle and ensure correct functioning of retard system.
5. Lack of engine power	Damaged diaphragm	Inspect, and replace if incorrectly fitted or damaged.
	Low fuel flow	Check discharge from fuel pump. Inspect needle valve seating.

NOTE: To ensure compliance with exhaust emission legislative requirements the following items MUST NOT be changed or modified in any way:

The fuel jet assembly· the air valve· the depression cover· the position of the fuel metering needle.

The following items must not be adjusted in service but should be replaced completely by factory-set units.

The temperature compensator· the air valve return spring· the by-pass unit· the starter assembly.

AIR CLEANER

– Remove and refit **19.10.01**

Remove

1. Remove the six bolts securing the air cleaner assembly to the carburetter intakes.
2. Lift off the air cleaner complete with gaskets.

Refitting

3. Reverse instructions 1 and 2 ensuring
   a) A new gasket is fitted between the air cleaner and carburetter intakes.
   b) The bolts are tightened evenly to 5 to 8 lbf ft (0·7 to 1·1 kgf m).

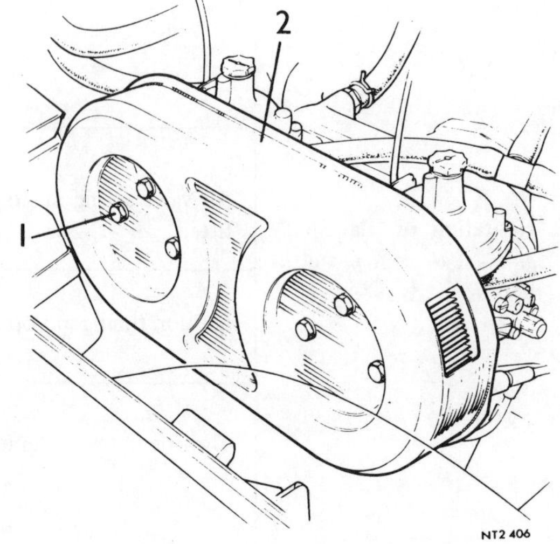

AIR CLEANER

– Renew elements **19.10.08**

Dismantling

1. Remove the air cleaner from the carburetter intakes 19.10.01.
2. Remove the back plate from the cover.
3. Remove and discard the paper elements.
4. Examine and if unsatisfactory, discard the four sealing rings.
5. Clean the casing assembly.

Re-assembling

6. Place two sealing rings in position on the back plate location.
7. Position the new paper elements on the back plate ensuring that they locate properly.
8. Position remaining two sealing rings on the cover locations and place the cover over the back plate. Ensure that the elements locate correctly.
9. Refit the air cleaner 19.10.01.

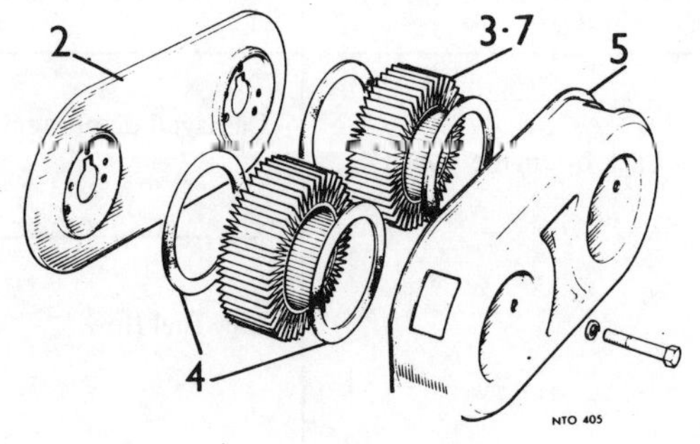

CARBURETTER – CAR SET

– Tune and adjust **19.15.02**

Special tool: S353

Mixture checking

1. Start the engine and run until normal operating temperature is achieved.
2. Stop the engine and remove the air cleaner 19.10.01.
3. Slacken the throttle interconnection, spring coupling nuts and bolts.
4. Unscrew the slow running screw on both carburetters.
5. Ensure that the mixture control knob on the fascia is pushed fully home and that there is clearance 'A' between the fast idle screw and the cam on both carburetters.
6. Turn both throttle adjusting screws approximately 1·1/2 turns to open the butterflies to give a datum setting.

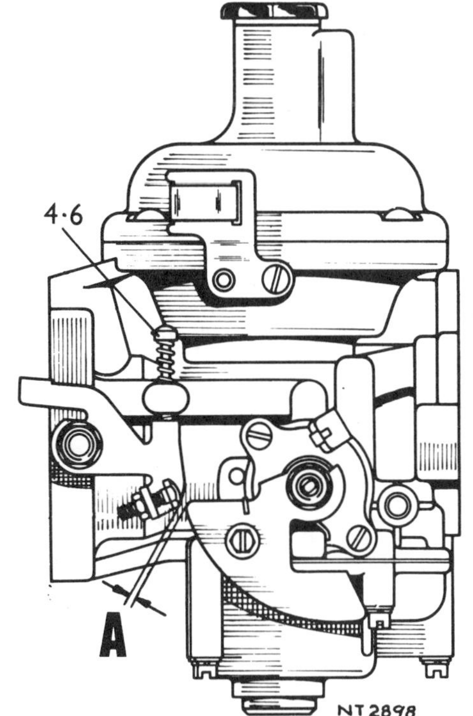

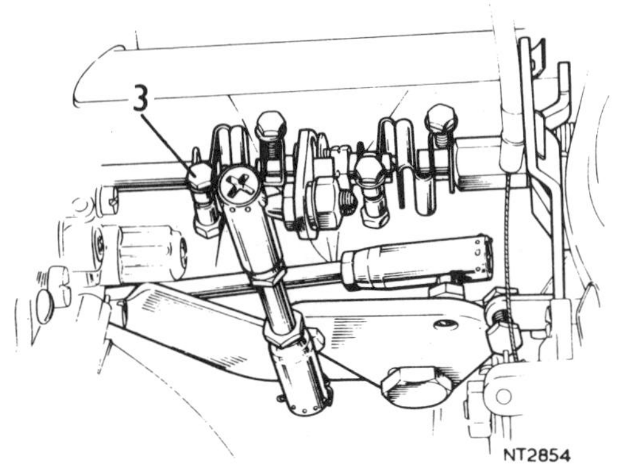

7. Start the engine and lift both carburetter pistons in turn approximately ¼ in (6 mm) and note the engine response as follows.
   - *a)* Immediate increase in r.p.m – rich mixture
   - *b)* Decrease in r.p.m. or stall – weak mixture
   - *c)* Slight increase in r.p.m. then return to normal – correct mixture.
8. Carry out a C.O. level check.

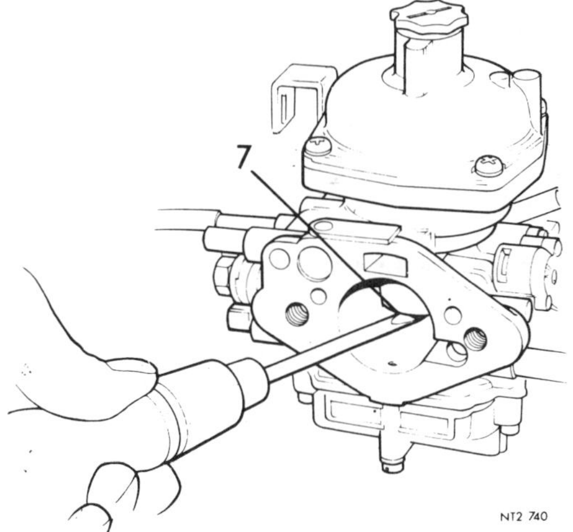

Continued

Mixture adjusting

NOTE: If the mixture in both carburetters is correct ignore the following instructions 9 to 11.

9. Remove the piston dampers from both carburetters or the damper from the carburetter that requires adjustment.
10. Insert the special jet adjusting tool and turn it clockwise to enrich or anti-clockwise to weaken the mixture and top-up dash pot and refit the damper.
11. Repeat instructions 7 and 8 until the mixture is correct.
12. Top up the piston dash-pot and refit the damper.

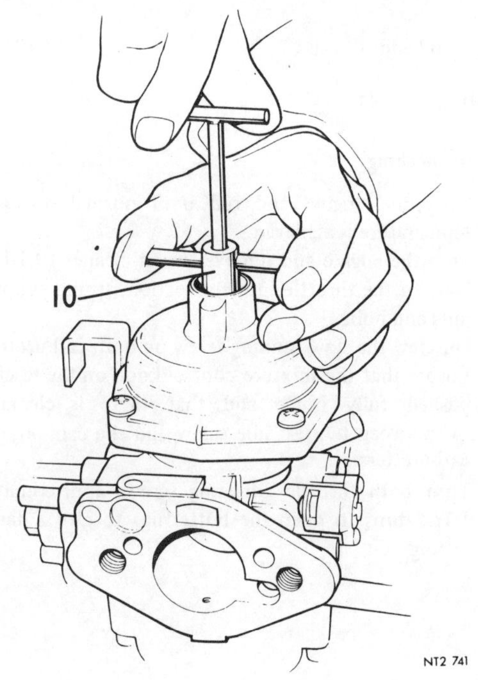

Idle speed setting and balancing

13. Using a synchro check meter against both carburetter intakes in turn, adjust the fast idle screws to give an r.p.m. of 800 to 850 whilst maintaining an identical air flow reading from both carburetters.
14. Stop the engine, check that the relay lever is against its stop and insert a 3/32 in (2·4 mm) drill shank between the tongue and the slot of the interconnection lever – and whilst holding it in this position tighten the interconnection spring coupling nuts and bolts. Remove the drill.
15. Start the engine and increase the r p m to 1500 and check the balance with the synchro check meter and if necessary adjust the idle screws to achieve an equal reading.
16. Recheck the balance at the correct idle speed.

Continued

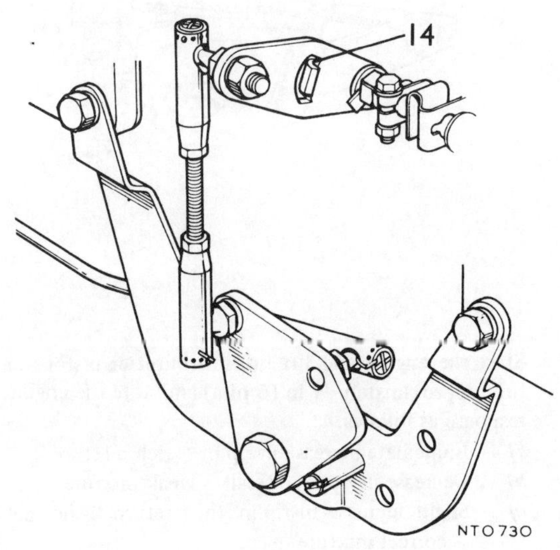

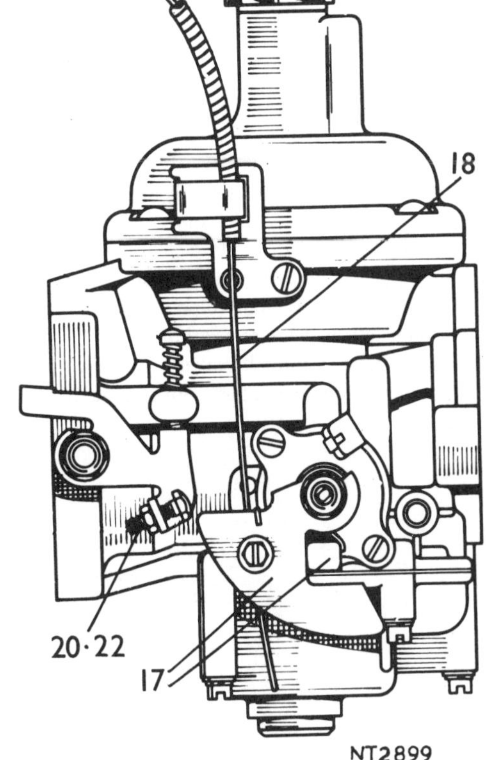

Fast idle speed setting

17. Check that the mixture control cam lever on both carburetters returns to its stop.
18. Ensure that the mixture control cables are so adjusted that they are not slack or too tight.
19. Pull the mixture control knob out on the fascia and insert a 5/16 in (7·937 mm) diameter bar between the cam and its stop on both carburetters in turn.
20. Slacken the fast idle screw lock nut on both carburetters and adjust the screws so that they just touch their respective cams.
21. Remove the bar, push the control knob home and pull the control knob out again to check that the setting gives a fast idle speed of 1100 – 1300 r.p.m. Make any necessary adjustments to the fast idle screw to achieve this setting whilst using the synchro check meter to maintain the carburetters in balance.
22. Tighten the lock nuts, stop the engine, push the control knob fully home and refit the air cleaner.

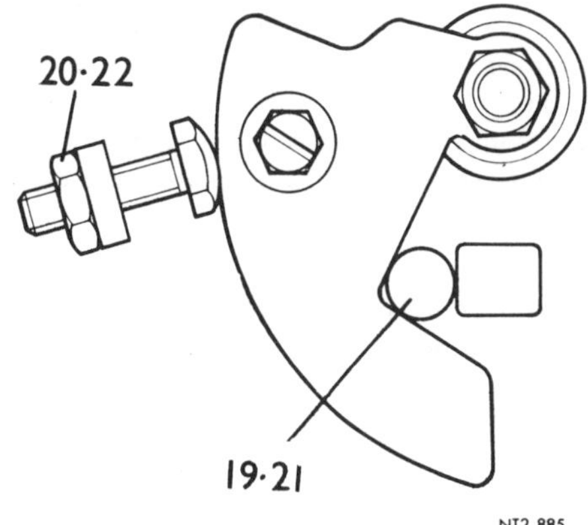

DATA

Idle speed	800 – 850 r.p.m.
Fast idle speed	1100 – 1300 r.p.m.

CARBURETTERS – CAR SET

– Remove and refit **19.15.11**

Removing

1. Remove the air cleaner assembly 19.10.01.
2. Disconnect the mixture control cables from both carburetters.
3. Disconnect the emission hoses from the carburetters.
4. Disconnect the vacuum pipe to the thermo static vacuum switch at the rear carburetter.
5. Disconnect the throttle linkage at the countershaft.
6. Disconnect the main fuel supply pipe to the carburetter.

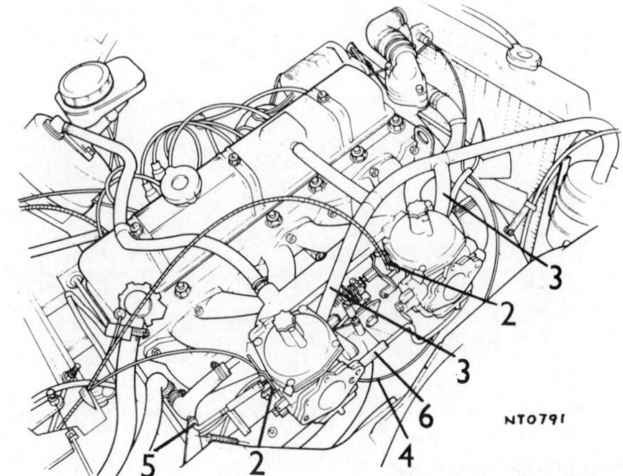

7. Remove the eight nuts and spring washers (four per carburetter) securing the carburetters to the inlet manifold.
8. Withdraw the carburetters complete with the linkage.
9. Remove the gaskets from the carburetter intakes.

Refitting

10. Fit new gaskets to both the inlet manifold intakes.
11. Reverse instructions 1 to 8.

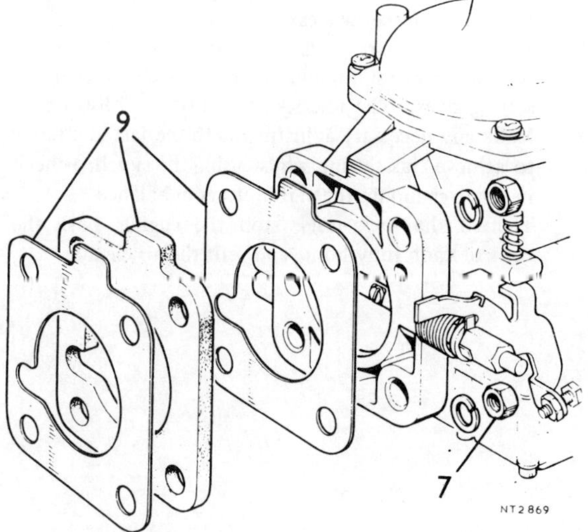

CARBURETTERS COMPLETE WITH INLET MANIFOLD

– Remove and refit **19.15.15**

Removing

1. Remove the air cleaner 19.10.01.
2. Disconnect the mixture control cables from both carburetters.
3. Disconnect the emission pipes from the carburetters and rocker cover.
4. Disconnect the vacuum pipe at the rear carburetter to the thermo static vacuum switch.
5. Disconnect the main fuel supply pipe to the carburetters.
6. Disconnect the throttle linkage at the countershaft.
7. Partially drain the cooling system.
8. Disconnect brake servo vacuum hose at the inlet manifold.
9. Disconnect the manifold heater hoses at the front and rear of the manifold.
10. Remove the three nuts and spring washers securing the inlet manifold to the cylinder head and the six nuts and plain washers securing the inlet and exhaust manifold to the cylinder head.
11. Withdraw the carburetters complete with the inlet manifold.

Refitting

12. Clean the manifold mating faces and offer up and secure the manifold to the cylinder head with the three nuts and spring washers and the six nuts and plain washers.

NOTE: If the manifold gasket is in any way damaged it should be replaced 30.15.01.

13. Reverse instructions 1 to 9.

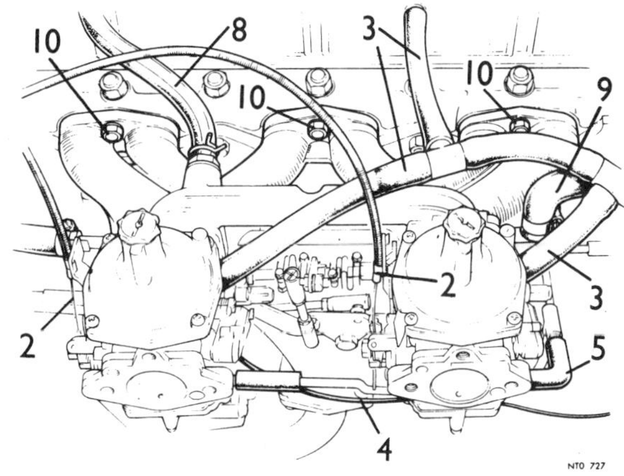

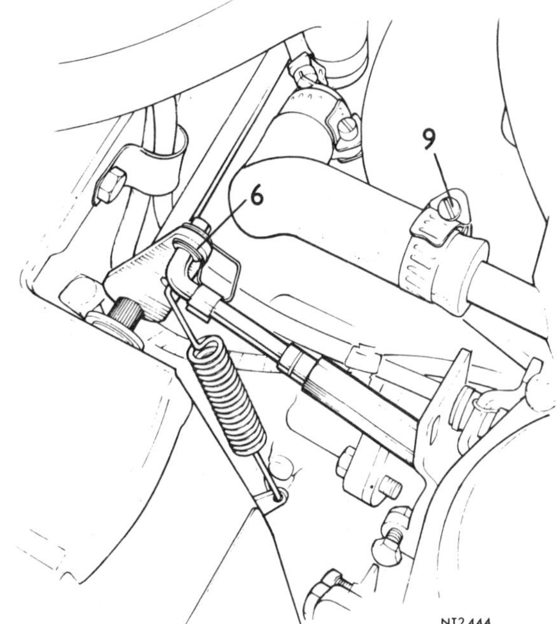

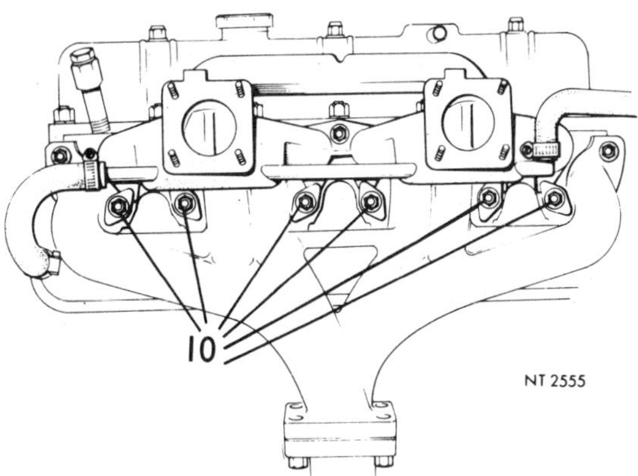

CARBURETTER – EACH

– Overhaul and adjust **19.15.17**

Service tool S353

1. Remove carburetters 19.15.11.
2. Remove damper.
3. Remove bottom plug. (lever-out).
4. Drain carburetter of oil and fuel.
5. Remove 'O' ring from plug.
6. Remove six screws securing float-chamber to body.
7. Remove float-chamber.
8. Remove float assembly by gently prising spindle from clip each end.
9. Remove needle valve.
10. Remove four screws securing top cover to body.
11. Remove top cover.
12. Remove spring.
13. Remove air valve assembly.
14. Remove four screws securing diaphragm and retaining ring to air valve assembly.
15. Remove diaphragm and retaining ring.
16. Slacken grubscrew in side of air valve.
17. Insert tool S353 in stem of air valve, turn anticlockwise approximately two turns, withdraw needle and housing by pulling firmly and straight with the fingers.
18. Remove two screws securing starter box to body.
19. Remove starter box.
20. Remove two screws securing the temperature compensator to body.
21. Remove the temperature compensator and two rubber washers of different diameters.
22. Remove three (slotted) screws securing the by-pass valve to body.
23. Remove the by-pass valve and gasket.
24. Remove two screws securing butterfly to spindle.
25. Turn spindle, remove butterfly.
26. Release spindle return spring.
27. Withdraw spindle and spring
28. Remove spindle seals from body by hooking out with small screwdriver.
29. Wash all components in clean fuel, allow to drain dry or use compressed air. Place all components on a clean surface. Discard all seals and gaskets.
30. Examine the condition of all components for wear, paying special attention to needle and seat, air valve and diaphragm which should be renewed unless in exceptionally good condition.
31. Use clean compressed air to blow through all ports, needle valve and starter box.

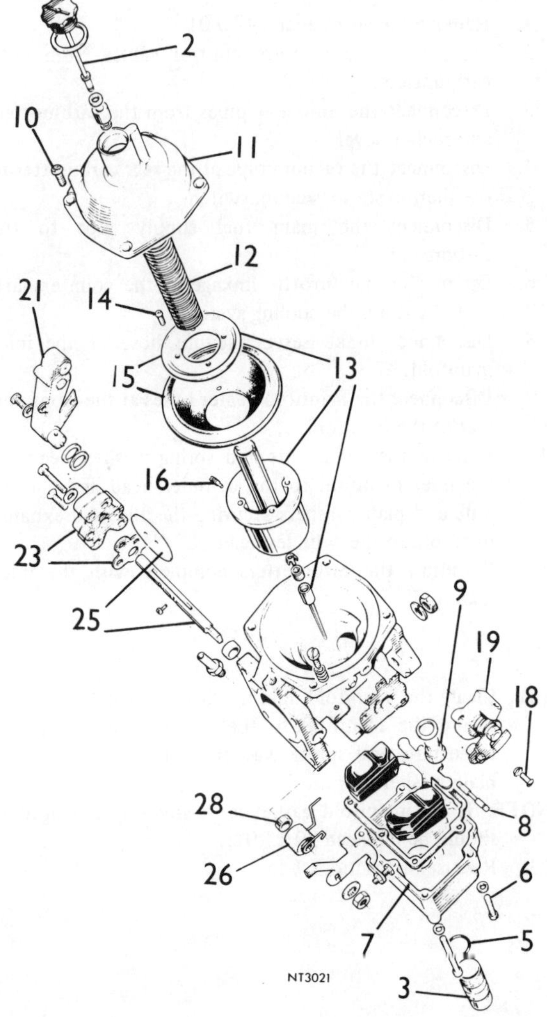

Continued

32. Fit spindle seals to body, tapping gently into position, with metal casing of seals flush with body of carburetter.
33. Insert spindle, loading and locating spindle return spring whilst so doing.
34. Insert butterfly with two protruding spots, outboard and below spindle, tighten screws.

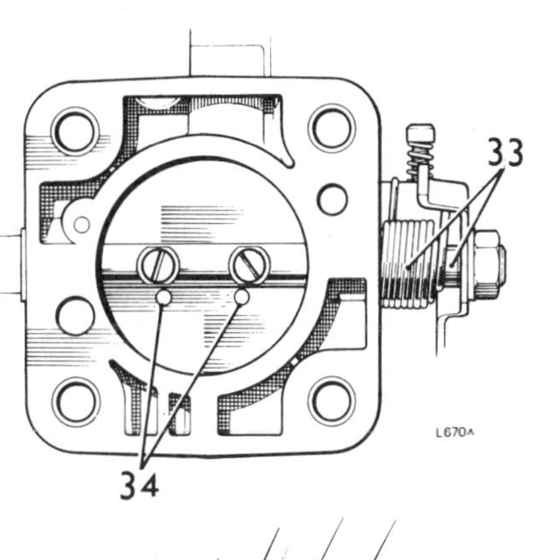

35. Fit starter box, tighten screws.
36. Fit by-pass valve and gasket, tighten screws.
37. Fit temperature compensator, tighten screws.
38. Insert needle housing assembly into the bottom of the air valve.
39. Fit tool S353, turning clockwise to engage threads of needle valve assembly with adjusting screw; continue turning until slot in needle housing is aligned with grub screw.
40. Tighten grub screw.

NOTE: The grub screw does not tighten on the needle housing but locates into the slot. This ensures that, during adjustment, the needle will remain in its operating position, i.e. biased, by a spring in the needle housing, towards the air cleaner side of the carburetter.

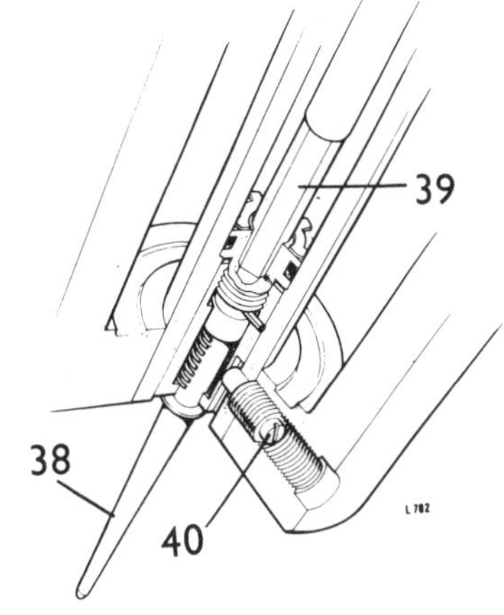

41. Fit diaphragm, locating inner tag into recess in air valve.
42. Fit diaphragm retaining ring; secure with four screws.
43. Fit air valve assembly, locating outer tag and rim of diaphragm in complementary recesses in carburetter body.
44. Fit carburetter top cover with bulge on housing neck towards air intake.
45. Fit and evenly tighten top cover screws.

Continued

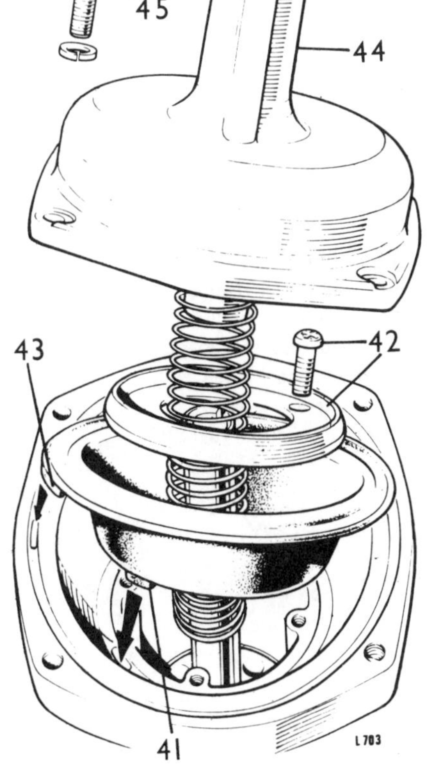

46. Fit needle valve and sealing washers; tighten.
47. Fit float assembly by levering pivot pin gently into position.
48. Check float height by measuring the distance between the carburetter gasket face and the highest point of the floats. See 19.15.32.

NOTE: The float heights must be equal and set to 0·625 to 0·672 in (16 to 17 mm). Adjust by bending tabs ensuring that tab sits on needle valve at right angles.

49. Fit float-chamber gasket.
50. Fit float-chamber, secure with six screws.
51. Fit 'O' ring to bottom plug.
52. Fit bottom plug. (Push fit).

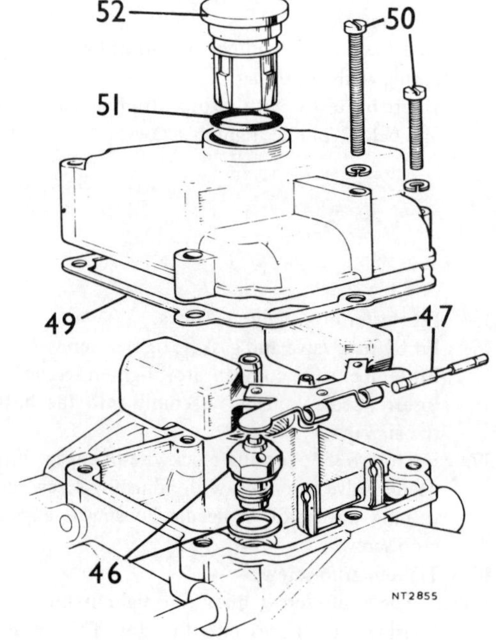

53. Fit carburetters 19.15.11.
54. Fill carburetter damper dashpot with seasonal grade of engine oil until, using the damper as a dipstick, the threaded plug is 0.25 in (6 mm) above the dashpot when resistance is felt.
55. Fit damper.
56. Tune carburetters 19.15.02.

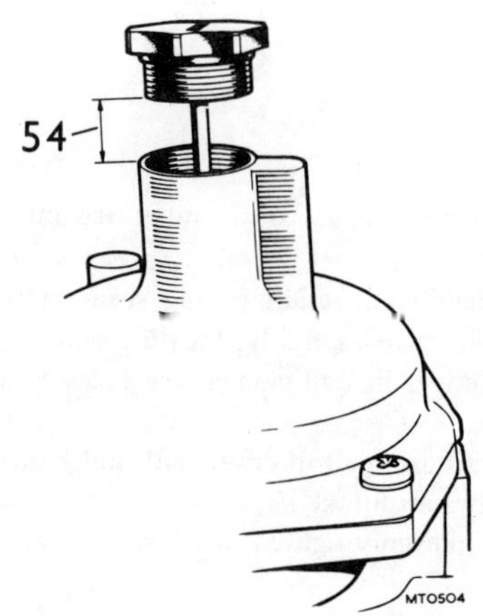

FLOAT CHAMBER NEEDLE VALVE

– Remove and refit **19.15.24**

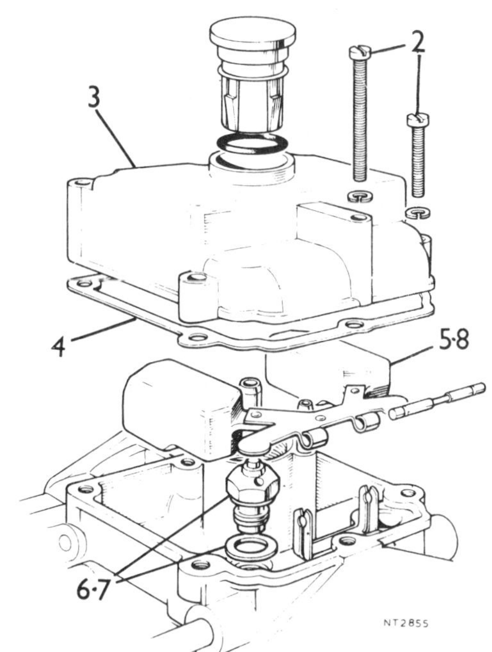

Removing

1. Remove the carburetters 19.15.11.
2. Remove the six screws securing the float chamber to the body.
3. Remove the float chamber.
4. Remove the gasket.
5. Remove the float assembly by gently prising the spindle from the locating clips.
6. Remove the needle valve and washer.

Refitting

7. Fit the needle valve and renew the washer.
8. Fit the float assembly.
9. Check and if necessary, adjust the height of both floats. Instruction 5, 19.15.32.
10. Renew the gasket and refit the float chamber.
11. Refit the carburetters.

FLOAT CHAMBER LEVELS

– Check and adjust **19.15.32**

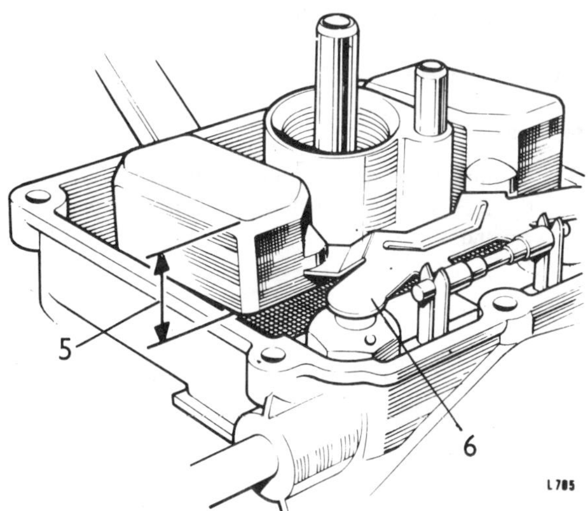

Check

1. Remove the carburetters 19.15.11.
2. Remove the six screws securing the float chamber to the body.
3. Remove the float chamber.
4. Remove the gasket.
5. With the carburetter in the inverted position check the distance between the gasket face on the carburetter body to the highest point of each float.

NOTE: The height of both floats must be the same i.e. 0·625 to 0·627 in (16 to 17 mm).

Adjust

6. Bend the tab that contacts the needle valve but ensure that it sits at right angles to the valve to prevent the possibility of sticking.
7. Fit a new gasket and reverse instructions 1 to 3.

DIAPHRAGM

– Remove and refit **19.15.35**

Removing

1. Remove the four screws securing the top cover to the carburetter body.
2. Lift off the top cover.
3. Remove the diaphragm spring.
4. Remove the diaphragm retaining plate.
5. Remove the diaphragm.

Refitting

6. Fit the diaphragm, locating the inner tag in the air valve recess.
7. Fit the retaining plate and ensure the correct diaphragm seating and tighten the screws.
8. Locate the diaphragm outer tag in the recess in the carburetter body.
9. Fit the top cover and evenly tighten the screws.

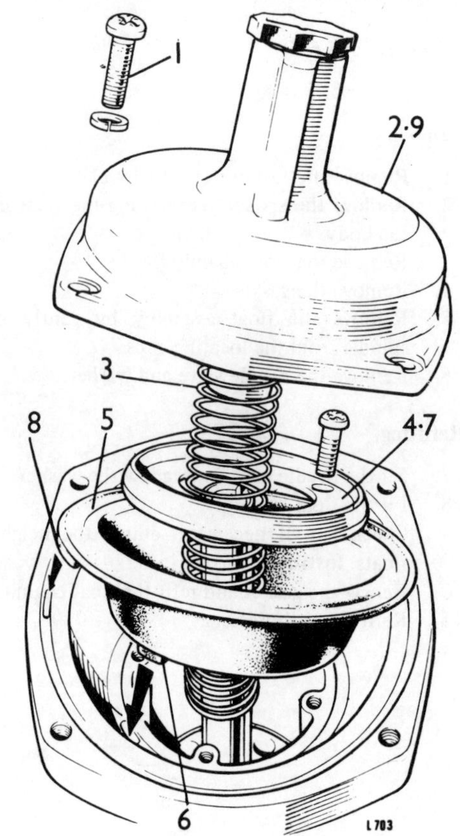

THROTTLE PEDAL AND COUNTER SHAFT

– Remove and refit **19.20.01.**

Removing

1. Working inside the car, pull back the carpet trim on the R.H. side of the bulkhead and remove the split pin and washer.

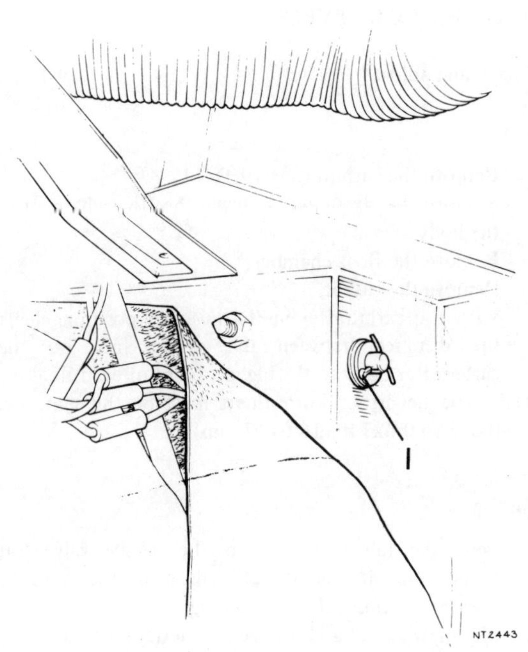

Continued

2. Within the engine compartment, disconnect the horizontal control rod from the countershaft lever.
3. Release the countershaft lever return spring.
4. Mark for reassembly the relationship of the countershaft to the lever.
5. Remove the countershaft lever clamp bolt and nut and remove the lever from the shaft together with the double spring and plain washer.
6. From inside the car, remove the throttle pedal and countershaft.
7. If necessary, remove the bushes in the bulkhead.

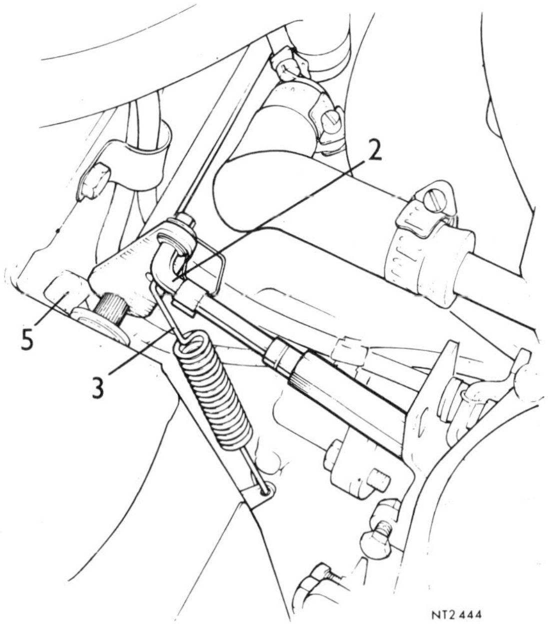

Refitting

8. Fit new bushes to the bulkhead if necessary.
9. Reverse instructions 1 to 6.

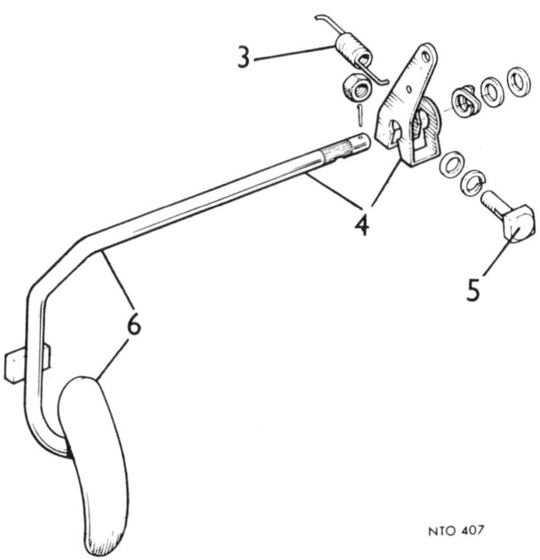

FUEL MAIN FILTER

– Remove and refit **19.20.02**

Removing

1. Clamp the inlet hose to the filter.
2. Disconnect the filter from the main line pipe.
3. Disconnect the filter from the inlet pipe to the pump and remove the filter.

****NOTE**: On later engines "Corbin" wire clips are fitted to secure the fuel pipe connections. New clips should be fitted when reassembling the fuel line.**

Refitting

4. Fit a new filter ensuring that the side of the filter marked 'in' faces the direction of flow.
5. Remove the clamp from the inlet pipe.

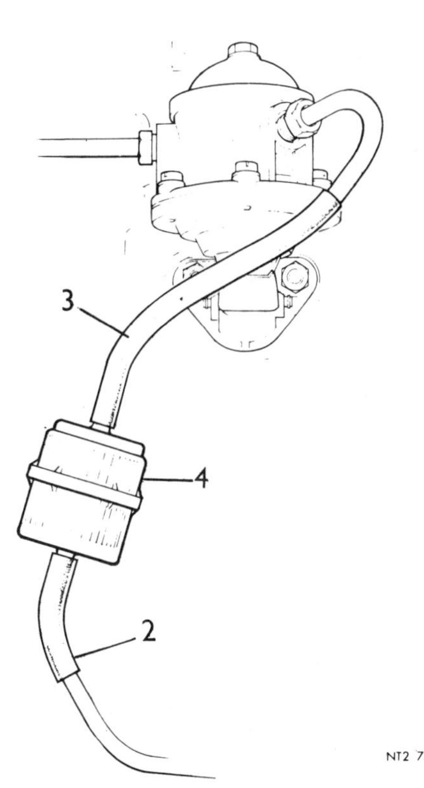

THROTTLE LINKAGE

– Remove and refit **19.20.07**

Removing

1. Disconnect the horizontal control rod from the throttle pedal countershaft lever.
2. Remove the relay lever support bracket from the carburetters.
3. Remove the nut and disconnect the short control rod from the interconnection lever.
4. Remove the throttle linkage complete.

Refitting

5. Check the length of the long horizontal and short vertical control rods – see DATA.
6. Refit the relay lever support bracket.
7. Fit the short vertical control rod assembly to the interconnection lever.
8. Slacken the spring coupling bolts.
9. Reconnect the long horizontal control rod to the throttle countershaft lever.
10. Check that the relay lever is against its stop.
11. Insert a 3/32 in (2·4 mm) drill shank between the tongue and slot of the throttle interconnection lever.
12. Tighten the spring coupling nuts and bolts.
13. Tune and adjust the carburetters 19.15.02.

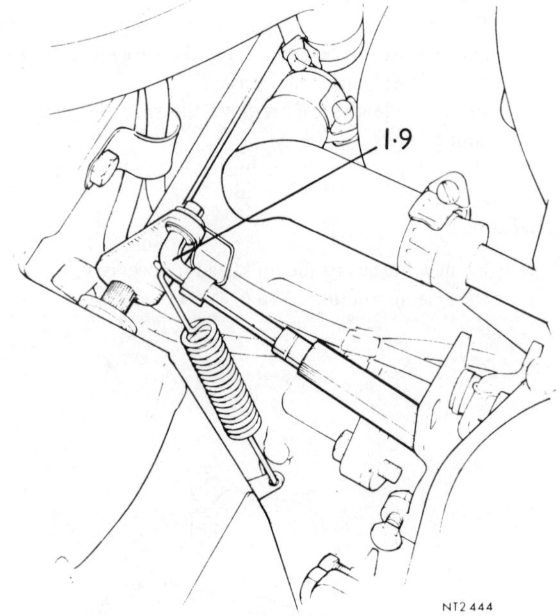

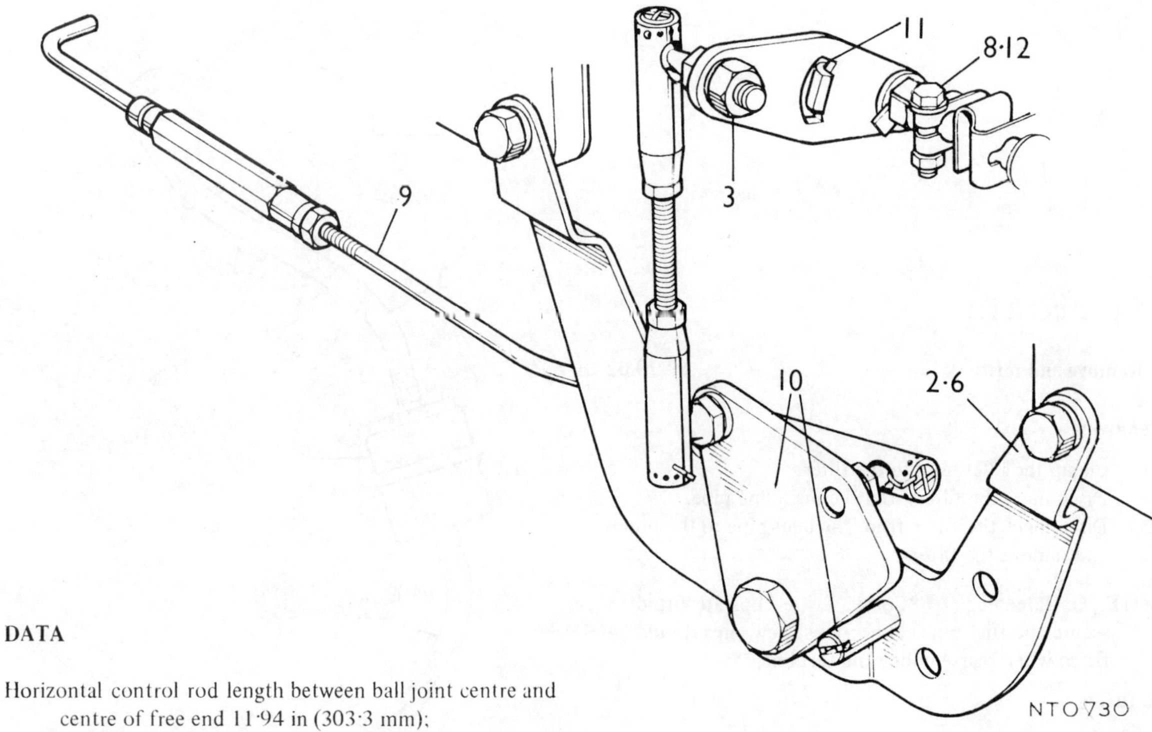

DATA

Horizontal control rod length between ball joint centre and centre of free end 11·94 in (303·3 mm);

Vertical control rod length between ball joint centres 3·18 in (80.8 mm)

MIXTURE CONTROL CABLE

– Remove and refit **19.20.13**

Removing

1. Disconnect the inner and outer cables from both carburetters.
2. Slacken the ferrule on the control panel (to facilitate the release of the locknut).
3. Unscrew the locknut behind the control panel and withdraw the cable complete through the locknut, the control panel and the bulkhead.

Refitting

4. Feed the cable complete through the control panel hole and pass the locknut over the cables.
5. Secure the outer cable assemblies to the control panel with the locknut and ferrule so that the end of the threaded part of the outer cable is flush with the ferrule on the control panel.
6. Feed the carburetter ends of the cable through the bulkhead and connect both inner and outer cables to the carburetters.

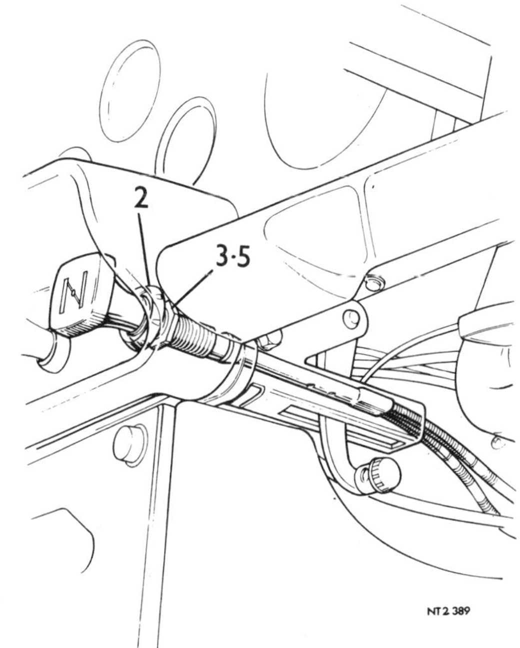

MIXTURE CONTROL CABLE – INNER

– Remove and refit **19.20.14**

Removing

1. Disconnect the inner cables from both carburetters.
2. Release the outer cables from the clips on the carburetters.
3. From within the car pull the mixture control knob out and withdraw the twin inner cables complete with the knob. – see 19.20.13.

Refitting

4. Feed the twin inner cables through the outer cables until the control knob is fully home.
5. Secure the outer cables to the clips on both carburetters.
6. Connect the inner cables to the carburetter trunnions.

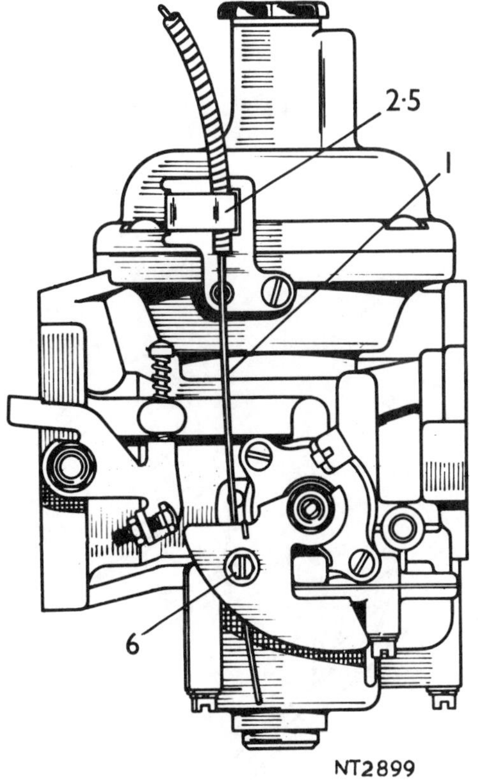

PETROL PIPE – MAIN LINE – REAR SECTION

– Remove and refit **19.40.02**

Removing

1. Place the car on a ramp.
2. Isolate the battery.
3. Drain the fuel tank 19.55.02.
4. Disconnect the pipe from the centre section as illustrated.
5. Remove the pipe from the fuel tank.

Refitting

6. Reverse instructions 1 to 5.

PETROL PIPE – MAIN LINE – CENTRE SECTION

– Remove and refit **19.40.03**

Removing

1. Place the car on a ramp.
2. Isolate the battery.
3. Drain the fuel tank 19.55.02.
4. Disconnect the centre pipe from the rear and engine end section as illustrated.

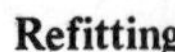

Refitting

5. Reverse instructions 1 to 4.

PETROL PIPE – MAIN LINE – ENGINE END SECTION

– Remove and refit **19.40.04**

Removing

1. Place the car on a ramp.
2. Isolate the battery.
3. Clamp the connector joining the centre section to the engine end section.
4. Disconnect the pipe from the centre section.
5. Disconnect the pipe from the fuel line filter.

Refitting

6, Reverse instructions 1 to 5.

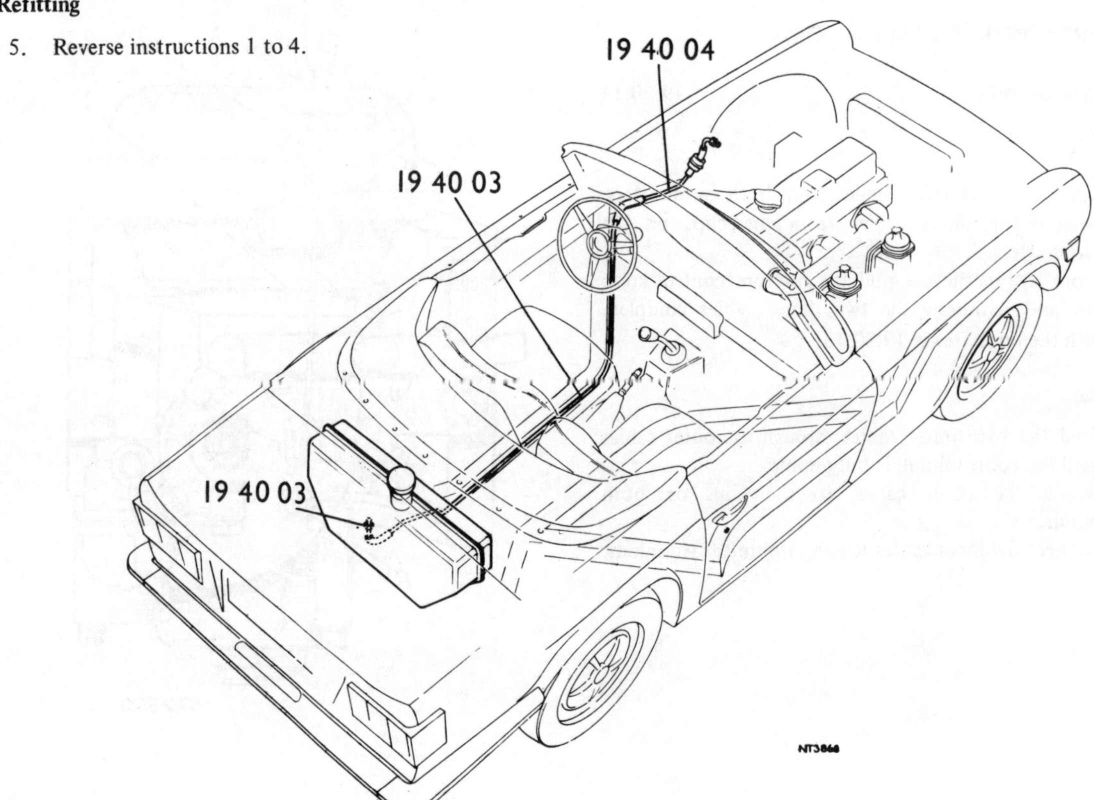

HOSE – FILLER TO TANK

– Remove and refit **19.40.19**

Removing

1. Remove the luggage compartment forward trim panel 76.13.17.
2. Remove the rear compartment trim panel 76.13.20.
3. Working from the rear compartment, slacken the top hose clip securing the filler cap assembly to the hose.
4. From the luggage compartment, slacken the hose clip securing the hose to the fuel tank.
5. Withdraw the filler cap assembly and the rubber sealing grommet.
6. Remove the filler hose complete with clips.

Refitting

7. Fit the filler hose to the fuel tank and secure with a hose clip.
8. Fit the filler cap securing clip to the hose, assemble the sealing grommet to the filler cap and fit the assembly to the tank filler hose. Secure with the hose clip.
9. Reverse instructions 1 and 2.

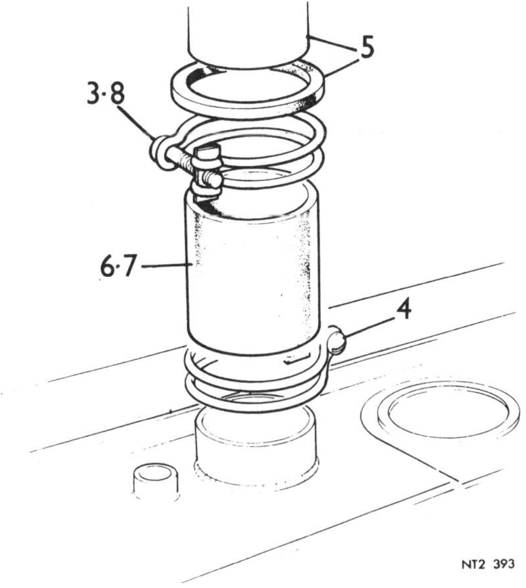

FUEL PUMP

– Test on vehicle **19.45.01**

1. Prime the fuel pump to fill the carburetter float chambers.
2. Connect a pressure gauge into the pump to carburetter fuel line.
3. Start the engine and allow it to run on the fuel remaining in the carburetters until the gauge reading on the scale ceases to rise.
4. Stop the engine and observe the gauge pressure which should remain at its highest reading for a short period. See Data for correct pressure.

NOTE: A rapid fall off indicates a leaking diaphragm or a sticking outlet valve. Failure to read within the tolerances in data suggests a defective pump or line blockage. Where the pressure is high it may be reduced by fitting extra paper washers between the pump and cylinder block. Where the pressure is low overhaul – 19.45.15 or renew the pump 19.45.15.

5. Remove the pressure gauge.

DATA

Fuel pump static pressure . . . . 1·5 p.s.i. minimum to 2·5 p.s.i. maximum

FUEL PUMP

– Clean filter 19.45.05

1. Remove the centre bolt and washer.
2. Remove the cover.
3. Remove the cover washer.
4. Remove the gauge filter and wash in petrol.
5. Loosen any sediment in the pump body and remove with compressed air. Avoid damage to the non-return valves.
6. Refit the gauze filter.
7. Refit the cover with a new cover washer and centre bolt washer. Do not overtighten the bolt.

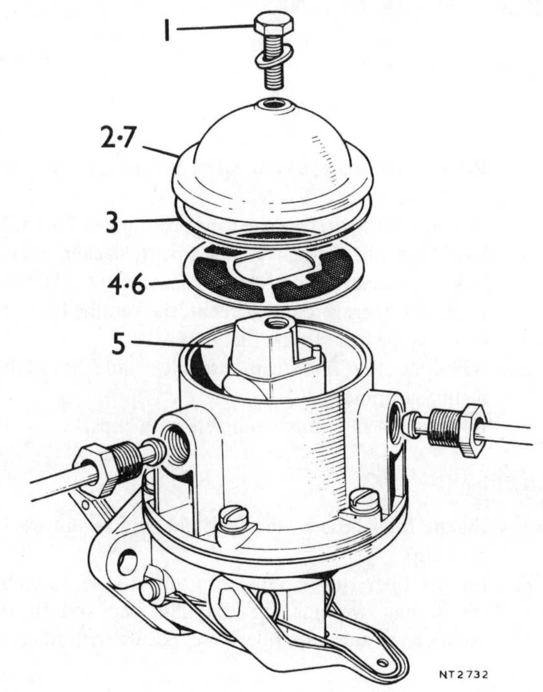

FUEL PUMP

– Remove and refit 19.45.08

Removing

1. Disconnect the main fuel supply pipe from the pump inlet connection..
2. Disconnect the pipe from the pump outlet.
3. Remove the two nuts and spring washers securing the pump to the cylinder block.
4. Remove the gasket.

Refitting

5. Clean the cylinder block and pump mating faces and fit a new gasket.
6. Reverse instructions 1 to 3 ensuring that the pump rocker arm is located correctly against the camshaft before tightening the attachment nuts.

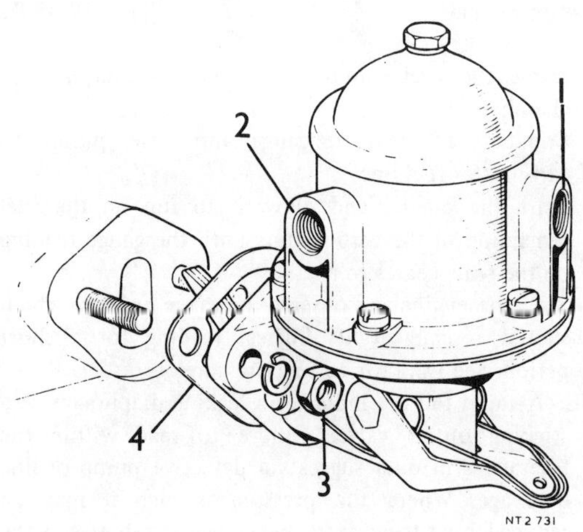

FUEL PUMP

– Overhaul **19.45.15**

Dismantling

1. Remove the fuel pump from the engine 19.45.08.
2. Remove the cover retaining bolt and washer and lift off the cover and sealing washer.
3. Remove the filter gauze.
4. Mark the relationship of the upper and lower body for re-assembly and remove the six screws and separate the two assemblies.
5. Remove the diaphragm and spring turning it through 90° and lifting it out of engagement with the link lever.
6. Remove the circlip securing the rocker arm pin.
7. Drive out the pin and remove the rocker and link lever.

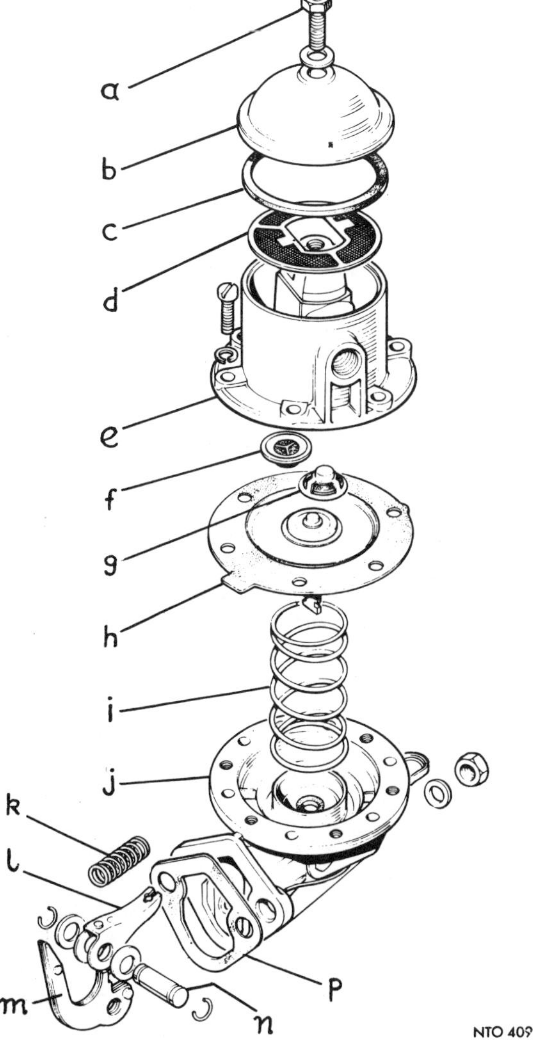

a. Cover retaining bolt
b. Cover
c. Cover washer
d. Filter gauze
e. Upper body
f. Inlet valve
g. Outlet valve
h. Diaphram
i. Diaphram spring
j. Lower body
k. Rocker return spring
l. Diaphram actuating lever.
m. Rocker
n. Rocker fulcrum pin
p. Gasket

Continued

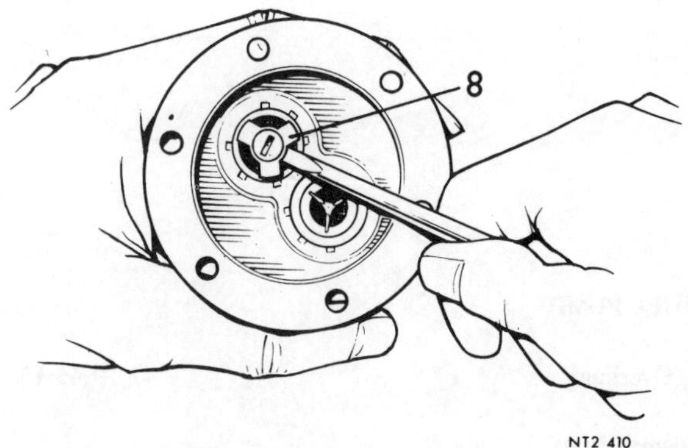

8. Remove from the upper body the inlet and outlet valves by prising them out with a screwdriver blade.

Examination

9. Clean all components in petrol and examine for wear and deterioration.
10. Check in particular the rocker and renew if wear is evident also the diaphragm and spring.
11. Check the upper and lower body mating faces for distortion and the engine mating face.

NOTE: Repair kits are available for this pump and it is advisable to fit all the new components supplied in the kit.

Re-assembling

12. Place a new washer in the base of each valve bore and fit the valves in the upper body by pressing them into the casting with a suitable tool (a piece of steel tubing 9/16 in (14·28 mm) inside diameter and 3/4 in (19·05 mm) outside diameter. Ensure that the valves are positioned correctly.
    a. Pump inlet valve pressed in with the concave side leading.
    b. Pump outlet to engine valve pressed in with the raised side leading.
13. Stake the casing round each valve in six places with a suitable punch.
14. Reverse instructions 1 to 7.

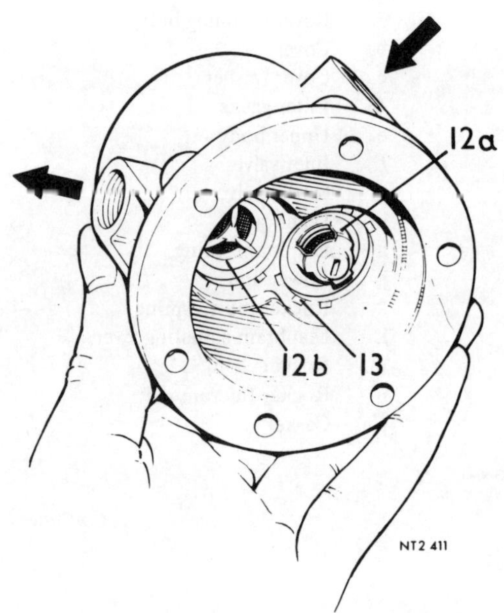

FUEL TANK

– Remove and refit **19.55.01**

Removing

1. Drain the fuel tank 19.55.02 instructions 1 and 2.
2. Remove the filler to tank hose 19.40.19.
3. Disconnect the fuel tank gauge unit leads.
4. Remove the six bolts complete with plain and spring washers securing the fuel tank to the body.
5. Withdraw the fuel tank and disconnect the evaporative emission control pipes.

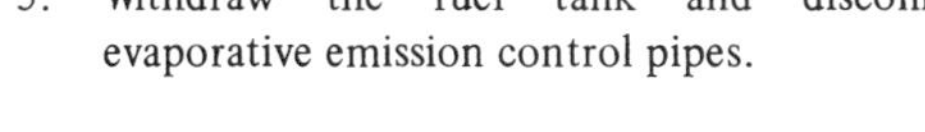

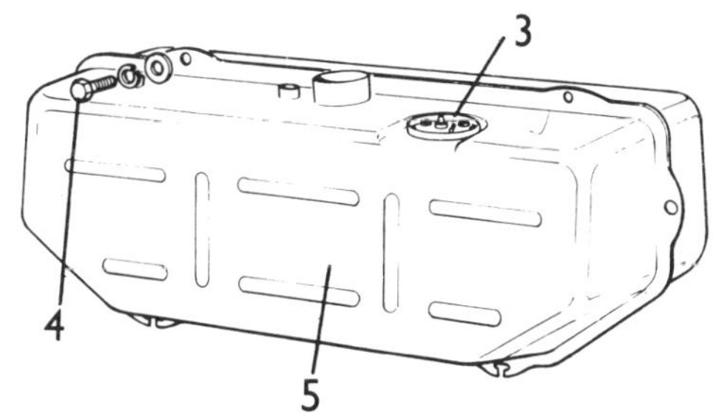

Refitting

6. Reverse instructions 1 to 5.

FUEL TANK

– Drain **19.55.02**

WARNING: Extinguish all naked lights.

1. Place the car on a ramp or over a pit.
2. Disconnect the rubber connection hose from the main line pipe and allow the fuel to drain into a suitable clean receptacle.
3. Reconnect the hose to the main line pipe.

CAUTION: If the fuel is to be returned to the tank, ensure that absolute cleanliness is observed during draining and storeage. Foreign matter or fluids in the fuel may cause damage or faults in the fuel system.

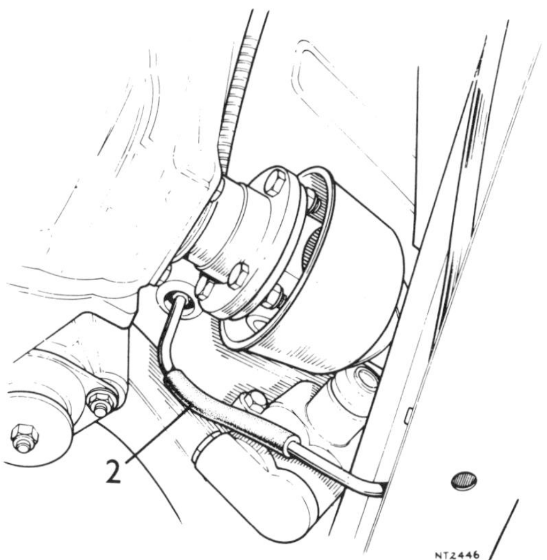

FUEL FILLER CAP

– Remove and refit **19.55.08**

Removing

1. Remove the rear compartment trim panel 76.13.20.
2. Working from the rear compartment slacken the hose clip securing the filler cap extension to the filler hose.
3. Withdraw the filler cap complete assembly.
4. Remove the rubber sealing ring.

Refitting

5. Assemble the rubber sealing ring to the filler cap extension.
6. Fit the assembly to the body ensuring, that the filler cap extension locates properly in the filler hose.
7. Secure the hose to the filler cap with the hose clip.
8. Refit the rear compartment trim panel 76.13.20.

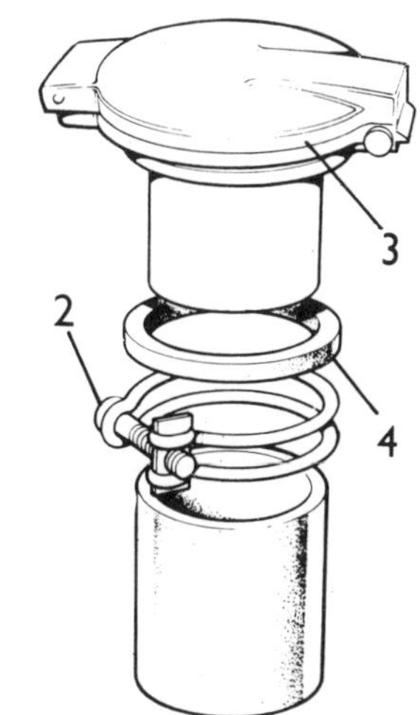

COOLING SYSTEM OPERATIONS

COOLANT

– Drain and refill 26.10.01

Drain

1. Set heater controls to HOT.
2. Remove the radiator cap. **CAUTION** If the engine is hot exercise care. Turn the cap slowly and release any pressure in the system before removing the cap.
3. Disconnect the radiator bottom hose at the radiator.
4. Remove the drain plug on the rear, right hand side of the cylinder block.
5. When system has drained, fit and tighten the drain plug and reconnect the radiator bottom hose.

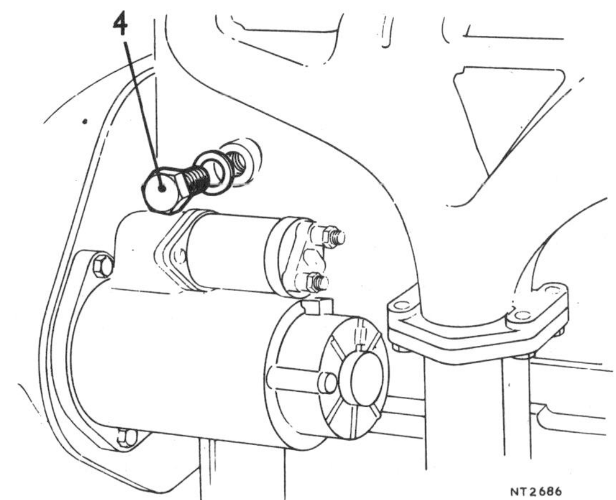

Refill

6. Fill the cooling system with clean soft water and, if required, anti-freeze.
7. Fit the radiator cap and run the engine at a fast idle for approximately 1 to 2 minutes.
8. Remove the radiator cap and top up as necessary.
9. Replace the radiator cap and check the system for leaks.
10. Top up the overflow bottle to the half full level.

COOLING SYSTEM

– Pressure Test 26.10.07

Radiator cap

1. Rinse the radiator filler cap in clean water and while it is still wet fit the cap to the pressure tester.
2. Pump up pressure until the gauge pointer ceases to rise. Reject the filler cap if the gauge does not register and maintain a pressure of 1 lb/in^2 (0·06 kg/cm^2) below the figure stamped on the filler cap for a period of at least ten seconds without further pumping.

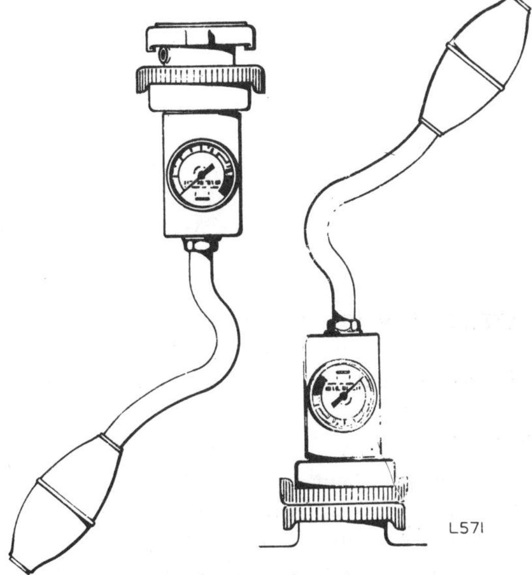

Radiator

3. Warm the engine.
4. Remove the radiator filler cap and top up the system if required.
5. Fit the pressure tester to the radiator.
6. Pump up pressure to the figure stamped on the filler cap, and check that this pressure can be maintained for approximately ten seconds without further pumping.
7. Check for leaks while system is pressurised. A pressure drop within ten seconds and no external leaks is indicative of internal leakage.

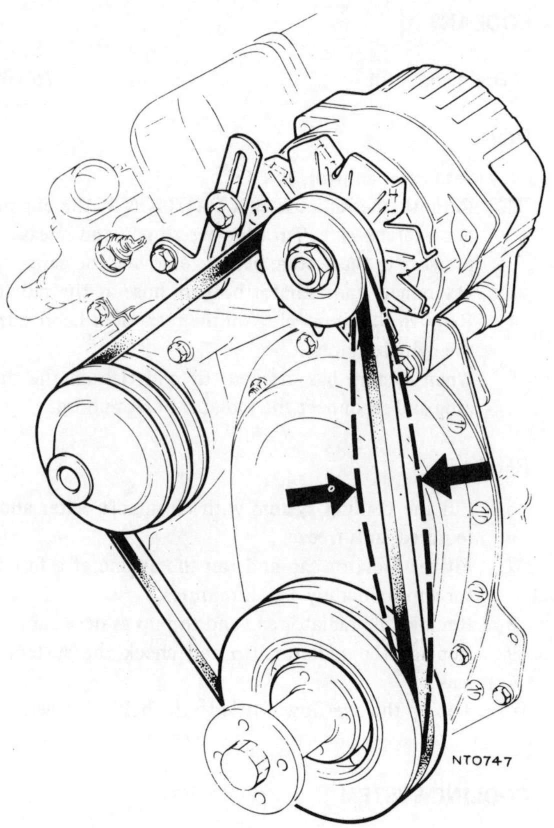

WATER PUMP BELT TENSION

– Check and adjust **26.20.01**

Checking

1. Check that the belt is capable of approximately ¾ to 1 in (19·1 to 25·4 mm) deflection at the mid- point of its longest run.

Adjusting

2. Slacken the alternator pivot bolt nut and the adjustment bracket bolt.
3. Pivot the alternator to obtain belt deflection as instruction 1.
4. Tighten the alternator pivot bolt nut and the adjustment bracket bolt.

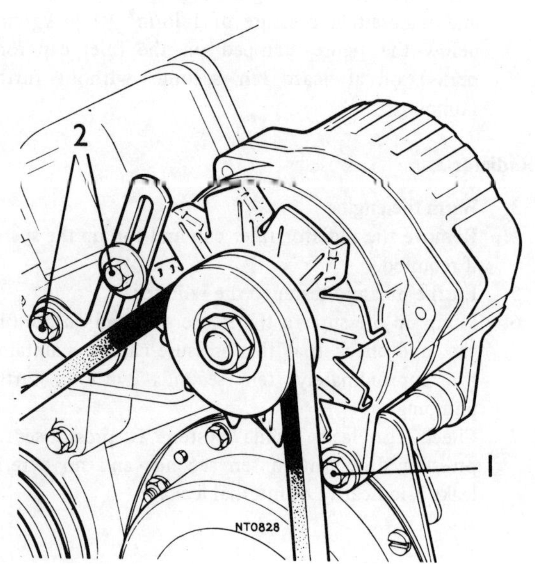

WATER PUMP BELT

– Remove and refit **26.20.07**

Removing

1. Slacken the alternator pivot and nut.
2. Slacken the adjustment bracket bolts.
3. Pivot the alternator towards the engine.
4. Release the belt from the alternator, water pump, and crankshaft pulley.
5. Remove the belt.

Refitting

6. Reverse instructions 1 to 5.

FAN (Carburetter engines)

– Remove and refit 26.25.06

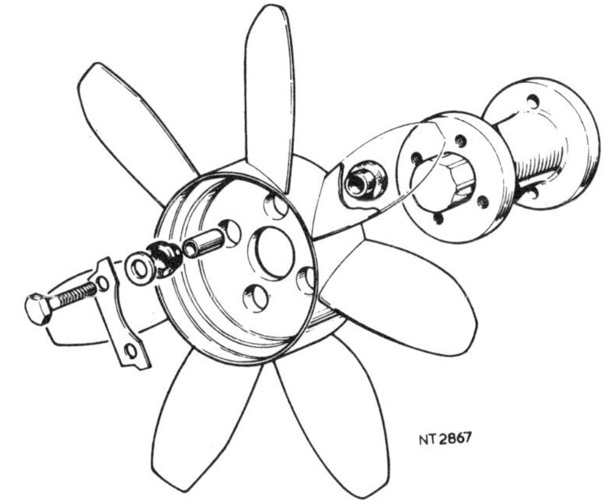

Removing

1. Remove the radiator 26.40.01.
2. Straighten the lock tabs of the fan securing bolts.
3. Remove the lockplates, four bolts and washers securing the fan to the crankshaft extension and withdraw the fan complete with bushes.

Refitting

4. Ensure that the mounting bushes and spacers are fitted and in sound condition.
5. Offer up the fan to the crankshaft extension and align the mounting holes. Note that the recessed faces of the fan hub must be fitted adjacent to the radiator.
6. Fit the four securing bolts and washers. Evenly tighten the bolts and bend over lock tabs.
7. Fit the radiator 26.40.01

FAN (P.I. Engines)

– Remove and refit 26.25.06

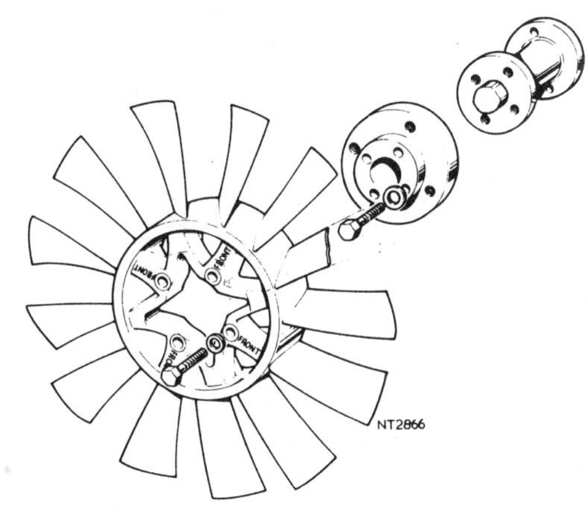

Removing

1. Remove the radiator 26.40.01.

2a. **To remove the fan only** remove the outer four bolts and washers securing the fan to the fan adaptor, and withdraw the fan.

2b. **To remove fan and adaptor** remove the inner four bolts and washers securing the fan adaptor to the crankshaft extension.

Refitting

Fan only

3a. Offer up the fan to the adaptor ensuring that the face marked FRONT is fitted adjacent to the radiator.

4a. Align the mounting holes and fit the four securing bolts and washers. Evenly tighten the bolts.

5a. Fit the radiator 26.40.01. and refill the cooling system.

Fan complete with adaptor

3b. Offer up the fan and adaptor to the crankshaft extension and align the mounting holes.

4b. Fit the four securing bolts and washers. Evenly tighten the bolts.

5b. Fit the radiator 26.40.01 and refill the cooling system.

HOSES

– Remove and refit

– Radiator – top	**26.30.01**
– Radiator – bottom	**26.30.07**
– Manifold to water pump pipe	**26.30.17**
– Heater to water pump	**26.30.18**
– Heater valve to heater	**26.30.40**
– Water pump housing to manifold	**26.30.46**

Removing

1. Drain the cooling system.
2. Slacken the hose clips.
3. Remove the hose.

Refitting

4. Reverse instructions 1 to 3.

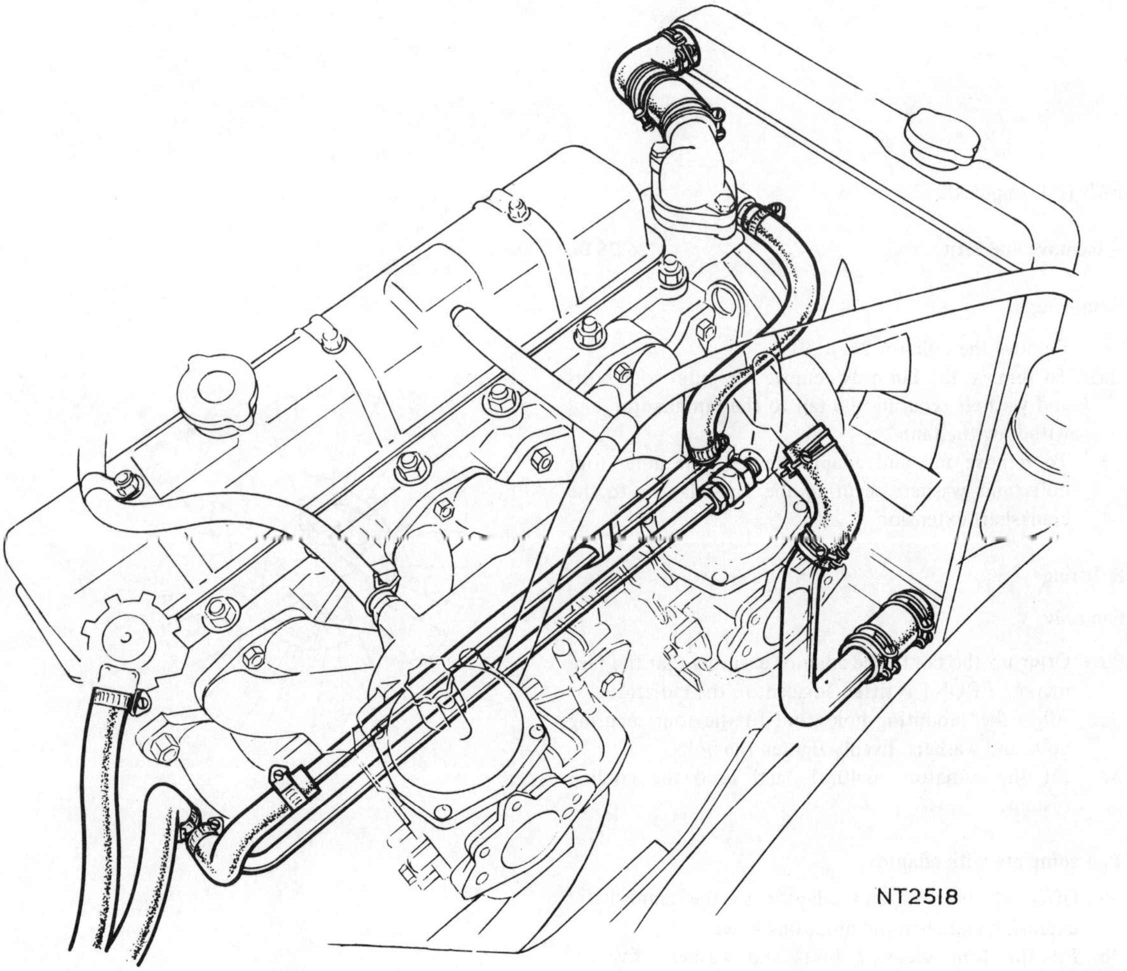

NT2518

OVERFLOW PIPE

– Remove and refit **26.30.31**

Removing

1. Detach the overflow pipe from the radiator.
2. Withdraw the overflow pipe from the filler cap of the overflow bottle.

Refitting

3. Reverse instructions 1 and 2. Ensure that the bottle end of the tube reaches to approximately 3/8 in (9·5 mm) of the bottom of the bottle.

RADIATOR

– Remove and refit **26.40.01**

Removing

1. Drain the cooling system.
2. Disconnect the top hose at the radiator.
3. Slacken the two bolts and nuts securing the lower end of the radiator stays to the tubular cross member.
4. Remove the two nuts and spring washers securing the upper end of the radiator stays to the radiator.
5. Detach the stays from the radiator.
6. Remove the two bolts and washers (earlier cars) *or* two nuts and washers (later cars) securing the radiator to the car. **
7. Withdraw the radiator and the two packing pieces.

Refitting

8. Locate the radiator in position on the car and fit the two packing pieces below the radiator mounting brackets. Fit the two mounting bolts and washers.
9. Reverse instructions 1 to 5.

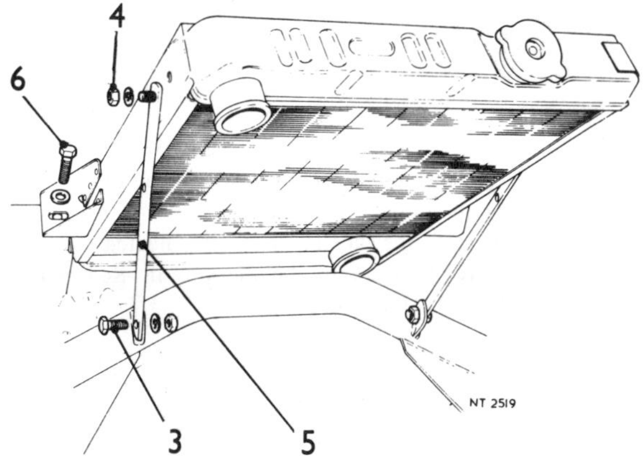

THERMOSTAT

– Remove and refit 26.45.01

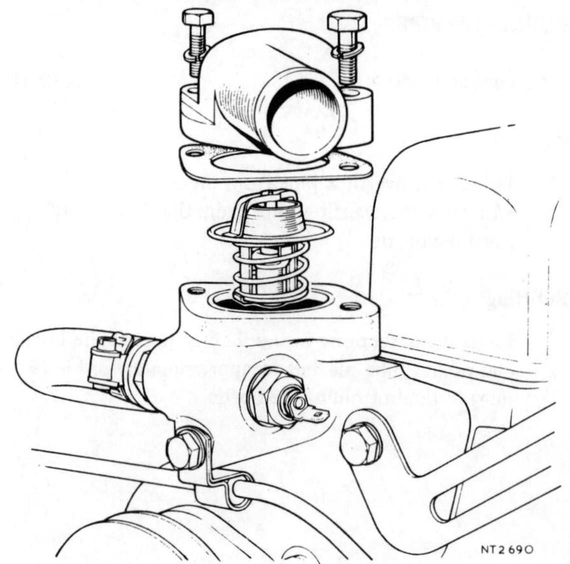

Removing

1. Drain the cooling system.
2. Remove the two bolts and spring washers securing the thermostat elbow to the water pump housing and withdraw the thermostat elbow.
3. Withdraw the thermostat.

Refitting

4. Clean the mating faces of the thermostat elbow and water pump housing.
5. Insert the thermostat in the water pump housing.
6. Fit a new gasket and the thermostat elbow. Tighten the two securing bolts.
7. Fill the cooling system.

THERMOSTAT

– Test 26.45.09

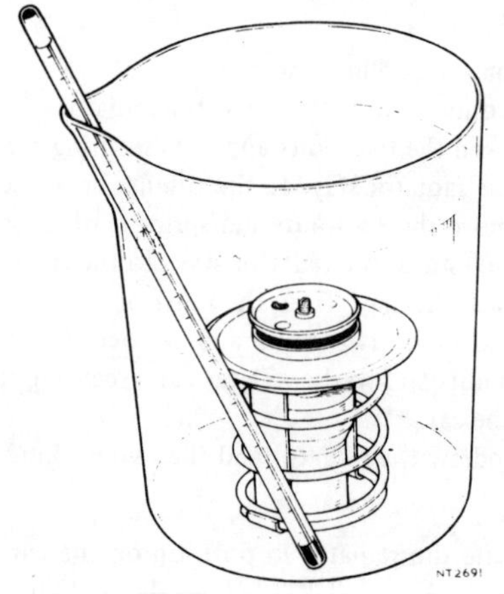

1. Determine the opening temperature of the thermostat stamped on the flange or base.
2. Immerse the thermostat in water heated to the opening temperature of the thermostat. Renew the thermostat if it fails to open.

WATER PUMP

– Remove and refit 26.50.01

Removing

1. Drain the cooling system.
2. Slacken the alternator mounting bolts, release the tension from the water pump/alternator drive belt, and slip the belt from the water pump pully.
3. Remove the three nuts and spring washers securing the water pump mounting flange to the water pump body.
4. Withdraw the water pump.

Refitting

5. Clean the water pump mounting faces and fit a new gasket.
6. Reverse instructions 1 to 3.

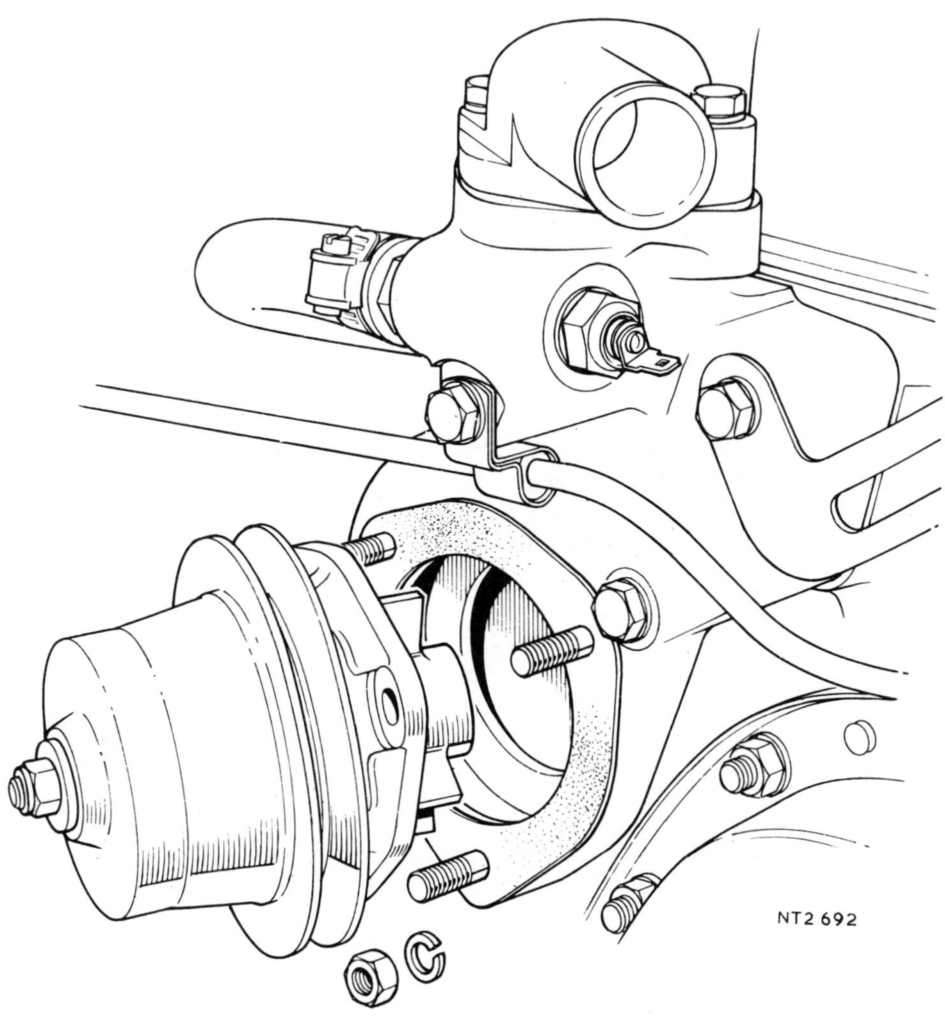

WATER PUMP HOUSING

– Remove and refit **26.50.03**

Removing

1. Drain the cooling system.
2. Disconnect the radiator top hose from the thermostat elbow.
3. Disconnect the bottom hose from the water pump housing.
4. Slacken the alternator mounting bolts, release tension from the water pump/alternator drive belt and slip the belt from the water pump pulley.
5. Disconnect the spade terminal from the temperature transmitter.
6. Remove the two bolts and spring washers securing the thermostat elbow to the water pump housing and withdraw the elbow and thermostat.
7. Disconnect the water pipe union at the rear of the water pump housing.
8. Remove the three bolts and spring washers securing the water pump housing to the cylinder head. The top right hand bolt also secures the alternator adjusting bracket. Note that the three bolts are of different lengths· Observe locations.
9. Withdraw the water pump housing.
10. Remove the water pump and temperature transmitter if required.

Refitting

11. Fit the water pump and temperature transmitter (if removed).
12. Ensure the mating faces of cylinder head and water pump housing are clean.
13. Using a new gasket offer the water pump housing to the cylinder head and engage the three securing bolts and spring washers. The alternator adjusting bracket is fitted to the top right hand bolt.
14. Fit the water pipe union to the water pump housing and tighten the housing securing bolts.
15. Reverse instructions 1 to 6.

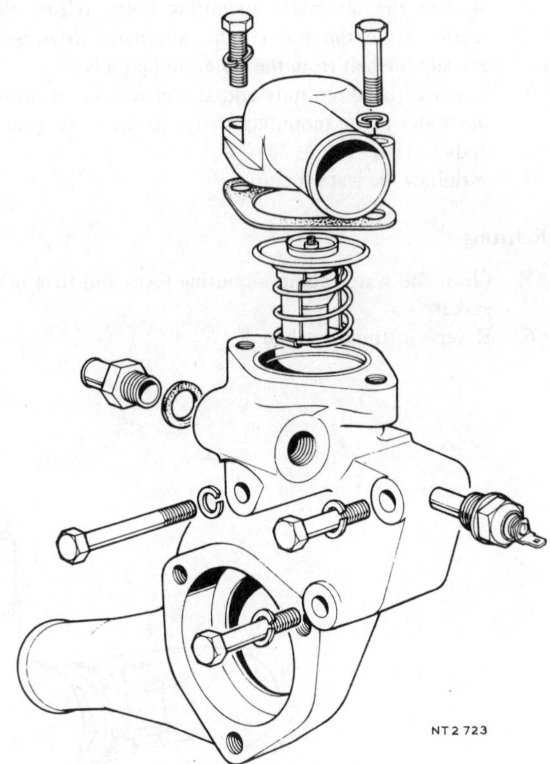

MANIFOLD AND EXHAUST SYSTEM OPERATIONS

EXHAUST SYSTEM 30.00.00

** On earlier carburetter engined cars the exhaust system differs from that shown in this Section in that it has a single exhaust pipe up to the silencer at the rear. **

EXHAUST SYSTEM COMPLETE

– Remove and refit 30.10.01

Removing

1. Slacken the two clips securing the front intermediate pipes to the rear intermediate pipes.
2. Remove the nut, bolt and clamp plate securing the tail pipes to the flexible mounting.
3. Remove the two nuts and washers from the clips securing the silencer assembly to the rear intermediate pipes and mounting bracket.
4. Remove the silencer assembly and rear intermediate pipes.
5. Remove the four nuts and lockwashers securing the front pipes to the manifold.
6. Remove the nut, bolt and lock washer securing the front intermediate pipes to the mounting bracket.
7. Remove the front pipes and front intermediate pipes.

Refitting

8. Fit new flange packing.
9. Reverse instructions 1 to 7, ensuring gas proof joints at all pipe connections.

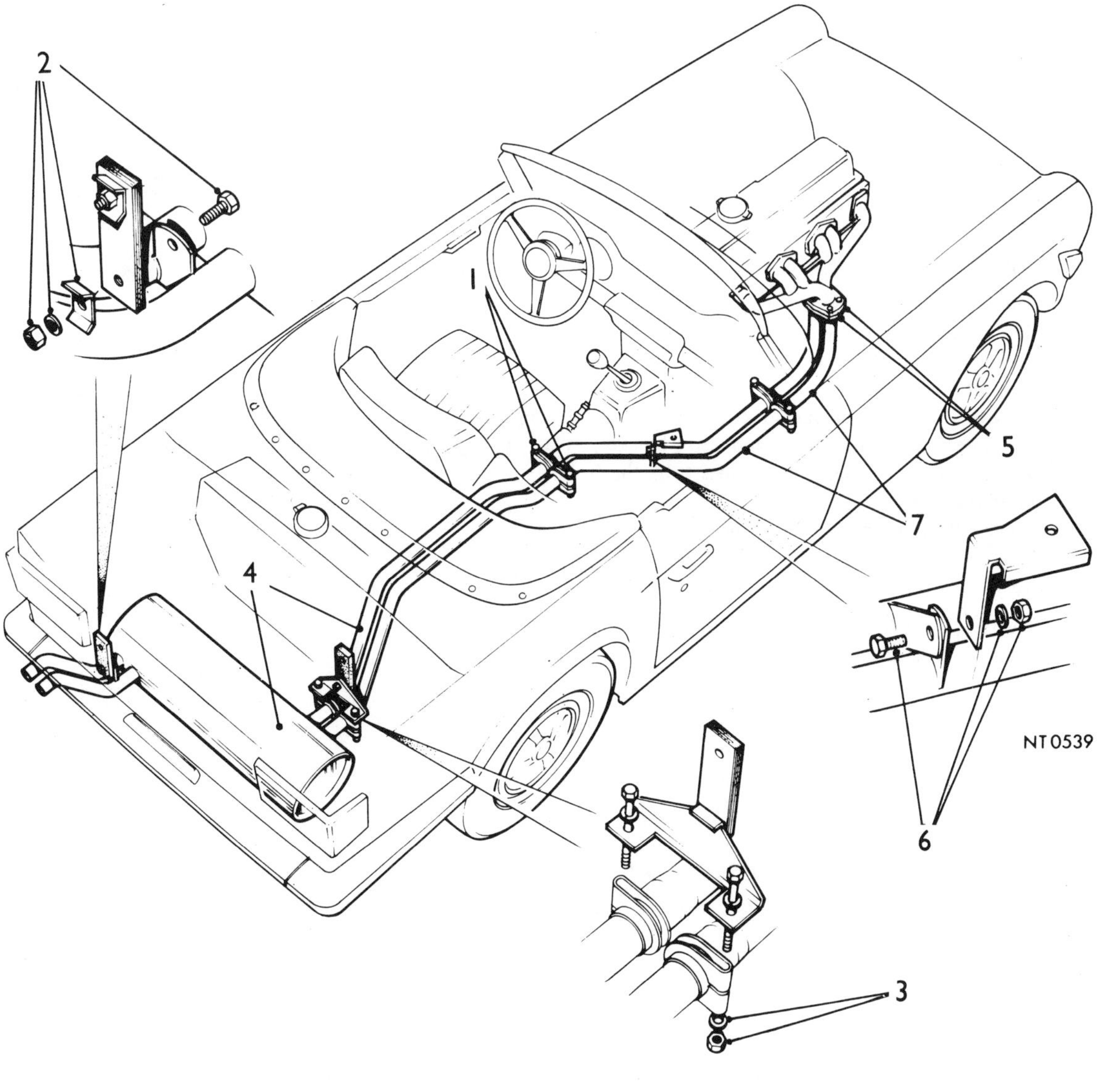

FRONT PIPES

– Remove and refit **30.10.09**

Removing

1. Remove the front intermediate pipes 30.10.11/30.10.12.
2. Remove the four nuts and lockwashers securing the front pipes to the manifold.
3. Remove the front pipes.

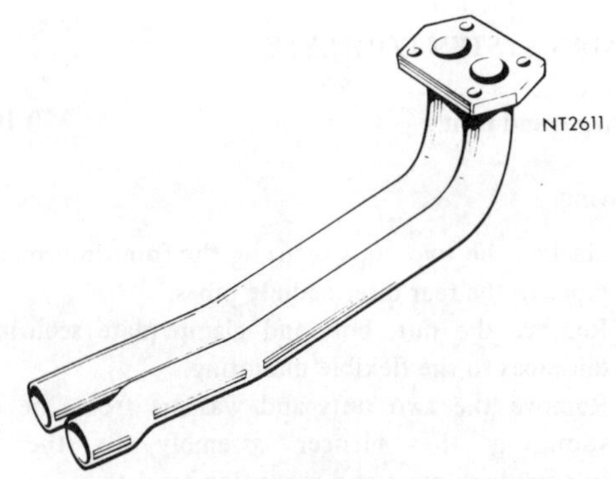

Refitting

4. Refit the front intermediate pipes but do not fully tighten the clips.
5. Slide the front pipes into the intermediate pipes sufficiently to ensure gas proof joints.
6. Fit the new flange packing.
7. Align the front pipes over the manifold studs and replace and tighten the nuts and lockwashers.
8. Tighten all clips, and fixings.

INTERMEDIATE PIPES – FRONT

– Remove and refit – L.H. **30.10.11**

– R.H. **30.10.12**

Removing

1. Slacken the two clips securing the front intermediate pipes to the rear intermediate pipes.
2. Slacken the two clips securing the front pipes to the front intermediate pipes.
3. Remove the nut, bolt and lockwasher securing the front intermediate pipes to the mounting bracket.
4. Disengage the rear intermediate pipes from the front intermediate pipes.
5. Remove the front intermediate pipes.

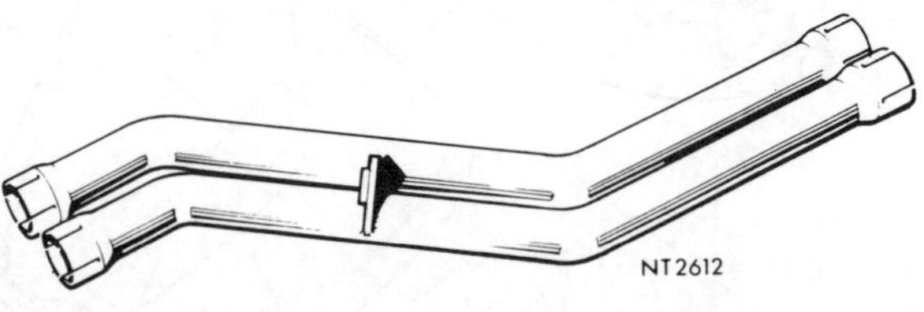

Refitting

6. Reverse instructions 1 to 5 ensuring gas proof joints at all pipe connections.

ˈILENCER ASSEMBLY

– Remove and refit **30.10.14**

Removing

1. Remove the nut, bolt and clamp plate securing the tail pipes to the flexible mounting.
2. Slacken the two clips securing the silencer assembly to the rear intermediate pipes and mounting bracket.
3. Remove the silencer assembly.

Refitting

4. Reverse instructions 1 to 3, ensuring gas proof joints at the pipe connections.

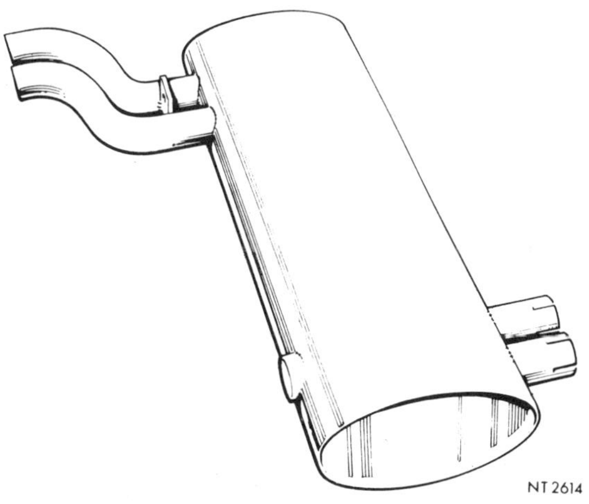

INTERMEDIATE PIPES – REAR

- Remove and refit – L.H. **30.10.24**

– R.H. **30.10.25**

Removing

1. Slacken the two clips securing the silencer assembly to the rear intermediate pipes and mounting bracket.
2. Slacken the two clips securing the front intermediate pipes to the rear intermediate pipes.
3. Disengage the silencer assembly from the rear intermediate pipes.
4. Remove the rear intermediate pipes.

Refitting

5. Reverse instructions 1 to 4, ensuring gas proof joints at all pipe connections.

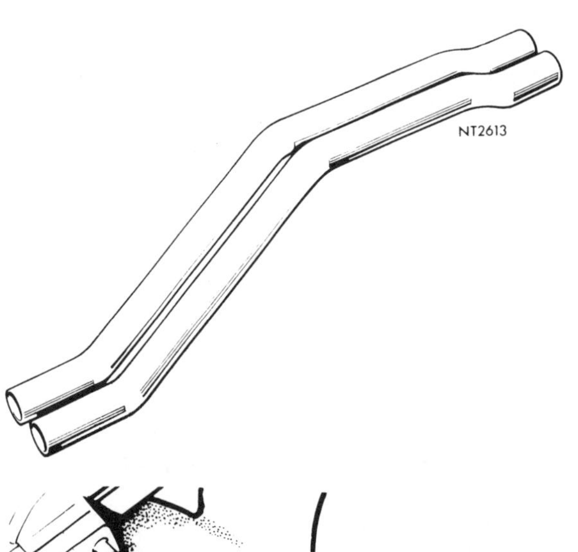

,OWN PIPE FLANGE PACKING

– Remove and refit **30.10.26**

Removing

1. Remove the nut and bolt securing the front intermediate pipes to the support bracket.
2. Remove the four nuts and lockwashers securing the front pipes to the manifold.
3. Pull down the pipes and remove the flange packing.

Refitting

4. Fit new flange packing.
5. Reverse instructions 1 and 2, ensuring that the stud nuts are tightened to 20 to 25 lbf ft (2·8 to 3·5 kgf m).

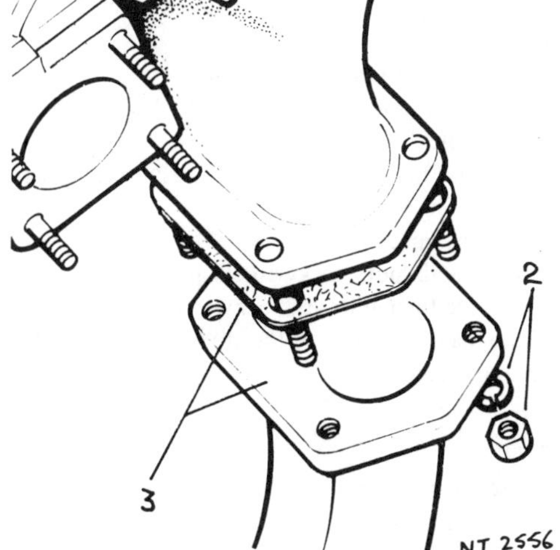

EXHAUST MANIFOLD

– Remove and refit **30.15.01**

Removing

1. Remove the nut and bolt securing the front intermediate pipes to the support bracket.
2. Remove the four nuts and lockwashers securing the front pipes to the manifold.
3. Pull down the pipes and remove the flange packing.
4. Remove the induction manifolds 30.15.02.
5. Remove the four nuts and lockwashers securing the exhaust manifold to the cylinder head.
6. Pull the manifold clear of the studs and remove it from the engine.

Refitting

7. Renew the flange packing.
8. Reverse instructions 1 to 6, ensuring that all stud nuts are tightened to 20 to 25 lbf ft. (2·8 to 3·5 kgf m).

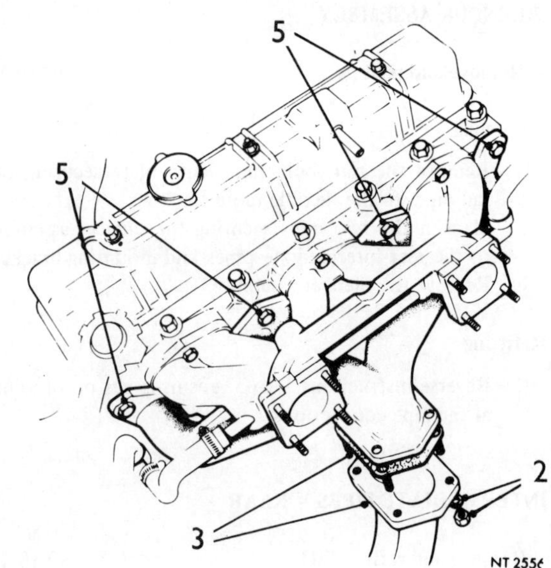

INDUCTION MANIFOLDS (PETROL INJECTION MODELS)
**** (Up to Engine No. CP 77609E) ****

– Remove and refit **30.15.02**

Removing

1. Remove the air intake manifold 19.70.01.
2. Disconnect the brake servo hose from the rear manifold.
3. Disconnect the metering control hose from the centre manifold.
4. Disconnect the air intake manifold hose from the front manifold – one corbin clip.
5. Remove the cold start cam return spring.
6. Slacken the trunnion bolt.
7. Remove the lower locknut and disconnect the cold start cable.
8. Remove the split pin and clevis pin.
9. Remove the lower locknut and disconnect the throttle cable.
10. Remove the three setscrews, lockwashers and clamp plates.
11. Remove the injectors.
12. Remove the six nuts, lockwashers and clamps.
13. Remove the three nuts and lockwashers.
14. Pull the manifolds clear of the studs and remove them from the engine.

Refitting

15. Reverse instructions 1 to 14, ensuring that all stud nuts are tightened to 20 to 25 lbf ft (2·8 to 3·5 kgf m).

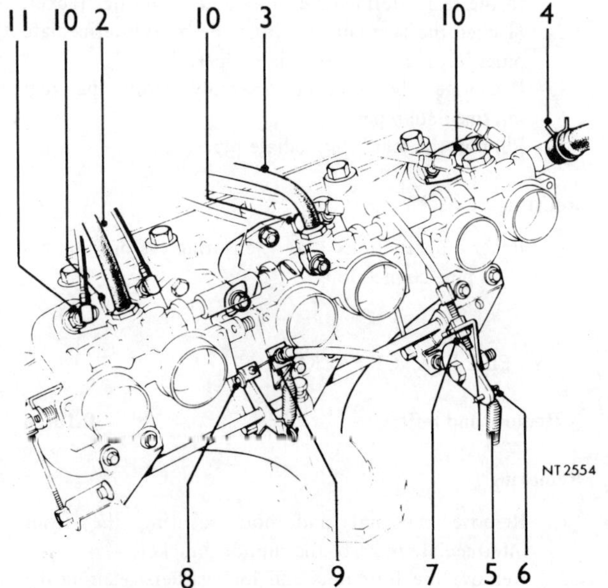

INDUCTION MANIFOLD (CARBURETTER MODELS)

– Remove and refit **30.15.02**

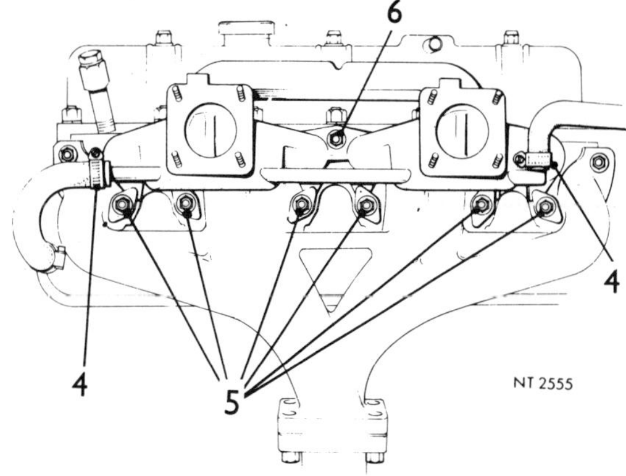

Removing

1. Remove the air cleaner 19.10.01.
2. Remove the carburetter 19.15.11.
3. Partially drain the cooling system.
4. Slacken the two clips and disconnect the hoses from the water pipe.
5. Remove the six nuts, lockwashers and clamps.
6. ** Remove the three nuts and lock washers and (later USA Markets cars only) release the Exhaust Gas Recirculation valve connection at the induction manifold. **
7. Pull the manifold clear of the studs and remove it from the engine.

Refitting

8. Reverse instructions 1 to 7, ensuring that all stud nuts are tightened to 20 to 25 lbf ft (2·8 to 3·5 kgf m).

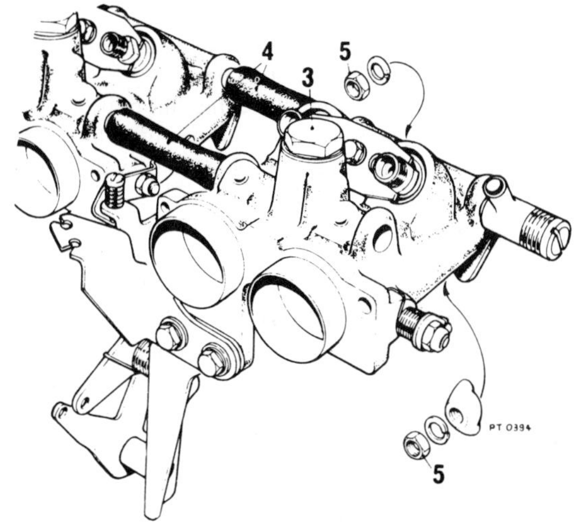

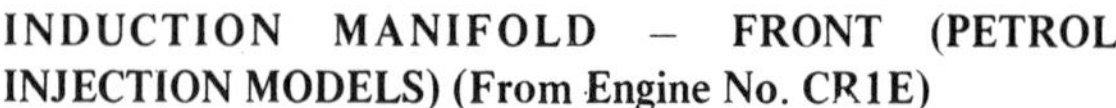

INDUCTION MANIFOLD – FRONT (PETROL INJECTION MODELS) (From Engine No. CR1E)

– Remove and refit **30.15.02**

Removing

1. Remove the air intake manifold. 19.70.01.
2. Disconnect the throttle cable from the throttle linkage.
3. Remove the clamp bolt and clamp and withdraw the two injectors.
4. Ease the rubber connectors to one side on
   a. the air rail
   b. the balance pipe.
5. Remove the three nuts and spring washers and the two clamps securing the manifold to the cylinder head.
6. Slacken the front throttle adjusting screw clear of the butterfly lever.
7. Withdraw the manifold complete with the throttle linkage.
8. Remove the two bolts, plain and spring washers securing the throttle linkage to the manifold and remove the linkage.

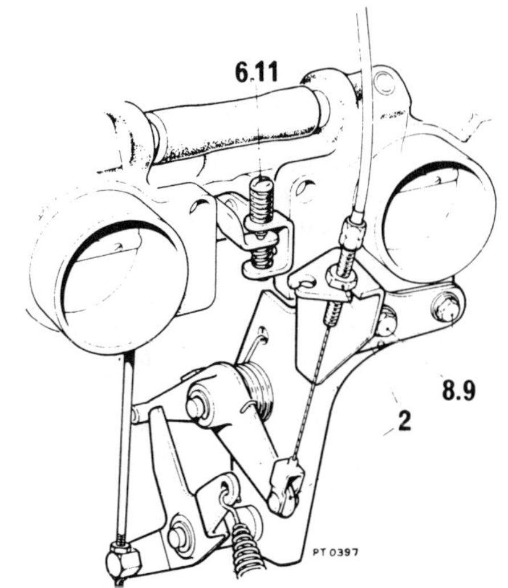

Refitting

9. Refit the linkage to the manifold.
10. Refit the manifold and loosely secure with the three nuts, spring washers and clamps.
11. Manoeuvre the manifold until the butterfly lever on the centre manifold is spaced equidistant between the fork lever of the front butterflies and tighten the manifold nuts.
12. Reverse instructions 2 to 4.
13. Adjust the throttle butterflies. 19.20.05

INDUCTION MANIFOLD – REAR (PETROL INJECTION MODELS) (From Engine No. CR1E)

– Remove and refit 30.15.03

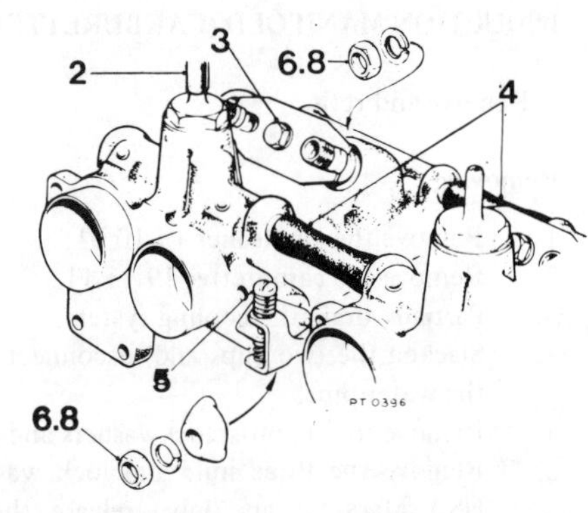

Removing

1. Remove the air intake manifold. 19.70.01.
2. Remove the brake servo vacuum hose from the manifold.
3. Remove the clamp bolt and plate and remove the two injectors.
4. Ease the rubber connectors to one side on
   a. the air rail
   b. the balance pipe.
5. Slacken the rear throttle adjusting screw clear of the butterfly lever.
6. Remove the three nuts, spring washers and two clamps securing the manifold to the cylinder head.
7. Withdraw the manifold.

Refitting

8. Refit the manifold loosely securing with the three nuts, spring washers and clamps.
9. Manoeuvre the manifold so that the butterfly lever is spaced equidistant between the fork lever of the centre manifold. Finally tighten the manifold nuts.
10. Reverse instructions 2 to 4.
11. Adjust the throttle butterflies. 19.20.05.

INDUCTION MANIFOLD – CENTRE (PETROL INJECTION MODELS) (From Engine No. CR1E)

– Remove and refit 30.15.04

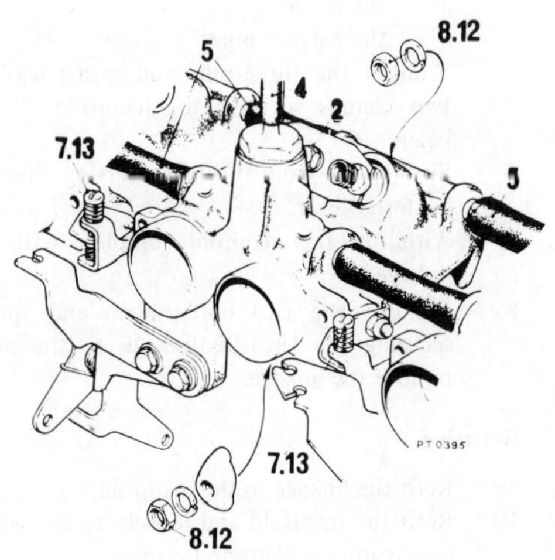

Removing

1. Remove the air intake manifold. 19.70.01.
2. Remove the clamp bolt and clamp and withdraw the two injectors.
3. Disconnect the cold start cable from the manifold linkage.
4. Disconnect the metering unit vacuum pipe from the manifold.
5. Ease the rubber connectors to one side on
   a. the air rail
   b. the balance pipe.
6. Disconnect the cold start cam return spring.
7. Slacken both throttle adjusting screws clear of the butterfly levers.
8. Remove the three nuts, spring washers and clamps securing the manifold to the cylinder head.
9. Withdraw the manifold complete with the cold start linkage.
10. Remove the two bolts, spring and plain washers securing the linkage to the manifold and withdraw the linkage.

Refitting

11. Fit the linkage to the manifold.
12. Fit and loosely secure the manifold with the three nuts, spring washers and two clamps.
13. Manoeuvre the manifold until the two butterfly levers are equidistant between the two fork levers and finally tighten the manifold nuts.
14. Reverse instructions 2 to 6.
15. Adjust the throttle butterflies. 19.20.05

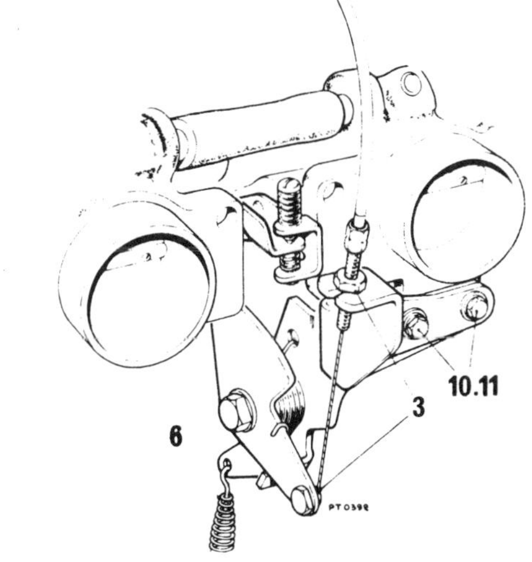

MANIFOLD GASKET

– Remove and refit **30.15.15**

Removing

1. Remove the induction manifold 30.15.02.
2. Remove the exhaust manifold 30.15.01.
3. Remove the gasket.

Refitting

4. Renew the gasket and fit with the metal side towards the manifold.
5. Reverse instructions 1 and 2, ensuring that all stud nuts are tightened to 20 to 25 lbf ft (2·8 to 3·5 kgf m).

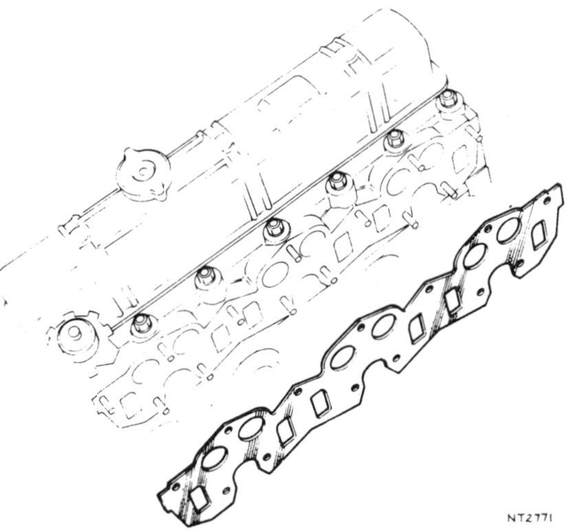

CLUTCH OPERATIONS

CLUTCH ASSEMBLY

– Remove and refit 33.10.01

Removing

1. Remove the gearbox 37.20.01.
2. Progressively slacken and remove the six bolts and spring washers securing the clutch to the flywheel.
3. Withdraw the clutch and the driven plate.

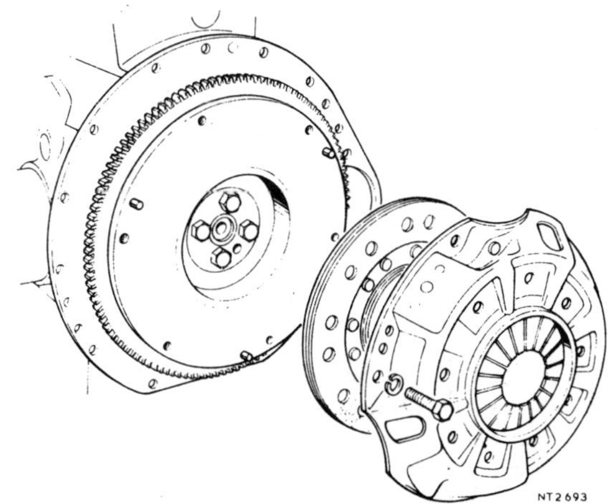

Refitting

4. Offer up the driven plate to the flywheel using a dummy input shaft. The longer boss of the driven plate hub must be fitted away from the flywheel.
5. Engage the clutch assembly in the three flywheel locating dowels.
6. Fit and evenly tighten the six securing bolts and spring washers. (torque 16 to 20 lbf ft – 2·2 to 2·8 kgf m).
7. Withdraw the dummy input shaft.
8. Refit the gearbox 37.20.01.

HYDRAULIC SYSTEM

– Bleed 33.15.01

1. Check the level of fluid in the master cylinder reservoir and top up as necessary.
2. Attach a bleed tube to the nipple on the slave cylinder. Allow the free end of the tube to hang submerged in brake fluid in a transparent container.
3. Slacken the bleed nipple (90 to 180 degrees is usually adequate).
4. Depress the clutch pedal and allow the pedal to return. Continue until fluid free of air issues from the slave cylinder. Hold the pedal depressed, close the bleed nipple and release the pedal.
5. Remove the bleed tube and container.
6. Top up the reservoir. It is necessary to ensure that the fluid in the reservoir is never permitted to fall to a level whereby air can be admitted to the system. When topping up the reservoir do not use the aerated and possibly contaminated fluid exhausted from the system during the process of bleeding.

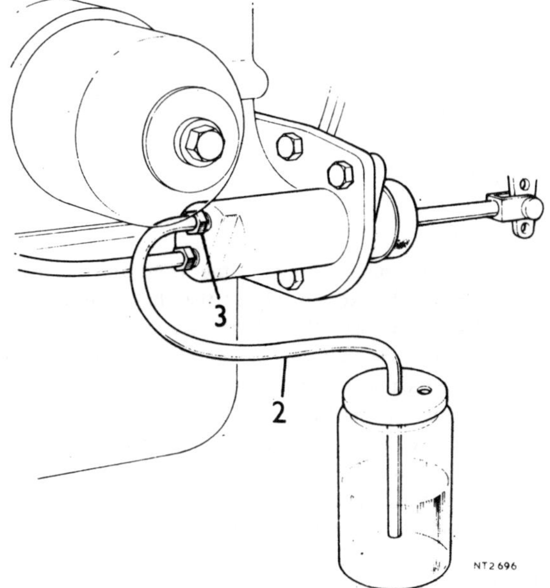

FLUID PIPE

– Remove and refit **33.15.09**

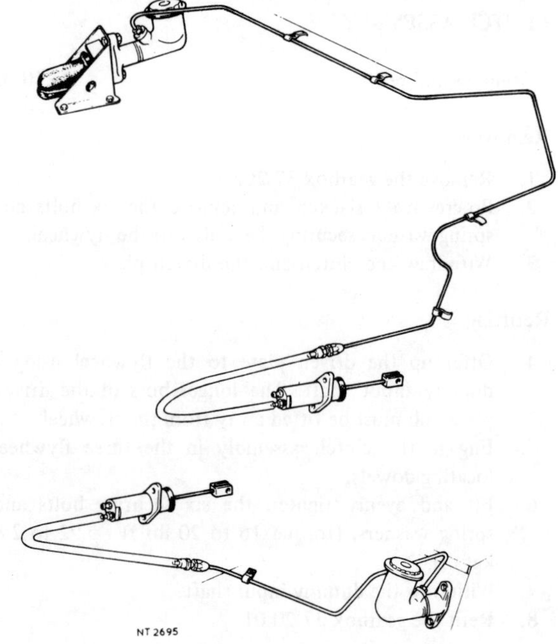

Removing

1. Disconnect the fluid pipe union from the clutch master cylinder.
2. Disconnect the fluid pipe union at the upper end of the flexible pipe.
3. Release the fluid pipe from its retaining clips and remove the pipe from the car.
4. Unscrew the flexible pipe union at the slave cylinder.

Refitting

5. Align the pipe in position on the car.
6. Screw the flexible pipe lower union to the slave cylinder.
7. Secure the pipe in its retaining clips.
8. Connect the pipe unions to the clutch master cylinder and the upper end of the flexible pipe.
9. Bleed the system 33.15.01.

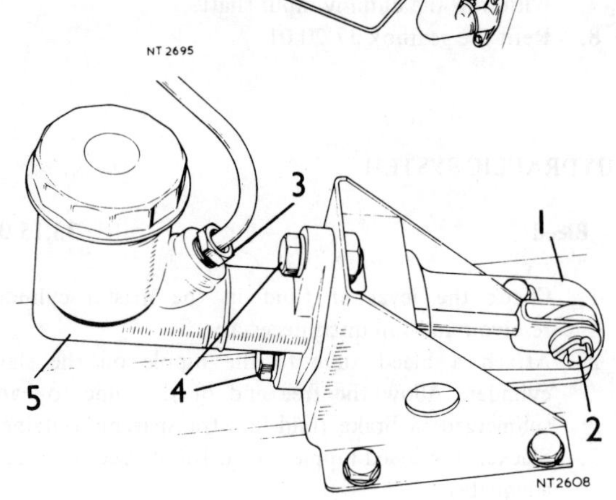

MASTER CYLINDER

– Remove and refit **33.20.01**

Removing

1. Lift the rubber boot at the front of the master cylinder bracket to expose the clutch pedal/master cylinder linkage. *(Right hand steering models only).*
2. Remove the split pin, washer and clevis pin securing the clutch pedal to the master cylinder push rod.
3. Disconnect the fluid pipe from the master cylinder.
4. Remove the two bolts and spring washers securing the master cylinder flange to the mounting bracket, or scuttle as appropriate.
5. Withdraw the master cylinder.

Refitting

6. Reverse instructions 1 to 5.
7. Bleed the system.

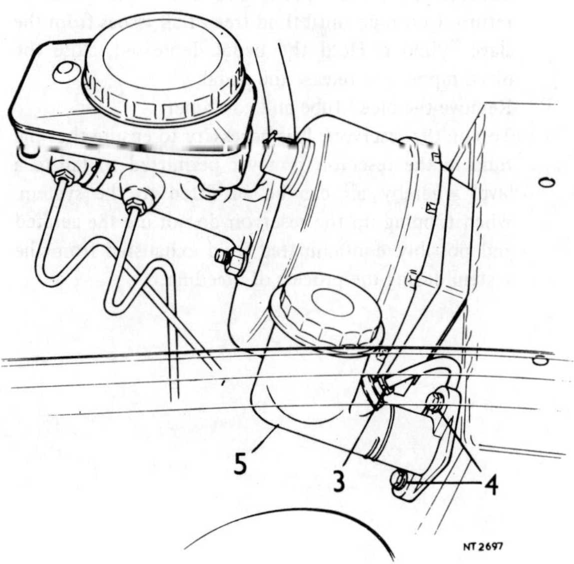

MASTER CYLINDER

– Overhaul **33.20.07**

1. Remove the master cylinder from the car 33.20.01
2. Drain the fluid reservoir.
3. Detach the rubber boot from the master cylinder and withdraw it from the push rod.
4. Remove the circlip retaining the push rod to the master cylinder and withdraw the push rod and washer.
5. Withdraw the piston, spring, and seal assembly.
6. Straighten the prong of the spring thimble and remove the thimble and spring from the piston.
7. Release the valve stem from the keyhole slot in the thimble.
8. Slide the valve seal spacer along the valve stem.
9. Remove the valve seal from the valve stem and fit a new seal.
10. Assemble the spacer, and thimble to the valve stem.
11. Remove the seal from the piston and fit a new seal (seal lip towards the spring).
12. Fit the spring thimble to the piston and carefully depress the thimble prong.
13. Lubricate the bore of the master cylinder with clean brake fluid and insert the seal assembly and piston.
14. Fit the push rod and washer to the master cylinder and secure with a circlip.
15. Fit a new rubber boot to the push rod and master cylinder.
16. Fit the cylinder to the car 33.20.01.
17. Bleed the system 33.15.01.

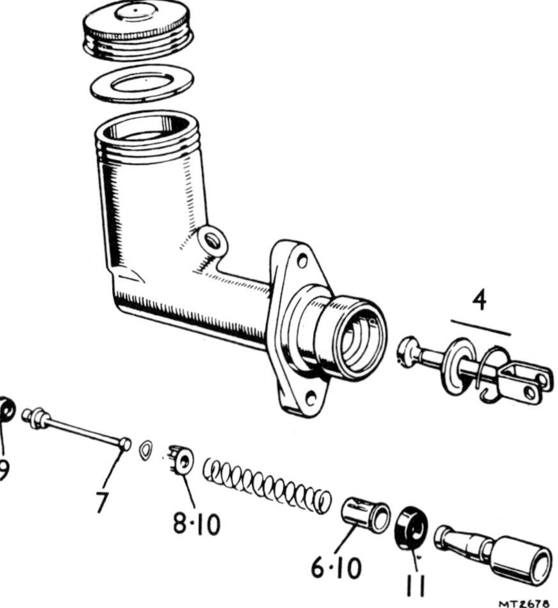

CLUTCH WITHDRAWAL MECHANISM

– Remove and refit **33.25.12**

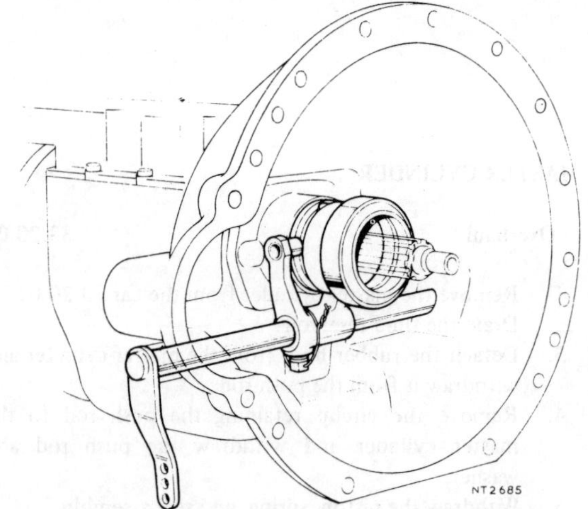

Removing

1. Remove the gearbox 37.20.01.
2. Withdraw the release bearing assembly from the gearbox front end cover.
3. Remove the locking wire from the square-headed pinch pin securing the withdrawal link to the withdrawal shaft.
4. Remove the pinch pin.
5. Remove the withdrawal shaft, anti-rattle spring and the withdrawal fork.

Refitting

6. Slide the release bearing assembly into position on the gearbox front end cover.
7. Fit the tapered coil anti-rattle spring to the withdrawal shaft (narrow end of taper adjacent to the drop arm).
8. Rotate the release bearing assembly to position the anti-rotation pin centrally above the gearbox primary shaft (12 o'clock position).
9. Engage the withdrawal fork in the release bearing assembly ensuring that the machined flats on the fork ends are located on the engine side of the withdrawal shaft.
10. **Slide the withdrawal shaft through the bushes and the withdrawal fork.**
11. Align the screwed boss of the withdrawal shaft and fit and tighten the square-headed pinchbolt.
12. Secure the pinchbolt with locking wire.
13. Fit the gearbox to the car 37.20.01.

NOTE: that the slave cylinder push rod should engage the centre hole in the withdrawal shaft drop arm.

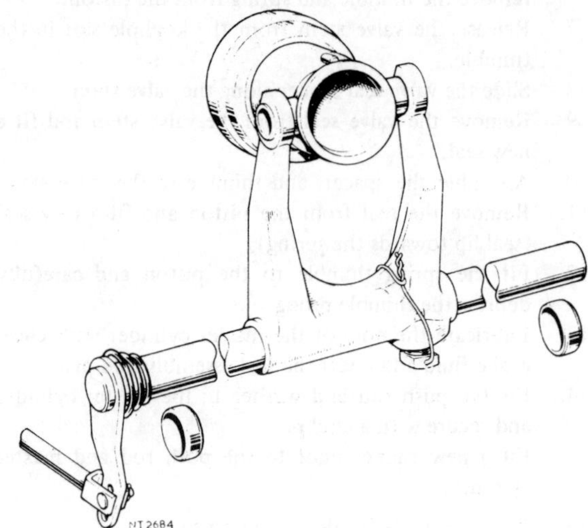

CLUTCH PEDAL

– Remove and refit **33.30.02**

Refer 70.35.01

CLUTCH PEDAL RETURN SPRING

– Remove and refit **33.30.03**

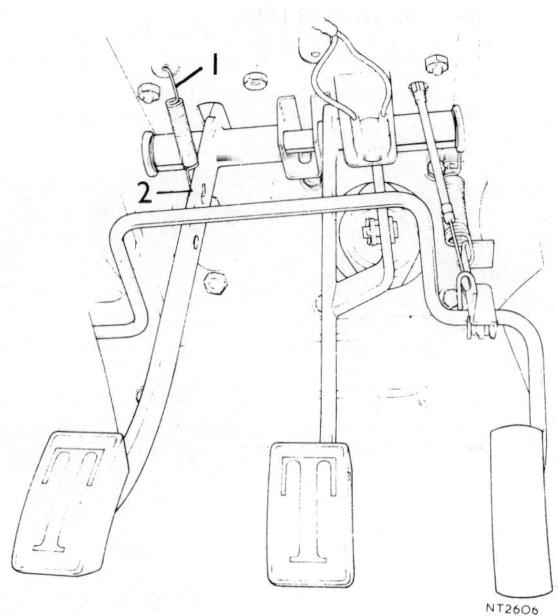

Removing

1. Release the spring hook from the pedal box.
2. Release the spring hook from the clutch pedal.

Refitting

3. Reverse instructions 1 and 2.

SLAVE CYLINDER

– Remove and refit 33.35.01

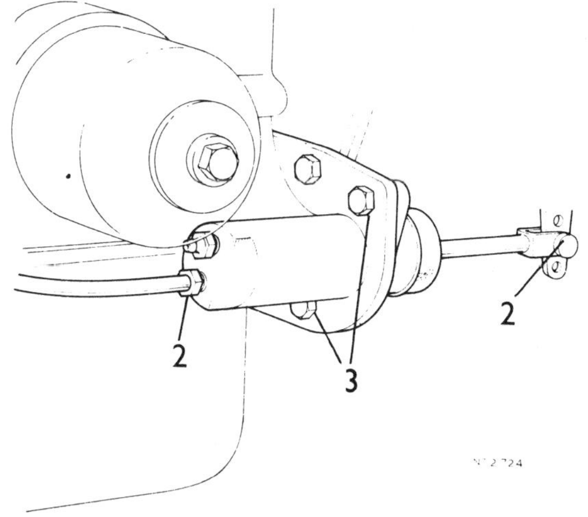

Removing

1. Disconnect the union at the upper end of the flexible pipe.
2. Unscrew the flexible pipe union from the slave cylinder and remove the clevis pin.
3. Remove the two nuts, spring washers and bolts securing the slave cylinder flange to the mounting bracket.
4. Withdraw the slave cylinder.

Refitting

5. Reverse instructions 1 to 4.

NOTE: that the slave cylinder push rod, should be fitted to the centre hole in the withdrawal shaft drop arm.

6. Bleed the system.

SLAVE CYLINDER

– Overhaul 33.35.07

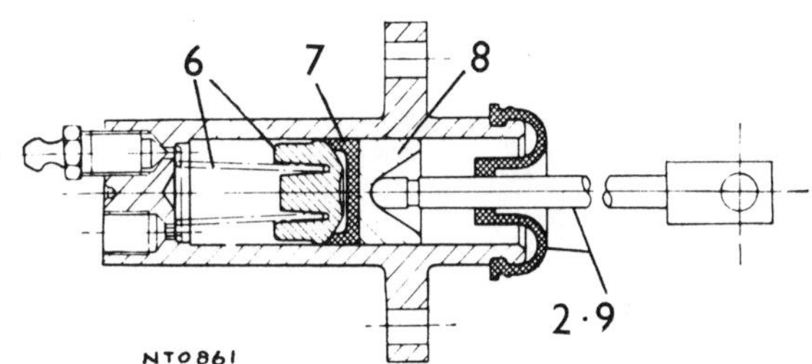

1. Remove the slave cylinder from the car. 33.35.01.
2. Withdraw the rubber boot and push rod.
3. Withdraw the piston, seal, filler block and spring.
4. Thoroughly clean all components and examine the cylinder bore, piston and filler block for signs of damage, scoring and corrosion. If doubt exists as to their serviceability a new slave cylinder assembly should be obtained.
5. Lubricate the cylinder bore with clean brake fluid.
6. Fit the spring to the filler block and enter the block (spring leading) into the bore.
7. Fit a new seal (lips leading).
8. Fit the piston (plain face leading).
9. Fit a new rubber boot and insert the push rod.
10. Fit the slave cylinder to the car 33.35.01.
11. Bleed the system 33.15.01.

SYNCHROMESH GEARBOX OPERATIONS

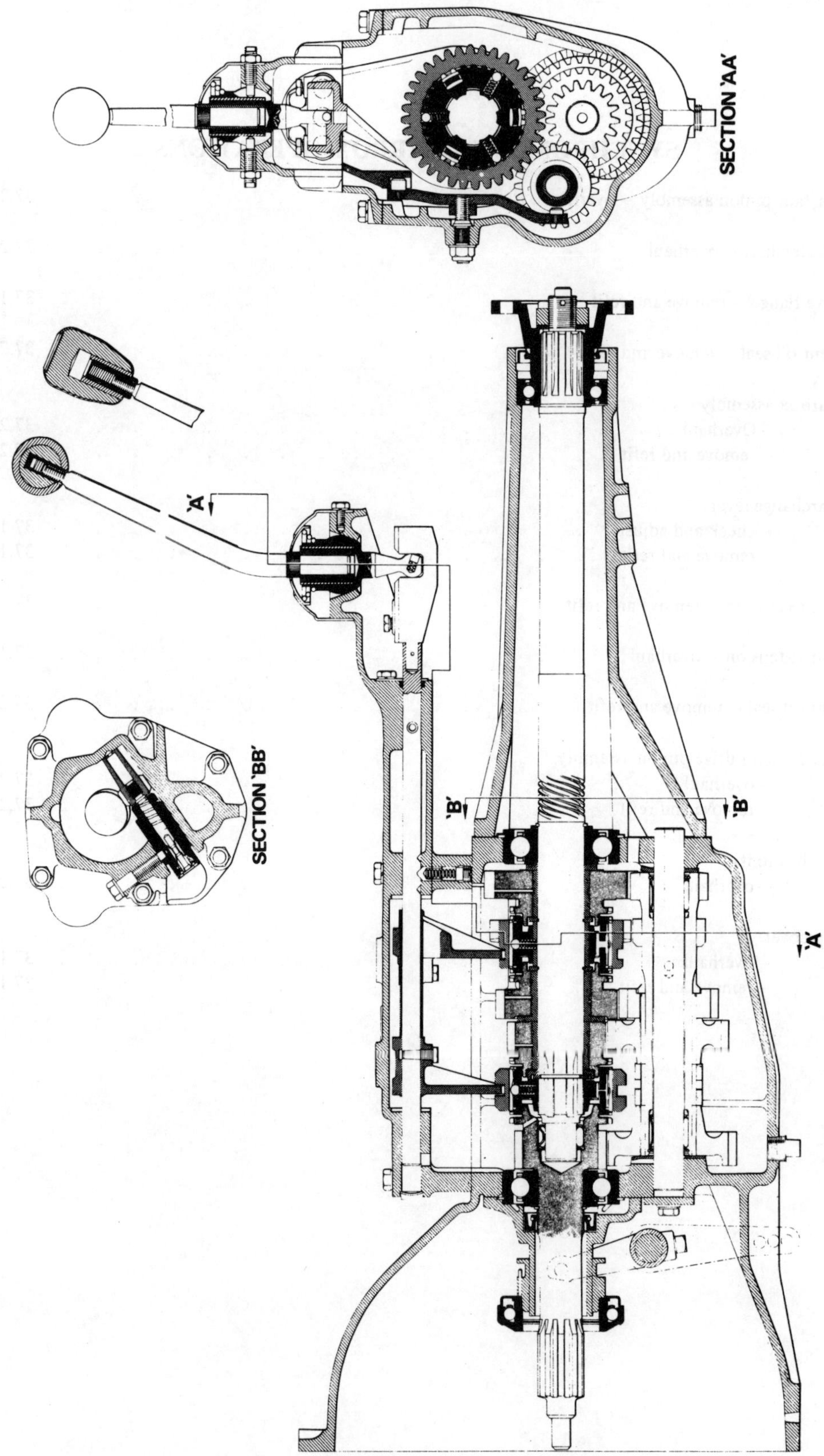

SECTION 'AA'

SECTION 'BB'

DRIVE FLANGE

– Remove and refit **37.10.01**

Service tools: RG421

Removing

1. Drive the vehicle onto a ramp and raise the ramp.
2. Remove the propeller shaft 47.15.01.
3. Using tool RG421 to retain the drive flange, unscrew and remove the nut and washer.
4. Remove the drive flange.

Refitting

5. Thoroughly clean the mainshaft and drive flange splines.
6. Fit the drive flange.
7. Refit the washer and nut.
8. Using tool RG421 to retain the flange, tighten the nut to 90 to 110 lbf ft (12·4 to 15·2 kgf m).
9. Refit the propeller shaft 47.15.01.

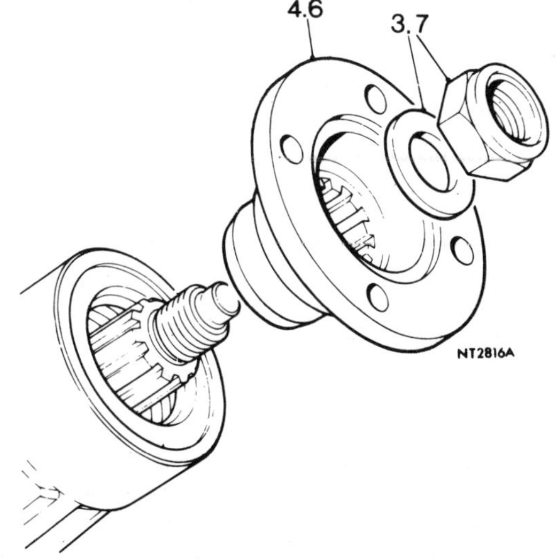

REAR EXTENSION

– Remove and refit **37.12.01**

Service tools: RG421

Removing

1. Drive the vehicle onto a ramp and raise the ramp.
2. Remove the exhaust intermediate pipes, silencer and tail pipes.
3. Remove the propeller shaft 47.15.01.
4. Using tool RG421 to retain the drive flange, unscrew and remove the nut and washer.
5. Remove the drive flange.
6. Unscrew and remove the peg bolt and washer.
7. Withdraw the speedometer drive cable and pinion assembly.
8. Using a ramp jack, support the gearbox and remove the rear mounting platform attachment bolts and nuts
9. Remove the two mounting bolts and nuts.
   Later Models. Swing the steady strap forward and clear of the rear extension.
10. Raise the gearbox and remove the mounting. Lower the gearbox.
11. Place a drip tray under the gearbox.
12. Unscrew and remove the bolts.
13. Withdraw the extension housing, thrust washer and gasket.

Refitting

14. Clean the mating faces of the gearbox casing and extension housing and fit a new gasket.
15. Refit the extension housing assembly and thrust washer.
16. Fit and tighten the extension housing bolts.
17. Refit the speedometer drive cable and pinion assembly.
18. Locate and tighten the peg bolt.
19. Refit the drive flange.
20. Fit the nut and washer.
21. Using tool RG421 to retain the flange, tighten the nut to 90 to 110 lbf ft (12·4 to 15·2 kgf m)
22. Refit the mounting.
23.** Refit the two mounting bolts and nuts and on later models the steady strap.**
24. Fit and tighten the four mounting bolts and nuts.
25. Refit the propeller shaft.
26. If necessary top up the gearbox, with oil.
27. Refit the exhaust system.

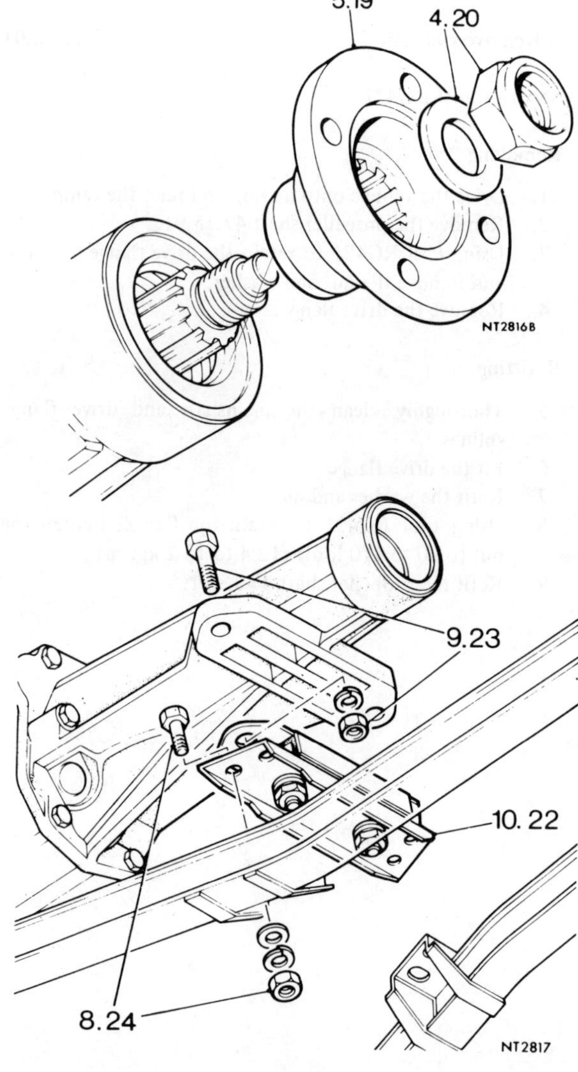

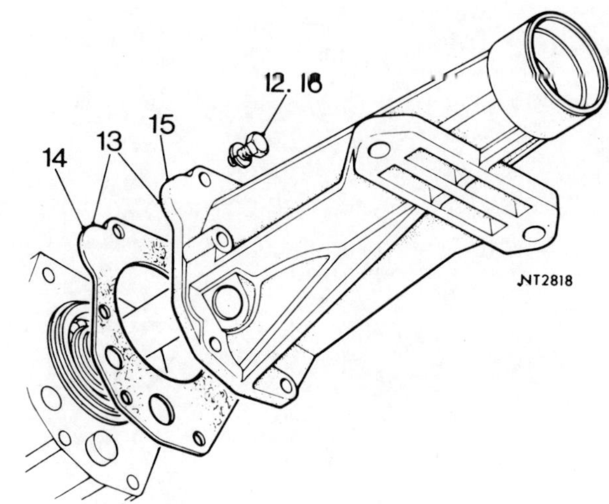

REAR EXTENSION

– Overhaul **37.12.04**

1. Remove the rear extension 37.12.01.

Dismantling

2. Prise out the oil seal.
3. Drive out the bearing.

Reassembling

4. Drift the bearing into the extension.
5. Press a new oil seal into the extension.
6. Refit the rear extension.

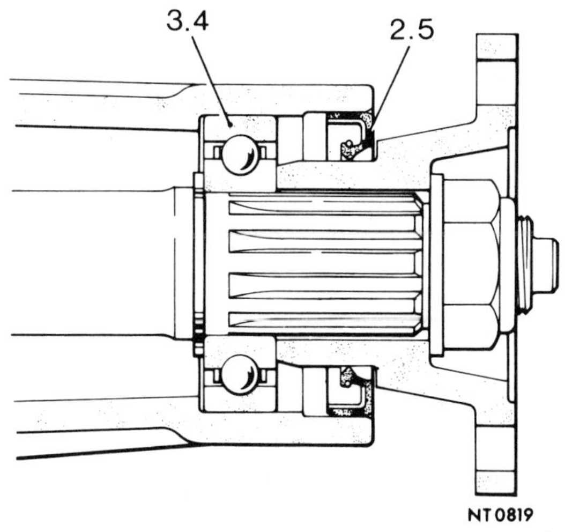

TOP COVER

– Remove and refit **37.12.16**

Removing

1. Remove the transmission cover panel 76.25.07 (includes gearlever removal 37.16.04).

** 2.(a) Disconnect the reverse lamp and overdrive isolator switch leads.
2.(b) Later Models – Release steady strap from top cover.**
3. Remove eight bolts.
4. Lift off the top cover assembly and the gasket.

Refitting

5. Apply grease to the abutment faces and fit the gasket.
6. Place the selector shafts in the neutral position and fit the top cover assembly. Ensure that the reverse lever is correctly engaged.
7. Secure the top cover with the following bolts, each fitted with a lock washer:
   a. Two bolts – 67 mm long – to front
   b. Two bolts – 73 mm long – to rear
   ** *c.* Four bolts to sides

8.(a) Connect the reverse lamp and overdrive isolator switch leads.
8.(b) Later Models – Connect the steady strap.**
9. Refit the transmission cover panel 76.25.07 (includes refitting gearlever 37.16.04).

**

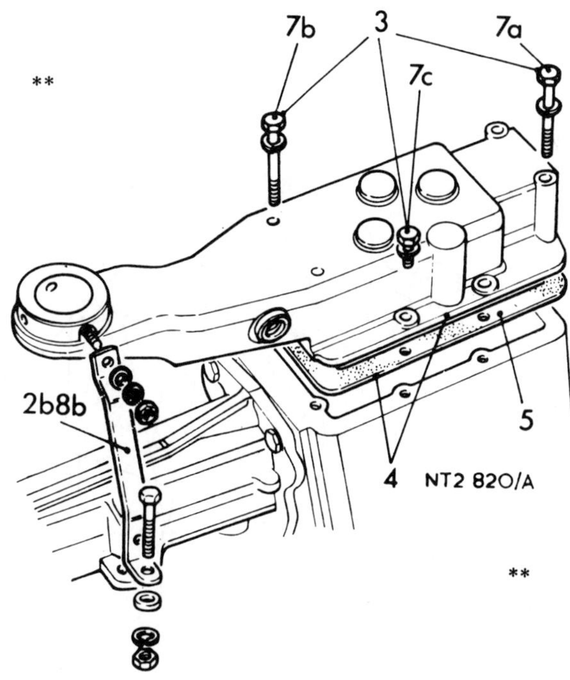

**

TOP COVER

– Overhaul **37.12.19**

1. Remove the top cover 37.12.16

Dismantling

2. Remove the reverse lamp switch and overdrive isolator switches (if fitted).
3. Remove the screwed plug, distance piece, spring and plunger – reverse detent.
4. Remove the screwed plug, spring and steel ball – 3rd/top detent.
5. Remove the screwed plug, spring and steel ball – 1st/2nd detent.
6. Remove three "wedglok" bolts – one from each selector shaft.
7. Move the three selector shafts into their neutral positions.
8. Withdraw the 1st/2nd selector shaft.
9. Remove the 1st/2nd selector fork and distance tube.
10. Withdraw the reverse selector shaft
11. Remove the reverse actuator and distance tube.
12. Withdraw the 3rd/top selector shaft.
13. Remove the 3rd/top selector fork and distance tube.
14. Remove the interlock plunger and interlock balls.
15. Unscrew two setscrews and remove the cover plate.
16. Remove the sealing rings.

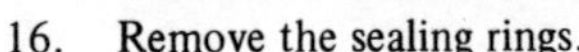

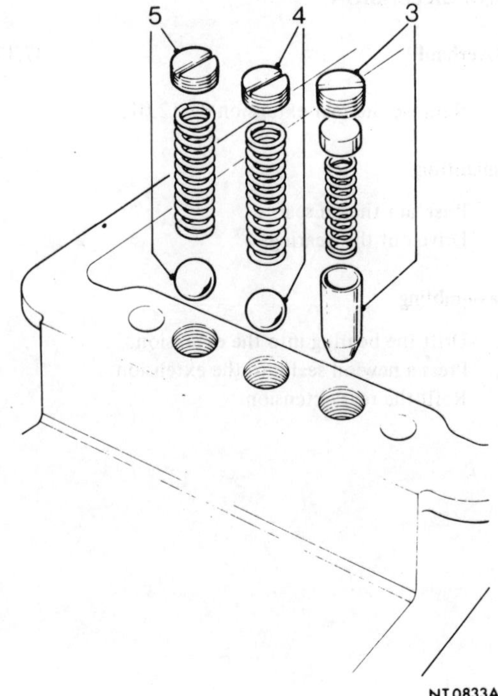

NT 0833A

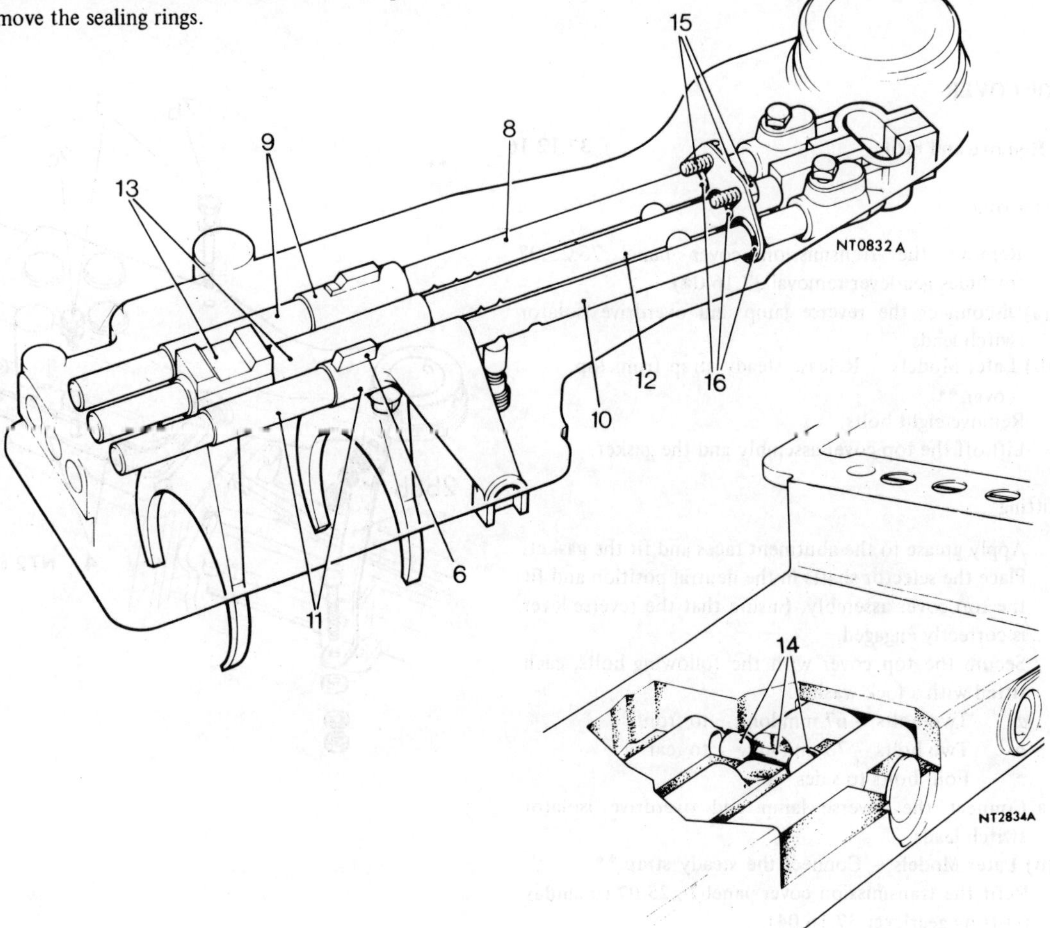

Reassembling

17. Fit a sealing ring into each bore.
18. Fit the cover plate and secure with two setscrews.
19. Fit the interlock plunger into the 3rd/top selector, shaft.
20. Fit the 3rd/top selector shaft, distance tube and fork into the top cover. Push the shaft into the neutral position.
21 Locate an interlock ball in-between the 3rd/top and reverse shaftbores and retain with grease.
22. Fit the reverse selector shaft, distance tube and actuator into the top cover. Push the shaft into the neutral position.
23. Locate an interlock ball in between the 3rd/top and 1st/2nd bores and retain with grease.
24. Fit the 1st/2nd selector shaft, distance tube and fork into the top cover.
25. Secure the forks and actuator to the shafts using new "wedglok" bolts.

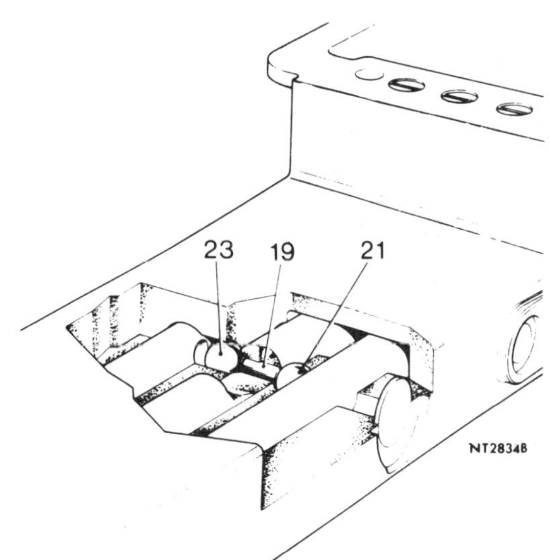

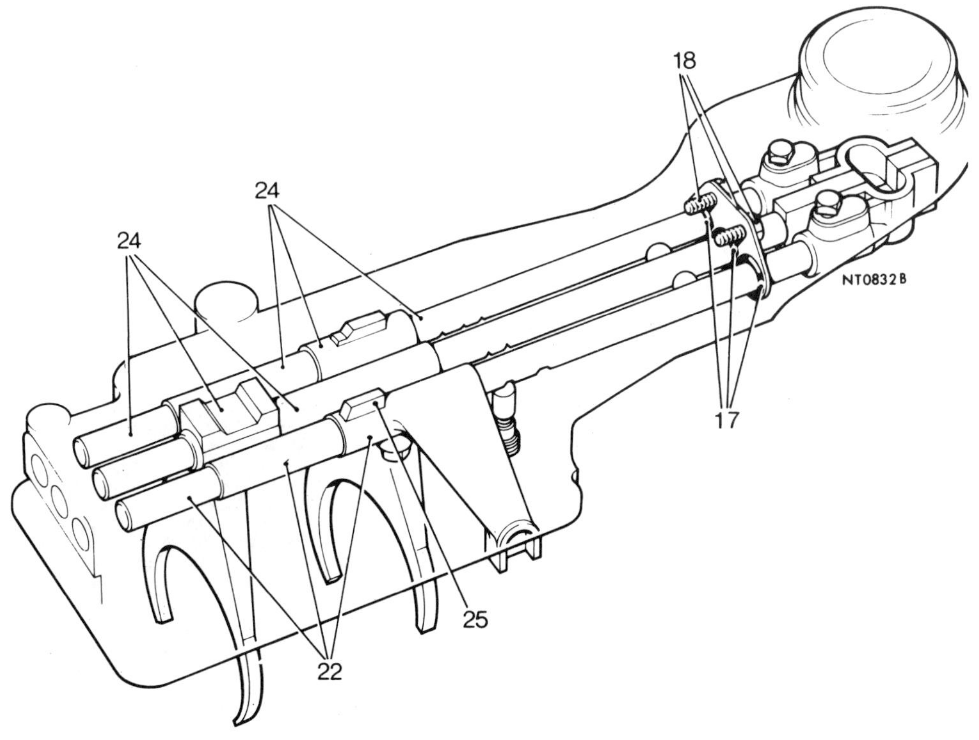

26. Refit the reverse detent plunger, spring distance piece and screwed plug.
27. Refit the 1st/2nd detent ball, spring and screwed plug.
28 Refit the 3rd/top detent ball, spring and screwed plug.
29. Check the pull off loads using a spring balance. 1st/2nd and 3rd/top ** – 32 to 34 lbsf (14·5 to 15·4 kgf.)
Reverse – 26 to 28 lbsf (11·8 to 12·7 kgf.) **
Insert shims or grind springs to adjust.
30. Refit the reverse lamp switch and overdrive isolator switches.
31. Refit the top cover assembly.

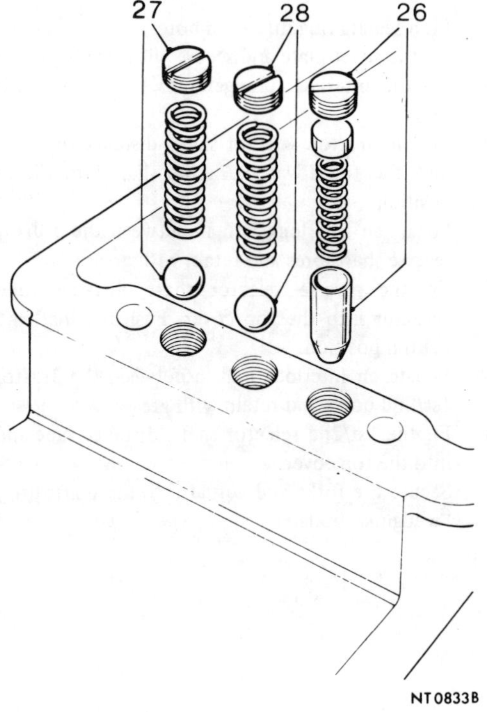

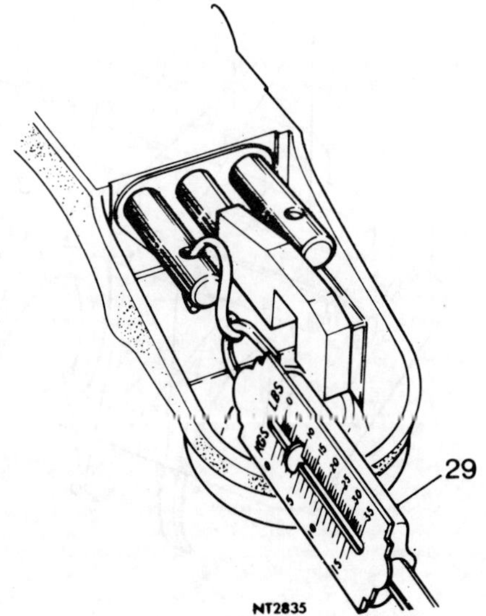

GEAR CHANGE LEVER

– Check and adjust 37.16.01

1. Remove the gearlever knob and locknut.
2. Remove the fascia support bracket.
3. Slacken the locknuts.
4. Place the lever in the 1st/2nd gate.
5. Tighten the right hand adjuster until it just moves the gearlever. Back off the adjuster a half turn and tighten the locknut.

** 6. Place the lever in the reverse gate. **

7. Tighten the left hand adjuster until it just moves the gearlever. Back off the adjuster a half turn and tighten the locknut.
8. Refit the fascia support bracket.
9. Refit the gearlever knob and locknut.

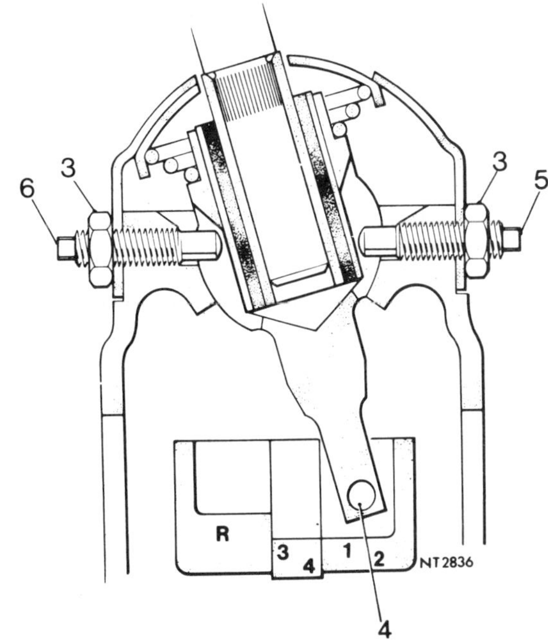

GEARCHANGE LEVER

– Remove and refit 37.16.04

Removing

1. Slacken the locknut and unscrew the gearlever knob.
2. Remove the fascia support bracket 76.46.09.
3. Remove the gearlever grommet.
4. Position the gearlever in neutral.
5. Take out the bolt.
6. Slacken the locknuts.
7. Depress and turn the gearlever cap, withdraw the cap, plate and spring.
8. Carefully withdraw the gearchange lever ensuring that the plunger and spring do not fall out.

Refitting

9. Using heavy grease to retain the plunger and spring, refit the gearchange lever.
10. Refit the spring, plate and cap.
11. Refit the bolt.
12. Adjust the gearchange lever 37.16.01.
13. Refit the grommet.
14. Refit the fascia support bracket.
15. Refit the gearlever knob and locknut.

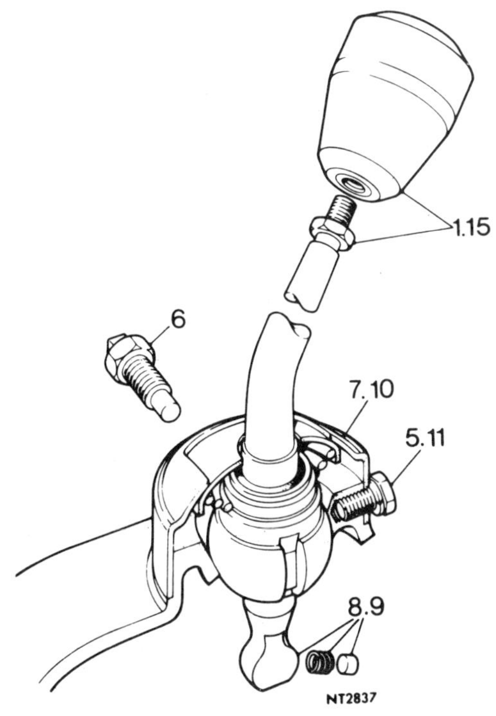

GEARBOX ASSEMBLY

– Remove and refit **37.20.01**

Removing

1. Drive the vehicle onto a ramp and isolate the battery.
2. Remove both front seats 76.70.04-05
3. Remove transmission side trim panels 76.13.06
4. Remove the fascia support bracket 76.46.09
5. Remove the gearlever 37.16.04.
6. Remove the carpet and the transmission cover panel. 76.25.07.
7. Disconnect the propeller shaft from the gearbox drive flange.
8. Disconnect the speedometer drive cable.
9. Unscrew and remove the mounting bolts and nuts.
   ** NOTE: On later models note the position of fixings for the steady bracket.**
10. Remove the exhaust support bracket.
11. Remove the mounting plate bolts.
12. Unscrew nine upper engine/bellhousing attachments.
13. Raise the ramp.
14. Disconnect the clutch slave cylinder push-rod from the cross-shaft lever.
15. Position a ramp jack under the engine and raise the engine/gearbox sufficient to remove the mounting plate assembly.
16. Remove the remaining (seven) engine/bellhousing attachments.
17. Lower the ramp and lift out the gearbox.

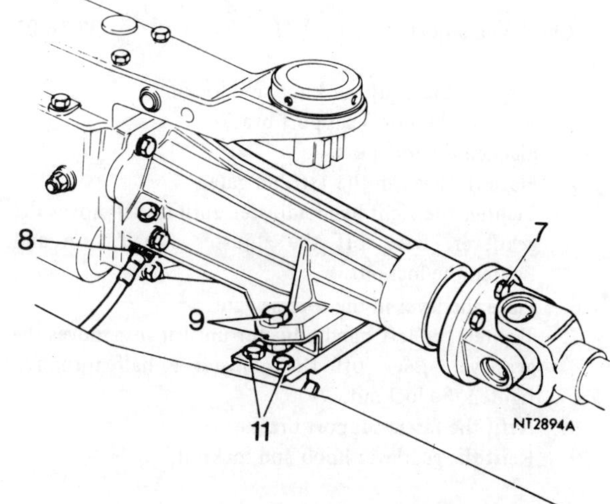

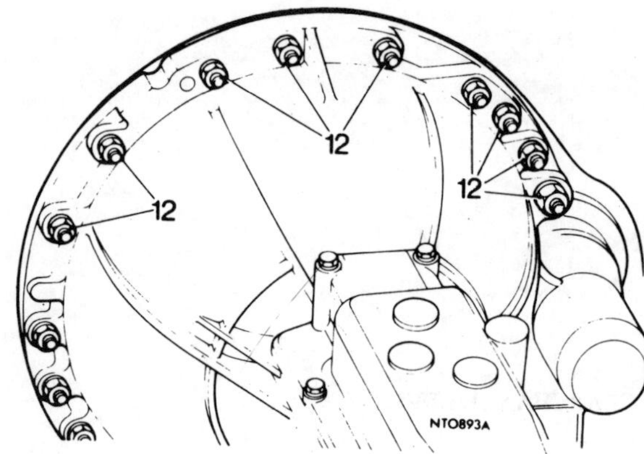

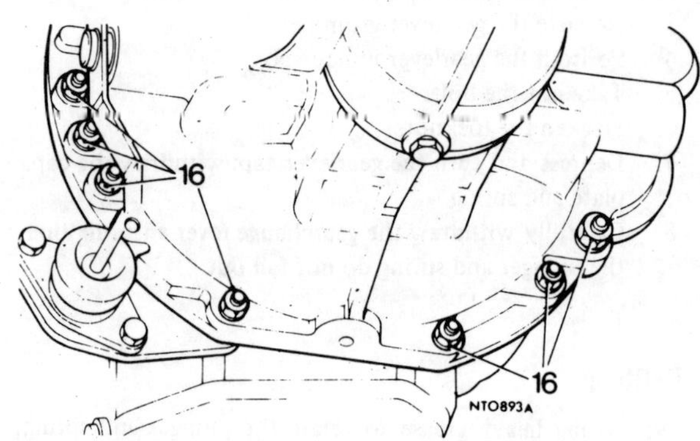

Refitting

18. Check the alignment of the clutch splines, move the clutch throwout bearing to the rear extent of its travel and engage top gear.
19. Manoeuvre the gearbox into position, if necessary rotating the drive flange to align the input shaft splines with those of the clutch.
20. Fit the upper (nine) engine/bellhousing attachments.
21. Raise the ramp and using the ramp jack, lift the engine.
22. Refit the lower (seven) engine/bellhousing attachments.
23. Place the mounting assembly in position and lower the ramp jack.
24. Refit the clutch slave cylinder push rod to the cross shaft lever.
25. Lower the ramp.
26. Secure the mounting plate to the chassis frame.
27. Refit the exhaust support bracket.
28.** Refit the two bolts and nuts and on later models the steady strap.**
29. Connect the speedometer cable to the gearbox.
30. Connect the propeller shaft to the gearbox drive flange.
31. Refit the transmission cover panel and carpet. 76.25.07
32. Refit the gearlever 37.16.04.
33. Refit the fascia support bracket 76.46.09.
34. Refit the transmission sidt trim panels 76.13.06
35. Refit both front seats 76.70.04-05
36. Re-connect the battery.

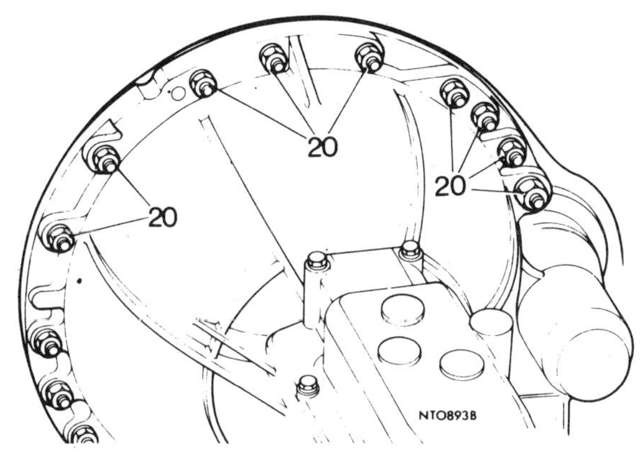

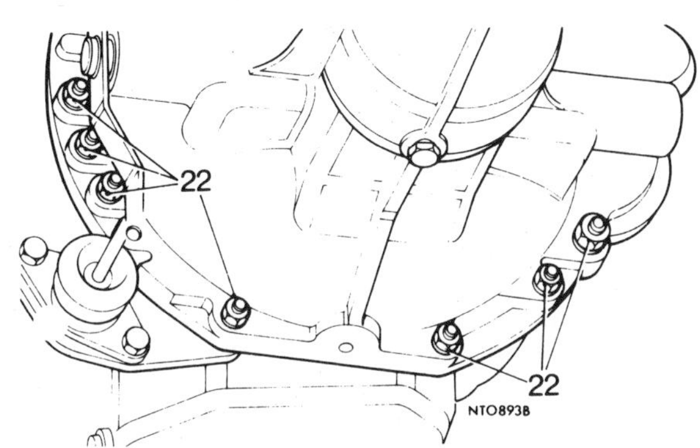

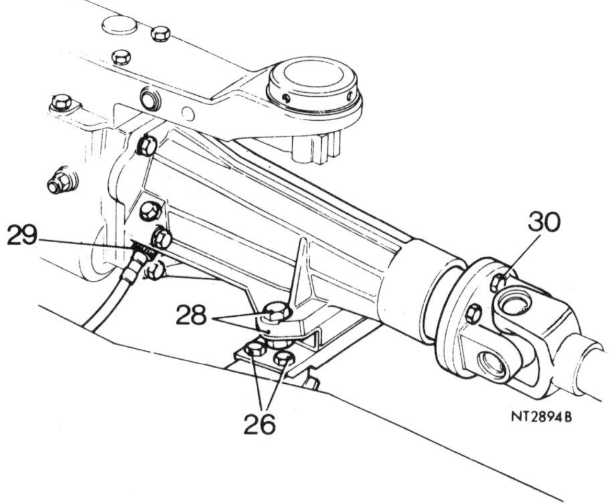

GEARBOX

– Overhaul **37.20.04**

Service tools: RG.421, S4235A-2, S314, S4221A-15A, S67A, S167.

1. Remove the gearbox 37.20.01 and drain the oil.

Dismantling

2. Unscrew and remove eight bolts.
3. Lift off the top cover and gasket.
4. Remove the clutch release mechanism 33.25.12.
5. Take out four setscrews and washers.
6. Tape over the constant pinion splines and remove the front bearing plate and gasket.
7. Remove the peg bolt and withdraw the speedometer drive pinion assembly (If overdrive is fitted, perform operation 40.20.07, remove the overdrive cam and adaptor plate and continue from para. 13).
8. Using tool No. RG421 to retain the flange, unscrew the nut.
9. Remove the flange.
10. Unscrew the bolts.
11. Remove the rear extension and gasket.
12. Remove the thrust washer.
13. Take out two screws.
14. Remove the countershaft front plate and gasket.
15. Take out the cross recessed head screw.
16. Remove the retaining plate.
17. Withdraw the countershaft spindle and allow the cluster to drop to the bottom of the box.
18. Using tool No. S4235A-2 withdraw the constant pinion assembly.
19. Fit the abutment tool No. S314.

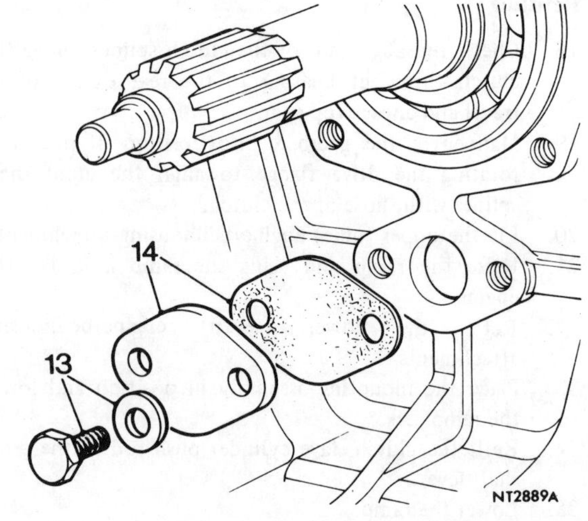

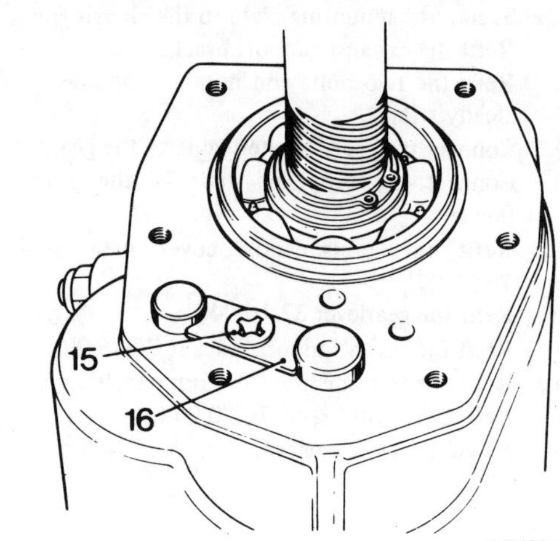

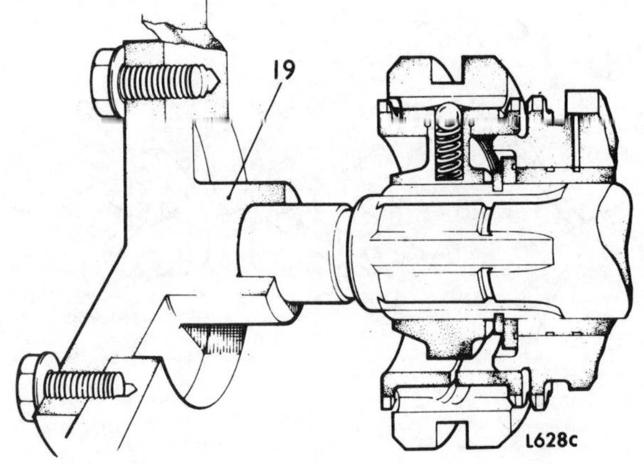

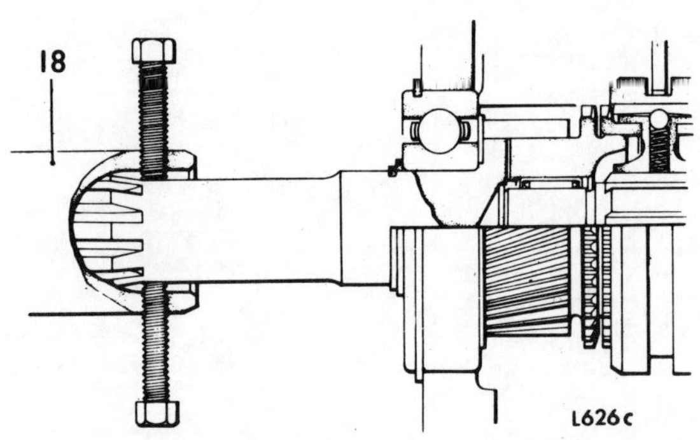

20. Remove the centre bearing circlip, washer and snap ring.
21. Using tool No. S4221A-15A, withdraw the centre bearing. Remove Tool S314.
22. Remove the mainshaft assembly through the top aperture.
23. Remove the 3rd/top synchro unit and cups.
24. Remove the washer, 1st gear and bush, washer, 1st/2nd synchro unit and cups.
25. Using tool S67A remove the circlip.

NOTE: The sectioned washer behind the circlip has three lugs that fit in alternate splines, the longer prongs on tool S69A fit in the splines between the lugs. Rotate circlip to ascertain position of lugs. Position circlip with ends on adjacent prongs of tool. With tool in position, gently prise between 2nd and 3rd gears to push circlip away from slot.

26. Remove the sectioned washer, 3rd gear and bush, washer, 2nd gear and bush, and washer.
27. Withdraw the reverse idler spindle, reverse gear, lever and pivot.
28. Remove the countershaft rear thrust washer.
29. Remove the countershaft assembly.
30. Remove the countershaft front thrust washer.

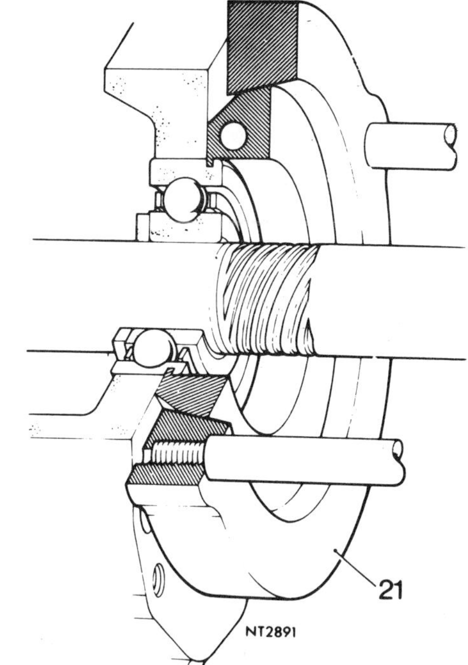

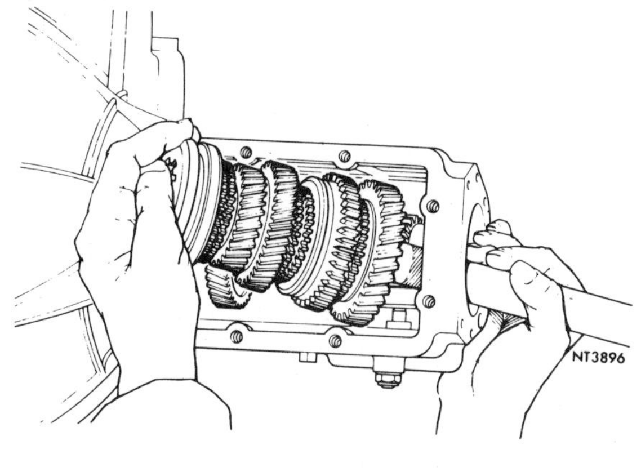

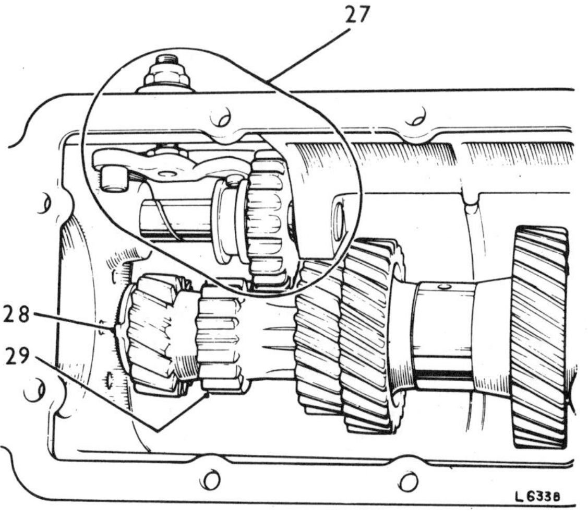

Reassembling

31. Refit the reverse lever with fulcrum pin, washer and nut to the gearbox.

NOTE: Position the lever on the pin so that two screw threads (approx) are visible between the gearbox and lever. Replace the reverse idler gear and shaft.

32. Using heavy grease to retain the thrust washers in position, fit the countershaft cluster.
33. Align the thrust washers and fit the spindle.
34. Check the countershaft end float. The end float should be 0·007 to 0·012 in (0·18 to 0·30 mm). Adjust by selective use of thrust washers or if necessary remove metal from the steel backing face of the thrust washer. Withdraw the spindle.
35. Check the end float of the 1st, 2nd and 3rd gears on their respective bushes. End float should be 0·004 to 0.008 in (0·1 to 0·2 mm).

NOTE: *i* Interchange of 1st and 3rd gear bushes is permissible to obtain these figures.

ii. If necessary reduce the bush length to reduce the end float or fit a new bush to increase the end float.

36. Check the total end float of the 2nd and 3rd gear bushes on the mainshaft.
    a. Temporarily fit to the front end of the mainshaft in order:
    i. Adjustment washer.
    ii. Bush – 2nd gear.
    iii. Thrust washer,
    iv. Bush – 3rd gear
    v. Thrust washer – fit reversed.
    iv. Sectioned washer – fit reversed.
    b. Insert the deeper portion of a discarded circlip in its groove in the mainshaft to retain the items.
    c. Measure the bush end float on the mainshaft using feeler gauges.
    d. End float is to be within 0·003 to 0·009 in (0·08 to 0·23 mm).
    e. Adjustment of end float is to be made by selection of the adjustment washer (a, i.) of appropriate thickness listed as follows:

Part No.	Colour	in ± 0·001	Thickness mm ± 0·25
129941	Metal	0·119	3·02
129942	Green	0·122	3·10
129943	Blue	0·125	3·17
129944	Orange	0·128	3·25
134670	Yellow	0·133	3·38

f. Remove the items from the mainshaft but suitably identify selected adjustment washer for association with 2nd gear.

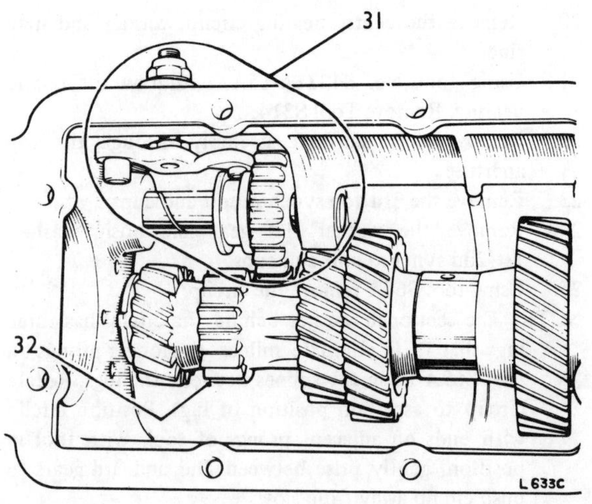

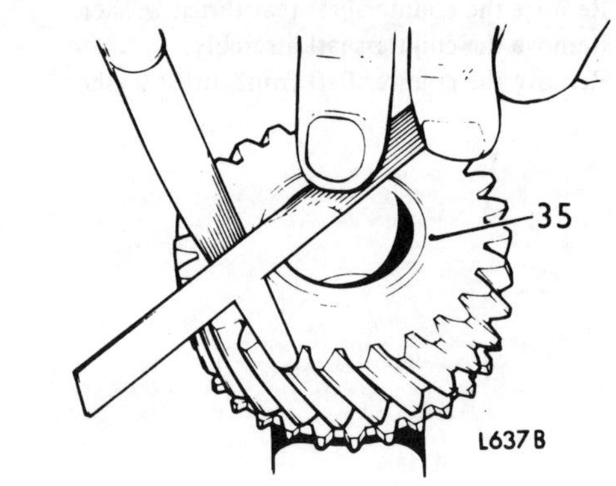

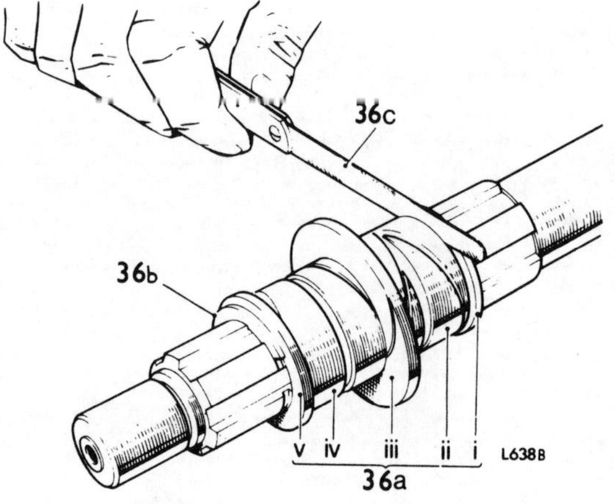

37. Check the end float of the 1st gear bush on the mainshaft.
    a. Temporarily fit the rear of the mainshaft in order:
    i. Adjustment washer.
    ii. Bush – 1st gear.
    iii. Thrust washer.
    iv. Ball bearing Tool S314.
    v. Washer.
    b. Insert the deeper portion of a discarded circlip in its groove in the mainshaft to retain the items.
    c. Drift the bearing into close abutment with the washer and circlip.
    d. Measure the bush end float on the mainshaft using feeler gauges.
    e. End float is to be 0·003 to 0·009 in (0·08 to 0·23 mm).
    f. Adjustment to end float is to be made by selection of the adjustment washer (a. i.) of appropriate thickness given in preceding list (36e).
    g. Remove the items from the mainshaft but suitably identify the selected adjustment washer for association with the 1st gear. Bearing extractor tool S4221A-15A.
38. Assemble each synchro cup on the respective gear and measure with feeler gauges the clearance between the gear and cup. Should the clearance be less than 0·030 in (0·76 mm) renew the cup.
39. Assemble the front of the mainshaft in order:
    a. Adjustment washer.
    b. Assembled 2nd gear and bush.
    c. Thrust washer.
    d. Assembled 3rd gear and bush.
    e. Sectioned washer.
    f. Circlip-Tool S176.
    g. 3rd/4th synchro unit fitted with synchro cups (short boss innermost).

NOTE: Ensure correct assembly of bush and gear (b and d) in that bush and gear oilways align.

40. Assemble to the rear of the mainshaft in order:

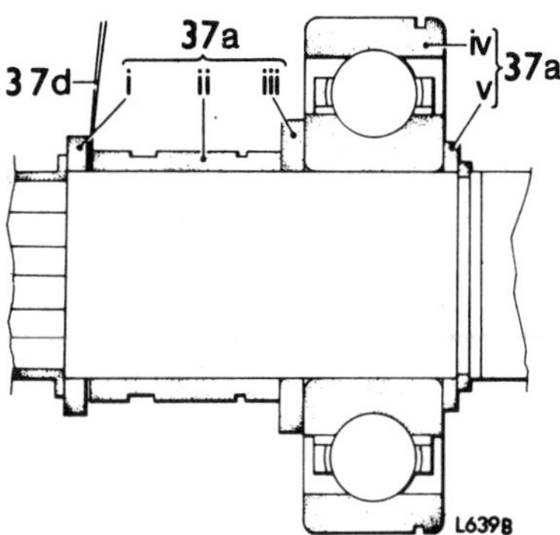

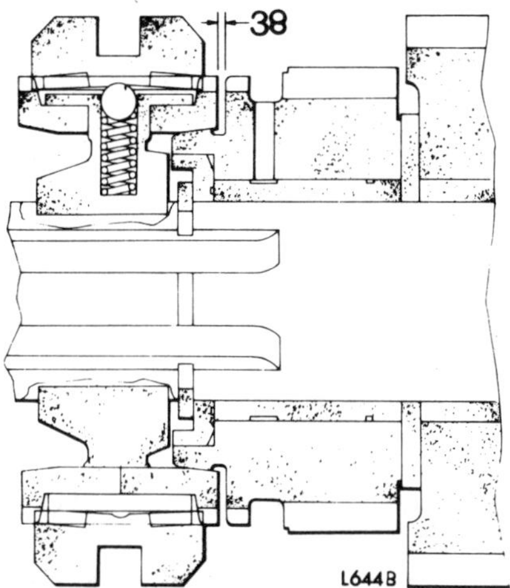

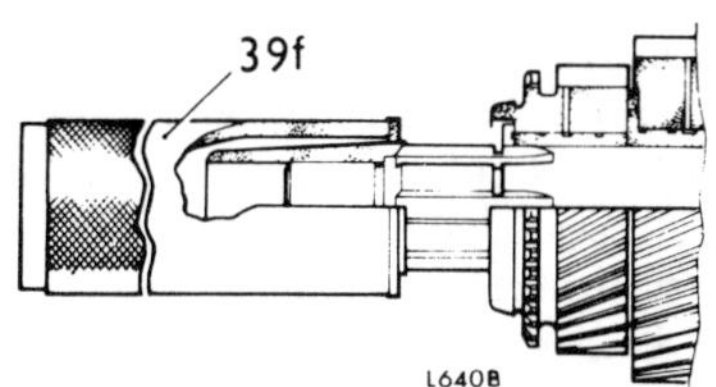

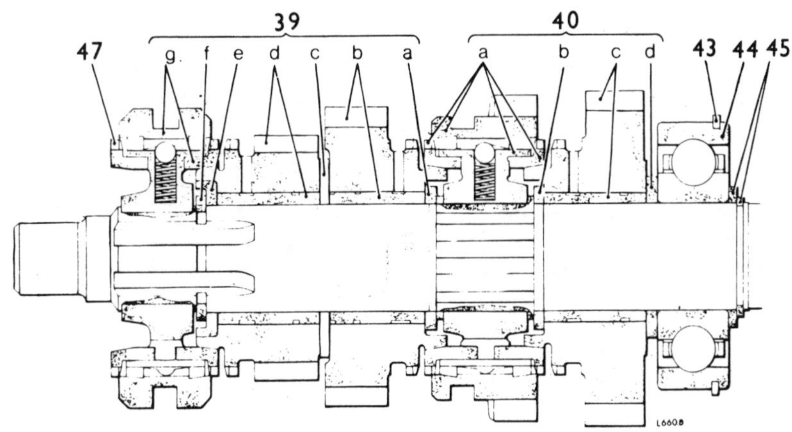

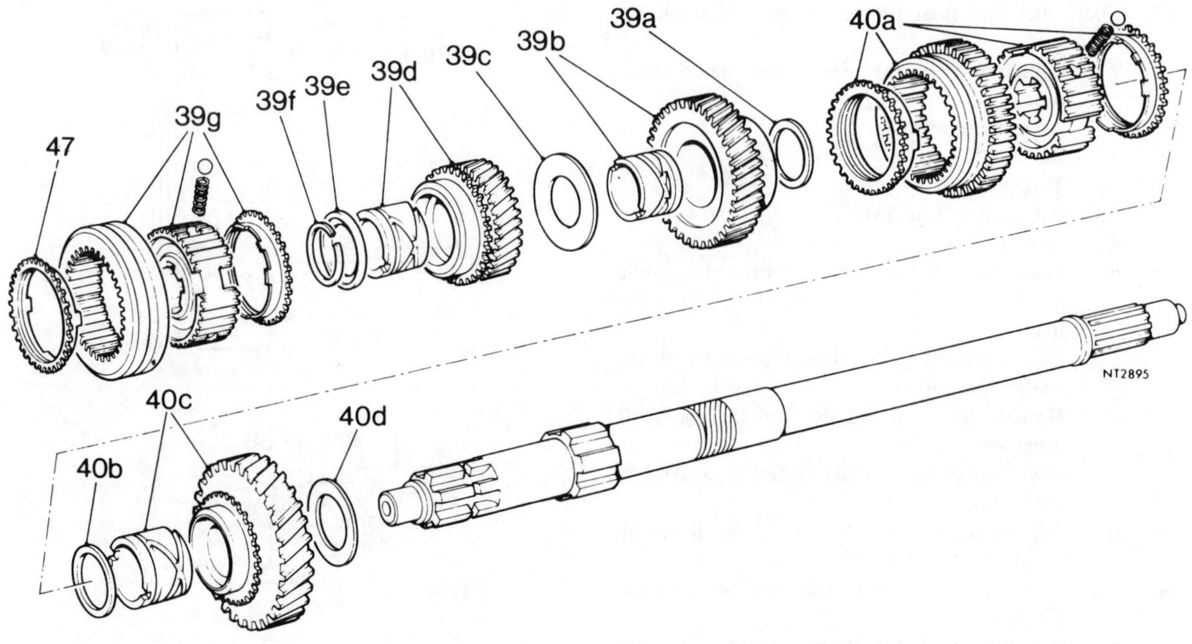

a. 1st/2nd synchro unit fitted with synchro cups.
b. Adjustment washer.
c. Assembled 1st gear and bush (see 39 Note).
d. Thrust washer.

WARNING: IT IS RECOMMENDED THAT SEVERAL WINDINGS OF CORD ARE LASHED AROUND MAINSHAFT TO REAR OF THE 1st GEAR TO PREVENT ITS MOVEMENT, THEREBY, AVOIDING ANY POSSIBILITY OF PERSONAL DAMAGE WHEN FITTING THE MAINSHAFT.

41. Enter the rear of the mainshaft through the top cover and rear apertures of gearbox, respectively, and manoeuvre mainshaft assembly into position.

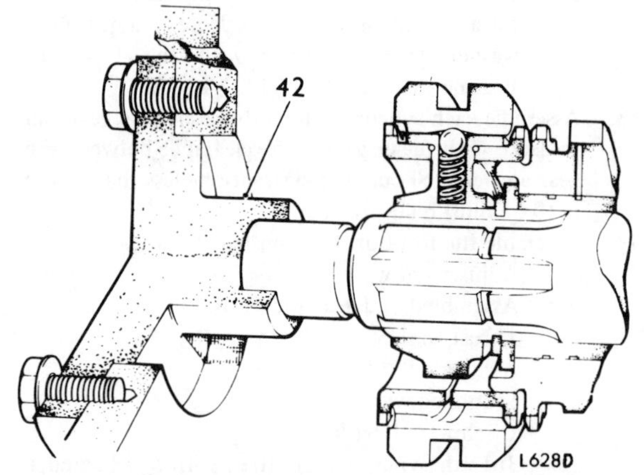

42. Fit tool S314 to the gearbox and engage the mainshaft spigot in the tool.
43. Fit the snap ring to the bearing.
44. Fit the bearing to the mainshaft and gearbox. Tool S314. Remove the tool.
45. Remove tool S314.
46. Fit the washer and circlip to the mainshaft. Protect the rear end of the mainshaft (hard brass block), then tap on the rear end until the inner face of the mainshaft bearing is in close abutment with the washer and circlip.
47. Fit the top gear synchro cup.
48. Fit the constant pinion assembly,
49. Prior to engaging the countershaft gears, free the synchro cups with a screwdriver.
50. Carefully invert the gearbox to engage the countershaft gears – rotating the mainshaft and constant pinion shaft as necessary.
51. Align the countershaft gears and thrust washers then press home countershaft spindle.

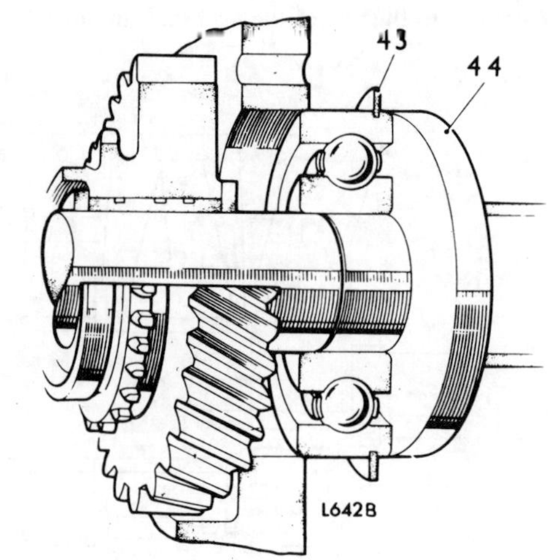

52. Refit the retaining plate, secure with cross recessed head screw.
** 53. Apply jointing compound to the front cover plate gasket, fit the plate and gasket and secure with two screws and copper washers. **
54. Refit the mainshaft rear thrust washer and locate the rear extension and gasket (if overdrive is to be fitted refit the adaptor plate and cam and continue from 59).
55. Secure the rear extension, six bolts.
56. Refit the drive flange.
57. Fit the washer and tighten the nut to a torque load of 90 to 110 lbf ft (12·4 to 15·2 kgf m) using tool No. R421 to retain the flange.
58. Refit the speedometer drive pinion assembly and secure with the peg bolt.
59. Refit the front bearing plate and gasket – 4 setscrews.
60. Refit the clutch release mechanism 33.25.12.
61. Refit the top cover assembly and gasket – secure with eight bolts.
62. Refit the gearbox.

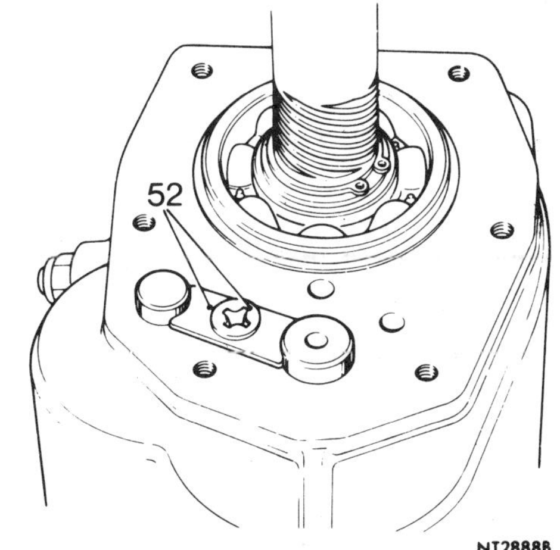

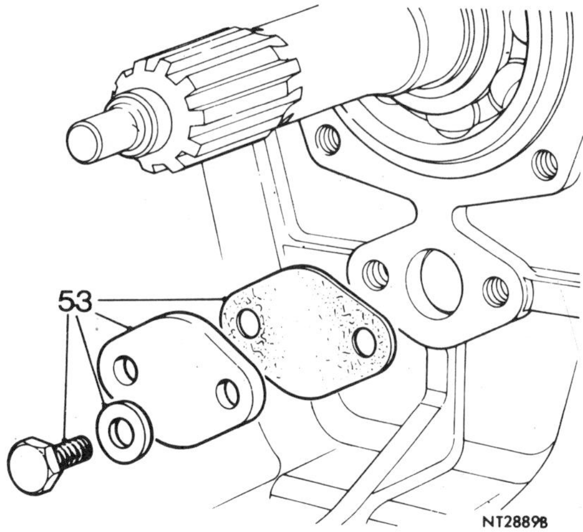

SYNCHRO UNITS

– Overhaul **37.20.08**

1. Remove the synchro units 37.20.04 (1 – 23).

Dismantling

2. Within the walls of a small box to prevent loss of components, carefully push the synchro hub through the sleeve.
3. Collect the three steel balls and springs.

Reassembling

4. Trial fit the sleeve to the hub. The fit should be free sliding.
5. Assemble three springs and steel balls to the hub.
6. Fit the sleeve.
7. Test, using a spring balance. The axial release load which should be:
   – 1st/2nd – 21 to 26 lbs (10·1 to 12·5 kg)

   – 3rd/top – 14 to 19 lbs (6·7 to 9·1 kg)
   If the release loads are below these limits, use new springs. If above, grind down the springs.
8. Refit the synchro units 37.20.04 (39 – 62).

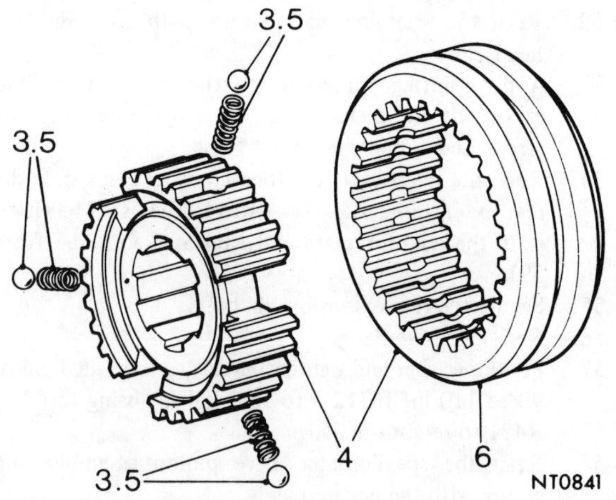

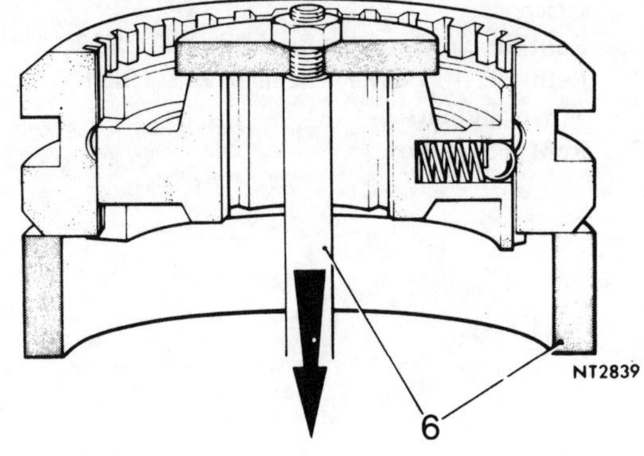

COUNTERSHAFT CLUSTER

– Overhaul 37.20.29

1. Remove the countershaft cluster 37.20.04 (1 – 23, 28 – 30).

Dismantling

2. Separate the 4th constant gear, spacer, 3rd and 2nd constant gears from the hub.
3. Remove the circlip.
4. Extract the roller bearings and backing washers from the hub.

Reassembling

5. Refit the backing washers and roller bearings.
6. Refit the circlips.
7. Assemble the 2nd and 3rd constant gears, spacer and 4th constant gear to the hub.
8. Refit the countershaft cluster 37.20.04 (32 – 62).

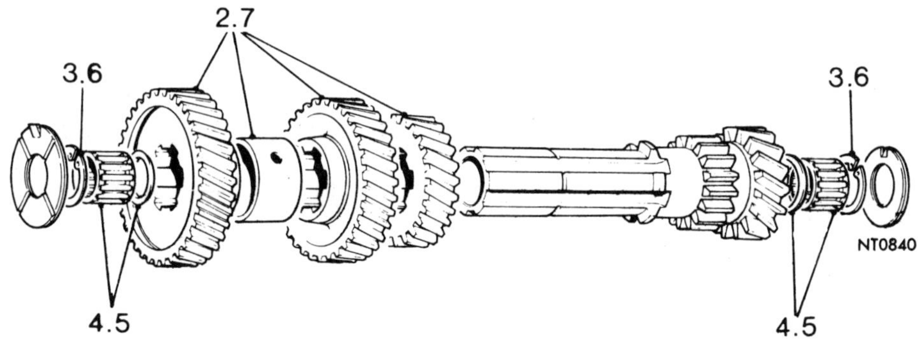

CONSTANT PINION ASSEMBLY

– Overhaul **37.20.54**

– Service tool S4221A – 15A.

1. Remove the constant pinion assembly 37.20.04 (1 – 18).

Dismantling

2. Remove the mainshaft spigot bearing.
3. Remove the circlip and washer.
4. Remove the snap ring.
5. Using tool No. S4221A-15A, withdraw the bearing.
6. Remove the oil thrower.

Reassembling

7. Fit the oil thrower over the shaft.
8. Using tool No. S4221A-15A fit the bearing ensuring that the oil thrower is centralised.
9. Fit the washer and a new circlip.
10. Refit the snap ring.
11. Refit the mainshaft spigot bearing.
12. Refit the constant pinion assembly 37.20.04 (48 – 62).

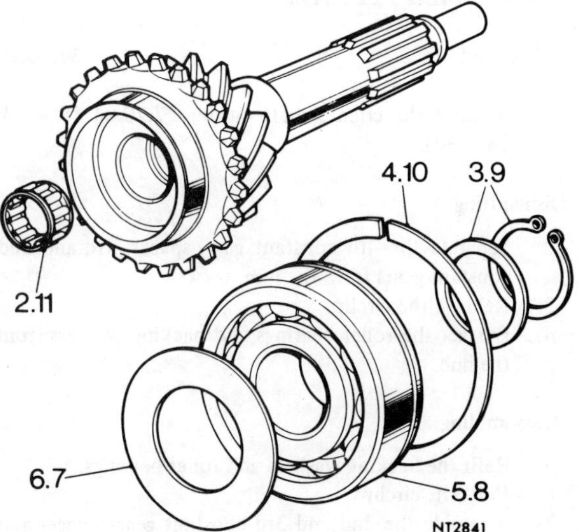

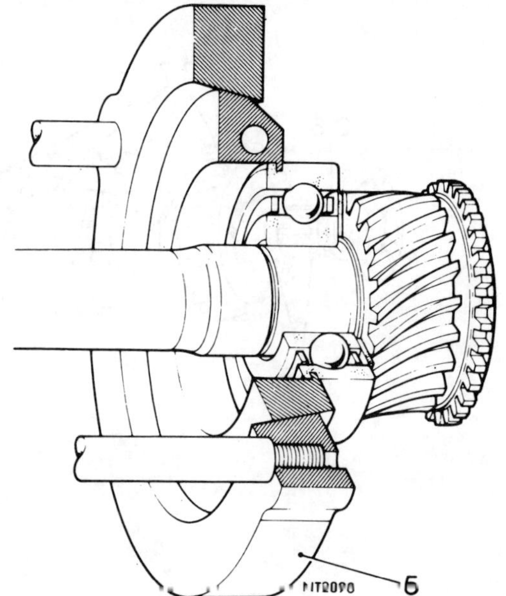

REAR OIL SEAL

Service tool RG.421

– Remove and refit **37.23.01.**

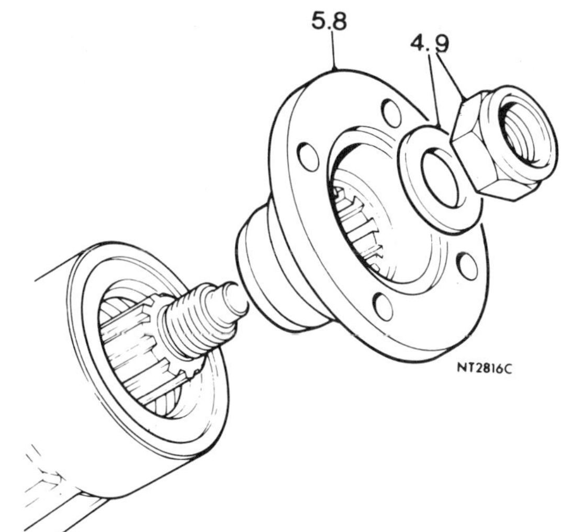

Removing

1. Drive the vehicle onto a ramp.
2. Remove the exhaust silencer and tail pipes and intermediate pipes 30.10.11 and 12.14.24-25.
3. Remove the propeller shaft 47.15.01.
4. Using tool No. RG.421 to retain the flange, unscrew and remove the nut.
5. Remove the drive flange.
6. Prise out the seal.

Refitting

7. Fit a new seal into the rear extension.
8. Refit the flange.
9. Using tool No. RG.421 to retain the flange, fit and tighten the nut to a torque load of 90 to 110 lbf ft (12·4 to 15·2 kgf m).
10. Refit the propeller shaft 47.15.01
11. Refit the exhaust intermediate pipes, silencer and tail pipes 30.10.11 and 12.14.24-25.

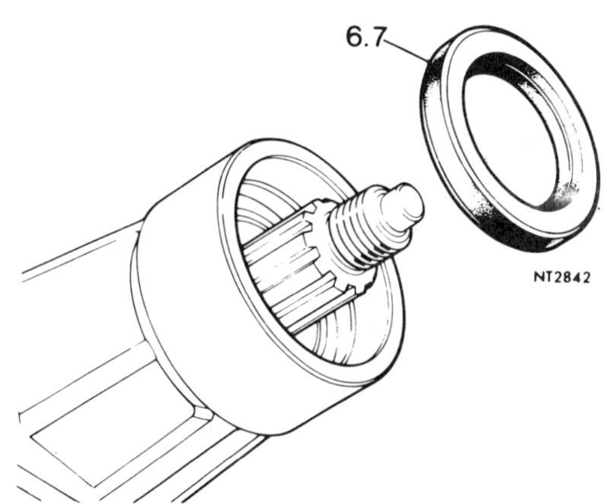

FRONT OIL SEAL

– Remove and refit **37.23.06**

Removing

1. Remove the gearbox 37.20.01.
2. Remove the clutch release mechanism 33.25.12.
3. Suitably mask the constant pinion shaft splines.
4. Remove the front bearing plate – four setscrews.
5. Prise out the oil seal.

Refitting

6. Press a new oil seal into the bearing plate.
7. Apply grease to the cover abutment face and fit the gasket.
8. With the constant pinion shaft splines covered (see 3), fit the front end cover - four setscrews and plain washers.
9. Remove the cover from constant pinion shaft splines.
10. Refit the clutch release mechanism 33.25.12.
11. Refit the gearbox 37.20.01.

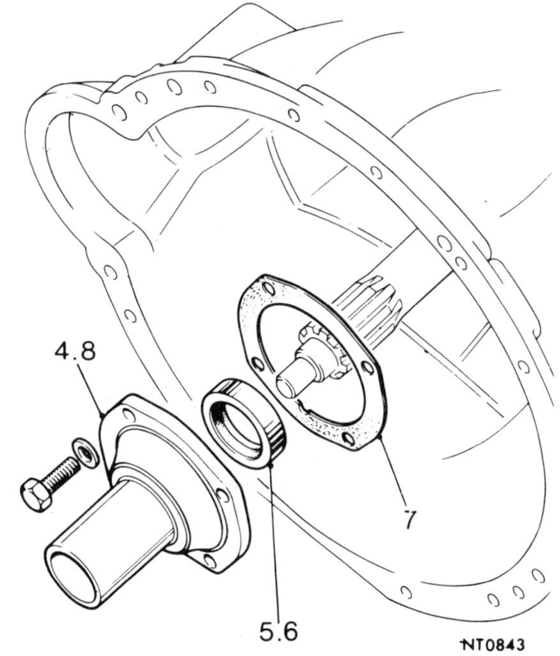

SPEEDOMETER DRIVE PINION ASSEMBLY

– Remove and refit **37.25.09**

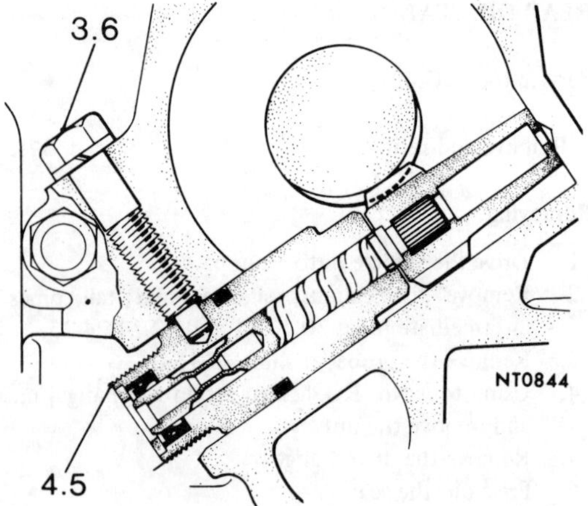

Removing

1. Drive the vehicle onto a ramp and raise the ramp.
2. Disconnect the speedometer cable from the gearbox.
3. Unscrew the peg bolt.
4. Withdraw the pinion assembly.

Refitting

5. Refit the pinion assembly.
6. Locate and tighten the peg bolt.
7. Connect the speedometer cable to the gearbox.

SPEEDOMETER DRIVE PINION ASSEMBLY

– Overhaul **37.25.13**

1. Remove the speedometer pinion assembly 37.25.09.

Dismantling

2. Withdraw the pinion from the housing.
3. Remove the 'O' ring.
4. Extract the oil seal.

Reassembling

5. Press a new oil seal into the housing.
6. Refit the 'O' ring.
7. Refit the pinion.
8. Refit the pinion assembly 37.25.09.

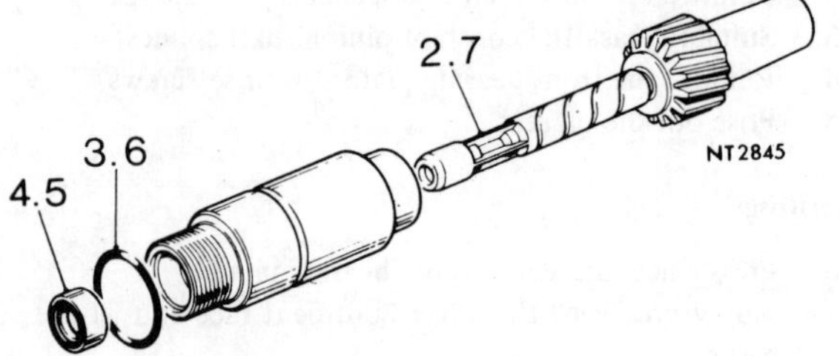

OVERDRIVE OPERATIONS 'A' TYPE

NOTE: The A type overdrive is fitted only to cars with the commission number prefix CP or CC.

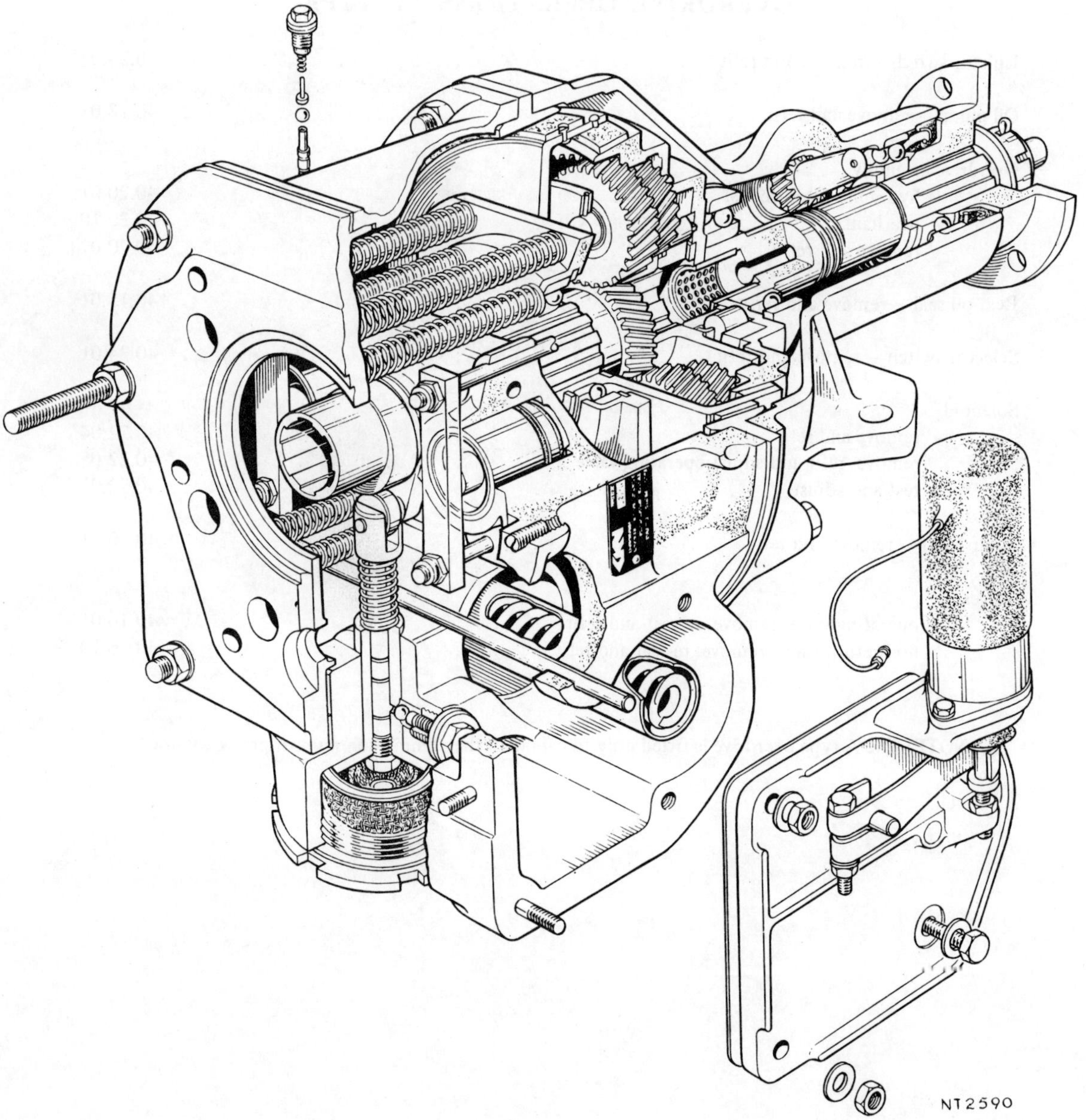

NT2590

FAULT DIAGNOSIS AND RECTIFICATION

Fault		Possible Cause	Remedy
OVERDRIVE DOES NOT ENGAGE	*a.*	Insufficient oil in unit	Top up gearbox/overdrive
	b.	Solenoid not energizing	Check circuit
	c.	Solenoid energized – not operating	Test and adjust. 40.22.01
	d.	Insufficient hydraulic pressure due to pump non-return valve not seating	Re-seat valve. 40.16.10
	e.	Insufficient hydraulic pressure due to worn accumulator	Overhaul unit. 40.20.10
	f.	Choked filter	Clean filter. 40.10.01
	g.	Pump damaged	Remove and check. 40.18.01
	h.	Operating valve leaking	Re-seat valve. 40.16.01
	j.	Internal damage	Overhaul unit. 40.20.10
*OVERDRIVE DOES NOT RELEASE	*a.*	Fault in electrical control circuit	Check circuit
	b.	Choked jet in operating valve	Check valve. 40.16.01
	c.	Solenoid/lever incorrect	Test and adjust. 40.22.01
	d.	Sticking clutch	See note †
	e.	Internal damage	Overhaul unit. 40.20.10
CLUTCH SLIP IN OVERDRIVE	*a.*	Insufficient oil in unit	Top up gearbox/overdrive
	b.	Solenoid lever out of adjustment	Adjust. 40.22.01
	c.	Insufficient oil pressure due to pump non-return valve not seating	Re-seat valve. 40.16.10
	d.	Insufficient oil pressure due to worn accumulator	Overhaul unit. 40.20.10
CLUTCH SLIP IN REVERSE AND FREE-WHEEL ON OVER-RUN	*a.*	Solenoid lever out of adjustment	Adjust. 40.22.01
	b.	Partially choked restrictor jet in operating valve.	Check valve. 40.16.01
	c.	Solenoid stop incorrectly set	Adjust. 40.22.01

*CAUTION: If, for any reason, the overdrive cannot be released **do not** reverse the vehicle as severe internal damage **will** result.

† NOTE: When a clutch is sticking on a new vehicle the probable cause is the linings not having bedded in sufficiently to release. Where this occurs the linings may usually be parted by striking the brake ring sharply with a hide mallet.

DATA

Clutch movement from direct to overdrive . . .	0·110 to 0·120 in
Hydraulic operating pressure	410 to 430 lb/in^2
Ratio	22%

**

SUMP FILTER (Laycock unit type 22/61753 – see identification plate)

– Remove and refit **40.10.01**

Removing

1. Raise car on ramp.
2. Place a container to receive oil.
3. Remove guard and drain plug.
4. Lift out filter.
5. Clean filter and plug.

Refitting

6. Insert filter.
7. Fit drain plug with magnetic washers and new sealing washer.
8. Fit drain plug guard.
9. Top up gearbox/overdrive oil level.
10. Lower vehicle.

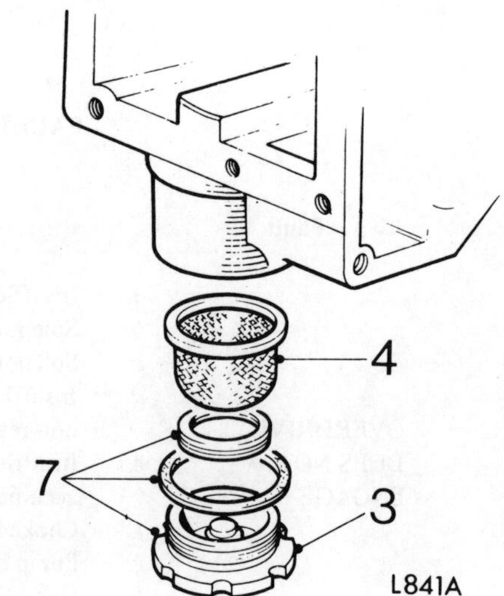

SUMP FILTER (Laycock unit type 22/61985 – see identification plate)

– Remove and refit **40.10.01**

Removing

1. Raise car on the ramp.
2. Place a container to receive the oil under the overdrive.
3. Remove the drain plug.
4. Lift out the filter.
5. Clean the filter, plug and magnetic rings.

Refitting

6. Insert the filter.
7. Fit the drain plug with magnetic washers and new sealing washer.
8. Top up gearbox/overdrive oil level.
9. Lower the vehicle.

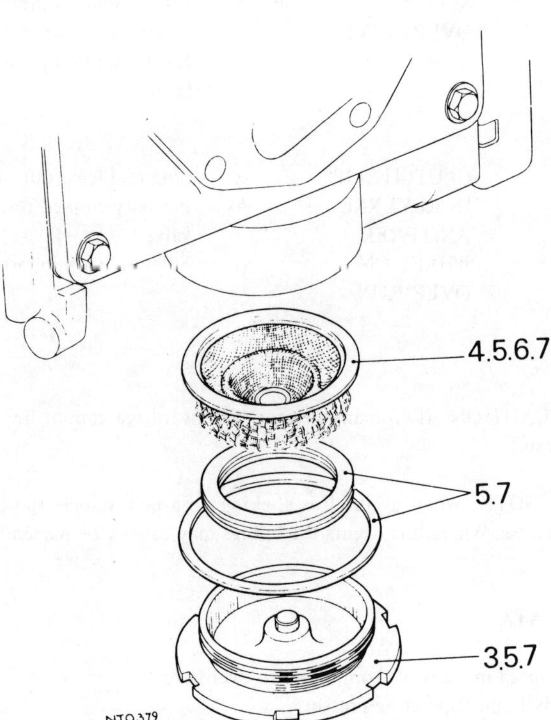

**

REAR OIL SEAL

– Remove and refit **40.15.01**

Service tool: L177A

Removing

1. Raise vehicle.
2. Remove propeller shaft. 47.15.01.
3. Remove split pin, nut, washer and drive flange.
4. Prise out oil seal.

Refitting

5. Fit oil seal squarely into position with lip facing inboard and abutting against shoulder in case tool L177A.
6. Fit drive flange, washer and nut, tightening to 90 to 110 lbf ft (12·4 to 15·2 kgf m). Secure with split pin.
7. Fit propeller shaft. 47.15.01.
8. Lower vehicle.

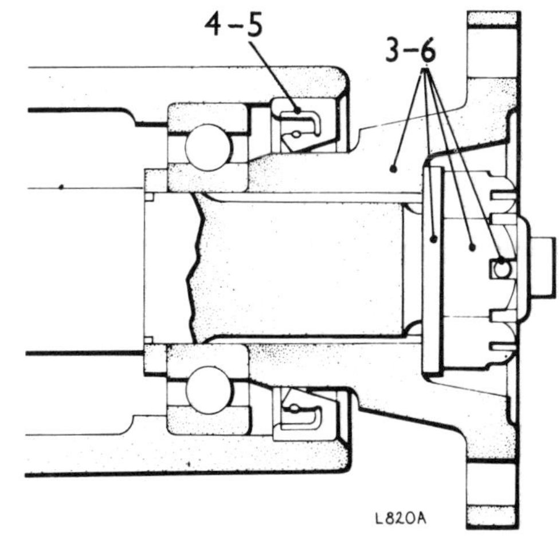

OPERATING VALVE

– Remove and refit **40.16.01**

Removing

1. Switch ignition ON, engage top gear, operate overdrive switch six times, switch off. This operation dissipates pressure in overdrive unit.
2. Lift front console tray, remove rubber grommet.
3. Use extension and socket to remove operating valve plug.
4. Use magnet to withdraw spring, plunger, ball and valve.
5. Insert ball into hole and onto its seal. Fit valve upside down so that the seat in the casing is facing the seat on the valve with the ball interposed.
6. Give the valve a sharp, gentle tap, remove the valve and ball.
7. Check the valve bore and outlet hole to ensure it is not choked.

Refitting

8. Reverse 1 to 4.

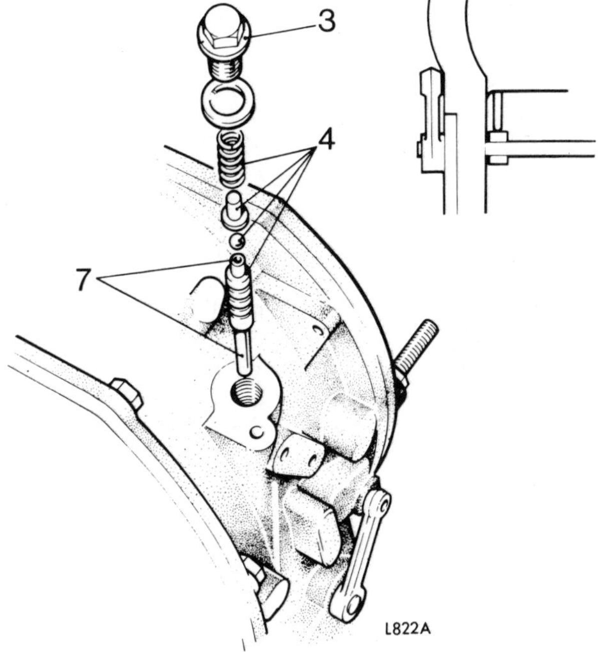

NON-RETURN VALVE

– Remove, re-seat and refit **40.16.10**

Operation 40.18.01, 1 to 9 and 21 to 33.

OIL PUMP

– Remove and refit **40.18.01**

Service tools: L183A, L183A1, L183A2, L184

Removing

1. Raise vehicle, drain oil from overdrive.
2. Remove two screws securing solenoid to bracket.
3. Withdraw solenoid and plunger.
4. Slacken clamp bolt, withdraw operating fork and spacer.
5. Remove two nuts on solenoid bracket studs.
6. Progressively unscrew two bolts, with red painted heads, securing solenoid bracket.
   WARNING: To avoid personal injury remove nuts (5) before bolts (6) to enable the greater length of the bolts to progressively relieve the tension of the accumulator spring.
7. Remove solenoid bracket, collect 'O' ring from bracket recess or operating lever cross-rod.
8. Remove non-return valve plug.
9. Withdraw non-return valve spring, plunger and ball.
10. Remove sump filter.
11. Remove hexagon plug and two screws.
12. Fit tool L183A1 to pump and withdraw pump body, spring and piston.

Refitting

13. Fit guide pegs into bottom pump face holes.
14. Assemble plunger, spring and pump body.
15. Insert pump assembly over guide pegs with:
    (a) Flat on plunger facing to the rear.
    (b) Hole in pump body flange adjacent to hole in casing.
16. Drift pump into position. Tool L184.
17. Remove guide pegs, fit two screws and hexagon plug.
18. Fit sealing washers, magnetic washers and filter to drain plug.
19. Fit and tighten drain plug.
20. Fit drain plug guard.
21. Fit non-return valve ball on seat and tap with copper drift to seat ball.
22. Fit valve components· ball, plunger and spring.
23. Fit plug and sealing washer.
24. Check that accumulator spring and shims (where fitted) are in position.
25. Fit 'O' ring to solenoid bracket recess.
26. Fit solenoid bracket and gasket.
27. Fit and evenly tighten the two red-headed screws.
28. Fit and tighten two nuts.
29. Fit spacer and solenoid operating lever.
30. Fit solenoid, inserting plunger in yoke of operating lever.
31. Fit and tighten two solenoid retaining screws.
32. Test and adjust solenoid. 40.22.01.
33. Top up gearbox and overdrive oil level, run vehicle and re-check oil level.

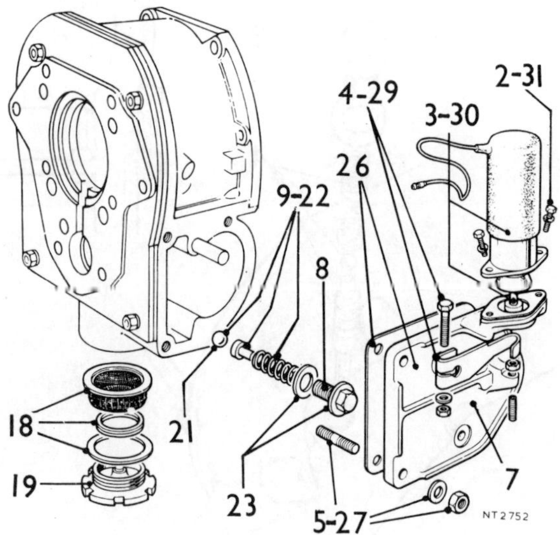

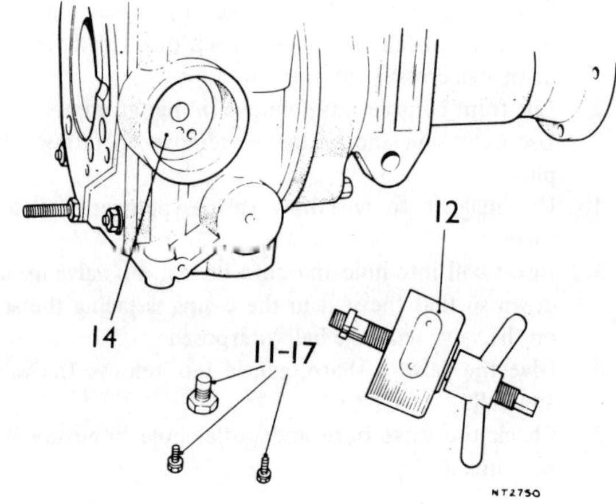

OPERATING VALVE

– Remove and refit 40.16.01

Removing

1. Switch ignition ON, engage top gear, operate overdrive switch six times, switch off. This operation dissipates pressure in overdrive unit.
2. Lift front console tray, remove rubber grommet.
3. Use extension and socket to remove operating valve plug.
4. Use magnet to withdraw spring, plunger, ball and valve.
5. Insert ball into hole and onto its seat. Fit valve upside down so that the seat in the casing is facing the seat on the valve with the ball interposed.
6. Give the valve a sharp, gentle tap, remove the valve and ball.
7. Check the valve bore and outlet hole to ensure it is not choked.

Refitting

8. Reverse 1 to 4.

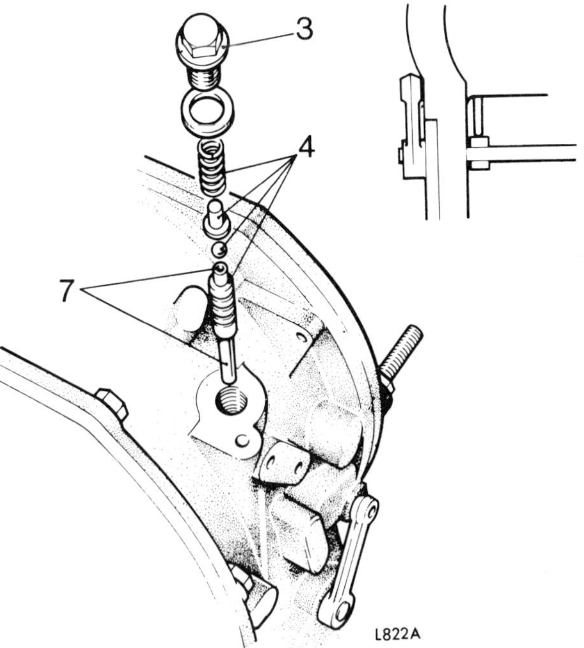

NON-RETURN VALVE

– Remove, re-seat and refit 40.16.10

Operation 40.18.01, 1 to 9 and 21 to 33.

OIL PUMP

– Remove and refit **40.18.01**

Service tools: L183A, L183A1, L183A2, L184

Removing

1. Raise vehicle, drain oil from overdrive.
2. Remove two screws securing solenoid to bracket.
3. Withdraw solenoid and plunger.
4. Slacken clamp bolt, withdraw operating fork and spacer.
5. Remove two nuts on solenoid bracket studs.
6. Progressively unscrew two bolts, with red painted heads, securing solenoid bracket.
   WARNING: To avoid personal injury remove nuts (5) before bolts (6) to enable the greater length of the bolts to progressively relieve the tension of the accumulator spring.
7. Remove solenoid bracket, collect 'O' ring from bracket recess or operating lever cross-rod.
8. Remove non-return valve plug.
9. Withdraw non-return valve spring, plunger and ball.
10. Remove sump filter.
11. Remove hexagon plug and two screws.
12. Fit tool L183A1 to pump and withdraw pump body, spring and piston.

Refitting

13. Fit guide pegs into bottom pump face holes.
14. Assemble plunger, spring and pump body.
15. Insert pump assembly over guide pegs with:
    (a) Flat on plunger facing to the rear.
    (b) Hole in pump body flange adjacent to hole in casing.
16. Drift pump into position. Tool L184.
17. Remove guide pegs, fit two screws and hexagon plug.
18. Fit sealing washers, magnetic washers and filter to drain plug.
19. Fit and tighten drain plug.
20. Fit drain plug guard.
21. Fit non-return valve ball on seat and tap with copper drift to seat ball.
22. Fit valve components: ball, plunger and spring.
23. Fit plug and sealing washer.
24. Check that accumulator spring and shims (where fitted) are in position.
25. Fit 'O' ring to solenoid bracket recess.
26. Fit solenoid bracket and gasket.
27. Fit and evenly tighten the two red-headed screws.
28. Fit and tighten two nuts.
29. Fit spacer and solenoid operating lever.
30. Fit solenoid, inserting plunger in yoke of operating lever.
31. Fit and tighten two solenoid retaining screws.
32. Test and adjust solenoid. 40.22.01.
33. Top up gearbox and overdrive oil level, run vehicle and re-check oil level.

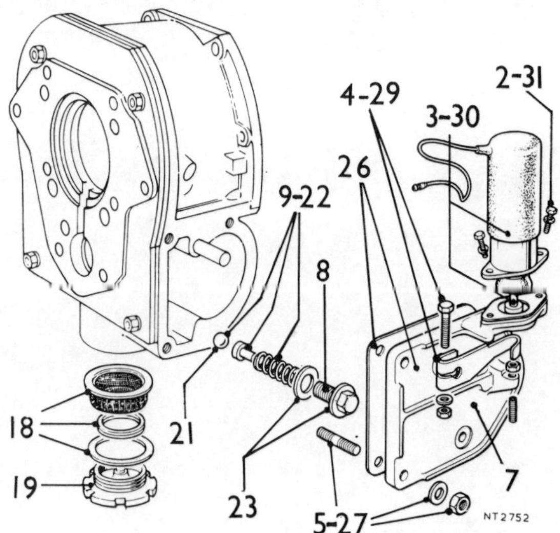

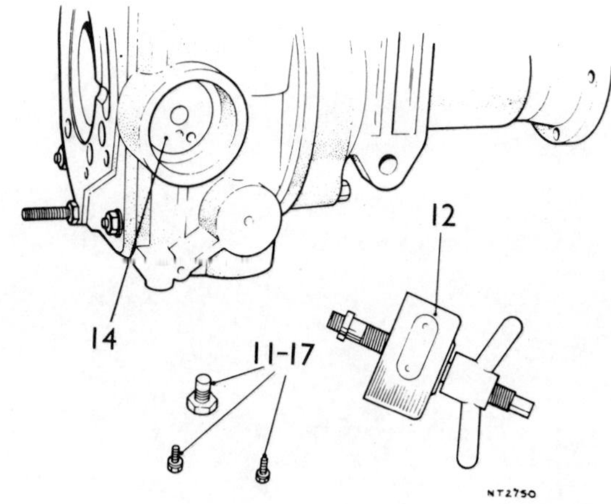

OVERDRIVE ASSEMBLY

– Hydraulic pressure test 40.20.01

Service tool: L188

1. Remove the gearbox tunnel cover – 17.01
2. Switch ignition ON, top gear, overdrive IN and OUT six times.
3. Use socket and extension to remove operating valve plug.
4. Fit hydraulic test gauge tool L188 to operating valve orifice.
5. Road-test or jack up vehicle and run engine with ans without overdrive.
6. Note the gauge reading which should be 410 to 430 lb/in^2.
7. Switch engine off, ignition on, top gear, overdrive in and out six times to dissipate oil pressure.
8. Remove gauge, refit operating valve plug.
9. Fit rubber grommet and front console tray.

NOTE: Lack of oil pressure when overdrive selected may indicate a fault in the pump non-return valve. 40.16.10.
Lack of oil pressure when overdrive not selected may indicate a fault in the operating valve. 40.16.01.

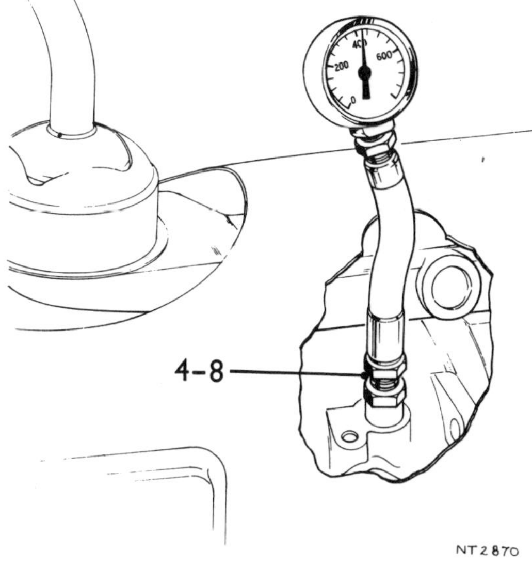

OVERDRIVE ASSEMBLY

– Remove and refit **40.20.07**

Removing

1. Remove gearbox. 37.20.01.
2. Drain gearbox and overdrive units of oil.
3. Place gearbox, bell housing flange down on bench.
4. Remove four nuts on *short* studs securing overdrive to gearbox.
5. Remove, evenly, the nuts on long studs securing overdrive to gearbox.
6. Lift off overdrive unit, collect eight overdrive clutch return springs.

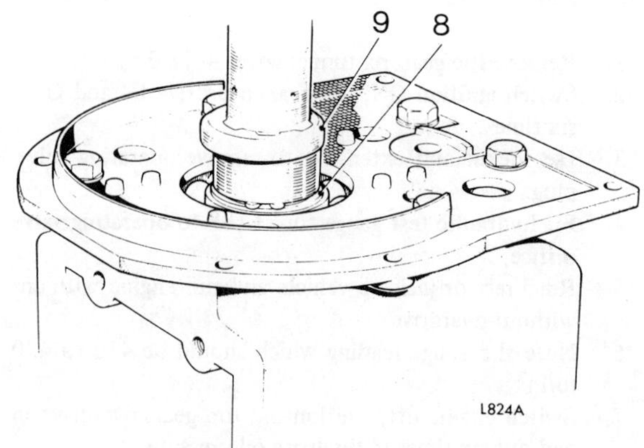

Refitting

7. Use a dummy mainshaft to ensure that the splines on the uni-directional clutch and the planet carrier are aligned.
8. Check that pump cam is fitted to mainshaft with long, plain end towards the gearbox.
9. Rotate mainshaft until narrowest part of cam is towards bottom of gearbox.
10. Thread a length of soft iron wire through the pump plunger and form it into a continuous loop just below sump level.
    NOTE: The plunger of the oil pump must be depressed whilst fitting the overdrive to allow it to come up below the drive cam when fitted.

Continued

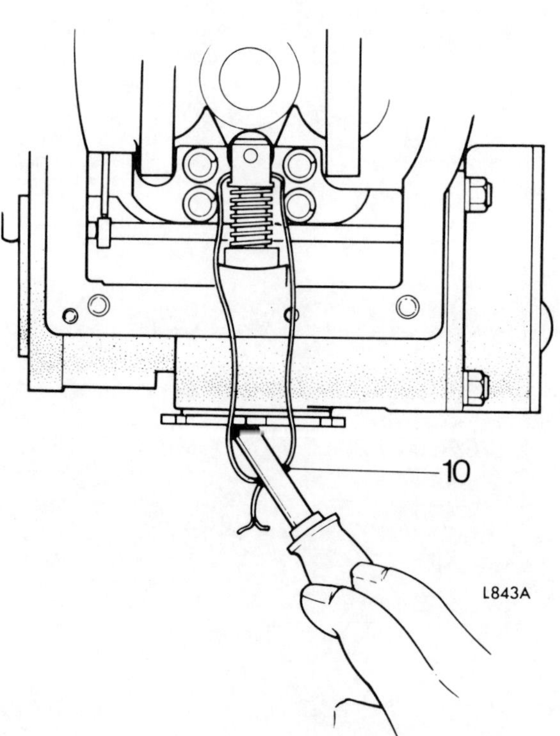

11. Fit gasket to adaptor plate.
12. Remove dummy mainshaft and position overdrive over mainshaft with the two long studs slightly misaligned to hold overdrive and gearbox apart.
13. Fit clutch return springs into position with shorter springs on inner posts and locating all springs on their posts and resting over bosses on adaptor plate.
14. Line up long studs and lower overdrive into position, turning drive flange to line up splines of mainshaft and planet carrier/uni-directional clutch.

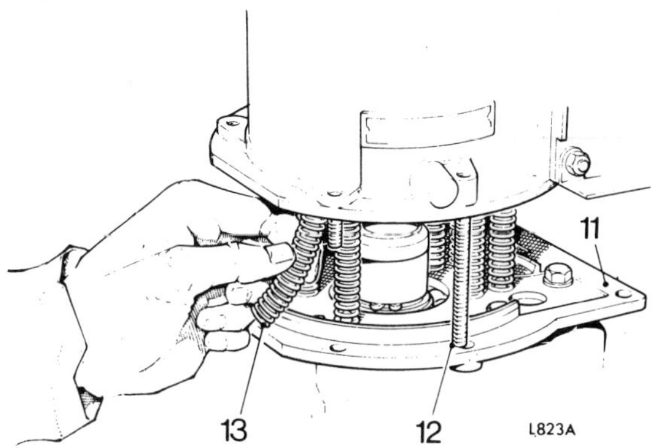

15. Fit nuts and washers to two long studs and evenly tighten whilst using a screwdriver through the loop of wire to depress pump plunger.
    CAUTION: Locking of the unit before it is tightened down indicates either *(a)* splines not aligned correctly or *(b)* cam and pump fouling. Do not try to force units together but slacken off, investigate cause, rectify and repeat.
16. When the faces are 0·20 in (5 mm) apart cut wire loop and pull out carefully ensuring that all of the wire is removed.
17. Tighten nuts, fit and tighten remaining nuts and washers.
18. Refit gearbox. 37.20.01.

OVERDRIVE ASSEMBLY

– Overhaul **40.20.10**

Service tools: L178. L182. L183A. L183A1. L183A2. L184. L185A. L188. L190A

CAUTION: The internal working parts and oil ways are particularly vulnerable to dirt: for this reason it is most important that a clinical standard of cleanliness is maintained throughout the following operation.

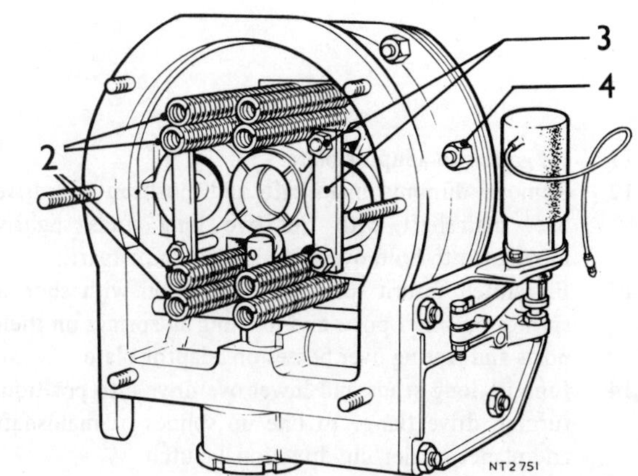

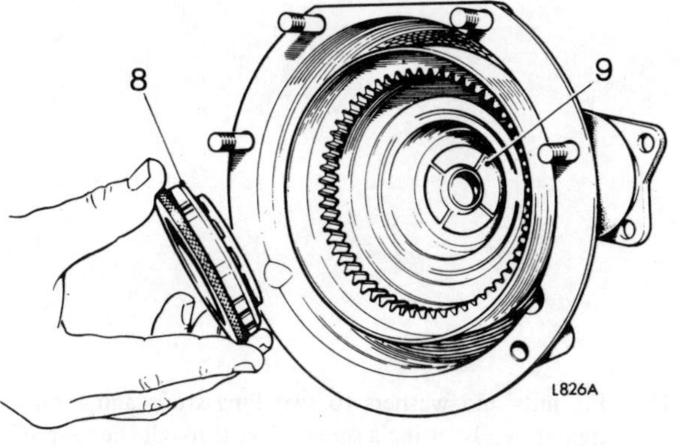

Dismantling

1. Remove the overdrive assembly. 40.20.07.
2. Remove eight clutch return springs.
3. Release lock washers, unscrew four nuts and remove the two bridge pieces.
4. Remove six nuts securing front to rear casings.
5. Separate casings and brake ring.
   CAUTION: The use of a lever or screwdriver to separate the casings will damage the mating faces and result in oil leakage, Use a hide hammer to cases that are tight.

Rear casing

6. Withdraw clutch sliding member.
7. Remove sun wheel and planet carrier.
8. Cover the uni-directional ckutch with tool L178 and and draw the clutch into the tool with the fingers.
9. Withdraw bronze thrust washer.
10. Remove split pin, nut and washer securing drive flange to tail shaft.
11. Withdraw drive flange.
12. Remove rear oil seal.
13. Remove speedometer drive pinion and housing.
14. Press annulus from rear casing.
15. Remove spacing washer from annulus tail shaft.
16. Remove front bearing from annulus.
17. Drive rear bearing from casing.

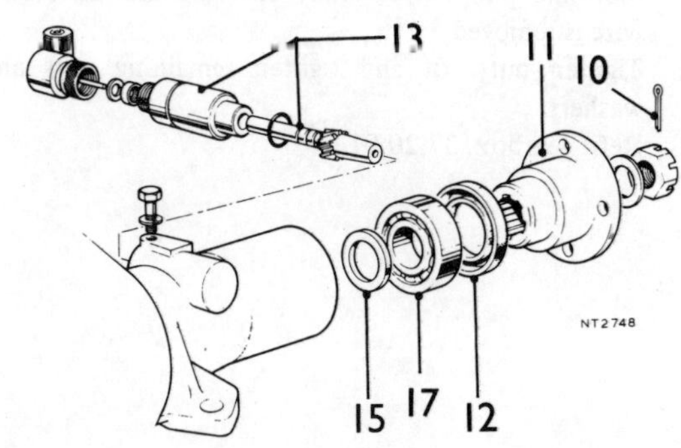

Continued

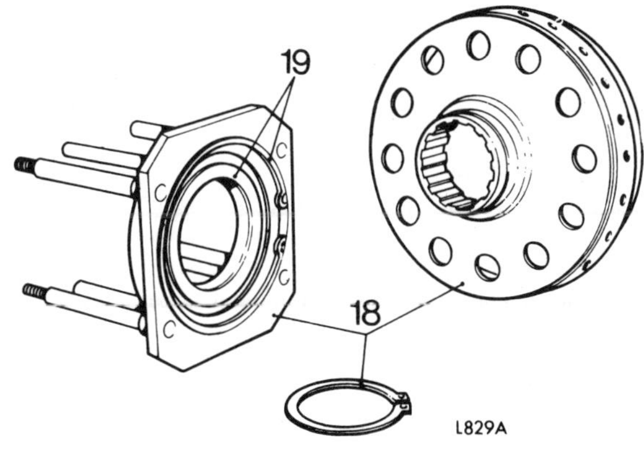

Clutch sliding member

18. Remove circlip and carefully separate clutch member and drive ring assembly.
19. Remove circlip and press bearing from drive ring.

Front casing

20. Remove bronze and steel thrust washers.

Operating valve

21. Remove operating valve plug a, copper washer b, and withdraw valve components – spring c, plunger d, ball e and valve f.
22. Remove operating pistons using grips and withdrawing with a rotary pull.

Solenoid

23. Remove two screws securing solenoid.
24. Remove solenoid, easing plunger from yoke of operating lever.
25. Release clamp bolt and remove operating lever and spacer.
26. Remove two nuts from studs securing solenoid bracket.

    WARNING: Remove the nuts (26) before slackening setscrews (27) as the accumulator spring, under tension, must be slackened progressively to avoid the risk of personal injury.
27. Progressively slacken the two setscrews with heads painted red securing solenoid bracket to casing.
28. Remove solenoid bracket.
29. Collect 'O' ring from cross-rod or solenoid bracket.

Continued

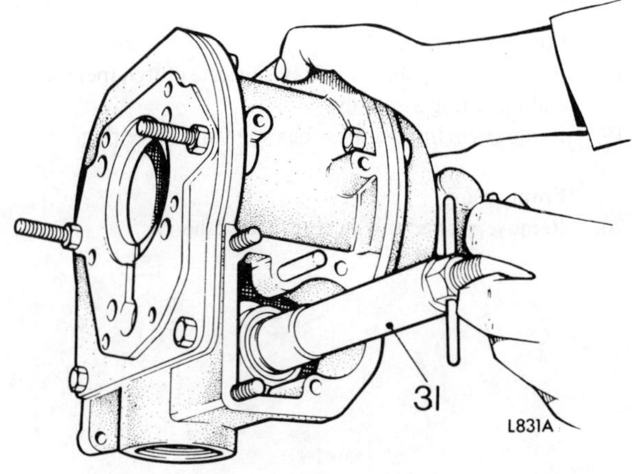

Accumulator

30. Remove accumulator spring, shim washers and tube.
31. Insert tool L182 into bore of accumulator sleeve, turn lower lever to lock in position, withdraw accumulator by turning and pulling upper lever.
32. Separate sleeve and piston.

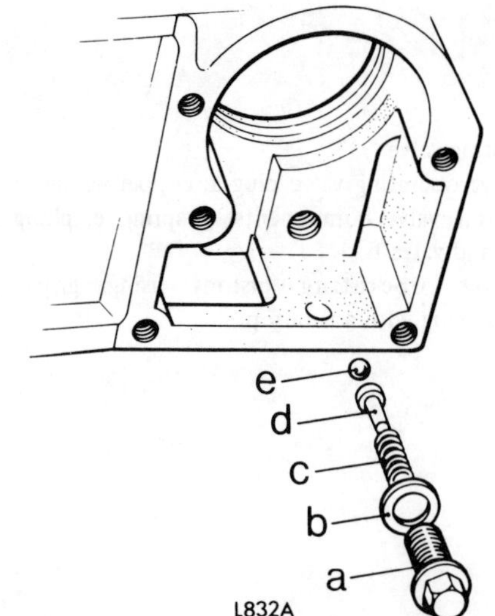

Non-return valve

33. Remove hexagon plug a, copper washer b and valve components – spring c, plunger d and ball e.

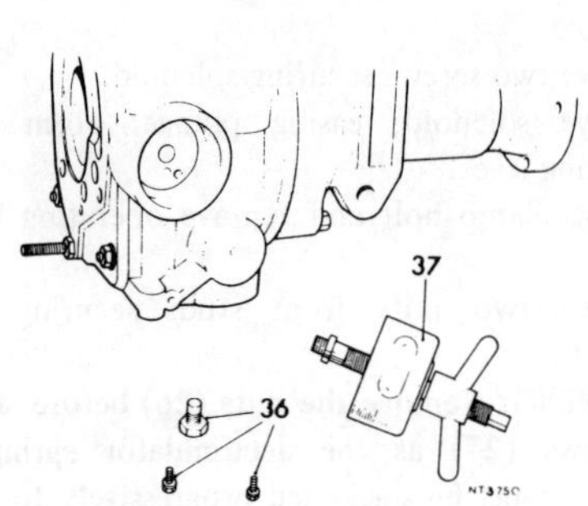

Pump

34. Remove sump plug, sealing washer and magnetic washers.
35. Remove filter.
36. Remove hexagon plug and two screws.
37. Fit tool L183A1 to pump and withdraw pump body a, spring b and piston c.

Inspection

38. Clean all components.
39. Inspect all gears, bearings, bushes, working surfaces and oilways for evidence of undue wear and blockage in accordance with good engineering practice. Renew as necessary.
40. Renew all 'O' rings, oil seals and gaskets. Lubricate all 'O' rings with petroleum jelly prior to fitting.

Continued

Reassembly

Front casing
Pump

41. Fit guide pegs into holes in bottom pump face.
42. Assemble plunger, spring and pump body.
43. Insert pump assembly over guide pegs with *(a)* flat on plunger against guide dowel (below centre bronze bush) and *(b)* hole in pump body flange adjacent to hole in casing.
44. Drift pump into position using L184 (drift).
45. Remove guide pegs, fit two screws and base plug.
46. Fit sealing washer, magnetic washers and filter to drain plug.
47. Fit and tighten drain plug and guard assembly.

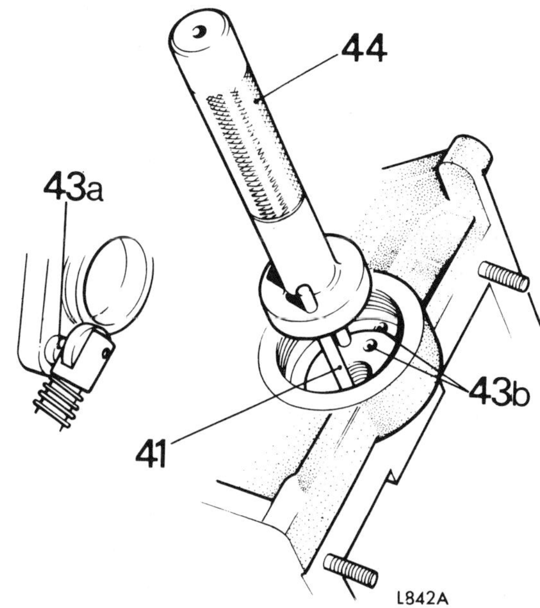

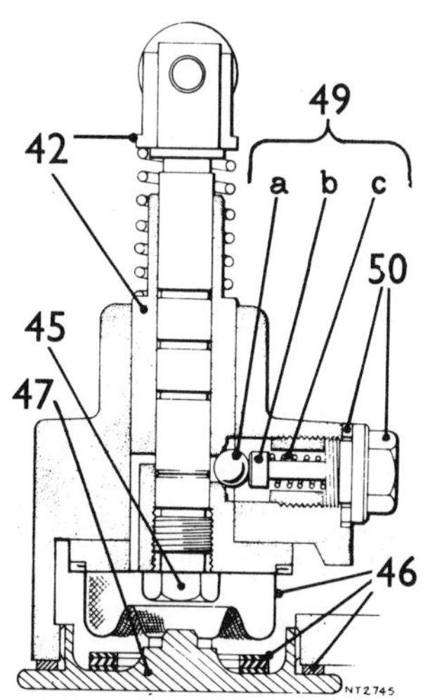

Non-return valve

48. Fit ball (0·25 in dia.) on seat and tap with copper drift to seat ball.
49. Fit valve components – *(a)* ball *(b)* plunger, *(c)* spring.
50. Fit and tighten copper washer and hexagon plug.

Continued

Accumulator

51. Fit rings to piston – two wide inners· four thin outers.
52. Fit piston to sleeve using tool L179.
53. Fit 'O' ring to sleeve.
54. Ease sleeve into bore and push home using accumulator tube.
55. Fit accumulator spring and shims (where fitted).
    CAUTION: When accumulator spring shims are fitted they must be replaced. Fitting washers of greater thickness can cause a pressure build-up where a spring becomes coil-bound and the blow-off holes are not uncovered by the piston.
56. Fit 'O' ring to solenoid bracket recess.
57. Fit solenoid bracket and gasket.
58. Fit and tighten evenly the two red-headed set screws.
59. Fit and tighten nuts and washers.

Solenoid

60. Fit spacers and solenoid-operating lever, securing with clamp bolt.
61. Fit solenoid, inserting plunger to yoke of operating lever.
62. Fit and tighten two solenoid retaining screws.
    NOTE: when the overdrive is rebuilt the solenoid will require adjustment (40.22.01).

Continued

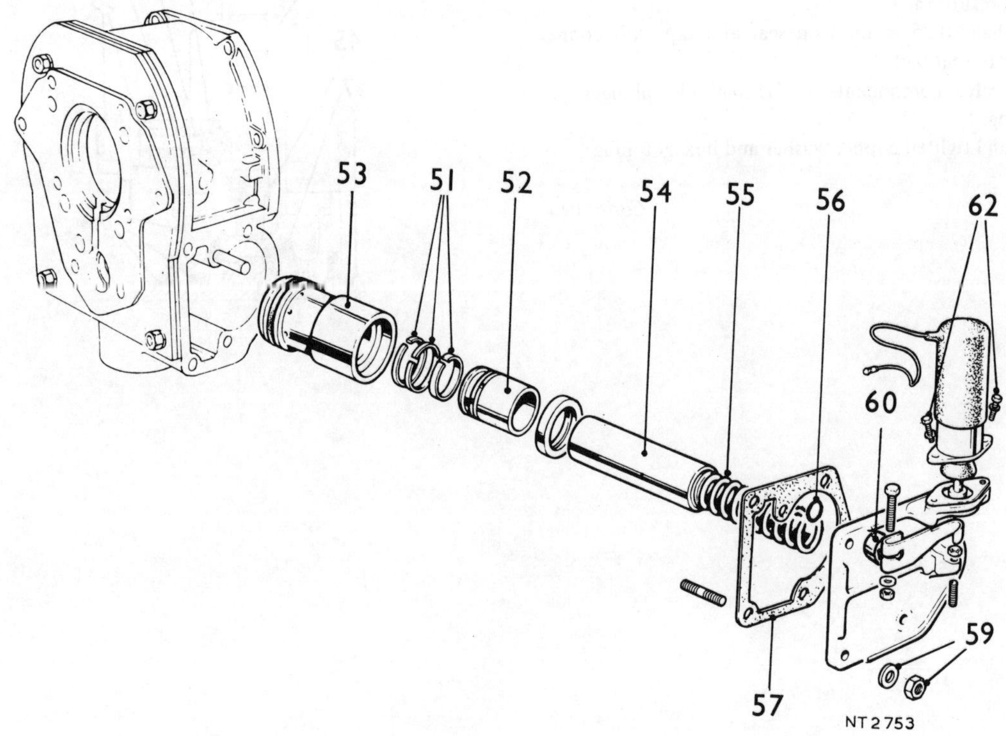

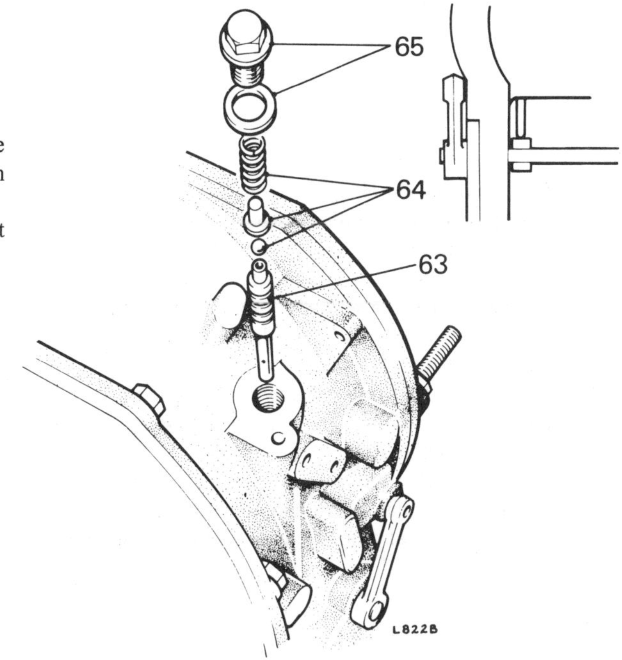

Operating valve

63. Insert valve into casing, ensuring that the hemispherical head engages on the flat of the cam on the operating cross-shaft.
64. Drop the 0·3125 in dia. ball *(a)* on its seat, insert plunger *(b)* and spring *(c)*.
65. Fit and tighten plug and copper washer.
66. Fit 'O' rings to operating pistons.
67. Fit pistons to bores.

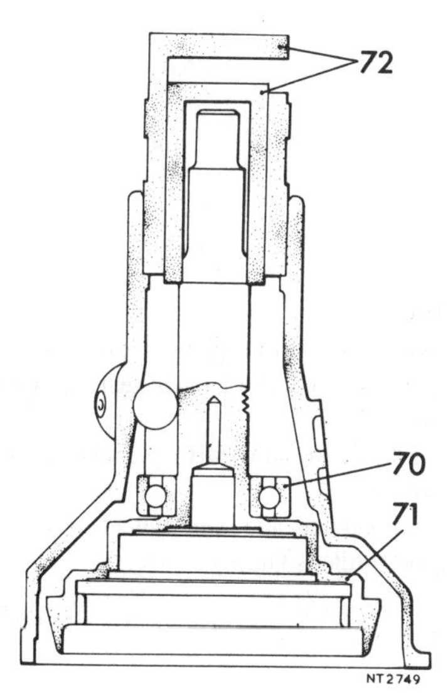

Rear casing

68. Press the front bearing into the rear casing until it abuts against the shoulder in the casing.
69. Press the annulus into the front bearing in casing.
70. Fit gauge L190A over the tailshaft until the outer member contacts the rear bearing shoulder in the casing.
71. Press down the inner member (L190A) and select a spacing washer which will just fit in slot in gauge.
    NOTE: Spacing washers are available as follows:
    Part No. 500623 suffix E 0·146 in; F 0·151 in; G 0·156 in; J 0·166 in.
72. Remove gauge, fit selected washer.
73. Drive rear bearing into position.
74. Fit rear oil seal squarely until it abuts on casing shoulder.
75. Fit rear drive flange, washer, nut and split pin.

Continued

Un-directional clutch

76. Assembly spring into roller cage.
77. Fit inner member and engage on other end of spring.
78. Engage the slots of the inner member with the tongues of the cage so that the spring rotates the cage and rollers (when fitted) up the inclined face of the inner member.
79. Place assembly, front end down, into tool L178 and insert rollers through slot in tool, turning clutch clockwise until all rollers are in place.
80. Fit thrust washer into annulus recess.
81. Fit uni-directional clutch and tool to annulus, slide clutch from tool into its outer bearing in annulus, remove tool.

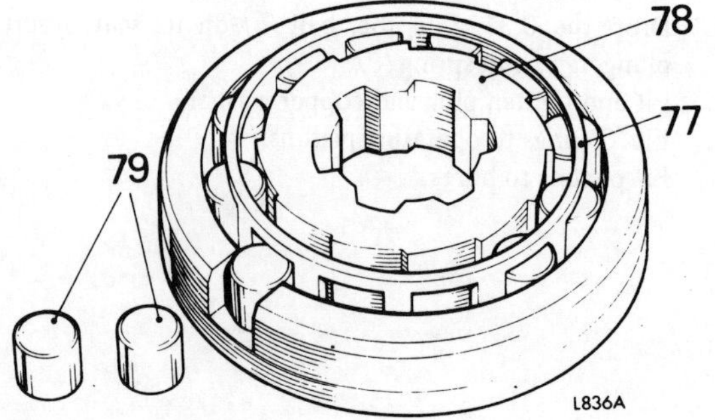

Planet carrier

82. Rotate each of the three planet gears until a spot, punched on the outside of each gear, is positioned radially outwards.
83. Insert sun wheel, meshing with planets and keeping dots in position.
84. Insert planet carrier and sun wheel into annulus, meshing gears whilst so doing.

Continued

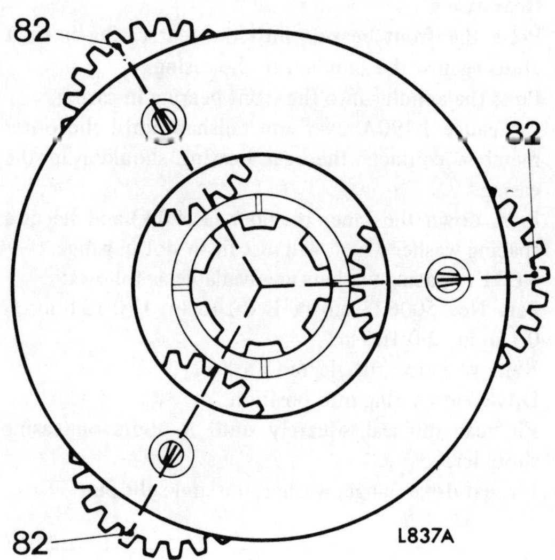

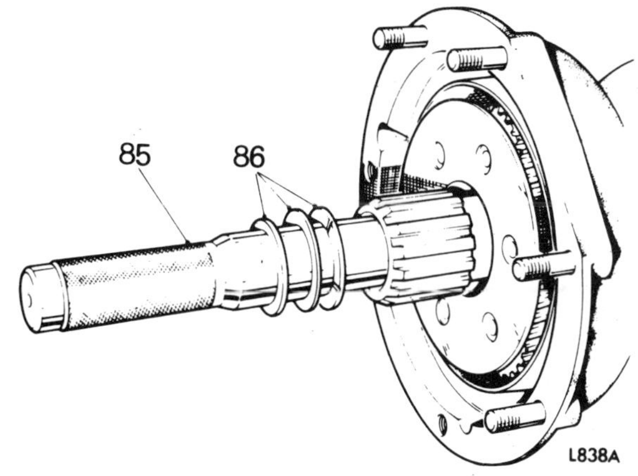

Sun wheel end-float

85. Insert dummy mainshaft tool L185A and turn sun wheel until shaft engages the planet carrier and uni-directional clutch splines.
86. Fit a thrust washer of known thickness plus steel and bronze thrust washers over dummy shaft until they rest on sun wheel.

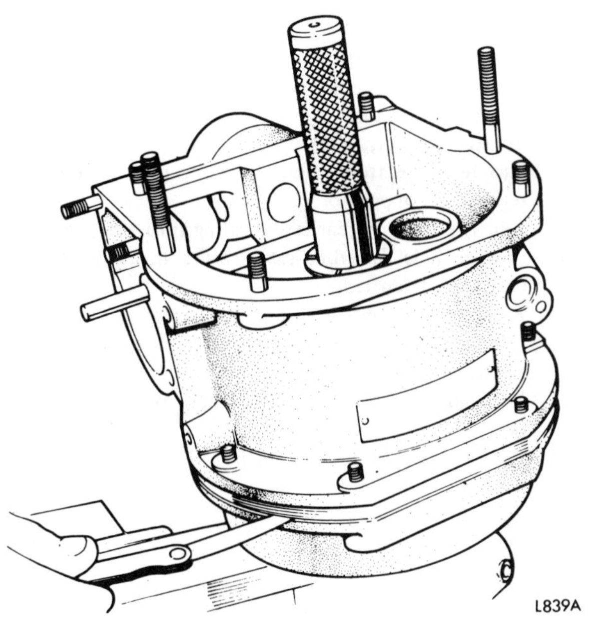

87. Fit brake ring to front casing, tap fully home.
88. Fit front casing to rear until abutted on washers on dummy shaft.
89. Use feeler gauges to measure gap between cases which should be the thickness of the additional washer fitted at 86 minus the required end-float 0·008 to 0·014 in (0·20 to 0·35 mm).

Example *(a)*:

Noted thickness of additional washer	0·125 in
Gap between flanges	0·114 in
End-float	0·011 in

As this end-float is within limits the existing washers are satisfactory.

Example *(b)*:

Noted thickness of additional washer	0·125 in
Gap between flanges	0.123 in
End-float	0·002 in

In this example 0·002 in end-float is not sufficient and a steel washer 0·006 to 0·012 in thicker than the existing washer must be fitted.

Washers are available in the following thicknesses in inches:

Part No. 500588 Suffix A. 0·113 to 0·114· B. 0·107 to 0·108; C. 0·101 to 0·102; D. 0·095 to 0·096; E. 0·089 to 0·090· F. 0·083 to 0·084; G. 0·077 to 0·078.

90. On selection of correct washer, separate casings.

Continued

Clutch sliding member

91. Press bearing evenly into thrust ring, secure with circlip.
92. Press thrust ring assembly on the hub of clutch sliding member, secure with circlip.
93. Fit sliding member assembly engaging with splines of sun wheel.

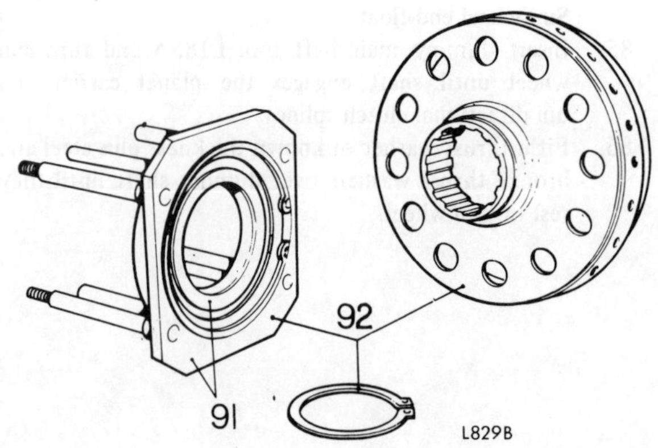

Re-assemble casings

94. Coat flanges of brake ring with jointing compound and fit to front case.
95. Fit steel washer, selected at 89, then bronze washer into recess in front case; use a smear of grease to retain them in position.
96. Join the front to rear case locating thrust ring posts through holes in front case, ensure thrust washers (95) are still located.
97. Fit and tighten nuts securing front to rear case.
98. Fit bridge pieces securing with nuts locked with new tab washers.
99. Fit eight clutch springs, four short ones on inner posts.
100. Fit overdrive assembly to gearbox.40.20.07.

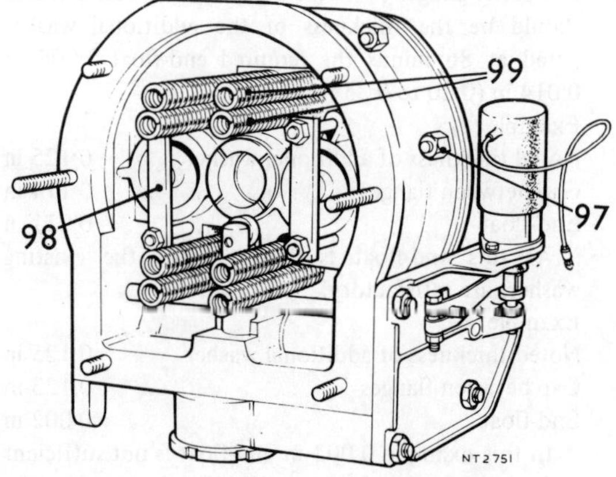

SOLENOID

– Test and adjust 40.22.01

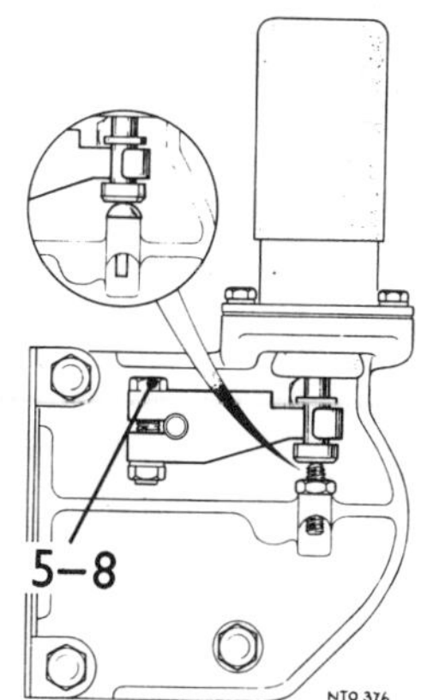

Testing

1. Raise vehicle.
2. Connect an ammeter into solenoid feed circuit.
3. Switch ignition ON, top gear, overdrive IN.
4. Note and act on the following accordingly.
   a. The setting lever will move to a position where its alignment hole is coincident with a hole in the casing (test alignment) by inserting a rod 3/16" dia. through hole in lever and into casing hole). The ammeter will drop to holding current of 1 to 2 amps immediately after switching on. Test satisfactory.
   b. No current to solenoid – check circuit.
   c. Setting lever correctly aligned, ammeter reading high – renew solenoid. 40.22.14.
   d. Setting lever incorrectly aligned, ammeter reading correct/incorrect – adjust operating lever.

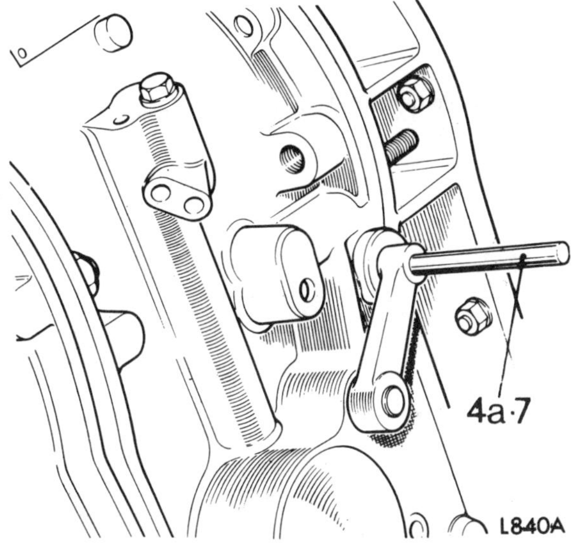

Adjusting operating lever

5. Slacken clamp bolt on operating lever.
6. Check, ignition ON, top gear, overdrive IN.
7. Position rod through hole in setting lever and alignment hole in case. Push plunger into solenoid to its limit, holding lever fork against collar of plunger.
8. Tighten clamp bolt on operating rod.
9. Switch off, re-check 4 till condition 4*a* exists.
10. Adjust the stop to provide 0·0625 in (1·6 mm) free movement by slackening locknut and turning grub screw with an Allen key.

SOLENOID

– Remove and refit **40.22.04**

Removing

1. Raise vehicle.
2. Disconnect solenoid cable.
3. Remove two screws securing solenoid to bracket.
4. Withdraw solenoid and plunger (release plunger from operating lever fork).

Refitting

6. Reverse instructions 1 to 4.

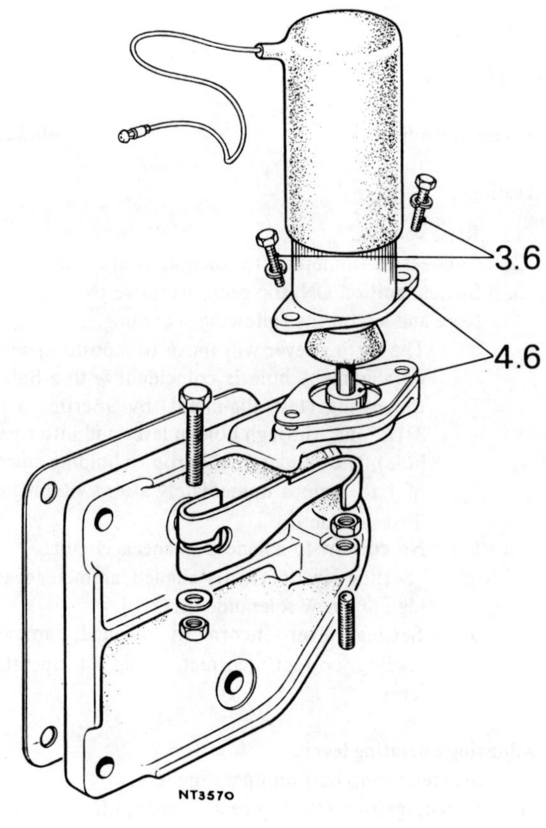

SOLENOID

– Remove, refit and adjust operating lever **40.22.05**

Operation 40.22.04 plus operation 40.22.01, 5 to 10.

LIST OF OPERATIONS

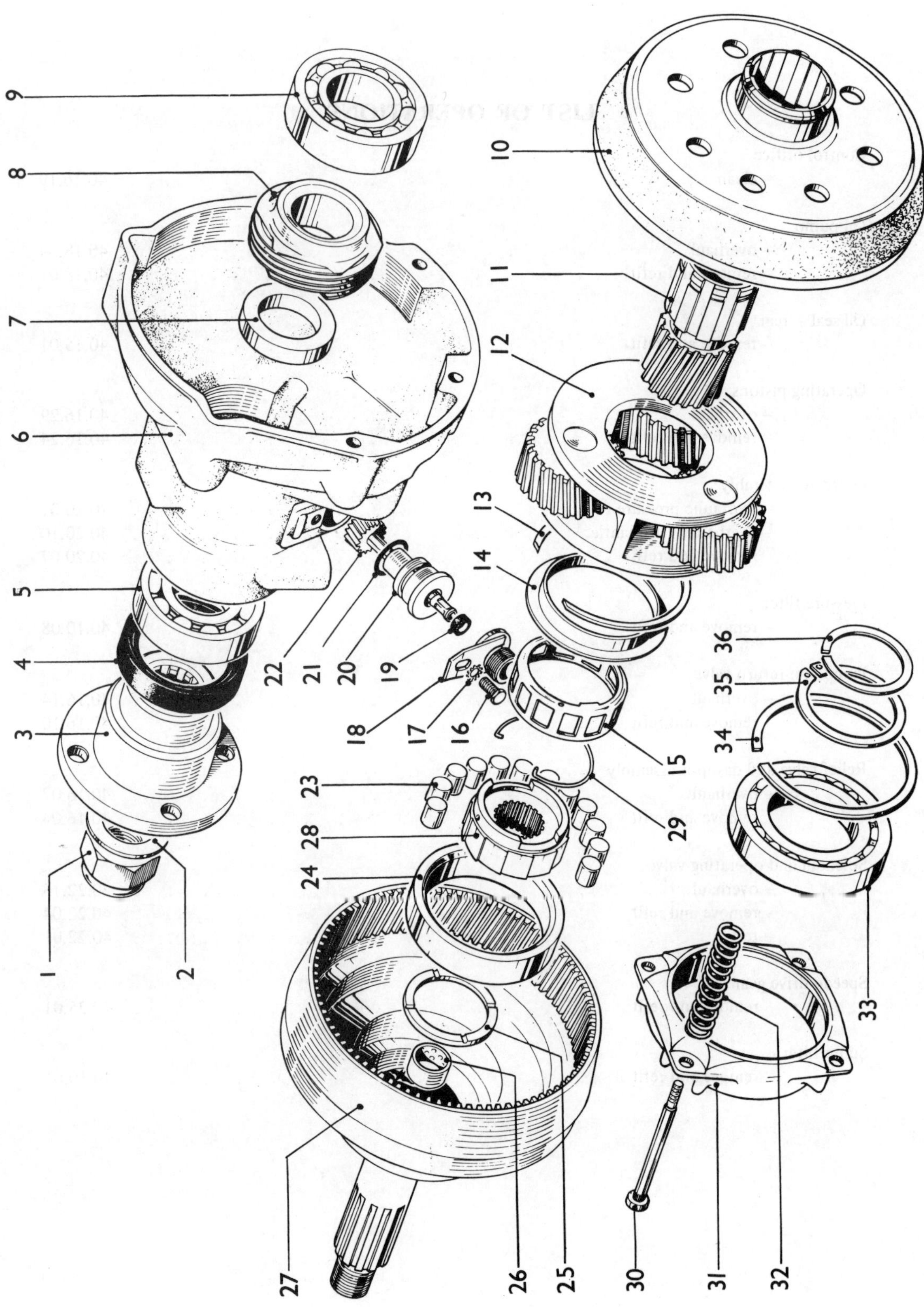
NT2919
1
2
3
4
5
6
7
8
9
10
11
12
13
14
15
16
17
18
19
20
21
22
23
24
25
26
27
28
29
30
31
32
33
34
35
36

J TYPE OVERDRIVE COMPONENTS

1. Locknut
2. Washer
3. Drive flange
4. Oil seal
5. Annulus rear ball race
6. Rear case
7. Spacer
8. Speedometer driving gear
9. Annulus front ball race
10. Clutch sliding member
11. Sun wheel
12. Planet carrier assembly
13. Circlip
14. Oil thrower
15. Unidirectional clutch cage
16. Bolt
17. Star washer
18. Speedometer retaining clamp
19. Oil seal
20. Speedo driven gear housing
21. 'O' ring
22. Speedometer driven gear
23. Unidirectional clutch rollers
24. Unidirectional clutch roller track
25. Thrust washer
26. Mainshaft bush
27. Annulus
28. Unidirectional clutch hub
29. Unidirectional clutch spring.
30. Thrust pin
31. Thrust ring
32. Clutch return springs
33. Thrust ball race
34. Retaining circlip
35. Circlip for sliding member
36. Circlip for sun wheel

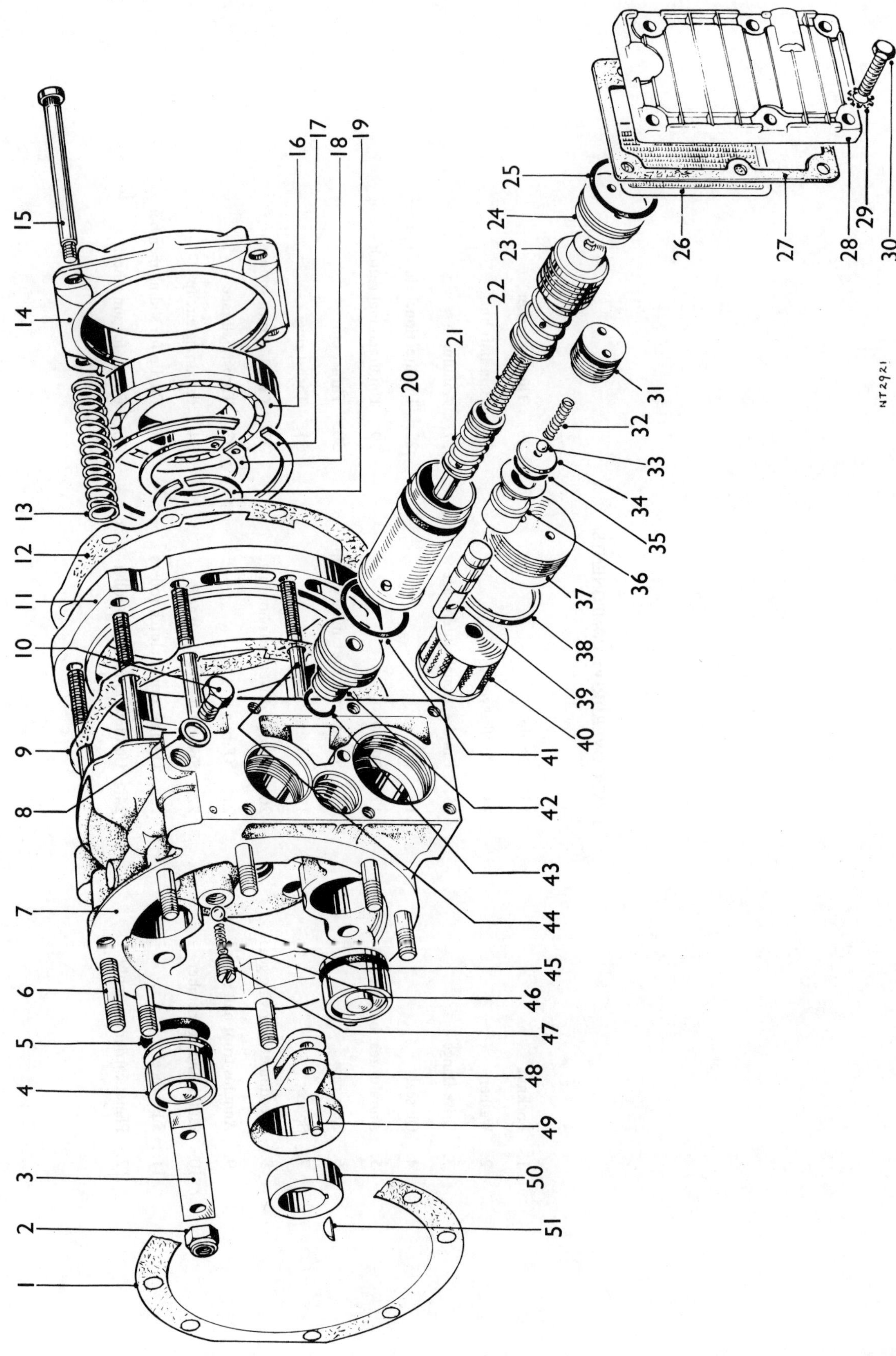
1
2
3
4
5
6
7
8
9
10
11
12
13
14
15
16
17
18
19
20
21
22
23
24
25
26
27
28
29
30
31
32
33
34
35
36
37
38
39
40
41
42
43
44
45
46
47
48
49
50
51
NT2921

J TYPE OVERDRIVE COMPONENTS

1. Gasket
2. Locknut
3. Bridge piece
4. Operating piston
5. 'O' ring
6. Stud
7. Main case
8. Washer (copper)
9. Gasket
10. Pressure tapping plug
11. Brake ring
12. Gasket
13. Clutch return spring
14. Thrust ring
15. Thrust pin
16. Thrust ball race
17. Retaining circlip
18. Circlip for sliding member
19. Circlip for sun wheel
20. Dashpot sleeve
21. Relief valve assembly
22. Double dashpot spring
23. Dashpot piston assembly
24. Dashpot plug
25. 'O' ring
26. Sump filter
27. Sump gasket
28. Sump
29. Star washer
30. Bolt
31. Pump plug
32. Non-return valve spring
33. Steel ball
34. Non-return valve seat
35. 'O' ring
36. Pump body
37. Pressure filter plug
38. Pressure filter washer
39. Pump plunger
40. Pressure filter
41. 'O' ring
42. Relief valve body
43. 'O' ring
44. Stud
45. Steel ball
46. Lubrication relief valve spring
47. Lubrication relief valve plug
48. Pump strap
49. Pump in
50. Cam
51. Woodruff key

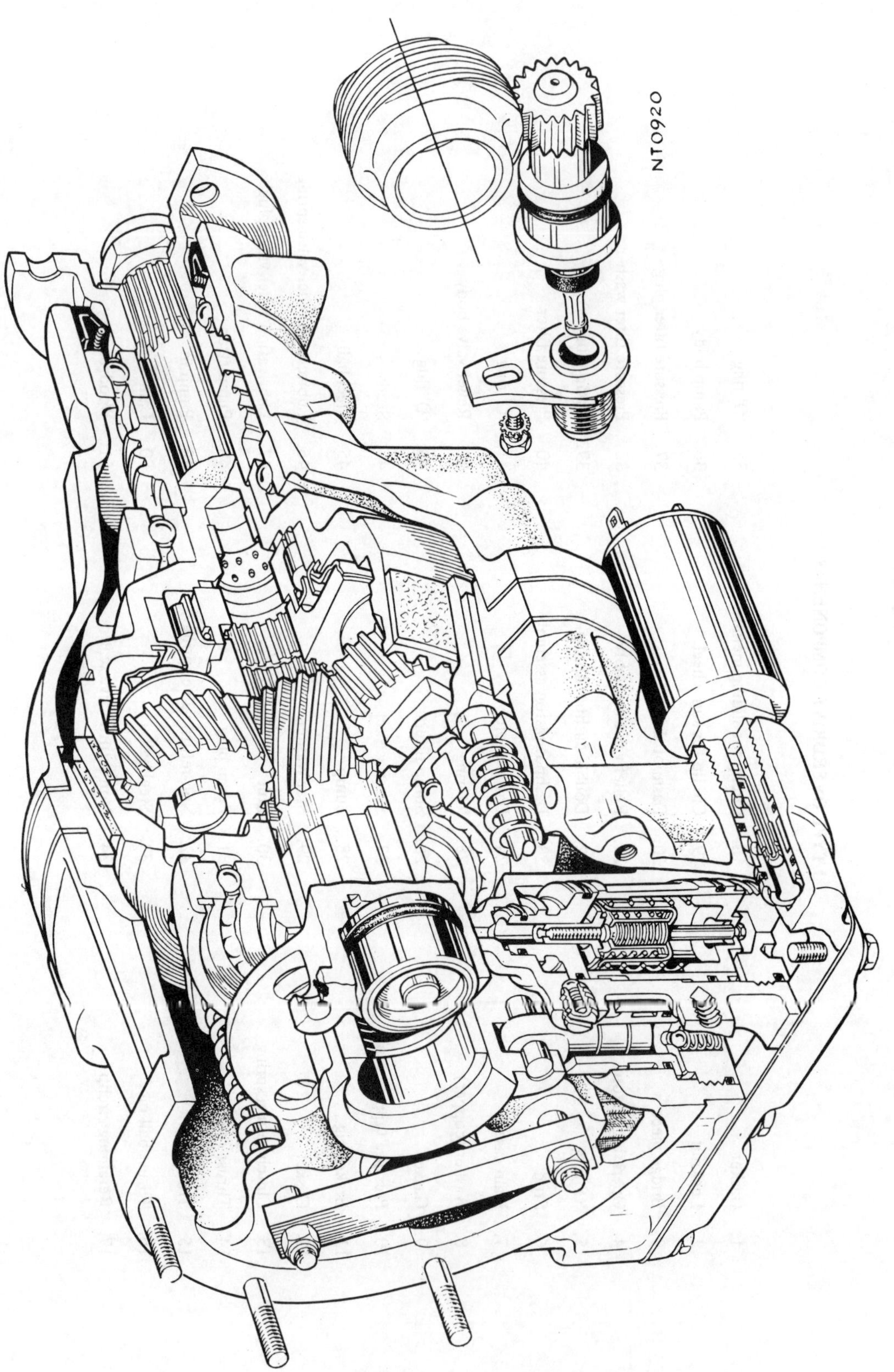

OVERDRIVE — J TYPE

INTRODUCTION

The overdrive is an additional gear unit between the gearbox and propeller shaft. When in operation it provides a higher overall gear ratio than that given by the final drive, crown wheel and pinion.

The primary object of an overdrive is to provide open road cruising at an engine speed lower than it would be in normal top gear. This reduced engine speed gives a considerable reduction in petrol consumption and increase in engine life. Overdrive may also be used on the indirect gears to enhance performance or to provide easy and clutchless gear changing, for example in town traffic.

The overdrive is operated by an electric solenoid controlled by a switch, fitted in the gear lever knob. An inhibitor switch is fitted in the electrical circuit to prevent engagement of overdrive in reverse, and some or all of the indirect gears.

Overdrive can be engaged or disengaged at will at any speed, but usually above 30 m.p.h. in top gear. It should be operated without using the clutch pedal and at any throttle opening because the unit is designed to be engaged and disengaged when transmitting full power. The only precaution necessary is to avoid disengaging overdrive at too high a road speed, particularly when using it in an indirect gear, since this would cause excessive engine revolutions.

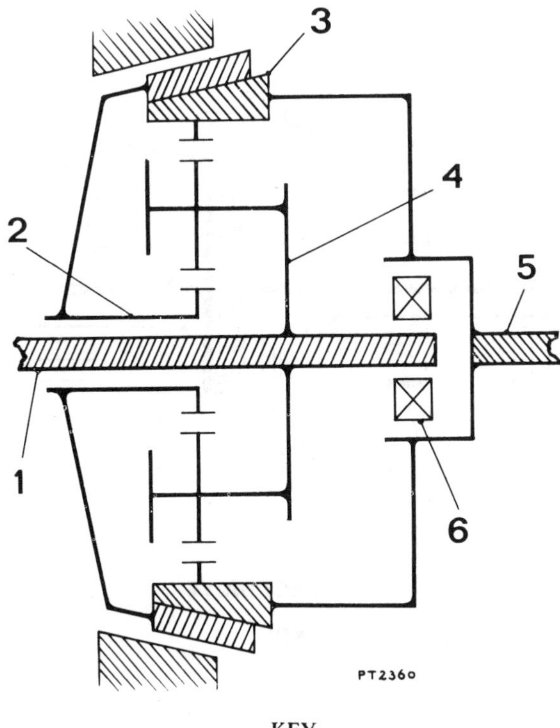

KEY

1. Input shaft connected to planet carrier.
2. Sun gear.
3. Annulus.
4. Planet carrier.
5. Output shaft connected to annulus.
6. Roller clutch.

WORKING PRINCIPLES

The overdrive gears are epicycle and consist of a central sunwheel meshing with three planet gears which in turn mesh with an internally toothed annulus. All gears are in constant mesh. The planet carrier is attached to the input shaft and the annulus is integral with the output shaft.

The unit is shown diagrammatically in PT 3355.

An extension of the gearbox mainshaft forms the overdrive input shaft. Forward direct drive (PT 3355) power is transmitted from this shaft to the inner member of uni-directional clutch and then to the outer member of this clutch through rollers which are driven up inclined faces and wedge between the inner and outer members. The outer member forms part of the combined annulus and output shaft.

The gear train is inoperative. A cone clutch is mounted on the externally splined extension of the sunwheel and is loaded in contact with the annulus by a number of springs which have their reaction against the casing of the overdrive unit. The spring load is transmitted to the clutch member through a thrust ring and ball bearing. This arrangement causes the inner friction lining of the cone clutch to contact the outer cone of the annulus and rotate with the annulus, whilst the springs and thrust ring remain stationary. Since the sunwheel is splined to the clutch member the whole gear train is locked, permitting over-run and reverse torque to be transmitted by the cone clutch, without which the uni-directional clutch would give a freewheel condition. Additional load is imparted to the clutch member, during over-run and reverse, by the sunwheel which, due to the helix angle of its gear teeth, thrusts rearward and has for its reaction member the cone clutch.

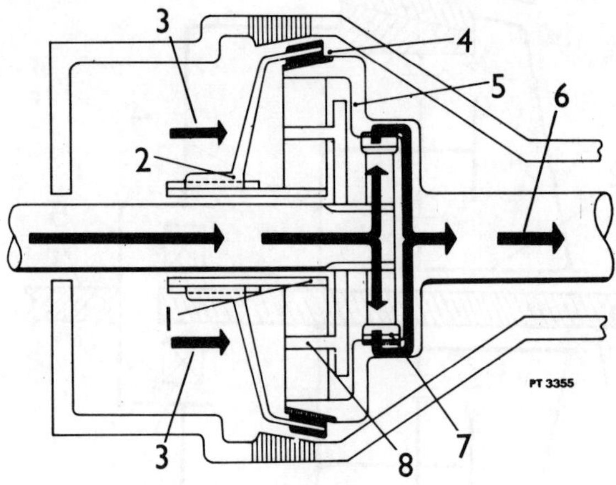

IN DIRECT DRIVE

KEY

1. Sunwheel.
2. Sliding cone clutch.
3. Spring pressure.
4. Annulus and sunwheel locked.
5. Annulus.
6. To propshaft.
7. Uni-directional roller clutch.
8. Planet wheels.

PT3356 shows the position of the cone clutch when overdrive is engaged.

It will be seen that it is no longer in contact with the annulus but has moved forward so that its outer friction lining is in contact with a brake ring forming part of the overdrive casing. The sunwheel to which the clutch is attached is therefore held stationary. The output shaft and annulus continue to rotate at the same speed, so the planet wheels rotate on their axes around the stationary sunwheel, reducing the planet carrier and input shaft speed. The uni-directional clutch permits the outer member to over run the inner member.

This condition gives a lower engine speed for a given road speed.

Movement of the cone clutch in a forward direction is effected by means of hydraulic pressure which acts upon two pistons when a valve is opened, by operating the driver controlled selector switch. This hydraulic pressure overcomes the springs which load the clutch member on to the annulus and causes the clutch to engage the brake ring with sufficient load to hold the sun wheel at rest. Additional load is imparted to the clutch in a forward direction due to the helix angle of the gear teeth.

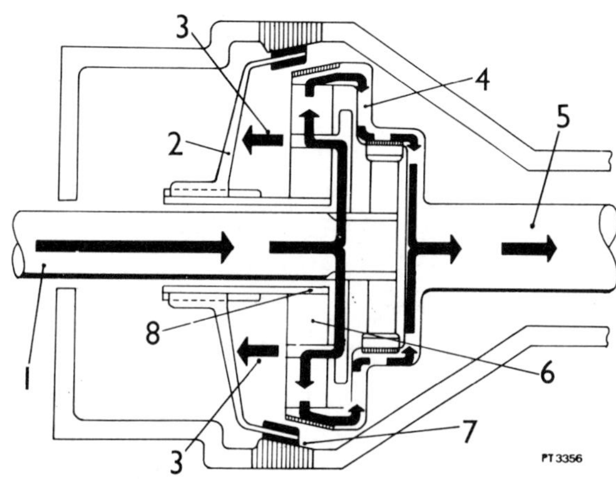

IN OVERDRIVE

KEY

1. From gearbox.
2. Sliding cone clutch.
3. Hydraulic pressure.
4. Annulus driven by planet gears.
5. To propshaft.
6. Planet wheels.
7. Locked cone clutch holds sunwheel.
8. Sunwheel.

SOLENOID AND OPERATING VALVE

Energising

The solenoid and operating valve are a self contained factory sealed unit, situated on the main case of the overdrive.

The solenoid has a single coil, encapsulated and completely waterproof, with a continuous current consumption of approximately 2 amperes. There are no electrical contacts in the solenoid.

In direct drive a residual pressure of approximately 20 p.s.i. maintains the system in primed condition and provides lubrication. This is achieved by the relief valve piston reacting on the residual pressure spring. When overdrive is engaged pressure increases to a pre-determined operating pressure of 430/460 p.s.i. When the solenoid is energised, its valve opens and oil which is at residual pressure is directed via passage 'Z' to the bottom of the dashpot piston. This causes the dashpot piston to rise and compress the dashpot spring causing a progressive increase in hydraulic pressure until the piston reaches its stop by which time the relief valve spring has been compressed to its working length, thus giving full operating pressure. This pressure causes the operating pistons to move forward overcoming the clutch springs and engages the cone clutch in the brake ring.

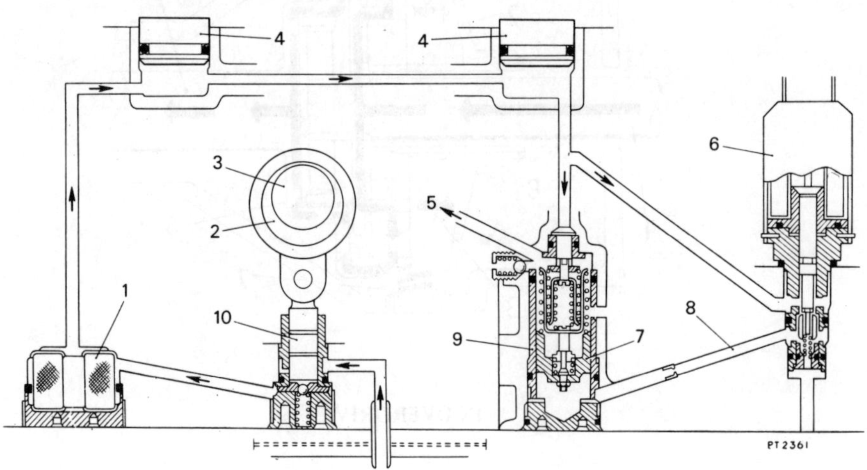

KEY

1. Pressure filter.
2. Cam.
3. Input shaft.
4. Operating pistons.
5. To central lubrication.
6. Solenoid valve.
7. Dashpot.
8. Passage Z.
9. Relief valve.
10. Pump.

De-energising

When the solenoid is de-energised its valve is closed by a spring, cutting off the oil supply from the pump to the dashpot. Oil is now exhausted via the control orifice in passage 'Z' which allows the relief valve spring to relax to its direct drive position. The dashpot spring moves the dashpot piston to its stop allowing the system pressure to progressively drop which enables the clutch springs to move the cone clutch gently into contact with the annulus.

The residual pressure of approximately 20 p.s.i. is now maintained in direct drive.

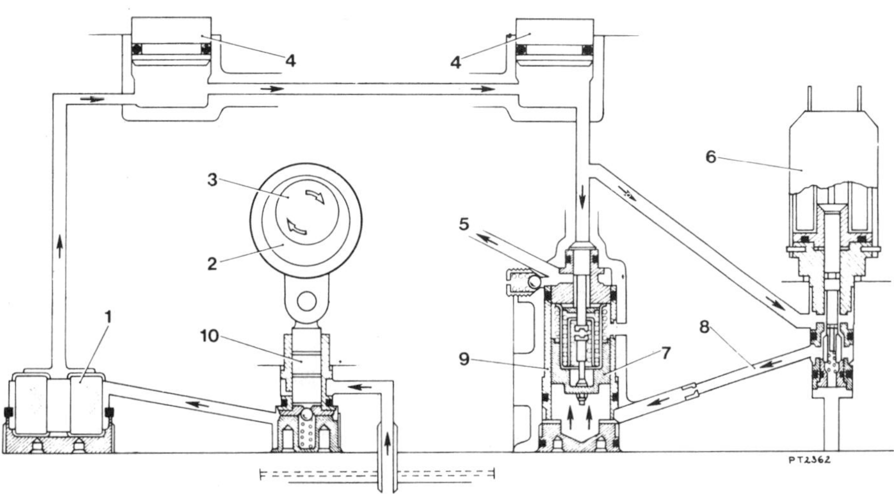

KEY

1. Pressure filter.
2. Cam.
3. Input shaft.
4. Operating pistons.
5. To central lubrication.
6. Solenoid valve.
7. Dashpot.
8. Passage Z.
9. Relief valve.
10. Pump.

HYDRAULIC SYSTEM

Hydraulic pressure is developed by a plunger type pump, cam operated from the input shaft. The pump draws oil from an air-cooled sump through a suction filter and delivers it via non-return valve, through a pressure filter to the operating pistons, solenoid valve and relief valve. Incorporated in the relief valve is a spring dashpot which ensures smooth overdrive engagement and disengagement under varying conditions.

LUBRICATION SYSTEM

Oil is discharged through the relief valve direct to an annular channel in the centre of the main casing and then through drillings in the mainshaft to the annulus spigot bearing. Immediately in front of the spigot bearing a radial drilling passes oil through the uni-directional clutch, from here it is directed by an oil thrower into a catcher disc on the planet carrier and to the planet bearings via the hollow planet bearing pins.

The pressure in the lubrication passage is controlled by the lubrication relief valve.

MAINTENANCE

The level of oil should be checked at the gearbox. To drain the sump of the overdrive must be removed as well as the gearbox drain plug. this will provide access to the suction and pressure filters, which should also be removed and cleaned before replenishing with new oil.

Following complete draining and refilling, run the transmission for a short period then re-check the oil level.

It is essential that only the approved lubricant is used for topping up and refilling. ON NO ACCOUNT SHOULD ANY ANTI-FRICTION ADDITIVES BE USED.

CLEANLINESS

Scrupulous cleanliness must be maintained throughout all servicing operations. Even minute particles of dust, dirt or lint from cleaning cloths may cause malfunction. When the overdrive and gearbox have a common oil supply, it is naturally as important that the same high standards of cleanliness must be maintained when servicing the gearbox.

Great care must be taken to avoid the entry of dirt when topping up or re-filling.

For cleaning use petrol or paraffin ONLY, and on no account should water be used.

FAULT DIAGNOSIS AND RECTIFICATION

Fault		Possible Cause	Remedy
OVERDRIVE DOES NOT ENGAGE	*a.*	Insufficient oil in unit.	Top up gearbox/overdrive.
	b.	Solenoid not energising.	Check electrical circuit.
	c.	Solenoid energising but not operating.	Remove solenoid and check operation of solenoid valve.
	d.	Insufficient hydraulic pressure	Fit pressure gauge and check operating pressure. Clean filters. Reseat pump non-return valve if necessary. Check relief valve operation. Clean control orifice DO NOT PROBE WITH WIRE.
	e.	Pump damaged.	Remove and check.
	f.	Internal damage.	Remove and examine overdrive.

THIS CALLS FOR IMMEDIATE ATTENTION. DO NOT REVERSE THE CAR, OR EXTENSIVE DAMAGE MAY BE CAUSED.

Fault		Possible Cause	Remedy
*OVERDRIVE DOES NOT RELEASE	*a.*	Fault in electrical control circuit.	Check electrical system for closed circuit.
	b.	Sticking solenoid valve.	Remove solenoid and check valve.
	c.	Residual pressure too high.	Fit pressure gauge and check residual pressure. If pressure is too high check for sticking relief valve.
	d.	Control orifice blocked.	Check and blow through with compressed air. DO NOT PROBE WITH WIRE.
	e.	Cone clutch sticking.	Tap the brake ring several times with a hide mallet.
	f.	Internal damage.	Remove and examine overdrive.
CLUTCH SLIP IN OVERDRIVE	*a.*	Insufficient oil in unit.	Top up gearbox/overdrive.
	b.	Operating pressure too low.	Fit the pressure gauge and check the pressure. Check the filters, pump non-return ball valve and relief valve. Check the control orifice is clear.
	c.	Sticking solenoid valve.	Remove solenoid and check operation of solenoid valve.
	d.	Worn or glazed clutch linings.	Remove overdrive and examine the linings or mechanical obstruction to movement of cone clutch.

(THESE SYMPTOMS MAY OCCUR TOGETHER OR SEPARATELY)

Fault		Possible Cause	Remedy
SLOW DIS-ENGAGEMENT OF OVERDRIVE FREE-WHEELING ON OVER-RUN SLIP IN REVERSE GEAR	*a.*	Sticking relief valve.	Check for sticking relief valve.
	b.	Sticking or partially blocked control valve	Remove solenoid and check.
	c.	Control orifice blocked.	Check to ensure the orifice is clear.
	d.	Internal damage.	Remove and examine overdrive.

DIMENSIONS AND CLEARANCES FOR PARTS WHEN NEW

	Dimensions New	Clearances New
CAM		
Outside Diameter of Cam	1·4590 in/1·4600 in	·0010 in/·0030 in
Inside Diameter of Pump Strap	1·4610 in/1·4620 in	
GEARBOX MAINSHAFT		
Diameter of Oil Transfer	·9640 in/ ·9650 in	·0010 in/·0030 in
Inside Diameter of Maincase at Oil Transfer	·9660 in/ ·9670 in	
Diameter at Sunwheel	·9410 in/ ·9430 in	·0040 in/·0080 in
Inside Diameter of Sunwheel Bush (Where Fitted)	·9470 in/ ·9490 in	
Diameter at Mainshaft Spigot	·5620 in/ ·5625 in	·0003 in/·0018 in
Inside Diameter at Spigot Bearing	·5628 in/ .5638 in	
OPERATING PISTONS		
Operating Piston Diameter	1·2492 in/1·2497 in	·0003 in/·0020 in
Operating Piston Bore Diameter	1·2500 in/1·2512 in	
RELIEF VALVE PUMP		
Pump Plunger Diameter	·4996 in/ ·5000 in	·0003 in/·0013 in
Pump Body Bore	·5003 in/ ·5009 in	
RELIEF VALVE		
Outside Diameter of Relief Valve Piston	·2496 in/ ·2498 in	·0002 in/·0009 in
Inside Diameter of Relief Valve Body	·2500 in/ ·2505 in	
Outside Diameter of Dashpot Piston	·9370 in/ ·9373 in	·0002 in/·0015 in
Inside Diameter of Dashpot Sleeve	·9375 in/ ·9385 in	
SPEEDO PINION		
Outside Diameter of Speedo Pinion	·3105 in/ ·3110 in	·0010 in/·0030 in
Inside Diameter of Speedo Bearing	·3120 in/ ·3135 in	
MISCELLANEOUS		
Sliding Member Travel from Direct Drive to Overdrive (Measured at Bridge Pieces).	·090 in/ ·115 in	

SUMP FILTER

– Remove and refit 40.10.01

Removing

1. Remove the six bolts and star washers holding the sump on.
2. Remove the sump.
3. Remove the sump gasket.
4. Pull the filter out.
5. Clean the filter in either paraffin or petrol.

Refitting

6. Push the filter back into position.
7. Refit the sump and gasket.
8. Refit the bolts and star washers and tighten to a torque of 6 lbf ft (0·8 kgf m).

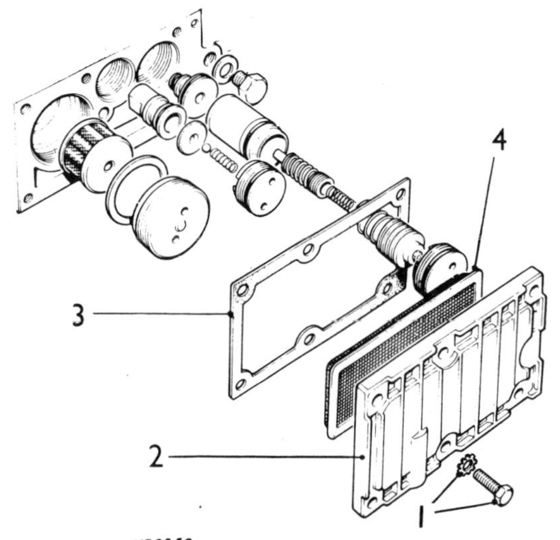

PRESSURE FILTER

– Remove and refit 40.10.08

Removing

1. Remove the sump and suction filter.
2. Remove the pressure filter base plug (largest plug), using tool L354; the filter element will come away with the plug.
3. Remove the aluminium washer which locates on the shoulder in the filter bore.
4. Remove foreign matter and wash the element in petrol or paraffin.
5. Renew the aluminium washer if there are any signs of damage or scoring.
6. Refit the filter and pressure filter base plug, using tool L354.
7. Tighten up until the plug is flush with the base, a torque loading of 16 lbf ft (2·2 kgf m).

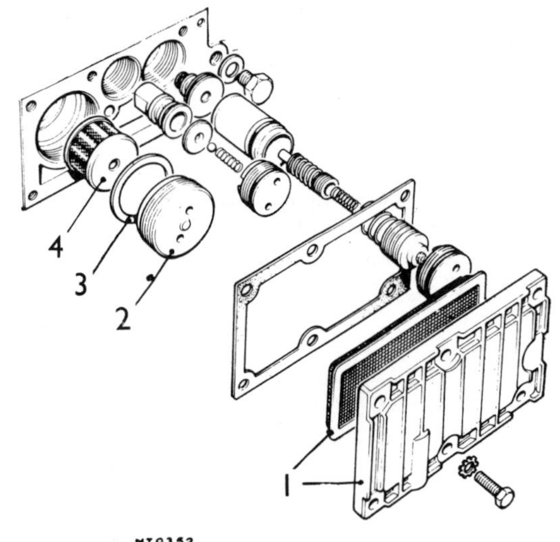

OIL SEAL – REAR

– Remove and refit **40.15.01**

Removing

1. Remove the nut.
2. Remove the washer.
3. Remove the drive flange.
4. Remove the rear oil seal, using special tool L176A with 7657.

Refitting

5. Fit the oil seal using special tool L177 with 550.
6. Refit the drive flange.
7. Refit the washer.
8. Fit a new self-locking nut and tighten to a torque of 80 to 130 lbf ft (11·1 to 18·0 kgf m).

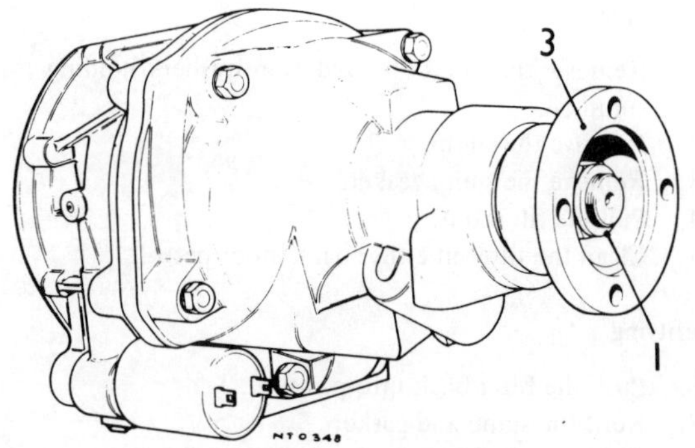

RELIEF VALVE AND DASHPOT ASSEMBLY

– Remove and refit **40.16.04**

NOTE: If the vehicle has been in recent use, care should be taken to avoid hot oil burning the skin.

1. Remove six bolts and star washers securing the sump to the main case.
2. Remove the gasket.
3. Remove the gauze filter.
4. Using Churchill tool L354, remove the relief valve plug.
5. Withdraw the dashpot piston complete with its component springs and cup.
6. Remove the residual pressure spring.
   NOTE: This is the only loose spring in the general assembly.

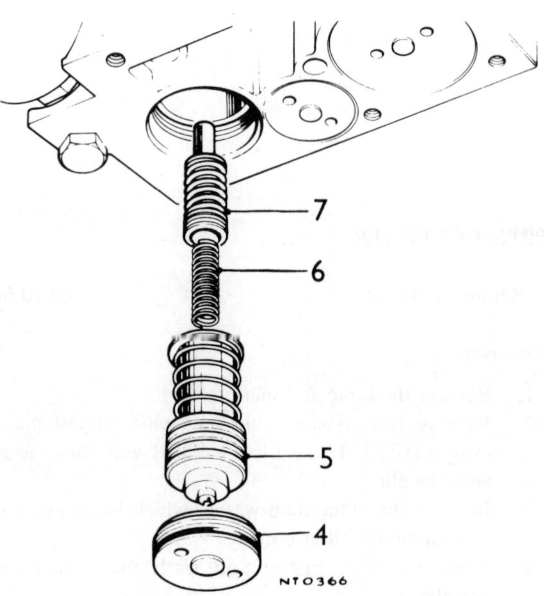

continued

7. The relief valve piston assembly can now be withdrawn by carefully pulling down with a pair of pliers.
8. Insert tool L401 into the now exposed relief valve bore (taking care not to damage this) and withdraw the relief valve together with the dashpot sleeve.
   NOTE: Do not dismantle the dashpot and relief valve piston assemblies otherwise the predetermined spring pressures will be disturbed.

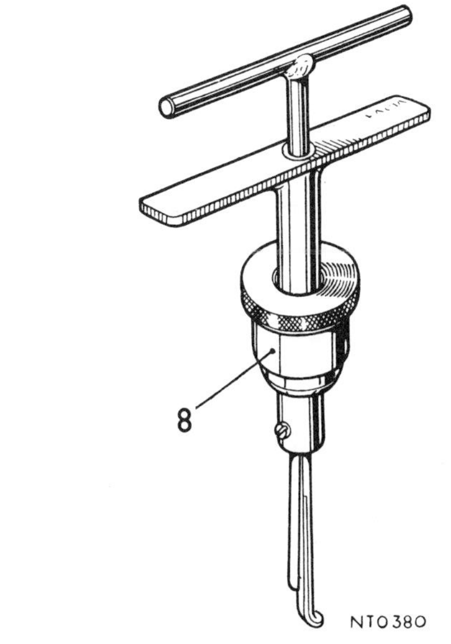

Refitting

9. Ensure that before assembly all the components are clean and lightly oiled.
10. Insert the relief body in the bore and, using the relief valve outer sleeve, push fully home.
    NOTE: The end with the 'O' ring is nearest to the outside of the casing.
11. Position the relief valve spring and piston assembly into the dashpot cup, ensuring that both ends of the residual pressure spring are correctly located.
12. Carefully positon these components in the relief valve outer sleeve, at the same time engaging the relief valve piston in its housing.
13. Fit the base plug and tighten it flush with the casing to a torque loading of 16 lbf ft (2·2 kgf m).

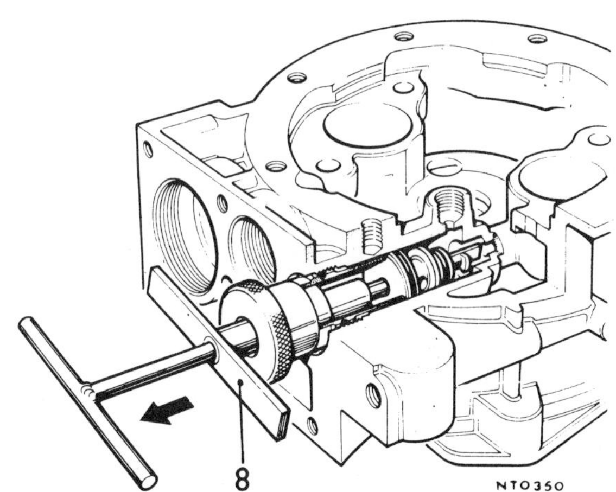

RELIEF VALVE AND DASHPOT ASSEMBLY

– Overhaul **40.16.07**

1. Remove the relief valve and dashpot assembly. 40.16.04.
2. Inspect the pistons and ensure that they move freely in their respective housings.
3. Inspect the 'O' rings and ensure that they are in good condition.
4. If they are damaged at all, the 'O' ring should be renewed.
5. Refit the relief valve and dashpot assembly. 40.16.04.

PUMP NON-RETURN VALVE

– Remove and refit 40.16.10

Removing

1. Remove the overdrive sump.
2. Remove the suction filler.
3. With Churchill tool L354, remove the pump plug (centre plug) taking care not to lose the non-return valve spring and ball.
4. Remove the non-return valve seat.

Refitting

5. Place the spring in the non-return valve plug.
6. Position the ball on the spring.
7. Locate the non-return seat on the ball.
8. Screw the complete assembly into the maincase, using tool L354.
9. Screw up flush with the case to a torque loading of 16 lbf ft (2·2 kgf m).

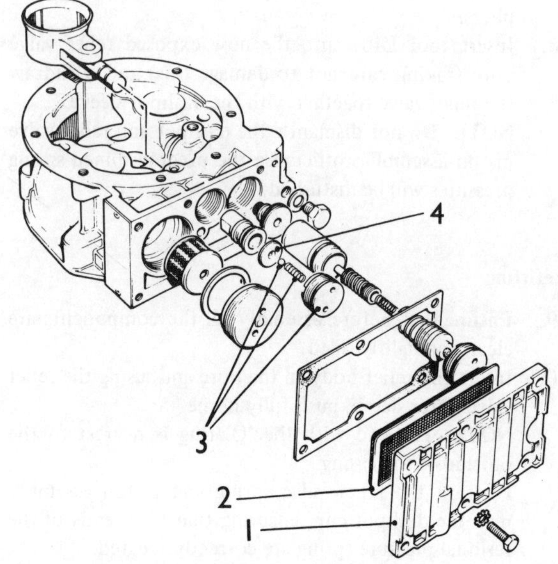

PUMP NON-RETURN VALVE

– Overhaul 40.16.14

1. Remove the pump non-return valve. 40.16.10.
2. Carefully inspect the non-return valve ball and valve seat. If necessary, reseat the ball on the seat by tapping gently with a copper drift.
3. Ensure that the 'O' ring is undamaged.
4. If the 'O' ring is damaged, renew it.
5. Refit the 'O' ring after smearing with petroleum jelly.
6. Refit the pump non-return valve. 40.16.10.

CONTROL ORIFICE

– Clean **40.16.19**

The control orifice is situated in the angled drilling between the relief valve and the solenoid control valve.

1. To gain access, remove the solenoid control valve. 40.22.04.
2. Remove the relief valve and outer sleeve. 40.16.04.
3. Clean the orifice with a high pressure air-line.
   NOTE: Do not attempt to clean the orifice with wire or its calibration may be impaired.
4. Refit the relief valve and outer sleeve. 40.16.04.
5. Refit the solenoid control valve. 40.22.04.

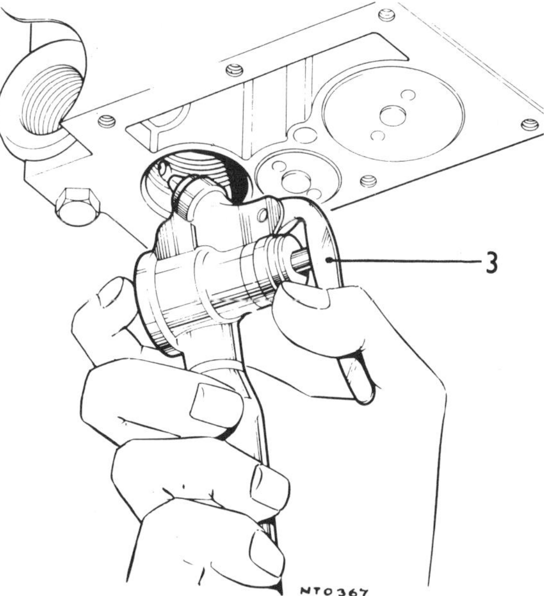

OPERATING PISTONS

– Remove and refit **40.16.24**

Removing

1. Remove the gearbox and overdrive from the car. 37.20.01.
2. Remove the overdrive from the gearbox. 40.20.07.
3. Remove four nuts.
4. Remove two bridge pieces.
5. With a pair of pliers, remove the operating pistons, identifying them with their respective cylinders.

Refitting

6. Lightly oil the operating pistons.
7. Push the pistons into the housings.
8. Fit the two bridge pieces.
9. Fit and tighten the four new nuts to a torque of 6 to 8 lbf ft (0·8 to 1·1 kgf m).
10. Refit the overdrive to the gearbox. 40.20.07.
11. Refit the gearbox and overdrive to the car. 37.20.01.

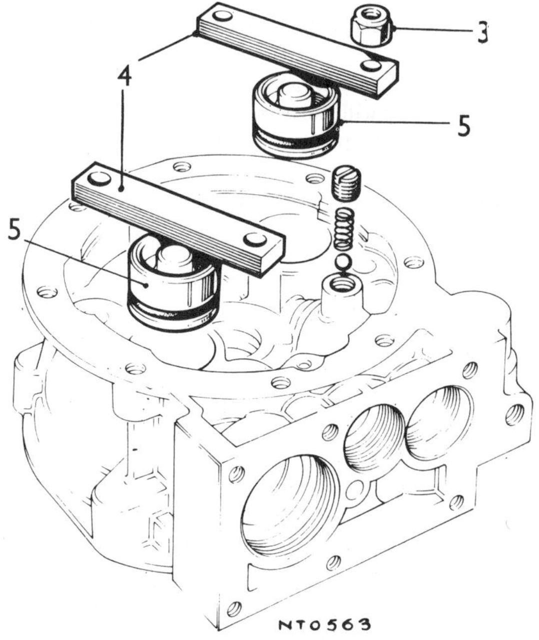

OPERATING PISTONS

– Overhaul **40.16.29**

1. Remove the operating pistons. 40.16.24.
2. Inspect each of the 'O' rings for any damage or wear.
3. If any damage is found the ring must be replaced and smeared with petroleum jelly.
4. Refit the operating pistons. 40.16.24.

OIL PUMP

– Remove and refit **40.18.01**

Removing

1. Remove the overdrive from the car. 40.20.07.
2. Remove the sump and filter. 40.10.01.
3. Remove the pump plug, using tool L354A.
4. Remove the non-return valve spring.
5. Remove the steel ball.
6. Remove the non-return valve seat.
7. Work the pump body out of the main casing.
8. Remove the pump plunger assembly.

Refitting

9. Position the pump plunger assembly in the main case.
10. Fit the pump body in the main casing, ensuring that the flat on the body faces towards the pressure filter housing.
11. Fit the non-return valve seat.
12. Fit the steel ball.
13. Fit the non-return valve spring into the pump plug.
14. Fit the plug and tighten to a torque of 16 lbf ft (2·2 kgf m).
15. Clean the sump filter and replace.
16. Fit the sump with a new joint.
17. Tighten the sump bolts to a torque of 6 lbf ft (0·8 kgf m).
18. Refit the overdrive to the car. 40.20.07.

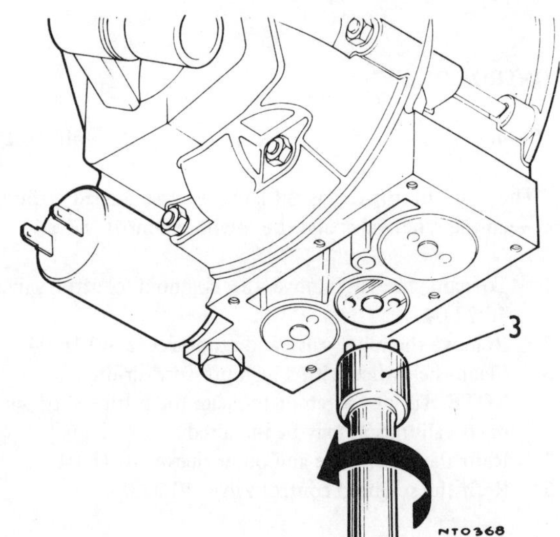

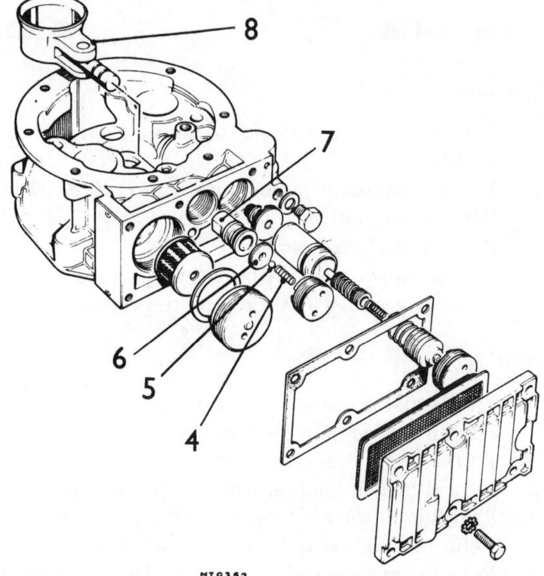

OIL PUMP

– Overhaul **40.18.04**

1. Remove the pump plunger assembly. 40.18.01.
2. Check that the strap is a good fit on the mainshaft cam.
3. Check that there is no excess play between the strap and the plunger.
4. If the pump plunger assembly is worn or damaged, this must be replaced as a complete assembly.
5 Check that the 'O' rings on the pump body and the plug are perfect; if not, these must be replaced.
6. Refit the pump plunger assembly. 40.18.01.

OVERDRIVE ASSEMBLY

– Hydraulic pressure test **40.20.01**

1. Check that the oil level in the gearbox is correct.
2. Remove the plug adjacent to the solenoid and fit a hydraulic pressure gauge (special tool L188) together with adaptor (L188–2).
3. Jack the car up and run the transmission at approximately 25 m.p.h. (40 km/h).
4. In direct drive the residual pressure should register on the gauge to approximately 20 lbf/in^2 (1·4 kgf/cm^2).
5. Engage the overdrive; a pressure of 430 to 460 lbf/in^2 (30·10 to 32·20 kgf/cm^2) should be recorded.
6. Disengage the overdrive and the gauge should return to show the residual pressure.

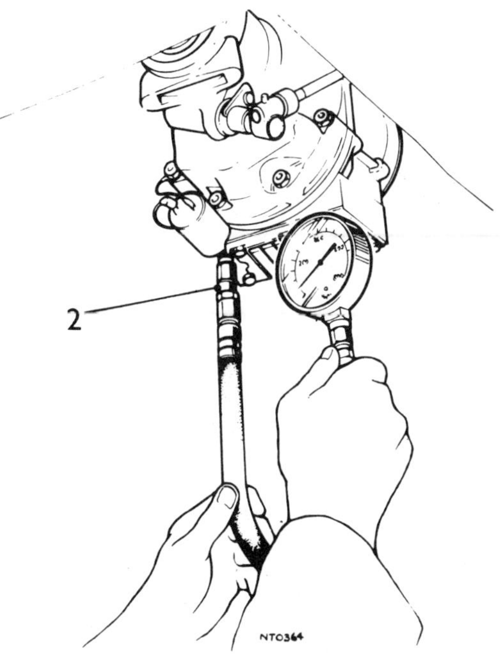

OVERDRIVE ASSEMBLY

– Remove and refit **40.20.07**

Removing

NOTE: Before commencing overdrive removal it is advisable to raise the rear wheels and run the transmission. Engage overdrive, then disengage with the clutch depressed leaving the overdrive ready for removal. This will release the spline loading between the planet carrier and the uni-directional roller clutch which could make removal difficult.

1. Remove the gearbox and overdrive from the car as operation number 37.20.01.
2. Remove the eight ½ in U.N.F. nuts securing the unit to the adaptor plate.
3. Remove the overdrive over the mainshaft, leaving the adaptor plate in position on the gearbox.
   If difficulty is experienced in separating the overdrive from the gearbox, use the following procedure: Remove the hexagon plug adjacent to the solenoid, and screw in and tighten tool L402. Energize the solenoid, then pressurize the unit by pumping clean oil through the nipple on the tool with a lubrication gun. This will release the spline loading on the mainshaft and permit easy removal. De-energize the solenoid when the overdrive has separated by about ¾ in (19 mm).
4. Use a screwdriver of suitable length to rotate the inner member of the uni-directional roller clutch (this is the innermost set of splines), in an anti-clockwise direction until the splines of this member are in line with the splines in the planet carrier.
5. Ensure that the pump cam and sun gear spring ring are correctly located on the mainshaft.
6. Rotate the gearbox mainshaft so that the peak of the pump cam is at the bottom to assist engagement with the pump strap.
7. Engage the bottom gear in the gearbox.
8. Fit a new joint to the front face of the overdrive.
9. Offer up the overdrive to the gearbox.
10. Rotate the output shaft of the unit in a clockwise direction.
11. At the same time apply slight pressure until the splines are engaged.
12. Ensure that the pump strap assembly rides smoothly onto the cam and that the overdrive pushes home to the adaptor plate face without excessive force.
13. Fit and tighten the eight nuts which secure the unit.
14. If the overdrive fails to meet the adaptor plate face by approximately 5/8 in (16 mm) it means that the planet carrier and the uni-directional roller splines have become mis-aligned. In this case remove the unit and re-align the splines.

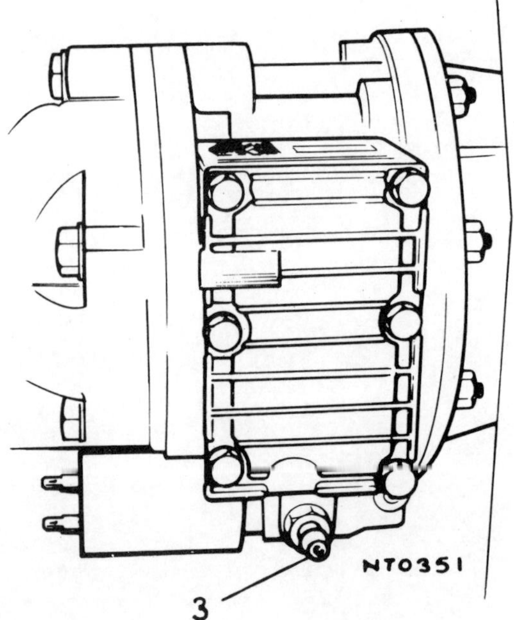

OVERDRIVE ASSEMBLY

– Overhaul or dismantle 40.20.10

1. Remove the gearbox and overdrive from the car. 37.20.01.
2. Remove the overdrive from the gearbox. 40.20.07.
3. Before starting to dismantle the overdrive assembly, the exterior of the casings must be thoroughly cleaned.
4. Mount the unit vertically in a vice with the use of 'soft' jaws.
5. Remove four nuts securing the bridge pieces.
6. Remove the bridge pieces.
7. Progressively release the six nuts around the main casing to release the clutch return spring pressure.
8. Note the position of the two copper washers which fit on the two studs at the top of the casing.
9. Remove all the washers from the casing.
10. Separate the main casing complete with the brake ring from the rear case.
11. Lift out the sliding member assembly complete with the sun wheel.
12. Lift out the planet carrier assembly, taking care not to damage the oil catcher which is attached to the underside of the carrier.
13. Tap the brake ring from its spigot in the main casing with a suitable drift.
14. Using a pair of pliers, withdraw the operating pistons.
15. Remove the sump and suction filter. 40.10.01.
16. Remove the relief valve assembly. 40.16.04.
17. Remove the pump non-return valve assembly. 40.16.10.
18. Remove the oil pump assembly. 40.18.01.
19. Remove the pressure filter. 40.10.08.
20. Remove the solenoid control valve. 40.22.09.
21. Inspect the main casing for cracks.
22. Examine the operating cylinder bores for scores or wear.
23. Check the operating pistons for wear.
24. Replace the sealing rings if there is any sign of damage.
25. Remove the circlip from the sun wheel extension.
26. Take out the sun wheel.
27. Remove the circlip from its groove on the cone clutch hub.
28. Tap out the clutch from the thrust ring bearing, using a hide mallet.
29. Extract the large circlip.
30. Press the bearing from its housing.
31. Examine the clutch linings on the sliding member for any signs of excessive wear or charring.
32. If there is any sign of this condition, the sliding member complete must be replaced.
    NOTE: It is not possible to fit new linings as these are precision machined after they are bonded.

continued

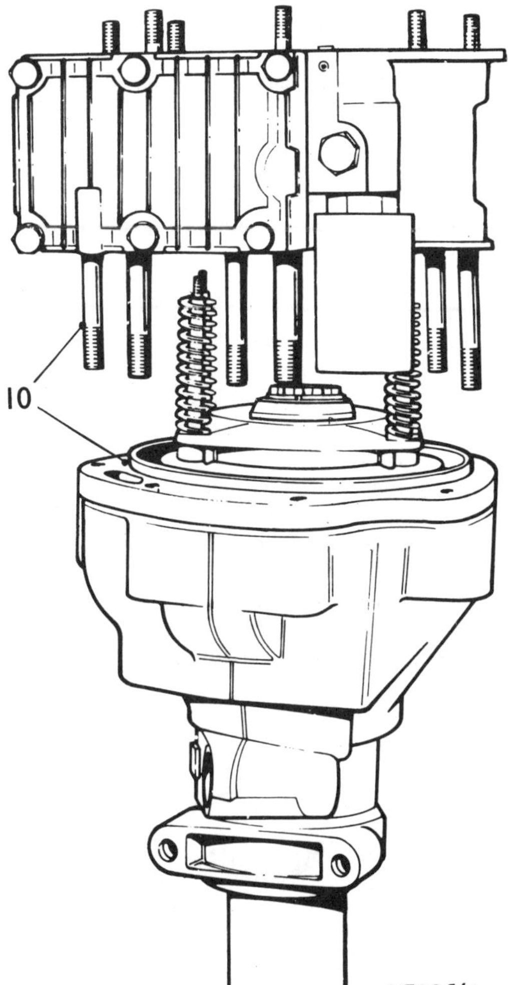

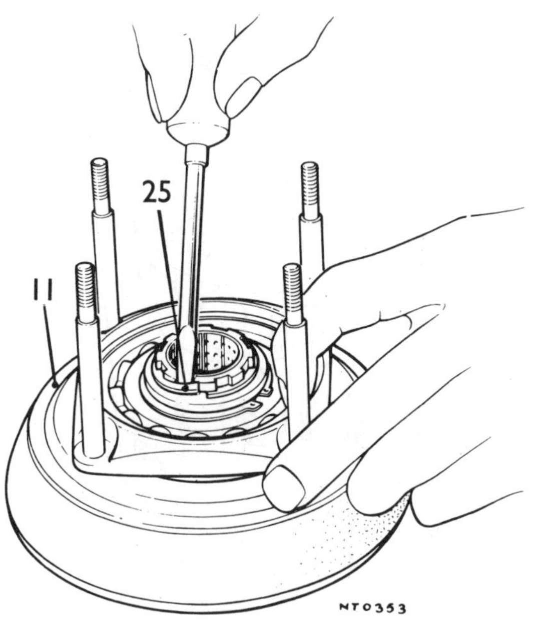

33. Check the ball race and ensure that it rotates smoothly as this can be a source of noise when running in direct drive.
34. Examine the clutch return springs for any signs of distortion or collapse.
35. Inspect the sun wheel teeth for wear or damage.
36. Inspect the planet gears for damage or wear.
37. Check the planet gear bearings for any excessive clearance.
38. Examine the oil thrower for damage.
39. Using a screwdriver blade, remove the circlip.
40. Lift out the oil thrower.
41. Place tool L178 over the exposed uni-directional roller clutch.
42. Lift the inner member complete with rollers into the special tool.
43. Remove the bronze thrust washer.
44. Remove the speedometer drive bolt.
45. Remove the speedometer driven gear clamp.
46. Pull the speedometer driven gear out with a pair of pliers; this will also remove the speedometer bush.

continued

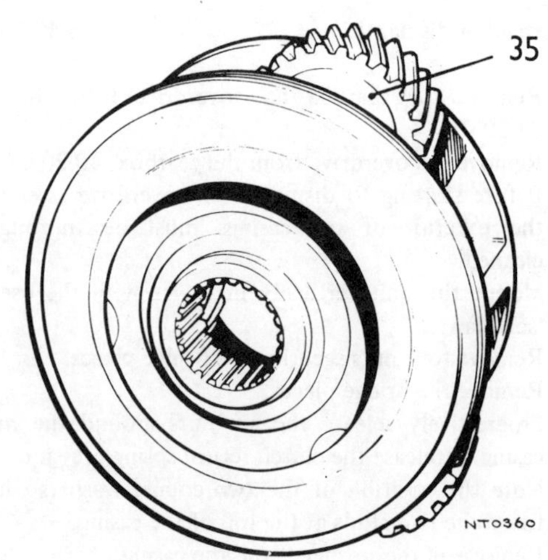

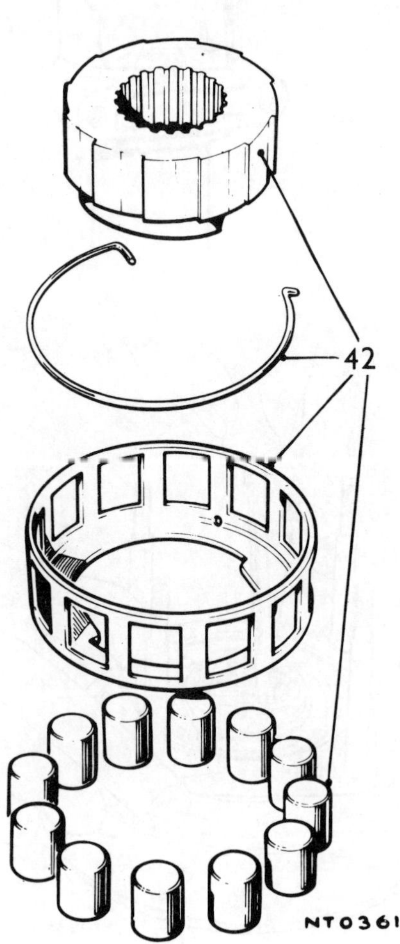

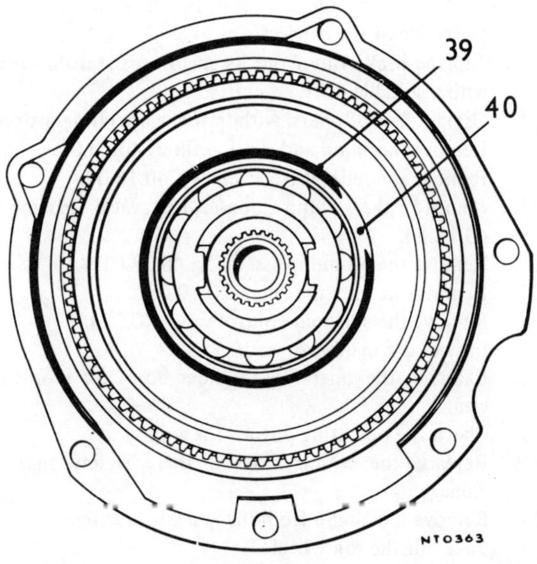

47. Separate the bush from the driven gear.
48. Remove the coupling flange nut and washer.
49. Withdraw the flange, using a suitable extractor.
50. Drift out the annulus, using a hide mallet applied to the end of the tail shaft.
51. The front bearing, speedometer drive gear and spacer will be withdrawn together with the annulus.
52. Remove the oil seal.
53. Drive out the rear bearing.
54. Check, and renew if necessary, all the 'O' rings.
55. Inspect the teeth and the cone surface of the annulus for wear.
56. Check that the uni-directional clutch rollers are not chipped.
57. Check that the inner and outer members are not damaged.
58. Examine the spring and cage for distortion.
59. The oil seal must be replaced.
60. Examine the speedometer drive and driven gears for wear and chafing; in either case they must be replaced.
61. Position the speedometer drive gear in the rear casing with its plain boss facing the front bearing.
NOTE: The speedometer drive gear cannot be fitted from the rear of the casing.

continued

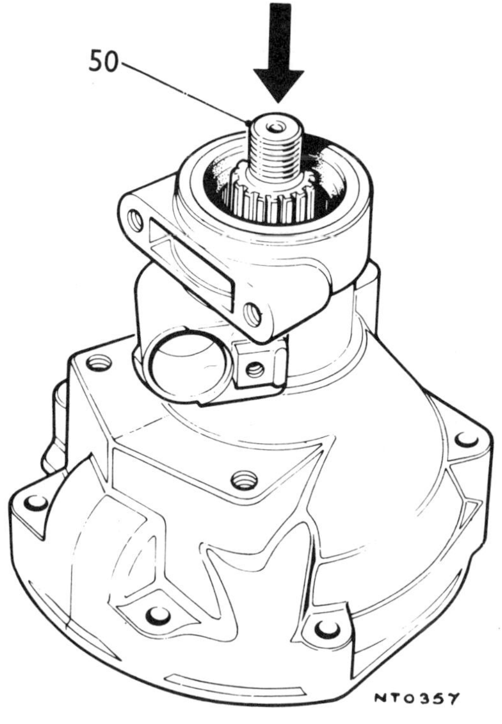

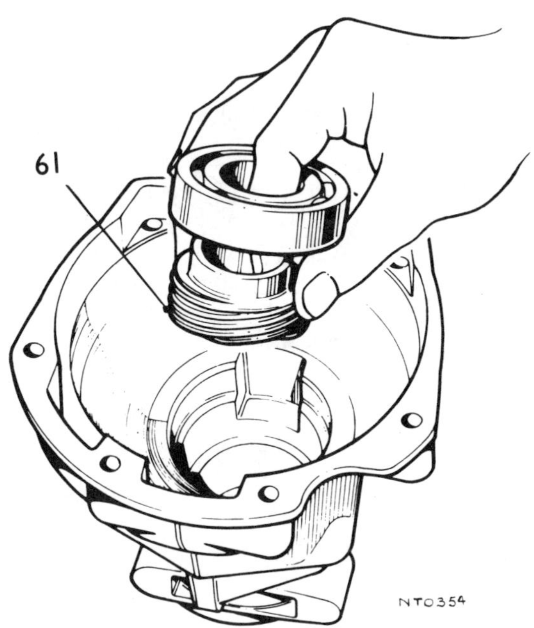

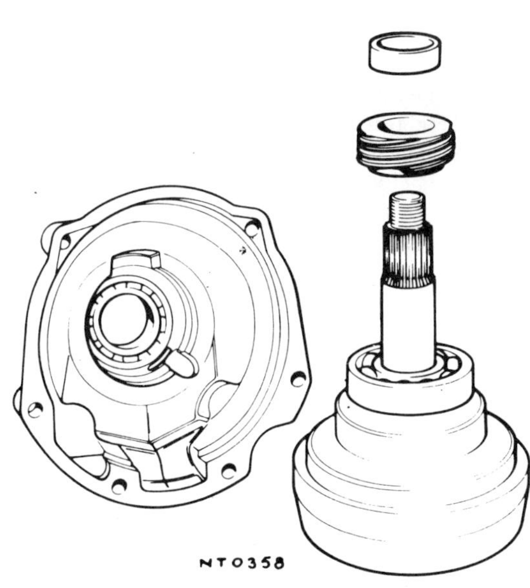

62. Press the front bearing into the rear casing.
63. Ensure that its outer track abuts against the shoulder in the casing.
64. Position the annulus with the inner face resting on a suitable packing piece.
65. Using tool L186, press the front bearing together with the rear casing and speedometer driving gear onto the annulus until the bearing abuts on the locating shoulder.
66. Fit the spacer onto the annulus.
67. Using tool L186, press the rear bearing onto the annulus and into the rear casing simultaneously.
68. Fit the oil seal, using tool L177 with 550.
69. Press on the coupling flange.
70. Fit the washer.
71. Tighten up the self-locking nut to a torque loading of 80 to 130 lbf ft (11·1 to 18·0 kgf m).
72. Position the spring and inner member of the uni-directional roller clutch into the cage.
73. Locate the spring so that the cage is spring loaded in an anti-clockwise direction when viewed from the front.
74. Place the assembly into tool L178, with the open side of the cage uppermost.
75. Move the clutch in a clockwise direction until all the rollers are in place.
76. Refit the bronze thrust washer in the recess in the annulus.
77. Transfer the uni-directional clutch assembly from the special assembly tool into its outer member up the annulus.
78. Position the oil thrower.
79. Secure with the circlip.
80. Check that the clutch rotates in an anti-clockwise direction only.

continued

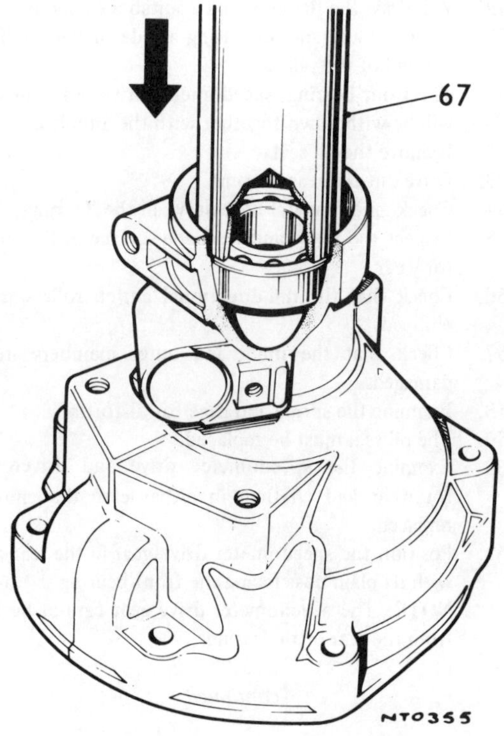

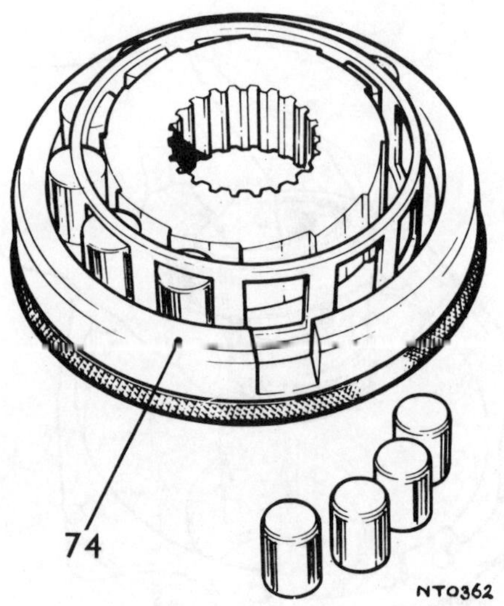

81. Fit the ball race into its housing.
82. Secure the ball race with the large circlip.
83. Position this assembly onto the hub of the cone clutch.
84. Secure with a circlip.
85. Ensure that the circlip locates properly in the groove.
86. Insert the sun wheel into the hub.
87. Fit the circlip on the sun wheel extension.
88. Lightly smear the operating pistons with oil.
89. Fit the pistons into their respective housings.
90. Refit the solenoid control valve. 40.22.09.
91. Refit the pressure filter. 40.10.08.
92. Refit the oil pump assembly. 40.18.01.
93. Refit the pump non-return valve assembly 40.16.10.
94. Refit the relief valve assembly. 40.16.04.

continued

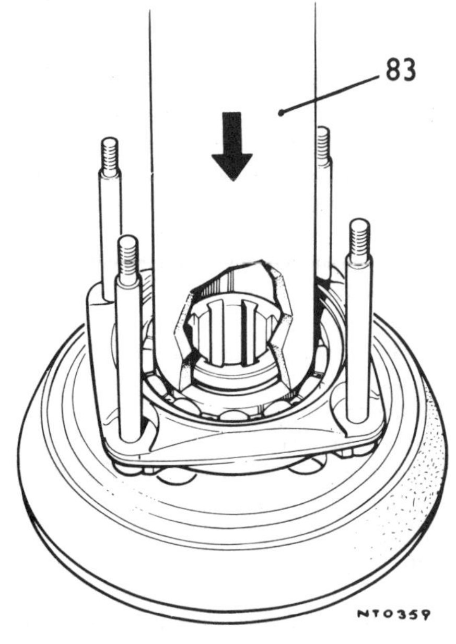

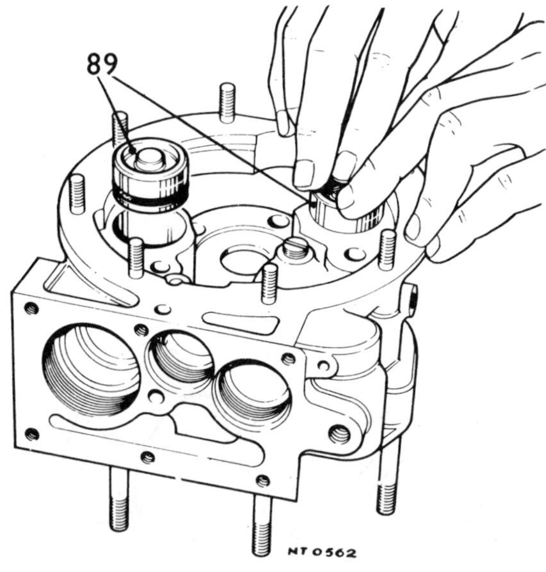

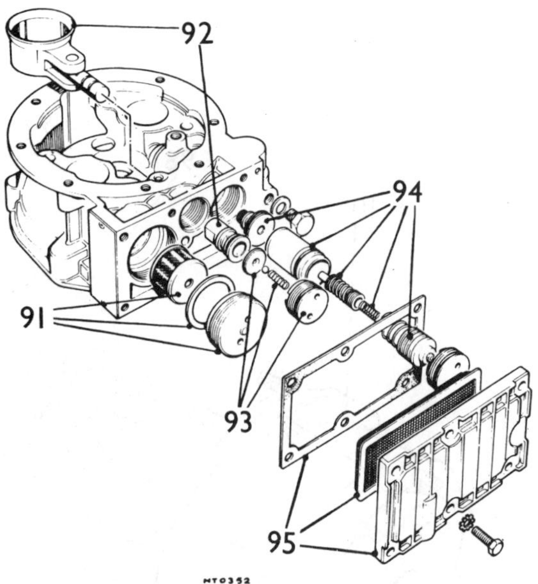

95. Refit the sump and suction filter. 40.10.01.
96. Mount the rear casing assembly vertically in a vice.
97. Insert the planet carrier assembly.
    NOTE: The gears can be meshed in any position.
98. Place the sliding member assembly complete with the clutch return springs onto the cone of the annulus.
99. Engage the sun wheel with the planet gears.
100. Apply Wellseal to new gaskets either side of the brake ring.
    NOTE: These gaskets are different.
101. Fit the brake ring onto its spigot in the tail casing, aligning the stud holes.
102. Position the main casing assembly over the thrust housing pins, at the same time entering the studs in the brake ring.
103. Fit and progressively tighten the six nuts securing the rear and main case assemblies to a torque setting of 13 to 15 lbf ft (1·8 to 2·1 kgf m).
104. Apply Wellseal to the two copper washers and threads of the two top studs.
105. Secure the earth lead to the stud above the solenoid aperture.
106. The clutch return spring pressure will be felt as the two casings go together.
107. Fit the two bridge pieces.
108. Secure with four new self-locking nuts to a torque setting of 6 to 8 lbf ft (0·8 to 1·1 kgf m).

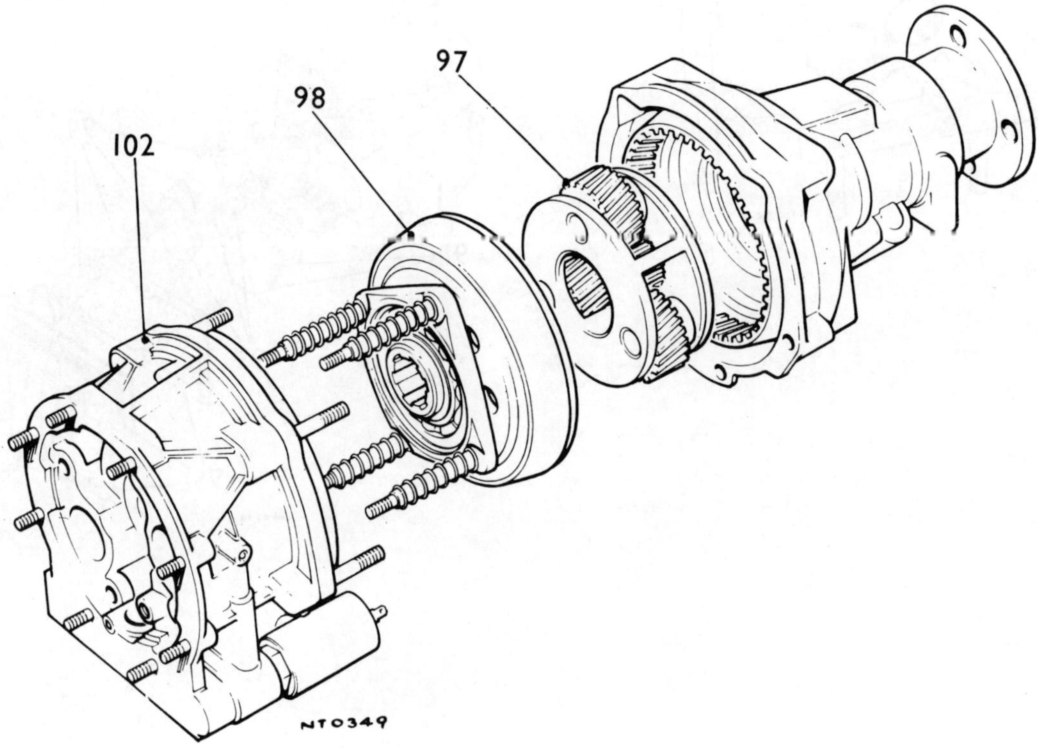

SOLENOID

– Test **40.22.01**

1. Connect the solenoid in series with a 12-volt battery and ammeter.
2. The solenoid should draw approximately 2 amps
3. Check that the plunger in the valve moves forward when the solenoid is energized.
4. Check that the plunger in the valve returns to its direct drive position by spring pressure when the solenoid is de-energized.
   NOTE: The solenoid does not operate with a loud click as the other types of overdrive.
5. If the solenoid is still faulty, the complete unit must be renewed.

SOLENOID OPERATING VALVE

– Remove and refit **40.22.04**

Removing

1. Disconnect the negative battery lead.
2. Disconnect the two Lucar connectors from the solenoid.
3. Using a 1 in (25 mm) A.F. open-ended spanner on the hexagon, loosen and unscrew the solenoid.
   NOTE: Do not attempt to remove the solenoid by gripping the cylindrical body as this is very easily damaged.

Refitting

4. Screw the solenoid into the casing.
5. Tighten with a spanner.
6. Connect Lucar connectors to the terminals; these can be connected either way round.
7. Connect the negative lead of the battery.

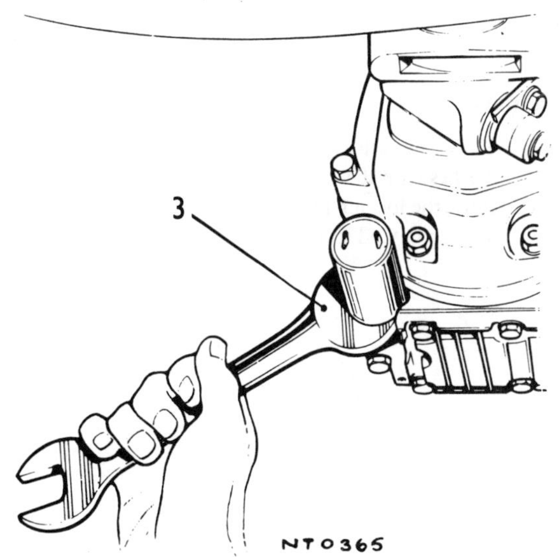

SOLENOID OPERATING VALVE

– Overhaul **40.22.13**

1. Remove the solenoid and operating valve. 40.22.04.
2. Should it be necessary to clean the operating valve, immerse this part of the solenoid valve in paraffin until the valve is clean.
3. Examine the 'O' rings on the solenoid valve for damage, and renew together with a sealing washer if necessary.
4. Fit the solenoid and operating valve. 40.22.04.

SPEEDO DRIVE GEAR

– Remove and refit **40.25.01**

Removing

1. Working from under the car, remove the locking plate screw.
2. Remove the drive pinion and holder.

Refitting

3. Refit the drive gear, ensuring that the drive gear meshes with the driven gear.
4. Refit the locking plate and screw.
5. Top up any oil lost.

PROPELLER SHAFT OPERATIONS

PROPELLER SHAFT

– Remove and refit **47.15.01**

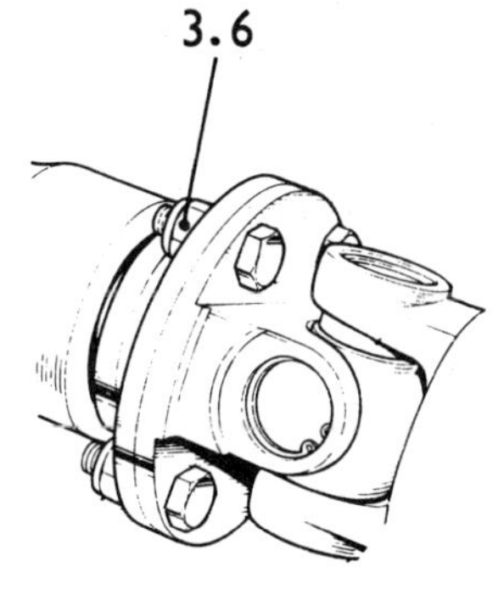

Removing

1. Place the car on a ramp or over a pit.
2. Remove the exhaust system 30.10.01, with the exception of the front pipes.
3. Mark for reassembly the relationship of the gearbox driving flange to the universal joint flange and remove the four securing nuts and bolts.
4. Mark for reassembly as in instruction 3 and remove the four nuts and bolts securing the rear end of the propeller shaft to the final drive flange and pull the propeller shaft forwards and downwards.

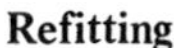

Refitting

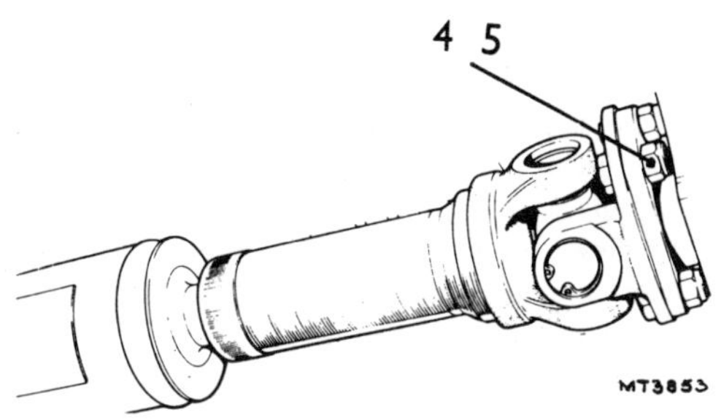

5. Offer up the propeller shaft to the final drive flange so that the identification marks line up and secure in position using new nyloc nuts. Tighten the nuts and bolts to 26 to 34 lbf ft (3·6 to 4·7 kgf m).
6. Offer up the propeller shaft to the gearbox flange so that the bolt holes line up and the identification marks coincide. Fit the bolts with new nyloc nuts and tighten as in instruction 5.
7. Reverse instructions 1 and 2.

UNIVERSAL JOINT

– Overhaul 47.15.18

Dismantling

1. Remove the propeller shaft 47.15.01.
2. Remove the paint, rust etc. from the vicinity of the bearing cups and circlips.
3. Remove the circlips.
4. Tap the yokes to eject the bearing cups.
5. Withdraw the bearing cups and spider.

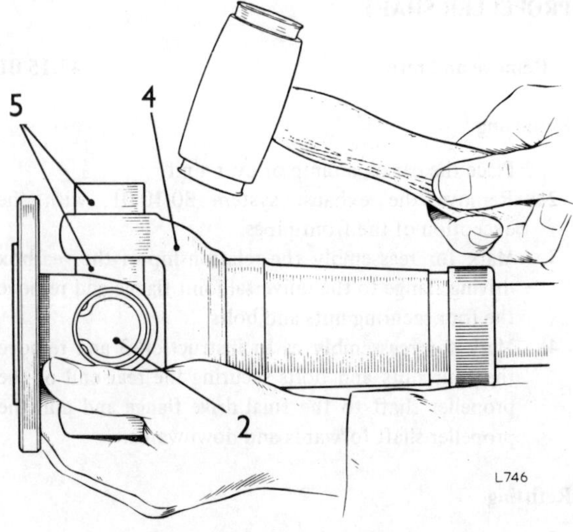

Reassembling

6. Remove the bearing cups from the new spider.
7. Ensure that the cups contain approved lubricant (one third full) and that the needle bearings are complete and in position.
8. Fit the spider to the propeller shaft yoke.
9. Engage the spider trunnion in the bearing cup and insert the cup into the yoke.
10. Fit the opposite bearing cup to the yoke and carefully press both cups into position, ensuring that the spider trunnion engages the cups and that the needle bearings are not displaced.
11. Using two flat faced adaptors of slightly smaller diameter than the bearing cups press the cups into the yokes until they reach the lower land of the circlip grooves. Do not press the bearing cups below this point or damage may be caused to the cups and seals.
12. Fit the circlips.
13. Refit the propeller shaft 47.15.01.

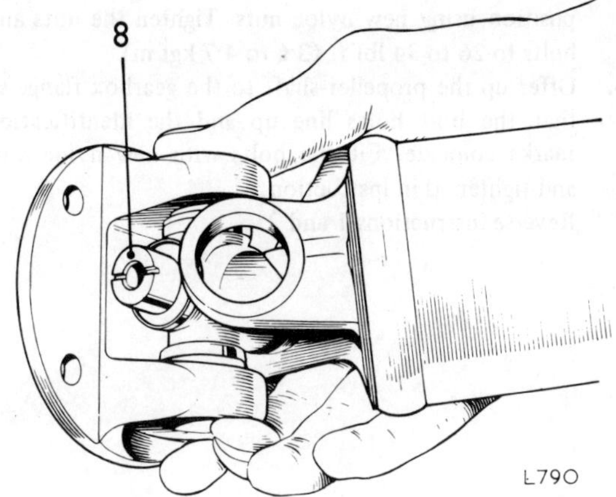

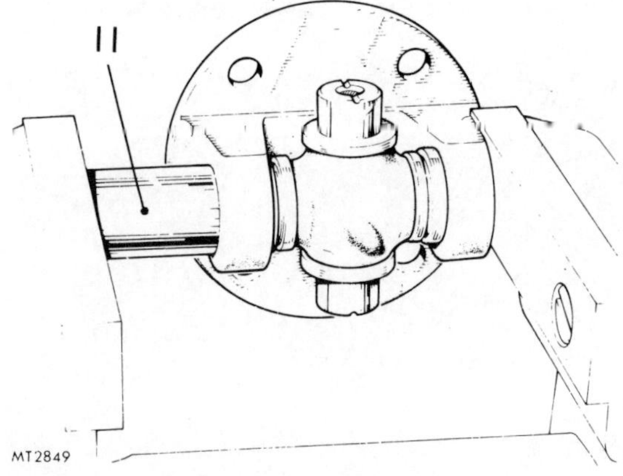

REAR AXLE OPERATIONS

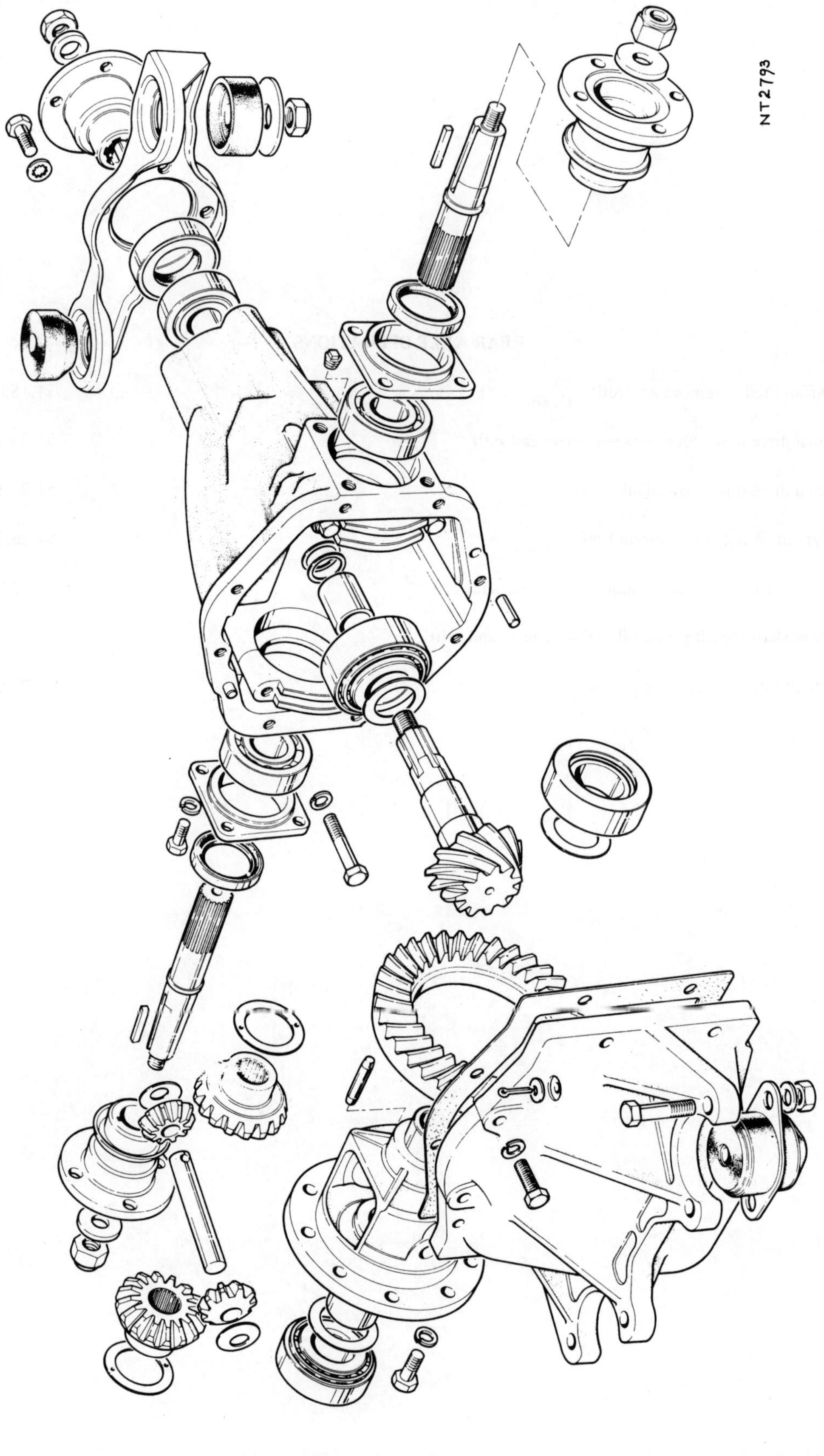

NT2793

INNER SHAFT BEARING AND OIL SEAL

– Remove and refit **51.10.02**

Removing

1. For right hand inner axle shaft, remove exhaust tail box and rear pipes 30.10.19.
2. Disconnect inner drive shaft from flange.
3. Remove four bolts and spring washers securing inner shaft oil seal housing to hypoid casing.
4. Withdraw inner shaft complete with driving flange, oil seal housing and ball race.
5. Remove nyloc nut and plain washer from shaft.
6. Withdraw driving flange, key and oil seal.
7. Remove ball race from shaft.
8. Extract oil seal from housing.

Refitting

9. Fit ballrace to shaft until outer face of ball race is approximately aligned with end of shaft taper.
10. Lay oil seal housing flat on bench with the smaller diameter uppermost. Insert oil seal (lip leading) into the housing until the plain face of the seal is flush with the housing.
11. Lubricate lip and slide seal over driving flange (plain face of seal leading). Ensure driving flange deflector seal is undamaged and will not foul the oil seal housing.
12. Fit key, driving flange and oil seal housing to the shaft.
13. Fit the plain washer and the nyloc nut to the shaft. Tighten the nut.
14. Enter the shaft into the hypoid casing engaging the splines in the sungear.
15. Fit and tighten the four spring washers and bolts securing the oil seal housing to the hypoid casing.
16. Connect up the drive shaft to the inner shaft.
17. For the right hand inner shaft, refit the tail box and rear pipes 30.10.19.
18. Top up the differential unit with oil.

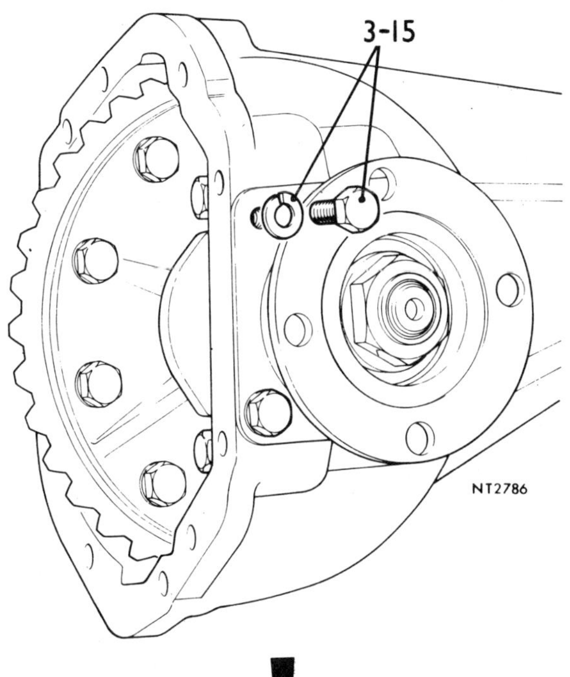

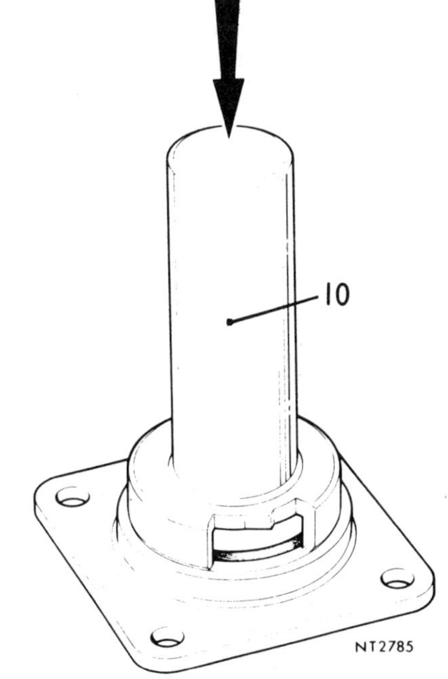

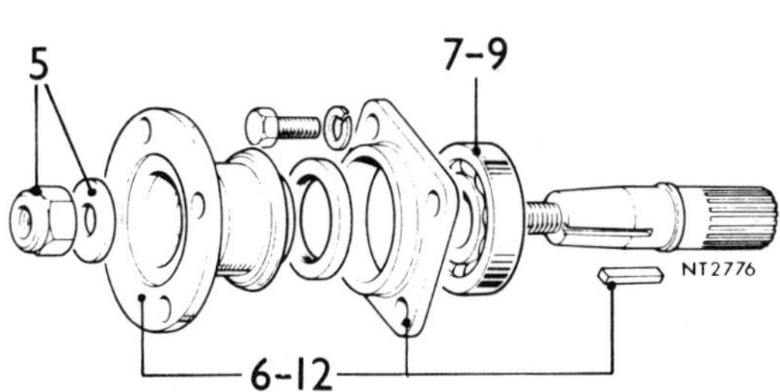

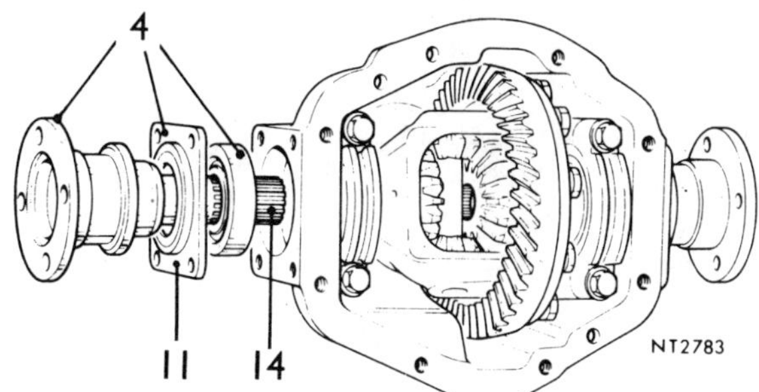

DIFFERENTIAL

– Remove and refit 51.15.01

Service tools S101

Removing

1. Remove the hypoid casing from the car 51.25.25.
2. Slacken the eight bolts and spring washers securing the rear cover to hypoid casing and allow oil to drain.
3. Remove the rear cover.
4. Remove the eight bolts (4 either side) securing the inner shaft housing to hypoid casing.
5. Withdraw the inner shafts complete with ballrace oil seal and flanges.
6. Note the location identity markings on carrier bearing caps. Remove four bolts and spring washers securing bearing caps and withdraw bearing caps. Do not intermix the bearing caps.
7. Tap the dowels flush with casing flange.
8. Fit the spreader tool (S101) adaptor plates to hypoid casing.
9. Mount the spreader tool on the adaptor and turn the jacking screw by hand to expand the spreader. A further half turn with a spanner will spread the casing sufficiently to release the differential unit.
   DO NOT over expand or damage will be caused to the hypoid casing.
10. Lift out the crown wheel and differential unit.

Refitting

11. Reverse instructions 1 to 10.

NOTE: Where the carrier bearing(s) and/or the crown wheel are renewed it is necessary to check the carrier bearing tolerances and the crown wheel/pinion backlash as is detailed under operation number 51.15.13.

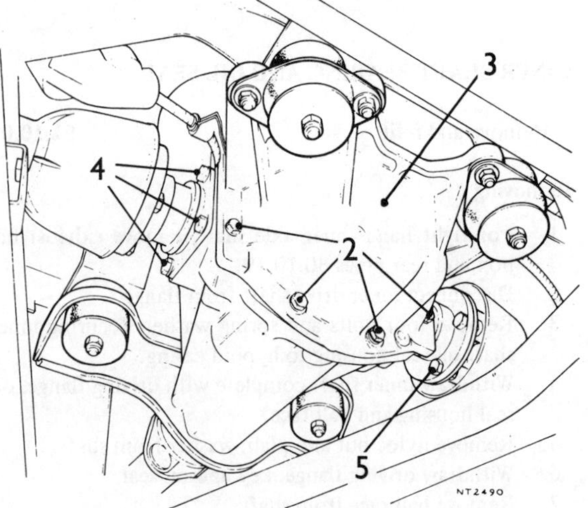

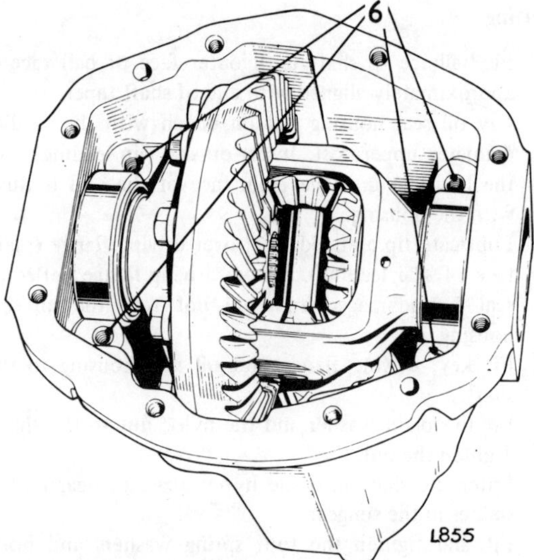

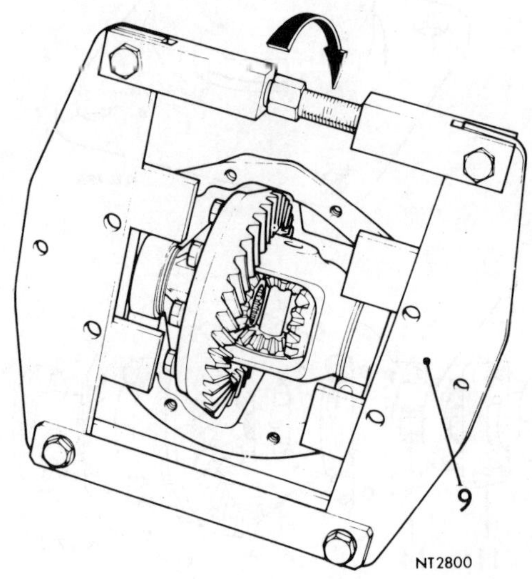

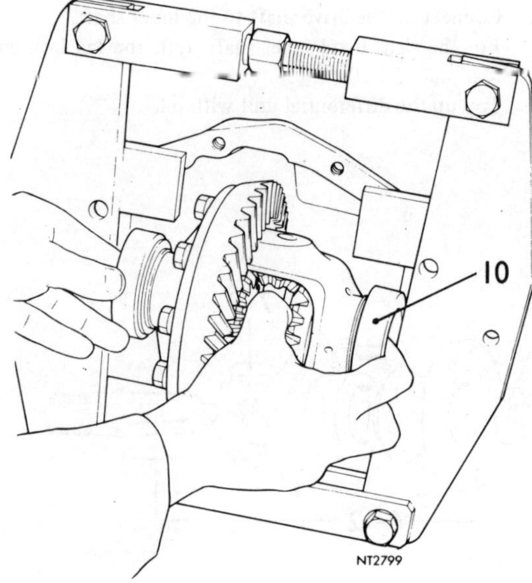

PINION OIL SEAL

– Remove and refit **51.20.01**

Removing

1. Remove the hypoid casing 51.25.25.
2. Remove the drive flange.
3. Withdraw the oil seal.

Refitting

4. Fit a new oil seal (lip towards the pinion).
5. Refit the drive flange.
6. Install the hypoid casing 51.25.25.

HYPOID CASING REAR COVER GASKET

– Remove and refit **51.20.07**

Removing

1. Drive the car onto the ramp and raise.
2. Remove the silencer and tail pipes 30.10.19.
3. Support the hypoid casing on a jack and slacken the two nyloc nuts and washers partially releasing the front mountings.
4. Remove the handbrake cable support bracket from the hypoid casing.
5. Remove the two rear mounting nuts.
6. Lower the jack and axle.
7. Remove the four nuts, bolts and spring washers and remove the two mounting rubbers.
8. Place a drip tray under the hypoid unit.
9. Slacken the seven bolts securing the rear cover to the hypoid casing. Ease the cover from the casing and allow the oil to drain.
10. Remove the cover.
11. Remove the gasket and clean the mating faces.

Refitting

12. Fit a new gasket and assemble the cover to the hypoid casing (seven bolts).
13. Place the four rear mounting bolts in the cover.
14. Raise the jack under the hypoid and locate the mounting rubbers to the studs.
15. Locate the rear mounting rubbers to the four mounting bolts in the rear cover and fit the four spring washers and nuts.
16. Fit the two plain washers and nyloc nuts.
17. Tighten the four nyloc nuts securing the front and rear rubber mountings.
18. Lower the jack.
19. Refit the handbrake support bracket.
20. Refill the hypoid casing with new oil.
21. Refit the silencer and tail pipes 30.10.19.
22. Lower the ramp and drive the car off.

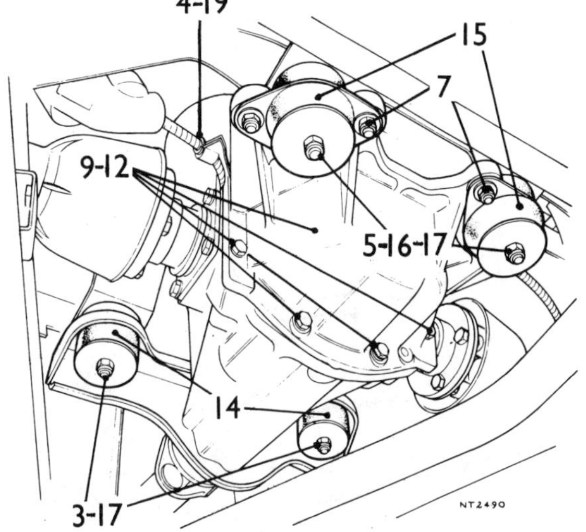

FINAL DRIVE UNIT

– Overhaul 51.25.19

Service Tools: S4221A-10-16, RG421, S123A, M84B-1, S316

NOTE: If slight damage to the crown wheel or the pinion necessitates replacement, discard both items and fit a new matched pair. These gears are lapped together during manufacture and etched with similar marking to identify them as a pair, therefore, before fitting, ensure that each gear is similarly marked as shown in NT 2784.

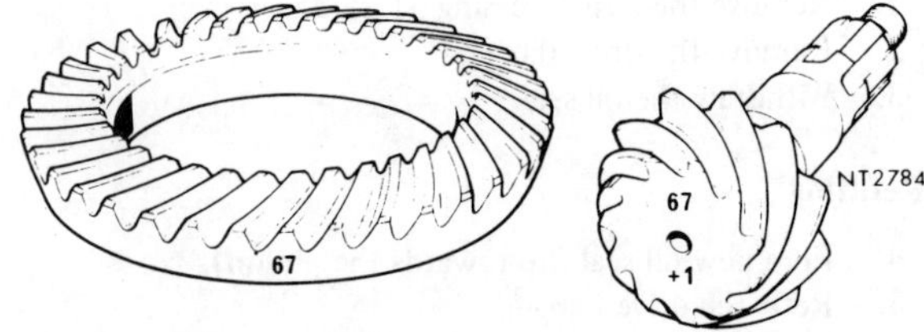

Dismantling

1. Withdraw crown wheel and differential unit from hypoid casing 51.15.01.
2. Remove the ten bolts and washers securing the crown wheel to the differential flange, withdraw the crown wheel.
3. With the crown wheel removed, install the differential unit in the hypoid casing and release all tension from the spreading tool.
4. Using a dial gauge check the crown wheel flange run-out, this should not exceed 0·003 in (0·08 mm). Excessive run out indicates a distorted crown wheel flange, differential or defective bearings.
5. Remove the differential unit from the hypoid casing.
6. Using the tools S4221A-10, withdraw the differential carrier bearings.

Continued

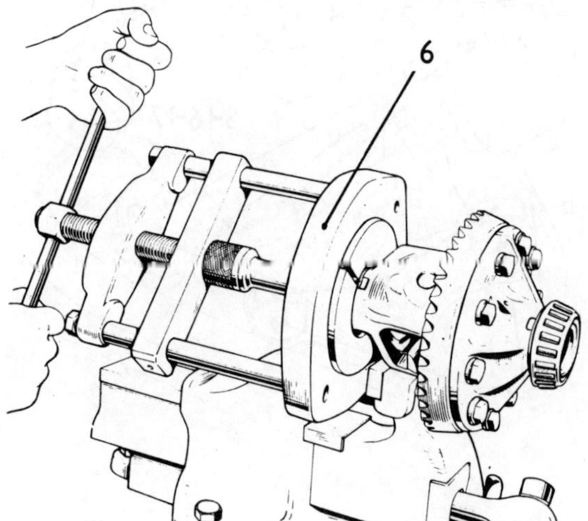

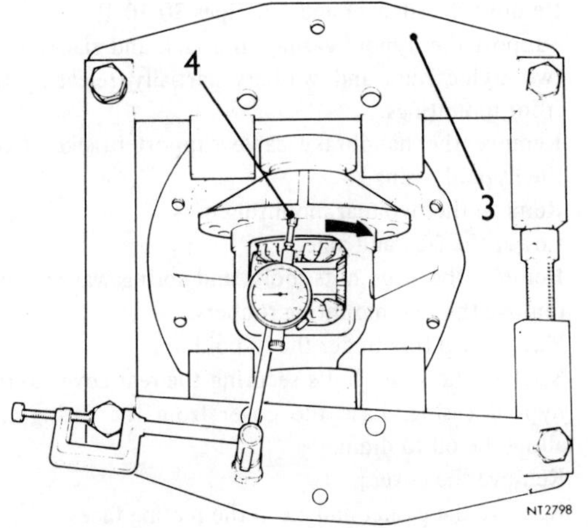

7. Drift out the cross shaft locking pin and the cross shaft.
8. Rotate the sun gears through 90° and extract the planet gears and thrust washers.
9. Withdraw the sun gears and thrust washers.
10. Remove the locking wire from the pinion shaft.
11. Using tool RG421 or S316 to hold the flange, remove the castellated nut and washer. Withdraw the flange.

** **NOTE**: Earlier units are fitted with a nyloc nut, Later units are fitted with a wired castellated nut. **

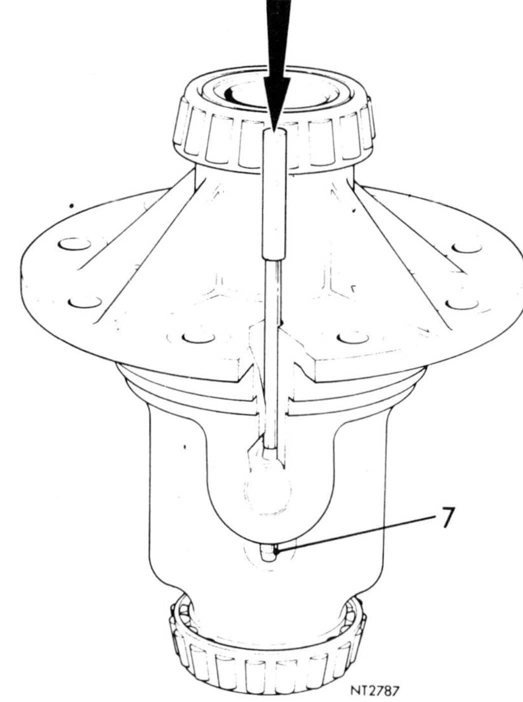

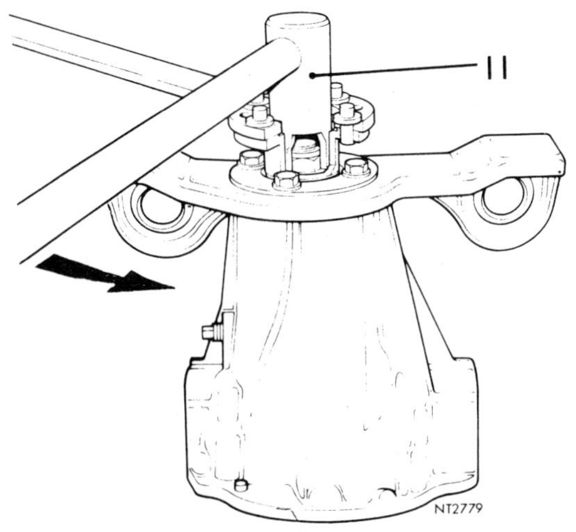

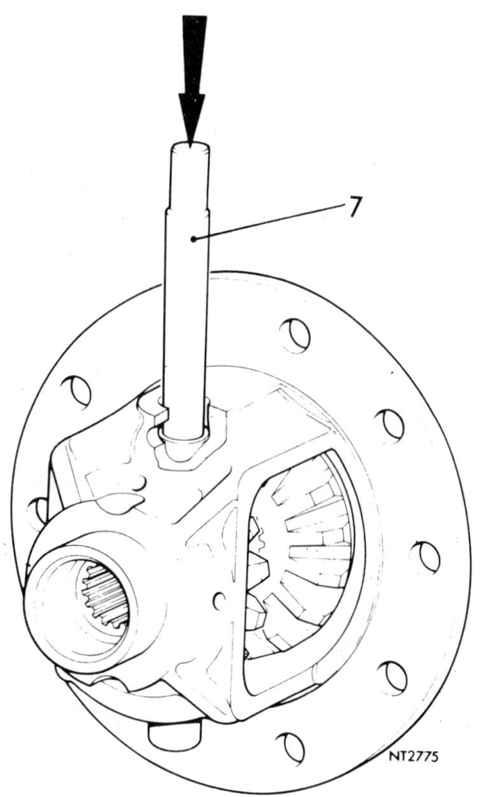

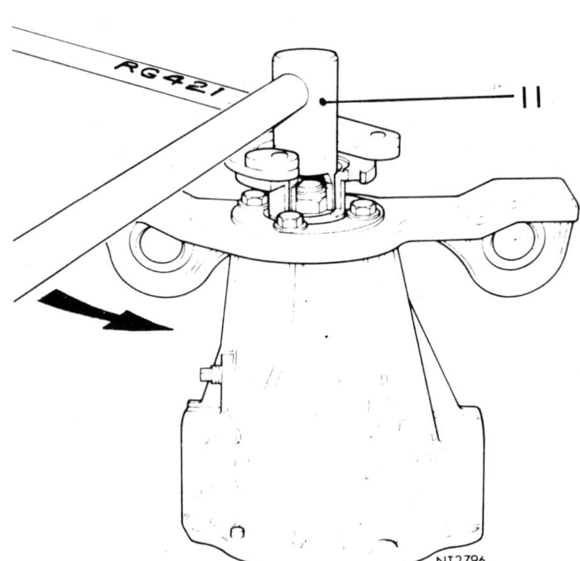

12. Remove the four bolts securing the front mounting bracket.
13. Remove the bracket.
14. Carefully drive out the pinion shaft complete with the inner bearing, bearing spacer and shim pack.
15. Extract the seal and the outer bearing.

Continued

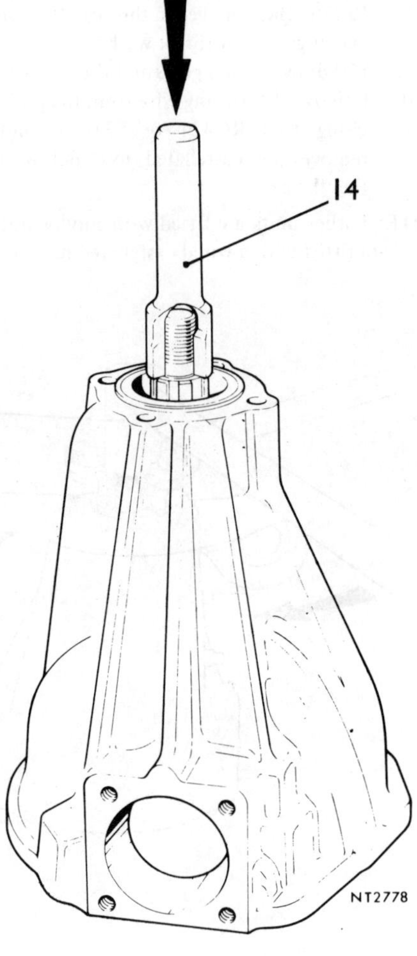

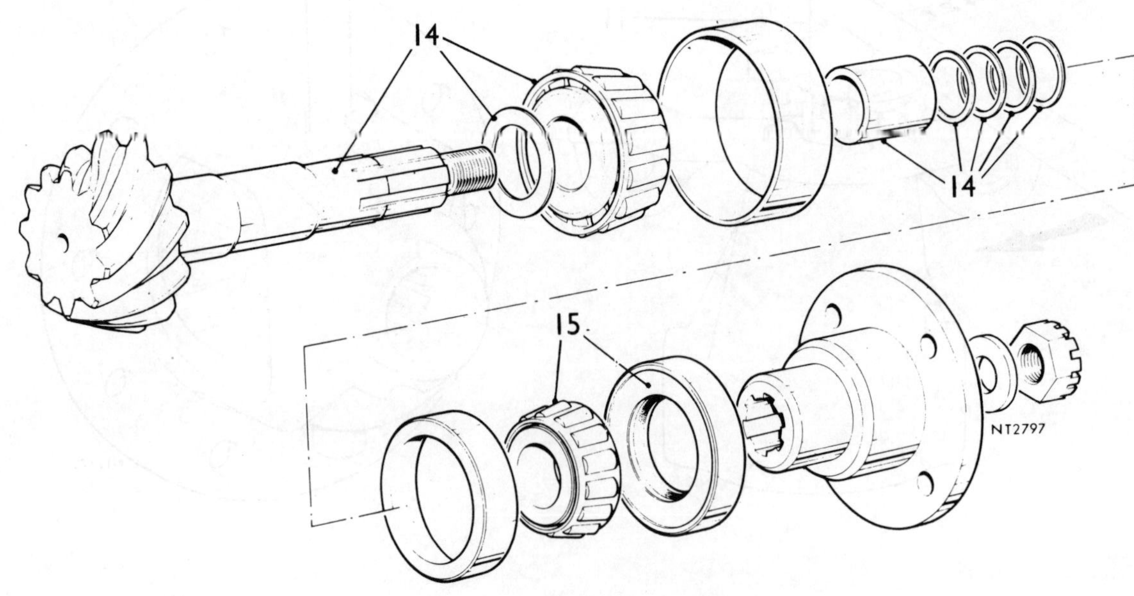

16. Remove the pinion shaft bearing outer tracks from the hypoid casing using tool **S123A**.
17. Using tool 4221A-16, install the pinion bearing outer tracks in the hypoid casing.

Continued

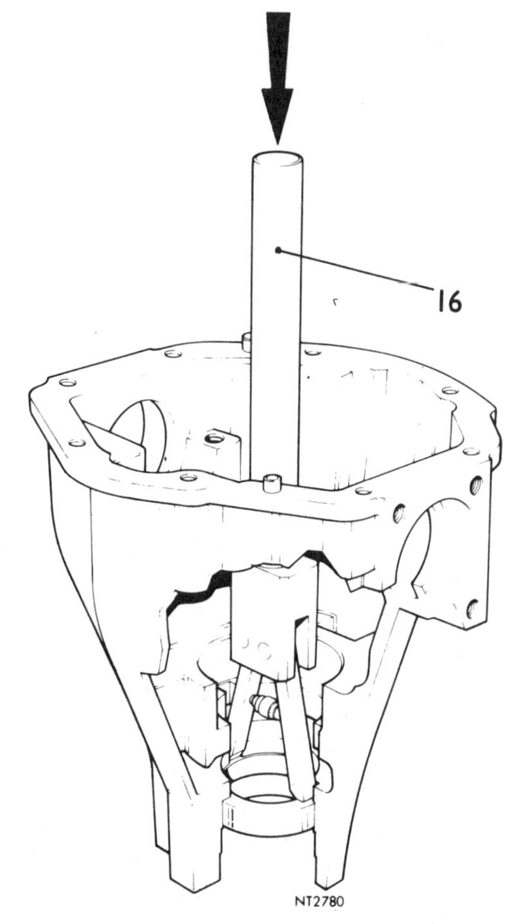

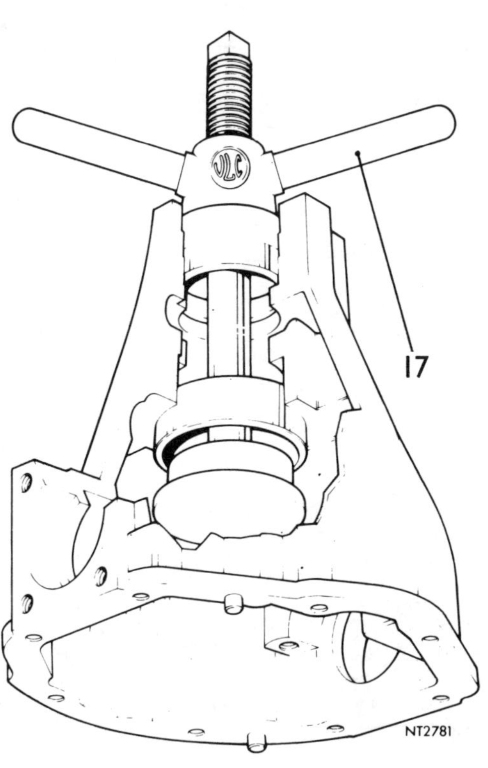

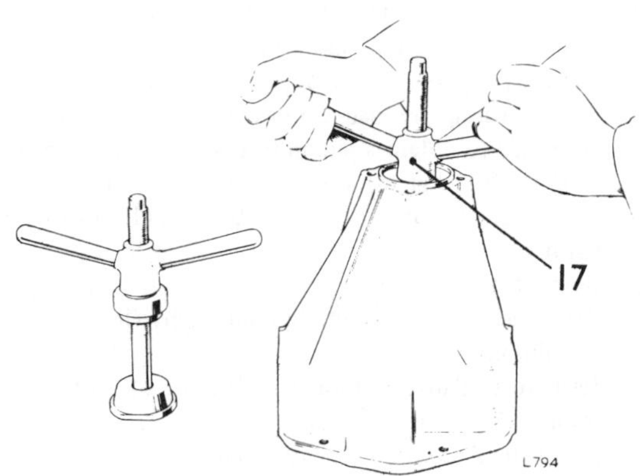

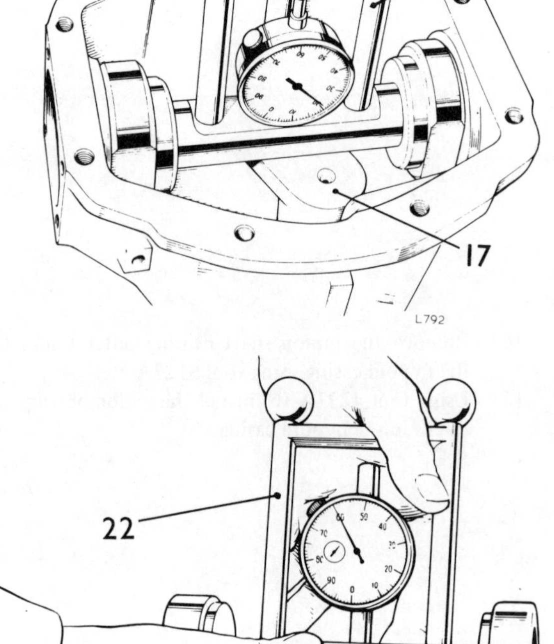

18. Install the pinion head bearing on the dummy pinion (tool M84B-1) and assemble it in the hypoid casing.
19. Fit the pinion tail shaft bearing, centralizing collar, flange, plain washer and slotted nut.
20. Tighten the slotted nut until a torque of 15 to 18 lbf in (0·17 to 0·21 kgf m) will just turn the pinion.
21. Set the pinion gauge (tool 84B) to zero.
22. Install the gauge and the dummy bearings in the hypoid casing.

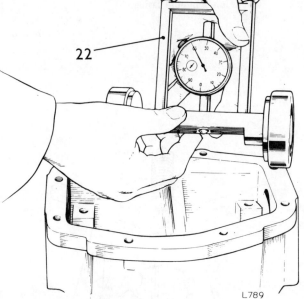

23. Maintaining slight pressure on the gauge body, rock the stylus across the dummy pinion, observe the gauge readings. The minimum valve is recorded when the stylus is parallel to the axis of the dummy pinion. This valve is the thickness of the shim(s) to be fitted between the pinion and the pinion head bearing.
24. Remove the gauge and the dummy pinion from the hypoid casing.
25. Fit the four bolts holding the mounting flange to the hypoid case 15 to 20 lbf in (2·1 to 2·8 kgf m).
26. Fit the required shim(s) to the pinion shaft and fit the pinion head bearing.
27. Install the pinion in the hypoid casing.
28. Fit the bearing spacer, tail shaft bearing drive flange, plain washer and castellated nut.

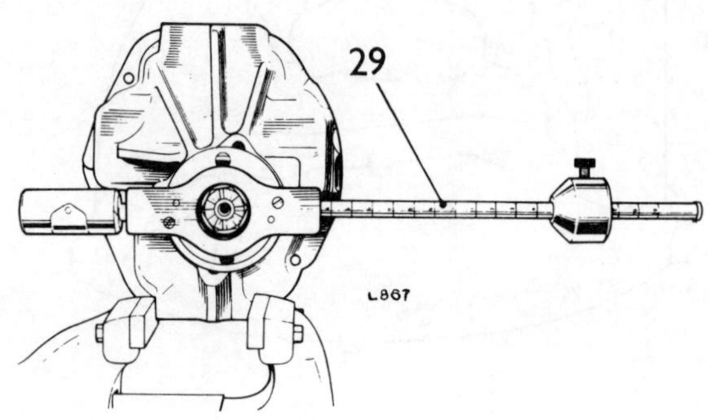

NOTE: Ensure that the tapered face of the bearing spacer is fitted adjacent to the tailshaft bearing.

29. Carefully tighten the castellated nut checking the pinion bearing pre-load. Shim the bearing spacer as is necessary to obtain a pinion torque of 15 to 18 lbf in (0·17 to 0·21 kgf m) when the castellated nut is tight to a torque loading of 90 to 120 lbf in (12·4 to 16·6 kgf m).
30. Remove drive flange.
31. Press the oil seal into the hypoid casing (lip towards the pinion).
32. Refit drive flange and nut to a loading of 90 to 120 lbf in (12·4 to 16·6 kgf m).
33. Fit the locking wire to the castellated nut.

Continued

34. Fit the thrust washers to the sun gears and slide these into the differential housing.
35. Assemble the thrust washers to the planet gears and mesh the planet gears with the sun gears (planet gears opposite each other).
36. Rotate the sun gears and slide both planet gears and thrust washers into position in the differential unit.
37. Insert the planet gear cross shaft.
38. Select and fit planet gear thrust washer as required to obtain zero backlash.
39. Fit the locking pin to the cross shaft and lightly peen to secure.
40. Fit the carrier bearing inner cones to the differential unit. Do not install any shims at this stage.
41. Refit the hypoid case spreader tool 51.15.01 operations 8 and 9.
42. Fit the outer bearing tracks to the cones and install the differential in the hypoid casing. Do not fit the bearing caps.
43. Using a dial gauge, check the total axial movement of the crown wheel flange. To the measurement obtained, must be added 0·003 in (0·0762 mm) carrier bearing pre-load. Thus the total amount of shims to be fitted to the carrier bearings is free movement + 0·003 in (0·0762 mm).
44. Remove the differential unit and fit crown wheel – 10 bolts and spring washers 38 to 46 lbf in (5·2 to 6·4 kgf m), ** apply loctite to bolts before fitting. **
45. Again install the differential unit in the hypoid housing.
46. Using a dial gauge check the total axial movement. This represents the crown wheel movement, zero backlash to maximum backlash.
Subtract an operational backlash of 0·004 to 0·006 in (0·1016 to 0·1524 mm) from the gauge reading. From these two dimensions can be found bearing shim thickness and location i.e.
Instruction 43. Total float WITHOUT crown wheel PLUS 0·003 in (0·0762 mm) bearing pre-load and
Instruction 46. Total float WITH crown wheel MINUS required backlash 0·004 to 0·006 in (0·1016 to 0·1524 mm). **
47. Remove the carrier bearing adjacent to the crown wheel from the differential unit and select the shim pack to the valve of instruction 46 (the total float with the crown wheel minus 0·004 to 0·006 in (0·1016 to 0·1524 mm). Fit this shim pack to the bearing.
48. Remove the carrier bearing farthest from the crown wheel. Subtract the dimension in instruction 46 from the dimension in instruction 40. Select the shim pack and fit the shims and bearing to the differential unit.

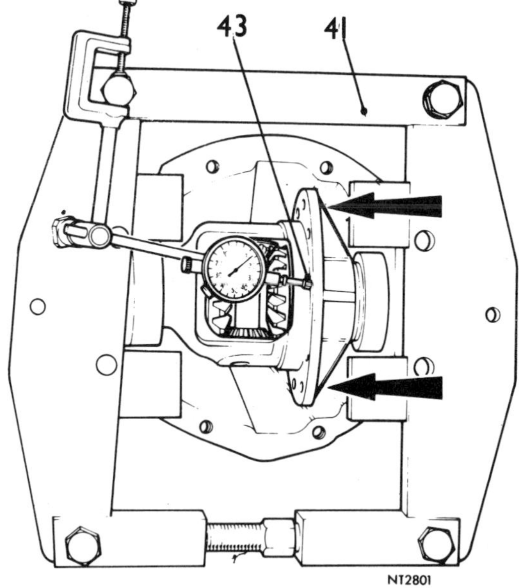

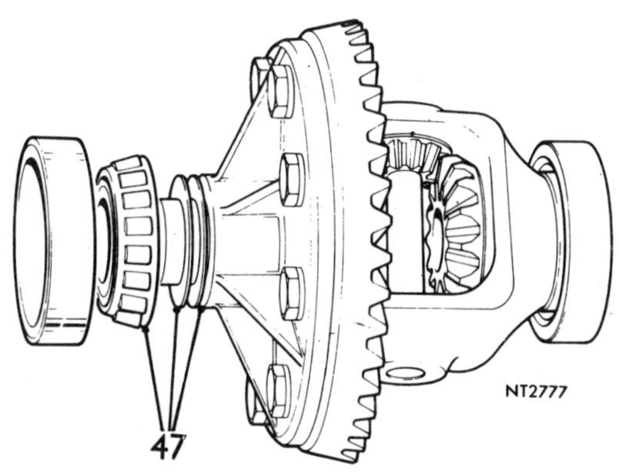

Continued

49. Insert the differential unit into the hypoid casing. Release the spreading tool and fit and tighten carrier bearing caps to a torque of 30 to 38 lbf in (4·1 to 5·2 kgf m).
50. Using a dial gauge, check the backlash at several points on the crown wheel if a mean reading of 0·004 to 0·006 in (0·1016 to 0·1524 mm) is not obtained, transfer shims from one carrier bearing to the other as required.
51. Refit a new rear cover gasket.
52. Tap the locating dowels back proud of the hypoid case.
53. Refit the rear cover (seven bolts).
54. Refit the hypoid casing to the car 51.25.25.

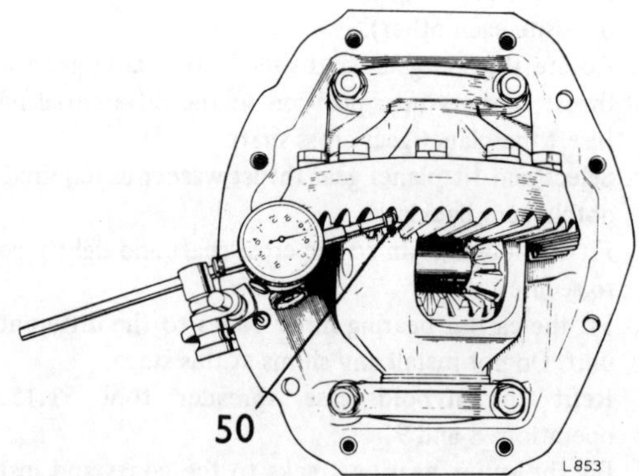

HYPOID CASING

– Remove and refit 51.25.25

Removing

1. Raise the car on a ramp, support the body on stands and locate a jack under the hypoid casing.
2. Remove exhaust tail box and rear pipe complete 30.10.19.
3. Roll back the rubber dust shields.
4. Disconnect the drive shafts from the inner axle shafts and propeller shaft from the pinion flange, four nuts and bolts on each.
5. Disconnect the nearside handbrake cable bracket, one bolt to the hypoid case.
6. Remove four nuts (two front mountings, two rear mountings) and heavy plain washers. Remove rubbers from front mountings only.
7. Carefully lower the jack until the two rear mountings are clear of the two chassis mounted studs.
8. Carefully withdraw the hypoid casing to the rear of the car, taking care not to damage the petrol pipes or brake fluid pipes.

Refitting

9. Carefully reposition the hypoid casing over the chassis studs.
10. Refit the rubbers over the front mountings.
11. Refit four heavy plain washers and nuts.
12. Connect up the nearside handbrake cable bracket to the hypoid housing.
13. Connect up the drive shafts to the inner axle shafts and the propeller shaft, four nuts and bolts on each.
14. Reposition the rubber dust shields over the universal joints.
15. Refit the exhaust tail box and rear pipes complete 30.10.19.
16. Remove the stands and lower the ramp.

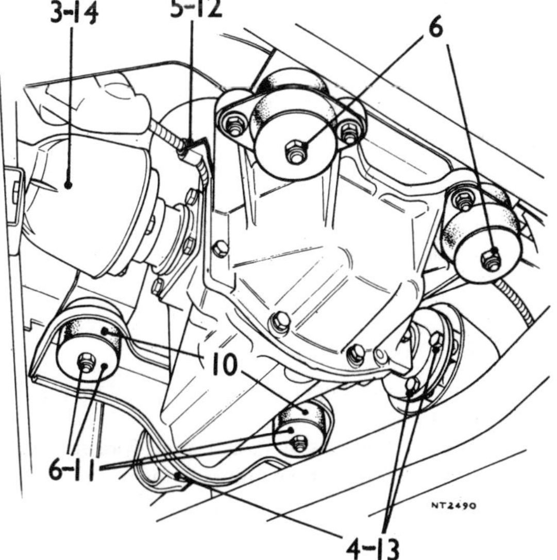

FINAL DRIVE UNIT MOUNTINGS

– Remove and refit **51.25.31**

Removing

1. Remove the hypoid casing from the car 51.25.25.
2. Remove the four nuts, bolts and spring washers securing the two rear mountings to the rear cover.
3. Remove the rear mountings.
4. Remove the two upper front rubber mountings from the chassis studs.

Refitting

5. Refit the two upper front rubber mountings to the chassis studs.
6. Refit the four nuts, bolts and spring washers securing the two rear rubber mountings to the rear cover.
7. Refit the hypoid casing to the car 15.25.25.

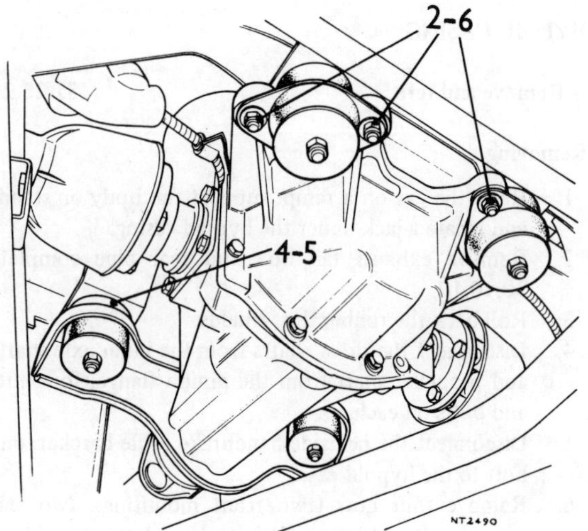

STEERING OPERATIONS

STEERING RACK AND PINION

– Remove and refit **57.25.01**

Service Tool: S341

Removing

1. Jack up the car and remove the front road wheels.
2. Disconnect the tie rod outer ball joints from the steering arms.
3. Remove the bolt, plain washer and nut securing the universal joint to the rack pinion.
4. Remove the plug from the damper plug and release the bonding strap.
5. Remove the four nuts, plain washers and two angle plates securing the rack 'U' bolts to the chassis.
6. Withdraw the 'U' bolts and bracket assemblies.
7. Slide the rack forward to release the pinion from the universal joint.
8. Remove the rack.
9. Remove the rack mounting rubbers.

Refitting

10. Fit the rack mounting rubbers on the inboard side of the rack flanges. Ensure the lip of the mountings engages the straight edges of the flanges.
11. Centralise the steering rack and place it in position on the chassis.
12. With the steering wheel centred engage the pinion in the universal joint.
13. Fit the 'U' bolt and bracket assemblies.
14. Fit the angle plates (angles inboard) plain washers and nuts to the 'U' bolts.
15. Using Tool S341, compress the mounting rubbers until approximately 1/8 in. (3 mm) remains exposed beyond the edge of the 'U' bolt brackets.
16. Ensure that the angle of the plates is in hard contact with the chassis and tighten the 'U' bolt nuts. Remove Tool S341.
17. Connect the tie rod ball joints to the steering arms.
18. Fit the clamp bolt, plain washer and nut to the universal joint and pinion. Tighten.
19. Fit the bonding strap and plug to the damper plug.
20. Fit the front wheels and remove the jack.
21. Check and adjust front wheel track.

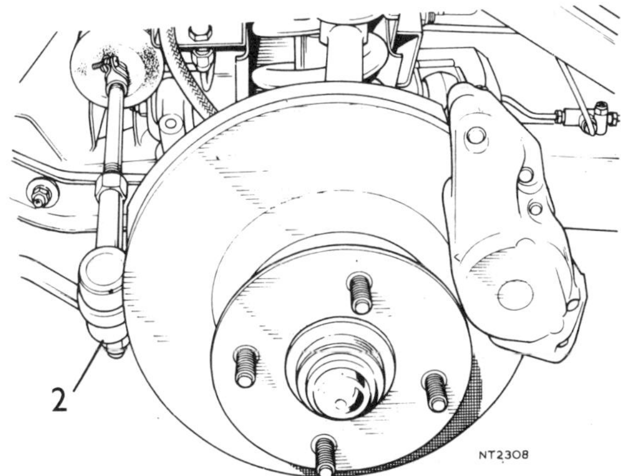

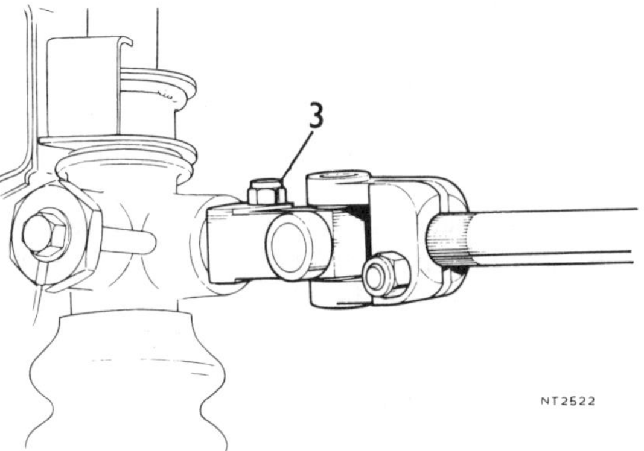

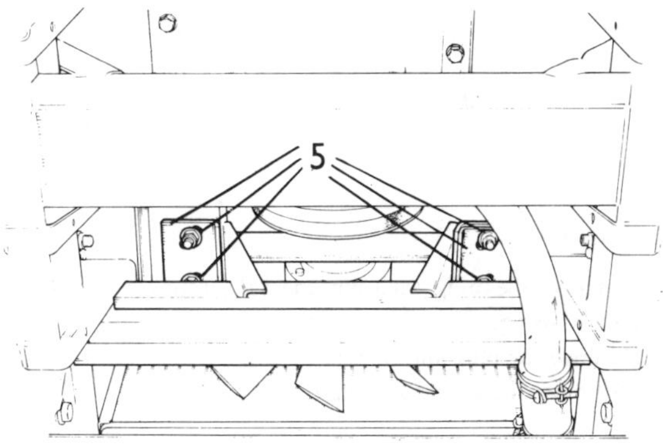

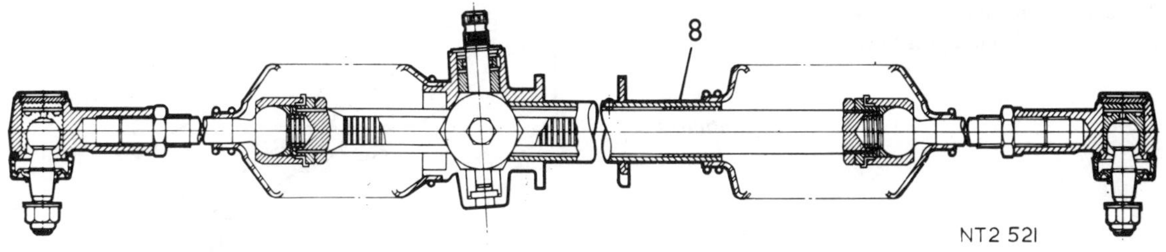

STEERING RACK GAITERS

– Remove and refit **57.25.02**

Removing

1. Remove the tie rod outer ball joints 57.55.02.
2. Remove the inner and outer clips securing the gaiters to the steering rack and the tie rods respectively.
3. Withdraw the gaiters.

Refitting

4. Lubricate the tie rod inner ball joints with fresh grease.
5. Slide the new gaiters complete with clips along the tie rods into position on the rack.
6. Fit the inner clips to the gaiters and the rack housing.
7. Fit the locknuts and outer ball joints to the tie rods.
8. Secure the outer ball joints to the steering arms and fit the road wheels.
9. Adjust the front wheel track and tighten the outer ball joint locknuts.
10. Tighten the outer clips on the gaiters ensuring that the gaiters are positioned to accommodate lock to lock movement of the tie rods.

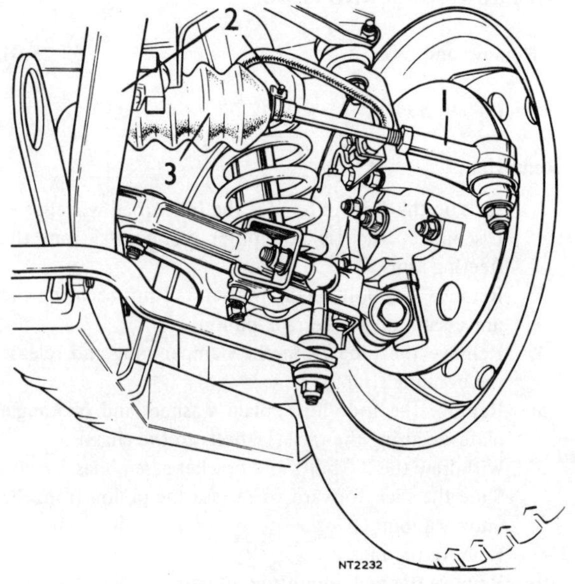

STEERING RACK AND PINION

– Overhaul **57.25.07**

1. Slacken the locknuts securing the tie rod outer ball joints.
2. Remove the rack from the car 57.25.01

Dismantling

Rack plunger

3. Unscrew the plug securing the rack plunger to the rack housing.
4. Remove the plug and shims.
5. Withdraw the spring and plunger.

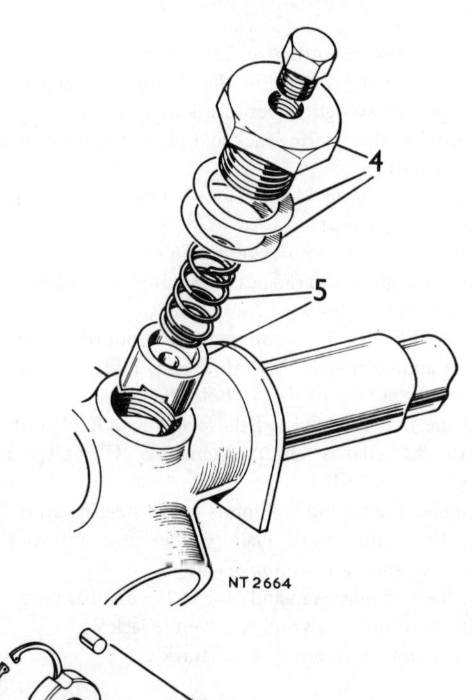

Pinion

6. Remove the circlip retaining the pinion to the rack housing.
7. Withdraw the pinion complete with plug end, locating pin, shims, bush and upper thrust washer.

Continued

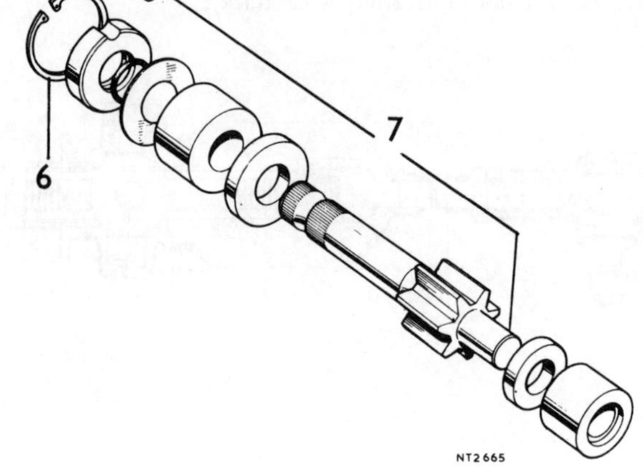

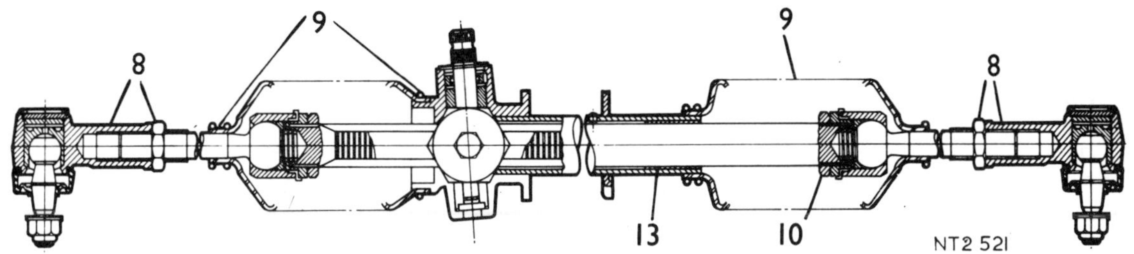

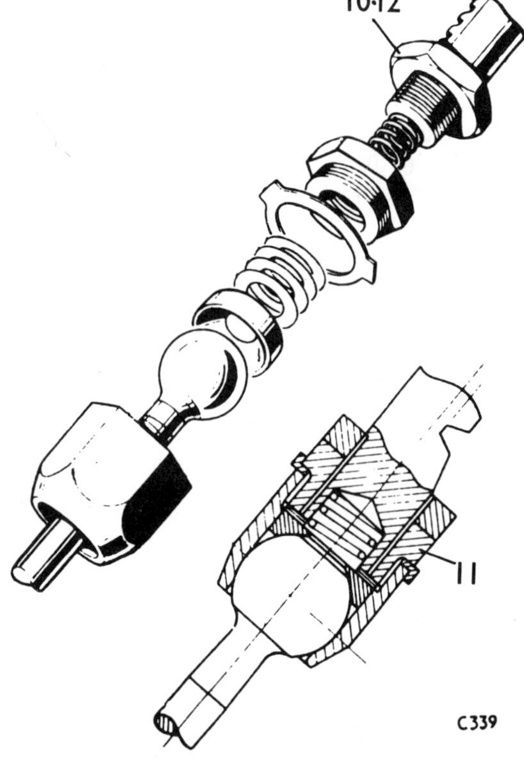

Tie rods and rack shaft

8. Remove the outer ball joints and locknuts.
9. Slacken the clips securing the gaiters to the rack housing and tie rods and remove the gaiters.
10. Slacken the locknuts securing the inner ball joint adaptors to the rackshaft.
11. Unscrew and remove the inner ball joint adaptors complete with tie rods and inner ball joint springs.
12. Remove the rack shaft locknuts and withdraw the rack shaft.

Rack housing bush

13. Remove the bush from the rack housing. (Fitted at end opposite to pinion location).

Pinion housing

14. Withdraw the pinion lower thrust washer.
15. Drive or press out the pinion end cover and the lower bush.

Assembling

Rack housing bush

16. Fit a new bush to the rack housing.

Pinion housing

17. Fit the end cover and the lower bush to the pinion housing ensuring that the recessed end of the bush is fitted adjacent to the end cover.

Rack shaft and tie rods.

18. Insert the pinion lower thrust washer in position above the pinion lower bush ensuring that the internal fillet faces away from the bush.
19. Insert the rack shaft in the housing ensuring that rack teeth are fitted to pinion end of housing.
20. Fit the locknuts to the rack shaft.
21. Fit both tie rods, springs and adaptors and secure with locknuts. (torque 80 lbf ft. – 11·1 kgf m).
22. Pack the inner ball joints with grease and fit the gaiters and clips.

Continued

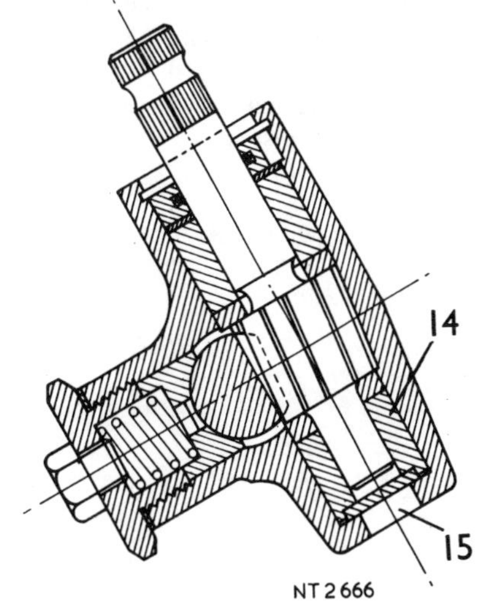

Pinion

23. Rotate the rack shaft until rack teeth will permit pinion engagement.
24. Engage the pinion in the pinion housing and rack shaft.
25. Fit the upper thrust washer, bush and shims.
26. Fit a new internal 'O' ring to the plug-end and fit the plug-end and locating pin.
27. Fit the circlip and check the pinion for end-float. End-float must not exceed 0·010 in (0·254 mm). Adjust the shim pack as necessary.

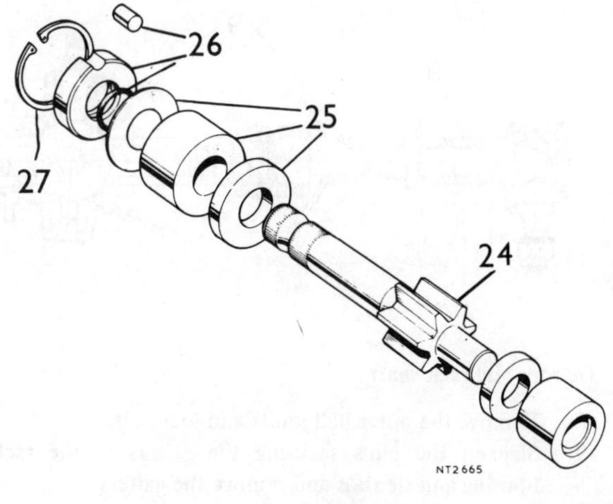

Rack plunger

28. Fit the plunger.
29. Fit the spring, shims and damper plug.
30. Check the rack shaft for side movement (90° to shaft axis). Side movement should be within 0·004 to 0·008 in (0·102 to 0·203 mm). Adjust as required by adding or removing shims as required.

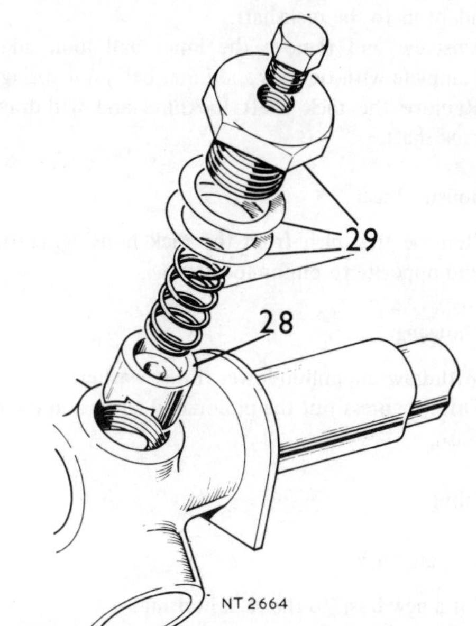

STEERING RACK DAMPER

– Remove and refit **57.35.10**

Removing

1. Disconnect the bonding strap at the damper plug.
2. Unscrew the damper plug and withdraw plug, shims, spring and plunger.

Refitting

3. Fit the plunger and spring.
4. Fit the shims and damper plug. Tighten the plug.
5. Check the rack shaft for movement (90° to rack axis). Side movement should be within 0·004 to 0·008 in (0·102 to 0·203 mm). Adjust as required by adding or removing shim(s) as necessary.
6. Connect the bonding strap.

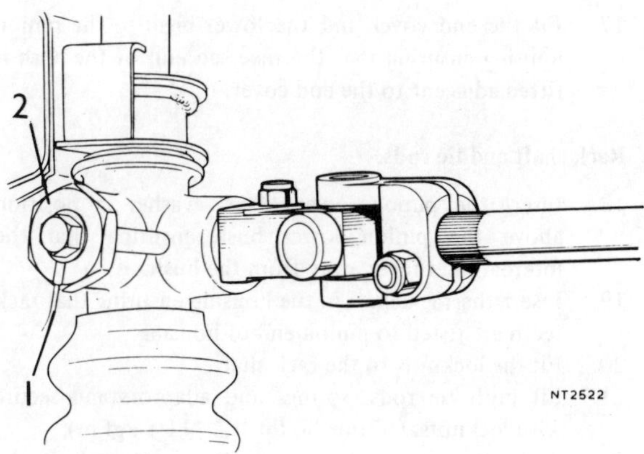

STEERING COLUMN ASSEMBLY

– Remove and refit 57.40.01

Removing

1. Disconnect the plug-in connectors for lights, horn, flashers, ignition and starter circuits.
2. Remove the steering wheel 57.60.01.
3. Remove the speedometer (LH Steer) *or* the tachometer (RH Steer). See 88.30.01 or 88.30.21 as appropriate.
4. Remove the pinchbolt securing the lower steering column to the flexible coupling.
5. Remove the two setscrews securing the steering column safety clamp and withdraw the clamp.
6. Remove the two bolts and nuts securing the forward end of the anti-torque strap to the scuttle.
7. Remove the domed protection covers from the steering column bracket bolts.
8. Remove the two bolts, nuts and washers securing the steering column bracket halves. Withdraw the harness cover.
9. Withdraw the anti-torque strap and the upper half of the column bracket.
10. Rotate the steering column to bring the shearbolts of the steering lock/ignition switch to an accessible position.
11. With a centre-punch mark the centre of the two shearbolts heads securing the steering lock/ignition bracket.
12. Using a small chisel, unscrew the shearbolts. If this proves unsuccessful drill the shearbolts and unscrew them using an 'Easiout' type extractor.
13. Remove the steering lock/ignition switch.
14. Withdraw the steering column.

Continued

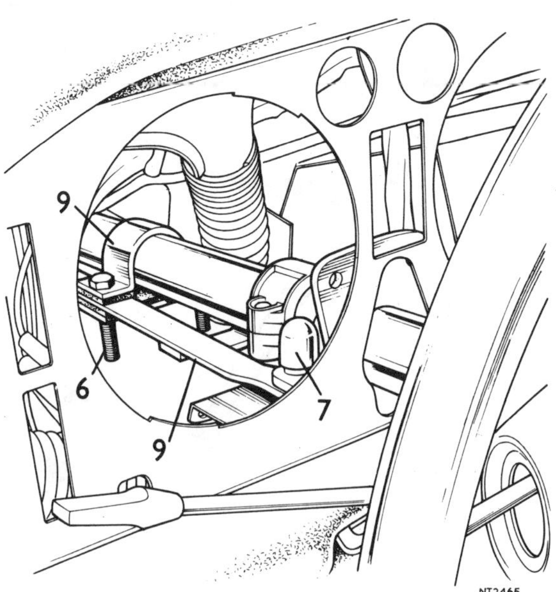

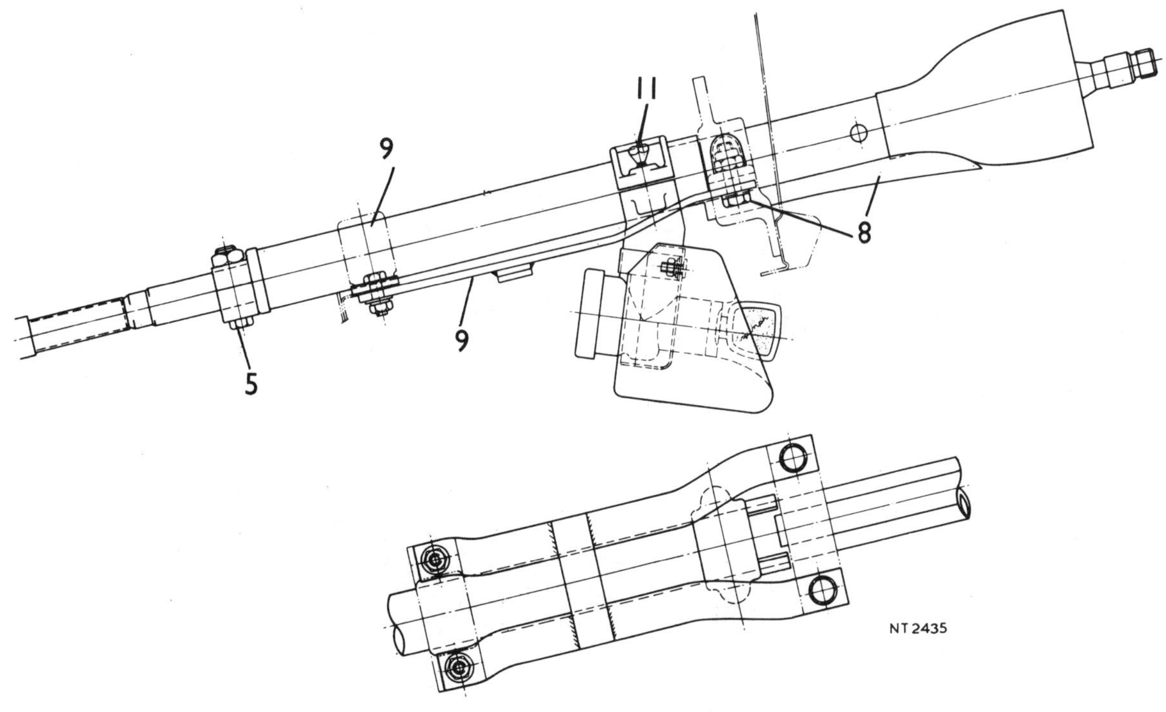

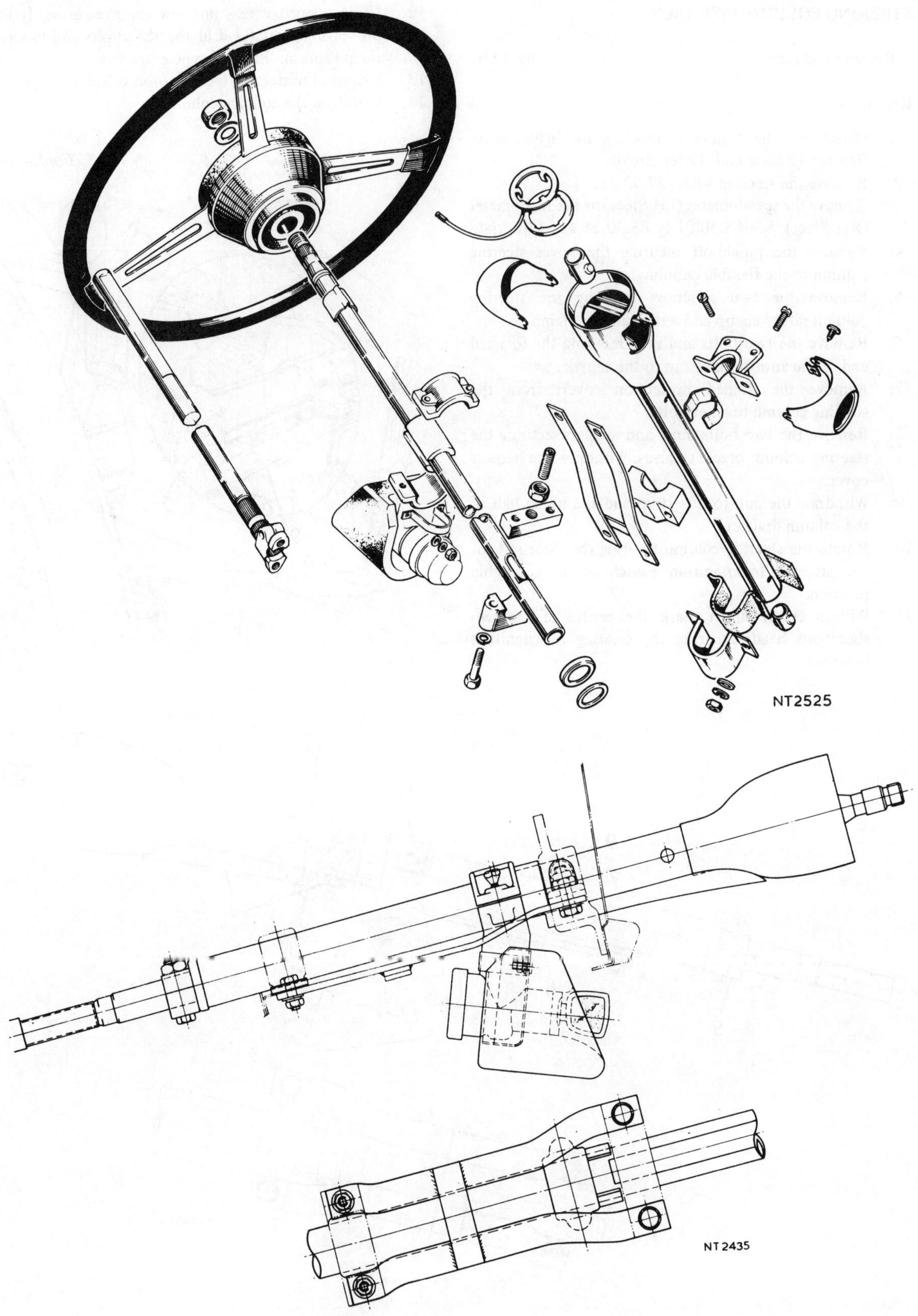
NT2525
NT 2435

Refitting

15. Locate the steering column in position in the car.
16. Offer up the steering lock/ignition switch to the steering column. Ensure that the spacer ring is **above** the steering lock/ignition switch.
17. Fit the steering lock/ignition switch clamp and secure the two new shearbolts.
18. Evenly tighten the shearbolts until the heads shear.
19. Ensuring that the front road wheels are in 'straight ahead' position and the steering wheel is centralised, engage the lower steering mast in the flexible coupling. Check that the steel tubular spacer, bullet and plastic washer are fitted to the lower mast.
20. Fit the pinchbolt to the lower column and flexible coupling.
21. Fit the harness cover to the steering column.
22. Engage the anti-torque strap on the underside of the column upper bracket. Fit the felt strip to the lower half of the bracket.
23. Fit the spring clip and the upper half of the steering column bracket and secure with two bolts, plain washers and nuts. Note that the left hand bolt is entered from below the bracket; The right hand bolt is entered from above the bracket. Fit the domed protective covers over the two nuts.
24. Align the slot in the upper mast with the flat on the lower mast. Slide the plastic washer upwards until it is in contact with the steering column housing.
25. Fit the safety clamp between the bullet and the plastic washer and secure with two bolts.
26. Connect the wiring sockets for lights, flashers and starter/ignition etc.
27. Fit and tighten the two bolts, washers and nuts securing the front of the anti-torque strap to the scuttle.
28. Fit the speedometer and tachometer to the facia. See 88.30.01 and 88.30.21.

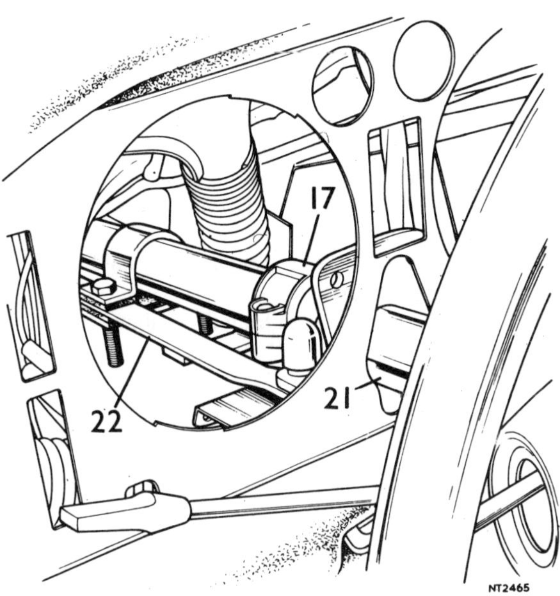

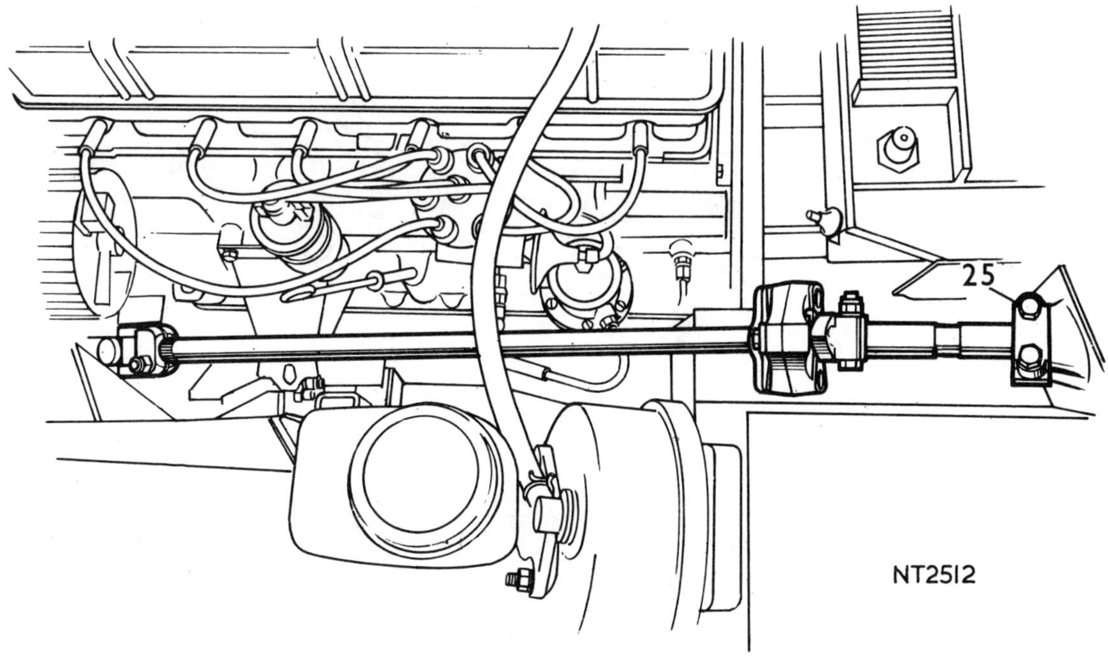

STEERING COLUMN – UPPER

– Remove and refit **57.40.02**

Removing

1. Remove the steering column assembly form the car 57.40.01.
2. Remove the steering wheel 57.60.01.
3. Remove the trafficator clip from the steering column.
4. Remove the tape securing the end cover at the lower end of the steering column housing and withdraw the end cover.
5. Slide the steering column downward until obstruction is felt.
6. Depress the dowls locating the steering column lower bush to release the bush from its location in the steering column housing.
7. Withdraw the steering column downward complete with the lower bush.
8. Remove the lower bush from the column.

Refitting

9. Enter the steering column from the lower end of the housing.
10. Fit the lower bush to the column (rubber dots on end face of bush trailing) and align the dowls with the drillings in the steering column housing.
11. Press the bush into the housing ensuring that the dowels engage the holes in the column.
12. Fit the end cover and secure with tape.
13. Fit the trafficator clip.
14. Fit the steering column assembly to the car 57.40.01.
15. Fit the steering wheel 57.60.01.

NT2435

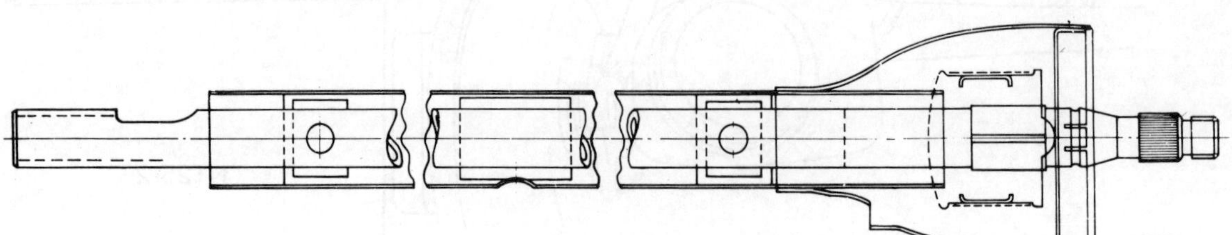

NT2523

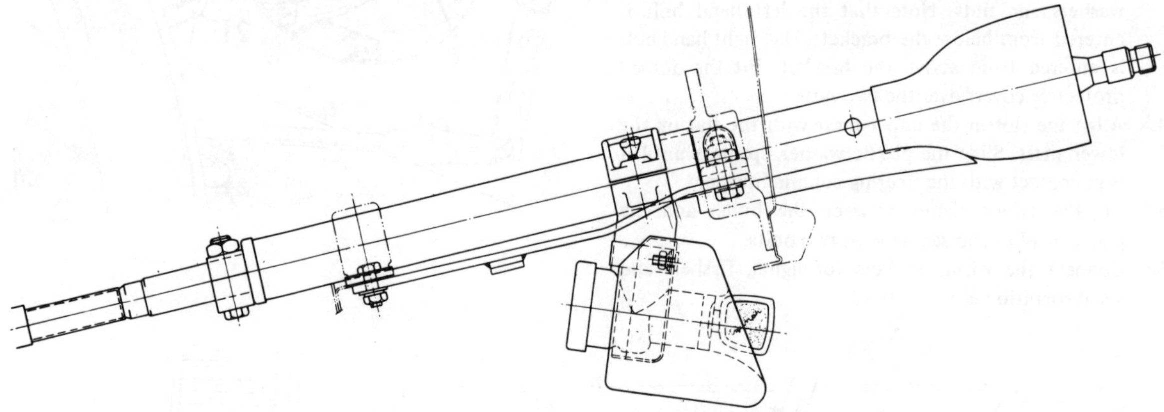

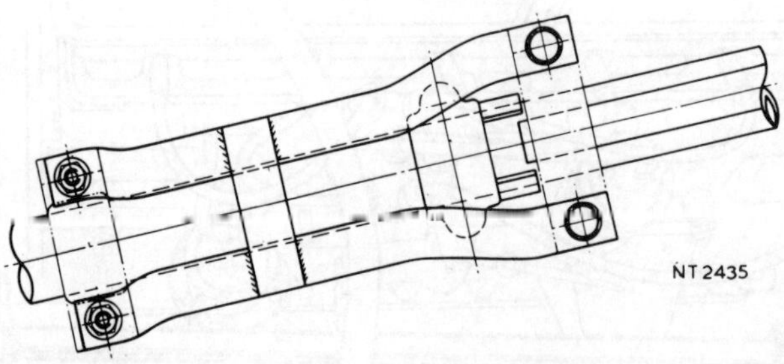

STEERING COLUMN – LOWER

– Remove and refit **57.40.05**

Removing

1. Remove the pinchbolt and nut securing the lower end of the intermediate shaft to the universal joint.
2. Remove the pinchbolt securing the flexible coupling yoke to the lower steering column.
3. Slacken the locknut and grubscrew on the safety clamp. Remove the two bolts and spring washers from the safety clamp and withdraw the safety clamp.
4. Detach the intermediate shaft from the universal joint and withdraw the intermediate shaft complete with the flexible coupling.
5. Remove the tubular distance piece and bullet from the lower steering column.
6. Withdraw the lower steering column.

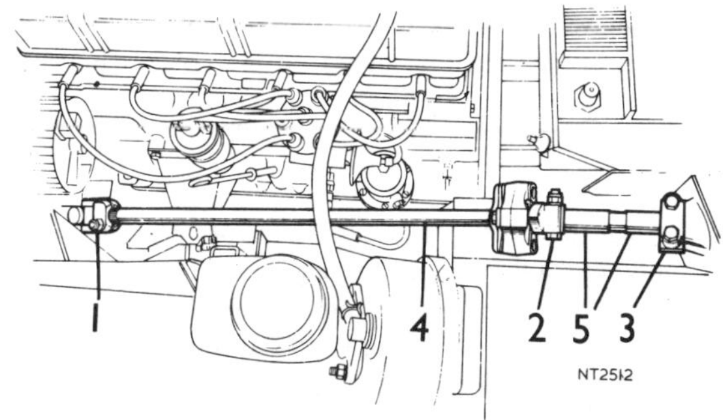

Refitting

7. Enter the lower steering column in the upper steering column and align the machined flat on the lower column with the cutaway section of the upper column.
8. Place the safety clamp and securing bolts and spring washers in position but do not tighten the bolts. Ensure that the plastic washer is fitted between the upper face of the safety clamp and the bottom of the steering column housing.
9. Slide the bullet, tapered face trailing, and the tubular distance piece over the lower column.
10. Align the flat on the lower end of the intermediate shaft with the pinchbolt location in the universal joint and enter the intermediate shaft in the universal joint. Fit the pinchbolt and nut but do not tighten at this stage.
11. With the road wheels and the steering wheel in 'straight ahead' position, enter the yoke of the flexible coupling in the lower column and fit the pichbolt washer and nut but do not tighten at this stage.
12. With light pressure on the steering wheel to prevent lift of the upper column slide the intermediate shaft upward to eliminate axial movement of the tubular distance piece and bullet.
13. Tighten both pinchbolt and the two bolts securing the safety clamp – torque 6 to 9 lbf ft (0·8 to 1·2 kgf m).
    Tighten the grubscrew –torque 18 to 20 lbf ft (2·5 to 2·8 kgf m). Tighten the locknut.

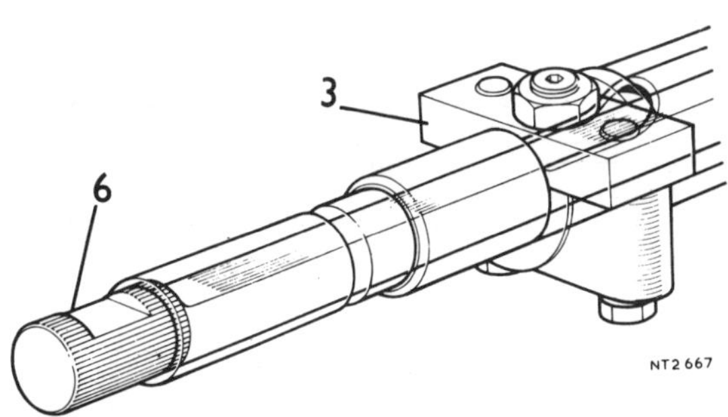

STEERING COLUMN BUSHES

– Remove and refit 57.40.18

Removing

1. Remove the upper steering column and the lower bush 57.40.02.
2. Remove the horn slip ring from the column housing.
3. Depress the locating dowls on the column housing upper bush and withdraw the upper bush.

Refitting

4. Align the locating dowls on the upper bush with the drillings in the column housing.
5. Insert the upper bush from the top of the column housing ensuring that the dots formed on the end face of the bush are leading. Press the bush into the housing and engage the dowels in the housing drillings.
6. Fit the horn slip ring to the column housing.
7. Fit the steering column and the lower bush. 57.40.02.

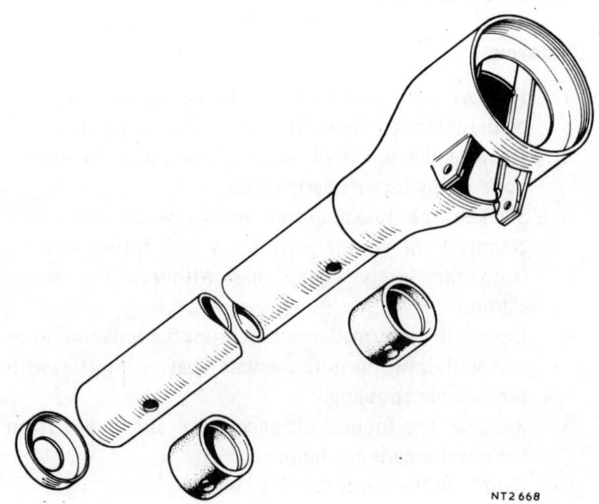

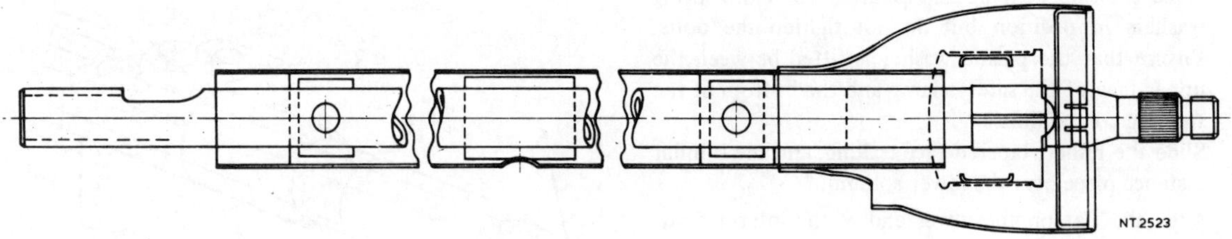

STEERING COLUMN INTERMEDIATE SHAFT

– Remove and refit 57.40.22

Removing

1. Set the road wheels to 'straight ahead' position.
2. Scribe the lower end of the intermediate shaft and the universal joint to ensure original spline location on reassembly.
3. Remove the pinch bolt and nut securing the universal joint to the intermediate shaft.
4. Remove the locking wire from the two bolts securing the upper end of the intermediate shaft to the flexible coupling and remove the two bolts.
5. Withdraw the intermediate shaft.

Refitting

6. Align the previously marked scribe lines and engage the lower end of the intermediate shaft in the universal joint. If the shaft was removed with the spline location unmarked, or a new shaft is being fitted, set the road wheels and the steering wheel to 'straight ahead' positions and align the flat of the lower end of the shaft with the pinch bolt location in the universal joint. Check that the upper two hole flange aligns with the flexible coupling, adjust spline location as necessary.
7. Fit the pinchbolt and nut to the universal joint. Do not tighten at this stage.
8. Fit the two bolts to the flexible coupling ensuring that the tail of the bonding clip is secured. Tighten the two bolts and secure with locking wire.
9. Tighten the universal pinchbolt.

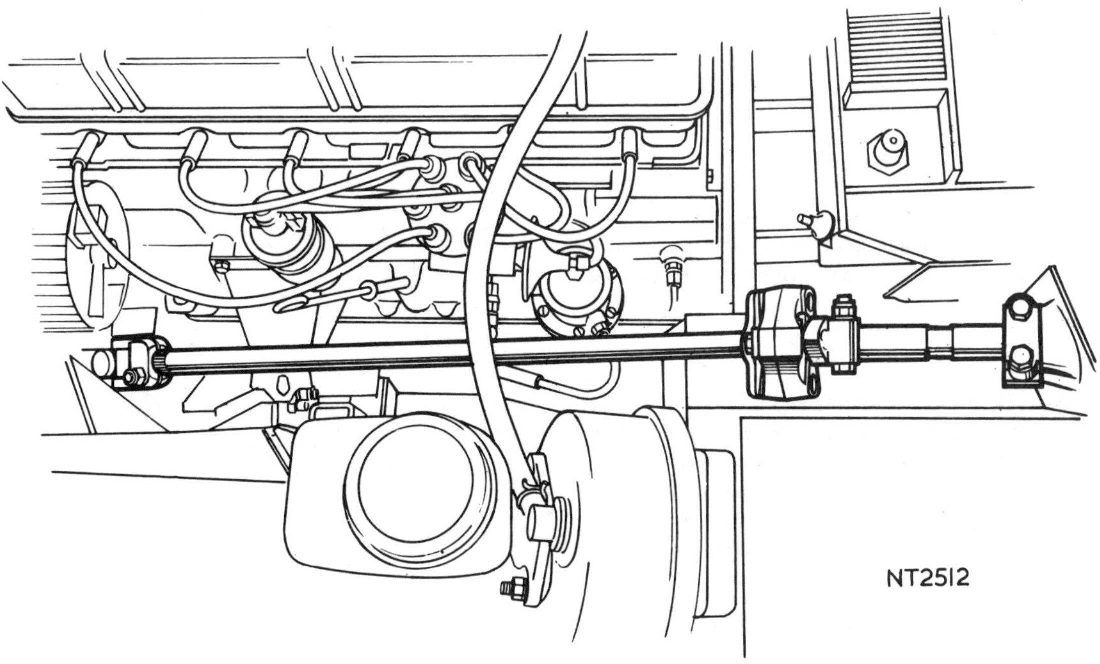

STEERING COLUMN UNIVERSAL JOINT/COUPLING – UPPER

– Remove and refit **57.40.26**

Removing

1. Removing the lock wires securing the flexible coupling securing bolts.
2. Remove the securing bolts (4).
3. Withdraw the flexible coupling and bonding strap.

Refitting

4. Reverse instructions 1 to 3. Ensure that the bonding strap is refitted.

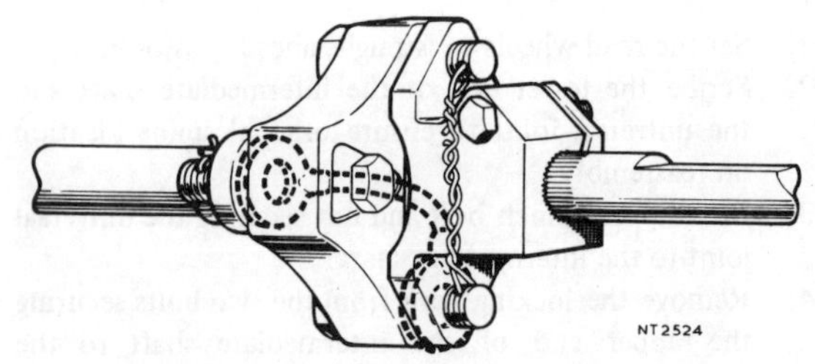
NT2524

STEERING COLUMN UNIVERSAL JOINT/COUPLING – LOWER

– Remove and refit **57.40.27**

Removing

1. Remove the intermediate shaft 57.40.22.
2. Remove the pichbolt securing the universal joint to the rack pinion shaft and withdraw the universal joint.

Refitting

3. Align the flat on the lower end of the intermediate shaft with the pinchbolt location in the yoke of the universal joint and fit the shaft to the universal joint.
4. With the road wheels and steering wheel in the 'straight ahead' positions, offer up the universal joint and intermediate shaft to the pinion shaft and check the upper flange of the intermediate shaft for alignment with the flexible coupling. Adjust as necessary on pinion shaft splines.
5. Fit the pinchbolt and nut to the pinion shaft and universal joint and tighten.
6. Fit the bolts and locking wire to the flexible coupling ensuring that the bonding strap is secured.
7. Fit and tighten the pinchbolt. Securing 'the intermediate shaft to the upper yoke of the universal joint.

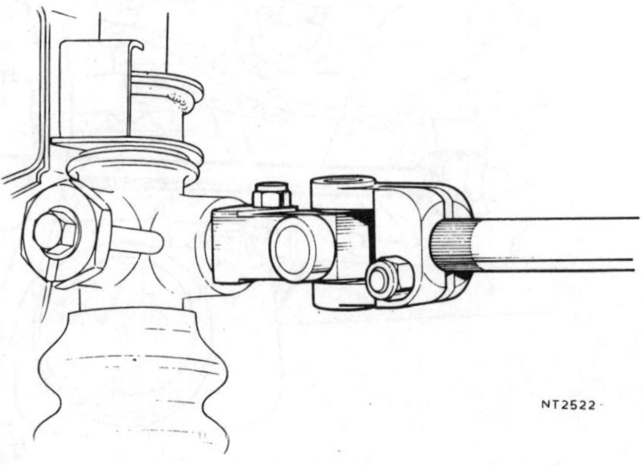
NT2522

STEERING COLUMN LOCK/IGNITION/ STARTER SWITCH

– Remove and refit **57.40.31**

Removing

1. Remove the speedometer and tachometer from the facia.
2. Release the wiring harness socket from the steering lock.
3. Remove the domed protective cover from the steering column upper bracket nuts.
4. Remove the nuts, plain washers and bolts from the steering column upper bracket.
5. Remove the top half of the steering column upper bracket.
6. Remove the nuts, spring washers and bolts securing the anti-torque strap to the scuttle.
7. Remove the cable harness cover from the underside of the steering column.
8. Withdraw the anti-torque strap from the steering lock.
9. Rotate the steering column 180° to expose the sheared heads of the two bolts securing the steering lock to the steering column.
10. Using a centre-punch mark the centre of the two shear bolt heads.
11. Using a small chisel unscrew the shear bolts. If this method proves unsuccessful drill the shearbolts and unscrew them with an 'Easiout' type extractor.
12. Remove the steering lock.

Refitting

13. Offer up the steering lock and clamp bracket to the steering column.
14. Fit two new shearbolts. Evenly tighten the shearbolts until the heads shear.
15. Reverse instruction 1 to 9.

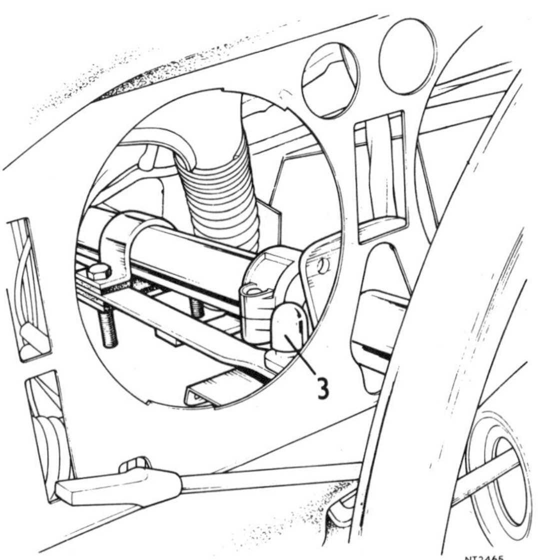

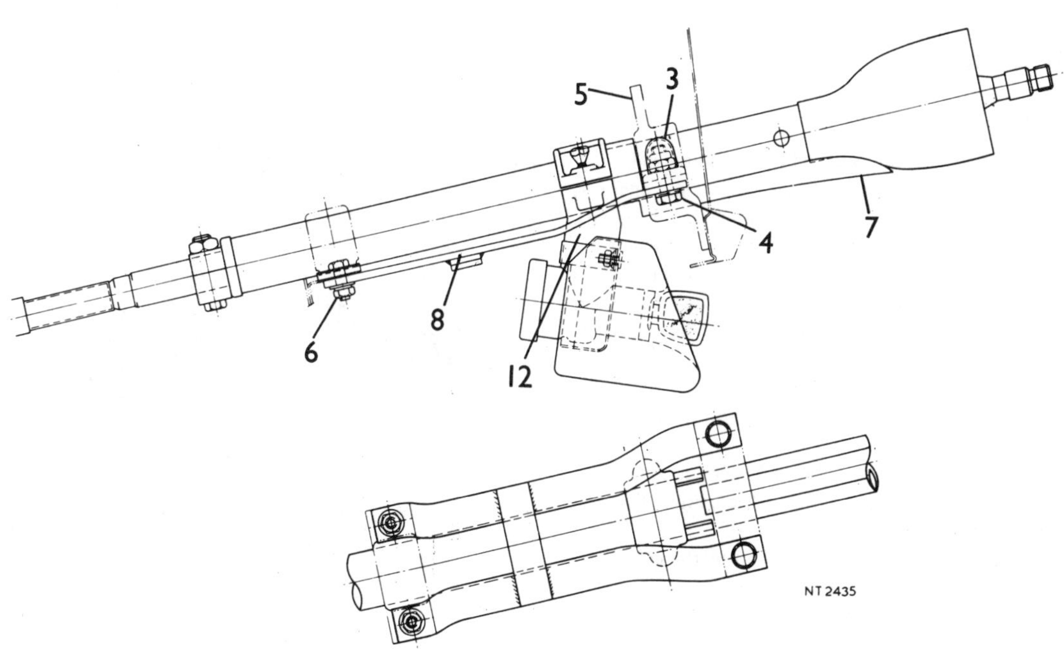

TIE ROD BALL JOINT – OUTER

– Remove and refit **57.55.02**

Removing

1. Remove the road wheel.
2. Slacken the locknut securing the outer ball joint.
3. Remove the nut and washer securing the ball joint to the steering arm.
4. Release the ball joint from the steering arm.
5. Unscrew the ball joint assembly from the tie rod.

Refitting

6. Reverse instructions 1 to 5.
7. Check and adjust front wheel track as necessary.

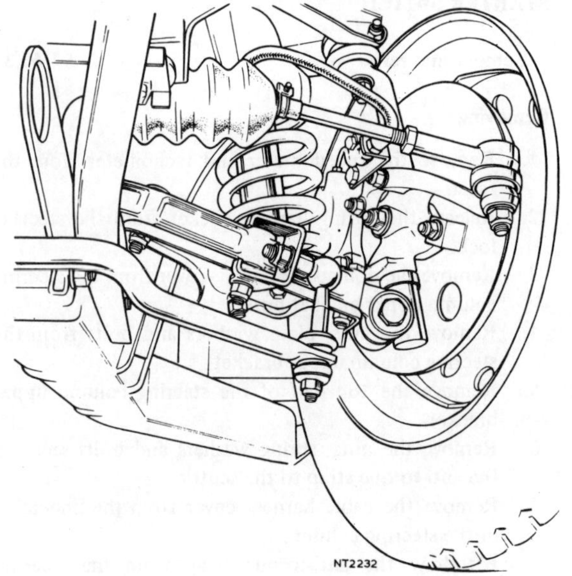

TIE ROD BALL JOINT – INNER

– Remove and refit **57.55.03**

Removing

1. Remove the rack from the car 57.25.01.
2. Remove the tie rod outer ball joint and locknut.
3. Release the gaiter clips and remove the gaiter.
4. Wipe the grease from the inner ball joint and slacken the rack shaft locknut securing the rack shaft to the ball joint adaptor. To prevent stress being applied to the pinion, the opposite adaptor should be held with a spanner.
5. Unscrew the tie rod assembly from the rack shaft.
6. Straighten the lock tabs securing the tie rod ball housing/adaptor.
7. Unscrew tha adaptor and withdraw spring, shims, ball seat and tie rod from the housing.

Refitting

8. Lubricate the ball housing and insert the tie rod.
9. Fit the ball seat, shim(s) new tab washer and adaptor.
10. Tighten the adaptor, torque 80 lbf ft (11·1 kgf m), and check the tie rod for end-float and articulation. End-float should be within 0·0005 to 0·003 in (0·013 to 0·076 mm). There must be no tight spots in articulation. Adjust by adding or removing shims as required.
11. Bend over the lock washer tabs.
12. Enter the spring in the ball housing and fit the tie rod assembly to the rack shaft.
13. Tighten the adaptor and the rack shaft locknut to a torque of 80 lbf ft (11·1 kgf m), ensuring that the pinion is not subjected to stress.
14. Smear the ball joint with grease and fit the gaiter and clips.
15. Fit the tie rod outer locknut and ball joint.
16. Fit the rack to the car 57.55.03.
17. Check and adjust front wheel track as required.

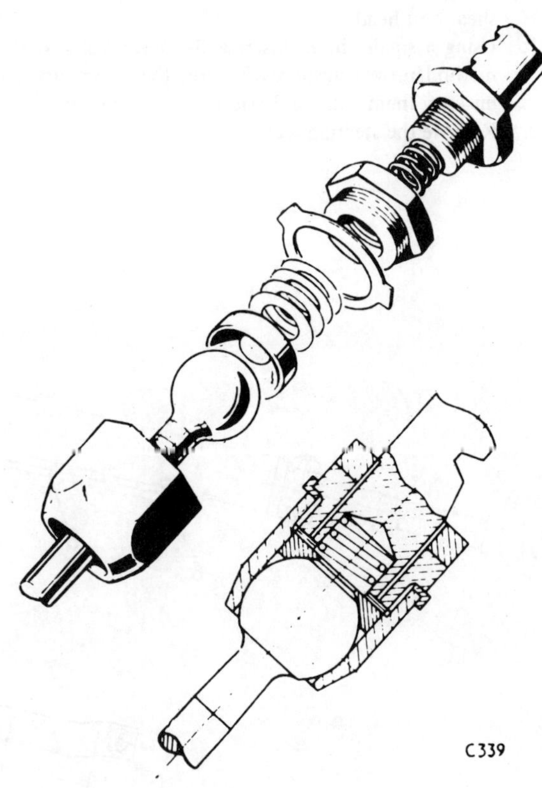

STEERING WHEEL

– Remove and refit **57.60.01**

Service tool S.3600

Removing

1. Remove the steering wheel pad.
2. Prise out the horn push.
3. Withdraw the horn connection brush.
4. Remove the nut and plain washer securing the steering wheel to the steering mast.
5. Scribe the top of the steering mast and the hub of the steering wheel to ensure spline re-engagement in original location.
6. Using Tool S3600, remove the steering wheel.

Refitting

7. Reverse instructions 1 to 6.
   When replacing the horn connection brush ensure that the spring end is entered in the wheel hub. If the wheel was withdrawn without spline location marks, set the road wheels to 'straight ahead' and fit the steering wheel with the top spokes horizontal.

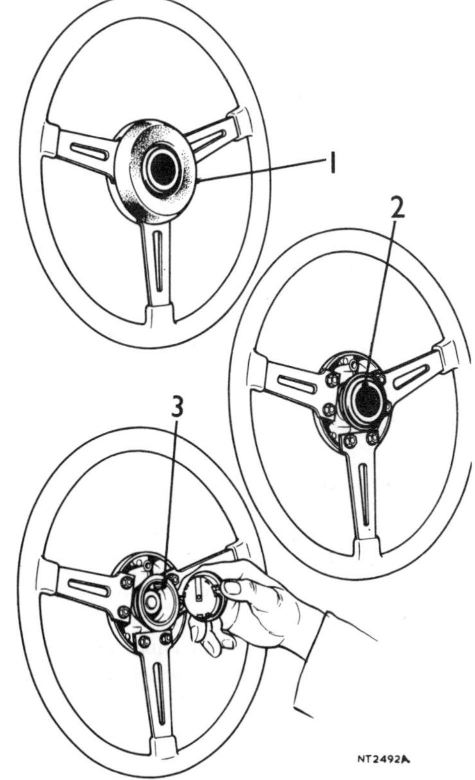

STEERING WHEEL HUB

– Remove and refit **57.60.02**

Removing

1. Remove the steering wheel and hub from the car 57.60.01.
2. Remove the six bolts and plain washers securing the steering wheel spokes to the hub.

Refitting

3. Reverse instructions 1 and 2.

STEERING GEOMETRY

57.65.00

Only two adjustments are possible: Front wheel alignment and Camber angle.

DATA		Kerb condition	Laden condition (2 up)
Camber – Carburetter		¼° pos ± 1°	¼° Neg ± ½°
–Petrol injection		½° pos ± 1°	0° ± ½°
Castor		2·3/4° ± 1°	2·3/4° ± ½°
King pin inclination – *Carburetter*		8·3/4° ± 1°	9·1/4° ± ¾°
– Petrol injection		8·1/2° ± 1°	9° ± ¾°
Toe in		1/16 – 1/8 in (1·6 –3·2 mm)	1/16 – 1/8 in (1·6 – 3·2 mm)

FRONT WHEEL ALIGNMENT

– Check and adjust **57.65.01**

Checking

1. Locate the car on level ground with the front wheels in 'straight ahead' position.
2. Using wheel alignment equipment check the front wheels for toe-in. Front wheel toe-in should be within 1/16 to 1/8 in (1·6 to 3·2 mm).

Adjusting

3. Slacken the outer clips on the rack gaiters.
4. Slacken the locknuts at the tie rod outer ends.
5. Shorten or extend both tie rods equally to obtain the required toe-in of 1/16 to 1/8 in (1·6 to 3·2 mm).
6. Tighten the locknuts at the tie rod outer ends.
7. Tighten the gaiter clips.

NOTE: Tie rods should be adjusted equally. Differences in tie rod lengths will result in incorrect wheel angles on turns.

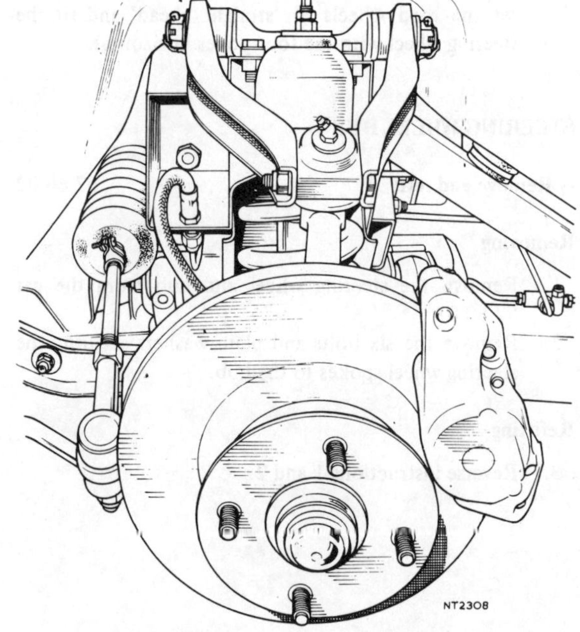

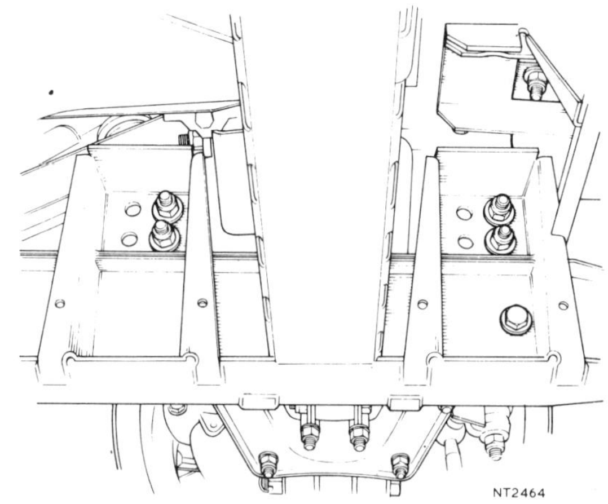

CAMBER ANGLE

– Check and adjust **57.65.05**

Checking

1. Using suitable equipment check the front wheels for camber angle. Front wheel camber should be within the following limits:
   Carburetter model ¼° pos ± 1° (kerb) ¼° neg ± ½° (laden – 2 up)
   P. I. Model ½° pos ± 1° (kerb) 0° ± ½° (laden – 2 up).
   Before altering camber angles, ensure that the cause is not attributable to wear in the ball joints, trunnions, wishbone bushes, or worn road springs.

Adjusting

2. Jack up the car and support the chassis on stands.
3. Slacken the four nuts securing the lower wishbone brackets to the chassis.
4. Remove or add shim(s) equally to both wishbone brackets as required. Add shim(s) to go negative: remove shim(s) to go positive. Repeat as necessary on opposite lower wishbone.
5. Tighten the nuts securing the wishbone brackets.
6. Remove the chassis stands.
7. Check and adjust front wheel track as necessary.

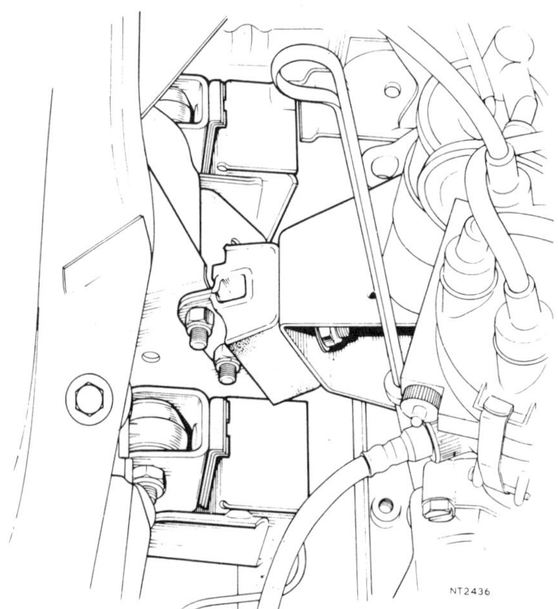

FRONT SUSPENSION OPERATIONS

ANTI-ROLL BAR

– Remove and refit **60.10.01**

Removing

1. Remove the nyloc nut and plain washer securing the anti-roll bar link to the lower wishbone bracket and detach the link from the bracket. Repeat on opposite side of car.
2. Remove the four nuts and plain washers securing the two 'U' bolts to the front crossmember.
3. Withdraw the 'U' bolts and brackets.
4. Withdraw the anti-roll bar.
5. Remove the nuts securing the lower end of the anti-roll bar links to the anti-roll bar. Detach the link and the rubber mountings, washers and distance tubes.
6. Remove the anti-roll bar mounting bushes.

Refitting

7. Reverse instructions 1 to 6. Ensure that the anti-roll bar is fitted centrally on the front crossmember.

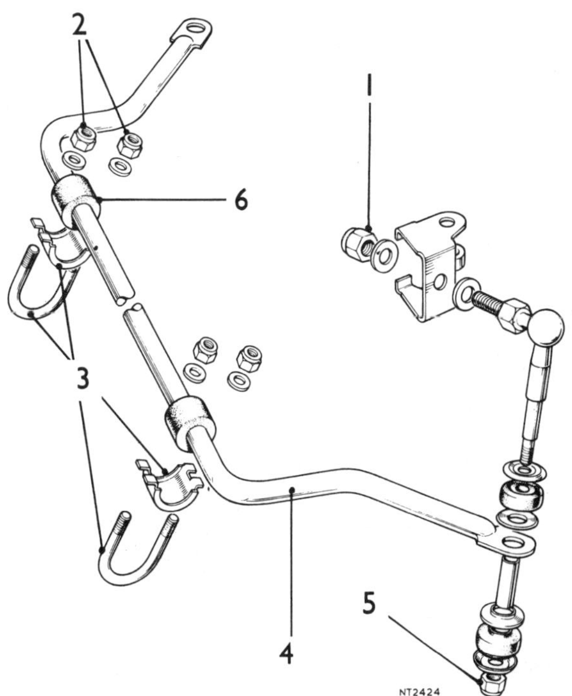

ANTI-ROLL BAR LINK

– Remove and refit **60.10.02**

Removing

1. Remove the nyloc nut and plain washer securing the anti-roll bar link to the lower wishbone bracket and detach the link from the bracket.
2. Remove the nyloc nut securing the lower end of the anti-roll bar link to the anti- roll bar and withdraw the anti- roll bar link, washers, rubbers and distance tube.

Refitting

3. Reverse instructions 1 and 2.

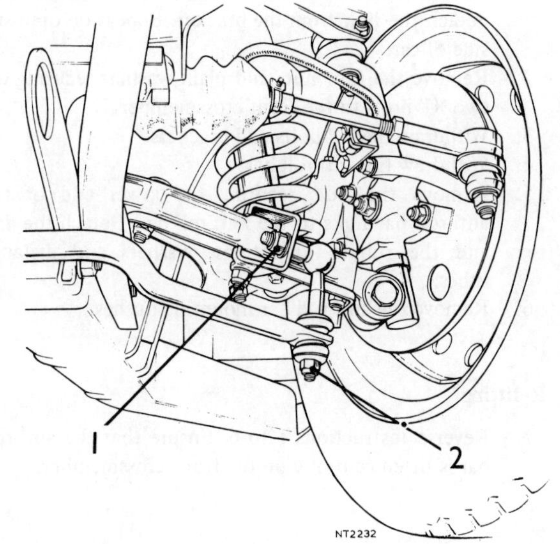

ANTI-ROLL BAR RUBBERS

– Remove and refit **60.10.04**

Removing

1. Remove the four nyloc nuts and plain washers securing the two 'U' bolts to the front crossmember.
2. Withdraw the 'U' bolts and mounting brackets.
3. Remove the mounting rubbers.

Refitting

4. Reverse instructions 1 to 3.

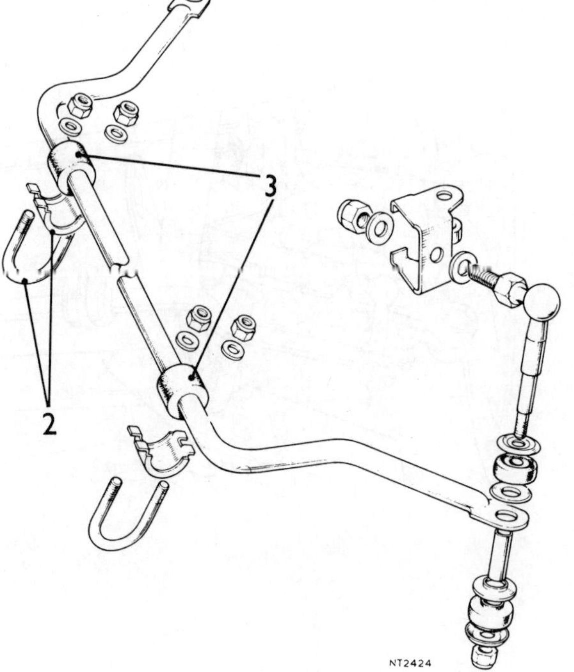

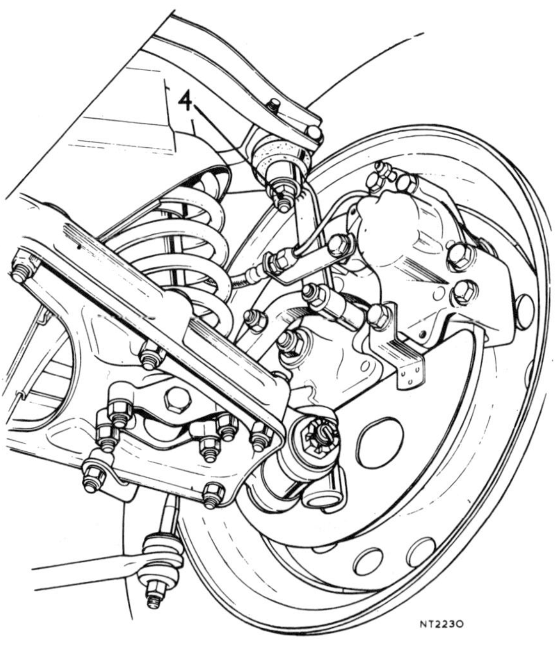

BALL JOINT

– Remove and refit **60.15.02**

Service tool S166

Removing

1. Jack up the car and support the chassis on stand(s).
2. Remove the front road wheel.
3. Locate a jack under the road spring pad on the lower wishbone and raise the jack sufficient to relieve the upper ball joint of spring tension.
4. Remove the nyloc nut and plain washer securing the ball joint to the vertical link.
5. Using Tool S166 release the ball joint from the vertical link.
6. Remove the two bolts, plain washers and nyloc nuts securing the ball joint housing to the upper wishbone. Note that the outer bolt is entered from the rear side of the wishbone and that the inner bolt is entered from the forward side of the wishbone.
7. Remove the ball joint and housing from the upper wishbone.

Refitting

8. Reverse instructions 1 to 4 and 6 to 7. Tightening torque for the bolts securing the ball joint housing to the upper wishbone is 24 to 32 lbf ft (3·3 to 4·4 kgf m.). Tightening torque for the nut securing the ball joint to the vertical link is 35 to 50 lbf f (4·8 to 6·9 kgf m.).

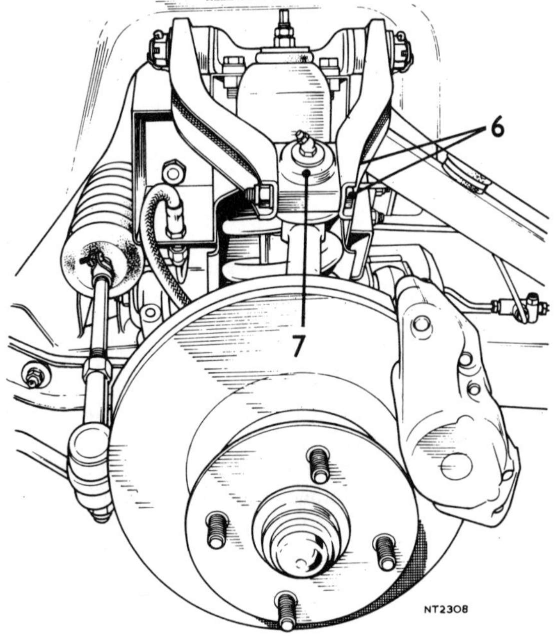

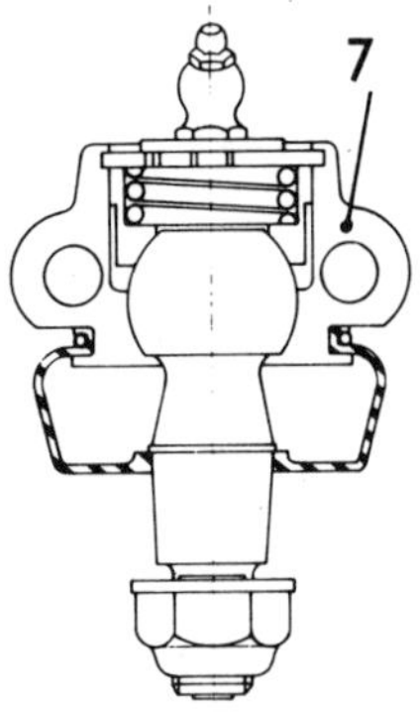

TRUNNION

– Remove and refit **60.15.03**

Removing

1. Jack up the car and support the chassis.
2. Remove the road wheel.
3. Remove the front hub 60.25.01/02.
4. Remove the disc shield. 70.10.18.
5. Locate a jack under the road spring pad on the lower wishbone and raise the jack sufficient to relieve the upper ball joint and trunnion of spring tension.
6. Remove the split pin from the slotted nut securing the trunnion to the lower wishbone.
7. Remove the slotted nut and bolt securing the trunnion to the lower wishbone.
8. Withdraw the trunnion washers and the vertical link from the lower wishbone.
9. Unscrew the trunnion from the vertical link.(Right hand vertical link – right hand thread: Left hand vertical link – left hand thread.)

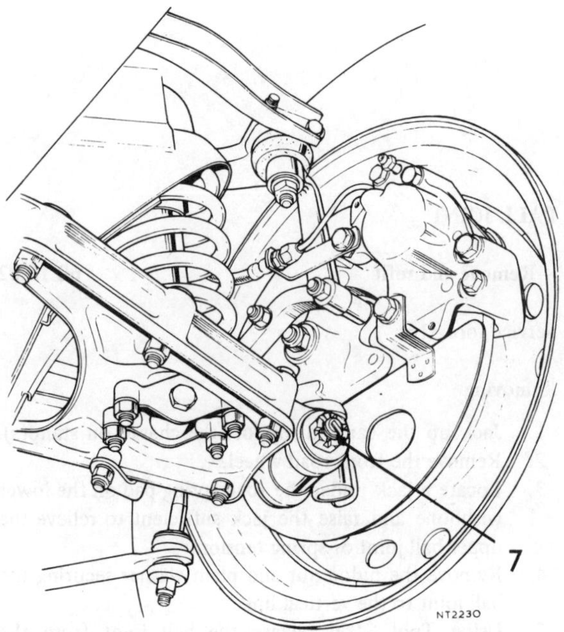

Refitting

10. Using a 90 S.A.E. EP lubricant partially fill (25%) the trunnion. Fit the rubber boot and screw the trunnion into position on the vertical link. (Right hand vertical link – right hand thread: Left hand vertical link – left hand thread).
11. Fit the vertical link washers and trunnion to the lower wishbone.
12. Reverse instructions 1 to 7. The slotted nut should be tightened to a torque of 50 to 65 lbf ft (4·8 to 9 kgf m).

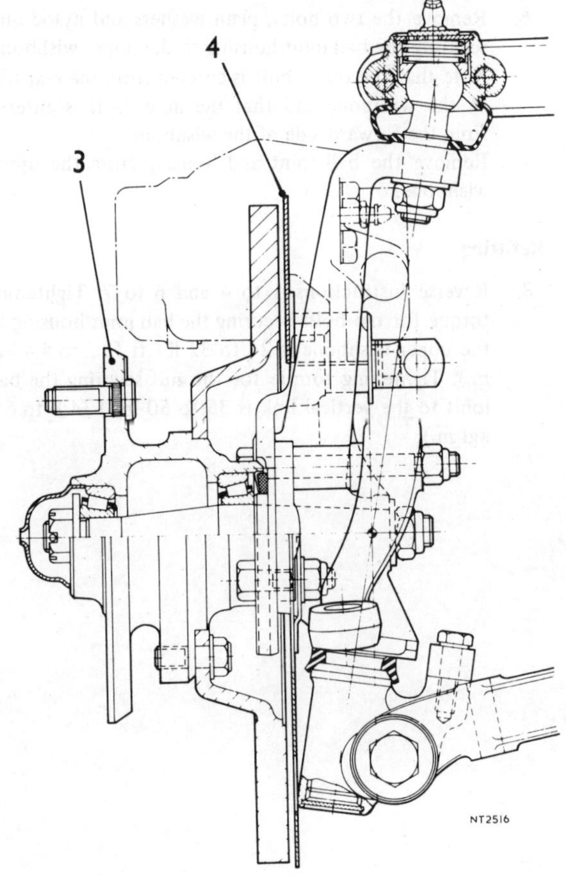

TRUNNION

– Overhaul **60.15.13**

1. Remove the trunnion from the car 60.15.03.

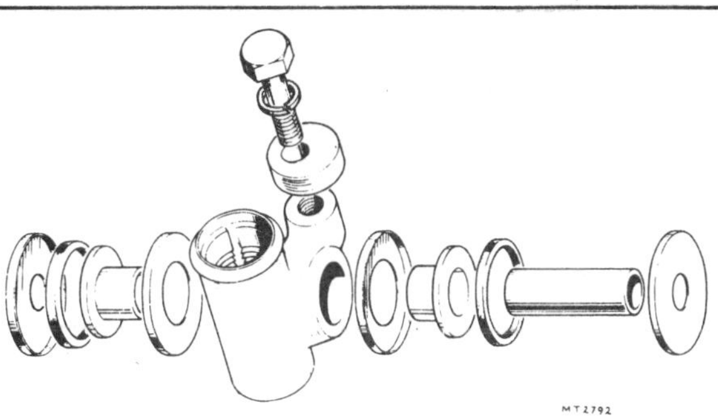

Dismantling

2. Remove the thrust washers.
3. Remove the nylon bushes and backing washers.

Assembling

4. Reverse instructions 2 to 3 using new components.
5. Fit the trunnion to the car 60.15.03.

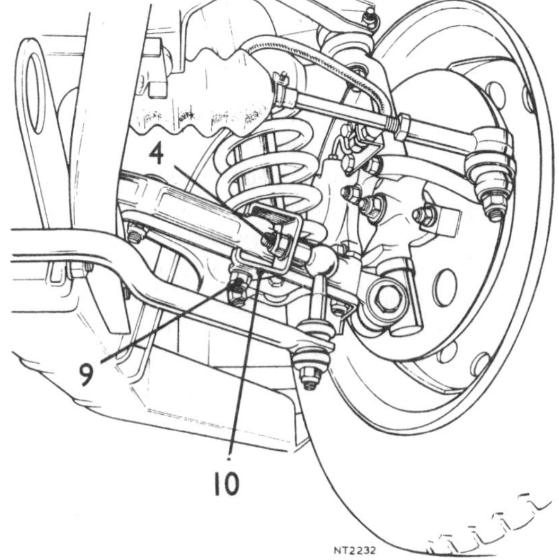

FRONT ROAD SPRING

– Remove and refit **60.20.01**

Removing

1. Jack up the car and support the chassis on stand(s).
2. Remove the front wheel.
3. Remove the front damper 60.30.02.
4. Disconnect the anti-roll bar link from the anti-roll bar.
5. Position a jack under the lower wishbone spring plate ensuring that the jack pad will not damage the damper mounting studs. Ensure also that the pad does not obstruct the spring plate securing bolts. The jack pad must be placed directly under the spring lower seat.
6. Raise the jack to partially compress the road spring and to relieve the vertical link joints of spring tension.
7. Remove the split pin, slotted nut, washers and bolt securing the trunnion to the lower end of the verical link.
8. Release the vertical link and trunnion from the outer ends of the lower wishbone.
9. Remove the nut, washer and bolt securing the anti-roll bar link bracket to the lower wishbone.
10. Withdraw the anti- roll bar link bracket and spacer from the wishbone.
11. Remove the five nuts, washers and three bolts securing the spring plate to the lower wishbone.
12. Separate the lower wishbone arms from the spring plate.
13. Carefully lower the jack taking care that the spring plate does not foul on the chassis. Continue lowering the jack until the road spring is relieved of tension.
14. Withdraw the spring plate and the road spring complete with upper and lower insulating rings.

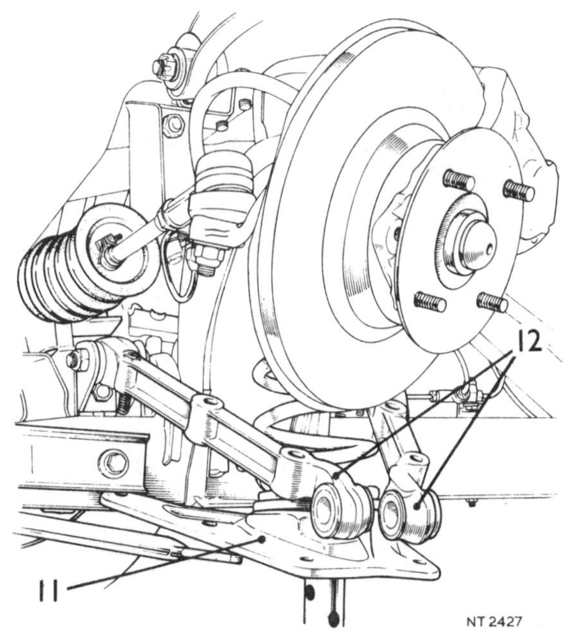

Continued

Refitting

15. Fit the insulating rings to the road spring: thin ring to top: thick ring to bottom.
16. Engage the top of the spring in the spring turret.
17. Engage the spring pan in the lower end of the spring.
18. Position the jack on the spring plate directly under the spring. Ensure that the jack pad will neither slip nor cause damage to the damper studs.
19. Carefully raise the jack and compress the road spring.
20. Align the spring plate with its location on the lower wishbone arms and enter the studs and five securing bolts. The bolt securing the anti- roll bar link bracket should be omitted at this stage.
21. Fit the five plain washers and nuts and evenly draw the spring plate into position on the wishbone arms.
22. Fit the anti- roll bar link bracket, spacer and securing bolt, plain washer and nut. Tighten the bolt and nut.
23. Tighten the other five nuts.
24. Engage and align the trunnion in the lower wishbone ensuring that the trunnion thrust washers are not omitted.
25. Fit the trunnion bolt, washers and slotted nut.
26. Tighten the slotted nut and secure with a new split pin.
27. Remove the jack from under the lower wishbone.
28. Fit the front damper 60.30.02.
29. Fit the anti- roll bar link.
30. Fit the front wheel and remove the stand(s) from the chassis.

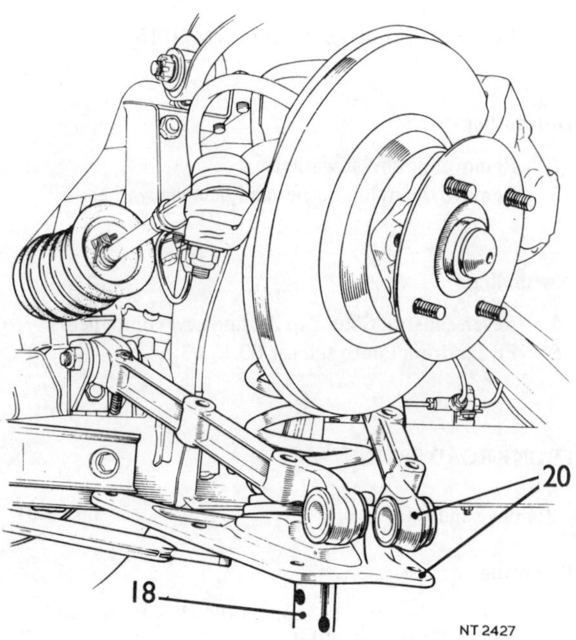

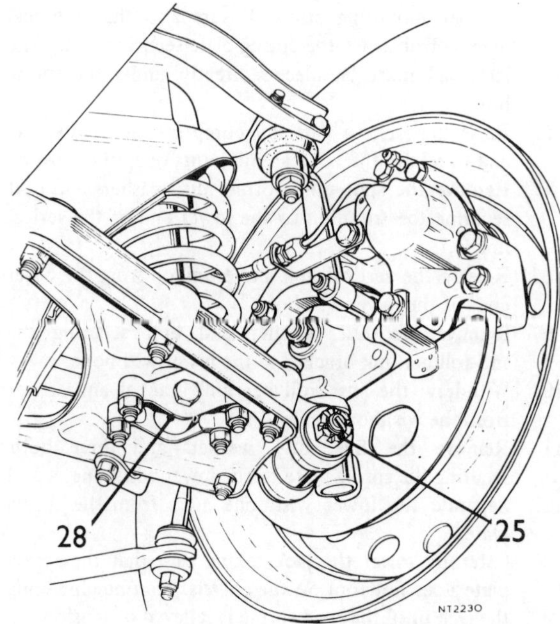

FRONT HUB

– Remove and refit **60.25.01**

Removing

1. Jack up the car and remove the front wheel.
2. *Wire wheels only.* Remove the four nuts securing the hub extension to the hub. Withdraw the hub extension.
   Remove the two bolts and spring washers se ~uring the caliper to the vertical link and ease the caliper clear of the disc. Support the caliper using string or wire. Ensure that strain is not imposed on the flexible brake hose.
4. Remove the hub cap.
5. Remove the split pin, slotted nut and washer securing the hub to the stub shaft.
6. Withdraw the hub complete with bearings, inner hub seal and disc.

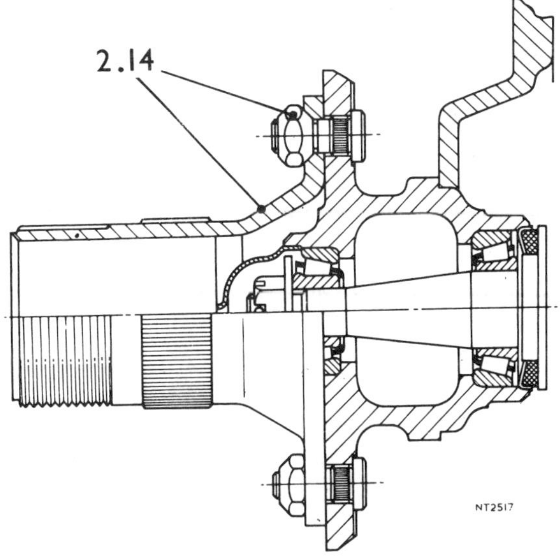

Refitting

7. Partially pack the hub with clean grease.
8. Ensure that the hub seal is installed on the inner side of the hub and fit the hub and bearings to the stub shaft.
9. Fit the washer and slotted nut to the stub shaft.
10. Tighten the slotted nut to 5 lbf ft (0·7 kgf m) and slacken the nut one flat to allow insertion of a new split pin. The required end-float is 0.003 to 0.005 ins (0·08 to 0·13 mm).
11. Fit the split pin.
12. Half fill the hub cap with clean grease and fit the cap to the hub.
13. Remove the string or wire supporting the caliper and fit the caliper. Note that the caliper upper bolt also secures the disc shield and the flexible hose support bracket.
14. *Wire wheels only.* Fit the hub extension.
15. Fit the road wheel and remove the jack.

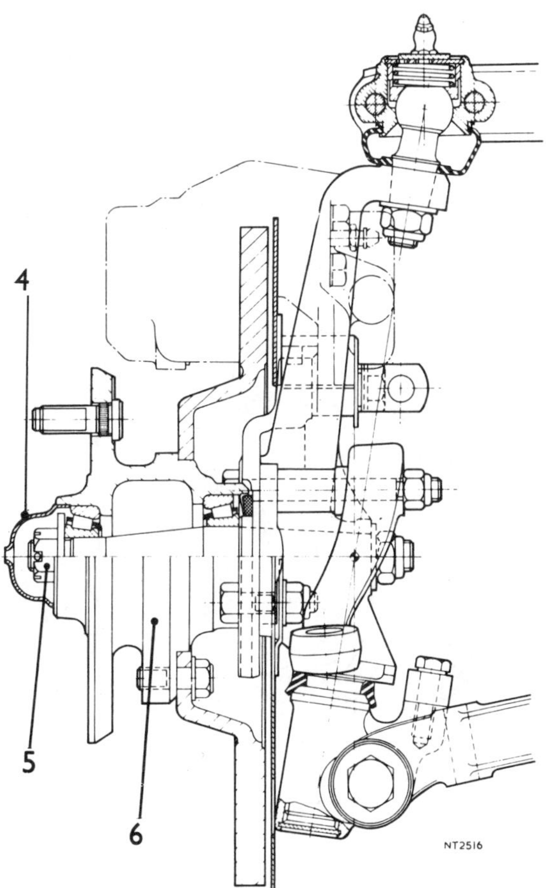

FRONT HUB

– Overhaul **60.25.07**

Dismantling

1. Remove the front hub 60.25.01/02.
2. Withdraw the outer bearing.
3. Withdraw the inner oil seal, inner bearing shield and inner bearing.
4. Extract the inner and outer bearing tracks.
5. Thoroughly clean all components.

Reassembling

6. Examine all components and renew as necessary.
7. Fit the bearing inner and outer tracks to the hub.
8. Insert the inner bearing.
9. Fit the inner bearing shield (lip of shield outward).
10. Partially fill the hub with clean grease.
11. Lubricate the new felt seal and install the seal in the inner side of the hub.
12. Insert the outer bearing.
13. Fit the hub to the car 60.25.01/02.

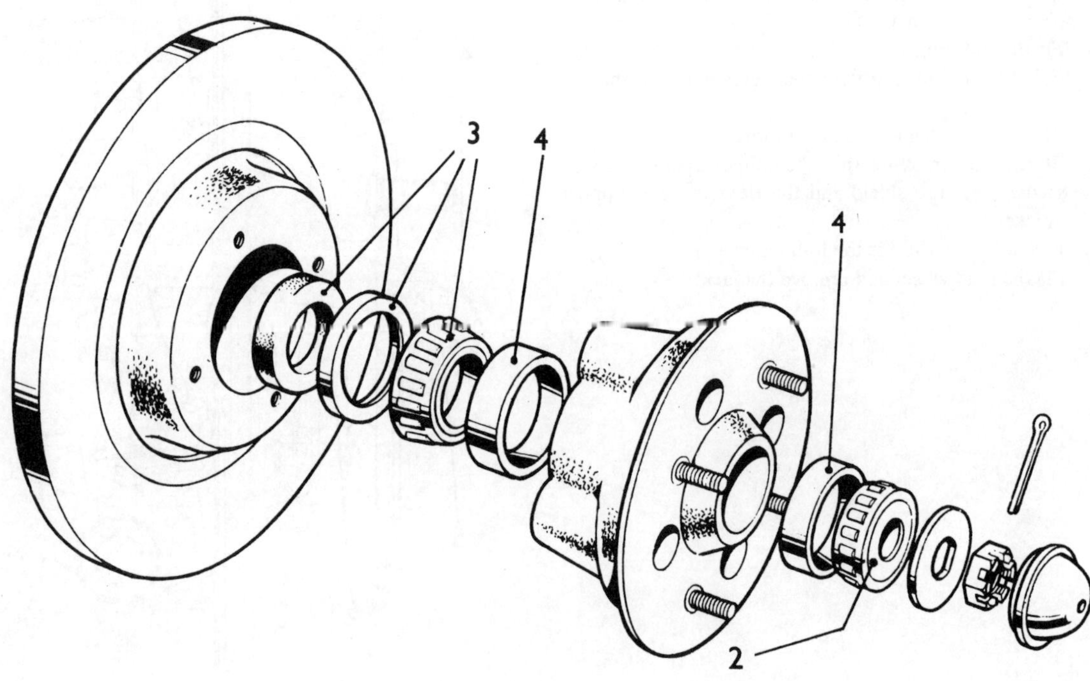

FRONT HUB BEARING END-FLOAT

– Check and adjust **60.25.13**

Checking

1. Jack up the car and remove the front wheel.
2. Remove the disc brake pads.
3. Check the front hub for bearing end-float. End-float should be within 0·003 to 0·005 in (0·08 to 0·13 mm).

Adjusting

4. *Wire wheels only.* Remove the hub extension.
5. Remove the hub cap.
6. Remove the split pin from the slotted nut.
7. Tighten or slacken the slotted nut as necessary to obtain 0·003 to 0·005 in (0·08 to 0·13 mm) bearing end-float.
8. Secure the slotted nut with a new split pin.
9. Clean the hub cap and partially fill it with fresh grease.
10. Fit the hub cap.
11. *Wire wheels only.* Fit the hub extension.
12. Fit the brake pads.
13. Fit the road wheel and remove the jack.

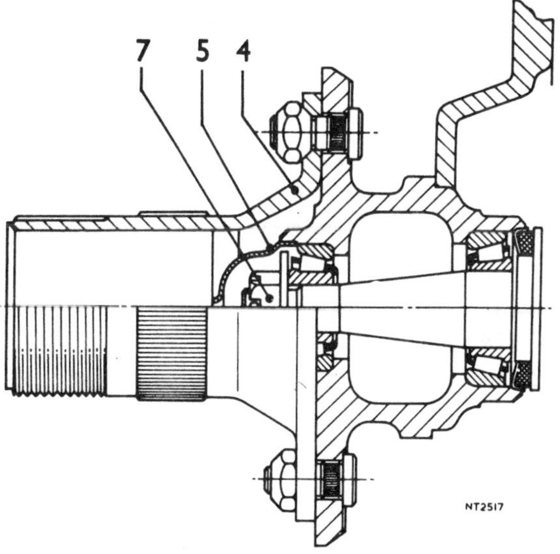

FRONT HUB BEARINGS

– Remove and refit **60.25.14**

As operation 60.25.07/08.

FRONT HUB OIL SEAL

– Remove and refit **60.25.15**

Removing

1. Remove the front hub 60.25.01/02.
2. Withdraw the oil seal.

Refitting

3. Partially pack the hub with clean grease.
4. Lubricate the new hub seal and enter the seal in the hub.
5. Fit the hub to the stub axle 60.25.01/02.

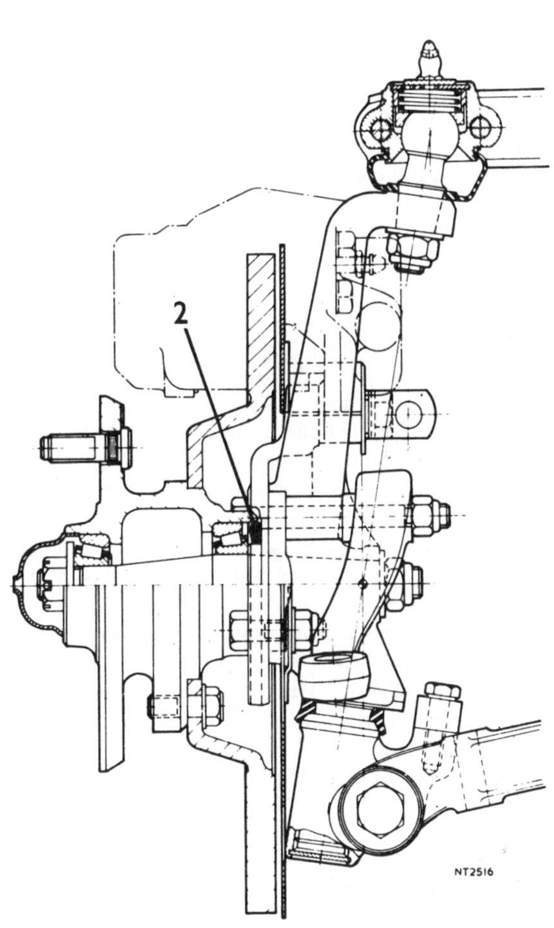

FRONT HUB STUB AXLE

– Remove and refit **60.25.22**

Removing

1. Remove the vertical link. 60.25.23.
2. Remove the nyloc nut and plain washer securing the stub axle to the vertical link.
3. Press the stub axle from the vertical link.

Refitting

4. Reverse instructions 1 to 3.

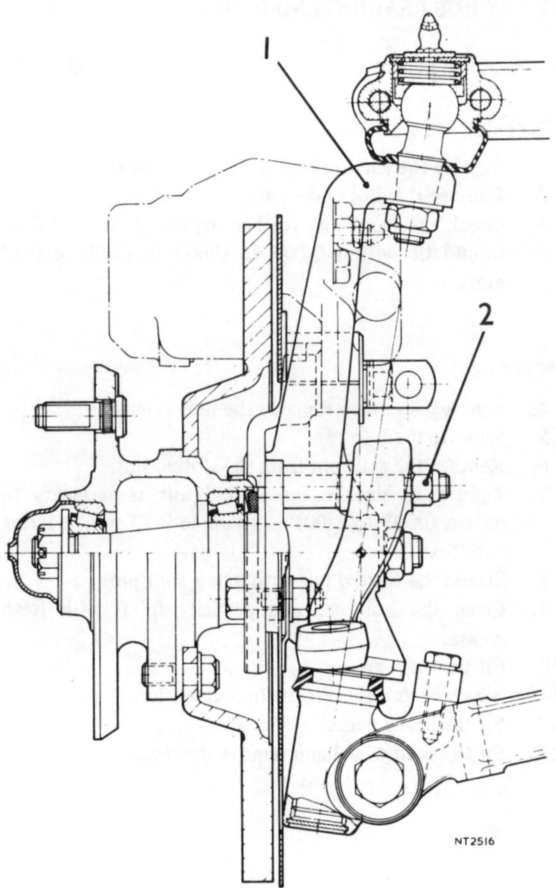

VERTICAL LINK

– Remove and refit **60.25.23**

Removing

1. Jack up the car and support the chassis on stand(s).
2. Remove the front wheel.
3. Locate a jack under the lower wishbone and compress the road spring to remove tension from the upper ball joint and the lower trunnion.
4. Remove the two bolts and spring washers securing the caliper to the mounting plate. Note that the upper bolt also secures the brake hose bracket.
5. Withdraw the caliper from the brake disc taking care that it is subsequently placed or tied in a position so that the weight of the caliper is **not** supported by the brake pipes or hose.
6. Remove the front hub and disc 60.25.01/02.
7. Remove the nyloc nut and bolt securing the disc lower bracket and mounting plate to the vertical link, and withdraw the disc shield.
8. Remove the two nyloc nuts, bolts and lock plates securing the mounting plate and steering arm to the vertical link.
9. Remove the remaining bolt and lock plate from the mounting plate and withdraw the mounting plate.
10. Remove the nyloc nut and plain washer from the upper ball joint and release the ball joint from the vertical link.
11. Unscrew the vertical link from the lower trunnion.

Refitting

12. Reverse instructions 1 to 11. Ensure that the mounting plate bolts are secured by the lock plates.

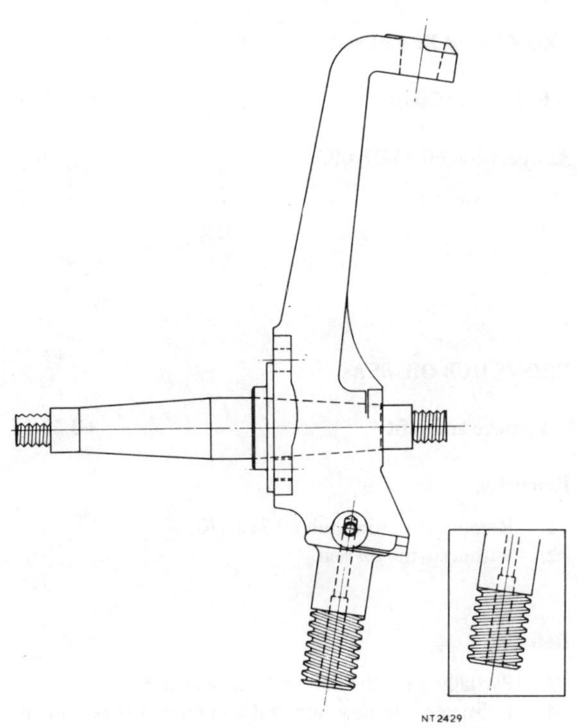

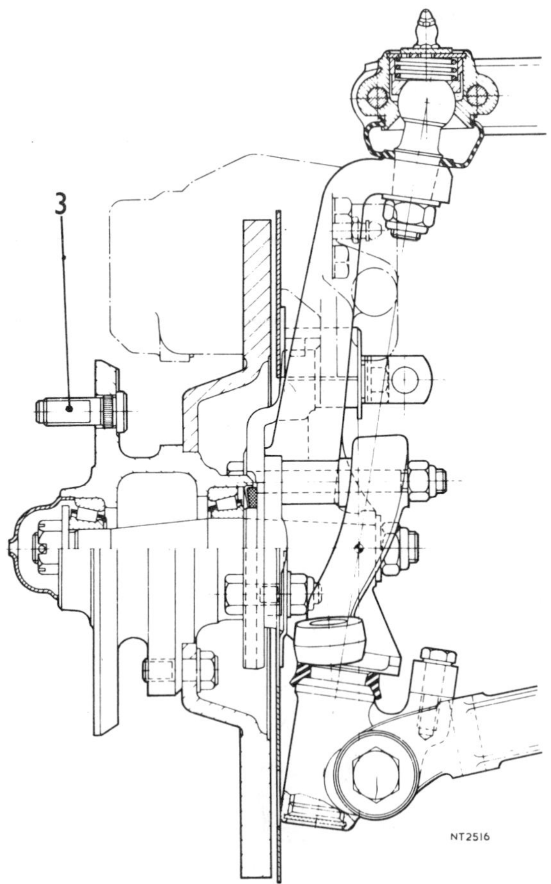

FRONT HUB WHEEL STUDS

– Remove and refit **60.25.29**

Removing

1. Jack up the car and remove the front wheel.
2. *Wire wheels only.* Remove the four nuts securing the hub extension to the hub and withdraw the hub extension.
3. Tap the wheel stud(s) towards the brake disc.
4. Withdraw the stud(s). Wheel stud removal is not advised unless renewal is intended.

Refitting

5. Ensure that the mating tapered faces of stud and hub flange are clean.
6. Enter the stud from the brake disc side of the hub.
7. Using suitable packing (e.g. a short length of steel tubing) draw the stud into position with the wheel nut or hub extension nut.
8. Remove the nut and packing.
9. Fit the road wheel (hub extension and road wheel – wire wheel models only) and remove the jack.

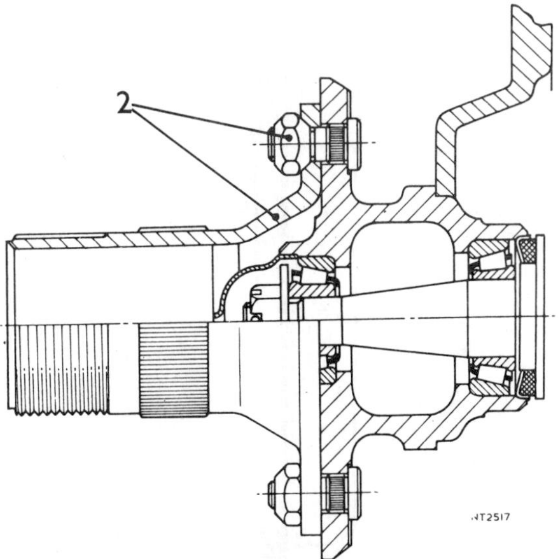

FRONT DAMPER

– Remove and refit **60.30.02**

Removing

1. Jack up the car and support the chassis.
2. Remove the road wheel.
3. Remove the four nuts and spring washers securing the damper lower mounting brackets to the underside of the lower wishbone.
4. Remove the locknut and nut, washer and upper rubber mounting from the top of the damper.
5. Withdraw the damper from the lower wishbone and remove the rubber mounting and washer from the damper rod.
6. Remove the bolt and nut securing the damper brackets to the damper.

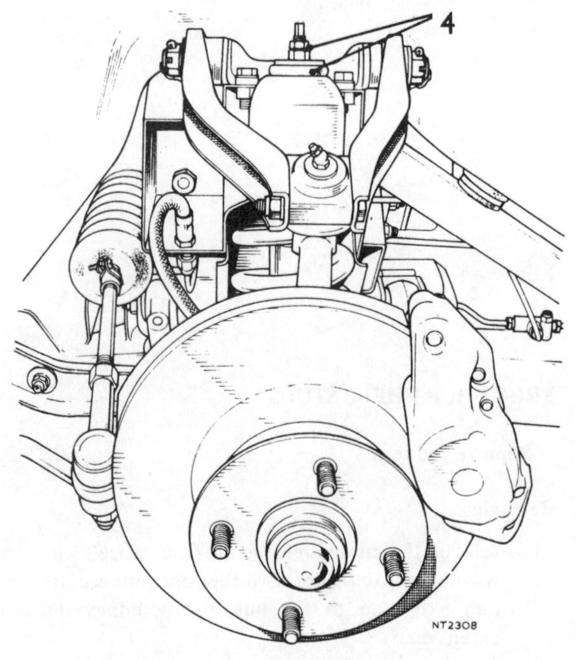

Refitting

7. Reverse instructions 1 to 6.

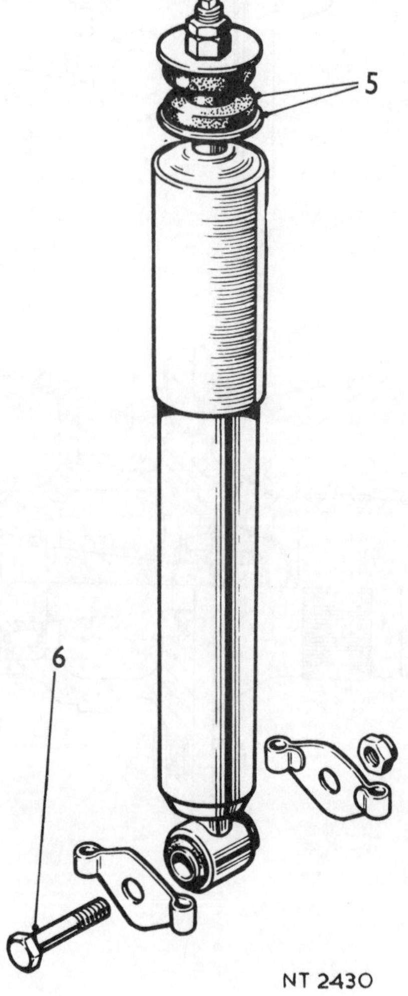

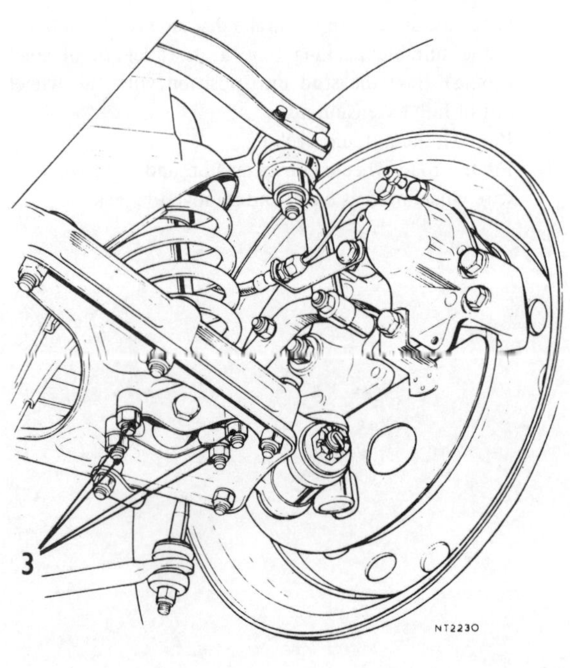

FRONT DAMPER BUSH

– Remove and refit **60.30.07**

Removing

1. Remove the damper from the car 60.30.02.
2. Remove the damper lower bush.

Refitting

3. Press new bush into position ensuring that it is centralised in the damper eye.
4. Refit the damper to the car 60.30.02.

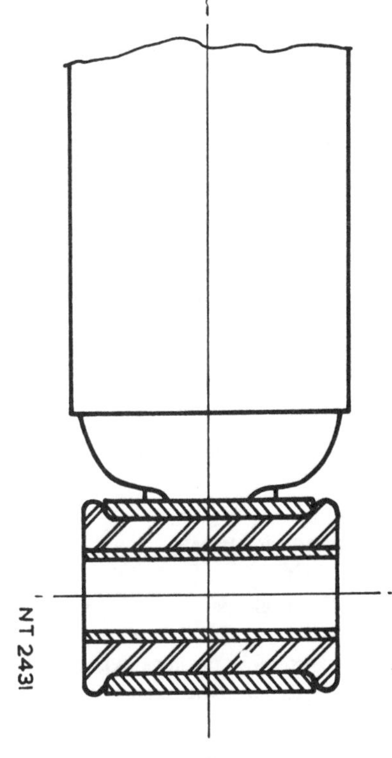

UPPER WISHBONE

– Remove and refit **60.35.01**

Removing

1. Jack up the car, support the chassis and remove the frontwheel.
2. Locate a jack under the spring pad of the lower wishbone and ráise the jack to relieve the upper wishbone of road spring tension.
3. Remove the two nuts, plain washers and bolts securing the outer end of the upper wishbone to the ball joint housing.
4. Detach the ball joint housing and the vertical link from the upper wishbone arms. Ensure that strain is not imposed on the front brake hose.
5. Remove the four bolts and spring washers securing the fulcrum bracket to the chassis.
6. Withdraw the fulcrum bracket complete with the upper wishbone arms.
7. Remove the split pins, slotted nuts and plain washers securing the wishbone arms to the fulcrum bracket.
8. Withdraw the wishbone arms complete with rubber bushes.

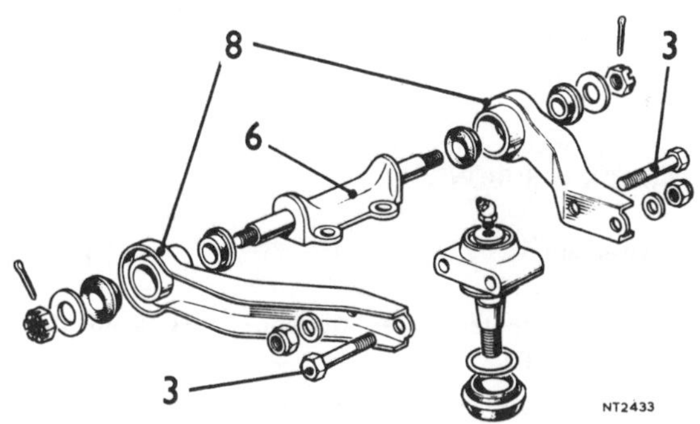

Refitting

9. Reverse instructions 1 to 8. When refitting the bolts securing the ball joint housing to the outer ends of the wishbone arms the outer bolt is entered from the rear: the inner bolt is entered from the front.

LOWER WISHBONE

– Remove and refit **60.35.02**

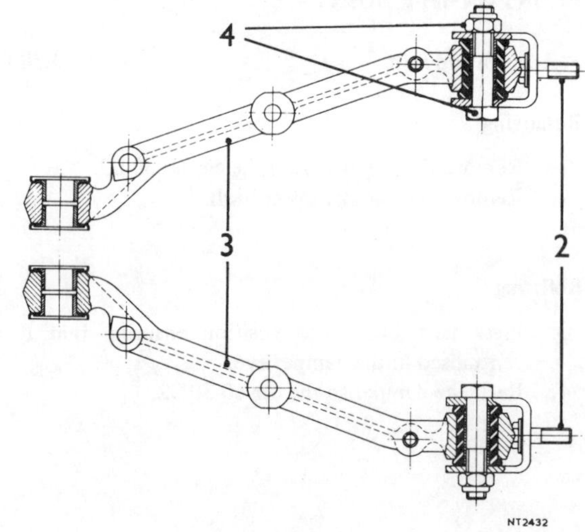

Removing

1. Remove the front road spring 60.20.01.
2. Remove the four nuts and plain washers securing the lower wishbone brackets to the chassis.
3. Withdraw the lower wishbone arms complete with mounting brackets and shims.
4. Remove the nuts and bolts securing the wishbone arms to the mounting brackets and remove the brackets.

Refitting

5. Reverse instructions 1 to 4.

UPPER WISHBONE

– Overhaul **60.35.08**

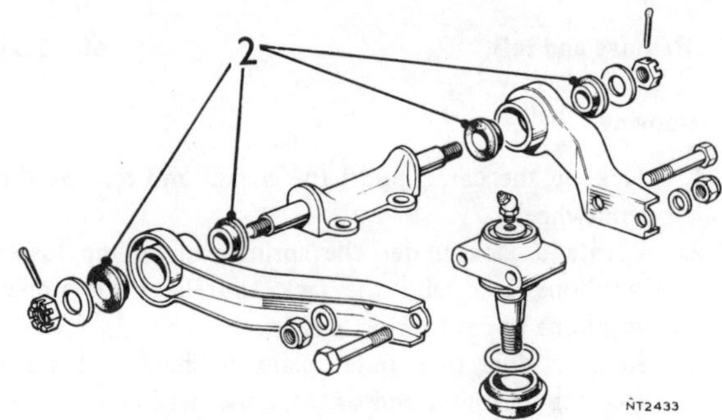

1. Remove the upper wishbone 60.35.01.
2. Remove the rubber bushes (4) from the wishbone arms.

Assembling

3. Fit new rubber bushes (4) to the wishbone arms.
4. Fit the wishbone arms, plain washers and slotted nuts to the fulcrum pin.
5. Tighten the slotted nuts and secure with new split pins.
6. Fit the fulcrum bracket and wishbone to the car 60.35.01.

LOWER WISHBONE

– Overhaul **60.35.09.**

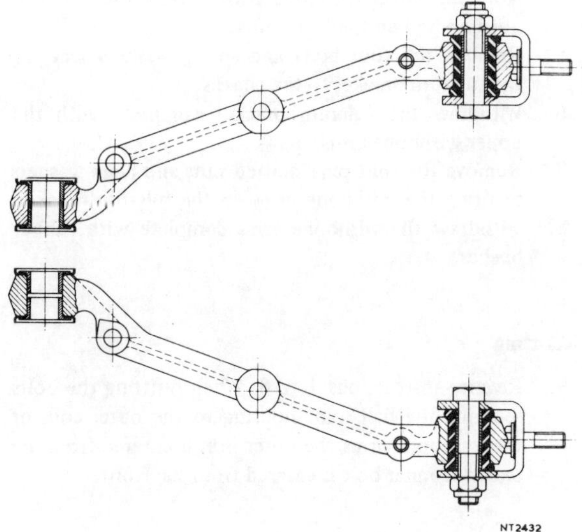

1. Remove the lower wishbone arms from the car 60.35.02.
2. Press out the rubber bushes.
3. Press in new bushes ensuring they are centred in the wishbone arms.
4. Fit the wishbone arms to the car 60.35.02.

REAR SUSPENSION OPERATIONS

REAR SUSPENSION OPERATIONS

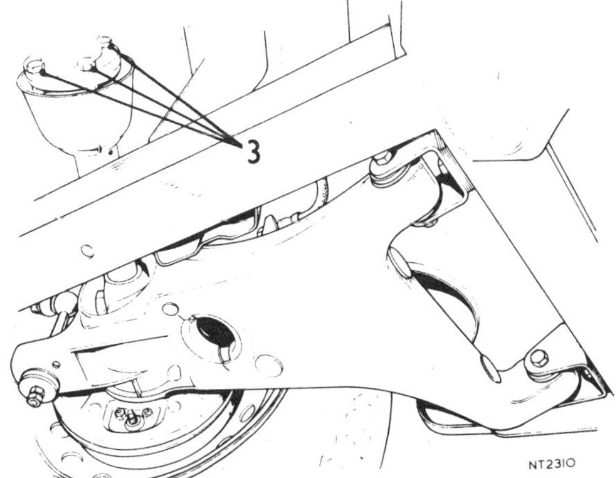

REAR HUB AND DRIVE SHAFT ASSEMBLY

– Remove and refit **64.15.01**

Removing

1. Jack up the car and remove the road wheel.
2. Release the handbrake.
3. Remove the four bolts and nyloc nuts securing the drive shaft inner flange to the differential flange.
4. Remove the brake drum.
5. Remove the six nyloc nuts securing the hub bearing housing to the trailing arm.
6. Withdraw the hub assembly and drive shaft complete.

Refitting

7. Reverse instructions 1 to 6.

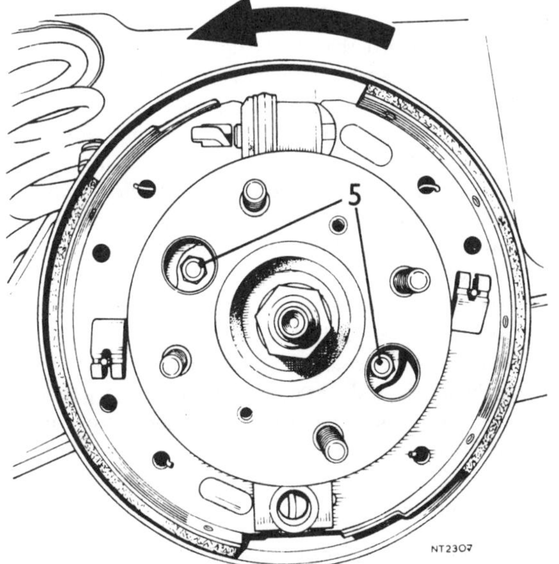

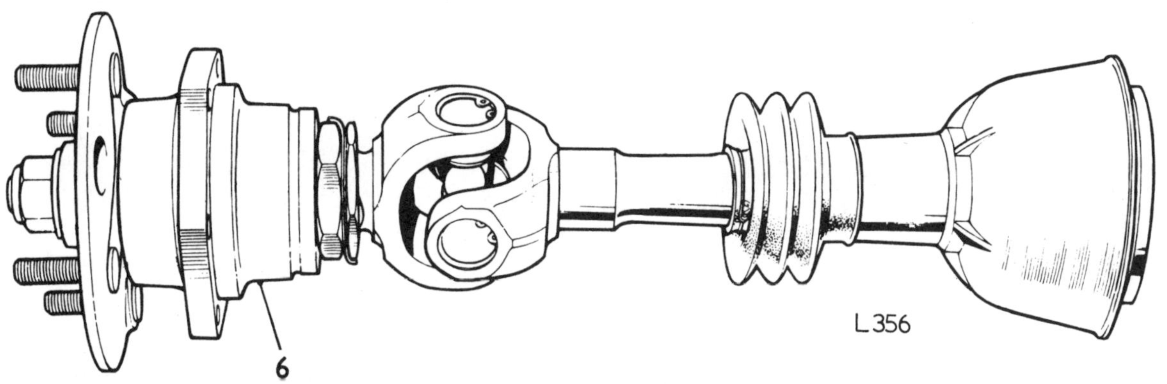

REAR HUB BEARING END-FLOAT

– Check and adjust 64.15.13

Checking

1. Jack up rear of car and remove the road wheel.
2. Release the handbrake and remove the brake drum.
3. Using a dial gauge with the stylus mounted to contact the hub flange check bearing end-float. Correctly adjusted, end-float should be within 0·002 to 0·005 in (0·051 to 0·13 mm).

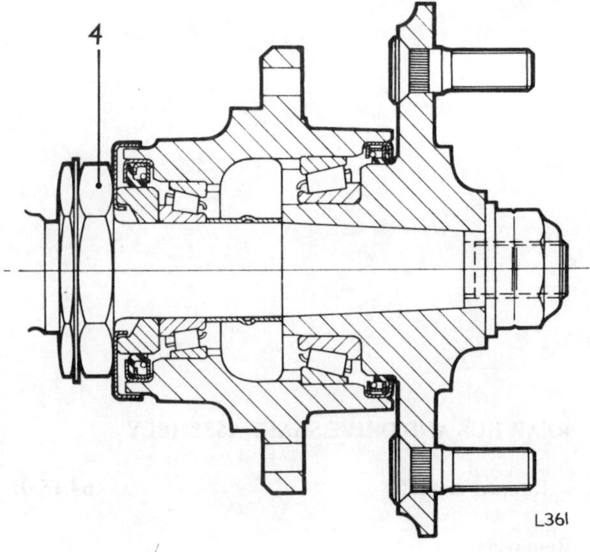

Adjusting

Service Tools S317, S318

Adjustment to the hub bearings is effected by means of the adjusting nut located behind the rear hub and necessitates the removal of the rear hub and drive shaft assembly from the car 64.15.01.

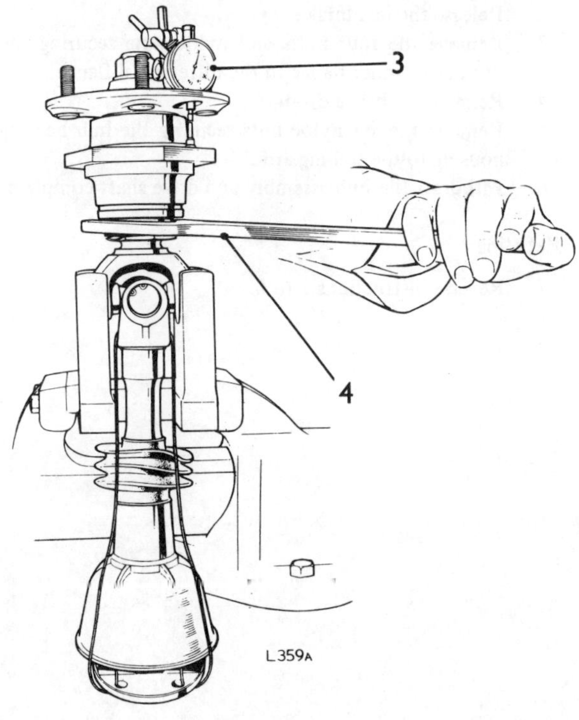

Reducing end-float

1. Locate the drive shaft in the holding jig S318.
2. Straighten the tabs on the lock washer.
3. Using a dial gauge check bearing end-float.
4. Screw the adjusting nut towards the hub until end Float of 0·002 in (0·051 mm), is obtained. Care must be taken not to reduce end-float below 0·002 in (0·051 mm). Should this occur the collapsible spacer fitted between the hub and the inner bearing must be renewed.
5. Tighten the locknut ensuring that the adjusting nut is held firmly. Bend the locking tabs over the adjusting nut and locknut and examine the condition of the locking tabs. If doubt exists as to their ability to hold the adjusting nut and locknut a new lock washer must be fitted.

Increasing end-float

1. Mount the drive shaft in holding jig S318.
2. Carry out instructions 3 to 9, 14 to 19 and 21 to 26, 64.15.14.

REAR HUB BEARINGS

– Remove and refit **64.15.14**

Service Tools S317, S318, M86C, S4221A and S4221A-16

Removing

1. Remove the rear hub and drive shaft assembly. 64.15.01.
2. Mount the hub and drive shaft assembly on tool S318.
3. Remove the nyloc nut and plain washer securing the hub to the stub shaft.

** NOTE: On later models a castellated nut and split pin is fitted.**

4. Using tool M86C withdraw the hub complete with the outer bearing.
5. Remove the key from the stub shaft.
6. Withdraw the bearing housing.
7. Remove the collapsible spacer, inner bearing and distance piece and stoneguard from the ttub shaft.
8. Straighten the locking tabs securing the bearing adjusting nuts and remove adjusting nut, tab washer and locknut.
9. Remove the inner and outer oil seals from the bearing housing.
10. Remove the inner and outer bearing tracks from the bearing housing. Bearing outer tracks should not be disturbed unless renewal is intended.
11. Remove the outer bearing (Tool S4221A and adaptor 16).
12. Thoroughly clean all components.

Continued

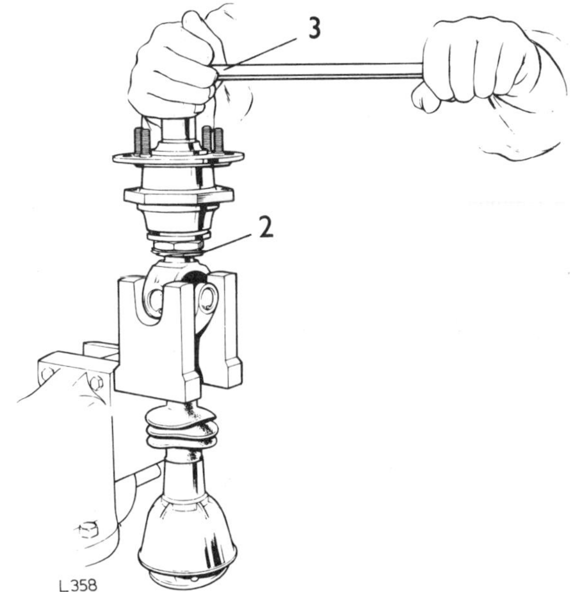

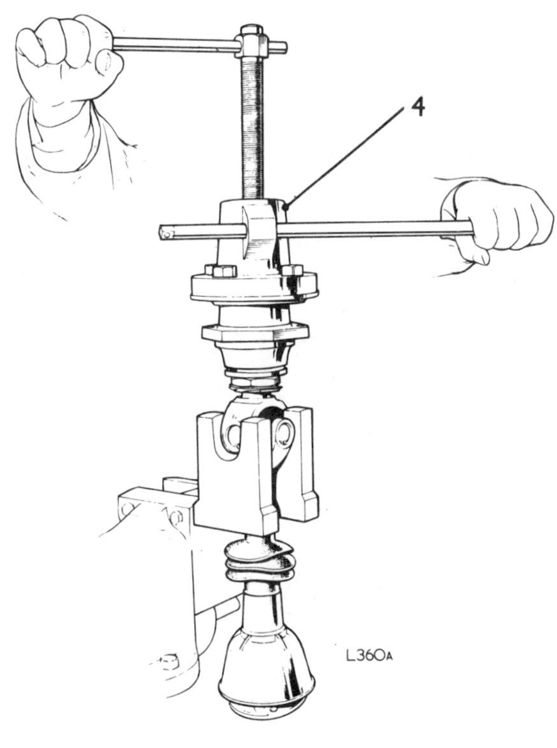

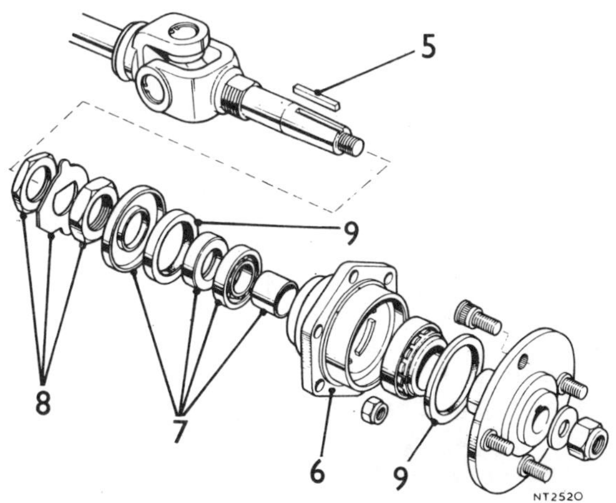

Refitting

13. Evenly press or drift the inner and outer bearing tracks into position in the bearing housing.
14. Fit new inner and outer oil seals to the bearing housing (Seal lip towards bearing track).
15. Fit the locknut, new tab washer and adjusting nut to the stub shaft, and screw both nuts as close to the universal joint as possible.
16. Fit the stoneguard, distance piece, inner bearing and a new collapsible spacer to the stub shaft.
17. Fit the key to the stub shaft.
18. Half fill the bearing housing with grease.
19. Install the bearing housing on the stub shaft.
20. Fit the outer bearing to the hub.
21.**Fit the hub, plain washer and nyloc nut (or castellated nut – later models) to the stub shaft. Tighten nut to the correct torque, see Page 06-4, and fit the split pin to the castellated nut on later models.**
22. Screw adjusting nut by hand towards the bearing housing until bearing end-float approaches 0·002 in (0·51 mm).
23. Using a dial gauge, check bearing end-float.
24. Using tool S317, carefully continue to screw the adjusting nut towards the bearing housing until bearing end float of 0·002 in (0·051 mm) is obtained. 0·13 mm) is obtained.

NOTE: Care must be taken not to reduce bearing end-float to less than 0·002 in (0·051 mm), as this will necessitate stripping the hub and renewing the excessively compressed collapsible spacer.

25. Ensure that the adjusting nut is not disturbed and tighten the locknut.
26. Bend the locking tabs over the adjusting nut and locknut.

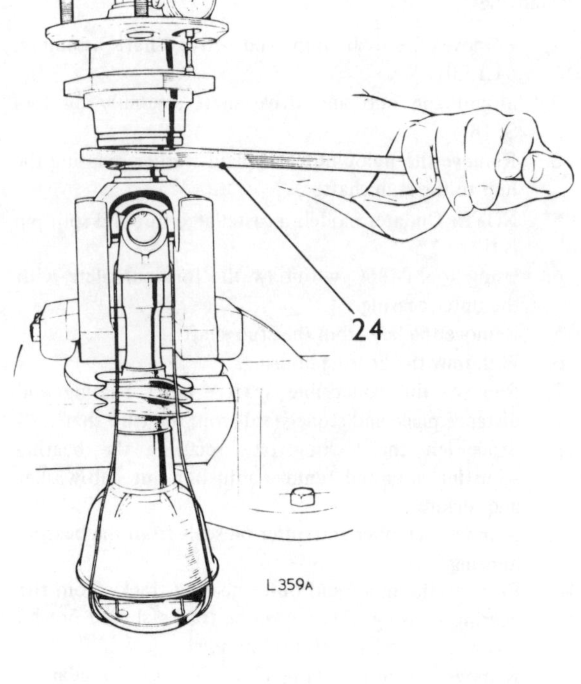

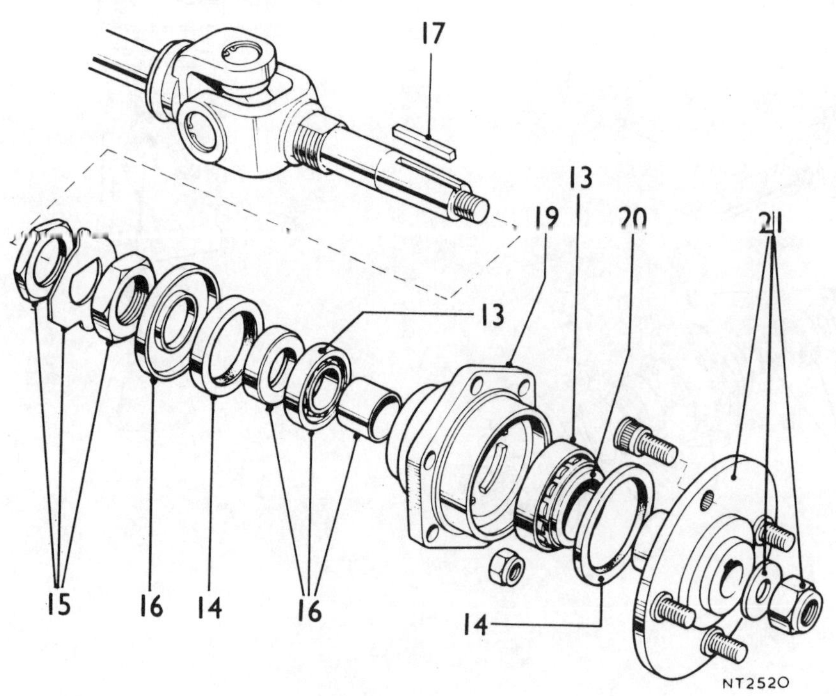

REAR HUB OIL SEALS

Service Tools S317, S318, M86C

– Remove and refit **64.15.15**

Instructions 1 to 9, 14 to 19 and 21 to 26, 64.15.14.

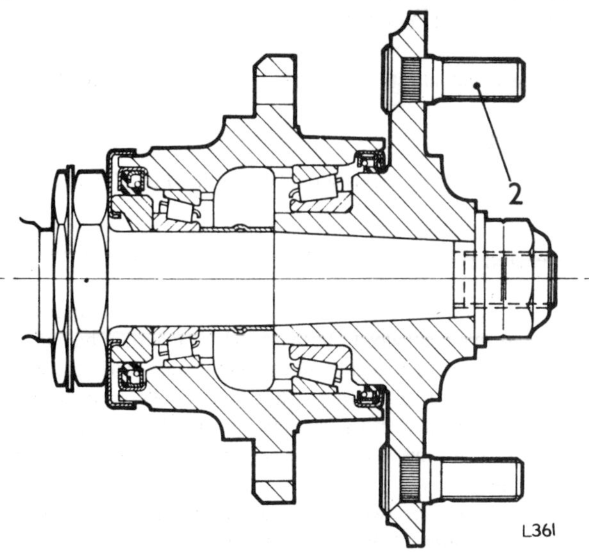

REAR HUB WHEEL STUD

– Remove and refit **64.15.26**

Removing

1. Remove the rear brake drum 70.10.03.
2. Tap the wheel stud towards the brake backplate until the stud splines are released from the hub flange.
3. Remove the stud.

Refitting

4. Enter the stud in the hub flange ensuring that the tapered faces are clean.
5. Using suitable packing (e.g. a short length of steel tubing and washers) draw the stub into position.
6. Remove the packing and fit the brake drum, and road wheel 70.10.03.

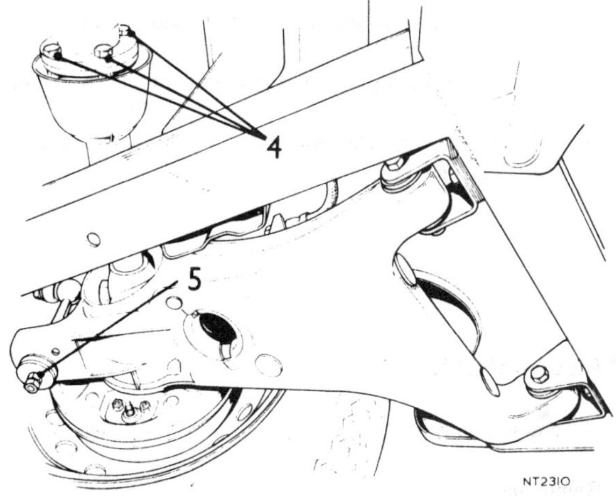

REAR SPRING

– Remove and refit **64.20.01**

Removing

1. Jack up the car and support the chassis on stand(s).
2. Remove the road wheel and release the handbrake.
3. Support the trailing arm with a jack.
4. Remove the locknut, nut, washers and rubbers securing the damper link to the trailing arm.
5. Carefully lower the jack under the trailing arm until the road spring is released of tension.
6. Withdraw the road spring and the upper and lower rubber insulating rings.

Refitting

7. Reverse instructions 1 to 7.

REAR SPRING SEAT RINGS

– Remove and refit **64.20.17**

As Operation 64.20.01.

REAR WHEEL ALIGNMENT

– Check and adjust **64.25.17**

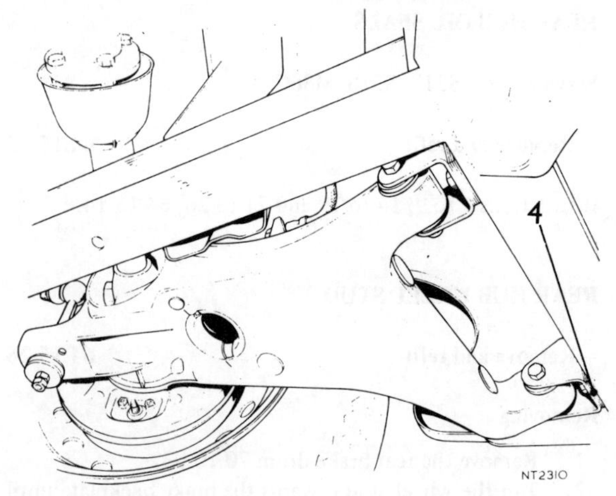

Checking

Rear wheel toe-in should be within 0 to 1/16 in (0 to 1·58 mm).

Adjusting

In contrast to the front wheel track where adjustment is made equally to both tie rods to maintain balanced steering lock angles, adjustment to rear wheel track is individual to either wheel and is determined by alignment with its respective front wheel to which it should have a tolerance of 0 to 1/32 in (0 to 0·313 mm) toe-in.

1. Slacken the two bolts and nuts securing the trailing arm **outer** bracket to the chassis.
2. Using a tyre lever, prise the trailing arm outer bracket away from the chassis.
3. Withdraw the shim pack,
4. Add shim(s) to reduce toe-in: remove shim(s) to increase toe-in.
5. Install the shim pack and tighten the bracket securing bolts.
6. Drive the vehicle forward or backward **before** rechecking rear toe-in.

REAR DAMPER

– Remove and refit **64.30.02**

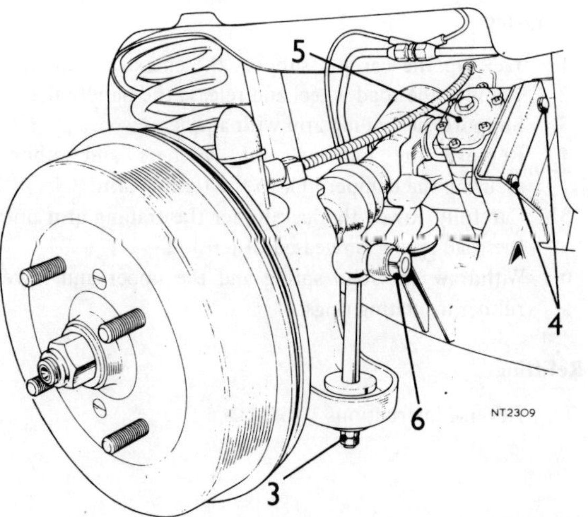

Removing

1. Jack up the car and support the chassis on stand(s) and remove the rear wheel.
2. Locate a jack under the trailing arm and raise the jack until the road spring is slightly compressed.
3. Remove the locknut, nut, washers and rubber securing the damper link to the trailing arm.
4. Remove the two bolts securing the damper to the chassis.
5. Withdraw the damper complete with damper link and upper washer and rubber.
6. Remove the nut and spring washer securing the link to the damper.
7. Release the link from the damper.

Refitting

8. Reverse instructions 1 to 7.

BUMP STOP

– Remove and refit **64.30.15**

Removing

1. Jack up the car and remove the rear wheel.
2. Unscrew the bump stop from the trailing arm.

Refitting

3. Reverse instructions 1 and 2.

REBOUND STOP

– Remove and refit **64.30.16**

Removing

1. Position a jack under the rear trailing arm and raise jack.
2. Remove the rear wheel.
3. Unscrew the rebound stop.

Refitting

4. Reverse instructions 1 to 5.

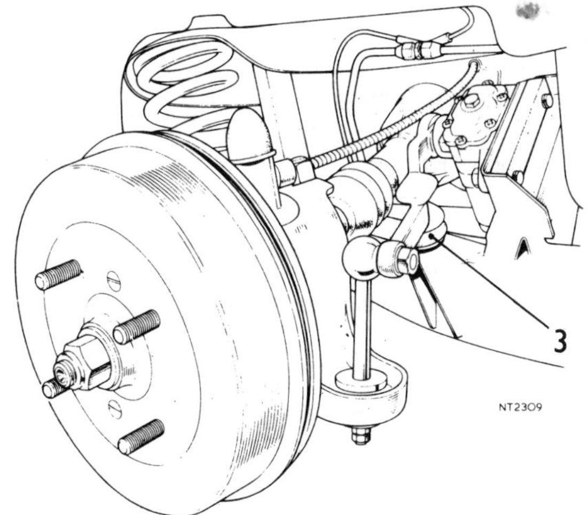

TRAILING ARM

– Remove and refit 64.35.02

Removing

1. Jack up rear of car and support chassis on stand(s).
2. Remove the road wheel and release the handbrake.
3. Disconnect the handbrake cable bracket from the trailing arm.
4. Position a jack under the trailing arm and partially compress the road spring taking care not to remove the weight from the chassis stand(s).
5. Remove the rear hub and drive shaft assembly 64.15.01.
6. Remove the locknut, nut, washer and rubber mounting from the lower end of the damper link.
7. Slacken the locknut securing the flexible hose to the trailing arm bracket, detach the hose and unclip the brake pipe from the trailing arm.
8. Carefully lower the jack and withdraw the road spring and the spring upper and lower insulating rings.
9. Remove the nut and bolt securing the trailing arm to the outer mounting bracket.
10. Remove the two nuts and washers securing the trailing arm inner mounting bracket to the chassis and withdraw the shim pack.
11. Withdraw the trailing arm complete with the inner mounting bracket.
12. Remove the bolt and nut securing the inner bracket to the trailing arm. If required remove the bump and rebound stops.

Refitting

13. Reverse instructions 1 to 12. Do not finally tighten the trailing arm pivot bolts until the car is resting on its wheels.

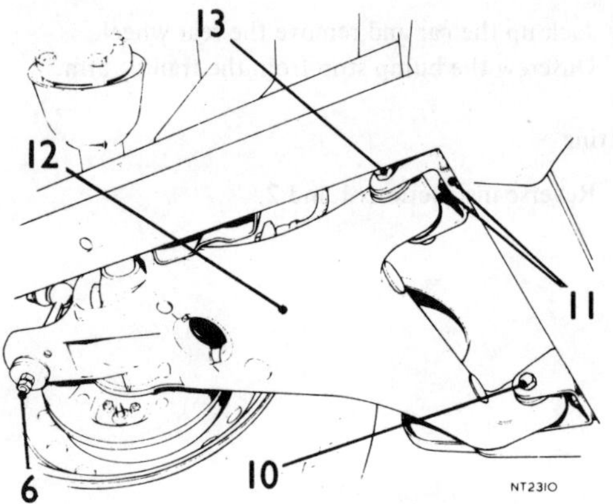

TRAILING ARM BUSHES

– Remove and refit 64.35.05

Removing

1. Remove the trailing arm 64.35.02.
2. Press out the trailing arm bushes.

Refitting

3. Press in new bushes to the trailing arm.
4. Fit the trailing arm to the car 64.35.02.
5. Bleed the brakes.

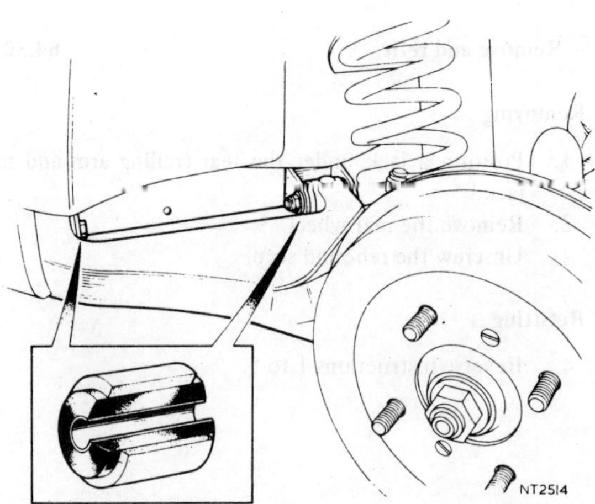

TRAILING ARM MOUNTING BRACKETS

– **Remove and refit** **64.35.20**

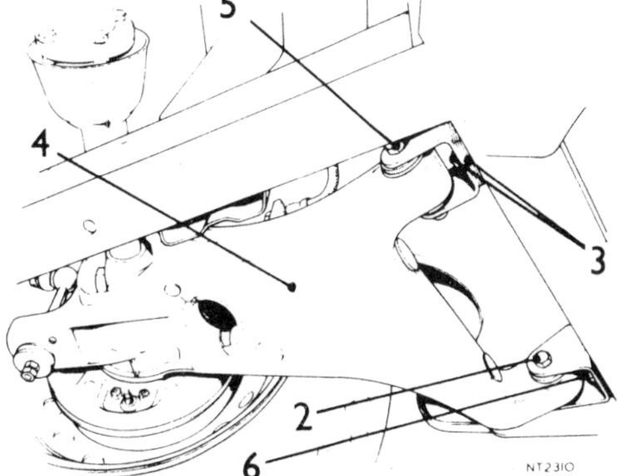

Removing

1. Remove the rear road spring 64.20.01.
2. Remove the outer pivot bolt and nut securing the trailing arm to the mounting bracket.
3. Remove the two nuts and washers securing the inner mounting bracket to the chassis and withdraw the shim pack.
4. Detach the trailing arm and outer bracket from the car.
5. Remove the nut and bolt securing the outer bracket to the trailing arm.
6. Remove the two nuts, washers and bolts securing the inner bracket to the chassis and withdraw the bracket and shim pack. Ensure shim packs are not intermixed.

Refitting

7. Reverse instructions 1 to 6. Do not finally tighten the trailing arm pivot bolts until the car is resting on its wheels.

BRAKE OPERATIONS

REAR BRAKE DRUM

– Remove and refit 70.10.03

Removing

1. Jack up the car and remove the rear wheel.
2. Release the handbrake.
3. Remove the two countersunk screws securing the brake drum to the hub.
4. Withdraw the brake drum.

Refitting

5. Align the countersunk holes in the drum with the tapped holes in the hub.
6. Engage the wheel studs in the drum.
7. Slide the brake drum into position. If the brake shoes were disturbed they may require to be centralised on the backplate to allow drum entry.
8. Fit and tighten the two countersunk screws.
9. Fit the road wheel and remove the jack.

FRONT DISC

– Remove and refit 70.10.10

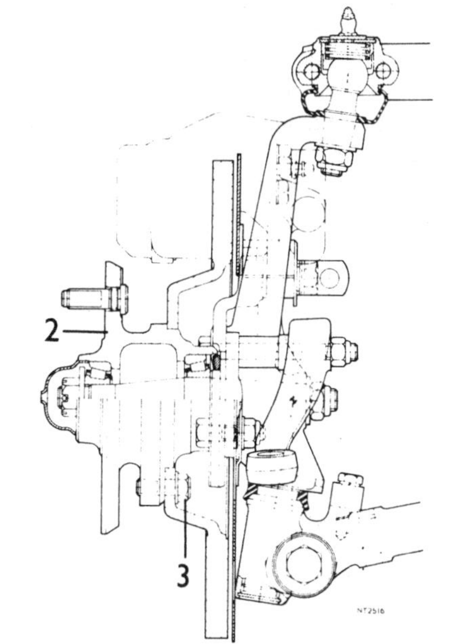

Removing

1. Jack up the car and remove the front wheel.
2. Detach the caliper and remove the front hub 60.25.01/02.
3. Remove the four bolts and spring washers securing the disc to the hub flange.
4. Withdraw the disc.

Refitting

5. Reverse instructions 1 to 4.

FRONT DISC SHIELD

– Remove and refit 70.10.18

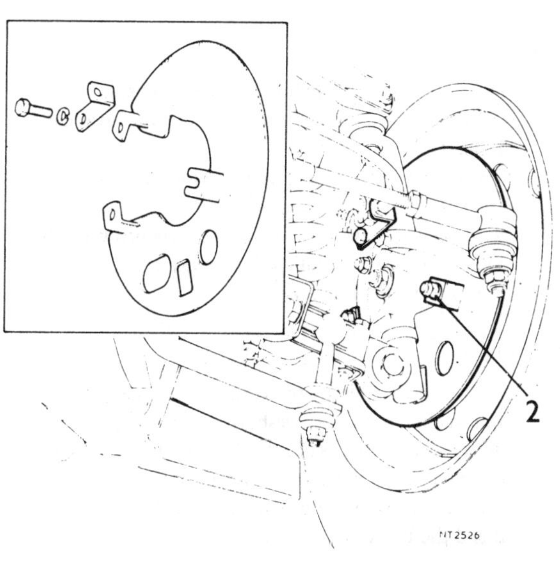

Removing

1. Remove the front hub 60.25.01/02.
2. Slacken the front lower nut, washer and bolt securing the disc mounting lug to the vertical link.
3. Withdraw the disc shield.

Refitting

4. Reverse instructions 1 to 3.

REAR BRAKE BACK PLATE

– Remove and refit **70.10.26**

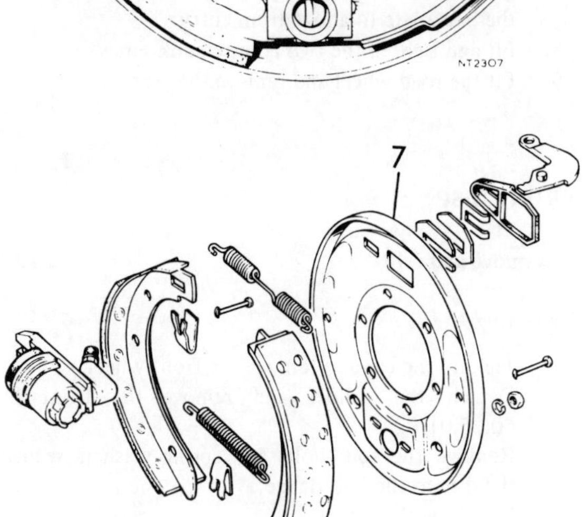

Removing

1. Remove the rear road wheel and brake drum 70.10.03.
2. Remove brake shoes. 70.40.03 and disconnect the handbrake cable at the backplate lever.
3. Disconnect the drive shaft flange at differential.
4. Disconnect the brake pipe at rear brake cylinder.
5. Remove the six nuts securing the rear hub and backplate to the trailing arm.
6. Withdraw the rear hub complete with drive shaft.
7. Withdraw the backplate.

Refitting

8. Reverse instructions 1 to 7.
9. Bleed the brakes.

FRONT HOSE

– Remove and refit **70.15.02/03**

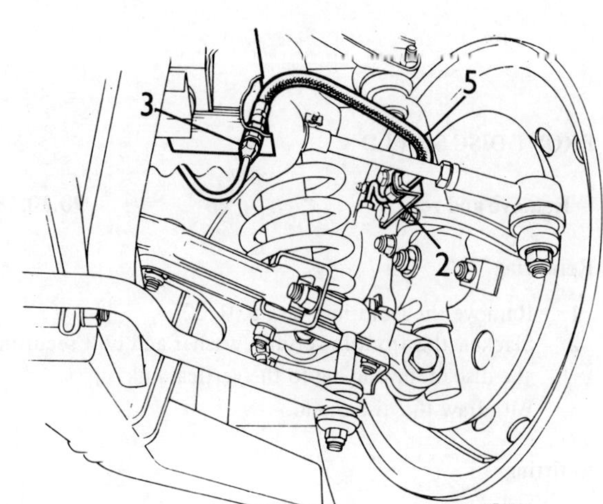

Removing

1. Jack up the car and remove the front wheel.
2. Disconnect the brake pipe union at hose/caliper bracket.
3. Disconnect the brake pipe union at the chassis bracket.
4. Remove the nuts and lockwashers securing the hose ends to the caliper and chassis brackets.
5. Remove the flexible hose.

Refitting

6. Fit the hose ends to the caliper and chassis brackets and secure with lockwashers and nuts. Ensure that the hose is neither kinked nor twisted on installation.
7. Fit the brake pipes to the hose ends.
8. Fit the road wheel and remove the jack.
9. Bleed the brakes.

REAR HOSE

– Remove and refit **70.15.17/18**

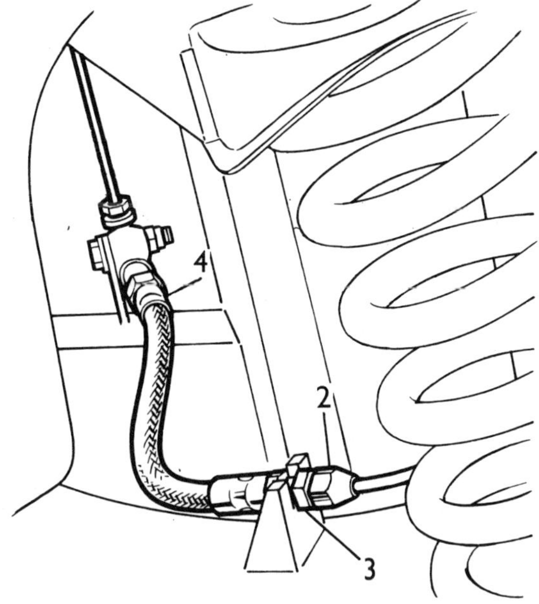

Removing

1. Jack up the car and remove the rear wheel.
2. Disconnect the brake pipe union and brake pipe from the wheel cylinder to the flexible hose.
3. Remove the nut and lockwasher securing the flexible hose to the trailing arm.
4. Disconnect the pipe union from the front end of the flexible hose. Remove the nut and lockwasher securing the hose to the chassis bracket and withdraw the hose.

or

Unscrew the hose from the 3-way connector.

Refitting

5. Fit the hose to the chassis bracket and secure with lockwasher and nut.
   Connect the brake pipe from the 3-way connector

   or

   Fit the hose to the 3-way connector.
6. Fit the hose to the trailing arm bracket and secure with lockwasher and nut. Ensure that the hose is neither kinked nor twisted on installation.
7. Connect the wheel cylinder pipe to the hose.
8. Fit the rear wheel and remove the jack.
9. Bleed the brakes.

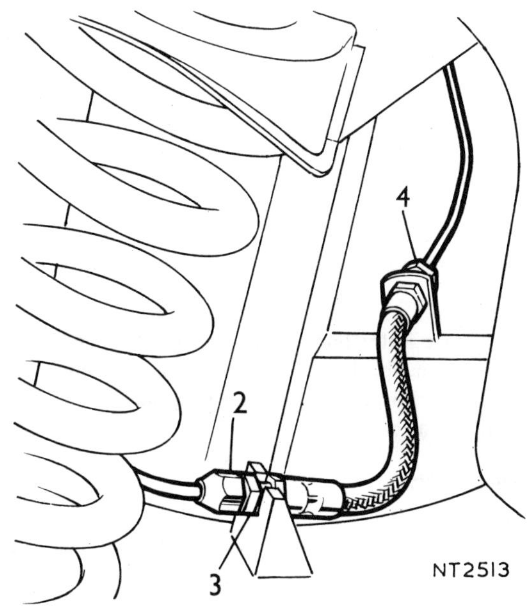

2-WAY CONNECTOR

– Remove and refit **70.15.32**

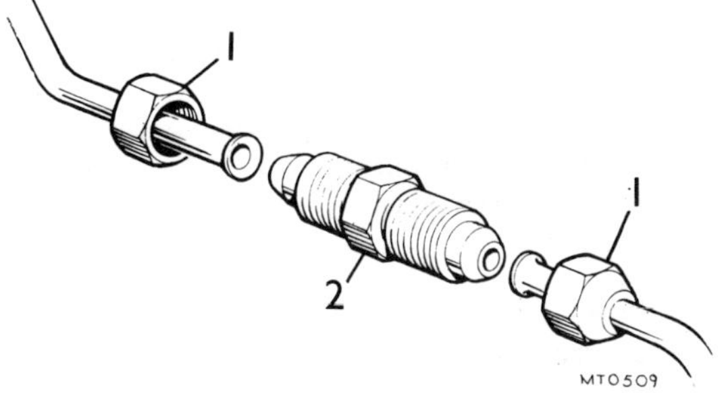

Removing

1. Disconnect the brake pipe unions from the connector.
2. Release the connector from the pipes.

Refitting

3. Reverse instructions 1 and 2.
4. Bleed the brakes.

3-WAY CONNECTOR – FRONT

– Remove and refit **70.15.33**

Removing

1. Disconnect brake pipe unions (3) and release the pipes from the connector.
2. Remove the nut and bolt securing the connector to the chassis bracket and withdraw the connector.

Refitting

3. Connect, but do not tighten the brake pipes and unions (3) to the connector.
4. Fit the connector to the chassis bracket and secure with nut and bolt.
5. Tighten the pipe unions (3).
6. Bleed the brakes.

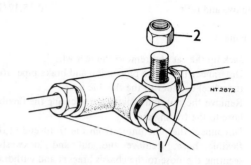

3-WAY CONNECTOR – REAR

– Remove and refit **70.15.34**

Removing

1. Jack up the car and remove the rear wheel on the driver's side of car.
2. Disconnect the brake pipe union from the flexible brake hose.
3. Remove the nut and lockwasher securing the hose to the trailing arm.
4. Unscrew the hose from the 3-way connector.
5. Disconnect the two brake pipe unions from the 3-way connector.
6. Remove the nut and bolt securing the connector to the chassis bracket and withdraw the connector.

Refitting

7. Reverse instructions 1 to 6. Ensure that the flexible hose is neither kinked nor twisted on installation.
8. Fit the rear wheel and remove the jack.
9. Bleed the brakes.

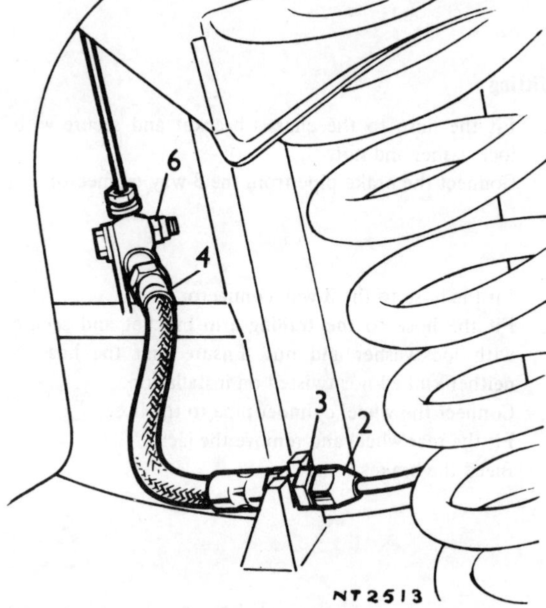

P.D.W.A. SWITCH

– Remove and refit **70.15.36**

Removing

1. Disconnect the electrical plug from the P.D.W.A. unit.
2. Disconnect the four brake pipes from the P.D.W.A. unit.
3. Remove the bolt and spring washer securing the P.D.W.A. unit to the car.
4. Remove the P.D.W.A. unit.

Refitting

5. Fit the P.D.W.A. unit to the car and secure with bolt and spring washer.
6. Fit the four brake pipes to the P.D.W.A. unit.
7. Connect the electrical plug to the P.D.W.A. unit.
8. Bleed the brakes.

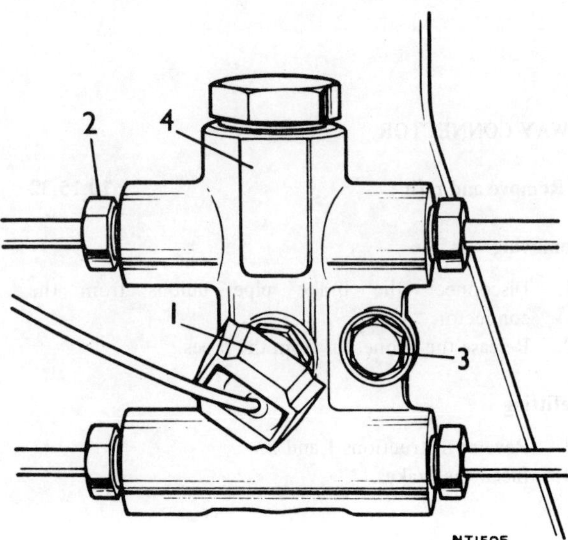

HYDRAULIC PIPES

– Remove and refit

Pipe – P.D.W.A. to 3-way – front	70.20.01
Pipe – 3-way – front – to L.H. hose	70.20.02
Pipe – 3-way – front – to R.H. hose	70.20.03
Pipe – hose to front caliper L.H.	70.20.08
Pipe – hose to front caliper R.H.	70.20.09
Pipe – 2-way connector to rear 3-way connector	70.20.14
Pipe – rear 3-way connector to rear hose R.H.	70.20.16
Pipe – hose to rear cylinder L.H.	70.20.17
Pipe – hose to rear cylinder R.H.	70.20.18
Pipe – P.D.W.A. to 2-way connector	70.20.27
Pipe – master cylinder to P.D.W.A. – front brakes	70.20.46
Pipe – master cylinder to P.D.W.A. – rear brakes	70.20.47.

Removing

1. Disconnect the brake pipe unions at pipe ends.
2. Release the pipe from securing clips (where fitted).
3. Withdraw the pipes.

Refitting

4. Locate the pipe in position on the car.
5. Connect the pipe unions at pipe ends to their respective components.
6. Secure the pipe to the pipe clips (where fitted).
7. Bleed the brakes.

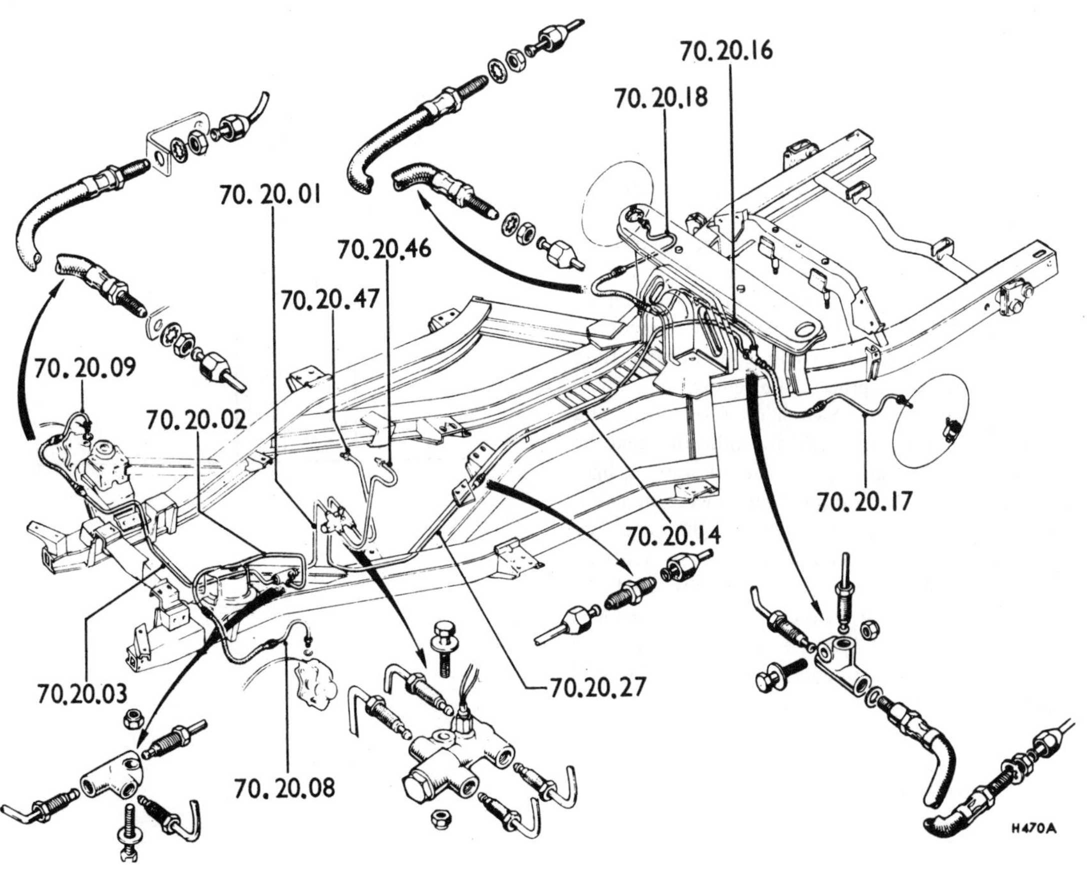

BRAKES – BLEED 70.25.02

1. Check the level of fluid in the master cylinder reservoir and top up as necessary.
2. Depress the brake pedal to destroy the vacuum in the servo. Do not bleed the brakes with the engine running.
3. Attach a bleed tube to the nipple of the rear wheel cylinder farthest (longest pipe run) from the master cylinder. Allow the free end of the tube to hang submerged in brake fluid in a trasparant container.
4. Slacken the bleed nipple (90° to 180° is usually adequate) and depress the brake pedal. On models fitted with a Pressure Differential Warning Actuator (P.D.W.A.) do not apply either hard pressure or full travel to the brake pedal in order to avoid moving P.D.W.A. shuttle out-of-centre.
5. Allow the brake pedal to return to its idle position and again depress. Continue until fluid discharge from the wheel cylinder is seen to be free of air bubbles.
6. Hold the brake pedal depressed, close the bleed nipple and remove the bleed tube.
7. Repeat above procedure on the opposite rear wheel cylinder.
8. Bleed the front calipers in similar manner commencing at the caliper farthest from the master cylinder.
9. Check the fluid level in the reservoir and top up. It is important to ensure that the reservoir fluid is never permitted to fall so low that air can be admitted to the master cylinder. When topping up the reservoir do not use the aerated and possibly contaminated fluid discharged during the process of bleeding.
10. *P.D.W.A. models only.* Switch on the ignition and observe the brake failure light for indication that the P.D.W.A. is centralised. (Both the oil warning light and the brake failure warning light glowing dimly). A brightly glowing brake failure light and no illumination from the oil warning light is indicative that the P.D.W.A. shuttle has been displaced. To re-centre the shuttle it is necessary to open the bleed nipple on the circuit opposite to that to which the shuttle has moved and depress the brake pedal until the brake failure light and the oil light glows.

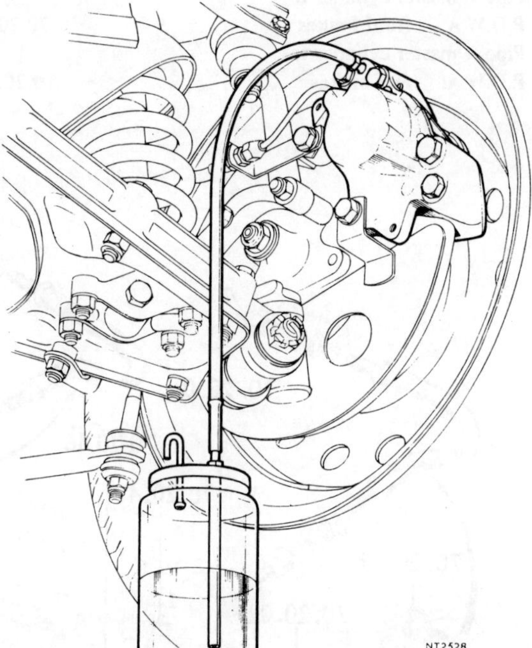

BRAKES

–Adjust 70.25.03

Front

The front brakes are hydraulically self-adjusting to compensate for brake pad wear. Manual adjustment is not provided.

Rear

A single wedge-type adjuster with a square-ended spindle is provided on the backplate.

1. Jack up rear of car until both wheels are free of ground contact.
2. Release the handbrake.
3. Rotate the adjuster spindle clockwise (viewed from the rear of backplate) until the wheel is locked.
4. Rotate the adjuster anti-clockwise until the wheel can be turned freely.
5. Repeat instructions 3 and 4 on opposite rear wheel. Failure of an adjuster to lock a rear wheel is indicative of excessively worn brake linings.
6. Remove the jack.

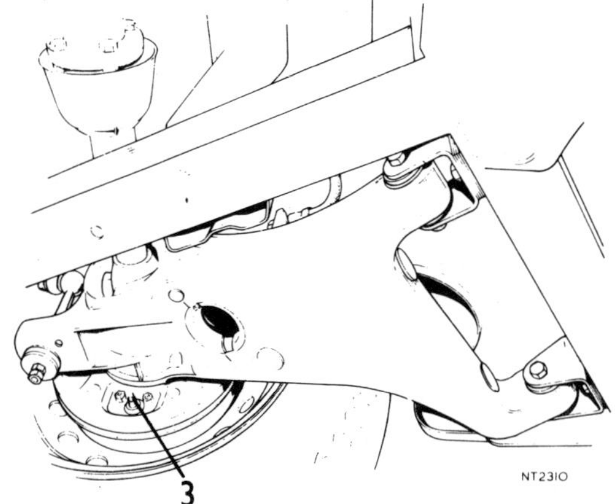

MASTER CYLINDER

– Remove and refit 70.30.08

Removing

1. Disconnect the two brake pipe unions from the master cylinder and seal the brake pipes to prevent ingress of foreign matter.
2. Remove the two nuts and spring washers securing the master cylinder to the servo.
3. Withdraw the master cylinder.

Refitting

4. Fit the master cylinder to the servo and secure with spring washers and nuts.
5. Connect the brake pipes to the master cylinder.
6. Top up the reservoir.
7. Bleed the brakes.

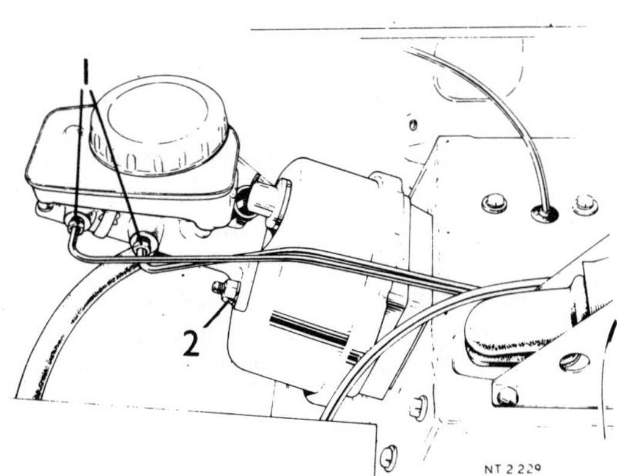

MASTER CYLINDER

– Overhaul 70.30.09

Dismantling

1. Remove the master cylinder from the servo 70.30.08 and drain the brake fluid.
2. Remove the four screws (underside of reservoir) securing the reservoir to the master cylinder and lift off the reservoir.
3. Withdraw the reservoir sealing rings (two).
4. Push the master cylinder secondary plunger slightly into the bore to allow the tipping valve to seat.
5. Maintaining slight pressure on the secondary plunger, remove the tipping valve. Release the plunger.
6. Withdraw the primary and secondary plungers complete with seals and springs.
7. Separate the plungers and the intermediate spring.
8. Prise up the leaf of the spring retainer and remove the spring and valve sub-assembly from the secondary plunger.
9. Withdraw the valve, spacer, spring washer and valve seal from the valve head.
10. Remove the seals from the primary and secondary plungers.
11. Thoroughly clean all components.
12. Examine the cylinder bore for wear, scoring and corrosion. If damage or wear is evident a new cylinder must be obtained.

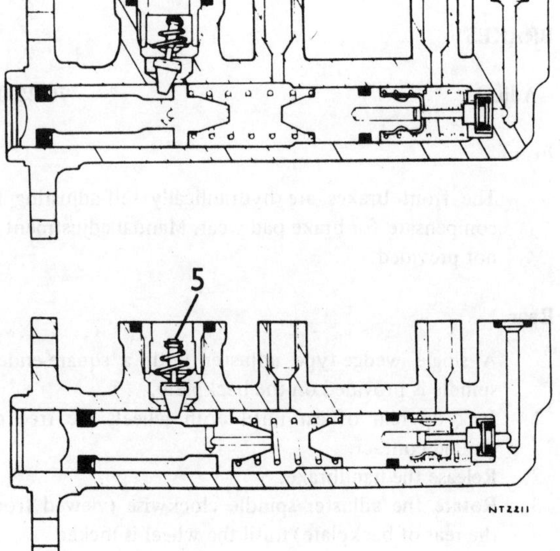

Assembling

13. Fit new seals to the primary and secondary plungers.
14. Fit a new valve seal to the valve head.
15. Place the spring washer on the valve stem (convex side of washer adjacent to the valve).
16. Fit the valve spacer, legs leading.
17. Fit the spring retainer to the valve stem, keyhole leading.
18. Slide the secondary spring over the spring retainer and offer up the secondary plunger.
19. Place the secondary plunger and valve assembly between the jaws of a vice covered with clean paper. Compress the spring and using a small screwdriver press the spring retainer hard against the secondary plunger. Holding the retainer in this position, depress the leaf of the spring retainer hard against the plunger. Remove the plunger and valve assembly from the vice and check that the retainer is firmly secured in the plunger.
20. Fit the intermediate spring between the primary and secondary plungers.
21. Generously lubricate the cylinder bore and plungers with clean brake fluid and insert the plungers in the cylinder.
22. Depress the secondary plunger and fit the tipping valve.
23. Renew the reservoir sealing rings and fit the reservoir.

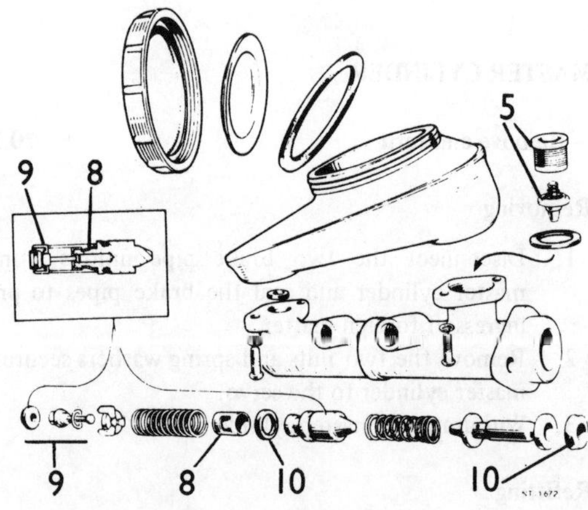

FLUID RESERVOIR

– Remove and refit **70.30.15**

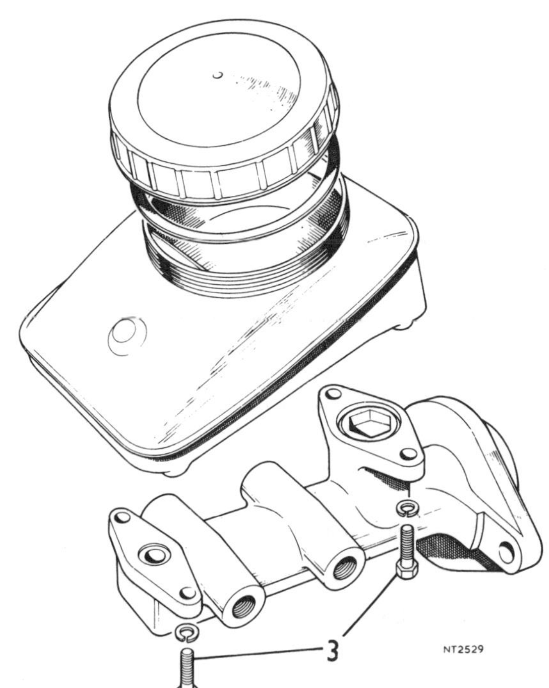

Removing

1. Remove the master cylinder 70.30.08.
2. Drain the reservoir and master cylinder.
3. Remove the four screws (underside of reservoir) securing the reservoir to the master cylinder.
4. Lift off the reservoir and remove the two sealing rings.

Refitting

5. Fit new sealing rings.
6. Fit the reservoir to the master cylinder and evenly tighten the four securing screws.

PEDAL ASSEMBLY

– Remove and refit **70.35.01**

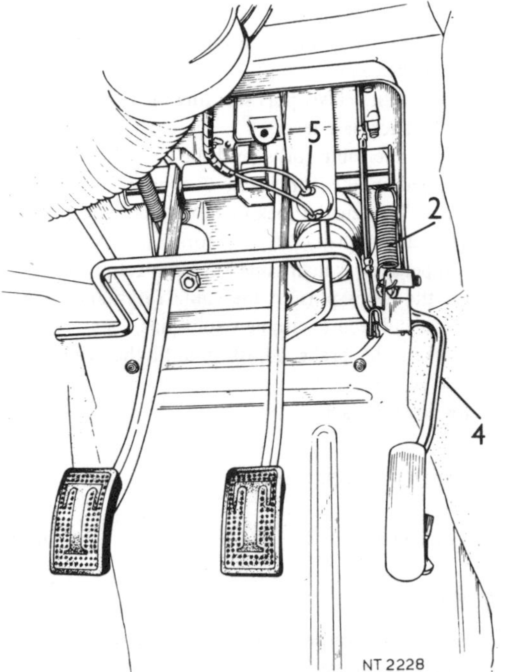

Removing

1. Remove the two nuts, spring washers and bolts securing the accelerator pedal bracket to the pedal box.
2. Release the accelerator pedal return spring.
3. Remove the spring clip and release the accelerator cable from the accelerator pedal.
4. Withdraw the accelerator pedal.
5. Disconnect the two spade terminals from the brake stop switch.
6. Remove the four nuts and plain washers securing the servo to the pedal box.
7. Remove the four bolts and spring washers securing the clutch master cylinder bracket to the scuttle.
8. Remove the seven bolts, plain washers and spring washers securing the pedal box to the scuttle.
9. Withdraw the pedal box assembly.

Refitting

10. Reverse instructions 1 to 9.

HANDBRAKE LEVER ASSEMBLY

– Remove and refit 70.35.08

Removing

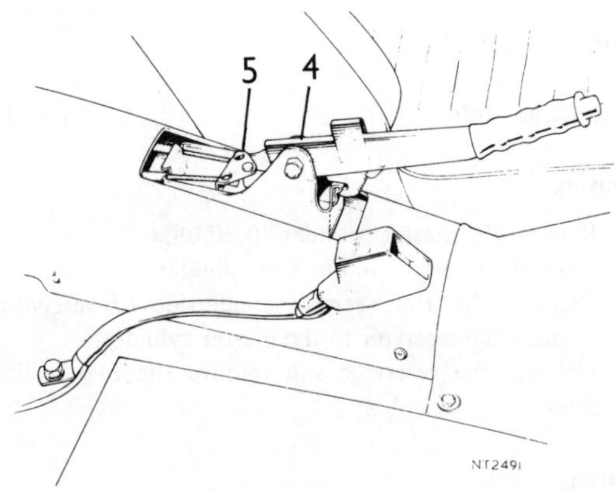

1. Release the handbrake.
2. Disconnect the handbrake cables from the backplate lever.
3. Remove the carpet from the rear of the transmission tunnel.
4. Remove the bolt and nut securing the handbrake lever to the transmission tunnel.
5. Release the handbrake cables from the handbrake compensator linkage and withdraw the handbrake lever assembly from the transmission tunnel.

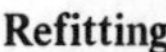

Refitting

6. Reverse instructions 1 to 5.

HANDBRAKE CABLE

– Adjust 70.35.10

1. Jack up the rear wheels and release the handbrake.
2. Tighten the brake adjusters on the rear backplates until both wheels are locked.
3. Slacken the locknuts securing the brake cable forks to the brake cable.
4. Remove the clevis pins securing the brake cable forks to the backplate levers.
5. Adjust the cable forks until the clevis pins can just be engaged in the forks and backplate levers without force. Tighten the locknuts. Note adjustment should be made equally to the forks in order that the compensator is maintained in a central position.
6. Fit the clevis pins to the cable forks and backplate levers and secure with new split pins.
7. Slacken the brake adjusters until the wheels rotate freely.
8. Remove the jack.

HANDBRAKE COMPENSATOR

– Remove and refit 70.35.11

Removing

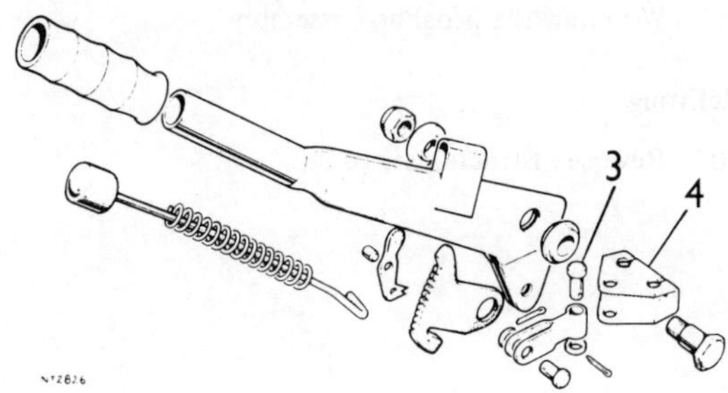

1. Remove the carpet from the rear of the transmission tunnel to expose the handbrake lever assembly.
2. Release the handbrake.
3. Remove the split pin, plain washer and clevis pin securing the compensator to the compensator link.
4. Release the handbrake cables and withdraw the compensator.

Refitting

5. Reverse instructions 1 to 4.

HANDBRAKE CABLE ASSEMBLIES – SET

– Remove and refit **70.35.16**

Removing

1. Remove the carpet from the rear of the transmission tunnel to expose the handbrake lever assembly.
2. Release the handbrake.
3. Jack up the rear wheels and support the chassis on stands.
4. Remove the clevis pins securing the cable forks to the backplate levers.
5. Remove the nuts and spring washers securing the brake cable supports to the trailing arms.
6. Release the brake cables from the handbrake compensator
7. Remove the brake cables.

Refitting

8. Fit the inner cables to the compensator and the outer casings to the trailing arms.
9. Tighten the brake adjusters on the rear backplates until the wheels are locked.
10. Adjust the brake cable forks equally until the clevis pins will just enter the forks and backplate levers without force.
11. Check that the compensator is central and if necessary readjust cable length by means of the cable forks.
12. Slacken the brake adjusters until the wheels rotate without brake drag.
13. Remove the stands and jack.
14. Fit the carpet to the rear of the transmission tunnel.

NT2825

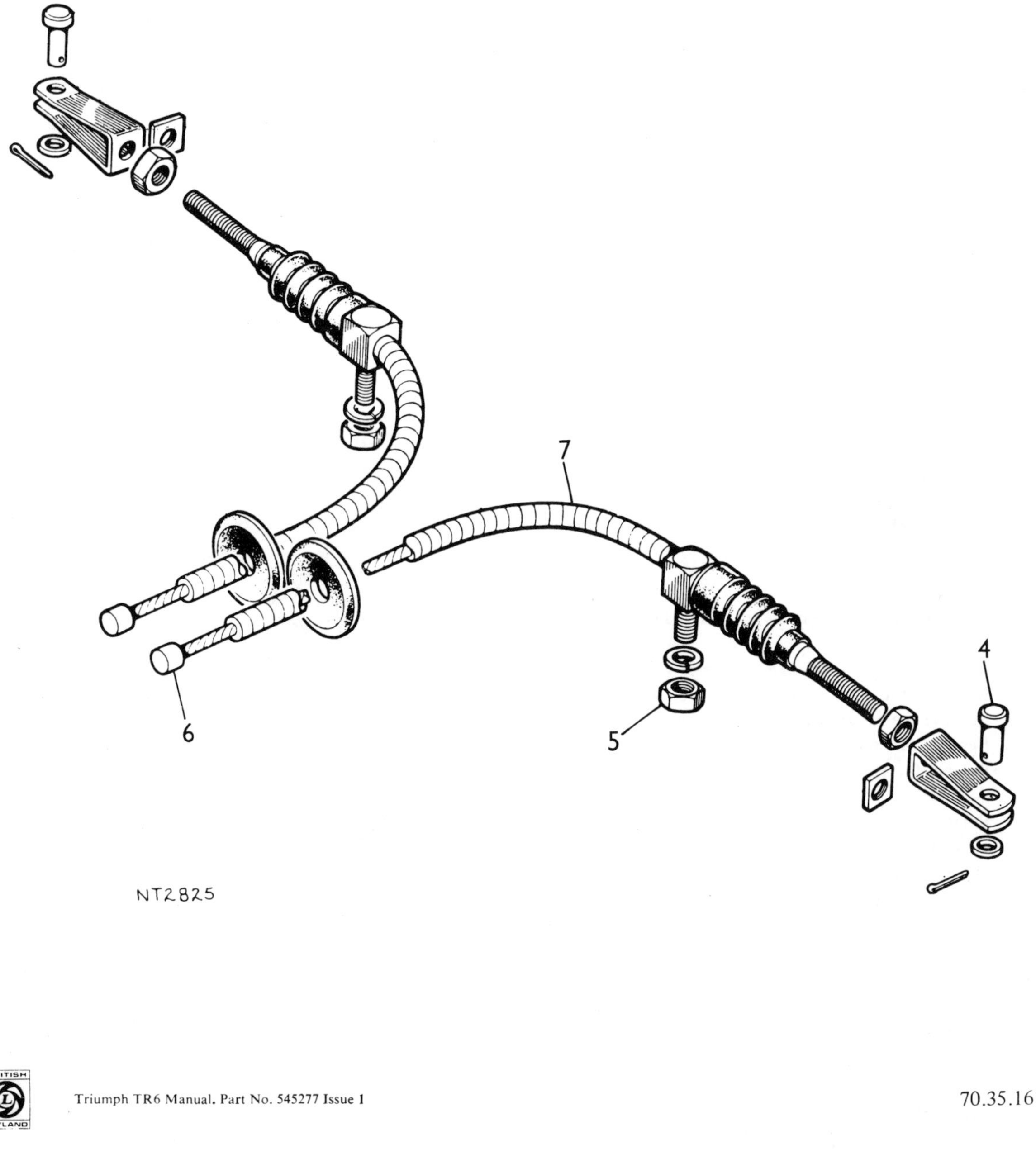

FRONT BRAKE PADS

– Remove and refit 70.40.01

Removing

1. Jack up the car and remove the front wheels.
2. Withdraw the spring pins (2) from the brake pad retaining pins.
3. Withdraw the brake pad retaining pins (2).
4. Lift out the brake pads complete with damping shims.
5. Repeat instructions 2 to 4 on opposite front wheel.

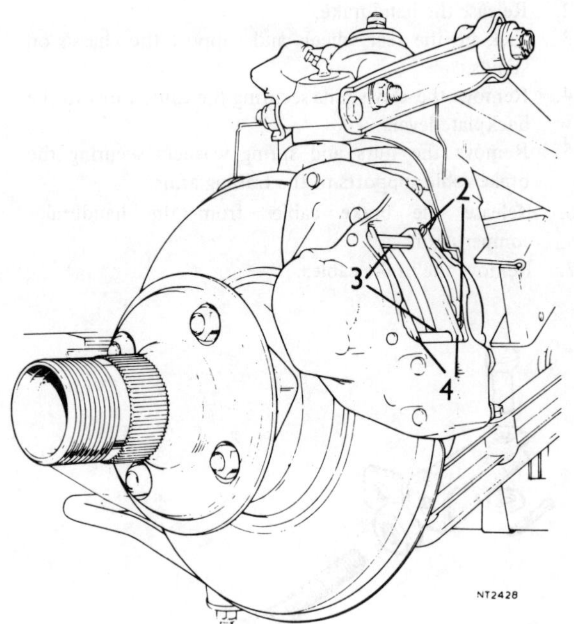

Refitting

6. Ease the caliper pistons into the bores to provide clearance to accommodate new brake pads, if necessary. This operation can be facilitated by applying pressure to the piston and at the same time opening the bleed nipple. Close the nipple when the piston has moved the required amount and repeat on the opposite piston in caliper. Provided the piston is not allowed to retract while the nipple is open, subsequent bleeding is not usually necessary.
7. Remove dust and clean the brake pad locations in the caliper.
8. Fit the brake pads and damping shims to the caliper ensuring that the arrow on the damping shims points in the direction of the forward disc rotation.
9. Engage the pad retaining pins in the caliper and secure with the spring pins.
10. Repeat instructions 6 to 9 on opposite front wheel.
11. Fit the road wheels and remove the jack.
12. Apply and release the brakes.
13. Check the level of fluid in the reservoir.

REAR BRAKE SHOES

– Remove and refit 70.40.03

Removing

1. Jack up the car and remove the road wheel.
2. Release the handbrake.
3. Fully slacken off the brake adjuster.
4. Remove the hub extension (wire wheels only). Remove the brake drum.
5. Remove the shoe-steady pins and springs.
6. Release the leading shoe from the adjuster and wheel cylinder.
7. Release the trailing shoe from the adjuster and wheel cylinder.
8. Unhook the brake shoe return springs and remove the shoes and springs.

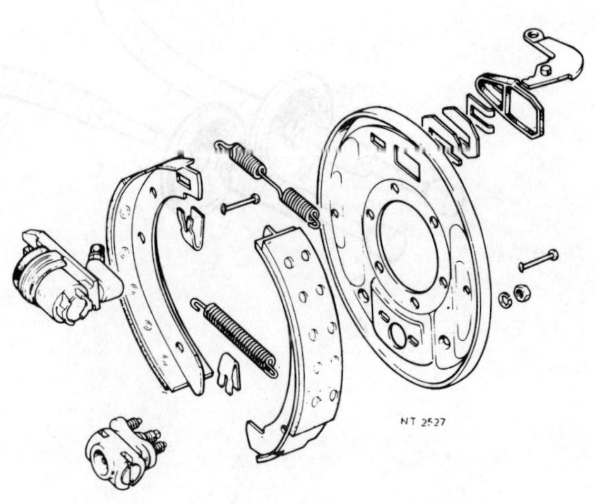

Continued

Refitting

9. Engage the hooks of the upper and lower return springs in the secondary brake shoe and offer up to the backplate. Do not fit the shoe to either the wheel cylinder or brake adjuster.
10. Engage return springs in the leading shoe.
11. Fit the leading shoe in position in the wheel cylinder and adjuster.
12. Fit the trailing shoe to the wheel cylinder and adjuster.
13. Check both return springs to ensure that hook ends are properly engaged in the shoes.
14. Fit the shoe-steady pins and springs. Note that the open end of the springs should lead in the direction of wheel rotation. See illustration for correct positions of brake shoes and shoe-steady springs.
15. Fit the brake drum. Fit the hub extension (wire wheels only).
16. Adjust the brake.
17. Fit the road wheel and remove the jack.

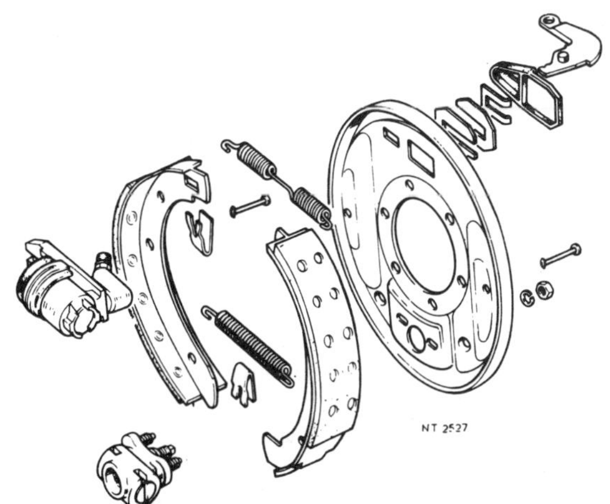

REAR BRAKE ADJUSTER

– Remove and refit **70.40.17**

Removing

1. Jack up the car and remove the road wheel.
2. Release the handbrake and remove the brake drum and brake shoes 70.40.03.
3. Remove the two nuts and spring washers securing the adjuster to the backplate and withdraw the adjuster.

Refitting

4. Reverse instructions 1 to 3.

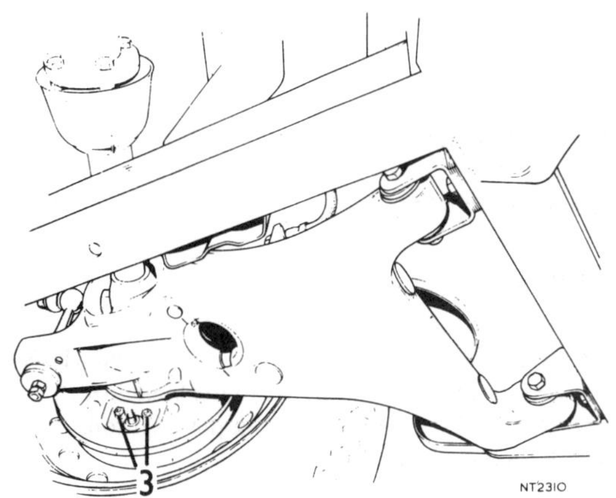

SERVO

– Remove and refit **70.50.01**

Removing

1. Disconnect the vacuum hose from the non-return valve.
2. Disconnect the two brake pipes from the master cylinder.
3. Remove the two nuts and spring washers securing the master cylinder to the servo and withdraw the master cylinder.
4. Remove the clevis pin securing the servo push rod to the brake pedal.
5. Remove the four nuts and spring washers securing the servo to the pedal bracket. And withdraw the servo.

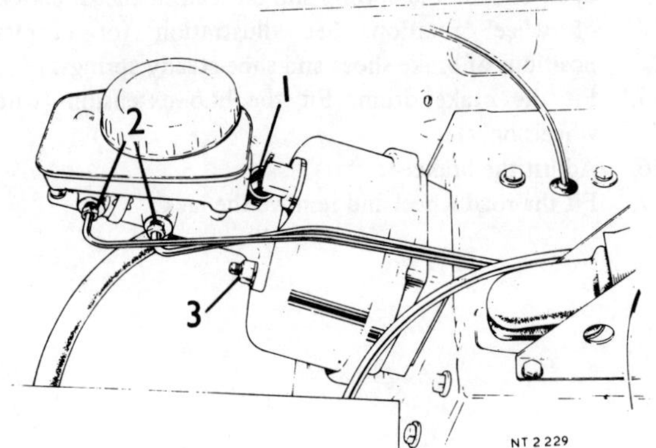

Refitting

6. Reverse instructions 1 to 5.
7. Bleed the brakes.

SERVO FILTER

– Remove and refit **70.50.25**

Removing

1. Remove the brake stop switch.
2. Remove the split pin, plain washer and clevis pin securing the servo push rod to the brake pedal.
3. Remove the rubber boot from the push rod.
4. Withdraw the filter.

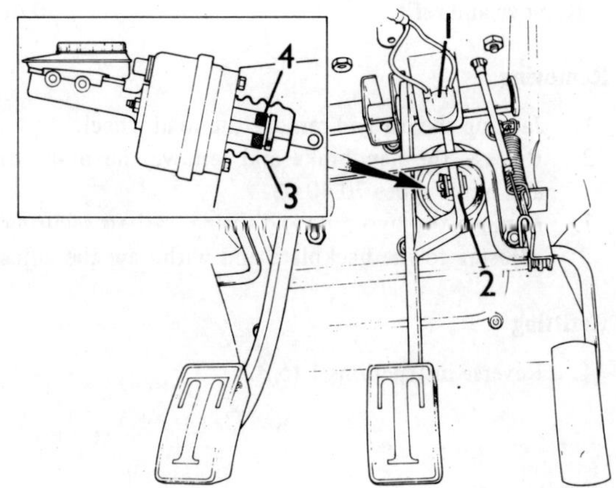

Refitting

5. Reverse instructions 1 to 4.

FRONT CALIPER

– Remove and refit 70.55.02

Removing

1. Jack up the car and remove the front wheel.
2. Disconnect the front caliper brake pipe union at the flexible hose.
3. Remove the two bolts and spring washers securing the caliper to the mounting disc.
4. Withdraw the caliper.

Refitting

5. Reverse instructions 2 to 4.
6. Bleed the brakes.

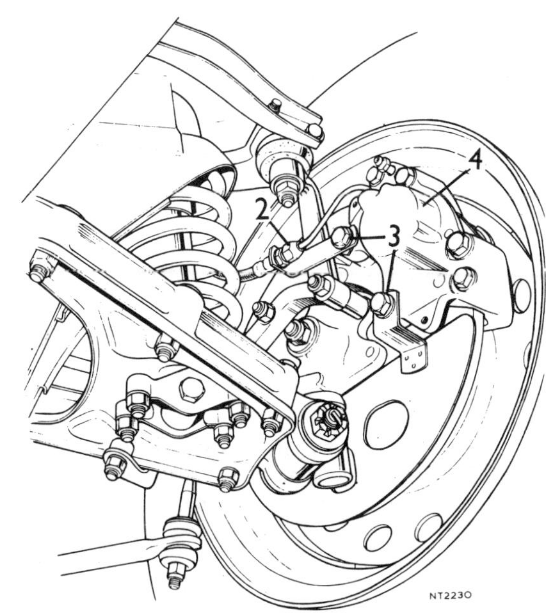

FRONT CALIPER

– Renew seals 70.55.13

Dismantling

1. Remove the caliper 70.55.02
2. Remove the brake pads and shims 70.40.01.
3. Remove the circlip retaining the piston dust covers and withdraw the dust covers.
4. Extract the caliper pistons. Piston removal may be effected using a low pressure air line. Do not interchange the pistons.
5. Prise out the cylinder seals taking care not to damage the cylinder bore.
6. Thoroughly clean the caliper and pistons.

Reassembling

7. Carefully install new seals in the cylinder bores and lubricate the bores with clean brake fluid.
8. Fit the pistons to the caliper.
9. Fit new dust covers and circlips.
10. Fit the caliper to the car 70.55.02.
11. Fit the brake pads and shims 70.40.01.
12. Bleed the brakes.

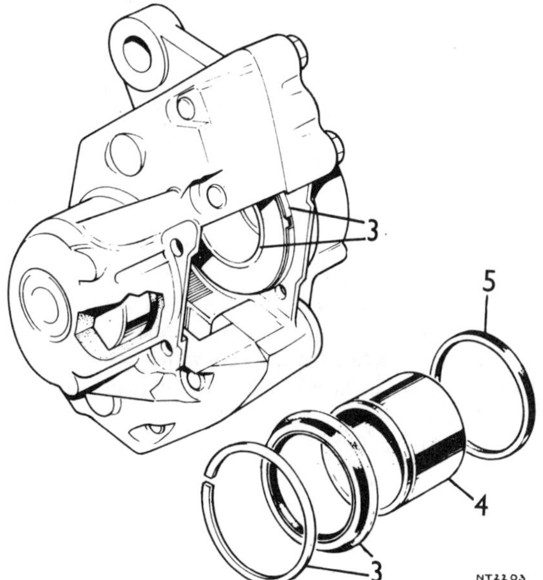

REAR WHEEL CYLINDER

– Remove and refit **70.60.18**

Removing

1. Remove the brake shoes 70.40.03.
2. Remove the clevis pin securing the backplate lever to the handbrake cable.
3. Disconnect the brake fluid pipe from the rear wheel cylinder.
4. Remove the outer plate (distance washer) in a forward direction.
5. Remove the locking plate in a rearward direction.
6. Remove the spring plate in a forward direction.
7. Remove the rubber boot at the rear of the backplate.
8. Withdraw the wheel cylinder and lever assembly from the front of the backplate.

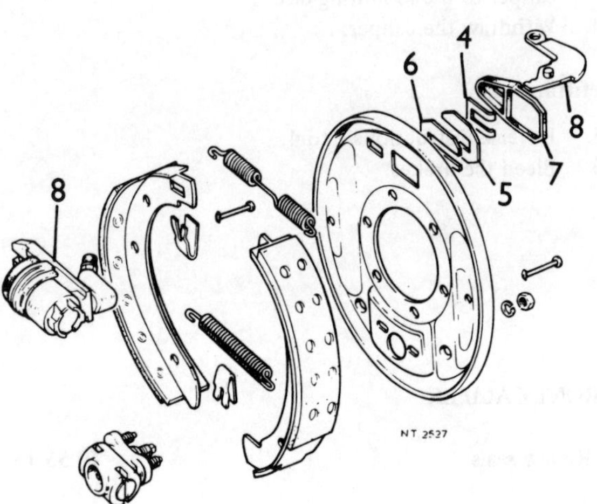

Refitting

9. Enter the wheel cylinder and lever assembly in the backplate.
10. Fit the rubber boot to the wheel cylinder at the rear of the backplate.
11. Fit the spring plate entering it in the slot in the wheel cylinder housing from the forward direction ensuring that the angled ends are inclined away from the backplate.
12. Fit the locking plate from the rear of the wheel cylinder ensuring that the slots in the rear face of the clip engages the angled tips of the spring plate.
13. Fit the outer plate (distance washer) from the forward direction.
14. Connect the brake pipes to the wheel cylinder.
15. Connect the handbrake cable to the wheel cylinder lever, and secure the clevis pin with a new split pin.
16. Fit the brake shoes, brake drum and road wheel.
17. Remove the jack.
18. Bleed the brakes.

REAR WHEEL CYLINDER

– Overhaul **70.60.26**

1. Jack up the car and remove the rear road wheel.
2. Remove the hub extension (wire wheels only). Remove the brake drum.
3. Remove the brake shoes.
4. Disconnect the handbrake cable from the backplate lever.
5. Remove the clip securing the rubber boot to the wheel cylinder.
6. Withdraw the rubber boot.
7. Withdraw the piston complete with seal from the wheel cylinder.
8. Examine the piston and cylinder bore for scoring, wear or damage. If either are damaged or worn or doubt exists, the cylinder assembly must be renewed.
9. Remove the seal from the piston.
10. Fit a new seal to the piston ensuring that the seal lip faces towards the closed end of the cylinder.
11. Fit the rubber boot to the piston, smear the piston and cylinder with clean brake fluid and insert the piston into the cylinder.
12. Ensure the rubber boot is fitted snugly to the cylinder and secure with the clip.
13. Fit the brake shoes, brake drum and hub extension if applicable.
14. Connect the handbrake cable to the backplate lever.
15. Fit the road wheel and remove the jack.
16. Bleed the brakes.

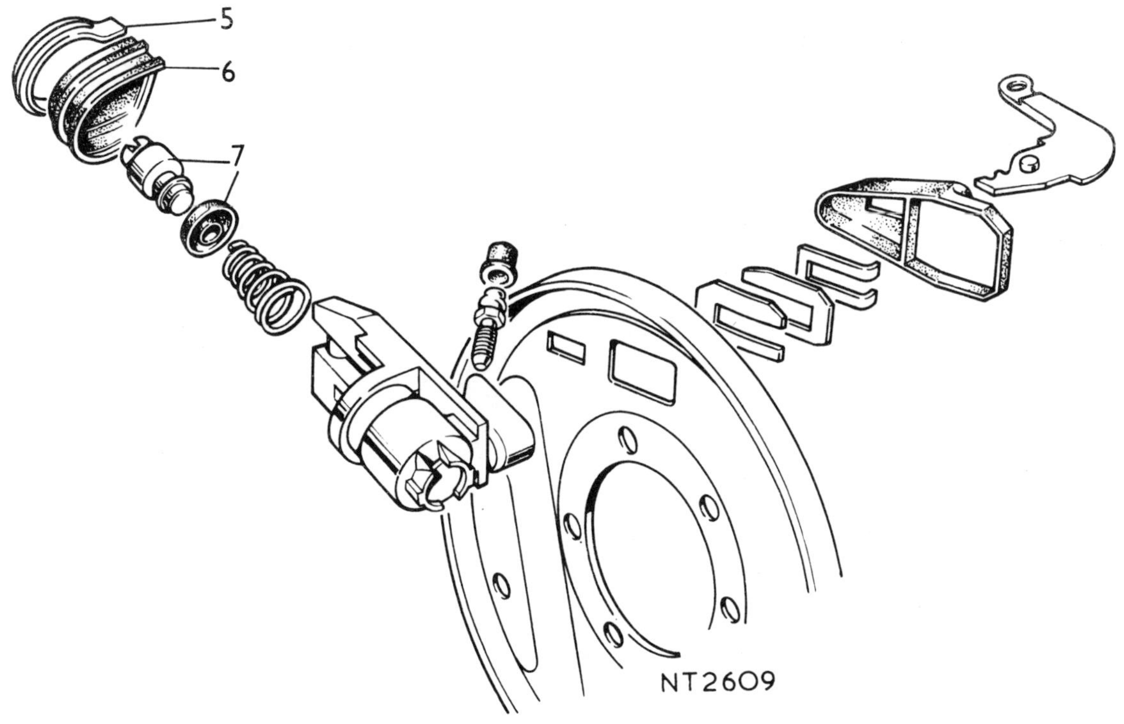

WHEEL AND TYRE OPERATIONS

Type	Size	Pressures			
		Front		Rear	
	**	lb/in²	kg/cm²	lb/in²	kg/cm²
Radial ply – Tubeless	165HR – 15 All Conditions	22	1·5	26	1·8
	High Speed	28	1·9	32	2·2
Tubes are fitted to wire wheels	185SR – 15 All Conditions	20	1·4	24	1·6
					**

Tyres of the correct type and dimensions at the correct cold inflation pressures are an integral part of the vehicle's design, therefore regular maintenance of tyres contributes not only to safety but to the designed functioning of the vehicle. Road holding, steering and braking are impaired by incorrectly pressurised, badly fitted, and worn tyres.

Tyres of the same size and type but of different make may have widely varying characteristics. It is therefore recommended that tyres of the same make and type are fitted to all wheels.

Radial tyres are fitted as original equipment. It is both dangerous and in the U.K. illegal to use on the public roads a vehicle fitted with unsuitable combinations of tyres. The following recommendations should therefore be observed.

1. Do not mix radial-ply and cross-ply tyres on the same axle.
2. Do not fit radial-ply tyres to the front wheels and cross-ply tyres to the rear wheels.
3. With suitable tyre pressure adjustments it may be possible to obtain acceptable handling with cross-ply tyres on the front wheels and radial-ply tyres on the rear wheels, but this combination is not recommended.

Tyre pressures

The tyre pressures recommended (refer chart), provide optimum ride and handling characteristics for all normal conditions. Tyre pressures should be checked and if necessary, adjusted weekly. This should be done with the tyres cold, i.e. not immediately following a run as pressures and temperatures increase when running. 'Bleeding' a warm tyre to the recommended pressure will result in under inflation which may be dangerous as well as harmful to the tyre. Pressure loss, with time, is normal, but if a pressure drop exceeds 2 lb/in² (0.14 kg/cm²) in a period of one week, investigation should be made. In the U.K. it is an offence to use a vehicle with tyres improperly inflated.

The spare wheel tyre should be maintained at rear tyre pressure and adjusted if fitted to the front of the car.

Wear

All tyres, fitted as original equipment, incorporate wear indicators in the tread pattern. When the tread has worn to a remaining depth of approximately 1.5 mm the wear indicators are exposed as bars which connect the tread pattern across the width of the tread. In the U.K. and some other countries it is illegal to use tyres when the tread is worn to a depth of less than 1 mm.

The properties of many tyres alter progressively with wear, particularly with regard to 'wet grip' and aquaplaning resistance, which are gradually but substantially reduced. Extra care and speed restriction should therefore be exercised on wet roads as the effective tread depth diminishes.

Tyre wear is influenced by driving techniques, incorrect inflation, types of road surface and also by misalignment and mechanical defects. Investigations into tyre wear must therefore consider a variety of factors.

Continued

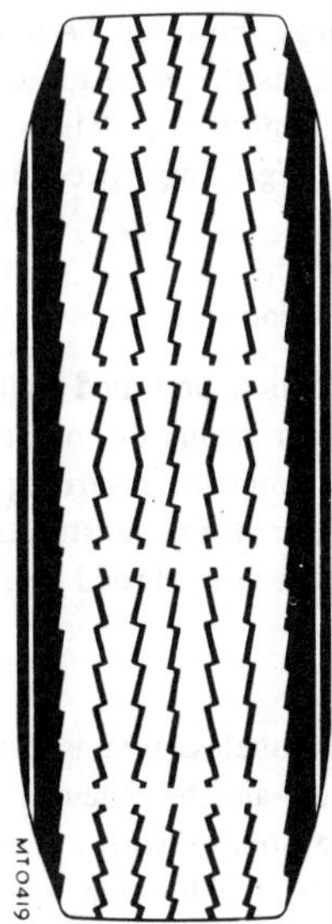

Damage

Excessive localised distortion such as is sometimes caused by severe contact with kerbs or stones can cause the tyre casing to fracture and may lead to premature tyre failure. Tyres should be periodically examined for cracks and cuts, exposed cords etc., and all imbeded objects such as stones and glass, removed from the treads. Oil or grease on the rubber should not be allowed to remain but should be removed by the sparing use of fuel. Do not use kerosene which has a detrimental affect on rubber.

Heat

When paint respraying is carried out and the car is subjected to a drying or baking oven it is recommended that the wheels be removed or at least that the weight of the car is relieved from the tyres.

Repairs – Tyres

A temporary repair can be made to tubeless tyres using a special kit, provided that the puncturing hole is small and is confined to the central tread area. The following precautions must be observed:

1. Use only one plug in each hole.
2. Following a temporary repair do not use the car at high speeds.
3. Remove the tyres from the wheel and make an internal, proper repair at the earliest opportunity.

Repairs – Tubes

A vulcanised repair must be made.

Winter tyres

Winter tyres are designed to provide improved traction and braking in mud and snow. Their performance on hard surfaces may, however, be inferior to normal road tyres and extra care is therefore required when using them under normal conditions. The tyre manufacturers recommendations regarding speed restrictions must be observed.

Racing and competition tyres

Should the vehicle be tuned to increase its maximum speed or be used for racing or competition work, consult the respective tyre company regarding the need for and use of tyres of special, or racing construction. Racing tyres are not recommended for normal road use.

Valves

When a new tubeless tyre is fitted the snap-in type valve housing should also be renewed. To facilitate fitting, lubricate the valve housing with a soap solution and use a special tool to enter the housing squarely into an airtight position in the wheel rim.

WHEELS AND TYRE BALANCE 74.15.00

The balancing of wheel and tyre assemblies is necessary to eliminate the undesirable and unpleasant effects of vibration which can be induced by the rotation of out-of-balance forces.

Balancing is advised when a tyre is renewed or if a tyre is removed for repair and refitted.

WHEELS

Wire Wheels 74.20.00

It is recommended that the servicing and reconditioning of wire wheels is entrusted only to those who are equipped to fulfil this specialist function. It is pointed out that the renewal of a single spoke may necessitate extensive readjustment to spoke tension throughout the wheel.

The average spoke torque in both rows should not be less than 60 lbf/in (0.69 kgf/m). With spokes fully tightened the nipples must not be at the extremities of the fitted flush with the nipple. **P.V.C. tape may be wrapped round the wheel over the nipple heads to give added protection for the tyre inner tube.**

Continued

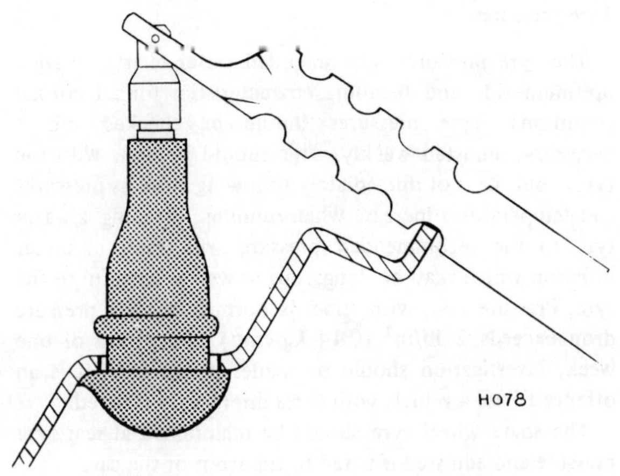

WHEEL TOLERANCES

Wire Wheels

Wobble

Lateral variation measured on the vertical inside face of the rim should not exceed 0.050 in (1.27 mm).

Eccentricity

On a truly mounted and revolving wheel the difference between the high and low points measured on either rim ledge should not exceed 0·050 in (1·27 mm).

Disc Wheel

Wobble

Lateral variation measured on the vertical inside face of the rim should not exeed 0·045 in (1·143 mm).

Eccentricity

On a truly mounted and revolving wheel the difference between the high and low points measured on either rim ledge should not exeed 0·045 in (1·143 mm).

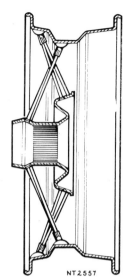

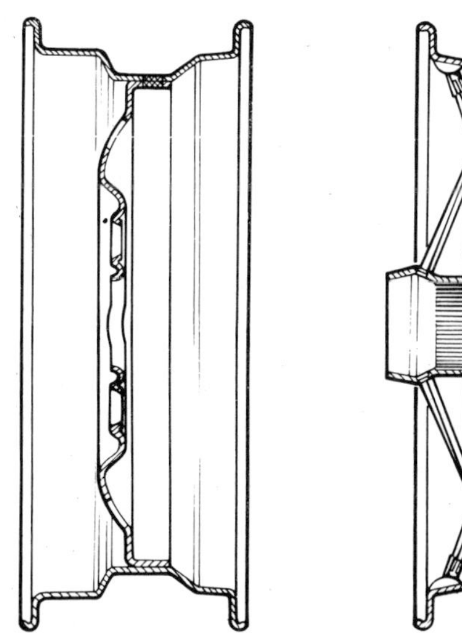

WHEELS

– Remove and refit **74.20.01**

Pressed steel wheels

5½J rims. Wheels are located and retained on the hubs by four 7/16 UNF studs and chrome-plated dome nuts tightened to 60 to 80 lbf/ft (8·3 to 11·1 kgf/m). Embellishment is provided by spring-loaded plastic hub covers fitted under the dome nuts.

Wire wheels

5½J rims, with 48 inner and 24 outer spokes. Wheel hub extensions are fitted. The wheels are splined to the hub extensions and are retained by a conical seating quick release type nut. The hub extensions and quick release nuts are screwed with right hand threads on the L.H. side of the car and with left hand threads on the R.H. side of the car. The quick release wheel retaining nuts are therefore *tightened* when rotated against the direction of forward wheel rotation. and *slackened* when rotated in the direction of forward wheel rotation. Hub extensions must not be interchanged left to right or vice versa.

When fitting the wire wheels to the car it is important to ensure that the conical seats on the hub extensions, road wheel, and retaining nuts are free of grit. Conical faces and splines must be coated with a P.B.C. (Poly Butyl Cuprasyl) base or an equivalent high temperature, low friction lubricant. It is necessary to ensure that wire wheels are fully tightened *before* lowering the wheel to the ground.

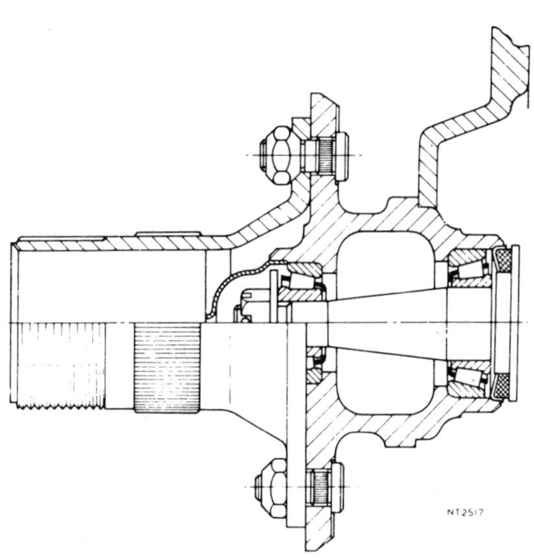

BODY OPERATIONS

continued

BODY OPERATIONS — *continued*

Continued

BODY OPERATIONS — *continued*

BODY OPERATIONS — continued

Operation	No.
[illegible] – remove and refit	[illegible]
[illegible] – remove and refit	[illegible]
Luggage compartment [illegible] – remove and refit	[illegible]
Luggage compartment [illegible] – remove and refit	[illegible]
Luggage compartment [illegible] – remove and refit	[illegible]
Luggage compartment lid lock striker – remove and refit	[illegible]
Luggage compartment [illegible] – remove and refit	[illegible]
Luggage compartment trim panels – remove and refit	[illegible]
[illegible] lock – remove and refit	[illegible]
Rear compartment trim panels – remove and refit	[illegible]
[illegible] – remove and refit	[illegible]
[illegible] – remove and refit	[illegible]
Seat cushion covers – remove and refit	[illegible]
Seat [illegible] – remove and refit	[illegible]
Seat [illegible] – remove and refit	[illegible]
Seat [illegible] – remove and refit	[illegible]
Seats [illegible] – remove and refit	[illegible]
Seat [illegible] – remove and refit	[illegible]
Valance [illegible] – remove and refit	[illegible]
[illegible] – remove and refit	[illegible]
Windscreen – glass – remove and refit	[illegible]
[illegible] – remove and refit	[illegible]

CHASSIS FRAME

– Alignment check 76.10.02

Whilst severe damage to the chassis is readily detected, less serious damage may cause distortion, that is not visually apparent. If steering and suspension checks indicate a fault which cannot be attributed to anything other than chassis distortion, the chassis frame should be checked for twist and squareness. Reference should be made to the appropriate sections of the manual where component removal is necessary for access to checking points.

Checking for twist

1. Position the vehicle on a clean level floor.
2. Place a jack under each jacking point and remove the road wheels 74.20.01.
3. Adjust the jacks until the following conditions are achieved:-
   Points 'A' are 24·97 in (63·40 cm) above the floor.
   Points 'F' are 24·94 in (63·35 cm) above the floor.
   This condition sets the datum 20 in (50·8 cm) above the floor.
   If the height of points 'A' cannot be equalised, the difference in height of points 'A' indicates the amount by which the chassis is twisted.

Checking for squareness

4. Transfer all the lettered points shown to the floor, using a plumb-bob and fine cord.
5. Letter the points on the floor and connect each pair by drawing a line between them.
6. Mark the central point of each line and place a straight edge along these mid points.
7. Check for squareness.
8. Using a straight edge mark the diagonals as shown.
9. Check for squareness. If the chassis is square then each pair of opposite diagonals must be equal in length and the points of intersection must lie on the same straight line.
10. The extent of lateral chassis distortion is assessed by the amount and direction by which any central point on the transverse line and/or the point of intersection of any pair of diagonals deviates from the centre line.

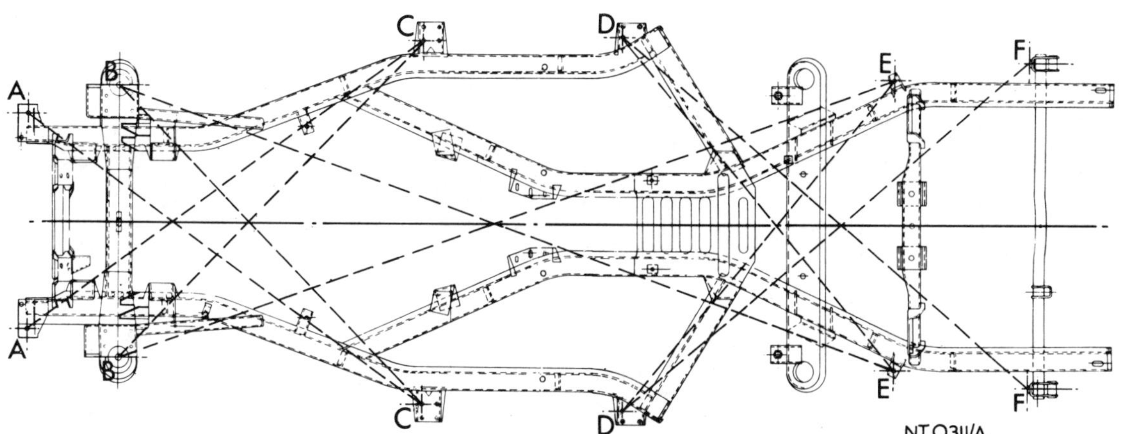

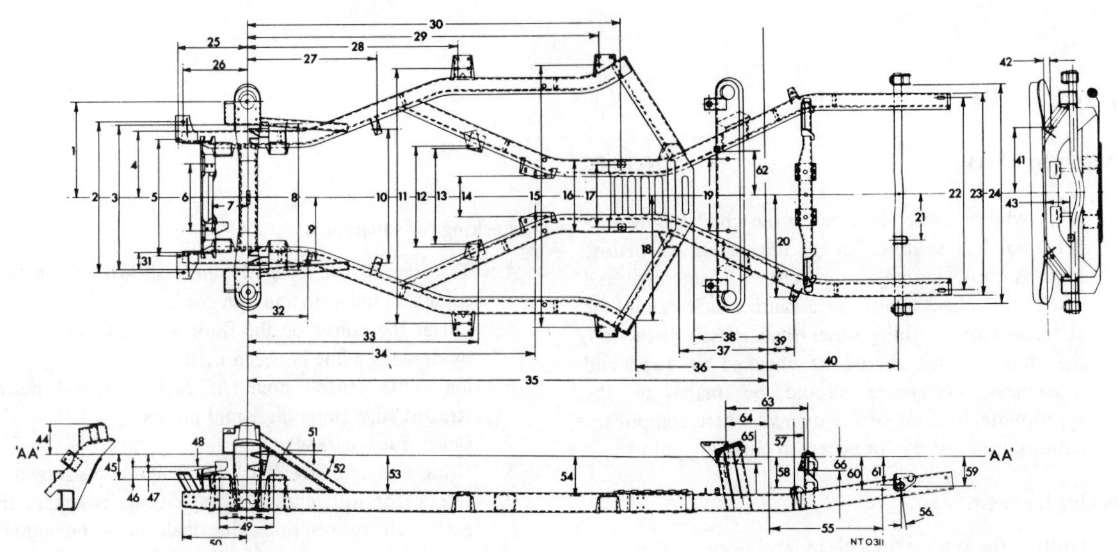

A A Datum line

	Inches	Centimetres		Inches	Centimetres		Inches	Centimetres
1	15·04	38.2	25	11·91	30·2	45	4·28	10·9
2	25·31	64·3		** 11·79	30·0		4·22	10·7
	25·19	63·9	26	11·06 **	28·1	46	2·03	5·2
3	24·03	61·0		10·94	27·8		1·97	5·0
	23·97	60·9	27	22·56	57·3	47	3·25	8·2
4	11·06	28·1		22·44	56·9		3·13	7·9
	10·94	27·8	28	36·25	92·1	48	5°	
5	19·56	49·7		36·13	91·8	49	9·53	24·2
	19·44	49·4	29	60·06	152·4		9·47	24·0
6	11·06	28·1		59·94	152·3	50	11·19	28·4
	11·00	27·9	30	63·63	161·8		11·06	28·2
7	** 5·53	14·0		63·50	161·4	51	0·69	1·8
	5·47	13·9 **	31	3·39	7·6		0·56	1·4
8	24·44	62·1		** 3·33 **	7·5	52	32°7′	
	24·31	61·7	32	10·69	27·1	53	6·06	15·4
9	10·56	26·8		10·56	26·8	54	6·53	16·6
	10·44	26·5	33	39·59	100·5		6·47	16·4
10	22·31	56·7		39·53	100·3	55	18·75	49·2
	22·19	56·4	34	**43·91	111·5} †	56	8°	
11	42·31	107·5		43·85	111·4}	57	1.70	4·3
	42·19	107·2		48·88	124·1}		1·64	4·2
12	16·71	42·4		48·82	124·0} †† **	58	5·25	13·3
	16·65	42·3	35	88·13	223·9		5·13	13·0
13	15·91	40·4		87·88	221·5	59	4·94	12·6
	15·85	40·3	36	21·92	55·7		4·81	12·4
14	** 7·81	19·8} †		21·87	55·5	60	5·38	13·7
	7·69	19·5}	37	14·71	37·3			
	6·56	16·6}		14·65	37·2	61	4·75	12·1
	6·44	16·3} ** ††	38	12.31	31·2	62	7·44	18·9
15	43·14	109·6		12·19	30·9		7·31	18·6
	43·02	109·3	39	4·38	11·1	63	13·23	33·6
16	11·94	30·3		4·25	10·8		13·17	33·4
	11·81	30·0	40	21·81	55·4	64	6·76	17·2
17	10·31	26·2		21·69	55·0		6·70	17·0
	10·19	26·0	41	10·72	27·2	65	1·34	3·4
18	20·36	51·7		10·66	27·0		1·28	3·3
	20·30	51·6	42	1·00	2·5	66	2·22	5·6
19	10·50	26·7		0·94	2·4		2·16	5·5
20	16·13	41·0	43	4·00	10·2			
	16·00	40·6		3·88	9·8			
21	10·62	27·0	44	4·97	12·6			
22	31·81	80·8						
	31·69	80·4						
23	33·50	85·1						
24	38·06	96·9						
	37·94	96·8						

†Two hole bracket up to Commission No. CF1 – Dimn., to centre line of forward hole.
††Three hole bracket from Commission No. CF1 – Dimn., 34 to centre line of middle slot.

FRONT CROSS MEMBER (TUBULAR)

– Remove and refit **76.10.05**

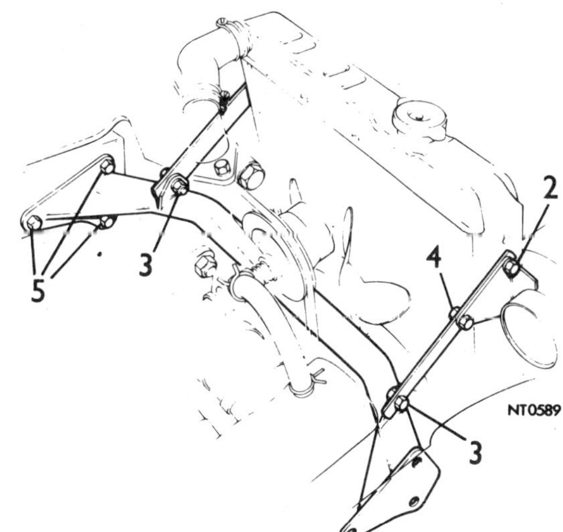

Removing

1. Relieve the load on the cross member using a jack positioned beneath the chassis frame.
2. Slacken the two nuts securing the support bracket to the radiator.
3. Remove the two nuts and bolts securing the support brackets to the cross member.
4. Remove the nut and bolt securing the air cleaner bracket to the support bracket.
5. Remove the six bolts securing the cross member to the chassis frame.
6. Pull the support brackets clear and remove the cross member from the vehicle.

Refitting

7. Reverse instructions 1 to 6.

FRONT VALANCE SPOILER

– Remove and refit **76.10.46**

** The spoiler fitted to later models is secured to the body by five bolts with plain washers and nuts. Note the location of the washers when removing the spoiler. **

GEARBOX TUNNEL COVER TRIM PAD

– Remove and refit **76.13.06**

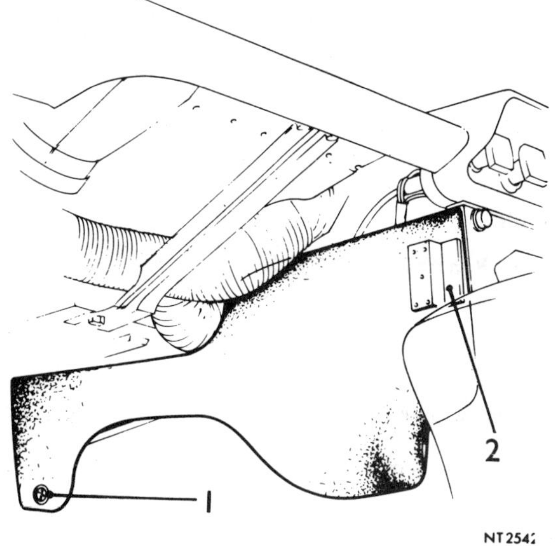

Removing

1. Remove the screw and cup washer securing the front end of the trim pad to the gearbox tunnel cover.
2. Disengage the rear end of the trim pad from the fascia support bracket. Lift off the trim pad.

Refitting

3. Reverse instructions 1 and 2.

LUGGAGE COMPARTMENT TRIM PAD

– Remove and refit **76.13.17**

Removing

1. Remove the luggage compartment carpet and floor.
2. Remove the luggage compartment lamp 86.45.16.
3. Remove the eight screws and washers securing the trim pad to the body. Lift out the trim pad.

Refitting

4. Reverse instructions 1 to 3.

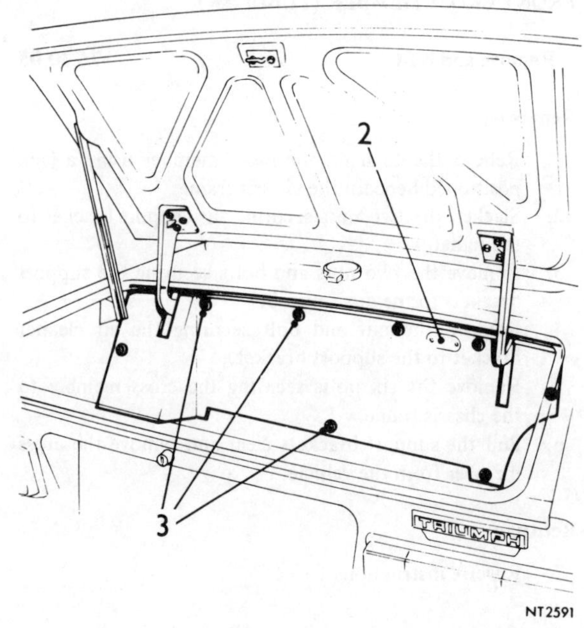

REAR COMPARTMENT TRIM PAD

– Remove and refit **76.13.20**

The rear compartment trim pad is secured to the body by eleven screws and cup washers.

AIR INTAKE VENT

– Remove and refit **76.15.17**

(Vehicles with hinged vent)

Removing

1. Remove the spring nut and detach the control rod from the lid.
2. Disconnect both ends of the spring from the lid.
3. Remove the three bolts and lockwashers securing the lid to the scuttle.
4. Lift off the lid.

Refitting

5. Reverse instructions 1 to 4.

AIR INTAKE VENT

– Remove and refit **76.15.17**

(Vehicles with fixed vent)

The air intake vent is secured to the scuttle by two screws.

BONNET

– Remove and refit 76.16.01

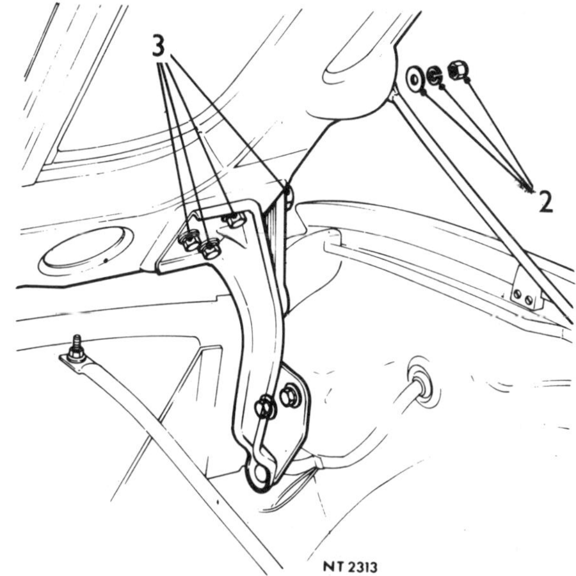

Removing

1. Raise and support the bonnet.
2. Remove the nut and washer securing the support stay to the bonnet.
3. Remove the eight bolts and washers securing the bonnet to the hinges.
4. Lift off the bonnet.

Refitting

5. Reverse instructions 1 to 4.

BONNET

– Adjust 76.16.02

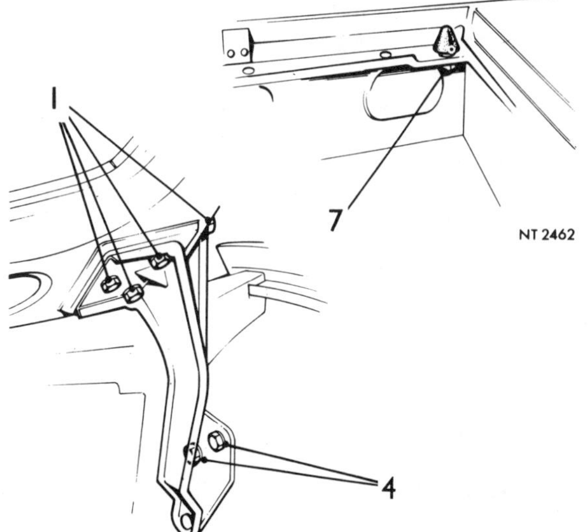

1. Slacken the eight bolts securing the hinges to the bonnet.
2. Adjust the bonnet fore and aft as required.
3. Retighten the bolts.
4. Slacken the four bolts securing the hinges to the wing valances.
5. Adjust the bonnet front upwards or downwards as required.
6. Retighten the bolts.
7. Slacken the two locknuts and screw the rubber buffers in or out to obtain correct height adjustment.
8. Retighten the locknuts.

BONNET HINGES

– Remove and refit 76.16.12

Removing

1. Remove the bonnet 76.16.01
2. Remove the two bolts and washers and lift off the hinges.

Refitting

3. Reverse instructions 1 and 2.

BONNET STAY

– Remove and refit 76.16.14

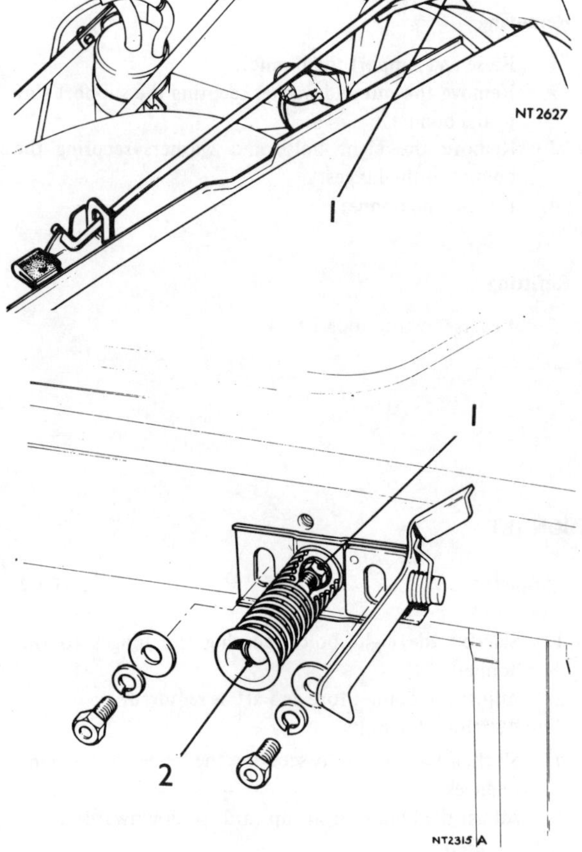

Removing

1. Raise and support the bonnet.
2. Remove the nut, plain washers and spring washer.
3. Detach the bonnet stay.

Refitting

4. Reverse instructions 1 to 3.

BONNET CATCH

– Adjust 76.16.20

To ensure positive locking and eliminate free movement at the closing face, adjust the bonnet catch as follows:-

1. Pull back the spring and slacken the locknut at the base of the shaft.
2. Using a screwdriver, screw the shaft in or out as required.
3. Retighten the locknut.
4. Check the bonnet closing action and repeat instructions 1 to 3 if necessary.

BONNET LOCK

– Remove and refit 76.16.21

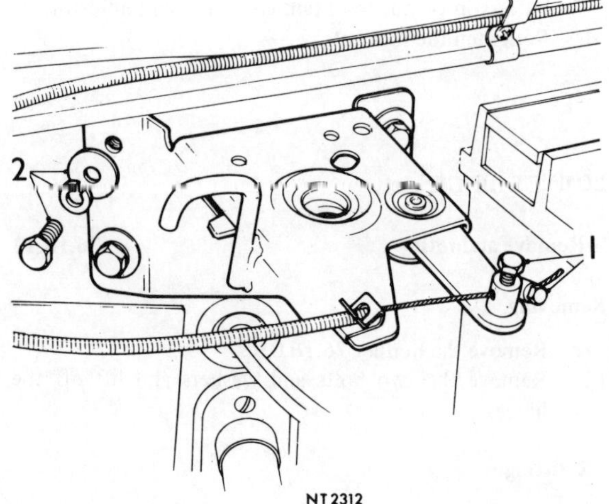

Removing

1. Slacken the trunnion bolts and detach the release cable.
2. Remove the four bolts and washers securing the lock to the bulkhead.

Refitting

3. Reverse instructions 1 and 2.

BONNET RELEASE CABLE

– Remove and refit **76.16.29**

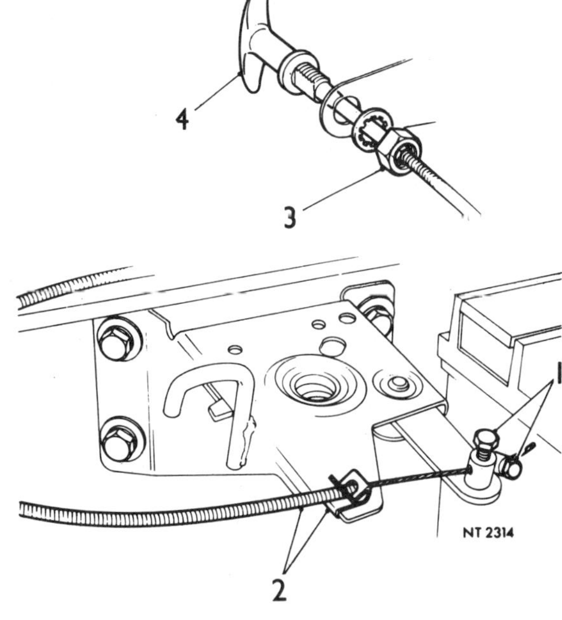

Removing

1. Slacken the trunnion bolts.
2. Pull the cable and clip from the lock.
3. Unscrew the nut.
4. Pull the cable out.

CAUTION: Do not close the bonnet whilst the cable is removed or loose.

Refitting

5. Reverse instructions 1 to 4.

BONNET CATCH

– Remove and refit **76.16.34**

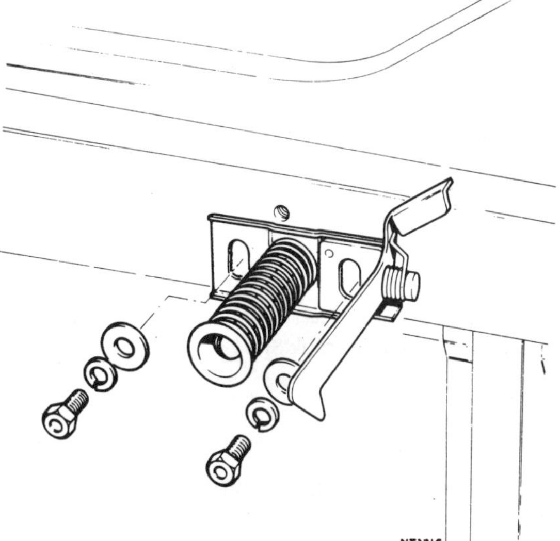

Removing

1. Remove the two bolts and washers securing the catch to the bonnet.

Refitting

2. Refit in reverse order and adjust if necessary 76.16.20.

LUGGAGE COMPARTMENT LID

– Remove and refit 76.19.01

Removing

1. Raise and support the lid.
2. Remove the bolt and washers securing the support stay to the lid.
3. Remove the six bolts and washers securing the hinges to the lid and lift off the lid.

Refitting

4. Reverse instructions 1 to 3.

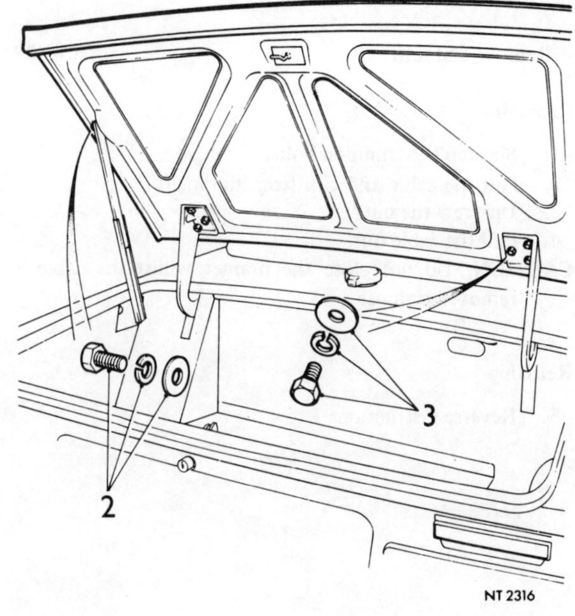

LUGGAGE COMPARTMENT LID SEAL

– Remove and refit 76.19.06

Removing

1. Free the seal from the body, using a suitable blunt tool if necessary.

Refitting

2. Ensure mating surfaces of seal and body are clean.
3. Fit seal, using Seelastik SR51.

LUGGAGE COMPARTMENT LID HINGES

– Remove and refit 76.19.07

Removing

1. Remove the luggage compartment trim pad. 76.13.17
2. Remove the luggage compartment lid 76.19.01.
3. Remove the four bolts and washers securing the hinges to the body.

Refitting

4. Reverse instructions 1 to 3, ensuring correct alignment of the lid.

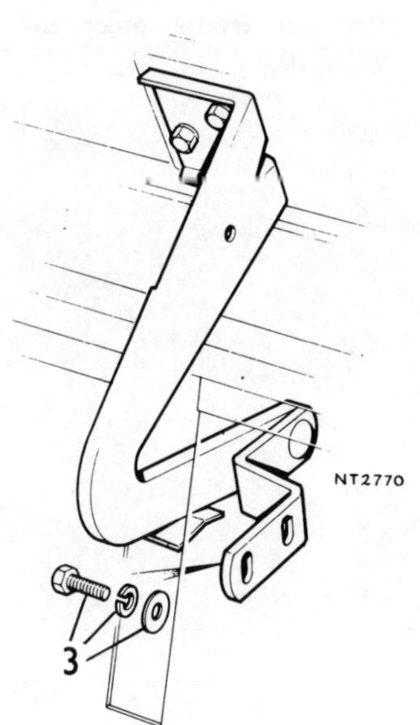

LUGGAGE COMPARTMENT LID LOCK

– Remove and refit **76.19.11**

Removing

1. Remove the four screws and washers securing the lock to the body.
2. Manoeuvre the lock clear of the body.
3. Drill out the two 1/8 in (3·17 mm) rivets securing the lock catch to the push button mounting plate.
4. Remove the two screws and washers securing the push button sub assembly to the mounting plate.
5. Extract the circlip and remove the retainer, spring and body.
6. Drive out the pin and withdraw the locking device.

Refitting

7. Reverse instructions 1 to 6.

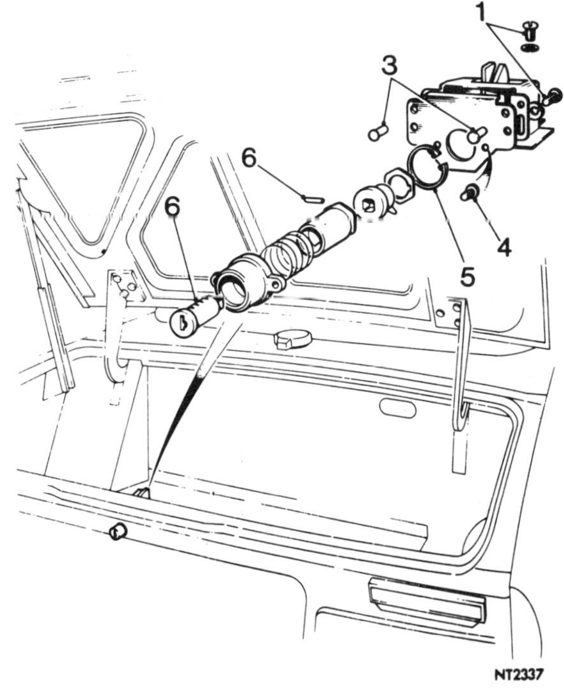

LUGGAGE COMPARTMENT LOCK STRIKER

– Remove and refit **76.19.12**

Removing

1. Remove the two bolts and washers securing the striker to the luggage compartment lid.

Refitting

2. Refit in reverse order ensuring correct alignment of the striker and lock.
3. Adjust, if necessary, to achieve positive locking by unscrewing the locknut and screwing the catch bolt in or out as required.
4. Retighten the locknut.

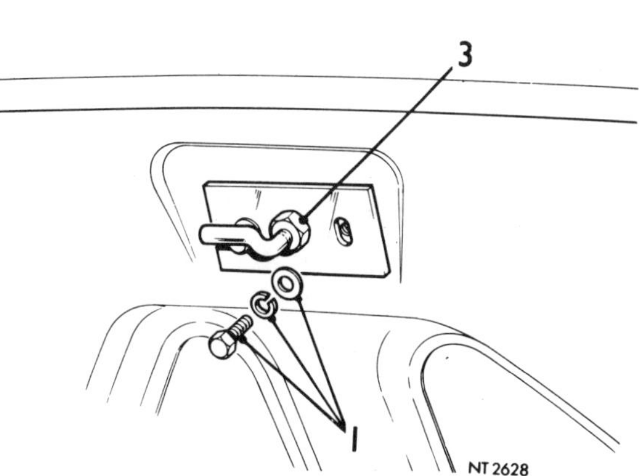

BUMPER – FRONT

– Remove and refit **76.22.08**

Removing

1. Remove the two bolts and washers securing the bumper to the body.
2. Remove the two bolts and washers securing the bumper to the brackets and lift off the bumper.

Refitting

3. Reverse instructions 1 and 2, ensuring that the rubber packing washers are in position between the body and the bumper.

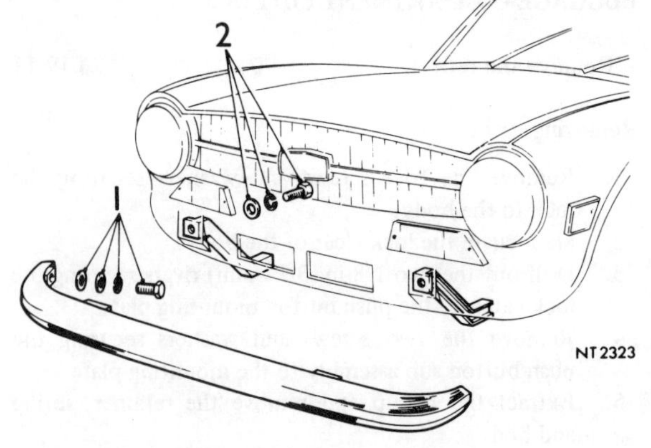

BUMPER – REAR

– Remove and refit **76.22.15**

Removing

1. Disconnect the two number plate leads. 86.40.86.
   Disconnect the two number plate leads. 86.40.86
   ** (Earlier Models only).**
2. Remove the two bolts and washers securing the bumper to the body and the side brackets.
3. Remove the two bolts and washers securing the bumper to the rear brackets and lift off the bumper.

Refitting

4. Reverse instructions 1 to 3, ensuring that the rubber packing washers are in position between the body and the bumper.

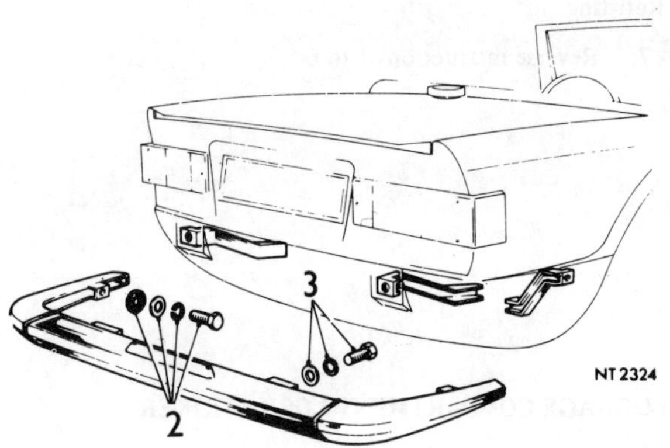

CONTROL COWL

– Remove and refit **76.25.03**

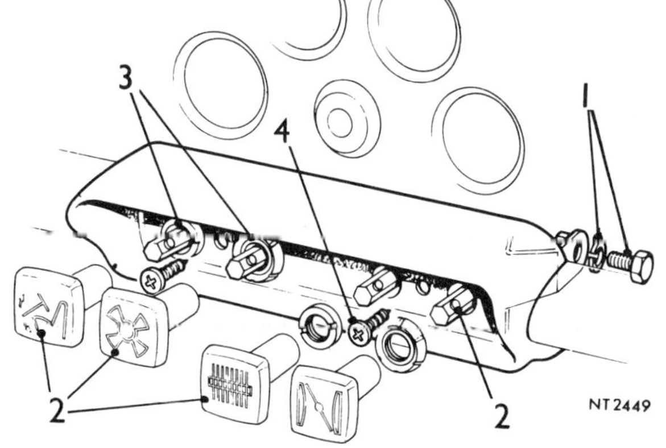

Removing

1. Remove the bolt and lockwasher securing the cowl reinforcement to the fascia.
2. Depress the four buttons and pull off the control knobs.
3. Unscrew and remove the four bezels.
4. Remove the two screws securing the cowl to the fascia.
5. Withdraw the cowl, noting the control positions for refitting.

Refitting

6. Reverse instructions 1 to 5.

GEARBOX TUNNEL COVER

– Remove and refit **76.25.07**

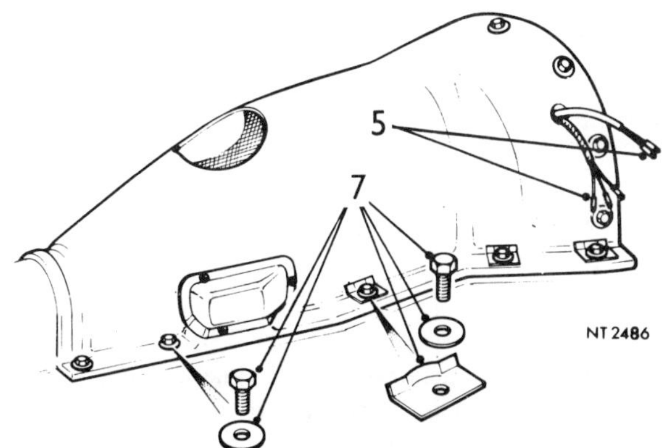

Removing

1. Remove the seats 76.70.04/76.70.05.
2. Remove the fascia support bracket 76.46.09.
3. Remove the front gearbox cover carpet 76.49.01.
4. Remove the rear gearbox cover carpet 76.49.05.
5. Disconnect the snap connectors (two on non-overdrive, five on overdrive models).
6. Remove the gear lever 37.16.04.
7. Remove the seventeen bolts and washers securing the cover to the floor and bulkhead.
8. Break the seal between the cover, floor and bulkhead and manoeuvre the cover over the gearbox.

Refitting

9. Apply Seelastik SR51 to mating surfaces of seals, cover, floor and bulkhead.
10. Reverse instructions 1 to 8.

DOOR

– Remove and refit **76.28.01**

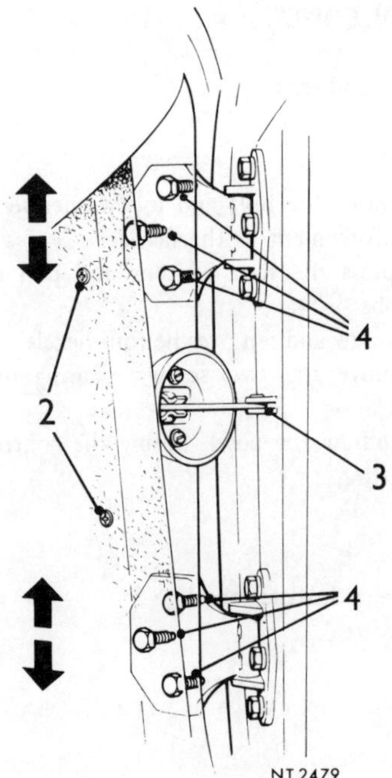

Removing

1. Isolate the battery.
2. Remove the three screws securing the dash side carpet to the 'A' post.
3. Remove the door check strap 76.40.27.
4. Support the door and remove the six bolts and washers securing the hinges to the 'A' post.

Refitting

5. Reverse instructions 1 to 4. Check the door closing action and adjust vertical alignment if necessary before fully tightening bolts 4.

NOTE: If adjustment in the lateral plane is required, refer to operation 76.28.42 instruction 3.

DOOR HINGES

– Remove and refit **76.28.42**

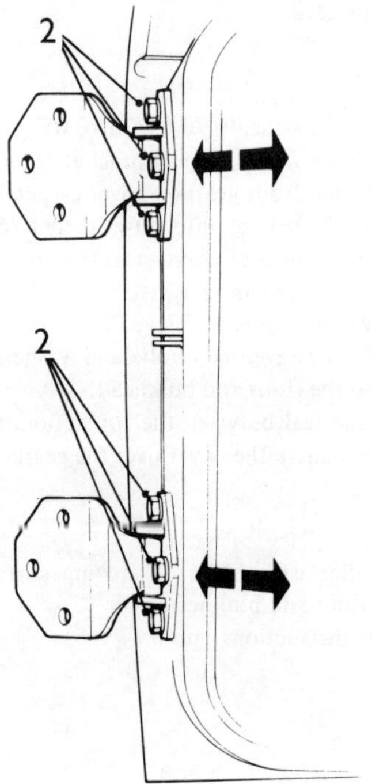

Removing

1. Remove the door 76.28.01
2. Remove the six bolts and washers securing the hinges to the door.

Refitting

3. Reverse instructions 1 and 2. Check door closing action and adjust lateral alignment if necessary before fully tightening bolts 2.

DOOR GLASS

– Remove and refit **76.31.01**

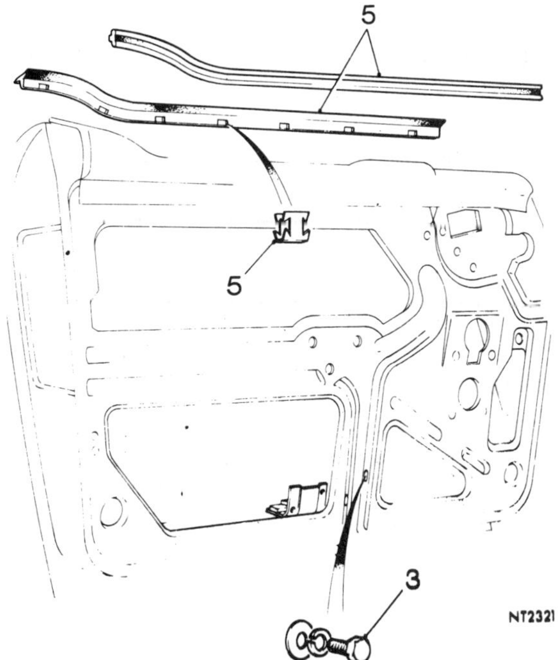

Removing

1. Remove the door trim pad 76.34.01.
2. Remove the door glass regulator 76.31.45.
3. Remove the two bolts and washers and push the glass stop to one side.
4. Fully lower the glass.
5. Detach the inner and outer door waist seals from the clips.
6. Carefully lift out the glass.

NOTE: Avoid scratching the glass on the seal clips during removal.

Refitting

7. Reverse instructions 1 to 6.

DOOR GLASS REGULATOR

– Remove and refit **76.31.45**

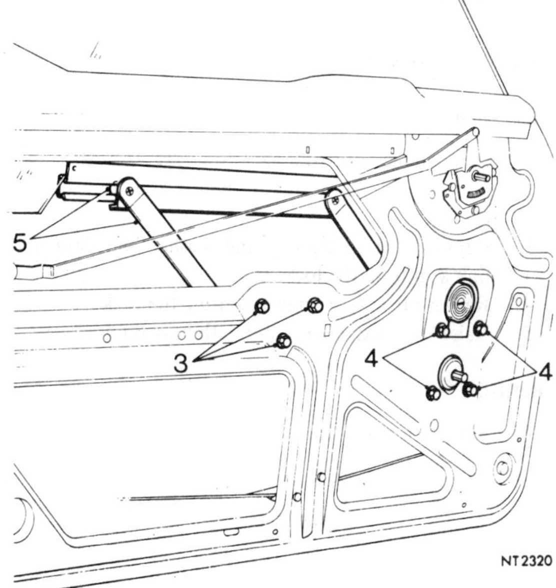

Removing

1. Remove the door trim pad.76.34.01.
2. Loosely refit the window winder handle and move the glass to the half open position.
3. Remove the three bolts and washers securing the bracket to the door.
4. Remove the four bolts and washers securing the mechanism to the door.
5. Support the glass and slide the regulator to release the studs from the glass lifting channel.
6. Withdraw the regulator from the door.

Refitting

7. Reverse instructions 1 to 6.

DOOR TRIM PAD

– Remove and refit **76.34.01**

Removing

1. Depress the bezel and press out the pin.
2. Remove the window winder handle and bezel.
3. Depress the bezel and press out the pin.
4. Remove the remote control handle and bezel.
5. Prise out the two buttons.
6. Remove the two screws and washers.
7. Prise off the trim pad – 15 clips.

Refitting

8. Reverse instructions 1 to 7, ensuring that the springs are in position on the window winder and remote control handle shafts before refitting the trim pad.

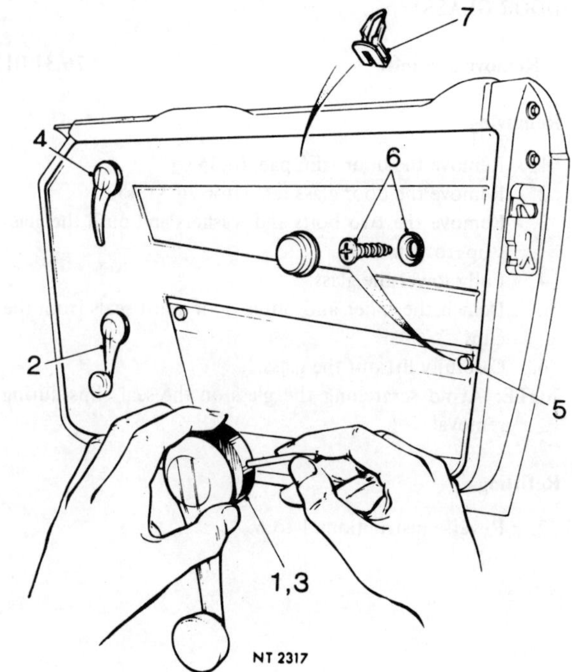

DOOR LOCK

– Remove and refit **76.37.12**

Removing

1. Remove the door trim pad. 76.34.01.
2. Loosely refit the regulator handle and fully raise the glass.
3. Remove the spring clip and washer and detach the link arm from the lock.
4. Remove the three screws securing the lock.
5. Raise the locking lever and withdraw the lock.

Refitting

6. Reverse instructions 1 to 5.

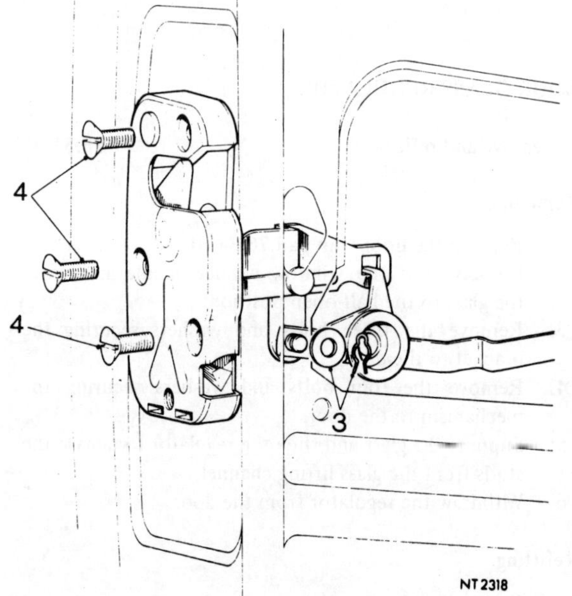

DOOR LOCK STRIKER

– Remove and refit **76.37.23**

Removing

1. Remove the three screws and lift off the striker.

Refitting

2. Reverse the above, adjusting if necessary to ensure correct door closing action.

DOOR LOCK REMOTE CONTROL

– **Remove and refit** **76.37.31**

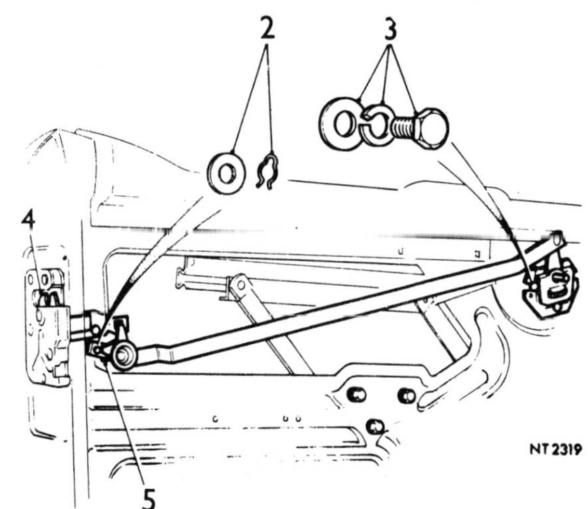

Removing

1. Remove the door trim pad 76.34.01.
2. Remove the spring clip and washer and detach the link arm from the lock.
3. Remove the three bolts and washers and lift off the remote control.

Refitting

4. Set the latch claw in the fully locked position as shown.
5. Reverse instructions 2 and 3. Position the unit so that the spring loaded lever just contacts the spring before tightening the three bolts.
6. Refit the trim pad 76.34.01.

DOOR PRIVATE LOCK

– **Remove and refit** **76.37.39**

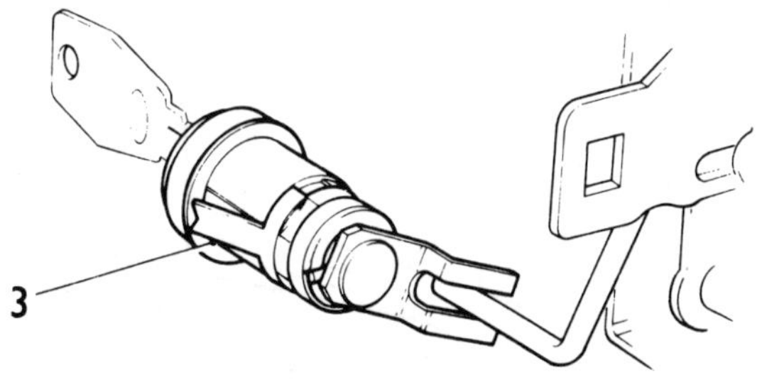

Removing

1. Remove the door trim pad. 76.34.01.
2. Loosely refit the regulator handle and fully raise the glass.
3. Using a suitable tool, compress the collar legs and withdraw the lock from the outside of the door.

Refitting

4. Press the lock into position ensuring that the collar legs are engaged inside the door and the operating fork is located on the door lock control rod.
5. Refit the door trim pad. 76.34.01.

DOOR CHECK STRAP

– **Remove and refit** **76.40.27**

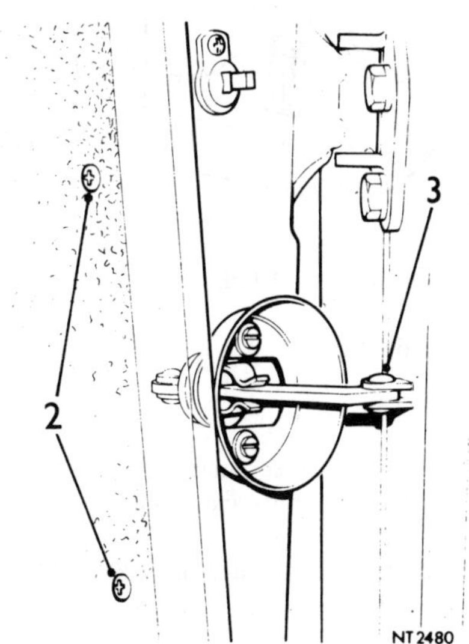

Removing

1. Isolate the battery.
2. Remove the three screws securing the dash side carpet to the 'A' post.
3. Drill out the rivet and remove the check strap.

Refitting

4. Reverse instructions 1 to 3.

FASCIA – VENEERED

– Remove and refit **76.46.01**

Removing

1. Isolate the battery.
2. Remove the speedometer 88.30.01.
3. Remove the tachometer 88.30.21.
4. Remove the two screws securing the glovebox lid to the check link.
5. Remove the five screws and cup washers securing the veneered fascia to the metal fascia.
6. Carefully lower the fascia to the service position to obtain access to the rear.
7. Pull off the rheostat knob.
8. Remove the windscreen wiper switch 86.65.38.
9. Remove the windscreen washer switch 86.65.40.
10. Remove the hazard warning light switch (if fitted) 86.65.50.
11. Pull out the hazard warning light indicator bulb holder (if fitted).
12. Pull out the brake line failure indicator bulb holder (if fitted).
13. Unscrew the nut securing the pipe to the oil gauge and pull out the bulb holder.
14. Disconnect the two Lucar connectors from the temperature gauge and pull out the bulb holder.
15. Disconnect the two Lucar connectors from the fuel gauge and pull out the bulb holder.
16. Pull out the bulb holder from the seat belt warning light (if fitted).
17. Disconnect the two Lucar connectors from the rheostat.
18. Disconnect the two Lucar connectors from the ammeter and pull out the bulb holder.
19. Remove the fascia from the car.

Refitting

20. Reverse instructions 1 to 19. Refer to Fascia Connections 86.00.01, to ensure correct reconnection of Lucar connectors.

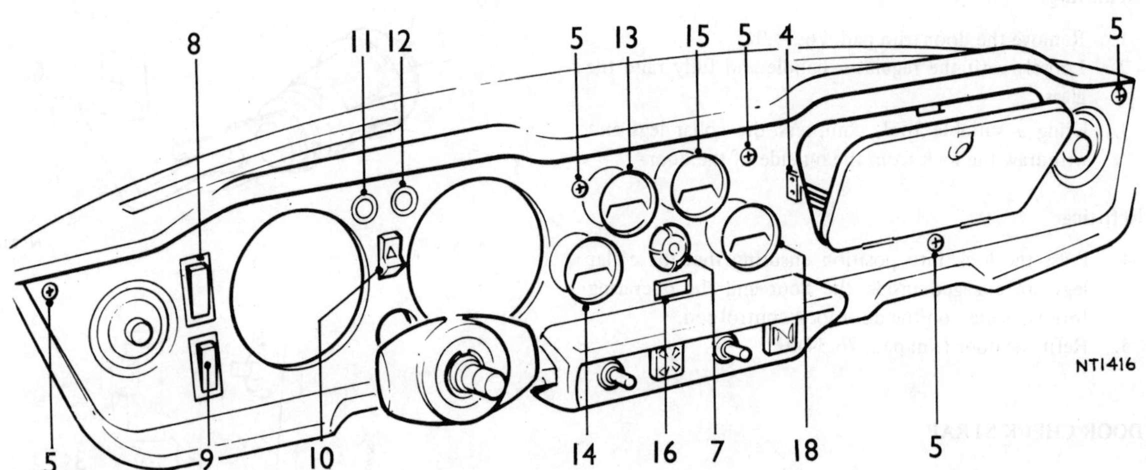

FASCIA CRASH PAD – UPPER

– Remove and refit **76.46.04**

Removing

1. Remove the veneered fascia 76.46.01.
2. Remove the five nuts and washers securing the metal fascia to the crash pad.
3. Remove the two demister ducts 80.15.03.
4. Remove the windscreen frame 76.81.02.
5. Remove the crash pad.

Refitting

6. Apply S758 adhesive to mating surfaces of the crash pad and the bulkhead panel.
7. Reverse instructions 1 to 5.

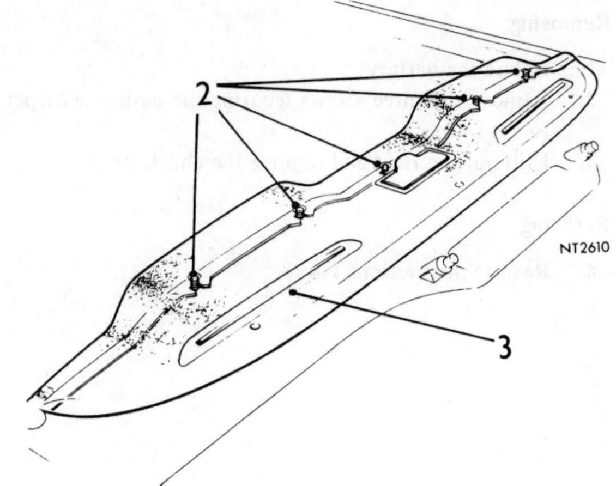

FASCIA SUPPORT BRACKET

– Remove and refit **76.46.09**

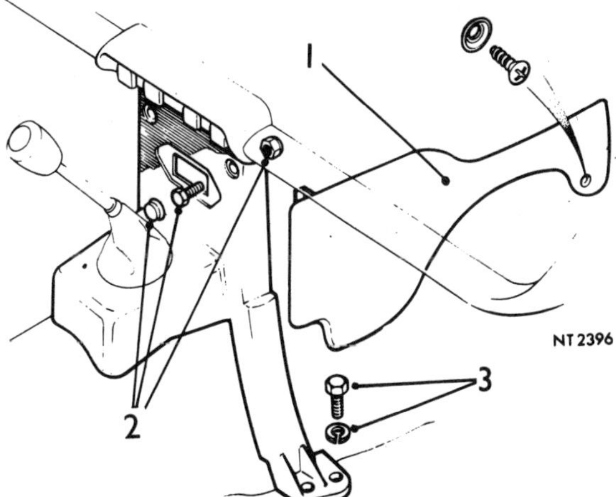

Removing

1. Remove the gearbox cover side trim pads 76.13.06.
2. Prise off the caps and remove the two nuts and bolts.
3. Remove the four bolts and washers securing the bracket to the floor.
4. Lift off the bracket.

Refitting

5. Reverse instructions 1 to 4.

FASCIA – METAL

– Remove and refit **76.46.10**

Removing

1. Remove the veneered fascia 76.46.01.
2. Remove the steering column 57.40.01.
3. Remove the two screws and washers securing the reinforcement bracket to the fascia.
4. Remove the control cowl 76.25.02.
5. Remove the fascia support bracket 76.46.09.
6. Slacken the two clips and disconnect the cold air hoses from the 'Y' pieces.
7. Pull the snap connector from the glovebox lamp switch and pull out the bulbholder.
8. Remove the buzzer (if fitted) 86.55.13.
9. Remove the two bolts and washers securing the fascia to the 'A' post.
10. Remove the five nuts and washers securing the fascia to the upper crash pad.
11. Remove the fascia from the car.

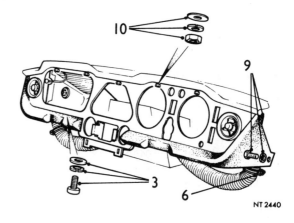

Refitting

12. Reverse instructions 1 to 11.

FASCIA CRASH PAD – LOWER

– Remove and refit **76.46.12**

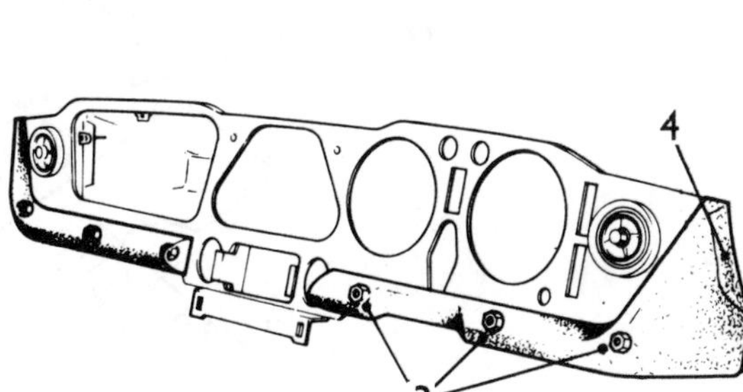
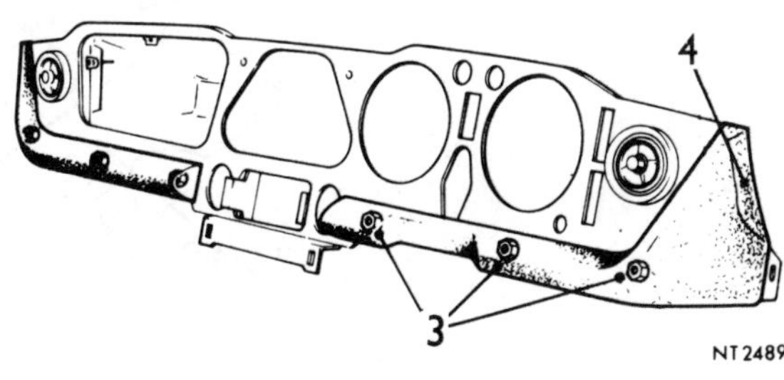

Removing

1. Remove the veneered fascia 76.46.01.
2. Remove the metal fascia 76.46.10.
3. Remove the three nuts and lock washers.
4. Pull the overlapping material away from the fascia and remove the crash pad.

Refitting

5. Reverse instructions 1 to 4, securing the material overlap to the fascia with Dunlop S758 adhesive.

CARPET – FRONT – GEARBOX COVER

– Remove and refit **76.49.01**

Removing

1. Remove the gearbox cover side trim side pads 76.13.06.
2. Remove the carpet – four fasteners.

Refitting

3. Reverse instructions 1 and 2.

CARPET – FRONT FLOOR

– Remove and refit **76.49.02**

The front floor carpets are each secured by four fasteners.

CARPET – REAR FLOOR

– Remove and refit **76.49.03**

Removing

1. Remove the seat 76.70.04/05.
2. Remove the seat runners 76.73.05.
3. Lift off the carpet.

Refitting

4. Reverse instructions 1 to 3.

CARPET – REAR – GEARBOX COVER

– Remove and refit **76.49.05**

Removing

1. Remove the fascia support bracket 76.46.09.
2. Lift off the carpet.

Refitting

3. Reverse instructions 1 and 2.

CARPET – TRANSMISSION TUNNEL

– Remove and refit **76.49.06**

Removing

1. Remove the transmission tunnel lamp 86.45.20.
2. Lift the carpet off over the handbrake lever.

Refitting

3. Reverse instructions 1 and 2.

CARPET – HEELBOARD AND SEAT PAN

– Remove and refit **76.49.07**

Removing

1. Remove the trim pad 76.13.20.
2. Lift off the carpet.

Refitting

3. Reverse instructions 1 and 2.

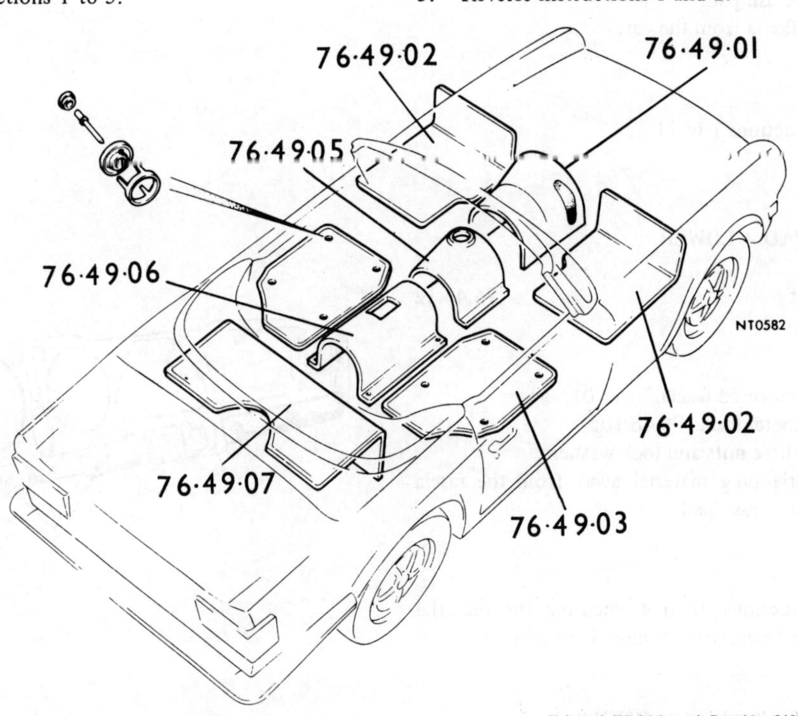

GLOVEBOX LID ASSEMBLY

– Remove and refit **76.52.02**

Removing

1. Remove the two screws securing the check link to the fascia.
2. Support the lid and remove the four screws securing the lid to the hinges. Remove the lid.

Refitting

3. Reverse instructions 1 and 2.

GLOVEBOX

– Remove and refit **76.52.03**

Removing

1. Isolate the battery.
2. Detach the bulb holder and snap connector from the glovebox.
3. Remove the fascia reinforcement bracket – one bolt and two screws.
4. Slacken the clip and disconnect the cold air hose from the heater.
5. Remove the two screws securing the floor level vent to the fascia.
6. Pull the cold air hoses and 'Y' piece away from the glovebox.
7. Remove the six screws securing the glovebox to the fascia.
8. Carefully push the glovebox downwards and remove it from beneath the fascia.

Refitting

9. Reverse instructions 1 to 8.

GLOVEBOX LOCK

– Remove and refit **76.52.08**

Removing

1. Remove the retainer – one screw and washer
2. Withdraw the lock.

Refitting

3. Reverse instructions 1 and 2.

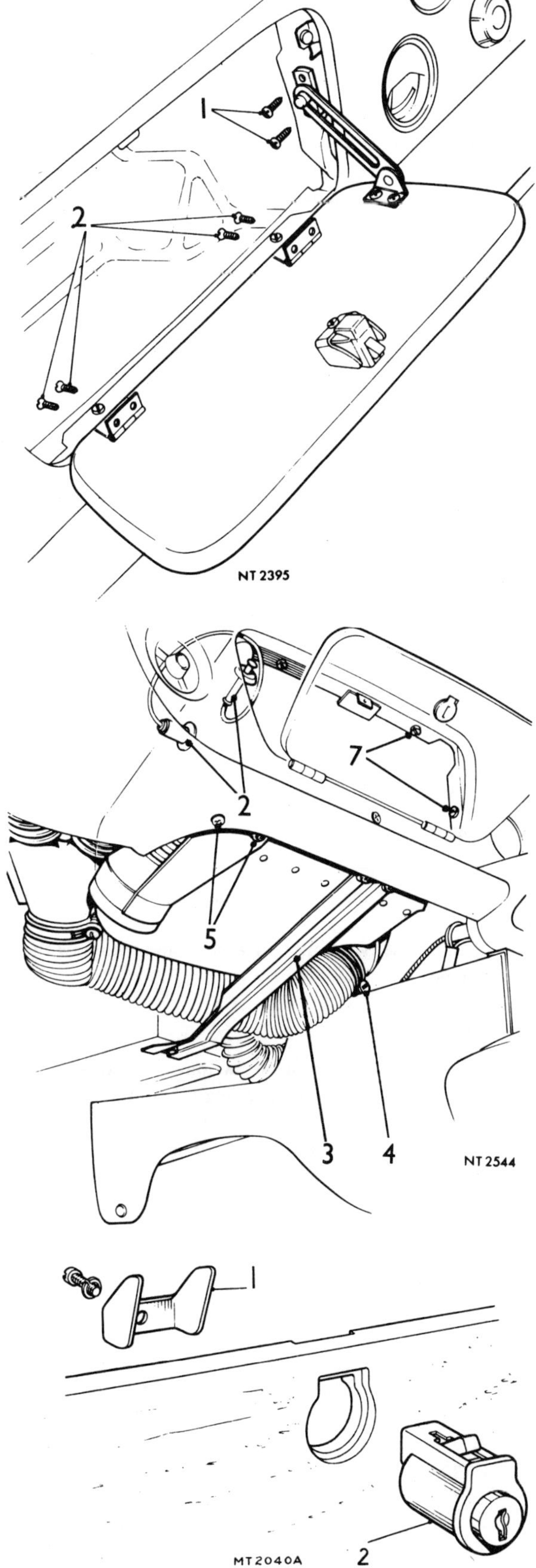

GRILLE FRONT

– Remove and refit **76.55.03**

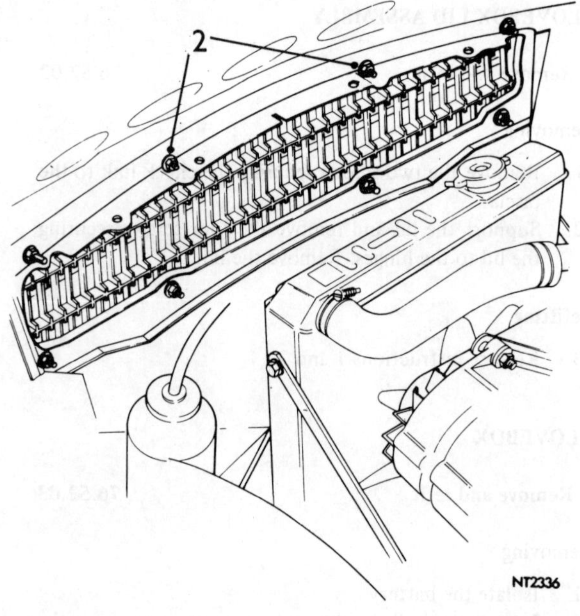

Removing

1. Remove the air intake valance 76.79.04.
2. Remove the eight nuts and washers and withdraw the grille assembly complete with motif.

Refitting

3. Reverse instructions 1 and 2

DOOR HANDLE

– Remove and refit **76.58.01**

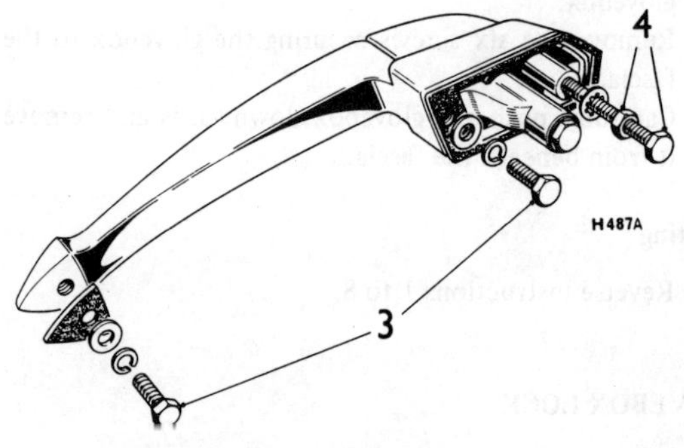

Removing

1. Remove the door trim pad 76.34.01.
2. Loosely refit the regulator handle and fully raise the glass.
3. Remove the two bolts and washers and withdraw the handle.

Refitting

4. Adjust the push button action if necessary by slackening the locknut, screwing the bolt in or out as required, then retightening the locknut.
5. Reverse instructions 1 to 3 ensuring that the seating washers are in position.

HARDTOP

– Remove and refit 76.61.01

Removing

1. Remove the two bolts and washers securing the roof to the header rail.
2. Remove the two bolts and washers securing the side bracket to the tie bar.
3. Remove the two bolts and washers securing the rear end to the rear deck.
4. Lift off the hardtop.

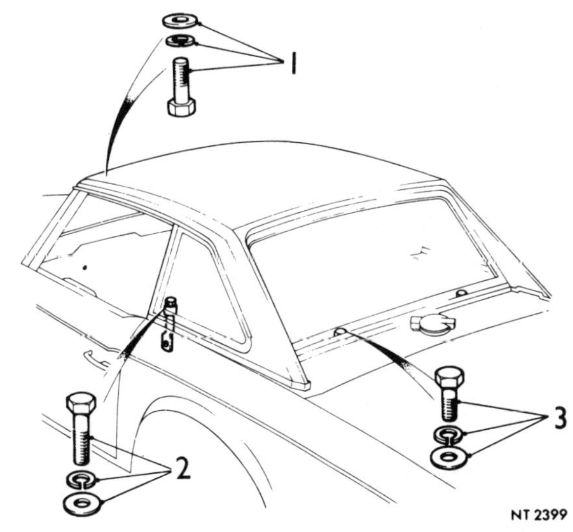

Refitting

5. Reverse instructions 1 to 4.

HOOD ASSEMBLY

– Remove and refit 76.61.08

Removing

1. Release the catch levers.
2. Disconnect the six fasteners.
3. Remove the five bolts and washers securing the angle bracket to the rear deck.
4. Remove the six screws securing the mounting brackets to the body.
5. Lift off the hood assembly.

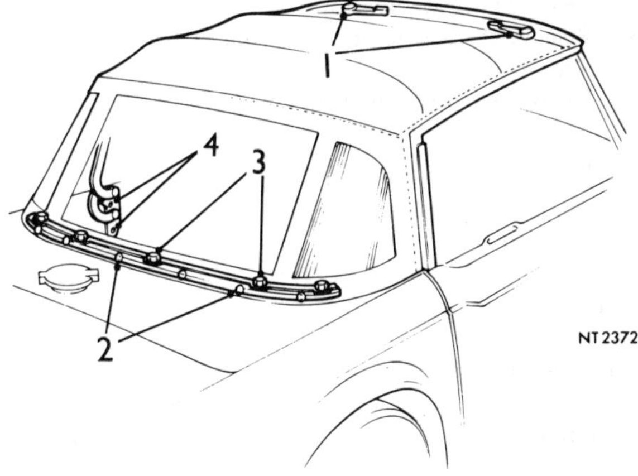

Refitting

6. Reverse instructions 1 to 5.

ASHTRAY

– Remove and refit 76.67.13

Removing

1. Pull the ashtray bowl out of the mounting bracket.
2. Straighten the mounting bracket legs and pull the bracket clear.

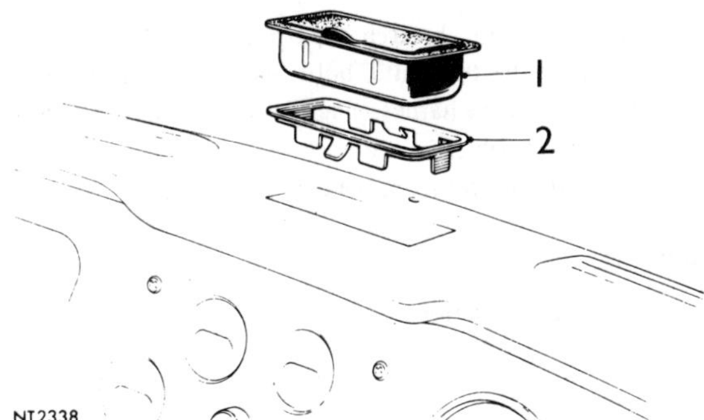

Refitting

3. Place the bracket in the ashtray aperture.
4. Bend the mounting bracket legs to secure it to the fascia.
5. Press the ashtray bowl into the mounting bracket.

SEAT CUSHION COVER

– Remove and refit **76.70.02**

Removing

1. Remove the seat 76.70.04/05.
2. Remove the cushion cover – eight clips.

Refitting

3. Reverse instructions 1 and 2.

SEAT SQUAB COVER

– Remove and refit **76.70.03**

Removing

1. Remove the seat 76.70.04/05.
2. Remove the seat catch 76.70.27.
3. Remove the seat reclining adjustment handle – one screw.
4. Pull off the cover – four clips.

Refitting

5. Reverse instructions 1 to 4.

SEATS

– Remove and refit

– Drivers seat **76.70.04**

– Passengers seat **76.70.05**

Removing

1. Release the squab catch and tip the seat forward.
2. Remove the two nuts, bolts and four plain washers.
3. Disconnect the harness plug (Passengers seat on U.S.A. post 1972 vehicles only)
4. Remove the seat from the car.

Refitting

5. Reverse instructions 1 to 4.

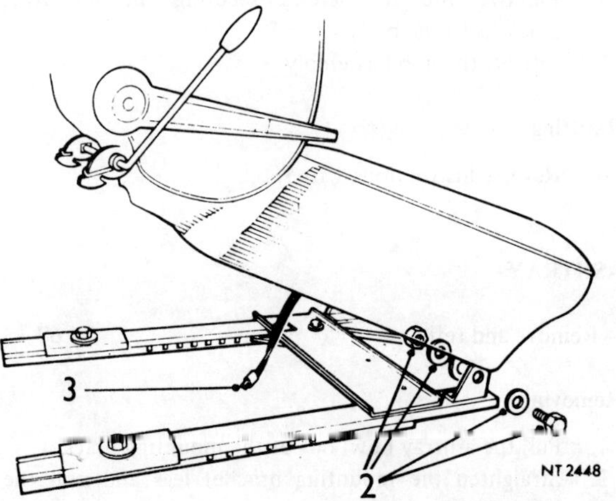

SEAT RUNNERS

– Remove and refit 76.70.21

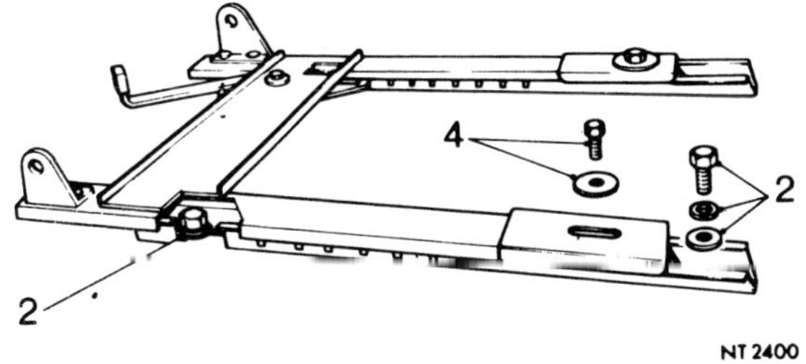

Removing

1. Remove the seat 76.70.04/05.
2. Remove the four bolts and washers.
3. Remove the seat runners.

Refitting

4. Reverse instructions 1 to 3. Adjust the catch plates if necessary, to ensure correct engagement of the seat squab catch.

SEAT SQUAB CATCH

– Remove and refit 76.70.27

The seat squab catch is secured to the seat frame by four screws, spring washers and plain washers.

SEAT BELTS – STATIC (EXCEPT U.S.A. MODELS)

– Remove and refit 76.73.02

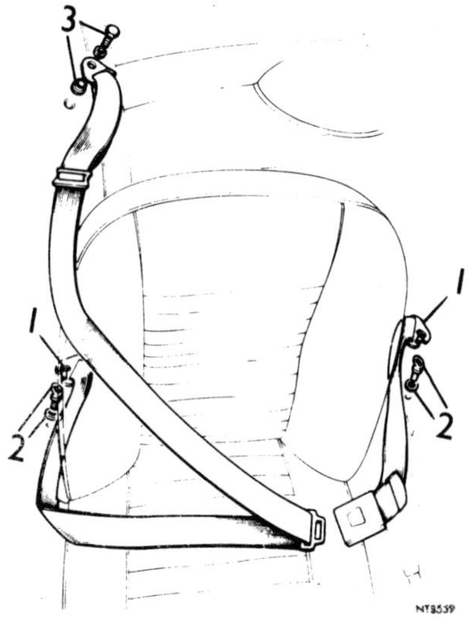

Removing

1. Disconnect the seat belts from the floor and 'B' post mountings.
2. Remove the eye bolts and plain washers.
3. Remove the two bolts, spring washers and spacers securing the swivel bracket to the wheelarch.

Refitting

4. Reverse instructions 1 to 3, ensuring that the swivel bracket is left free to swivel.

SEAT BELTS – AUTOMATIC (U.S.A. MODELS)

– Remove and refit 76.73.10

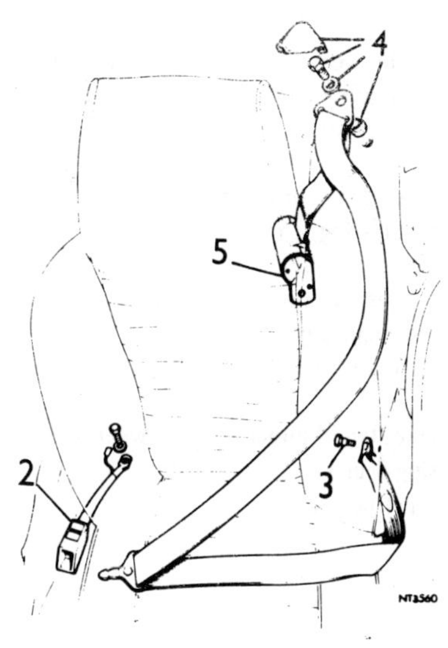

Removing

1. Isolate the battery.
2. Remove the buckle unit. 86.65.31/2.
3. Remove the bolt securing the swivel bracket to the 'B' post.
4. Remove the cap, bolt, plain washer, cover and spacer securing the swivel bracket to the wheelarch.
5. Remove the bolt securing the reel to the body.

Refitting

6. Reverse instructions 1 to 5, ensuring that the swivel brackets are left free to swivel.

VALANCE – AIR INTAKE

– Remove and refit **76.79.04**

Removing

1. Disconnect the overflow pipe from the radiator filler neck.
2. Slacken the two nuts securing the stay rods to the wheel arches.
3. a. (Carburetter vehicles) Remove the four bolts and washers.
   b. (P.I. vehicles) Remove the three bolts and washers.
   c. (P.I. vehicles) remove the nut and washer securing the air cleaner support strap.
4. Lift out the valance.

Refitting

5. Reverse instructions 1 to 4.

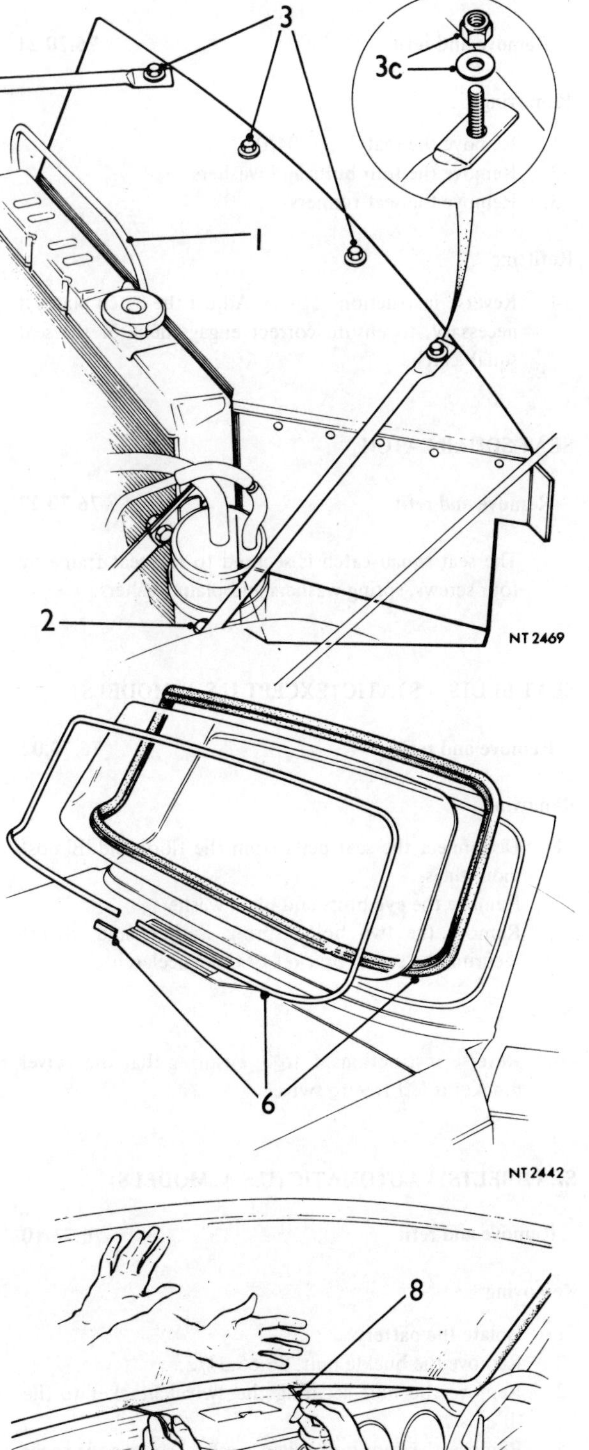

WINDSCREEN

– Remove and refit **76.81.01**

Removing

1. Remove the wiper arms 84.15.01.
2. Remove the interior mirror.
3. Remove the sun visors.
4. Break the seal, using a suitably blunt tool.
5. Push the glass outwards.

CAUTION: Take care to avoid scratching the glass, which must be steadied by an assistant.

6. Remove the finisher moulding, clip and weatherstrip noting positions for refitting.

Refitting

7. Assemble the weatherstrip finisher moulding and clip to the glass, using a new weatherstrip if necessary and applying Seelastik to the glass channel before fitting.
8. Insert a strong cord into the weatherstrip inner channel, allowing the ends to protrude from the lower edge.
9. Have an assistant position the glass centrally in the frame and maintain a steady pressure whilst the cord ends are pulled to locate the weatherstrip on the body flange.
10. Seal the outer channel of the weatherstrip to the body using Seelastik.
11. Reverse instructions 1 to 3.

WINDSCREEN FRAME ASSEMBLY

– Remove and refit 76.81.02

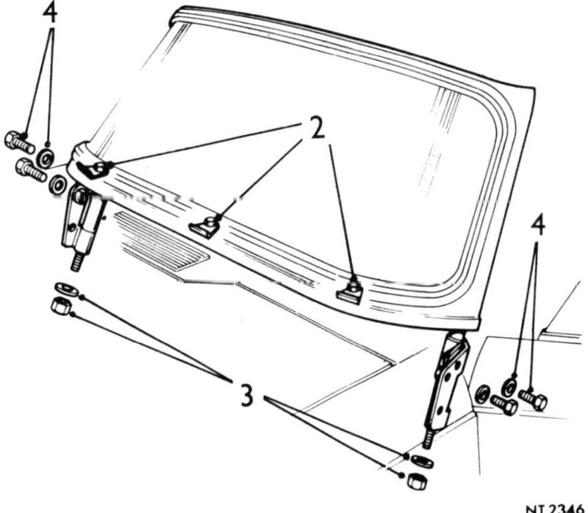

Removing

1. Pull the weatherstrip away from the screen pillars.
2. Remove the three bolts and cover plates.
3. Remove the two nuts and washers from the screen pillars.
4. Slacken the six nuts and bolts securing the screen pillar mounting brackets.
5. Lift out the windscreen frame assembly.

Refitting

6. Remove all traces of sealing compound from mating surfaces of the weatherstrip and scuttle panel and apply new Seal-a-strip.
7. Reverse instructions 1 to 5, ensuring uniform clearance between the door glass and windscreen frame before tightening nuts 4.

HEATING AND VENTILATION OPERATIONS

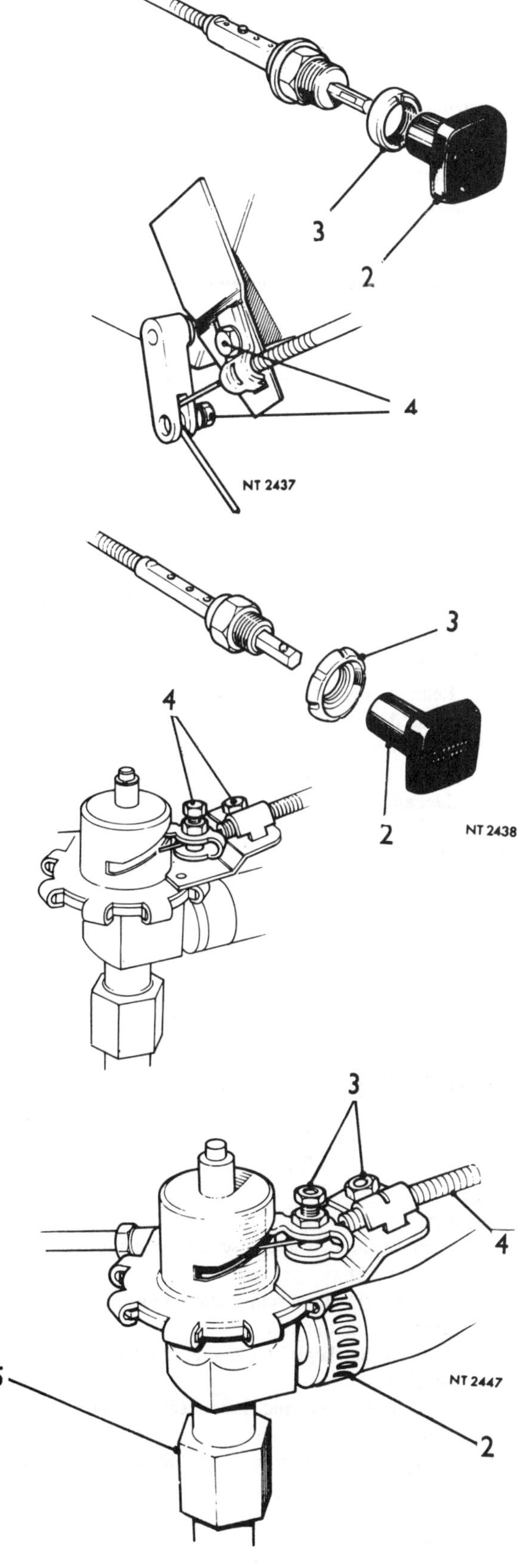

AIR FLOW CONTROL CABLE

– Remove and refit **80.10.06**

Removing

1. Remove the gearbox cover trim pad. 76.13.06.
2. Depress the retainer and pull off the control knob.
3. Unscrew the bezel.
4. Slacken the trunnion bolt and cable clamp bolt.
5. Remove the cable.

Refitting

6. Reverse instructions 1 to 5, ensuring that the cable is positioned to allow full operation of the flap valve.

WATER VALVE CONTROL CABLE

– Remove and refit **80.10.07**

Removing

1. Remove the gearbox cover side trim panel 76.13.06.
2. Depress the retainer and pull off the control knob.
3. Unscrew the bezel.
4. Slacken the trunnion bolt and cable clamp bolt.
5. Withdraw the cable.

Refitting

6. Reverse instructions 1 to 5, ensuring that the cable is positioned to allow full operation of the water valve.

WATER VALVE

– Remove and refit **80.10.16**

Removing

1. Drain coolant from the system 26.10.01.
2. Slacken the clip and disconnect the hose.
3. Slacken the trunnion bolt and clamp bolt.
4. Detach the control cable.
5. Unscrew the water valve.

Refitting

6. Reverse instructions 1 to 5 using 'Hermetite' sealing compound on the water valve threads.

DEMISTER HOSES

– Remove and refit **80.15.01**

Removing

1. Remove the gearbox cover side trim pads 76.13.06.
2. Slacken the two clips and disconnect the hoses from the heater.
3. Remove the glovebox (passenger side hose only) 76.52.03.
4. Pull the hoses from the demister ducts.

Refitting

5. Reverse instructions 1 to 4.

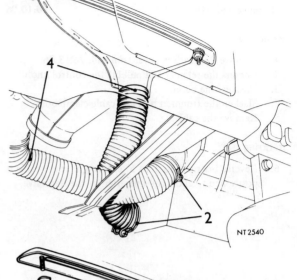

DEMISTER DUCTS

– Remove and refit **80.15.03**

Removing

1. Remove the glovebox (passenger side duct only) 76.52.03.
2. Disconnect the hose from the duct.
3. Remove the two nuts and. washers. Withdraw the duct and lift off the finisher.

Refitting

4. Reverse instructions 1 to 3.

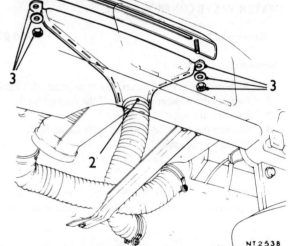

SWIVELLING COLD AIR VENTS

– Remove and refit – L.H. **80.15.22**
–R.H. **80.15.23**

Removing

1. Remove the two screws securing the support bracket to the fascia.
2. Slacken the hose clip and remove the vent and bracket from the hose.
3. Slacken the clamp bolt and remove the vent from the bracket.
4. Slacken the clip and disconnect the hose from the vent.
5. Compress the three retaining lugs and withdraw the vent and sealing ring.

Refitting

6. Reverse instructions 1 to 5.

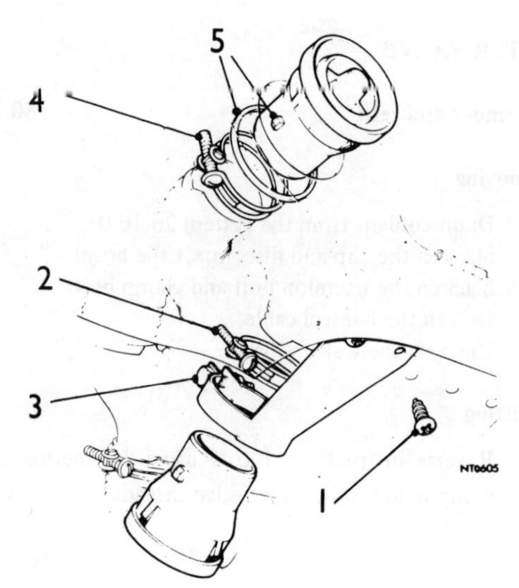

HEATER UNIT

– Remove and refit **80.20.01**

Removing

1. Drain the coolant 26.10.01.
2. Disconnect the hose from the water valve and blow through it to expel coolant from the heater matrix.
3. Remove the veneered fascia 76.46.01.
4. Remove the glovebox 76.52.03.
5. Remove the gearbox tunnel cover trim pads 76.13.06.
6. Slacken the clips and disconnect the four ventilation hoses from the heater.
7. Slacken the clips and disconnect the two water hoses from the heater.
8. Slacken the trunnion bolt and clamp bolt securing the flow control cable to the heater. Detach the cable.
9. Disconnect the two Lucar connectors from the blower switch.
10. Remove the nut securing the blower earht lead to the steering column.
11. Remove the nut and washers securing the heater to the bulkhead.
12. Support the heater and remove the three bolts, washers and spacers securing it to the plenum chamber.
13. Remove the heater from the car taking care to avoid spillage of coolant from the matrix.

Refitting

14. Reverse instructions 1 to 13.

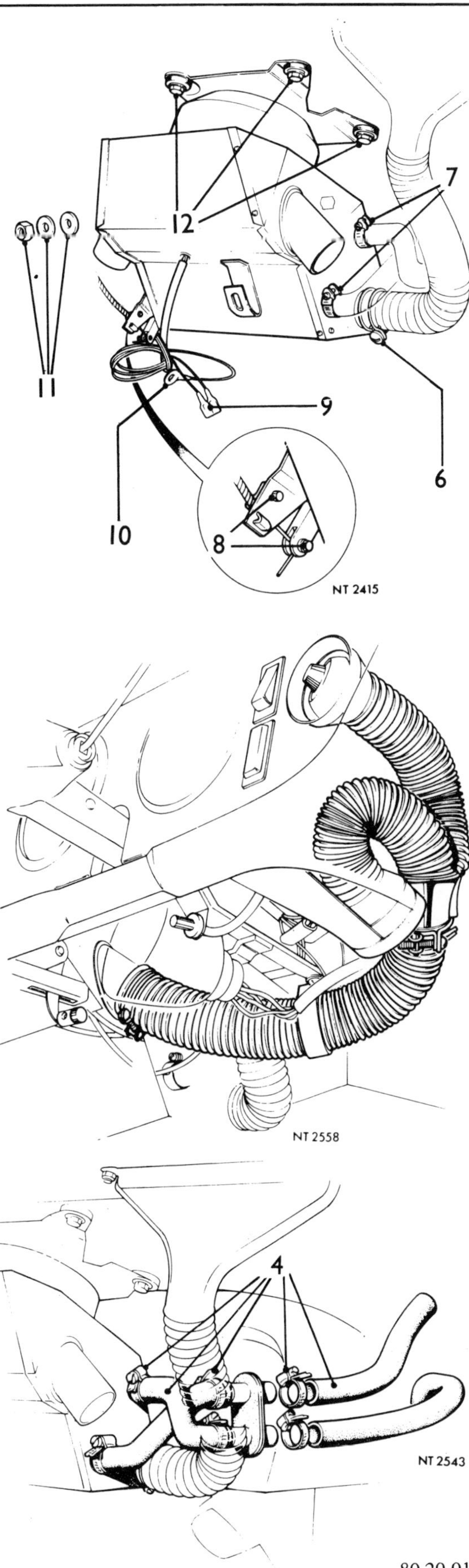

COLD AIR HOSES

– Remove and refit **80.25.01**

The cold air hoses are each secured by two clips. Remove the gearbox cover trim pads 76.13.06 to facilitate access to hoses connected to the heater unit.

WATER HOSES

– Remove and refit

Hoses – heater to engine **80.25.07**
Hoses – water valve to heater **80.25.09**

Removing

1. Drain the cooling system 26.10.01.
2. Remove the glovebox tunnel cover trim pad 76.13.06.
3. Remove the glovebox 76.52.03.
4. Slacken the clips and remove the hoses.

Refitting

5. Reverse instructions 1 to 4.

HEATER UNIT

Remove and refit 80.20.01

Removing

1. Drain the coolant 26.10.01.
2. Disconnect the hose from the water valve and blow through it to expel coolant from the heater matrix.
3. Remove the ventilated fascia 76.46.01.
4. Remove the glovebox 76.52.03.
5. Remove the gearbox tunnel cover trim pads 76.13.06.
6. Slacken the clips and disconnect the four ventilation hoses from the heater.
7. Slacken the clips and disconnect the two water hoses from the heater.
8. Slacken the trunnion bolt and clamp bolt securing the flow control cable to the heater. Detach the cable.
9. Disconnect the two Lucar connectors from the blower switch.
10. Remove the nut securing the blower earth lead to the steering column.
11. Remove the nut and washers securing the heater to the bulkhead.
12. Support the heater and remove the three bolts, washers and spacers securing it to the plenum chamber.
13. Remove the heater from the car taking care to avoid spillage of coolant from the matrix.

Refitting

14. Reverse instructions 1 to 13.

COLD AIR HOSES

Remove and refit 80.15.01

The cold air hoses are each secured by two clips. Remove the gearbox cover trim pads 76.13.06 to facilitate access to hoses connected to the heater unit.

WATER HOSES

Remove and refit

Hoses — heater to engine 80.25.07
Hoses — water valve to heater 80.25.09

Removing

1. Drain the cooling system 26.10.01.
2. Remove the gearbox tunnel cover trim pad 76.13.06.
3. Remove the glovebox 76.52.03.
4. Slacken the clips and remove the hoses.

Refitting

5. Reverse instructions 1 to 4.

WINDSCREEN WIPERS AND WASHERS OPERATIONS

WINSCREEN WASHER JET

– Remove and refit **84.10.09**

Removing

1. Use a pair of pliers to grip the metal jet nozzle and carefully pull it from the rubber moulding.
2. Remove the wheelbox spindle nut.
3. Carefully break the seal between the rubber moulding and vehicle body.
4. Carefully withdraw the rubber moulding. Ensure that the plastic tube is not detached from the metal pipe and lost in the body wheelbox cavity as retrieval may be difficult.
5. Pull the plastic tube from the metal pipe.

Refitting

6. Reverse instructions 1 to 5. Seal the rubber moulding to the vehicle body using an approved sealer.

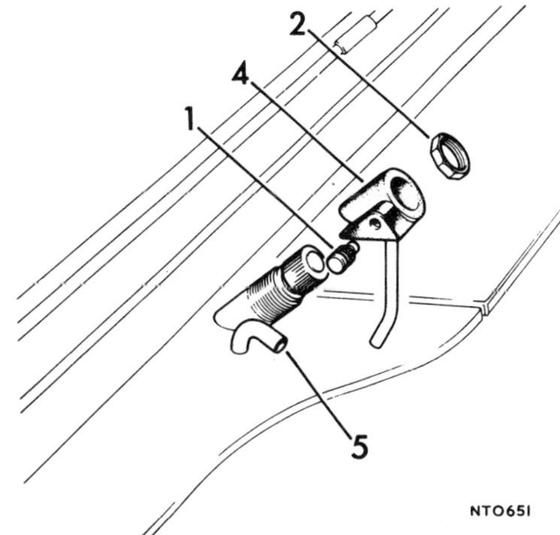

WINDSCREEN WASHER PUMP AND RESERVOIR

– Remove and refit **84.10.21**

Removing

1. Disconnect two Lucar connectors.
2. Early vehicles with Lucas 5SJ unit only – pull off the outlet pipe.
3. Later vehicles with Lucas 9SJ unit only – remove the cover. Pull off the outlet pipe and withdraw it from the cover. Refit the cover.
4. Manoeuvre the unit upwards from the carrier.

Refitting

5. Reverse instructions 1 to 4. To ensure that the motor runs in the correct direction observe polarity. Connect the Lucar connectors as follows:
   Light green/black wire to the positive terminal.
   Black wire to the negative terminal.

WINDSCREEN WASHER PUMP AND RESERVOIR – LUCAS TYPE 5SJ

– Overhaul **84.10.24**

Dismantling

1. Rotate the cover anti-clockwise to release the bayonet fitting. Lift the pump assembly from the reservoir.
2. Remove the screw and lift the motor from its mounting spigots.
3. Remove the coupling.
4. Using a pair of long-nosed pliers to secure the shaft, use a second pair of pliers to withdraw the coupling drive.
5. Remove two screws. Withdraw the bearing plate and rubber gasket.
6. Hold the clamping member in position during operations 7 to 9.
7. Remove the shaft distance tube
8. Remove the two terminal screws, spring washers, connector blades and nuts.
9. Using a pair of long-nosed pliers carefully lift out the two brushes.
10. Lift out the clamping member.
11. Lift out the armature and permanent magnet. Separate the two components against the action of the permanent magnet.

Brushes

12. Clean the brushes with a petrol-moistened cloth.
13. Check the brush length. Renew the brushes if less than the length given in Data.
14. Check that the brushes bear firmly against the commutator. If the pressure is low, renew the brushes.

Commutator

15. Clean the commutator with a petrol-moistened cloth. If the unit is in good condition it will be smooth and free from pits or burned spots. If necessary, polish with fine glass-paper. If excessively worn, replace the armature.

Reassembling

16. Lubricate the motor case bearing by filling the recess with Rocol Molypad molybdenized grease. Wiper excess grease from the boss.
17. Position the permanent magnet. To ensure that the motor runs in the correct direction the narrower pole must be adjacent to the terminal position. Ensure that the poles locate correctly around the circular spigot.
18. Position the clamping member.
19. Hold the clamping member in position during operations 20 to 23.
20. Insert the armature and locate to the motor case bearing against the action of the permanent magnet.
21. Using a pair of long-nosed pliers, carefully position the two brushes. Ensure that the arm ends are inserted in the slits provided in the motor case. To achieve this the brush positions cannot be inter-changed.
22. Fit the two nuts, connector blades, spring washers and terminal screws.
23. Fit the shaft distance tube.
24. Reverse instructions 1 to 5.

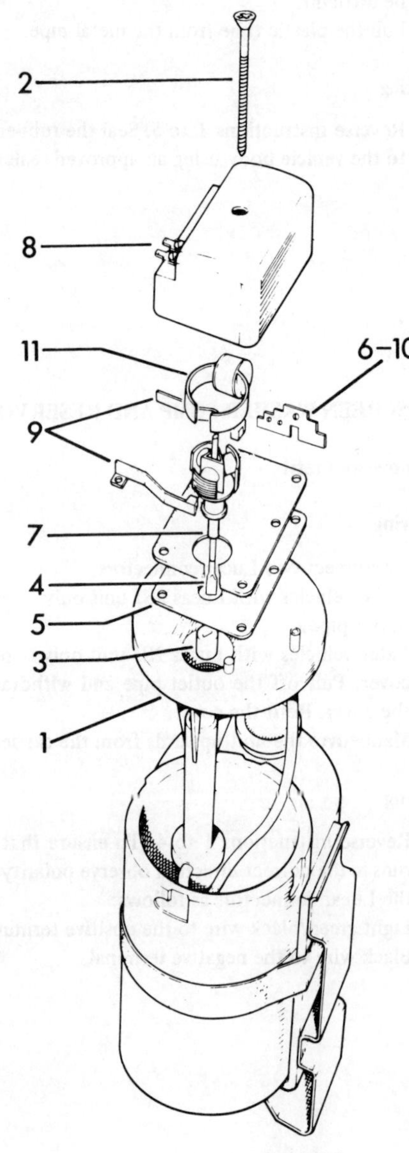

WINDSCREEN WASHER PUMP AND RESERVOIR – LUCAS TYPE 9SJ

– Overhaul 84.10.24

It is not advisable to attempt to overhaul the pump assembly. If the pump operation is suspect repair by replacement of the complete pump and cover assembly.

The motor is a sealed unit and can not be serviced. It is possible to dismantle and clean the interior of the pump as detailed below but no individual Stanpart spare parts are available.

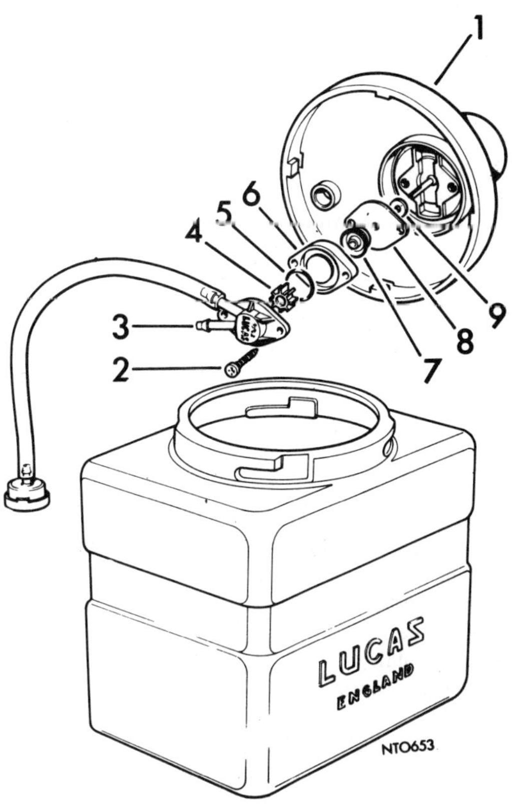

Dismantle

1. Rotate the cover anticlockwise to release the bayonet fitting. Lift the pump and cover assembly from the reservoir.
2. Remove two screws.
3. Lift off the pump housing.
4. Carefully withdraw the rotor and rotor drive plate.
5. Lift out the rubber 'O' ring.
6. Lift off the seal housing.
7. Withdraw the seal from the shaft.
8. Remove the plate.
9. Withdraw the small rubber disc from the shaft.

Assemble

10. Reverse instructions 1 to 9.

WINDSCREEN WIPERS AND WASHERS

WINDSCREEN WIPER SYSTEM

Data and description **84.15.00**

Motor

Manufacturer	Lucas
Type	14W
Lucas Part No.: motor minus gear assembly	75664
gear assembly – R.H. Steer	54702597
– L.H. Steer	54702584
Stanpart No.: motor minus gear assembly	517621
gear assembly – R.H. Steer	517622
– L.H. Steer	517646
Running current – after 60 seconds from cold with connecting rod removed:	
Normal speed	1·5 amp
High speed	2·0 amp
Running speed – final gear after 60 seconds from cold with connecting rod removed:	
Normal speed	46 to 52 rev/min
High speed	60 to 70 rev/min
Armature end-float	0·002 to 0·008 in (0·05 to 0·02 mm)
Brush length – normal speed: new	0·380 in (9·65 mm)
renew if less than	0·180 in (4·76 mm)
high speed: new	0·380 in (9·65 mm)
renew if less than	0·280 in (7·11 mm) (i.e. when narrow section is worn to step into full-width section)
earth: new	0·380 in (9·65 mm)
renew if less than	0·180 in (4·76 mm)
Brush spring pressure – when compressed so brush bottom is aligned with brushbox slot end	5 to 7 oz (140 to 200 g)
Maximum permissible force to move cable rack in tubing – arms and blades removed	6 lb (3 kg)

The unit consists of a two speed permanent magnet motor and a gearbox unit which drives a cable rack mechanism. Rotation of the motor armature is converted to a reciprocating motion of the cable rack by a single stage worm and gear, a connecting rod and a crosshead contained in a guide channel.

Two speed operation is provided by a third brush. When high speed is selected the positive supply is transferred from the normal speed brush to the high speed brush.

A switching feature stops the blades in the park position irrespective of their position when the fascia switch is selected off. This is effected by a two stage limit switch unit attached to the gearbox. The contacts are actuated by a cam on the final gear.

When the fascia switch is selected off the motor will continue to run until the limit switch first stage contacts open. A momentary period follows during which no contact is made. The second stage contacts then close causing regenerative braking of the armature which maintains consistent parking of the blades.

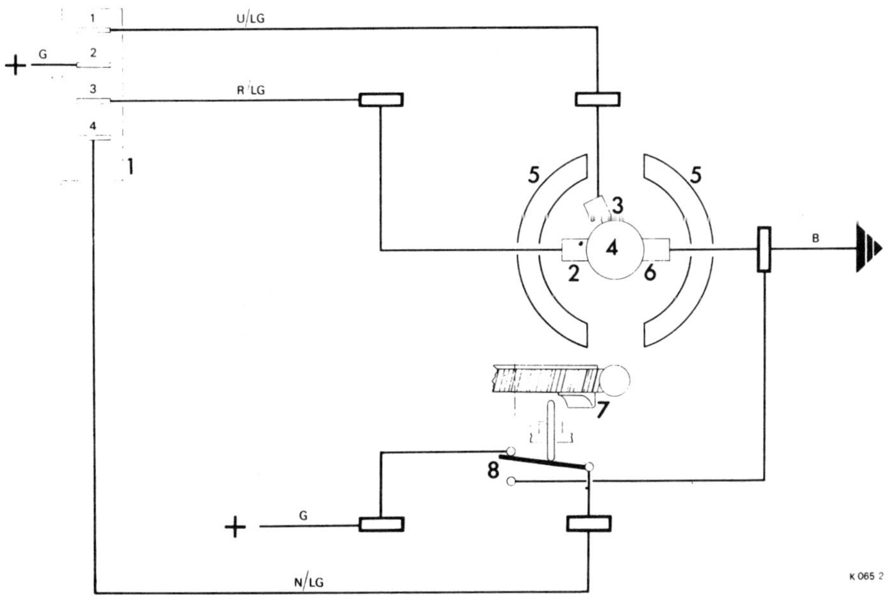

- \+ Supply
- 1 Fascia switch

OFF	3 connected to 4
NORMAL	2 connected to 3
HIGH	2 connected to 1

- 2 Normal speed brush
- 3 High speed brush
- 4 Commutator
- 5 Permanent magnet
- 6 Earth brush
- 7 Final gear cam
- 8 Limit switch unit

Component and switch wiring diagram

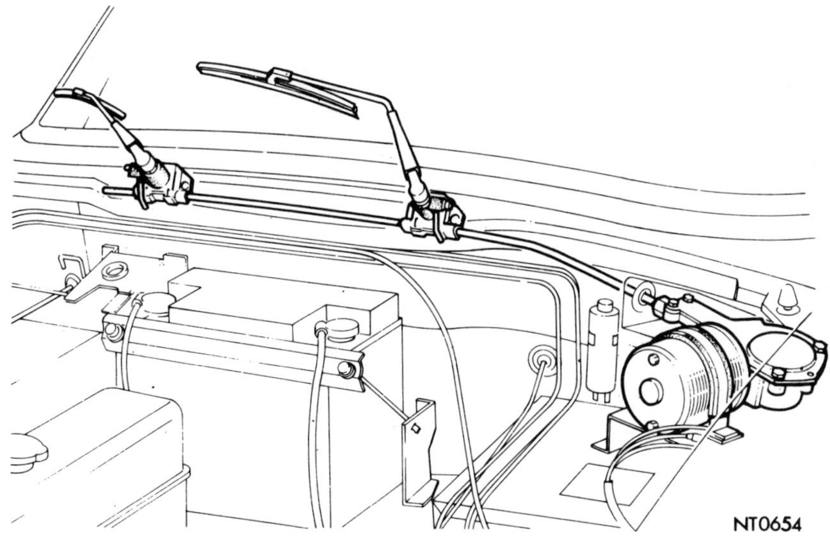

General arrangement

WINDSCREEN WIPER ARM

– Remove and refit **84.15.01**

Removing

1. Lift the wiper arm and blade from the screen so that it falls into its service position.
2. Position a screwdriver as shown and impart a twisting action to lift the clip from the spindle groove.
3. The assembly may now be removed by hand.

Refitting

4. Ensure that the spindles are in the 'park' position.
5. Hinge the wiper arm against the spring to adopt its service position.
6. Locate the splines for a suitable 'park' position. Push on to engage the clip to the spindle groove.
7. Lower the wiper arm to the screen.

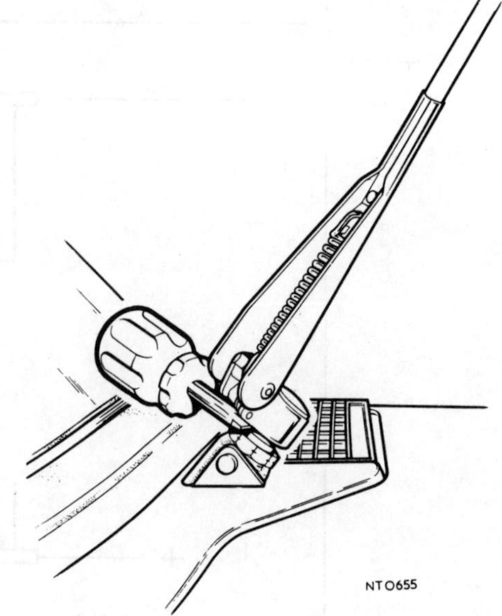

WINSCREEN WIPER BLADE

– Remove and refit **84.15.05**

Removing

1. Lift the wiper arm and blade from the screen so that it falls into its service position.
2. Simultaneously lift the clip 'A', tilt cage 'B' and gently pull the wiper blade from the arm.

Refitting

3. Locate the cage and clip assembly to the wiper arm. Push on to engage 'pip'.
4. Lower the wiper arm to the screen.

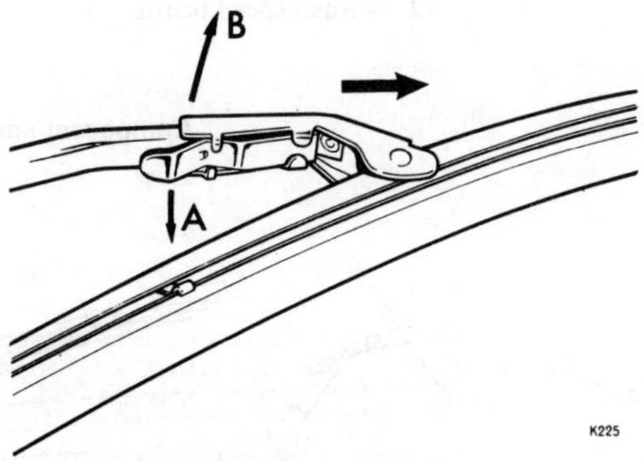

WINDSCREEN WIPER MOTOR

Remove and refit 84.15.12

Removing

1. Remove the harness plug from the limit switch.
2. Remove four screws. Lift off the gearbox cover.
3. Remove the crankpin spring clip by withdrawing sideways.
4. Remove the washer.
5. Carefully withdraw the connecting rod.
6. Remove the washer.
7. Remove two bolts, spring washers and washers. Remove the strap and rubber sleeve. Collect up the rubber pad.
8. Manoeuvre the motor to allow the cross-head, rack and tube assembly to be released. Remove the motor from the vehicle.

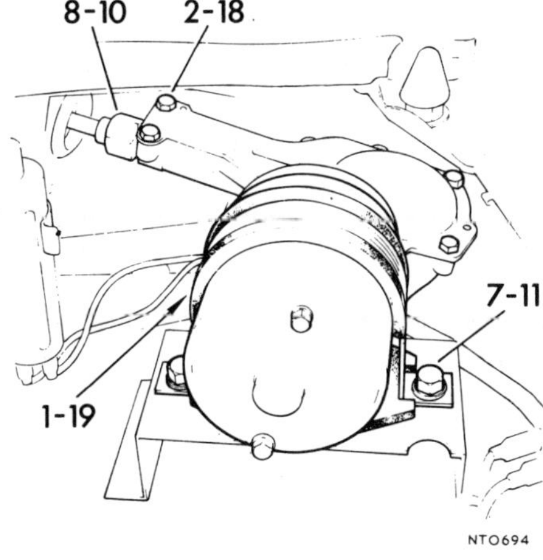

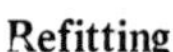

Refitting

9. Ensure that the connecting rod is removed as detailed above.
10. Position the motor so that the cross-head, rack and tube assembly are correctly located to the motor guide channel.
11. Position the rubber pad. Locate the strap and rubber sleeve. Secure with two bolts, spring washers and washers.
12. Fit the washer.
13. Lubricate the final gear crankpin with Shell Turbo 41 oil.
14. Lubricate the cross-head end of the connecting rod, including the pin, with Ragosine Listate grease.
15. Carefully insert the connecting rod.
16. Fit the washer.
17. Fit the spring clip by inserting sideways.
18. Position the gearbox cover. Secure with four screws.
19. Fit the harness plug to the limit switch.

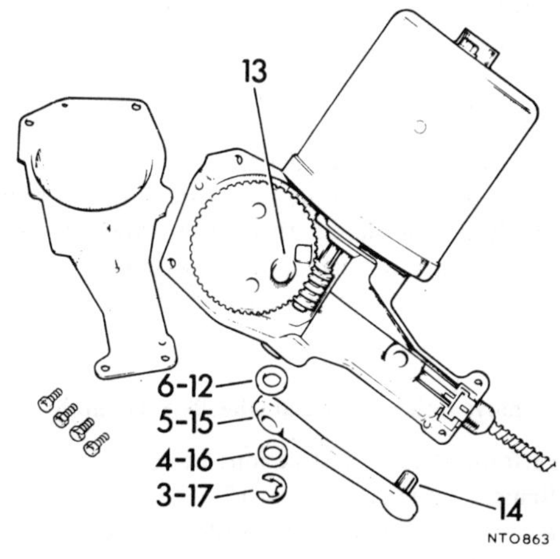

WINDSCREEN WIPER MOTOR

Overhaul 84.15.18

General

If the motor is not operating correctly, check the electrical supply of 12 volts on terminal 5 with normal speed selected and terminal 3 with high speed selected. Also check the electrical earth on terminal 1.

If the electrical supply and the earth is satisfactory, perform the following operations to determine if the fault is in the motor or in the rack, tube and wheelbox assembly, resulting in the motor being required to drive an excessive load.

Running current

1. Perform 84.15.12 instructions 2 to 6.
2. Connect an ammeter suitable for the running current (see data) in the supply circuit.
3. Allow the motor to run for 60 seconds. The ammeter reading should then be as given in data for normal speed and high speed respectively.
4. If the reading is not as stated, a fault in the motor is indicated.

Running speed

5. Perform 84.15.12 instructions 2 to 6.
6. Allow the motor to run for 60 seconds. The speed of the final gear should then be as given in data for normal speed and high speed respectively.
7. If the speed is not as stated, a fault in the motor is indicated.

Force to move rack in tube and wheelbox assembly

8. Perform 84.15.12 instructions 2 to 6.
9. Remove the wiper arms 84.15.01.
10. Attach a suitable spring scale to the hole in the cross-head. The maximum permissible force to move the rack is given in data.
11. If the required force is greater than stated, a fault in the rack, tube and wheelbox assembly is indicated.

Dismantle

12. Perform 84.15.12 instructions 2 to 6.
13. Remove the final gear shaft spring clip by withdrawing sideways. Remove the washer. Ensure that the shaft is burr free and withdraw it. Remove the dished washer.
14. Remove the through bolts.
15. Carefully withdraw the cover and armature about 0·200 in (5 mm). Continue withdrawal allowing the brushes to drop clear of the commutator. Ensure that the brushes are not contaminated with grease.
16. Pull the armature from the cover against the action of the permanent magnet.
17. Remove five screws to release the brush assembly and limit switch unit. Remove both units joined together by the wires.

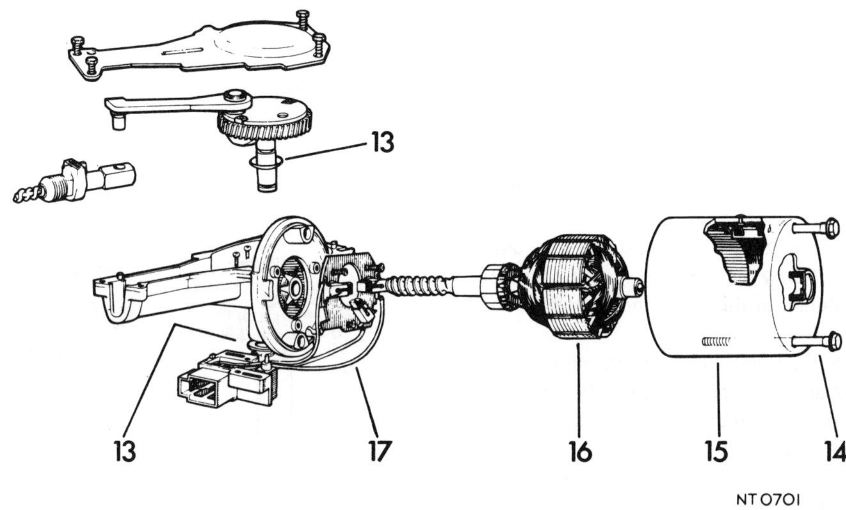

Assemble

Note that the following lubricants are used during assembly:

Shell Turbo 41 oil
Ragosine Listate grease

18. Position the brush assembly and limit switch unit joined together by the wires. Secure with five screws.
19. Lubricate the cover bearing and saturate the cover bearing felt washer with Shell Turbo 41 oil. Position the armature to the cover against the action of the permanent magnet.
20. Lubricate the self aligning bearing with Shell Turbo 41 oil. Carefully insert the armature shaft through the bearing. Ensure that the brushes are not contaminated with lubricant. Push the three brushes back to clear the commutator.
21. Seat the cover against the gearbox. Turn the cover to align the marks shown. Fit the through bolts.
22. Fit the thrust screw or the thrust screw and locknut as fitted.
23. If a non-adjustable thrust screw is fitted check the armature end-float as follows:
    Position a feeler gauge between the armature shaft and the thrust screw.
    Push the armature towards the cover. End-float should be 0·002 to 0·008 in.
    In the unlikely event of adjustment being required end-float may be increased by fitting shim washer/washers under the thrust screw head or reduced by mounting the thrust screw in a lathe and removing metal from the underside of the head.
24. If an adjustable thrust screw and locknut is fitted, adjust the armature end-float as follows:
    Slacken the locknut. Screw the thrust screw in until resistance is felt. Screw the thrust screw out a quarter of a turn – maintain in this position and tighten the locknut.
25. Note that the final gear is serviced only as an assembly. Normally the crankpin mounting plate is not separated from the moulded gearwheel. If they should become parted assemble so that the relationship of the crankpin to the cam is as shown.
26. Lubricate the final gear bushes with Shell Turbo 41 oil. Lubricate the final gear cam with Ragosine Listate grease. Fit the dished washer with its concave surface facing the final gear. Insert the shaft. Fit the washer. Fit the spring clip by inserting sideways.
27. Pack Ragosine Listate grease around the worm gear, final gear and into the crosshead guide channel.
28. Perform 84.15.12 instructions 12 to 18.

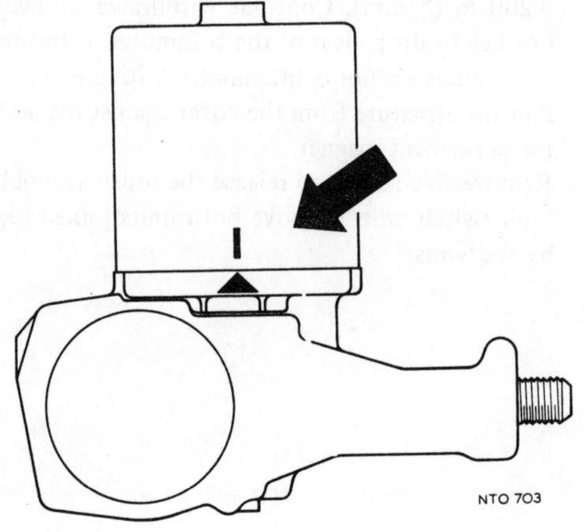

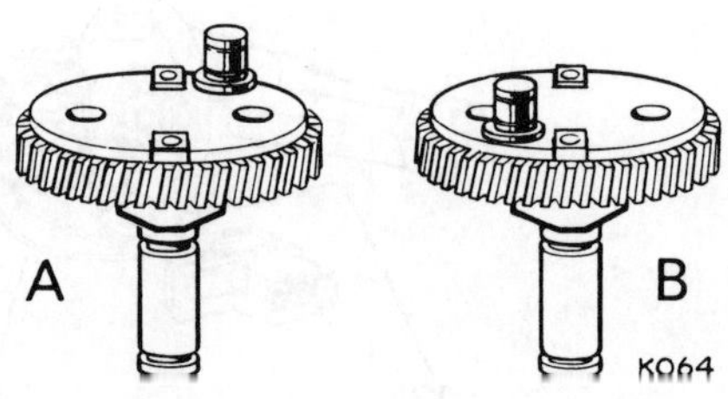

A Park position – cable rack retracted – RH Steer vehicles

B Park position – cable rack extended – LH Steer vehicles

Relationship of crankpin to cam for correct park position

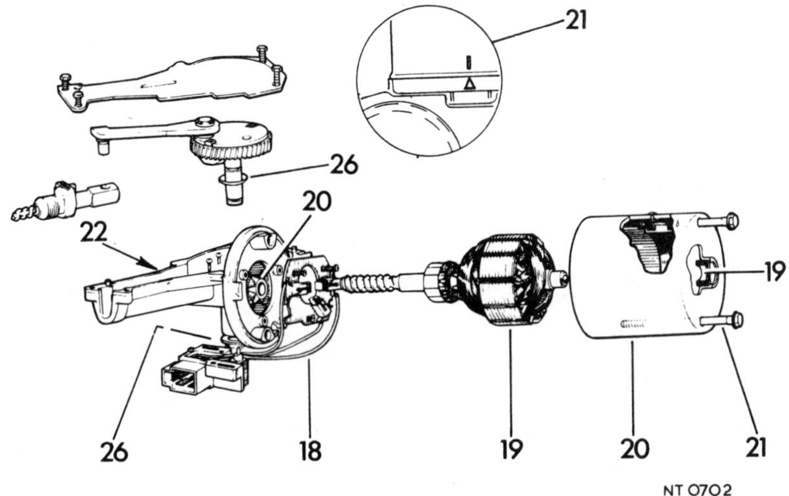
21
26
20
22
19
26
18
19
20
21
NT 0702

WINDSCREEN WIPER RACK

– Remove and refit 84.15.24

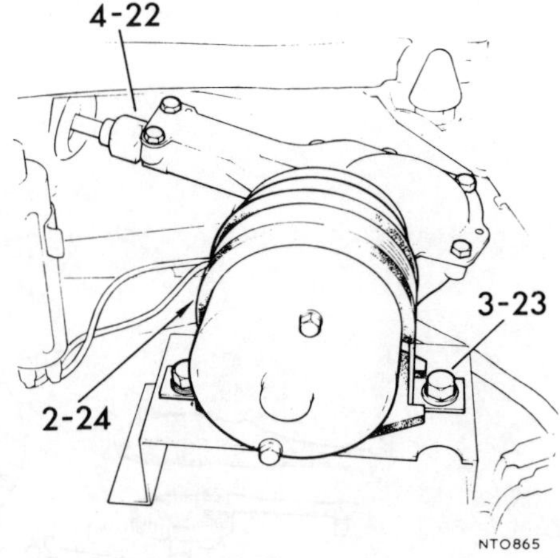

Removing

1. Remove two wiper arms 84.15.01.
2. Remove the harness plug from the limit switch.
3. Remove two bolts, spring washers and washers. Remove the strap and rubber sleeve. Collect up the rubber pad.
4. Unscrew the tubing nut.
5. Withdraw the motor and rack assembly.
6. Remove four screws. Lift off the gearbox cover.
7. Remove the crankpin spring clip by withdrawing sideways.
8. Remove the washer.
9. Carefully withdraw the connecting rod.
10. Remove the washer.
11. Remove the crosshead and rack assembly.

Refitting

12. Position the crosshead and rack assembly to the motor.
13. Fit the washer.
14. Lubricate the final gear crankpin with Shell Turbo 41 oil.
15. Lubricate the crosshead end of the connecting rod, including the pin, with Ragosine Listate grease.
16. Carefully insert the connecting rod.
17. Fit the washer.
18. Fit the spring clip by inserting sideways.
19. Position the gearbox cover. Secure with four screws.
20. Lubricate the rack with Ragosine Listate grease.
21. Insert the motor and rack assembly. It may be necessary to slightly rotate each wheelbox spindle by hand to facilitate the rack engagement.
22. Screw on the tubing nut.
23. Position the rubber pad. Locate the strap and rubber sleeve. Secure with two bolts, spring washers and washers.
24. Fit the harness plug to the limit switch.
25. Fit two wiper arms 84.15.01.

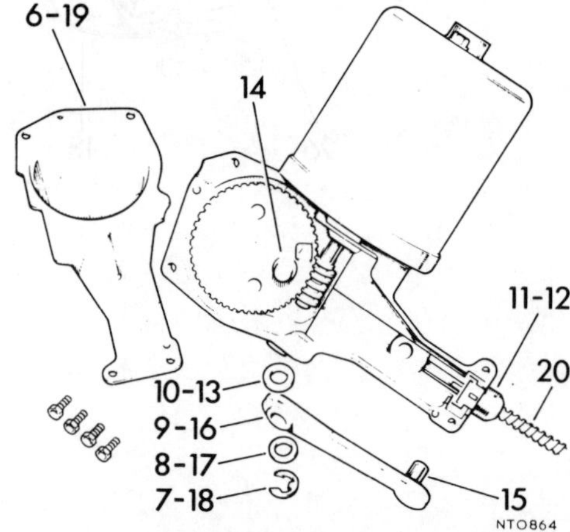

WINDSCREEN WIPER WHEELBOX

– Left hand – remove and refit **84.15.28**

– Right hand – remove and refit **84.15.29**

Removing

1. Isolate the battery.
2. Perform 84.15.24 operations 1 to 5.
3. To improve access remove the air inlet vent 76.15.17.
4. To improve access remove the drivers seat 76.70.04 or the passengers seat 76.70.05 as required.
5. Drivers side only – Remove the tachometer 88.30.21.
6. Passengers side only – Remove the cubby box 76.52.03 and the demister duct 80.15.03.
7. Remove four screws. Break the seal and remove the access plate.
8. Left hand side only – Remove two nuts and remove the wheelbox backplate.
9. Right hand side only – Action to prevent losing the short tubing in the plenum chamber. Slacken two nuts unequally as shown just enough to push the wheelbox to wheelbox tubing from position. Tighten two nuts to firmly trap the short tubing.
10. Remove the wheelbox spindle nut.
11. Carefully break the seal between the rubber moulding and vehicle body. Withdraw the rubber moulding. Ensure that the plastic tube is not detached from the metal pipe.
12. Withdraw the wheelbox through the access aperture.
13. Right hand side only – Dismantle two nuts, wheelbox backplate, short tubing and wheelbox.
14. Remove the rigid tube from the wheelbox spindle.

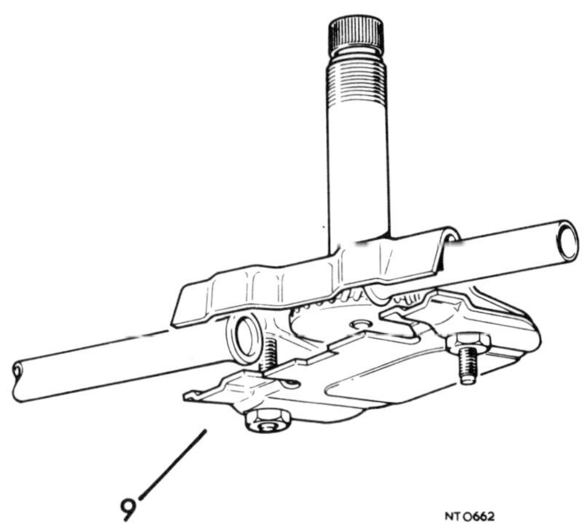

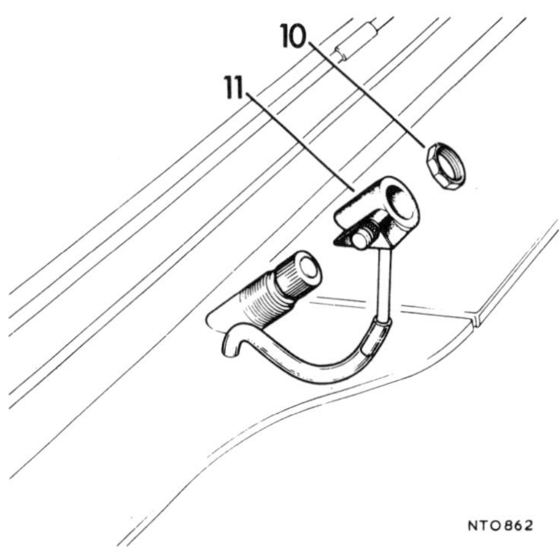

Refitting

15. Fit the rigid tube to the wheelbox spindle.
16. Right hand side only –
    Assemble the wheelbox, short tubing, wheelbox backplate and two nuts.
17. Insert the wheelbox through the access aperture.
18. Position the rubber moulding. Ensure a good seal by using an approved sealer.
19. Fit the wheelbox spindle nut.
20. Left hand side only –
    Position two lengths of tubing to the slots provided on the wheelbox. Position the wheelbox backplate and secure with two nuts.
21. Right hand side only –
    Action to prevent losing the short tubing in the plenum chamber. Slacken two nuts unequally as shown just enough to push the wheelbox to wheelbox tubing into position. Tighten two nuts.
22. Position the access plate. Ensure a good seal by using an approved sealer. Secure with four screws.
23. Drivers side only –
    Fit the tachometer 88.30.21
24. Passengers side only –
    Fit the demister duct 80.15.03 and the cubby box 76.52.03.
25. Fit the drivers seat 76:70.04 or the passengers seat 76.70.05 as required.
26. Fit the air inlet vent 76.15.17.
27. Perform 84.15.24 operations 20 to 25.
28. Connect the battery.

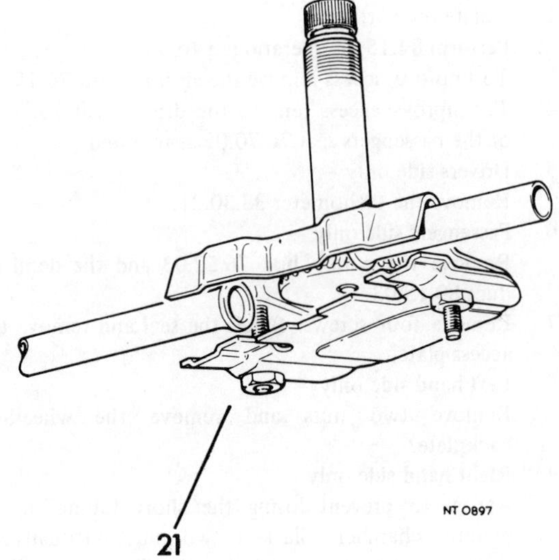

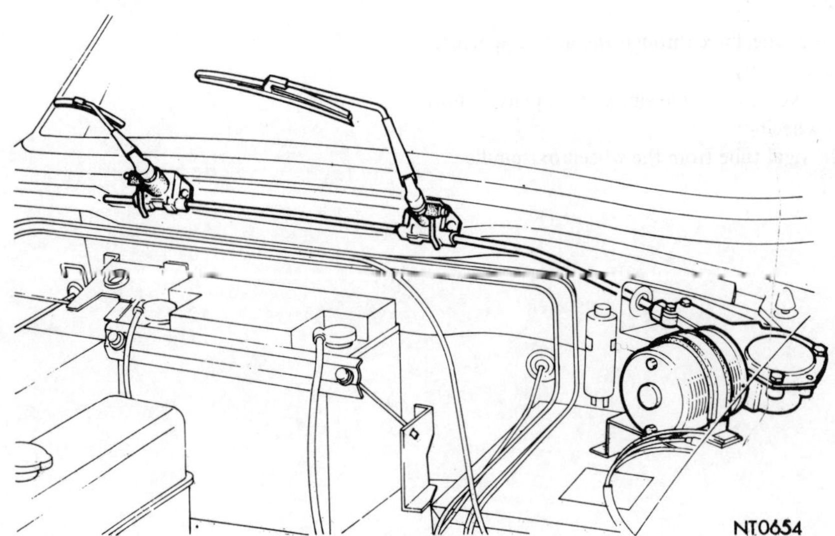

ELECTRICAL OPERATIONS

Switches

brake line failure switch – remove and refit	[illegible]
bonnet light switch – remove and refit	86.65.[illegible]
cubby box illumination switch – remove and refit	86.65.[illegible]
data	86.65.00
[illegible] switch – remove and refit	86.65.[illegible]
door switch – remove and refit	86.65.15
fuel pump inertia cut-out switch – data and description	86.65.58
fuel pump inertia cut-out switch – remove and refit	86.65.[illegible]
fuel pump inertia cut-out switch – reset	86.65.59
hazard switch – remove and refit	86.65.50
heater switch – remove and refit	86.65.[illegible]
horn push – remove and refit	86.65.18
ignition/starter switch – remove and refit	86.65.[illegible]
key switch – remove and refit	57.40.31
luggage boot lamp switch – remove and refit	86.65.22
oil pressure switch – remove and refit	86.65.30
overdrive manual switch – remove and refit	86.65.33
overdrive gearbox switches – remove and refit	86.65.[illegible]
panel rheostat – remove and refit	86.65.12
reverse lamp switch – remove and refit	86.65.[illegible]
seat belt – drivers belt switch – remove and refit	86.65.[illegible]
seat belt – gearbox switch – remove and refit	86.65.[illegible]
seat belt – passengers belt switch – remove and refit	86.65.[illegible]
seat belt – passengers seat switch – remove and refit	86.65.[illegible]
stop lamp switch – remove and refit	86.65.51
transmission tunnel lamp switch – remove and refit	86.65.[illegible]
turn signal switch – remove and refit	86.65.[illegible]
windscreen washer switch – remove and refit	86.65.[illegible]
windscreen wiper switch – remove and refit	86.65.[illegible]

Wiring diagrams

left hand steer – except U.S.A.	86.00.[illegible]
right hand steer	86.00.[illegible]
U.S.A. – from introduction of 1972 model year	86.00.[illegible]
U.S.A. – up to end of 1971 model year	86.00.[illegible]

BULB CHART

Lamp	Unipart No.	Stanpart No.	Specification		
			Reference No.	Watts	
Headlamps – L.H. dip	GLU 101	512231	54521872	60/45	*
R.H. dip – Normal	GLB 410	510213	410	45/40	
or	GLU 114	215735	54523079	60/50	*
France	GLB 411	510219	411	45/40	
U.S.A.	–	–	54522231	50/40	*
Front flasher lamps	GLB 382	502379	382	21	
Front parking lamps	GLB 989	59467	989	6	
Front flasher and parking lamps	GLB 380	502287	380	5/21	
Flasher repeater lamps	–	518220	233	4	
Front marker lamps	–	501436	222	4	
Rear marker lamps	–	501436	222	4	
Rear flasher lamps	GLB 382	502379	382	21	
Tail/stop lamps	GLB 380	502287	380	5/21	
Reverse lamps	GLB 382	502379	382	21	
Plate illumination lamps	GLB 207	57591	207	6	
Luggage boot lamp	GLB 256	57599	256	3	
Transmission tunnel lamp	GLB 254	59897	254	6	
Cubby box illumination	GLB 987	59492	987	2·2	
Instrument illumination	GLB 987	59492	987	2·2	
Warning lights	GLB 987	59492	987	2·2	
Seat belt warning light	GLB 281	513000	281	2	

* Sealed beam light unit

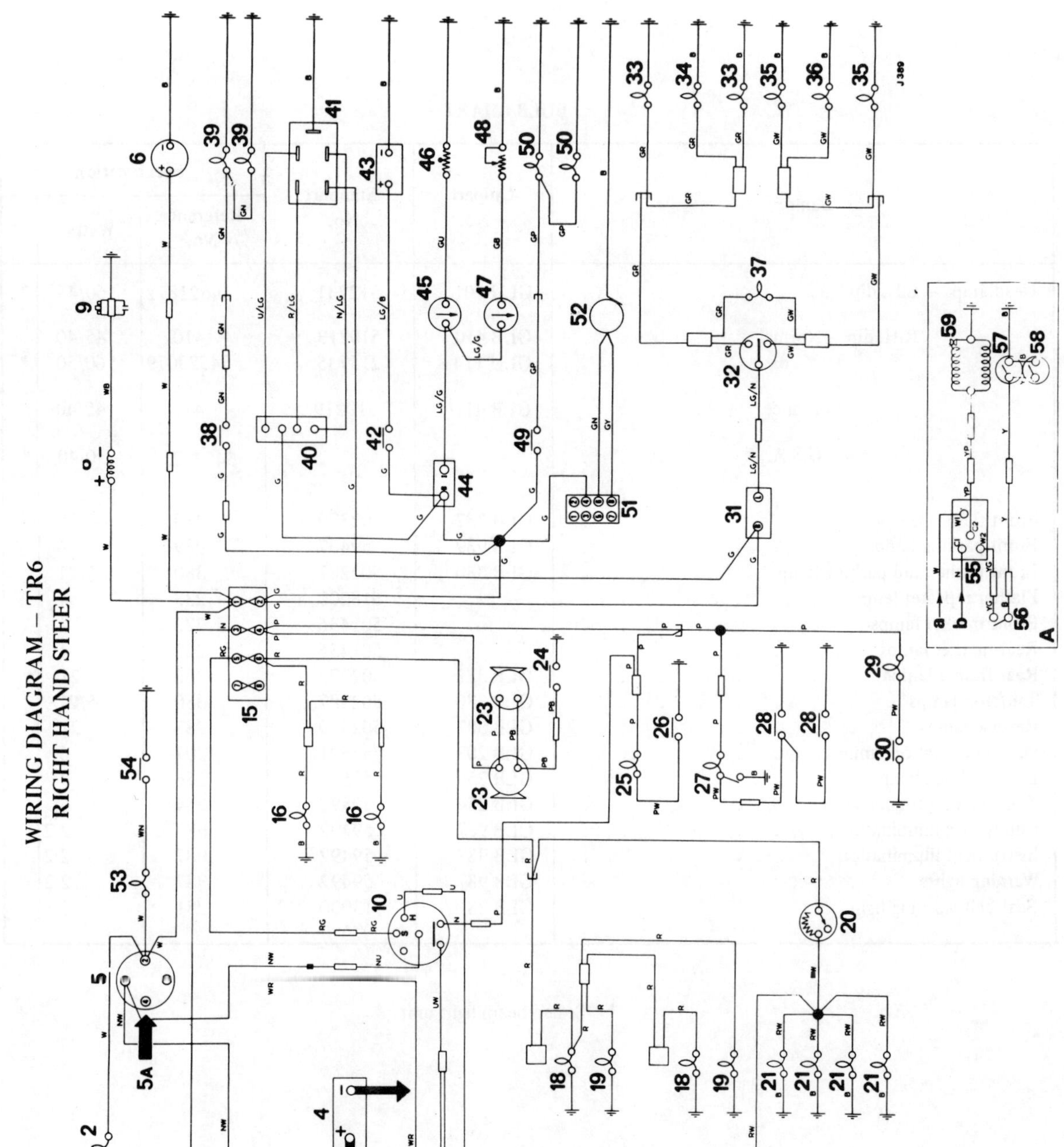

WIRING DIAGRAM – TR6
RIGHT HAND STEER

J 389

KEY TO WIRING DIAGRAM – TR6
RIGHT HAND STEER

1. Alternator
2. Ignition warning light
3. Ammeter
4. Battery
5. Ignition/starter switch
5A. Ignition/starter switch – radio supply connector
6. Petrol pump
7. Starter motor
8. Ignition coil
9. Ignition distributor
10. Column light switch
11. Dip switch
12. Main beam warning light
13. Main beam
14. Dip beam
15. Fuse box
16. Front parking lamp

18. Tail lamp
19. Plate illumination lamp
20. Panel rheostat
21. Instrument illumination
22. Connector block
23. Horn
24. Horn push
25. Cubby box illumination
26. Cubby box illumination switch
27. Transmission tunnel lamp
28. Transmission tunnel lamp door switch
29. Luggage boot lamp
30. Luggage boot lamp switch
31. Turn signal flasher unit
32. Turn signal switch
33. L.H. Flasher lamp
34. L.H. Flasher repeater lamp
35. R.H. Flasher lamp
36. R.H. Flasher repeater lamp
37. Turn signal warning light
38. Reverse lamp switch
39. Reverse lamp
40. Windscreen wiper switch
41. Windscreen wiper motor
42. Windscreen washer switch
43. Windscreen washer pump
44. Voltage stabilizer
45. Temperature indicator
46. Temperature transmitter
47. Fuel indicator
48. Fuel tank unit
49. Stop lamp switch
50. Stop lamp
51. Heater switch
52. Heater motor
53. Oil pressure warning light
54. Oil pressure switch

A Overdrive (optional extra)

55. Overdrive relay
56. Overdrive column switch
57. Overdrive gearbox switch- 2nd gear ON
58. Overdrive gearbox switch- 3rd and 4th gear ON
59. Overdrive solenoid

a From fuse box
b From fuse box

COLOUR CODE

N.	Brown	**LG.**	Light Green
U.	Blue	**W.**	White
R.	Red	**Y.**	Yellow
P.	Purple	**S.**	Slate
G.	Green	**B.**	Black

WIRING DIAGRAM – TR6
LEFT HAND STEER – EXCEPT U.S.A.

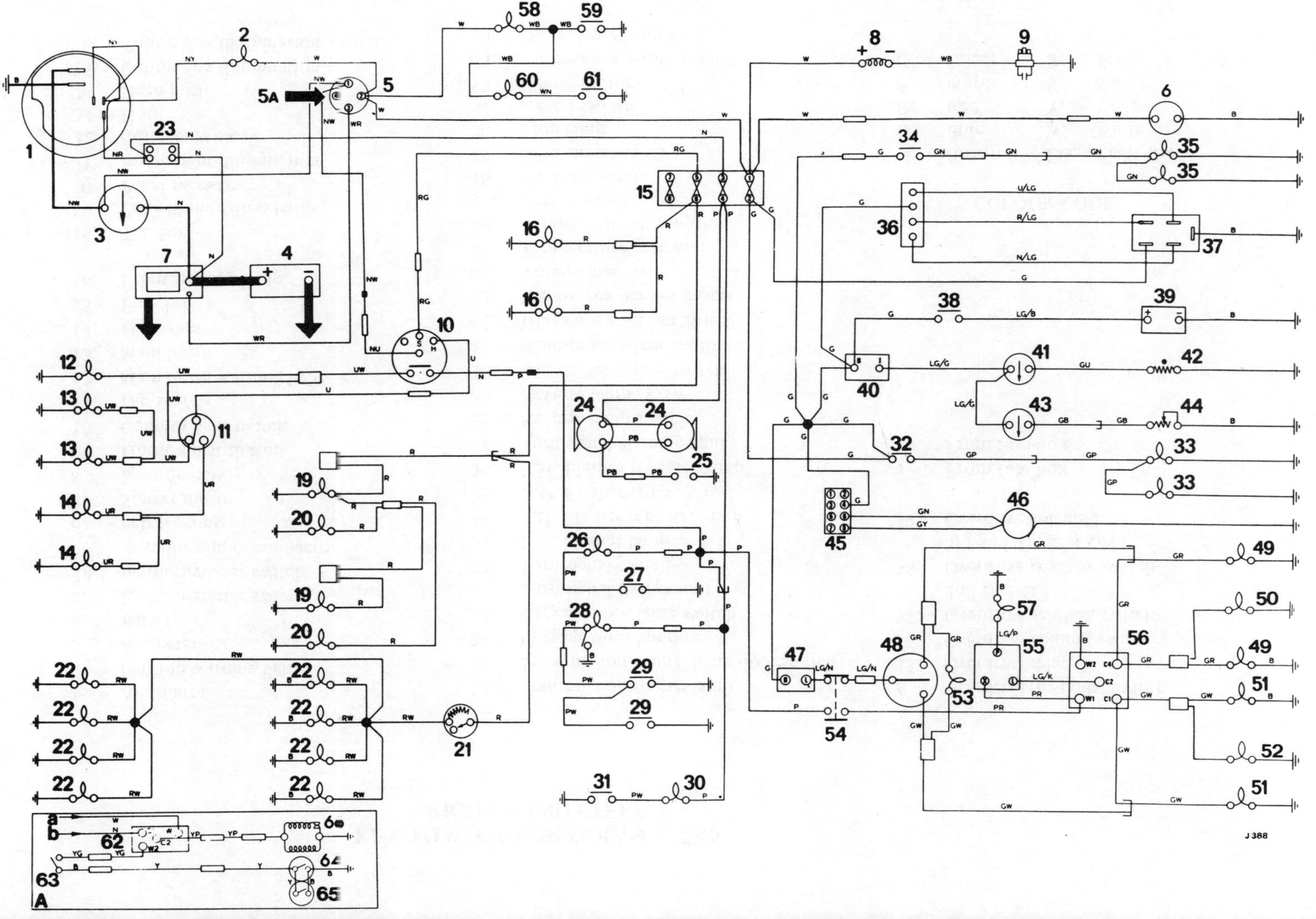

KEY TO WIRING DIAGRAM – TR6
LEFT HAND STEER – EXCEPT U.S.A.

1. Alternator
2. Ignition warning light
3. Ammeter
4. Battery
5. Ignition/starter switch
5A. Ignition/starter switch – radio supply connector
6. Petrol pump
7. Starter motor
8. Ignition coil
9. Ignition distributor
10. Column light switch
11. Dip switch
12. Main beam warning light
13. Main beam
14. Dip beam
15. Fuse box
16. Front parking lamp

19. Tail lamp
20. Plate illumination lamp
21. Panel rheostat
22. Instrument illumination
23. Connector block
24. Horn
25. Horn push
26. Cubby box illumination
27. Cubby box illumination switch
28. Transmission tunnel lamp
29. Transmission tunnel lamp door switch
30. Luggage boot lamp
31. Luggage boot lamp switch
32. Stop lamp switch
33. Stop lamp
34. Reverse lamp switch
35. Reverse lamp
36. Windscreen wiper switch
37. Windscreen wiper motor
38. Windscreen washer switch
39. Windscreen washer pump
40. Voltage stabilizer
41. Temperature indicator
42. Temperature transmitter
43. Fuel indicator
44. Fuel tank unit
45. Heater switch
46. Heater motor
47. Turn signal flasher unit
48. Turn signal switch
49. L.H. Flasher lamp
50. L.H. Flasher repeater lamp
51. R.H. Flasher lamp
52. R.H. Flasher repeater lamp
53. Turn signal warning light
54. Hazard switch
55. Hazard flasher unit
56. Hazard relay
57. Hazard warning light
58. Brake line failure warning light
59. Brake line failure switch
60. Oil pressure warning light
61. Oil pressure switch

A. Overdrive (optional extra)

62. Overdrive relay
63. Overdrive column switch
64. Overdrive gearbox switch-2nd gear ON
65. Overdrive gearbox switch-3rd and 4th gear ON
66. Overdrive solenoid

a From fuse box
b From fuse box

COLOUR CODE

N.	Brown	**LG.**	Light Green
U.	Blue	**W.**	White
R.	Red	**Y.**	Yellow
P.	Purple	**S.**	Slate
G.	Green	**B.**	Black

WIRING DIAGRAM – TR6
U.S.A. – UP TO END OF 1971 MODEL YEAR

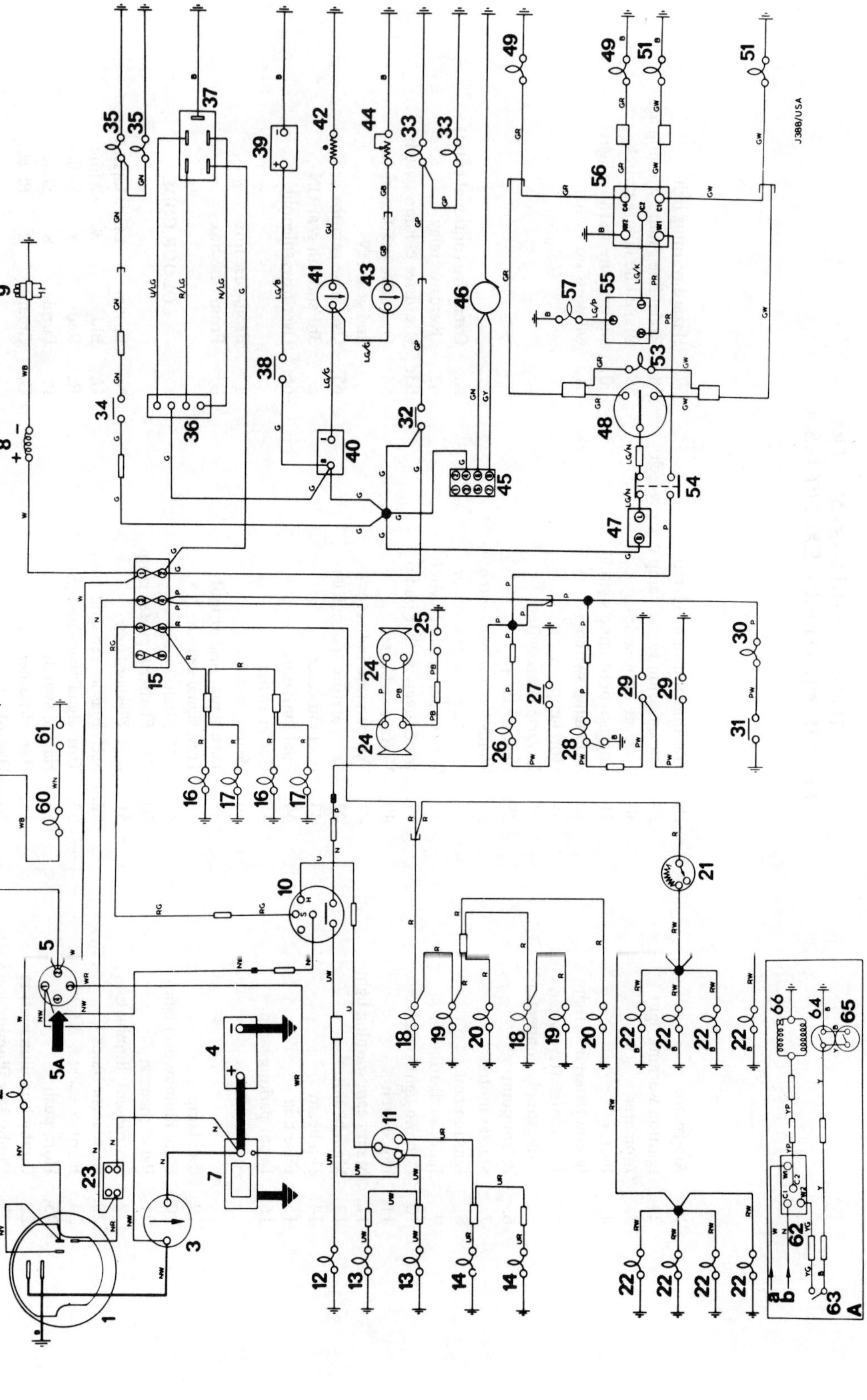

J388/USA

KEY TO WIRING DIAGRAM – TR6
U.S.A. – UP TO END OF 1971 MODEL YEAR

1. Alternator
2. Ignition warning light
3. Ammeter
4. Battery
5. Ignition/starter switch
5A. Ignition/starter switch-radio supply connector

7. Starter motor
8. Ignition coil
9. Ignition distributor
10. Column light switch
11. Dip switch
12. Main beam warning light
13. Main beam
14. Dip beam
15. Fuse box
16. Front parking lamp
17. Front marker lamp
18. Rear marker lamp
19. Tail lamp
20. Plate illumination lamp
21. Panel rheostat
22. Instrument illumination
23. Connector block
24. Horn
25. Horn push
26. Cubby box illumination
27. Cubby box illumination switch
28. Transmission tunnel lamp
29. Transmission tunnel lamp door switch
30. Luggage boot lamp
31. Luggage boot lamp switch
32. Stop lamp switch
33. Stop lamp
34. Reverse lamp switch
35. Reverse lamp
36. Windscreen wiper switch
37. Windscreen wiper motor
38. Windscreen washer switch
39. Windscreen washer pump
40. Voltage stabilizer
41. Temperature indicator
42. Temperature transmitter
43. Fuel indicator
44. Fuel tank unit
45. Heater switch
46. Heater motor
47. Turn signal flasher unit
48. Turn signal switch
49. L.H. Flasher lamp

51. R.H. Flasher lamp

53. Turn signal warning light
54. Hazard switch
55. Hazard flasher unit
56. Hazard relay
57. Hazard warning light
58. Brake line failure warning light
59. Brake line failure switch
60. Oil pressure warning light
61. Oil pressure switch

A. Overdrive (optional extra)

62. Overdrive relay
63. Overdrive column switch
64. Overdrive gearbox switch-2nd gear ON
65. Overdrive gearbox switch-3rd and 4th gear ON
66. Overdrive solenoid

a From fuse box
b From fuse box

COLOUR CODE

N.	Brown	**LG.**	Light Green
U.	Blue	**W.**	White
R.	Red	**Y.**	Yellow
P.	Purple	**S.**	Slate
G.	Green	**B.**	Black

WIRING DIAGRAM – TR6
U.S.A. – FROM INTRODUCTION OF 1972 MODEL YEAR

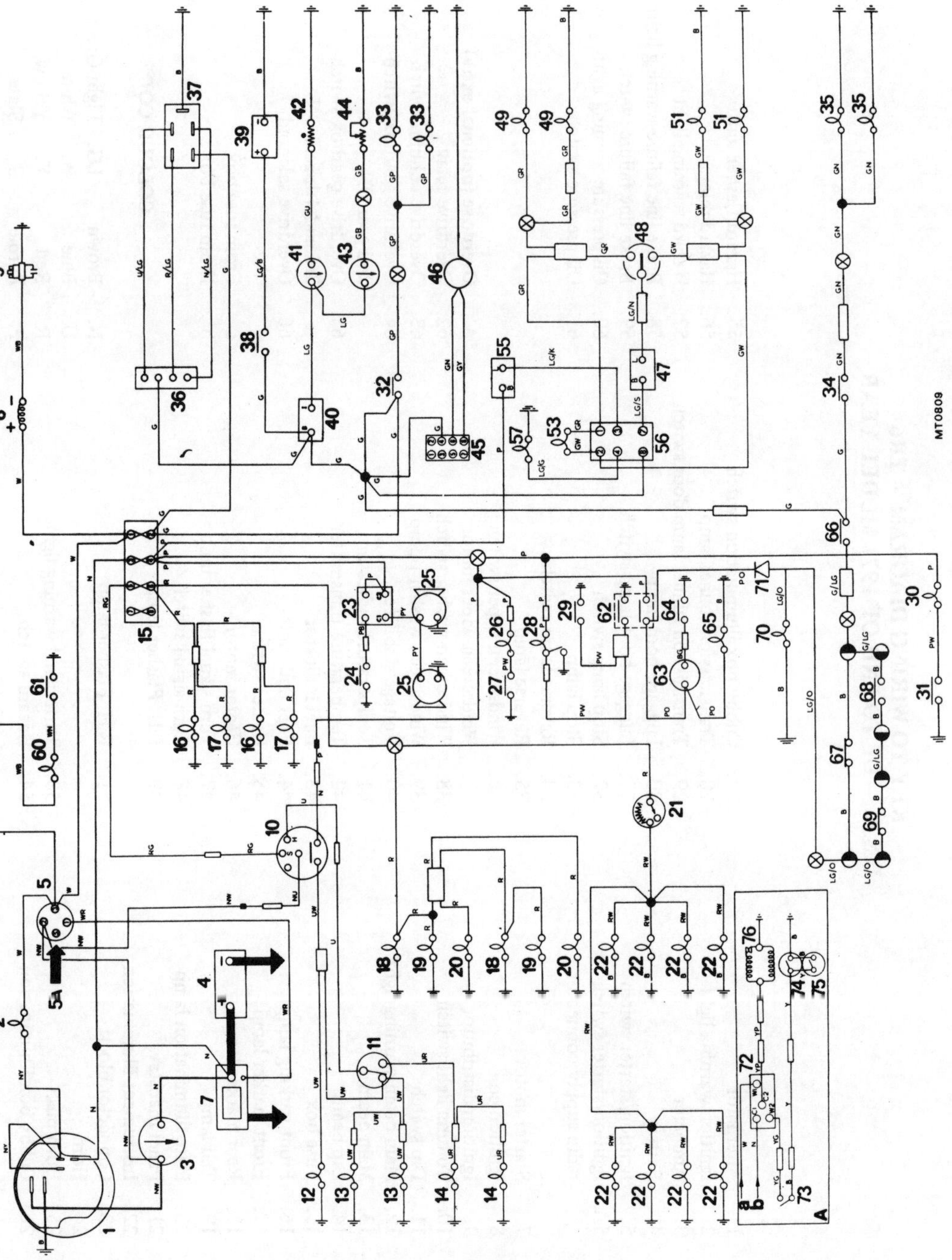

MT0809

KEY TO WIRING DIAGRAM – TR6, U.S.A. – FROM INTRODUCTION OF 1972 MODEL YEAR

1. Alternator
2. Ignition warning light
3. Ammeter
4. Battery
5. Ignition/starter switch
5A. Ignition/starter switch- radio supply connector
7. Starter motor
8. Ignition coil
9. Ignition distributor
10. Column light switch
11. Dip switch
12. Main beam warning light
13. Main beam
14. Dip beam
15. Fuse box
16. Front parking lamp
17. Front marker lamp
18. Rear marker lamp
19. Tail lamp
20. Plate illumination lamp
21. Panel rheostat
22. Instrument illumination
23. Horn relay
24. Horn push
25 Horn
26. Cubby box illumination
27 Cubby box illumination switch
28. Transmission tunnel lamp
29. Transmission tunnel lamp door switch
30. Luggage boot lamp
31. Luggage boot lamp switch
32. Stop lamp switch
33. Stop lamp
34. Reverse lamp switch
35. Reverse lamp
36. Windscreen wiper switch
37. Windscreen wiper motor
38. Windscreen washer switch
39. Windscreen washer pump
40. Voltage stabilizer
41. Temperature indicator
42. Temperature transmitter
43. Fuel indicator
44. Fuel tank unit
45. Heater switch
46. Heater motor
47. Turn signal flasher unit
48. Turn signal switch
49. L.H. Flasher lamp
51. R.H. Flasher lamp
53. Turn signal warning light
55. Hazard flasher unit
56. Hazard switch
57. Hazard warning light
58. Brake line failure warning light
59. Brake line failure switch
60. Oil pressure warning light
61. Oil pressure switch
62. L.H. door switch
63. Buzzer
64. Key switch
65. Key light
66. Seat belt warning gearbox switch
67. Drivers belt switch
68. Passengers seat switch
69. Passengers belt switch
70. Seat belt warning light
71. Diode

A. Overdrive (optional extra)
72. Overdrive relay
73. Overdrive column switch
74. Overdrive gearbox switch – 2nd gear ON
75. Overdrive gearbox switch – 3rd and 4th gear ON
76. Overdrive solenoid

a. From fuse box
b. From fuse box

COLOUR CODE

N.	Brown	**LG.**	Light Green
U.	Blue	**W.**	White
R.	Red	**Y.**	Yellow
P.	Purple	**S.**	Slate
G.	Green	**B.**	Black

HARNESS

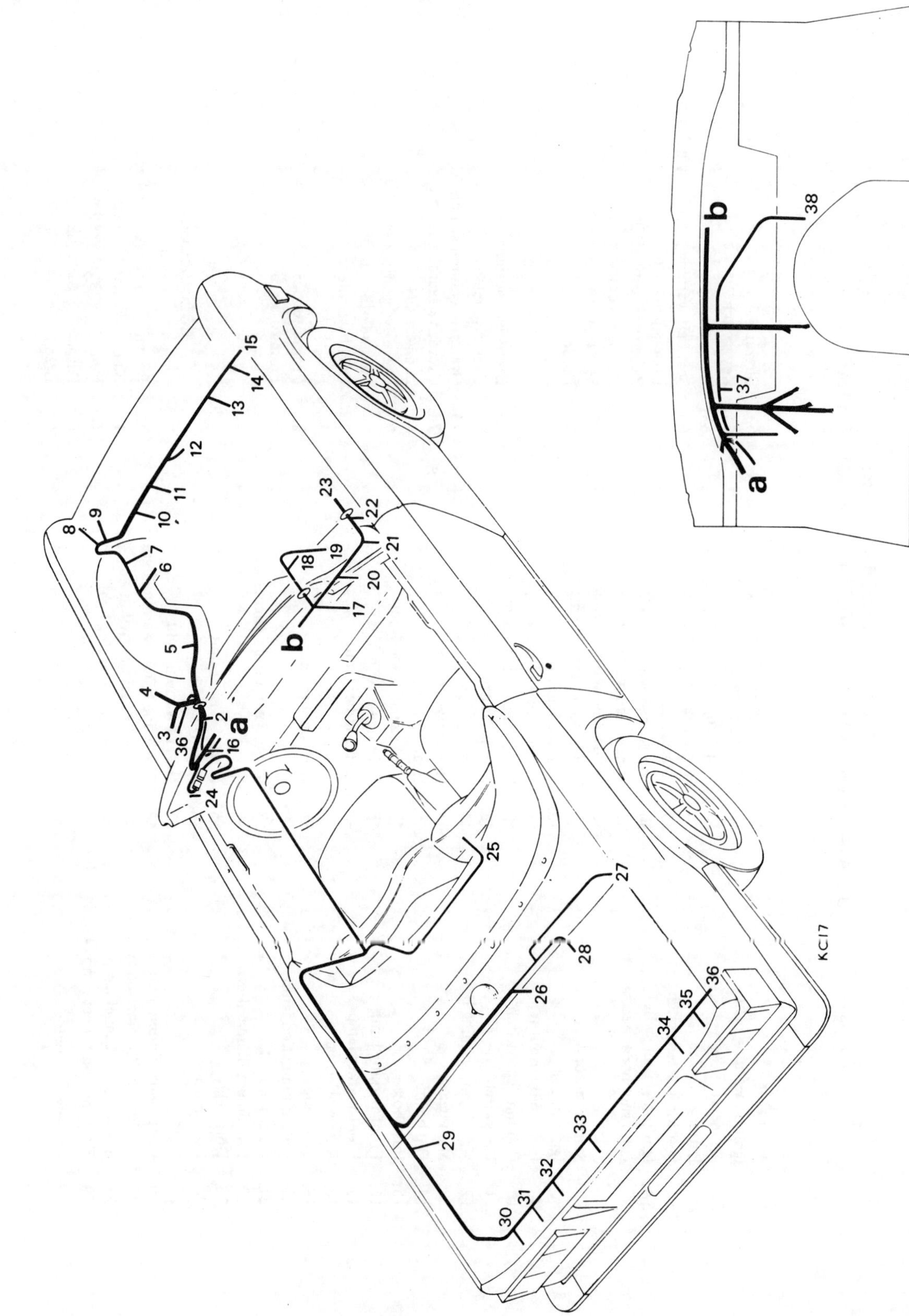

a
b
1
2
3
4
5
6
7
8
9
10
11
12
13
14
15
16
17
18
19
20
21
22
23
24
25
26
27
28
29
30
31
32
33
34
35
36
37
38
KC17

KEY TO HARNESS

MAIN HARNESS

1 Plug connection to body harness

2 Dip switch

3 Windscreen wiper motor
Hazard relay – left hand steer only
Fuse box

4 Fuse box
Connector block
Hazard flasher unit – left hand steer only

5 Brake line failure switch – left hand steer only

6 Alternator
Ignition coil
Temperature transmitter
Oil pressure switch

7 Horn push – earth return wire connected to steering unit

8 Harness earth

9 Front parking lamp
Front flasher lamp
Flasher repeater lamp

10 Headlamp

11 Horn

12 Harness earth

13 Horn

14 Headlamp

15 Front parking lamp
Front flasher lamp
Flasher repeater lamp

16 Transmission tunnel lamp door switch

a Refer to Fascia connections 88.00.01 to 88.00.05 for continuation

b Refer to Fascia connections 88.00.01 to 88.00.05 for continuation

17 Reverse lamp switch

18 Harness earth

19 Starter motor

20 Cubby box illumination

21 Transmission tunnel lamp door switch

22 Turn signal flasher unit

23 Windscreen washer pump

BODY HARNESS

24 Plug connection to main harness

25 Transmission tunnel lamp

26 Fuel tank unit

27 Luggage boot lamp switch

28 Luggage boot lamp

29 Petrol pump

30 Rear flasher lamp

31 Tail/stop lamp

32 Reverse lamp

33 Plate illumination lamp

34 Reverse lamp

35 Tail/stop lamp

36 Rear flasher lamp

OVERDRIVE HARNESS (Optional extra)

36 Fuse box
Overdrive relay

37 Overdrive column switch

38 Overdrive gearbox switch – 2nd gear ON
Overdrive gearbox switch – 3rd and 4th gear ON
Overdrive solenoid

NOTE: Early left hand steer vehicle shown – other TR6 vehicles similar.

ALTERNATOR DATA CHARTS

CAUTION: The alternator contains polarity sensitive components that may be irreparably damaged if subjected to incorrect polarity.

Do not connect or disconnect any part of the charging circuit – including the battery leads – while the engine is running. Run the alternator with all connections made or with the unit disconnected.

NOTE: Three Lucas alternators and two Delco Remy alternators have been fitted to the TR6 model range up to the end of the 1972 model year. Identify the unit on the specific vehicle to ensure that information obtained from this manual refers to the appropriate alternator.

Manufacturer	Lucas		Lucas		Lucas	
Type	15 ACR Battery sensed with small lugs		15 ACR Machine sensed with large lugs		17 ACR Machine sensed with large lugs	
Part numbers –	**Lucas Part No.**	**Stanpart No.**	**Lucas Part No.**	**Stanpart No.**	**Lucas Part No.**	**Stanpart No.**
assembly	——	216970	——	217771	——	217692
–comprising–						
alternator	23562	215346	23634	217772	23635	217988
fan	54217652	147990	54217652	147990	54217652	147990
pulley	54218695	154334	54218695	154334	54219467	155948
Polarity	Negative earth only		Negative earth only		Negative earth only	
Brush length – new	0·5 in (12·70 mm)		0·5 in (12·70 mm)		0·5 in (12·70 mm)	
– renew if less than	0·2 in (5·00 mm) protrudes from brushbox when free		0·2 in (5·00 mm) protrudes from brushbox when free		0·2 in (5·00 mm) protrudes from brushbox when free	
Brush spring pressure	9 to 13 oz (255 to 370g) at face flush with brushbox		9 to 13 oz (255 to 370g) at face flush with brushbox		9 to 13 oz (255 to 370g) at face flush with brushbox	
Rectifier pack–output rectification	6 diodes (3 live side and 3 earth side)		6 diodes (3 live side and 3 earth side)		6 diodes (3 live side and 3 earth side)	
–field winding supply rectification	3 diodes		3 diodes		3 diodes	
Stator windings	Three phase – star connected		Three phase – star connected		Three phase – star connected	
Field winding rotor: poles	12		12		12	
maximum permissible speed	12,500 rev/min		12,500 rev/min		12,500 rev/min	
shaft thread	9/16 in – 18 U.N.F.		9/16 in – 18 U.N.F.		9/16 in – 18 U.N.F.	
Field winding resistance at 20°C	4·33 ± 5% ohm		4·33 ± 5% ohm		4·165 ± 5% ohm	
Nominal output: condition	Hot		Hot		Hot	
alternator speed	6000 rev/min		6000 rev/min		6000 rev/min	
engine speed	2200 to 2900 rev/min – variations of ratio occur according to current market specification requirements		2200 to 2900 rev/min – variations of ration occur according to current market specification requirements		2200 to 2900 rev/min – variations of ratio occur according to current market specification requirements	
control voltage	14 volt		14 volt		14 volt	
amp	28 amp		28 amp		36 amp	

	Delco Remy Part No.	Stanpart No.	Delco Remy Part No.	Stanpart No.
Manufacturer	Delco Remy		Delco Remy	
Type	Delcotron DN 460 Battery sensed		Delcotron DN 460 Battery sensed	
Part numbers – assembly	7982648	217456	7982652	218042
—comprising —	——	——	——	——
alternator	7982515	519667	7982515	519667
fan				
pulley	7982645	217464	7982655	156364
Polarity	Negative earth only		Negative earth only	
Brush length – new	0·5 in (12·70 mm)		0·5 in (12·70 mm)	
– renew if less than	0·2 in (5·00 mm)		0·2 in (5·00 mm)	
Brush spring pressure	8 to 13 oz (225 to 370g) at normal working position		8 to 13 oz (225 to 370g) at normal working position	
Rectifier pack—output rectification	6 diodes (3 live side and 3 earth side)		6 diodes (3 live side and 3 earth side)	
—field winding supply rectification	3 diodes		3 diodes	
Stator windings	Three phase – star connected		Three phase – star connected	
Field winding rotor: poles	14		14	
maximum permissible speed	Continuous 12000 rev/min – flighting 16000 rev/min		Continuous 12000 rev/min – flighting 16000 rev/min	
shaft thread	0·669 – 20NS – 2A		0·669 – 20NS – 2A	
Field winding resistance at 20°C	2·65 to 2·95 ohm		2·65 to 2·95 ohm	
Nominal output: condition	Hot		Hot	
alternator speed	5000 rev/min		5000 rev/min	
engine speed	1800 to 2400 rev/min – variations of ratio occur according to current market specification requirements		1800 to 2400 rev/min – variations of ratio occur according to current market specification requirements	
control voltage	14 volt		14 volt	
amp	35 amp		35 amp	

ALTERNATOR WIRING DIAGRAM – LUCAS TYPES 15ACR AND 17ACR

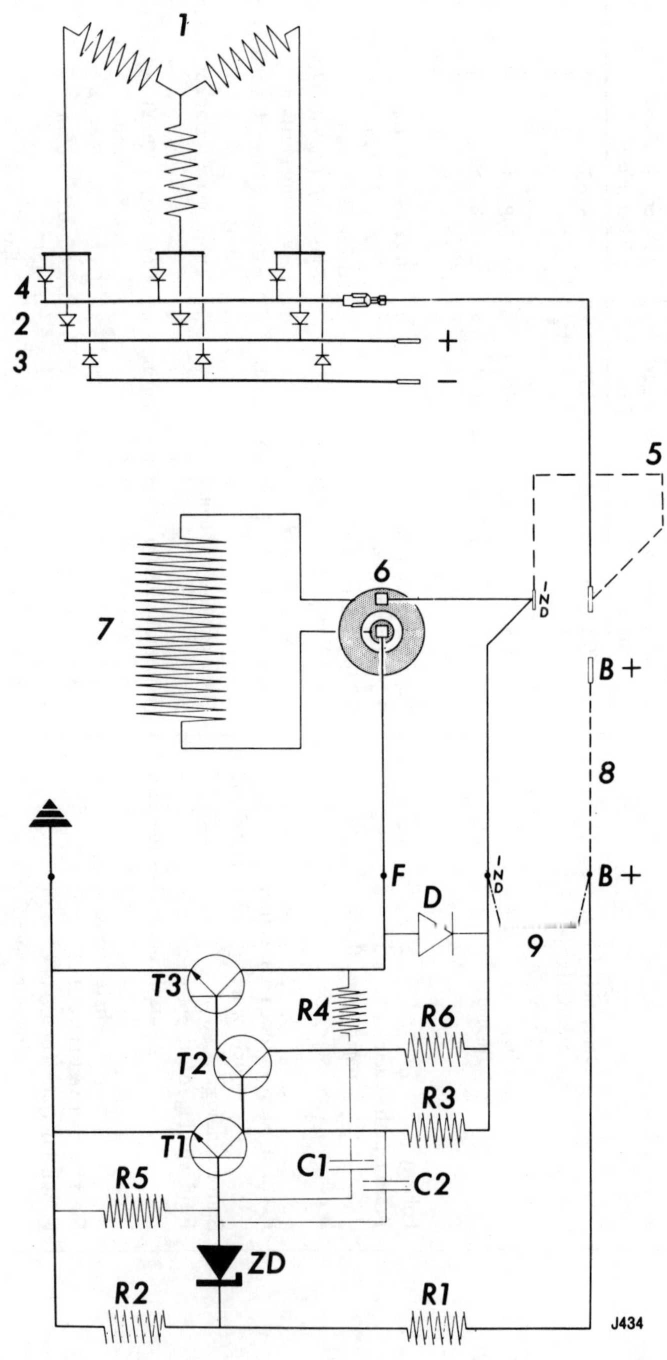

KEY TO ALTERNATOR WIRING DIAGRAM – LUCAS TYPES 15ACR AND 17ACR

1	Stator windings	
2	Live side output diodes	
3	Earth side output diodes	
4	Field winding supply diodes	
5	Harness loop	Circuit is made when multi-socket connector is fitted and broken when connector is removed
6	Brushes and slip rings	
7	Field winding	
8	Connection to external harness wire	Alternative to item 9. Fitted to battery sensed units
9	Internal B+ connection	Alternative to item 8. Fitted to machine sensed units
R3	Resistor	Restricts T2 base current supplied from 'field winding supply' diodes
T2	Intermediate transistor	Controls T3 base current direct
R6	Resistor	Restricts T3 base current supplied from 'field winding supply' diodes
T3	Output transistor	Controls field winding earth return circuit
R1 and R2	Potential divider	Senses battery reference voltage
ZD	Zener diode	Voltage sensitive component. Opposes passage of current until breakdown voltage – approximately 8 volts – is reached. Controls T1 base current direct
T1	Input transistor	Controls T2 base current by diverting current passing through R3 to earth when ZD is conducting
C1 and R4	Capacitor and Resistor	Prevents transistor overheating by providing positive feed back circuit to ensure quick switching of transistors from 'fully on' to 'fully off'
R5	Resistor	Path for small leakage current which may pass through ZD at high temperatures
D	Surge quench diode	Connected across field winding. Protects T3 from field winding high induced voltage surge and smooths field winding current
C2	Condenser	Radio interference suppression

ALTERNATOR WIRING DIAGRAM – DELCO REMY TYPE DN460

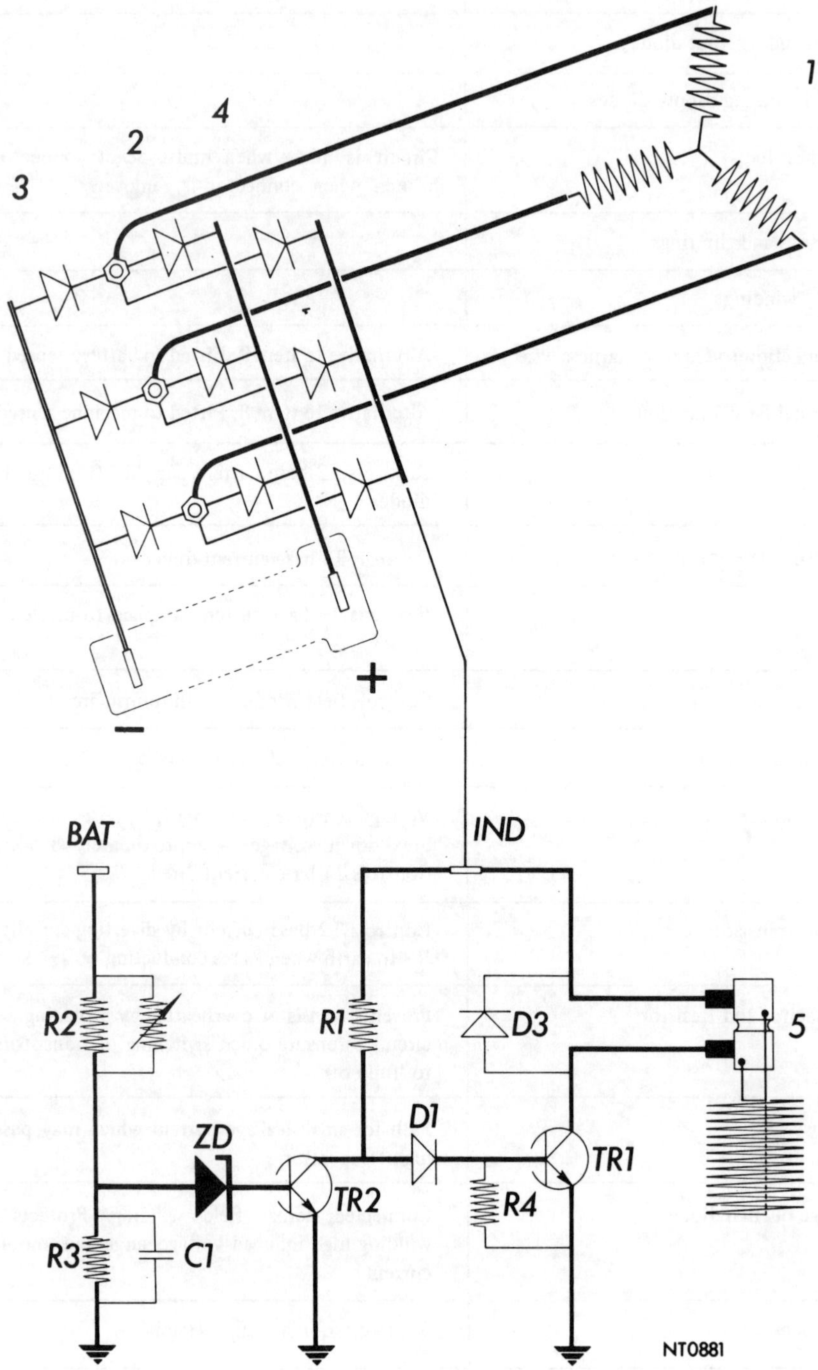

1
4
2
3
+
–
BAT
IND
R2
R1
D3
5
D1
ZD
TR1
6
TR2
R4
R3
C1
NT0881

KEY TO ALTERNATOR WIRING DIAGRAM
DELCO REMY TYPE DN460

1	Stator windings	
2	Live side output diodes	
3	Earth side output diodes	
4	Field winding supply diode trio	
5	Brushes and slip rings	
6	Field winding	
R1	Resistor	Restricts TR1 base current supplied from diode trio
TR1	Transistor	Controls field winding earth return circuit
R2 R3	Resistor and thermistor Resistor	Potential divider which senses battery reference voltage. Thermistor causes voltage to vary with temperature.
ZD	Zener diode	Voltage sensitive component. Opposes passage of current until breakdown voltage is reached. Controls TR2 base current.
TR2	Transistor	Controls TR1 base current by diverting current passing through R1 to earth when ZD is conducting
C1	Capacitor	Smooths voltage across R3
R4	Resistor	Prevents excessive current through TR1 at high temperatures
D3	Surge quench diode	Connected across field winding. Protects TR1 from field winding high induced voltage surge and smooths field winding current.
D1	Diode	Provides a fixed voltage drop which together with the voltage drop across the base emitter of TR1 ensures that the saturation voltage of TR2 will completely turn off TR1

ALTERNATOR – LUCAS TYPES 15ACR AND 17ACR

– Functional check 86.10.01

This operation must be performed in two parts. The first is to prove the alternator's capacity to produce current, while the second is to prove the performance of the integral control unit.

Check capacity to produce current

NOTE: The stated output may be exceeded slightly when the alternator is cold. To avoid misleading results, the check should be performed with the unit as near to its normal operating temperature as possible.

1. Check drive belt adjustment. 86.10.05
2. Disconnect the multi-socket connectors.
3. Remove the moulded cover.
4. Provide a test circuit as shown.
   CAUTION: The alternator contains polarity-sensitive components that may be irreparably damaged if subjected to incorrect polarity. Observe polarity of alternator and battery terminals.
5. Do not connect the variable resistor across the battery for longer than is necessary to perform the check.
6. Run the engine.
7. Gradually increase the speed. At 1,500 alternator rev/min (550 to 720 engine rev/min – variations of ratio occur according to current market specification requirements) the light should be extinguished.
8. Hold the speed at approximately 6000 alternator rev/min (2200 to 2900 engine rev/min). Adjust the variable resistor so that the voltmeter reads 14 volts. The ammeter reading should now be approximately equal to the nominal output given in data for the appropriate alternator.
9. If the ammeter reading is not correct, the indication is that the alternator requires overhaul or replacement.

continued

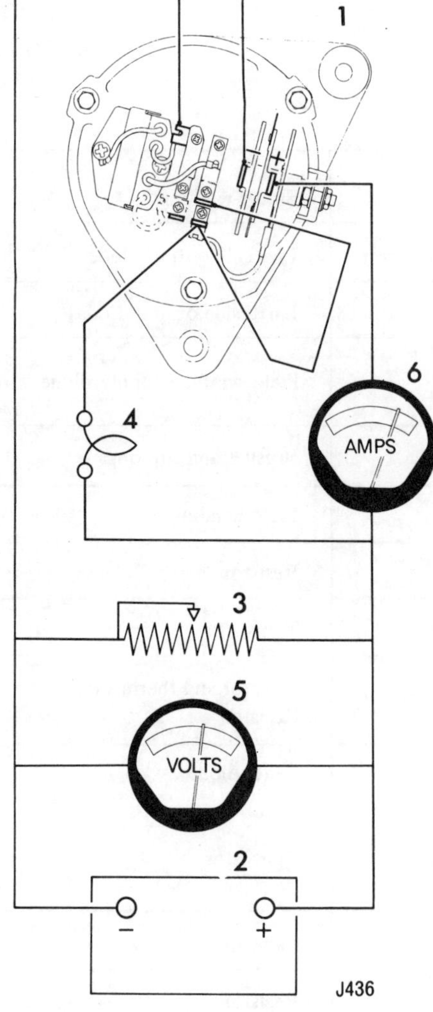

1. Alternator
2. Battery . . 12 volt
3. Variable resistor . 0-15 ohm – 35 amp
4. Light . . . . 12 volt – 2·2 watt
5. Voltmeter . . 0-20 volt
6. Ammeter . . 0-40 amp

Check control unit

NOTE: The stated output may be exceeded slightly when the alternator is cold. To avoid misleading results, the check should be performed with the unit as near to its normal operating temperature as possible.

10. Check drive belt adjustment. 86.10.05.
11. Disconnect multi-socket connectors.
12. Provide test circuit as shown.
    CAUTION: The alternator contains polarity-sensitive components that may be irreparably damaged if subjected to incorrect polarity. Observe polarity of alternator and battery terminals.
13. Run the engine.
14. Gradually increase the speed. At 1,500 alternator rev/min (550 to 720 engine rev/min) the light should be extinguished.
15. Hold the speed at approximately 6,000 alternator rev/min (2200 to 2900 engine rev/min). The voltmeter reading should now be steady at 14·0 to 14·4 volts.
16. If the voltmeter reading is not steady at the above figure – and a satisfactory 'Check capacity to produce current' has been performed – the indication is that the control unit should be replaced.

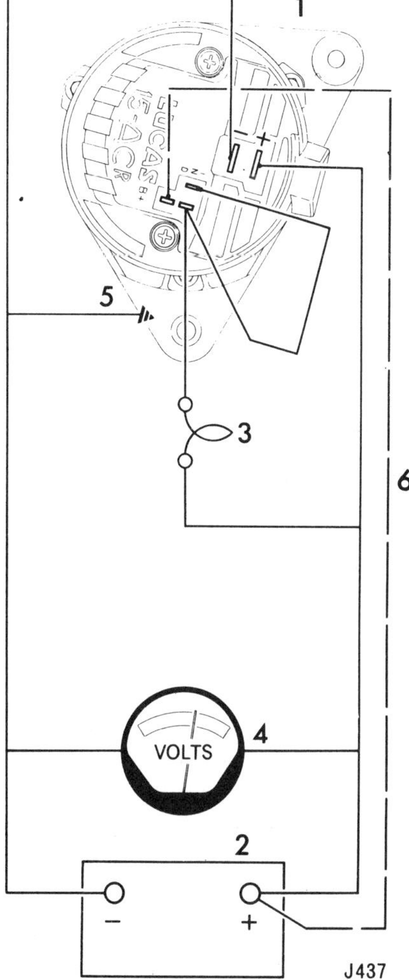

1. Alternator
2. Battery . . . 12 volt
3. Light . . . 12 volt – 2·2 watt
4. Voltmeter . . 0-20 volt
5. Earth connection to alternator body
6. This wire is only necessary for Lucas battery sensed 15 ACR alternators. It is not required for Lucas machine sensed 15 ACR and 17 ACR alternators.

ALTERNATOR – DELCO REMY TYPE DN 460

– Functional check 86.10.01

1. Check drive belt adjustment 86.10.05.
2. Disconnect the multi-socket connectors.
3. Provide a test circuit as shown.

   CAUTION: The alternator contains polarity sensitive components that may be irreparably damaged if subjected to incorrect polarity. Observe polarity of alternator and battery terminals.
4. Do not connect the variable resistor into the test circuit until instructed and do not connect it across the battery for longer than is necessary to perform the check.
5. Run the engine.
6. If the voltmeter reading fluctuates with speed and exceeds 15.5 volt the indication is that the regulator should be replaced.
7. If the voltmeter reading is steady below 15.5 volt connect the variable resistor into the test circuit as shown.
8. Hold the speed at approximately 5000 alternator rev/min (1800 to 2400 engine rev/min). Adjust the variable resistor to obtain the maximum ammeter reading.
9. The ammeter reading should now be within 10% of the nominal output given in data.
10. If the ammeter reading is not correct the indication is that the alternator requires overhaul or replacement.

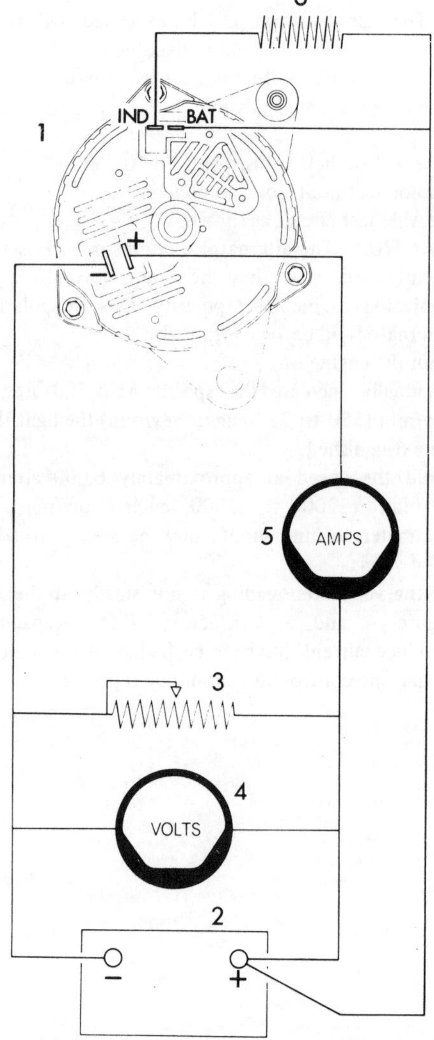

1. Alternator
2. Battery . . . 12 volt
3. Variable resistor
4. Voltmeter . . 0-20 volt
5. Ammeter . . 0-40 amp
6. Resistor . . 10 ohm – 6 watt or more

ALTERNATOR

– Remove and refit 86.10.02

Removing

1. Isolate the battery.
2. To improve access to the link bolt disconnect the Lucar connector from the temperature transmitter.
3. Disconnect two multi-socket connectors.
4. Remove the adjustment bolt lock nut.
5. Slacken the link bolt.
6. Remove the adjustment bolt and two washers.
7. Remove the main mounting bolt nut.
8. Support the weight of the alternator and withdraw the main mounting bolt and washer.
9. Lift and manoeuvre the alternator from the engine mounting bracket and drive belt.
10. Collect up the large spacer and the small spacer.

Refitting

11. To facilitate the operation tap the bush in the alternator rear mounting lug slightly rearwards.
12. Assemble the main mounting bolt, washer, alternator and large spacer together. Position the assembly to the engine mounting bracket and drive belt. Insert the main mounting bolt into the engine mounting bracket to stabilize the assembly.
13. Position the small spacer and insert the main mounting bolt fully.
14. Fit the main mounting bolt nut.
15. Fit the adjustment bolt with two washers positioned either side of the link.
16. Adjust the drive belt 86.10.05.
17. Connect two multi-socket connecters.
18. Connect the battery.

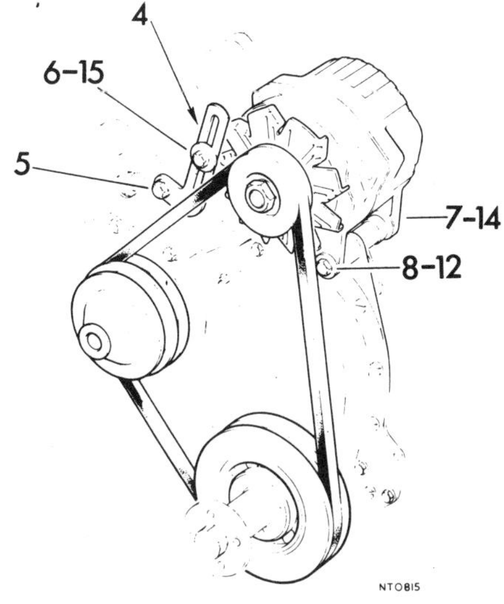

ALTERNATOR

– Drive belt – adjust **86.10.05**

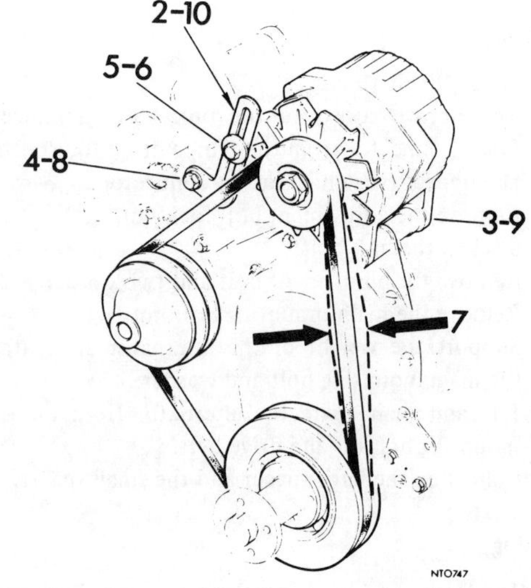

1. To improve access to the link bolt disconnect the Lucar connector from the temperature transmitter.
2. Remove the adjustment bolt lock nut.
3. Slacken the main mounting bolt.
4. Slacken the link bolt.
5. Slacken the adjustment bolt.
6. Carefully lever the alternator away from the engine to tension the belt. Tighten the adjustment bolt.
   CAUTION: To prevent bearing damage when tensioning the belt use a lever of soft material – preferably wood – applied to the alternator drive-end bracket. Do not lever on any other part of the alternator.
7. Check the belt tension. Total movement should be 0·75 to 1·00 in (20 to 25 mm) at the mid-point of the longest run.
8. Tighten the link bolt.
9. Tighten the main mounting bolt.
10. Using a spanner to hold the head of the adjustment bolt, fit the adjustment bolt lock nut.
11. Connect the Lucar connector to the temperature transmitter.

ALTERNATOR – LUCAS TYPES 15 ACR AND 17 ACR

– Overhaul 86.10.08

Dismantling

1. Remove the moulded cover.
2. Remove the brush box and control unit assembly by disconnecting the Lucar type connector from the rectifier pack and unscrewing three screws.
3. If required, the control unit may be detached from the assembly. Note the position of the three wire eyelets. Withdraw the screw to release the control unit and three screws to release the wire eyelets.
4. Note the position of the three stator wires on the rectifier pack.
5. Unsolder the three stator wire connections. Do not overheat the diodes or bend the diode pins. Solder quickly and provide a heat sink by gripping the diode pin with pliers.
6. Slacken the nut and withdraw the rectifier pack.
7. Remove the through-bolts.
8. Provide an extractor tool as shown.
9. To remove the slip-ring end bracket, position the extractor tool to engage with the outer journal of the slip-ring end bearing. Employ a second operator to support the slip-ring end bracket by hand. Carefully tap the extractor tool to drive the bearing from the housing.
   NOTE: It may be necessary to carefully file away surplus solder from the two field winding connections on the slip-ring moulding if the extractor tool will not pass over the moulding.
10. The rubber 'O' ring fitted in the slip-ring end bracket bearing housing may remain *in situ* unless replacement is contemplated.
11. Remove the stator windings from the drive end bracket.
12. Prevent the rotor turning by wrapping a scrap fan belt round the pulley and retaining by hand or vice. Remove the nut, spring washer, pulley and fan. If necessary, use a suitable extractor.
13. Remove the key.
14. Using a suitable press, remove the rotor from the drive end bracket.
    CAUTION: Do not attempt to remove the rotor by applying hammer blows to the shaft end. Such action may burr over and damage the thread.

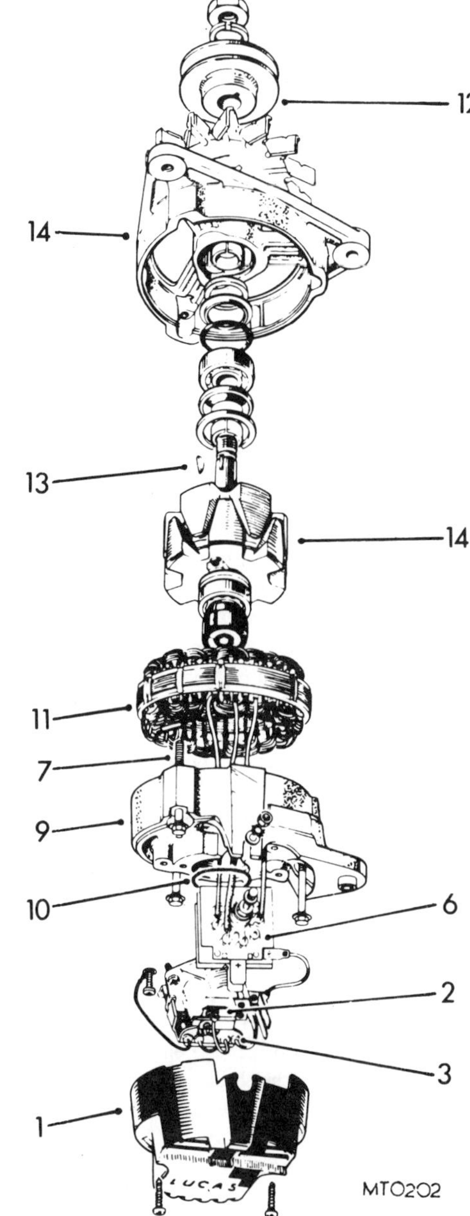

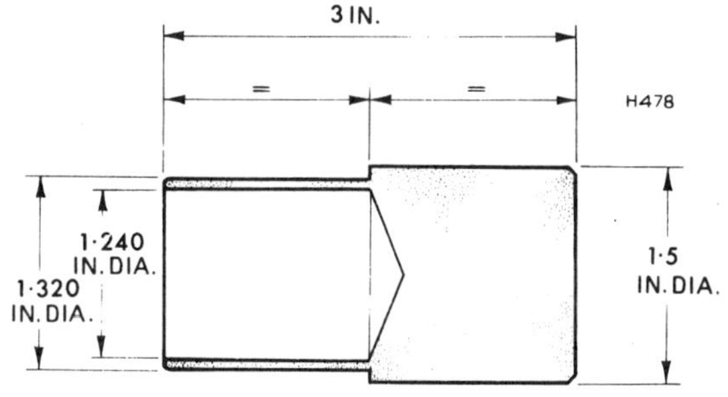

Reassembling

15. Using the spacer (arrowed) and a suitable tube, fit the rotor to drive end bracket by applying pressure to the bearing inner journal.
    CAUTION: Do not use the drive end bracket as a support while fitting the rotor. If the spacer is not employed, the felt ring may be damaged.
16. Fit the key.
17. Fit the fan, pulley, spring washer and nut. Prevent the rotor turning by wrapping a scrap fan belt round the pulley and retaining by hand or vice. Torque load the nut to 25 to 30 lb ft (3·46 to 4·15 kgf m).
18. Observe the relationship of the stator windings to the drive end bracket determined by the stator wire connections, the rectifier pack position on the slip-ring end bracket, the alignment of the mounting lugs on the end brackets and the through-bolt clearances on the stator windings.
19. Position the stator windings to the drive end bracket.
20. Ensure that the rubber 'O' ring is fitted correctly in the slip-ring end bracket bearing housing.
21. Fit the slip-ring end bracket by carefully pushing the bearing into the housing.
22. Fit the through-bolts, tightening evenly.
23. Ensure that the rubber locating piece is correctly fitted to the rectifier pack. Position the rectifier pack and secure it with the nut.
24. Position the three stator wires on rectifier pack as noted operation 4.
25. Solder the three stator wire connections. Note the precautions stated in operation 5 and use 'M' grade 45-55 tin-lead solder.
26. If required, attach the control unit to the brush box. Position the three wire eyelets on the brush box as noted in operation 3. Insert the screw to secure the control unit and the three screws to secure the wire eyelets.
27. Ensure that the brushes are entered correctly in the brush box. Fit the brush box and control unit assembly by inserting three screws and connecting the Lucar type connector to the rectifier pack.
28. Fit the moulded cover.

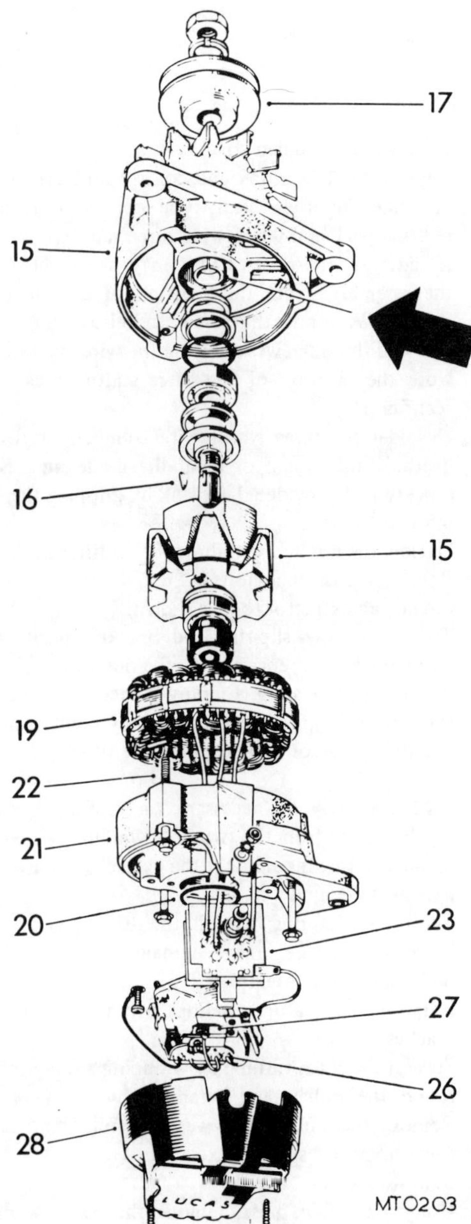

ALTERNATOR – DELCO REMY TYPE DN 460

– Overhaul **86.10.08**

Dismantle

1. Scribe a line across the drive end frame, stator and slip ring end frame to facilitate assembly.
2. Remove three through bolts.
3. Separate the drive end frame and rotor assembly from the slip ring end frame and stator assembly.
4. The brush springs will push the brushes from the brushbox as the rotor is withdrawn. Collect up two brush springs.
5. Remove three nuts. Withdraw the stator taking care that the three wire tags withdraw freely from the studs.
6. Incorrect assembly of screws, washers and insulation components removed during operations 7 to 12 may affect the operation of the alternator and cause irreparable damage to components. To ensure the correct assembly of all screws, washers and insulation components it is suggested that the individual components of each screw assembly are taped together and identified with the appropriate operation number before the next operation is performed.
7. Remove single screw, washer and insulation washer. An insulation sleeve may also be fitted to the screw. Lift out the diode trio.
8. Remove single screw, washer and insulation washer. An insulation sleeve may also be fitted to the screw. Lift out the brushbox.
9. Remove short red earthing screw and washer. Lift out the regulator.
10. Remove single screw and washer securing the earth side of the rectifier bridge.
11. Remove single screw, washer and insulation washer securing the live side of the rectifier bridge. Lift out the rectifier bridge.
12. The insulation piece fitted to the rectifier bridge live side slot may remain in situ unless replacement is contemplated.
13. Mark the forward face of the pulley and fan to facilitate assembly.
14. Prevent the rotor turning by using a 5/16 in. AF hexagon wrench in the shaft socket. Remove the nut, spring washer, pulley and fan.
15. Withdraw the rotor shaft from the drive end frame bearing.
16. Remove the spacer.

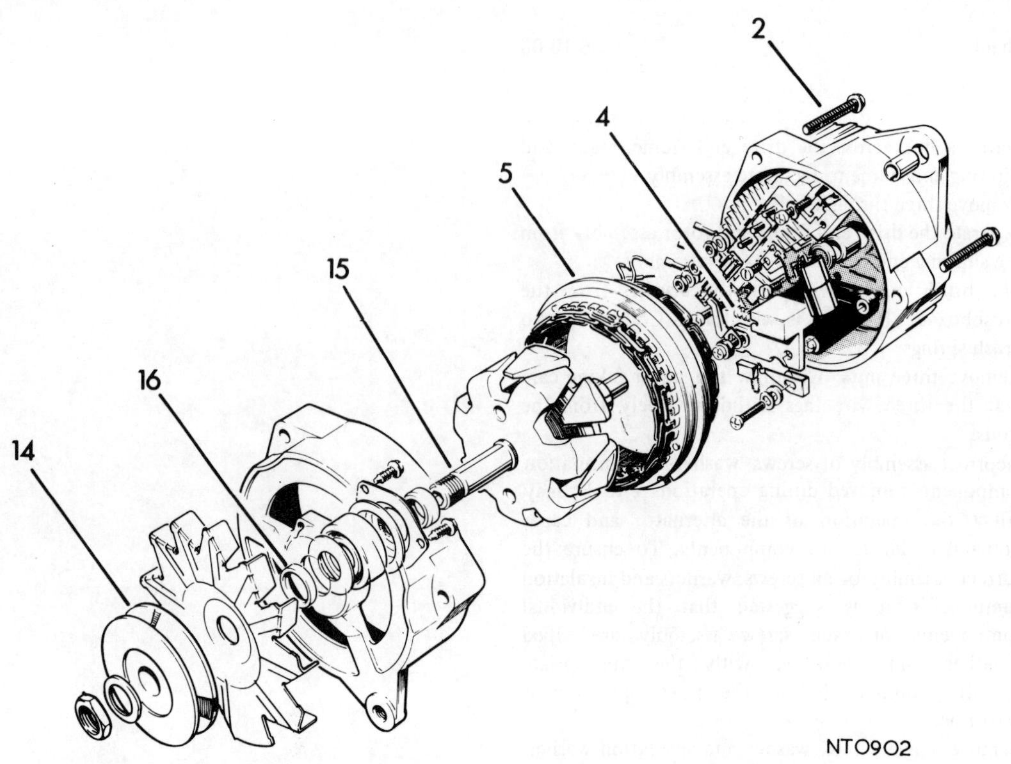
2
4
5
15
16
14
NTO902

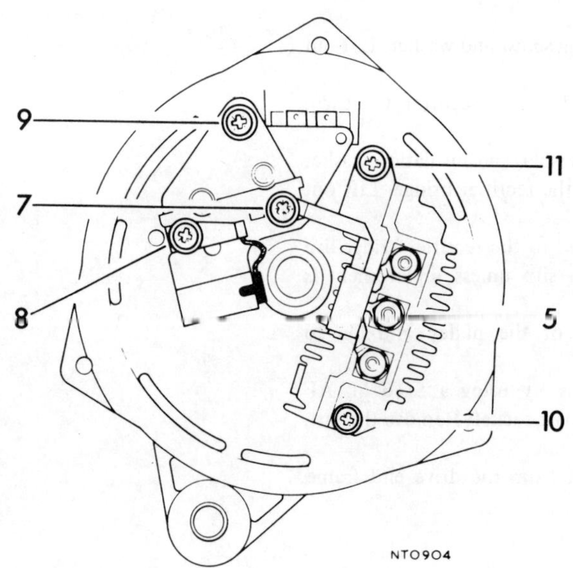
9
11
7
8
5
10
NTO904

Assemble

17. Fit the spacer.
18. Ensure that the rotor shaft is clean. Insert the rotor shaft through the drive end frame bearing.
19. Fit the fan, pulley, spring washer and nut. Prevent the rotor turning by using a 5/16 in. AF hexagon wrench in the shaft socket. Torque load the nut to 40 to 60 lbf ft (5·5 to 8·3 kgf m).
20. Ensure that the insulation piece is fitted correctly to the rectifier bridge live side slot so that its flange will be assembled against the slip ring end frame.
21. Position the rectifier bridge. Use screw assembly identified operation 11. Fit single screw, washer and insulation washer to secure the live side of the rectifier bridge.
22. Use screw assembly identified operation 10. Fit single screw and washer to secure the earth side of the rectifer bridge.
23. Position the regulator. Use screw assembly identified operation 9. Fit short red earthing screw and washer.
24. Position the brushbox. Use screw assembly identified operation 8. Fit single screw, washer and insulation washer. An insulation sleeve may also be fitted to the screw.
25. Position the diode trio. Use screw assembly identified operation 7. Fit single screw, washer and insulation washer. An insulation sleeve may also be fitted to the screw.
26. Provide a suitable probe to hold back the brushes. Fit the far brush spring and brush. Insert the probe through the slip ring end frame to hold back the brush. Fit the near brush spring and brush. Insert the probe further to hold back both brushes.
27. Insert the stator taking care that the three wire tags locate freely to the studs. Fit three nuts.
28. Ensure that the rotor shaft and slip rings are clean. Carefully position the drive end frame and rotor assembly to the slip ring end frame and stator assembly.
29. Align the scribe lines made at operation 1 above.
30. Fit three through bolts tightening evenly.
31. Withdraw the probe to allow the brushes to drop onto the slip rings.

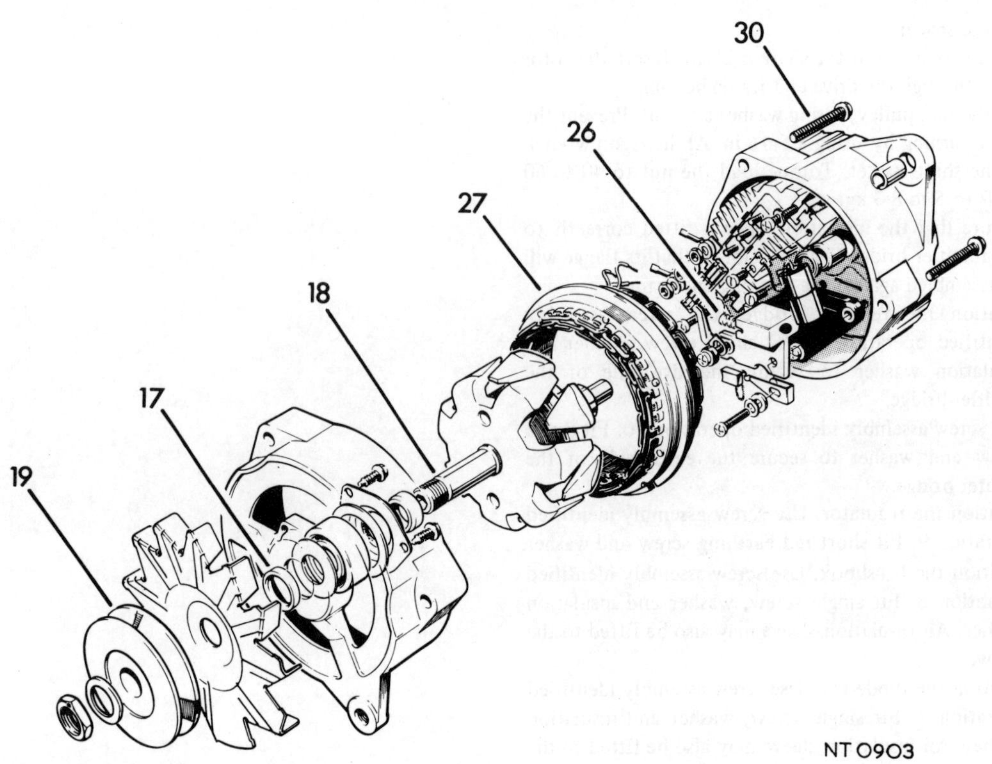
30
26
27
18
17
19
NT O903

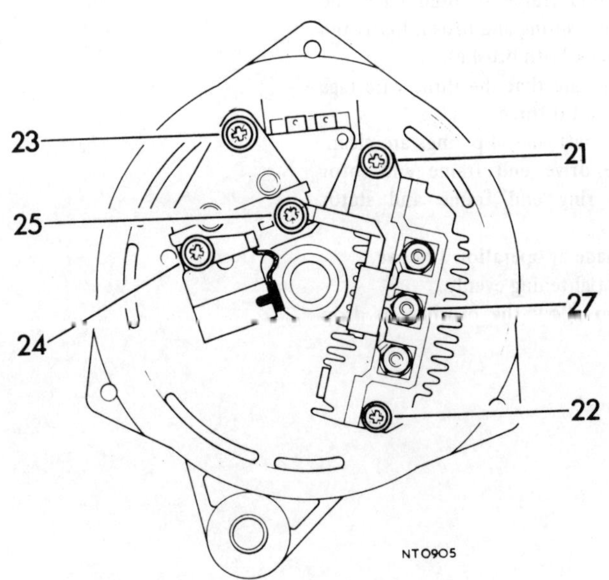
23
21
25
27
24
22
NTO9O5

BATTERY

– Remove and refit **86.15.01**

Removing

1. Remove the battery leads.
2. Slacken the nuts and swing down the battery retaining assembly.
3. Lift the battery from the vehicle

Refitting

4. Lift the battery into the tray.
5. Swing up the battery retaining assembly. Tighten the nuts.
6. Fit the battery leads. Ensure that the earth lead is connected to the battery negative terminal. Do not hammer the terminals to the terminal posts.
7. Coat the terminals with petroleum jelly (vaseline) to prevent corrosion.

HORN SLIP RING

– Remove and refit **86.30.02**

Removing

1. Perform 86.65.17 operations 1 to 5.
2. Disconnect one snap connector.
3. Remove the horn push 86.65.18.
4. Remove the steering wheel 57.60.01.
5. Bend up two metal tags. Remove the slip ring with its wire.

Refitting

6. Thread the wire through the appropriate steering column apertures, fascia panel aperture and steering column clamp aperture. Do not disturb the position of the felt strip located below the wires in the lower half of the steering column clamp. Position the slip ring and secure by bending down two metal tags. Note that two spare metal tags are provided for use if one of the original tags should break.
7. Apply petroleum jelly (Vaseline) to the slip ring contact surface.
8. Fit the steering wheel 57.60.01
9. Fit the horn push 86.65.18.
10. Ensure that the felt strip is correctly located and rectify if necessary.
11. Connect one snap connector. Purple/black slip ring wire to purple/black main harness wire.
12. Perfrom 86.65.17 operations 14 to 18.

IGNITION DISTRIBUTOR APPLICABILITY, IGNITION TIMING AND FEATURES CHART

	Normal Market – Petrol Injection Vehicle	U.S.A. Market – Carburetter Vehicle				
	1969 to 72 Engine units	1969 to 70 Engine units		1971 Engine units		1972 Engine units
	Fitted from Engine No. CP 25001 HE	Fitted from Engine No. CC 25001 HE				Fitted from Engine No. CC75001
	Fitted up to commencement of CR series Engine Nos.					Fitted up to commencement of CD series Engine Nos.
Stanpart No.	214459	308460	308460	308460	217521	218100
Lucas part No.	41219	41202	41306	41306 Modified by Triumph to be suitable for 1971 U.S.A. engine units. Action of vacuum advance deleted by sealing pipe with protective plug.	41352	41385
Ignition timing – static	11 degree B.T.D.C.	12 degree B.T.D.C.	12 degree B.T.D.C.	12 degree B.T.D.C.	4 degree B.T.D.C.	12 degree B.T.D.C.
Ignition timing – at idle	–	4 degree A.T.D.C.	4 degree A.T.D.C.	4 degree A.T.D.C.	4 degree A.T.D.C.	4 degree A.T.D.C.
Idle speed	–	800 to 850 rev/min	800 to 850 rev/min	800 to 850 rev/min	800 to 850 rev/min	800 to 850 rev/min
Centrifugal advance	√	√	√	√	√	√
Vacuum advance	No	√	√	No	No	No
Retard unit	No	√	√	√	√	√
Micrometer adjustment nut	√	No	No	No	No	No

IGNITION DISTRIBUTOR

Data

Manufacturer	Lucas
Type	22D6
Lucas part No.	41219
Stanpart No.	214459
Contact gap	0·014 to 0·016 in.
Rotation – viewed on rotor	Anticlockwise
Firing angles	60 ± 1 degrees
Dwell angle	35 ± 3 degrees
Open angle	25 ± 3 degrees
Moving contact spring tension	18 to 24 ozs.
Capacitor capacity	0·20 microfarad
Engine firing order	1 - 5 - 3 - 6 - 2 - 4

Centrifugal advance

Check at decelerating speeds

Distributor r.p.m.	Degrees distributor advance		Crankshaft r.p.m.	Degrees crankshaft advance	
	Minimum	Maximum		Minimum	Maximum
Below 175	No advance to occur		Below 350	No advance to occur	
450	0	2·0	900	0	4
800	2·5	4·5	1600	5	9
1300	6·0	8·0	2600	12	16
2000	6·0	8·0	4000	12	16

IGNITION DISTRIBUTOR

Data

Manufacturer	Lucas
Type	22D6
Lucas part No.	41202
Stanpart No.	308460
Contact gap	0·014 to 0·016 in.
Rotation – viewed on rotor	Anticlockwise
Firing angles	60 ± 1 degrees
Dwell angle	35± 3 degrees
Open angle	25 ± 3 degrees
Moving contact spring tension	18 to 24 ozs.
Capacitor capacity	0·20 microfarad
Engine firing order	1 - 5 - 3 - 6 - 2 - 4

Centrifugal advance

Check at decelerating speeds

Distributor r.p.m.	Degs. distributor advance		Crankshaft r.p.m.	Degs. crankshaft advance	
	Minimum	Maximum		Minimum	Maximum
Below 375	No advance to occur		Below 750	No advance to occur	
450	0	1	900	0	2
850	4	6	1700	8	12
1500	6	8	3000	12	16
2500	9	11	5000	18	22
3000	9	11	6000	18	22

Vacuum advance

Ins. of mercury vacuum	Degs. distributor advance		Degs. crankshaft advance	
	Minimum	Maximum	Minimum	Maximum
Below 2·5	No advance to occur			
3	0	0·5	0	1
4	0	2·5	0	5
6	2·5	7·0	5	14
8	6·0	9·0	12	18
15	7·0	9·0	14	18

Retard unit

Ins. of mercury vacuum	Degs. distributor retard		Degs. crankshaft retard	
	Minimum	Maximum	Minimum	Maximum
Below 1·5	No retard to occur			
2·5	0	1	0	2
4·0	0	3	0	6
8·0	5	8	10	16
15·0	7	9	14	18

IGNITION DISTRIBUTOR

Data

Manufacturer	Lucas
Type	22D6
Lucas part No.	41306
Stanpart No.	308460
Contact gap	0·014 to 0·016 in.
Rotation – viewed on rotor	Anticlockwise
Firing angles	60 ± 1 degrees
Dwell angle	35 ± 3 degrees
Open angle	25 ± 3 degrees
Moving contact spring tension	18 to 24 ozs.
Capacitor capacity	0·20 microfarad
Engine firing order	1 - 5 - 3 - 6 - 2 - 4

Centrifugal advance

Check at decelerating speeds.

Distributor r.p.m.	Degs. distributor advance		Crankshaft r.p.m.	Degs. crankshaft advance	
	Minimum	Maximum		Minimum	Maximum
Below 375	No advance to occur		Below 750	No advance to occur	
450	0	1	900	0	2
850	4	6	1700	8	12
1500	6	8	3000	12	16
2500	9	11	5000	18	22
3000	9	11	6000	18	22

Vacuum advance

Later distributors of this part number were modified by Triumph to be suitable for 1971 U.S.A. engine units. Action of vacuum advance deleted by sealing pipe with protective plug.

Ins. of mercury vacuum	Degs. distributor advance		Degs. crankshaft advance	
	Minimum	Maximum	Minimum	Maximum
Below 2·5	No advance to occur			
3	0	0·5	0	1
4	0	2·5	0	5
6	2·5	7·0	5	14
8	6·0	9·0	12	18
15	7·0	9·0	14	18

Retard unit

Ins. of mercury vacuum	Degs. distributor retard		Degs. crankshaft retard	
	Minimum	Maximum	Minimum	Maximum
Below 1·5	No retard to occur			
2·5	0	1	0	2
4·0	0	3	0	6
8·0	5	8	10	16
15·0	7	9	14	18

IGNITION DISTRIBUTOR

Data

Manufacturer	Lucas
Type	22D6
Lucas part No.	41352
Stanpart No.	217521

Contact gap	0·014 to 0·016 in.
Rotation – viewed on rotor	Anticlockwise
Firing angles	60 ± 1 degrees
Dwell angle	35 ± 3 degrees
Open angle	25 ± 3 degress
Moving contact spring tension	18 to 24 ozs
Capacitor capacity	0·20 microfarad
Engine firing order	1 - 5 - 3 - 6 - 2 - 4

Centrifugal advance

Check at decelerating speeds.

Distributor r.p.m.	Degs. distributor advance		Crankshaft r.p.m.	Degs. crankshaft advance	
	Minimum	Maximum		Minimum	Maximum
Below 500	No advance to occur		Below 1000	No advance to occur	
650	1·0	3·5	1300	2	7
900	6.5	9·0	1800	13	18
1100	8·5	10·5	2200	17	21
2200	12·0	14·0	4400	24	2[illegible]
2800	13·0	15·0	5600	26	30

Retard unit

Ins. of mercury vacuum	Degs. distributor retard		Degs. crankshaft retard	
	Minimum	Maximum	Minimum	Maximum
Below 1	No retard to occur			
3	1·0	4·0	2	8
4	2·5	5·0	5	10
5	3·0	5·0	6	10
8	3·0	5·0	6	10

IGNITION DISTRIBUTOR

Data

Manufacturer	Lucas
Type	22D6
Lucas part No.	41385
Stanpart No.	218100
Contact gap	0·014 to 0·016 in.
Rotation – viewed on rotor	Anticlockwise
Firing angles	60 ± 1 degrees
Dwell angle	35 ± 3 degrees
Open angle	25 ± 3 degrees
Moving contact spring tension	18 to 24 ozs
Capacitor capacity	0·20 microfarad
Engine firing order	1 - 5 - 3 - 6 - 2 - 4

Centrifugal advance

Check at decelerating speeds.

Distributor r.p.m.	Degs. distributor advance		Crankshaft r.p.m.	Degs. crankshaft advance	
	Minimum	Maximum		Minimum	Maximum
Below 400	No advance to occur			No advance to occur	
600	1·0	3·0	1200	2	6
900	4·0	6·0	1800	8	12
1200	6·0	8·0	2400	12	16
2200	10·5	12·5	4400	21	25
2800	12·0	14·0	5600	24	28

Retard unit

Ins. of mercury vacuum	Degs. distributor retard		Degs. crankshaft retard	
	Minimum	Maximum	Minimum	Maximum
Below 1	No retard to occur			
2	0	0·5	0	1
4	0	3·5	0	7
8	4·0	7·0	8	14
15	6·0	8·0	12	16

IGNITION DISTRIBUTOR

– Contact assembly – remove and refit 86.35.13

Removing

1. Remove the cover and rotor.
2. Remove the nut.
3. Remove the low tension wire eyelet and capacitor wire eyelet from the post.
4. Remove the lock screw, spring washer and washer.
5. Lift out the Quikafit contact assembly.

Refitting

6. Wipe preservative from the new contact faces.
7. Position the Quikafit contact assembly.
8. Fit the lock screw, spring washer and washer.
9. Position the capacitor wire eyelet and low tension wire eyelet to the post.
10. Fit the metal nut to the nylon thread finger tight. Tighten by rotating half a turn only with a spanner.
11. Adjust the contact gap. 86.35.14.

IGNITION DISTRIBUTOR

– Contact gap – adjust 86.35.14

1. Remove the cover and rotor.
2. Rotate the crankshaft to position the contact heel on a cam peak.
3. If the contact gap is correct, a 0·014 to 0·016 in (0·36 to 0·41 mm) feeler gauge will just slide between the contacts.
4. When the contact gap is correct operations 5 to 8 may be ignored.
5. If a correction is required, slacken the lock screw.
6. Move the fixed contact about the pivot to adjust the gap. This may be facilitated by inserting a screwdriver in the slots and twisting to position the fixed contact.
7. Tighten the lock screw.
8. Check that the correct gap has been maintained.
9. Fit the rotor and cover.

IGNITION DISTRIBUTOR

– Ignition timing – adjust 86.35.15

Static

1. Adjust the contact gap. 86.35.14.
2. Disconnect the distributor lead from the coil.
3. Provide a test lamp circuit as shown.
4. Rotate the crankshaft in engine run direction to approximately align the timing cover pointer with the 24 degree BEFORE on the crankshaft pulley scale. The test lamp should now be illuminated.
5. Carefully rotate the crankshaft further until the lamp just goes out.
6. If the timing is correct the pointer will be aligned with the scale at the ignition timing – static figure given in the chart 86.35.00.
7. When the timing is correct operations 8 to 12 may be ignored.

Operations 8 to 10 apply only when the distributor is fitted with a micrometer adjustment nut.

8. If a small correction is required, rotate the micrometer adjustment nut to advance or retard the timing.
9. If a large correction is required centre the micrometer adjustment nut and slacken the clamp bolt. Align the pointer with the scale at the 'ignition timing – static' figure given in the chart 86.35.00. Rotate the distributor body anticlockwise past the test lamp illumination position. Carefully rotate clockwise until the lamp just goes out. Tighten the clamp bolt with unit in this position.
10. Repeat operation 4 onwards.

Operations 11 to 12 apply only when the distributor is not fitted with a micrometer adjustment nut.

11. Slacken the clamp bolt. Align the pointer with the scale at the 'Ignition timing – static' figure given in the chart 86.35.00. Rotate the distributor body anticlockwise past the test lamp illumination position. Carefully rotate clockwise until the lamp just goes out. Tighten the clamp bolt with unit in this position.
12. Repeat operation 4 onwards

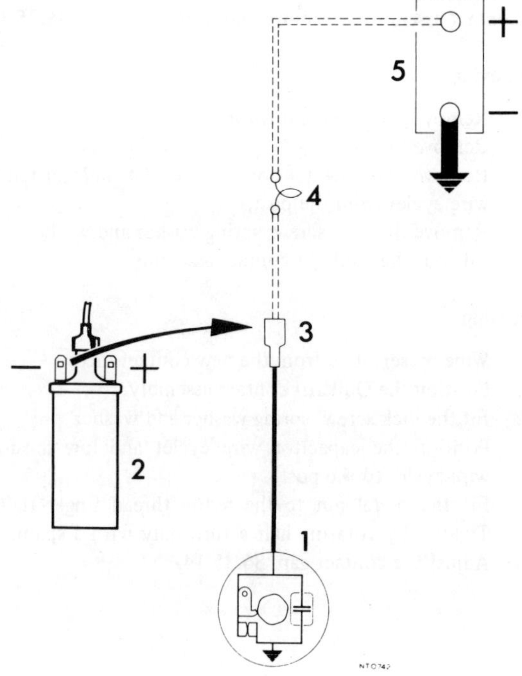

1. Distributor – diagrammatic layout
2. Ignition coil
3. Distributor fly lead removed from coil
4. Test lamp – 12 volt
5. Vehicle battery

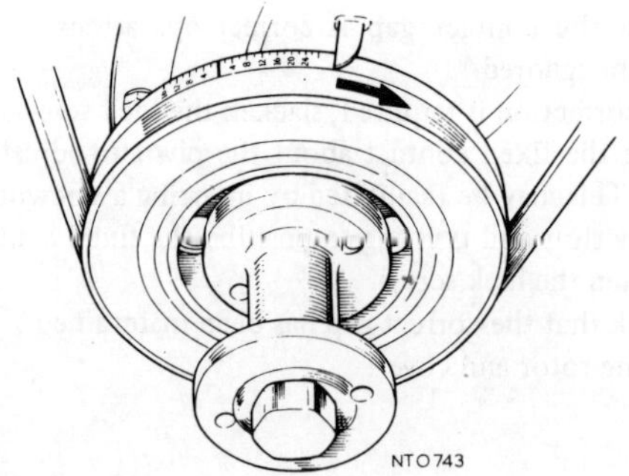

Dynamic

** *U.S.A. market vehicles only.*

13. Adjust the contact gap 86.35.14.
14 Connect the timing light as instructed by the manufacturer. This engine is timed on No. 1 cylinder which is located at the front.
15 Run the engine at the 'idle speed' given in the chart 86.35.00. Position the timing light to illuminate the timing cover pointer and the crankshaft pulley scale.
16 If the timing is correct the equipment will show the pointer to be aligned with the scale at the 'ignition timing – at idle' figure given in the chart 86.35.00.
17 When the timing is correct operations 18 to 22 may be ignored.

Operations 18 to 20 apply only when the distributor is fitted with a micrometer adjustment nut to advance or retard the timing.

18 If a small corection is required, rotate the micrometer adjustment nut to advance or retard the timing.
19 If a large correction is required stop the engine. Centre the micrometer adjustment nut. Slacken the clamp bolt. Carefully rotate the distributor body as required. Tighten the clamp bolt.
20 Repeat operation 15 onwards.

Operations 21 to 22 apply only when the distributor is not fitted with a micrometer adjustment nut.

21 Stop the engine. Slacken the clamp bolt. Carefully rotate the distributor body as required. Tighten the clamp bolt.
22 Repeat operation 15 onwards.**

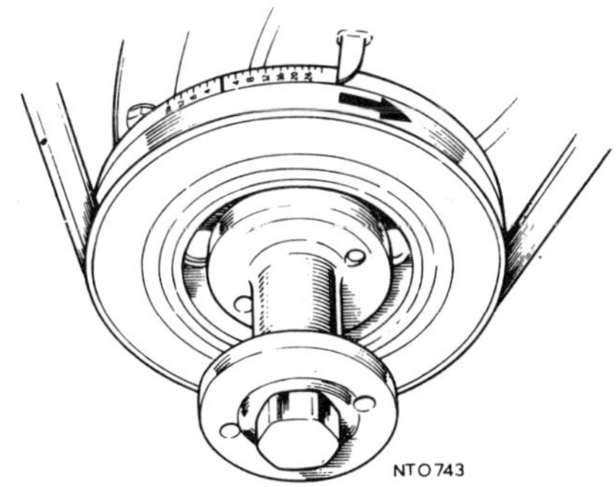

IGNITION DISTRIBUTOR

– Lubrication 86.35.18

1. Remove the cover and rotor.
2. Apply a few drops of engine oil to lubricate the cam spindle bearing.
3. Inject a few drops of engine oil through the apertures to lubricate the centrifugal timing control.
4. Lightly grease the cam with Mobilgrease No. 1 or equivalent.
5. If the moving contact is removed from the post lightly grease post with Shell Retinax A or equivalent.

IGNITION DISTRIBUTOR

Remove and refit 86.35.20

Removing

1. Pull off the high tension connection to the ignition coil.
2. Pull off the six high tension connections to the spark plugs.
3. Remove the distributor cover.
4. Disconnect the low tension Lucar connector from the distributor.
5. Pull off the vacuum advance pipe if fitted.
6. Pull off the retard unit pipe if fitted.
7. Unscrew the knurled nut and withdraw the tachometer drive cable.
8. Remove single bolt, spring washer and washer to release the clamp plate from the pedestal.
9. Withdraw the distributor from the pedestal.

Refitting

10. Insert the distributor into the pedestal. Ensure that the coupling offset key locates correctly in the drive gear slot.
11. Reverse 1 to 8.
12. Adjust the ignition timing. 86.35.16.

IGNITION DISTRIBUTOR

– Overhaul **86.35.26**

Due to the number of ignition distributors fitted to the TR6 vehicle range a precise overhaul instruction for every unit connot be included in this manual.

By referring to this general overhaul instruction service personnel should be able to successfully overhaul the distributor of any specific vehicle.

Dimantling

1. Remove the contact assembly. 86.35.13.
2. Remove the screw and lift out the capacitor.
3. Remove the two side screws and spring washers.
4. Withdraw the terminal block. Lift off the link. Withdraw the plate assembly.
5. Some units fitted with micrometer adjustment nut – Prise off the circlip. Unscrew the micrometer adjustment nut and remove the spring. Withdraw the internal component with any vacuum capsules attached. Push off the ratchet spring.
6. Some units fitted with advance unit and retard unit – Using a small screwdriver force in the retaining spring and push the vacuum advance unit against the body. With the lugs clear of the slots unscrew the retard unit. Withdraw the vacuum advance unit with the spring. Push off the retaining spring.
7. Some units fitted with retard unit but no advance unit –
   Using a pin punch tap out the small pin. Withdraw the retard unit.
8. Remove two screws and spring washers. Withdraw the cover, gasket and tachometer drive gear.
9. Tap out the coupling pin. Remove the coupling and thrust washer. Ensure that the shaft is burr-free and withdraw it.
10. Remove the control springs, exercising care not to distort the springs.
11. Remove the cam spindle screw. Withdraw the cam spindle.
12. Remove the weights.

Assembly

13. Lubricate the action plate sliding surfaces and cam surfaces with Rocol 'Moly pad'. Position the weights on the action plate.
14. Lubricate the cam spindle bearing and cam spindle weight pillars with Rocol 'Moly pad'. Fit the cam spindle either way round to the weights and secure it with the cam spindle screw.
15. Fit the control springs, exercising care not to distort the springs.
16. Lubricate the shaft with Rocol 'Moly pad' and insert it into the body. Fit the thrust washer and coupling. Ensure that the coupling is the correct way round so that the relationship of the coupling offset key to the rotor will be as shown. Secure with the coupling pin.
17. Lubricate the tachometer drive gear with engine oil. Insert the tachometer drive gear, gasket and cover. Secure with two screws and spring washers.
18. Reverse operation 5, operation 6 or operation 7 as appropriate.
19. Insert the plate assembly. Lift on the link. Insert the terminal block.
20. Fit the two side screws and spring washers. Include the moving plate earth lead tag in the appropriate screw assembly.
21. Position the capacitor and secure it with the screw.
22. Fit the contact assembly. 86.35.13.
23. Lubricate. 86.35.18.

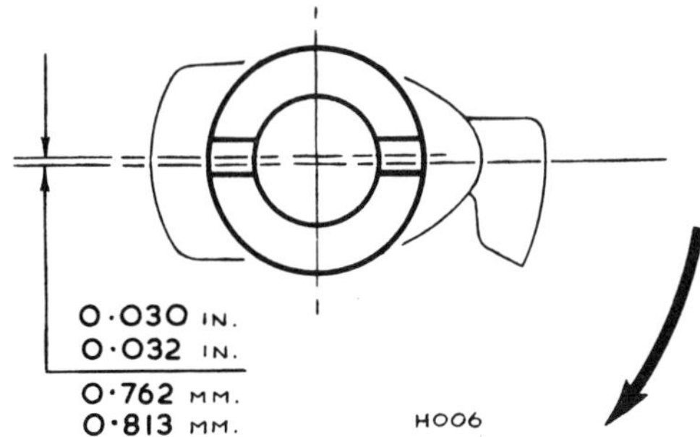

LAMPS

– Headlamp – remove and refit 86.40.02

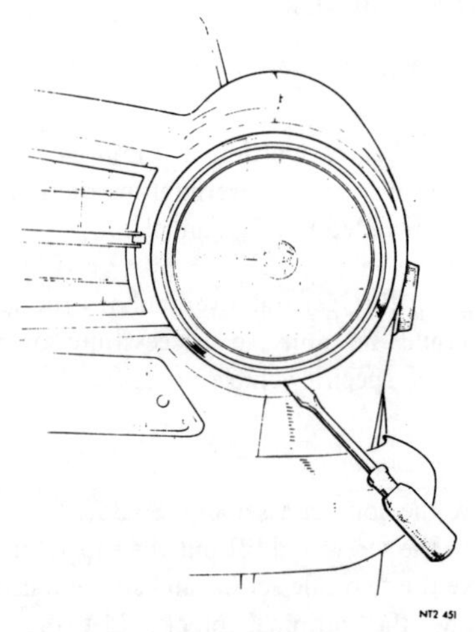

Removing

1. Insert a large screwdriver behind the rim adjacent to the clip as shown. Twist the screwdriver to release the rim from the clip.
2. Lift the rim from the upper retainers.
3. Remove three screws to release the retaining rim and light unit.
4. Pull the connector block from the light unit.

Refitting

5. Reverse instructions 3 to 4.
6. Ensure that neither of the rim clip components are bent.
7. Position the rim so that the clip components are aligned. Locate the rim behind the upper retainers and push to engage the clip.

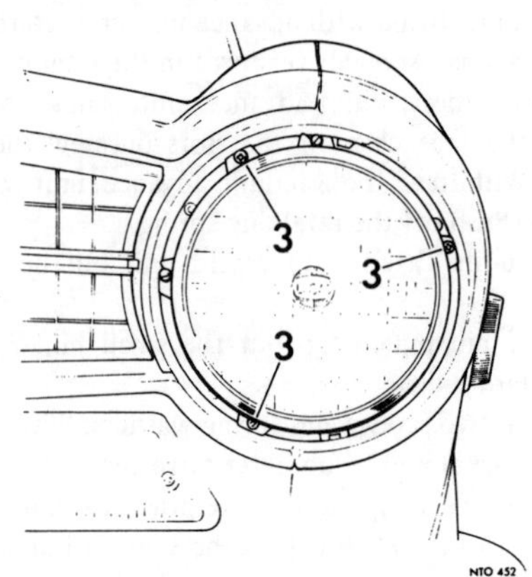

LAMPS

Headlamp – beam aiming 86.40.17

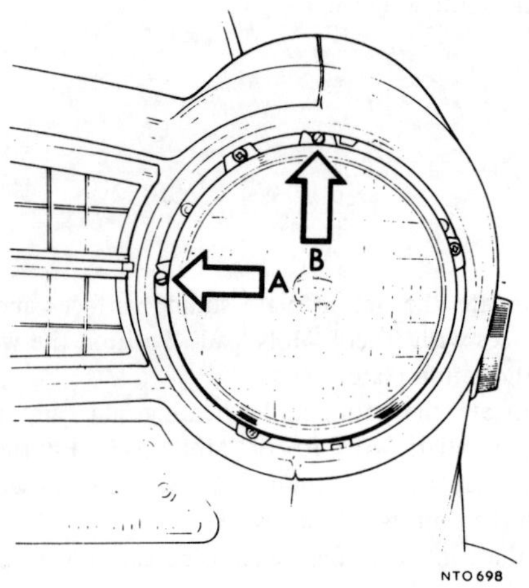

Beam aiming can best be accomplished using equipment such as Lucas 'Beamsetter', 'Lev-L-Lite' or 'Beam tester'. This service is available at Triumph distributors or dealers and will ensure maximum road illumination with minimum discomfort to other road users.

1. Insert a large screwdriver behind the rim adjacent to the clip as shown. Twist the screwdriver to release the rim from the clip.
2. Lift the rim from the upper retainers.
3. Screw 'A' positions the beam in the horizontal plane.
4. Screw 'B' controls beam height.

LAMPS

– Front parking and flasher lamp – remove and refit 86.40.26

Removing

1. Remove two screws and withdraw the lens.
2. Remove the bulb/bulbs (according to market) from the bayonet fitting/fittings.
3. Remove the air intake valance 76.79.04.
4. Locate the appropriate harness break out and disconnect three snap connectors.
5. Remove two nuts, spring washers and washers.
6. Withdraw the lamp assembly from the panel.

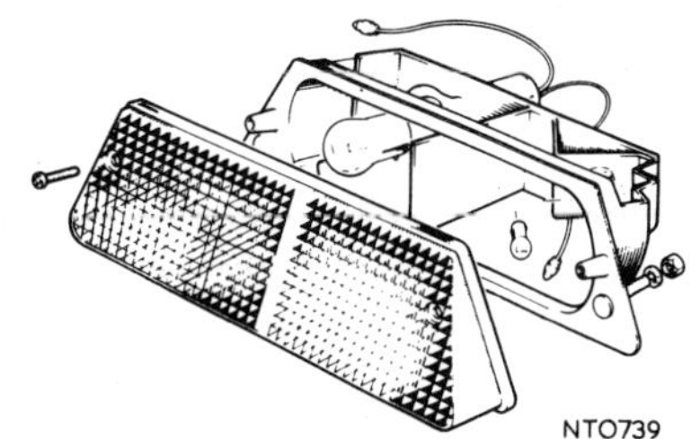

Refitting

7. Reverse instructions 1 to 6. Note that the lamp green wire should be connected to the harness green/red wire for the left hand lamp and to the harness green/white wire for the right hand lamp.

LAMPS

– Front marker lamp – remove and refit 86.40.59

Removing

1. Remove two screws and withdraw the lens.
2. Remove the bulb from the bayonet fitting.
3. Remove the air intake valance 76.79.04.
4. Locate the appropriate harness break out and disconnect two snap connectors.
5. Remove two nuts and washers.
6. Withdraw the lamp assembly from the panel.

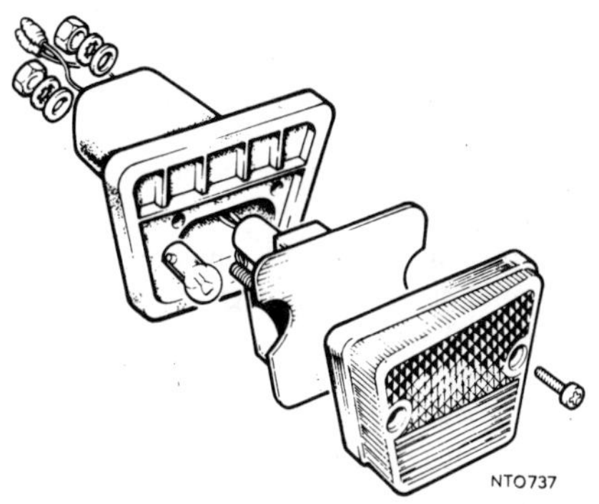

Refitting

7. Reverse instructions 1 to 6.

LAMPS

Rear lamp assembly – remove and refit 86.40.70

Removing

1. Open the luggage boot lid.
2. Remove the floor carpet.
3. Remove the spare wheel cover panel.
4. Remove six screws and withdraw the appropriate small rear trim panel.
5. Turn back the side trim panel on the appropriate side.
6. Pull four bulb holders from the lamp base.
7. Disconnect six Lucar connectors.
8. Remove the bulbs from the bayonet fittings.
9. Remove six nuts, spring washers and washers.
10. Withdraw the lamp from the panel.
11. The four lenses are attached to the lamp base with Posidrive screws. A lens may be replaced individually after removing the lamp.

Refitting

12. Reverse instructions 1 to 11. Connect the Lucar connectors as shown.

NTO736

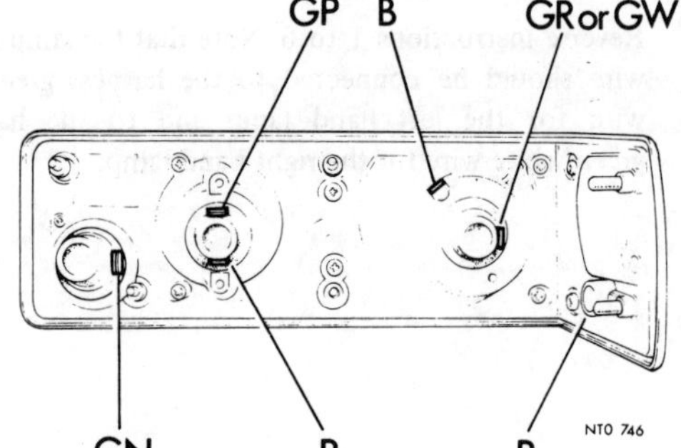

GP Green/purple wire
B Black wire
GR Green/red wire
GW Green/white wire
R Red wire
GN Green/brown wire

LAMPS

Plate illumination lamp – remove and refit 86.40.86

Removing

1. Remove two screws and lift off the chrome cover.
2. Disengage the small lens lugs from the rubber moulding.
3. Remove the two bulbs from the bayonet fittings.
4. Open the luggage boot lid.
5. Locate the plate illumination lamp wires at a harness brake out point accessible through an aperture in the rear valance panel.
6. Disconnect two wires from the four-way snap connector.
7. To facilitate refitting tie a suitable length of cord firmly to the wires.
8. Carefully pull the wires and cord through the panel grommet.
9. Remove two nuts, spring washers and washers. Remove the lamp base from the bumper.

Refitting

10. Reverse instructions 1 to 9. If any difficulty is experienced positioning the wires or panel grommet remove the floor carpet, spare wheel cover panel and spare wheel. A rubber plugged access hole exists on the inner panel in line with the panel grommet position.

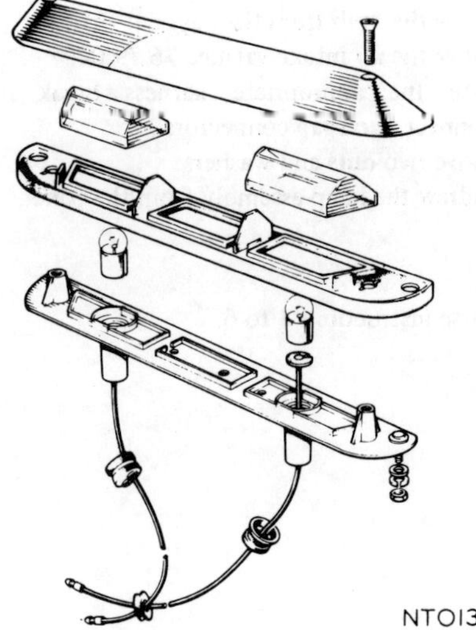

LAMPS

Luggage boot lamp – remove and refit 86.45.16.

Removing

1. Open the luggage boot lid.
2. Remove two screws.
3. Withdraw the lamp assembly from the petrol tank trim panel.
4. Disconnect two Lucar connectors.
5. Remove the elastic band and separate the two components of the lamp.
6. Carefully lever out the festoon bulb.

Refitting

7. Reverse instructions 1 to 6. Connect the Lucar connectors either way round.

LAMPS

– Transmission tunnel lamp – remove and refit 86.45.20

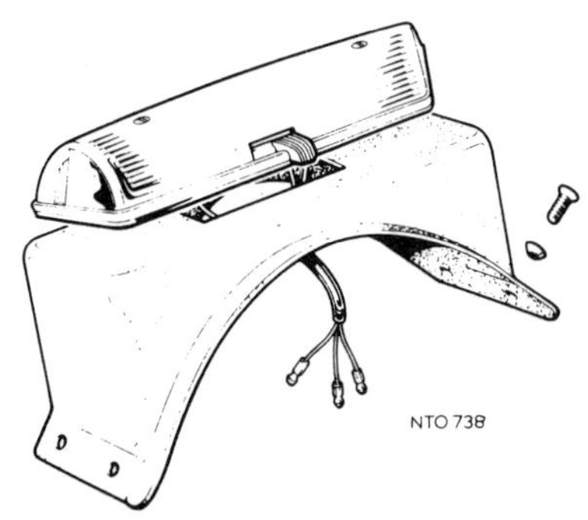

Removing

1. Remove two screws and lift off the cover/lens assembly.
2. To renew the festoon bulb, carefully lever the bulb from the contacts.
3. Remove two screws and lift off the lamp base assembly.
4. Remove two screws on the left hand side of the plinth. Lift the plinth slightly to locate and free the harness.
5. Disconnect three snap connectors.

Refitting

6. Reverse instructions 1 to 5.

LAMPS

– Seat belt – warning light – remove and refit 86.45.75

Later U.S.A. market vehicles only.

Removing

1. Isolate the battery.
2. Remove single screw and washer and withdraw the gearbox cover side trim panel on the passenger side of the vehicle.
3. Pull out the bulb holder from the projection of the 'FASTEN BELTS' unit.
4. If required remove the bulb from the bayonet fitting.
5. Push out the 'FASTEN BELTS' unit from the fascia.

Refitting

6. Reverse instructions 1 to 5.

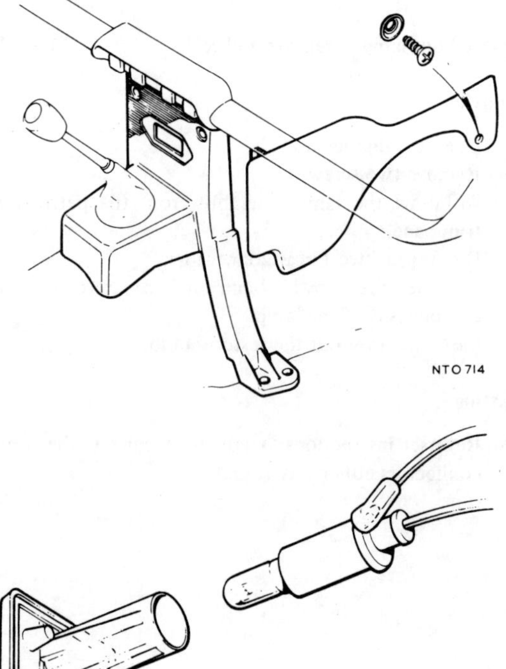
NTO 714

NTO 773

LAMPS

– Hazard warning light – remove and refit 86.45.76

– Brake line failure warning light – remove and refit 86.45.77

Left hand steer vehicles only.

Removing

1. Isolate the battery.
2. To gain access remove either the speedometer 88.30.01 or the tachometer 88.30.21. The choice depends entirely on which operation is prefered by the individual fitter.
3. Pull out the bulb holder from the housing.
4. If required unscrew the bulb from the holder.
5. Unscrew the lens bezel from the housing.

Refitting

6. Reverse instructions 1 to 5.

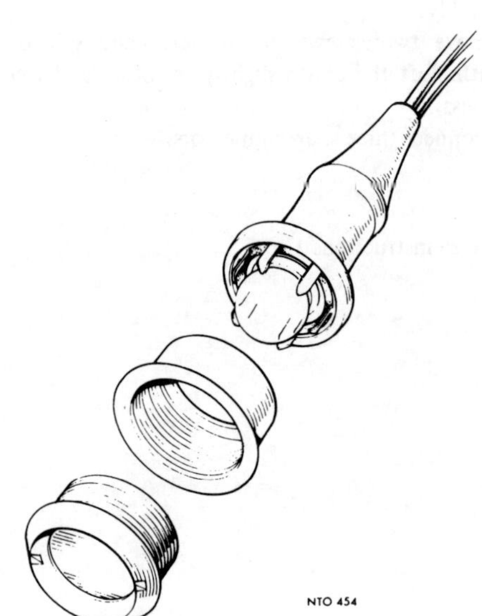
NTO 454

LAMPS

– Key light – remove and refit **86.45.78**

Later U.S.A. market vehicles only.

Removing

1. Locate the key light adjacent to the steering column lock assembly.
2. Pull out the bulb holder from the bracket.
3. If required unscrew the bulb from the holder.

Refitting

4. Reverse instructions 2 to 3.

RADIO FACILITY

Description **86.50.00**

Early vehicles with ignition/starter switch fitted to central control cowl.

The ignition/starter switch includes a facility for this optional extra item. The two Lucar blades which make up terminal 4 provide a positive 12 volt radio supply controlled by the ignition/starter key.

To locate the terminal refer to the appropriate 86.65.02 operation.

Later vehicles with ignition/starter switch fitted to steering column lock assembly.

The ignition/starter switch includes a facility for this optional extra item. The two Lucar blades which make up terminal 5 provide a positive 12 volt radio supply controlled by the steering column lock key.

To locate the terminal refer to the appropriate 86.65.02 operation.

RELAYS

– Hazard relay – remove and refit **86.55.02**

Early left hand steer vehicles with hazard circuit using relay.

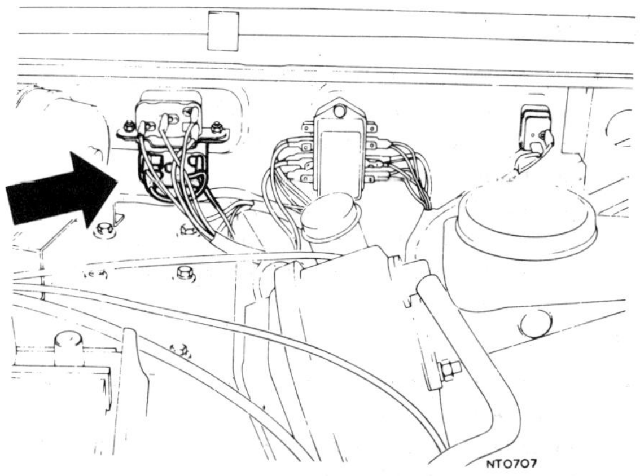

Removing

1. Lift the bonnet and locate the hazard relay on the left hand front wheelarch closing panel. The hazard relay is identified by being connected to the wires listed in operation 4.
2. Disconnect five Lucar connectors.
3. Remove two nuts, spring washers, washers and screws. Lift the relay from the vehicle.

Refitting

4. Reverse instructions 1 to 3. Connect the Lucar connectors as follows:
   Purple/red wire to terminal W1
   Black wire to terminal W2
   Green/white wire to terminal C1
   Light green/pink wire to terminal C2
   Green/red wire to terminal C4

RELAYS

Overdrive relay – remove and refit **86.55.04**

Overdrive vehicles only.

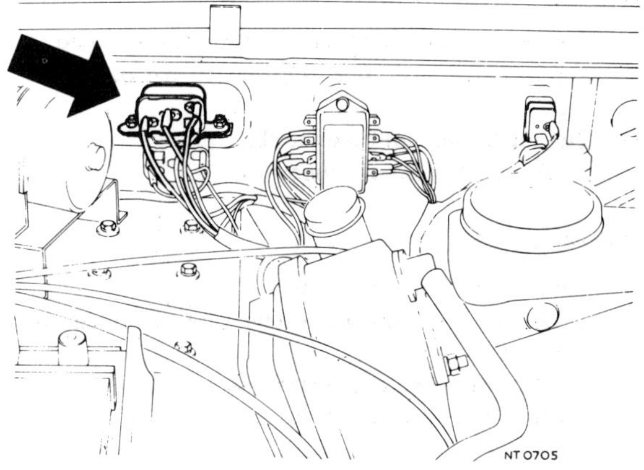

Removing

1. Lift the bonnet and locate the overdrive relay on the left hand front wheelarch closing panel. The overdrive relay is identified by being connected to the wires listed in operation 4.
2. Disconnect four Lucar connectors.
3. Remove two nuts, spring washers, washers and screws. Lift the relay from the vehicle.

Refitting

4. Reverse instructions 1 to 3. Connect the Lucar connectors as follows:
   White wire to terminal W1
   Yellow/green wire to terminal W2
   Brown wire to terminal C1
   Yellow/purple wire to terminal C2

RELAYS

Horn relay – remove and refit 86.55.09

Later vehicles only.

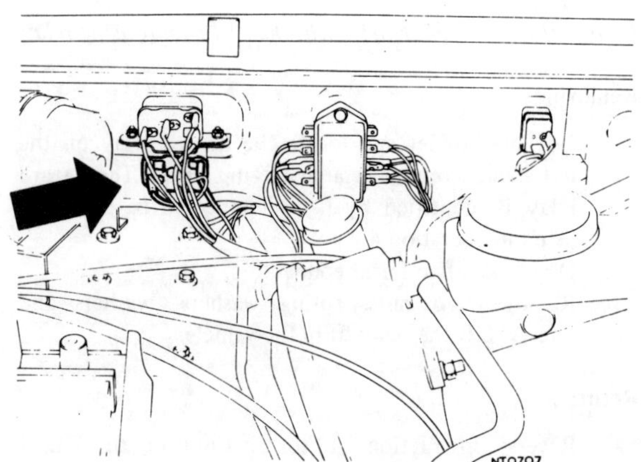

Removing

1. Lift the bonnet and locate the horn relay on the left hand front wheelarch closing panel. The horn relay is identified by being connected to wires with purple as the primary colour.
2. Disconnect four Lucar connectors.
3. Remove two nuts, spring washers, washers and screws. Lift the relay from the vehicle.

Refitting

4. Reverse instruction 1 to 3. Connect the Lucar connectors as follows:
   Purple/black wire to terminal W1
   Purple wire to terminal W2
   Purple/yellow wire to terminal C1
   Purple wire to terminal C2

FLASHER UNIT

Turn signal flasher unit – remove and refit 86.55.11

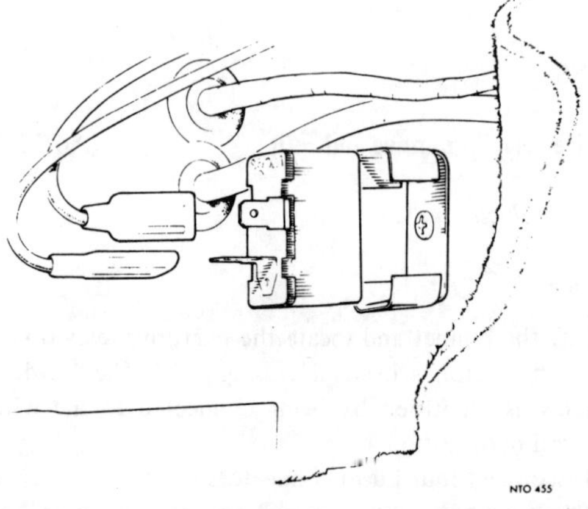

Removing

1. Locate the flasher unit mounted in a clip attached to the bulkhead end panel adjacent to the passengers feet.
2. Pull the flasher unit from the clip
3. Disconnect two Lucar connectors.

Refitting

4. Connect two Lucar connectors
   Green wire or light green/slate wire (as fitted) to terminal B.
   Light green/brown wire to terminal L.
5. Fit the flasher unit to the clip.

FLASHER UNIT

Hazard flasher unit – remove and refit 86.55.12

Left hand steer vehicles only.

Removing

1. Locate the flasher unit mounted in a clip attached to the left hand front wheelarch closing panel.
2. Pull the flasher unit from the clip.
3. Disconnect the Lucar connectors.

Refitting

4. Connect the Lucar connectors as detailed on the appropriate wiring diagram.
5. Fit the flasher unit to the clip.

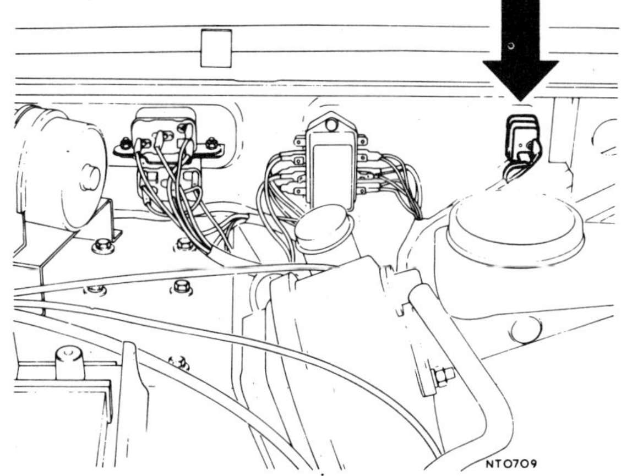

BUZZER

– Remove and refit 86.55.13

Later U.S.A. market vehicles only.

Removing

1. Locate the buzzer unit mounted to the lower edge of the fascia below the tachometer.
2. Remove single screw and spring washer.
3. Disconnect two Lucar connectors.

Refitting

4. Reverse instructions 2 to 3. Connect the Lucar connectors either way round.

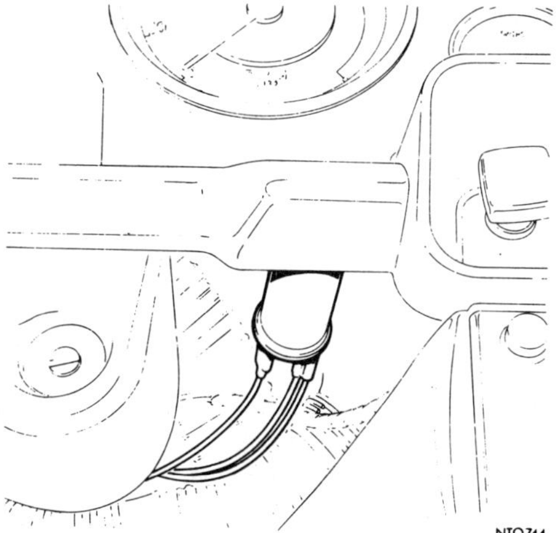

SEAT BELT WARNING SYSTEM

– Description **86.57.00**

Later U.S.A. market vehicles only.

This system is designed to discourage driving the vehicle without the seat belts being in use.

The system is actuated by selection of any gear other than neutral. When the system is actuated a 'FASTEN BELTS' warning light on the fascia illuminates and a buzzer provides an audible intrusion.

With the driver only in the vehicle the system is cancelled when the drivers seat belt is fastened.

With the driver and a passenger in the vehicle, a switch built into the passengers seat is actuated. The system is then cancelled when both the drivers and passengers seat belts are fastened.

A diode in the circuit (see appropriate wiring diagram) enables the seat belt warning system and the key warning system to use the same audible buzzer unit.

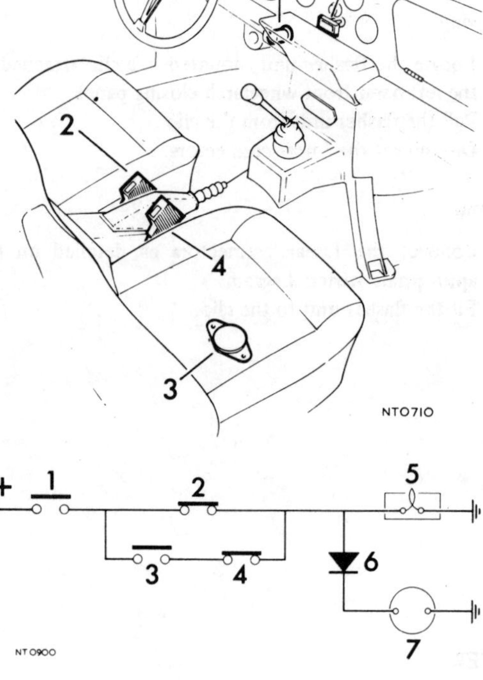

+ Supply
1. Gearbox switch
2. Drivers belt switch
3. Passengers seat switch
4. Passengers belt switch
5. Warning light
6. Diode
7. Buzzer

DIODE

– Remove and refit **86.57.10**

Later U.S.A. market vehicles fitted with seat belt warning system only.

Removing

1. Isolate the battery.
2. Locate the diode taped to the harness in a position above the bonnet release handle.
3. Unwind the tape to release the diode.
4. Disconnect two Lucar connectors. Remove the diode from the vehicle.
5. Remove the insulating sleeve.

Refitting

6. Fit the insulating sleeve over the female connector.
7. Position the diode the correct way round indicated by the connectors. Connect two Lucar connectors as follows:
   Light green/orange wire to diode male connector.
   Purple/orange wire to diode female connector.
8. Apply the tape to secure the diode.
9. Connect the battery.

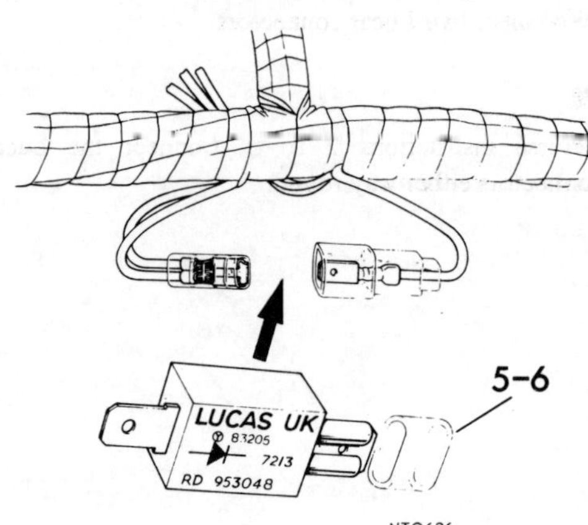

KEY WARNING SYSTEM

– Description **86.58.00**

Later U.S.A. market vehicles only.

This system is designed to discourage leaving the ignition key in the lock with the vehicle unattended. While it should prevent the encouragement of theft it is not a comprehensive anti-theft device.

The system is actuated by opening the drivers door when the ignition key is still in the lock. When the system is actuated a buzzer provides an audible intrusion.

The system is cancelled when the ignition key is removed from the lock or when the drivers door is closed.

The drivers door switch in the circuit is a 'double function' component with two individual contact sets. One set controls the electrical supply to the key warning circuit and key light circuit. The second set provides an earth return for the transmission tunnel lamp circuit.

The key switch is built into the steering column lock unit. Failure of the switch would necessitate replacement of the steering column lock.

A diode in the circuit enables the key warning system and the seat belt warning system to use the same audible buzzer unit.

BRAKE LINE FAILURE AND OIL PRESSURE WARNING SYSTEM

– Description **86.59.00**

Left hand steer vehicles only.

The brake line failure indication system consists of a warning light mounted on the fascia panel and a switch which is a component part of the pressure differential warning actuator incorporated in the brake system.

The oil pressure indication system consists of a warning light housed in the tachometer and a switch fitted to the cylinder block. The switch is in communication with the main oil gallery.

The brake line failure indication circuit is amalgamated with the oil pressure indication circuit so that when the ignition circuits are energised both warning lights will illuminate faintly to indicate no bulb filament failure.

When the engine is started the oil pressure will rise causing the oil pressure switch diaphragm to be actuated outwards. The contact plate is isolated from earth. Both warning lights will extinguish.

Should pressure loss occur in either front or rear brake lines the brake line failure switch will actuate. The 'BRAKE' warning light will illuminate brightly.

Should the oil pressure fall below the saft operating pressure while the engine is running the oil pressure switch will actuate. Both the 'OIL' and the 'BRAKE' warning lights will illuminate faintly.

BRAKE AND OIL WARNING LIGHT SUMMARY

Condition	'BRAKE' warning light	'OIL' warning light
Ignition on – Engine not running	ON FAINT	ON FAINT
Engine running	OFF	OFF
Engine running – Brake line pressure low	ON BRIGHT	OFF
Engine running – Oil pressure low	ON FAINT	ON FAINT

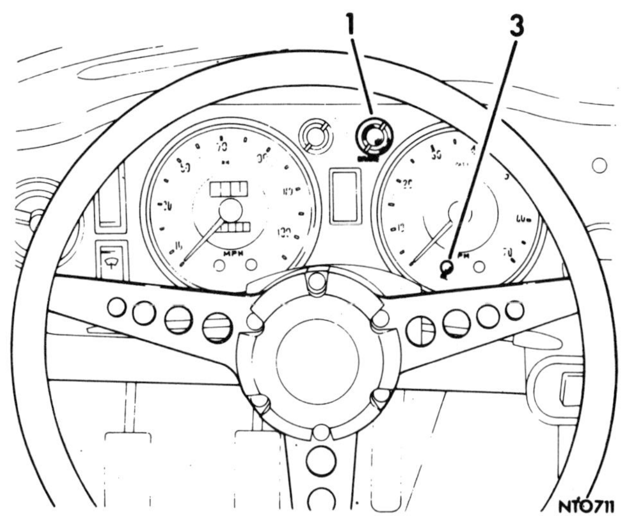

1. Brake line failure warning light
2. Brake line failure switch
3. Oil pressure warning light
4. Oil pressure switch

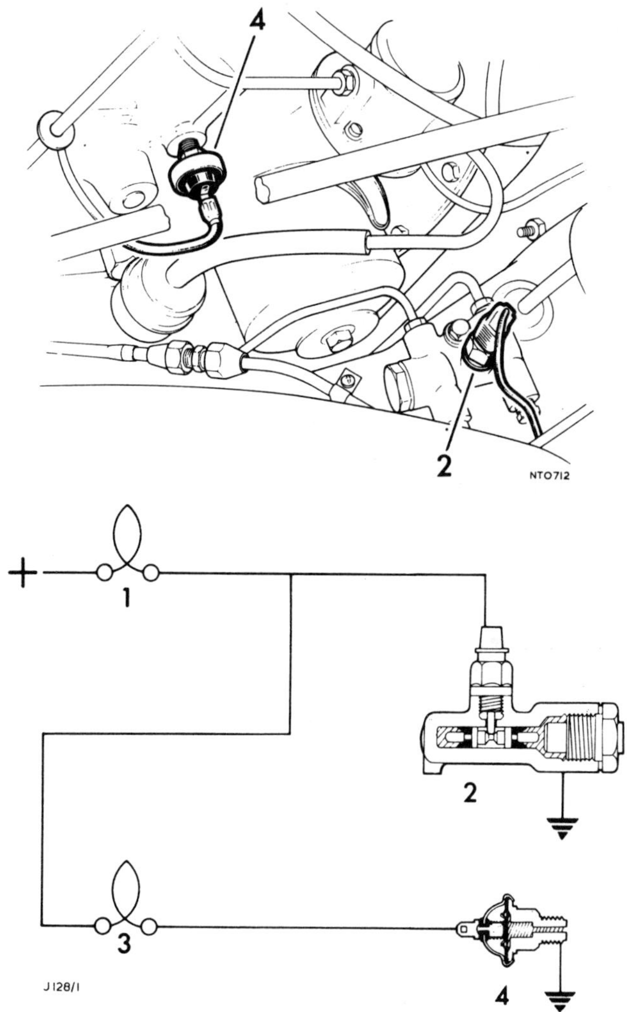

STARTER MOTOR – TYPE M418G PE

Data and description 86.60.00

Note that two starter motors have been fitted to the TR6 model range. Ensure that information obtained from this manual refers to the appropriate starter motor for the specific vehicle. A Lucas type M418G PE unit was fitted up to engine numbers CP 53636 and CC63894. A Lucas type 2M100 PE unit was fitted from engine numbers CP 53637 and CC 63895.

Data

Manufacturer	Lucas
Type	M418G PE
Lucas Part No.	25626
Stanpart	214914

Motor

Yoke diameter	4·187 to 4·218 in (106·35 to 107·14 mm)
Light running – speed	5500 to 8000 rev/min
current	80 amp
torque	Not stated
Load running – speed	1000 rev/min
current	280 amp
torque	7 lbf ft (0·97 kgf m)
Locked – speed	Nil
current	465 amp
torque	15 lbf ft (2·1 kgf m)
Commutator minimum skimming diameter	1·530 in (38·90 mm)
Brush length – new	0·559 in (14·19 mm)
renew if less than	0·310 in (7·90 mm)
Brush spring tension	36 oz f (1000 gf)
Bearing renewal mandrel diameter:	
Commutator end cover bearing	0·5005 to 0·4995 in (12·713 to 12·687 mm)
Drive end bracket bearing	0·4734 to 0·4724 in (12·024 to 11·999 mm)

Solenoid

Pull-in winding resistance – measured between unmarked 'WR wire' connector and 'STA' terminal	0·13 to 0·15 ohm
Hold-in winding resistance – measured between unmarked 'WR wire' connector and unit body	0·63 to 0·73 ohm

Motor

A conventional, four pole, four brush motor with a shaft which carries a roller clutch drive.

The armature shaft rotates in two porous bronze bushes. The armature features a conventional cylindrical commutator.

Shaft end float is controlled at the commutator end bracket by a steel thrust washer and a fabric thrust washer.

The yoke has four windows and is fitted with an external cover band. The yoke and commutator end bracket are secured by two through bolts which screw into tappings provided in the fixing bracket.

Solenoid and roller clutch drive

The starter solenoid is integral with the starter motor. The solenoid contains a heavy pull-in winding and a light hold-in winding. Applying battery voltage to the unmarked 'WR wire' connector initially energizes both windings. The combined action of both windings pulls in the plunger to cause engagement of the pinion and contact of the main terminals. The pull-in winding is now shorted-out leaving the hold-in winding to maintain the plunger position.

Contact of the main terminals energizes the motor. The roller clutch drive locks up and the engine is cranked.

Firing of the engine rotates the pinion at high speed. The roller clutch drive is over-ridden and damaging high-speed rotation of the armature does not occur.

Driver release of the ignition/starter switch allows the solenoid plunger to move out under spring pressure. Contact of the main terminals is broken and disengagement of the pinion occurs.

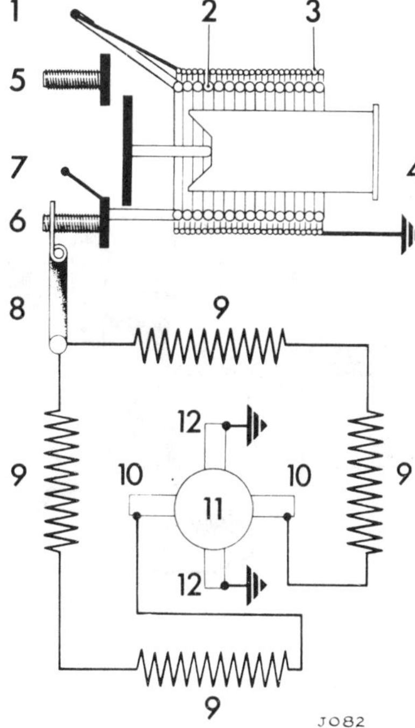

1. Unmarked 'WR wire' connector
2. Pull in winding
3. Hold in winding
4. Plunger
5. Solenoid battery terminal
6. STA terminal
7. IGN connector for ballast ignition when fitted
8. Motor lead
9. Field windings
10. Field winding brushes
11. Commutator
12. Earth brushes

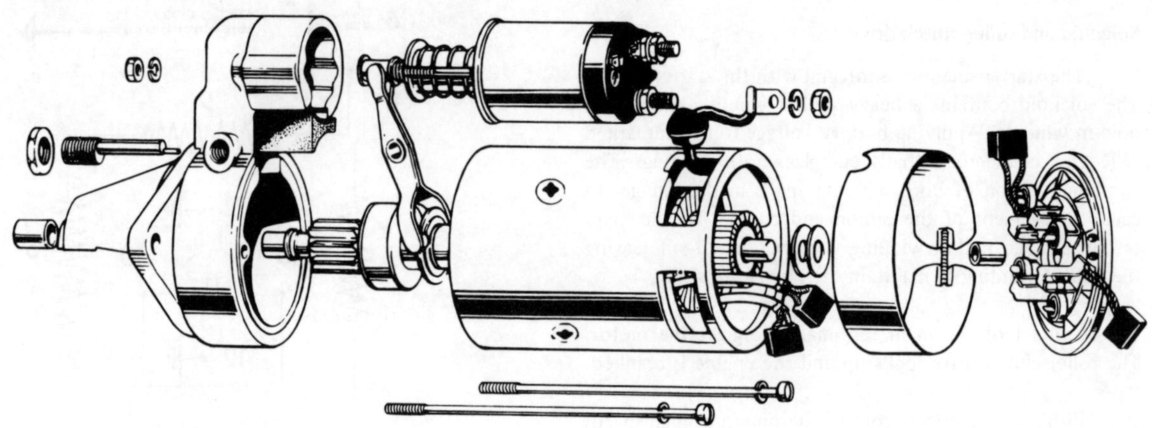

NTO910

STARTER MOTOR – TYPE 2M100 PE

Data and description 86.60.00

Note that two starter motors have been fitted to the TR6 model range. Ensure that information obtained from this manual refers to the appropriate starter motor for the specific vehicle. A Lucas type M418G PE unit was fitted up to engine numbers CP 53636 and CC 63894. A Lucas type 2M100 PE unit was fitted from engine numbers CP 53637 and CC 63895.

Data

Manufacturer	Lucas
Type	2M100 PE
Lucas part No.	25647
Stanpart No.	218053

Motor

Yoke diameter	4 in (101·60 mm)
Light running – speed	6,000 rev/min
current	40 amp
torque	Not stated
Load running – speed	1,000 rev/min
current	300 amp
torque	7·3 lbf ft (1·01 kgf m)
Locked – speed	Nil
current	463 amp
torque	14·4 lbf ft (1·99 kgf m)
Commutator minimum skimming thickness	0·140 in (3·56 mm)
Brush length – new	0·710 in (18·03 mm)
renew if less than	0·375 in (9·53 mm)
Brush spring tension	36 ozf (1000 gf)
Shaft end-float: maximum between bush and spire retaining ring	0·010 in (0·25 mm)
Bearing renewal mandrel diameter:	
Commutator end cover bearing	0·4377 in (11·118 mm)
Drive end bracket bearing	0·4729 in (12·012 mm)

Solenoid

Pull-in winding resistance – measured between unmarked 'WR wire' connector and 'STA' terminal	0·25 to 0·27 ohm
Hold-in winding resistance – measured between unmarked 'WR wire' connector and unit body	0·76 to 0·80 ohm

Motor

A series-wound, four-pole, four-brush motor with a shaft which carries a roller clutch drive.

The armature shaft rotates in two porous bronze bushes. The armature features a face-type moulded commutator.

Shaft end-float is controlled at the commutator end cover by the internal thrust washer and the position of a Spire retaining ring fitted on the shaft extension.

A plastic brush box is riveted to the commutator end cover. It holds four wedge-shaped brushes and captive coil springs. The brushes are keyed to ensure correct fitting.

The field winding is four joined strips. One end is attached to two brush flexibles, while the other is attached to a single flexible which is earthed to the yoke.

The yoke is windowless. The yoke and commutator end cover are secured by two through bolts which screw into tappings provided in the drive-end bracket.

Solenoid and roller clutch drive

The starter solenoid is integral with the starter motor. The solenoid contains a heavy pull-in winding and a light hold-in winding. Applying battery voltage to the unmarked 'WR wire' connector initially energizes both windings. The combined action of both windings pulls in the plunger to cause engagement of the pinion and contact of the main terminals. The pull-in winding is now shorted-out leaving the hold-in winding to maintain the plunger position.

Contact of the main terminals energizes the motor. The roller clutch drive locks up and the engine is cranked.

Firing of the engine rotates the pinion at high speed. The roller clutch drive is over-ridden and damaging high-speed rotation of the armature does not occur.

Driver release of the ignition/starter switch allows the solenoid plunger to move out under spring pressure. Contact of the main terminals is broken and disengagement of the pinion occurs.

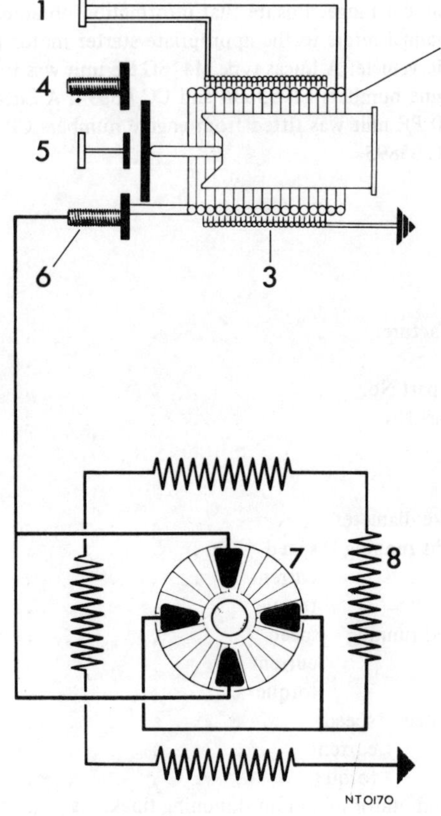

1. Unmarked 'WR wire' connector
2. Pull in winding
3. Hold-in winding
4. Solenoid battery terminal
5. IGN. connector for ballast ignition when fitted
6. Solenoid motor terminal
7. Brushes and commutator
8. Field windings

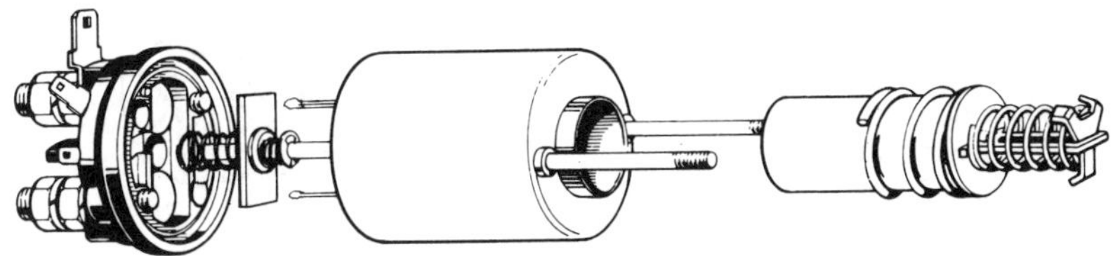

NTO150

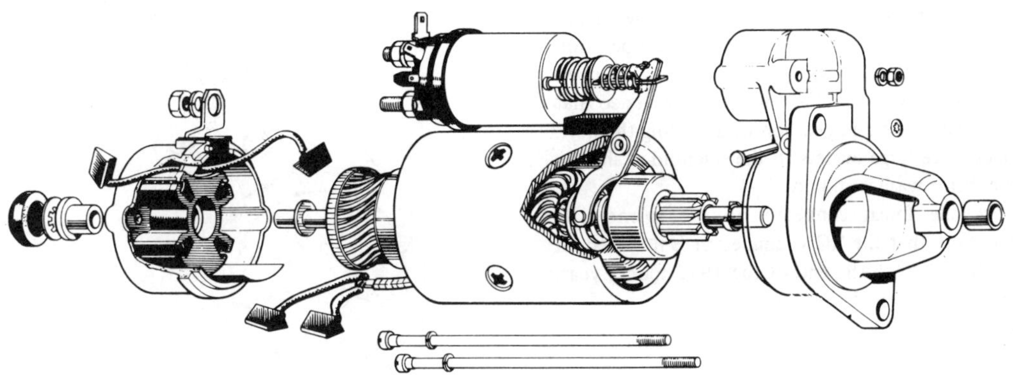

NTO214

STARTER MOTOR – TYPES M418G PE AND 2M100 PE

Remove and refit **86.60.01**

Removing

1. Drive the vehicle onto a ramp.
2. Isolate the battery.
3. Petrol injection vehicles only – Remove the air intake manifold 19.17.01.
4. Carburetter vehicles only – Remove the air cleaner 19.10.01.
5. Disconnect one Lucar connector.
6. Remove the nut and spring washer. Disconnect three large eyelets from the solenoid.
7. Working from above the engine, remove the upper mounting nut, spring washer and bolt.
8. Raise the ramp.
9. Working from below the engine, remove the lower mounting nut, spring washer and bolt.
10. Employ a second operator. With one fitter above the engine and one below, carefully manoeuvre the starter motor upwards from the vehicle.

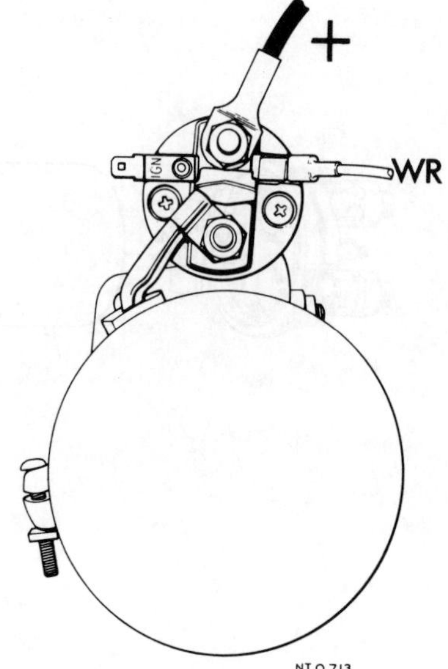

Refitting

NOTE: Include an earthing star washer under either bolt head.

11. Reverse instructions 8 to 10.
12. Working from above the engine, fit the upper mounting bolt, spring washer and nut. This operation may be facilitated by securing the nut to an open jawed spanner with suitable adhesive or sealer so that the nut may be held in position while fitting the bolt.
13. Connect three large eyelets to the solenoid as shown. Fit the spring washer and nut.
14. Connect one Lucar connector to the solenoid as shown. Note that the 'IGN' connector is not used on TR6 vehicles up to the end of the 1972 model year.
15. Reverse instructions 1 to 4.

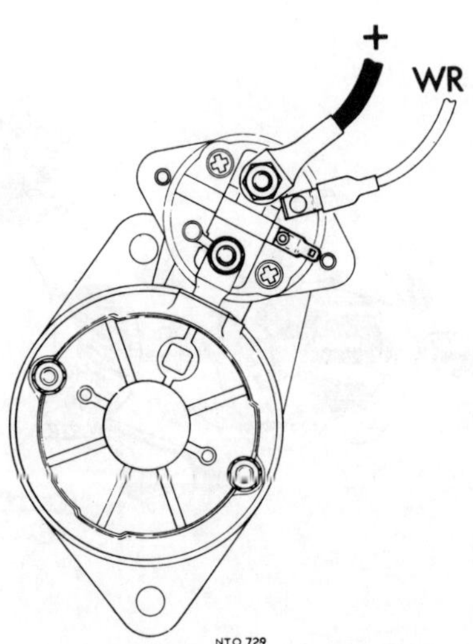

\+ Battery lead
WR White/red wire

STARTER MOTOR – TYPES M418G PE AND 2M100 PE

– Roller clutch drive – remove and refit 86.60.07

Removing

1. Dismantle the starter motor. 86.60.13.
2. Provide a special punch as shown.
3. Position the special punch over the shaft end and tap the thrust collar from the jump-ring towards the roller clutch drive.
4. Prise the jump-ring from the shaft groove.
5. Remove the thrust collar.
6. Remove the roller clutch drive

Refitting

7. Lubricate the splines and pinion bearing with grease.
8. Fit the roller clutch drive.
9. Fit the thrust collar with the open side facing the shaft end as shown.
10. Prise the jump-ring into the shaft groove.
11. Force the thrust collar over the jump-ring.

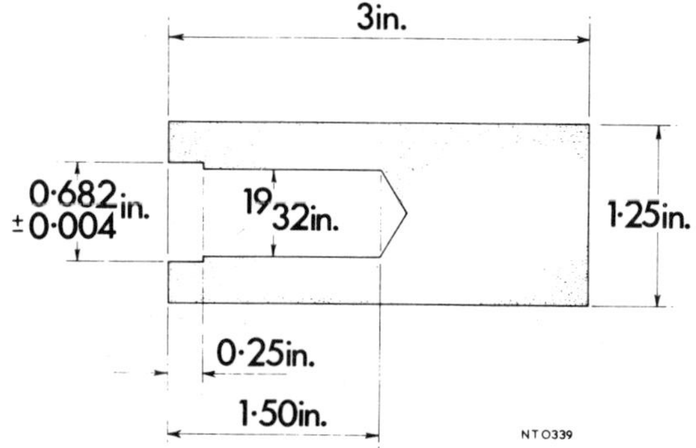

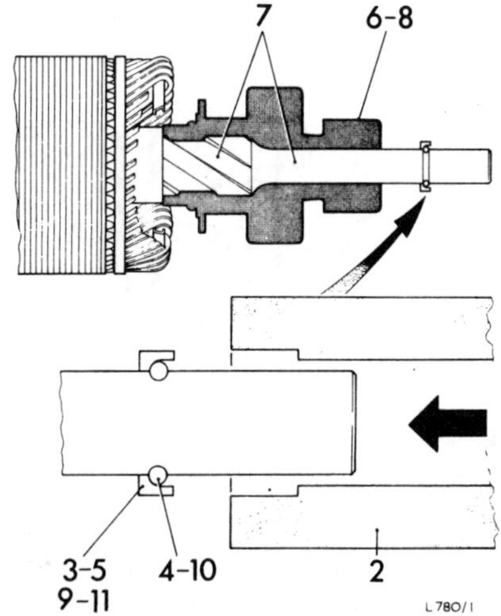

STARTER MOTOR – TYPE M418G PE

Overhaul 86.60.13

Note that two starter motors have been fitted to the TR6 model range. Ensure that information obtained from this manual refers to the appropriate starter motor for the specific vehicle. A Lucas type M418G PE unit was fitted up to engine numbers CP 53636 and CC 63894. A Lucas type 2M100 PE unit was fitted from engine numbers CP 53637 and CC 63895.

Dismantling

1. Remove the nut and spring washer. Disconnect the motor lead from the solenoid 'STA' terminal.
2. Remove two nuts and washers. Withdraw the solenoid leaving the plunger attached to the engaging lever.
3. Remove the return spring.
4. Remove the plunger from the engaging lever.
5. Slacken the locknut. Unscrew and withdraw the eccentric pin.
6. Remove the cover band.
7. Withdraw the brushes from the holders.
8. Remove two through bolts.
9. Carefully tap the fixing bracket mounting lugs to separate the yoke from the fixing bracket.
10. Separate the commutator end bracket from the yoke.
11. Remove the steel thrust washer and the fabric thrust washer.
12. Remove the rubber moulding.
13. Withdraw the armature and starter drive assembly. Remove the engaging lever.
14. Remove the thrust washer.

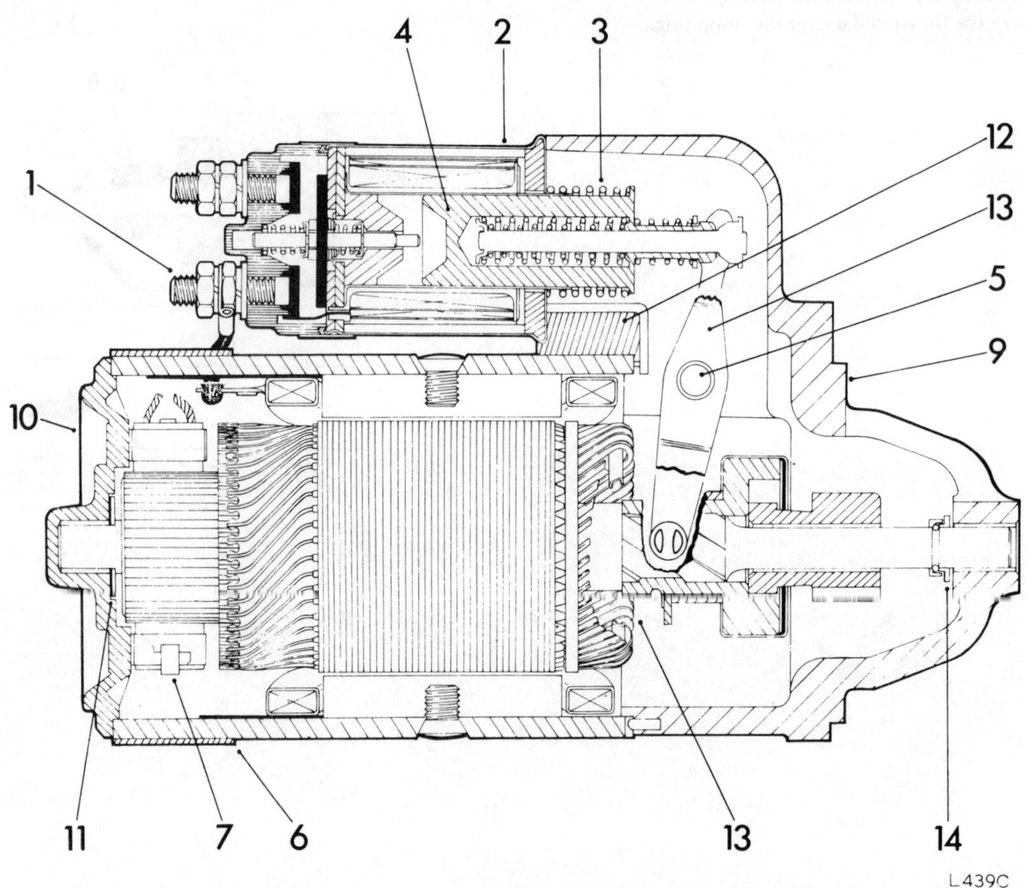

Bearings

15. Inspect the porous bronze bearing bushes for wear.
16. If necessary renew either bush as follows:
    Extract the fixing bracket bush using a suitable press and mandrel. Extract the commutator end bracket bush using a suitable extractor or by screwing a 9/16 in. tap squarely into the bush and withdrawing. Prepare the porous bronze bush by immersing it in thin engine oil for 24 hours or thin engine oil heated to 100° C for two hours. Fit the bush, using a suitable press and a highly polished, shouldered mandrel of the appropriate dimension given in Data. Do not ream the bush after fitting or its porosity may be impaired.

Brushes

17. Clean the brushes and holders with a petrol moistened cloth.
18. Check that the brushes move freely in the holders.
19. Check the brush spring tension as shown. Brush spring tension should be as given in Data. Repeat for the remaining three springs. If the tension is low renew the spring set.
20. Check the brush length. Renew the brushes if less than the length given in Data.
21. If necessary, renew the field winding brushes. Unsolder the flexibles from the field windings. Position the ends of the new flexibles. Squeeze up and solder.
22. If necessary, renew the earth brushes. Unsolder the flexibles from the clips on the commutator end bracket. Open the clips and position the ends of the new flexibles. Squeeze up and solder.

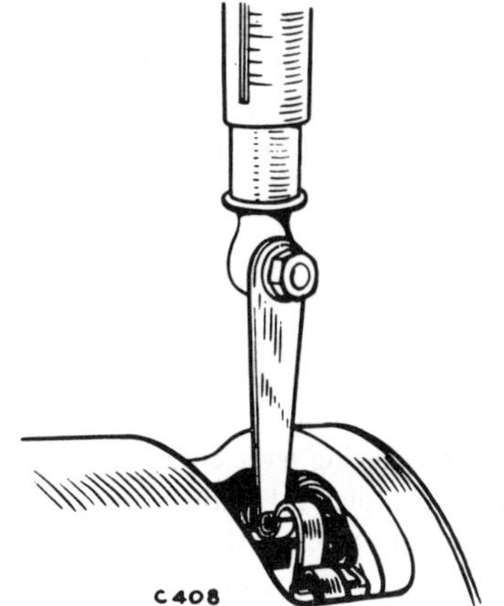

Commutator

23. Clean the commutator with a petrol-moistened cloth. If the commutator is in good condition it will be smooth and free from pits or burned spots.
24. If necessary, polish the commutator with fine glass-paper.
25. If necessary, skim the commutator. Separate the armature from the roller clutch drive by performing 86.60.07. Mount the armature in a lathe and rotate at high speed. Using a very sharp tool, take a light cut. Polish with fine glass-paper. Do not cut below the minimum skimming diameter given in Data. Do not undercut insulators between segments.

Roller clutch drive

26. Do not wash the roller clutch in petrol as such action would remove lubricant from the sealed unit. It may be cleaned by wiping with a petrol-moistened cloth.
27. Check that the clutch locks in one direction and rotates smoothly in the other. The unit should move freely round and along the armature shaft splines.
28. The roller clutch is a sealed unit. If the above conditions are not met, repair by replacement of the roller clutch unit.

Solenoid

29. Assembly of the starter solenoid involves soldering and sealing complications. It is therefore not advisable to attempt to service this unit. If the solenoid operation is suspect, repair by replacement of the solenoid unit.
30. The plunger is matched with the solenoid body. The spares unit of purchase is a matched solenoid and plunger and the box also contains a return spring. All three items should be fitted as a set.

Assemble

31. Fit the thrust washer to the shaft with the lip facing the starter drive as shown.
32. Position the engaging lever either way round to the drive operating plate. Lightly lubricate the fixing bracket bearing bush with engine oil. Insert the armature and starter drive assembly with the engaging lever into the fixing bracket.
33. Position the rubber moulding.
34. Position the yoke to the fixing bracket.
35. Fit the steel thrust washer and the fabric thrust washer to the shaft as shown.
36. Lightly lubricate the commutator end bracket bearing bush with engine oil. Ensure that no brushes are inserted in the holders. Position the commutator end bracket.
37. Fit the through bolts.
38. Insert the brushes into the holders.
39. Fit the cover band.
40. Lightly grease the eccentric pin bearing surface. Insert the eccentric pin. Ensure to align it through the engaging lever. Screw it in to maintain position only.
41. Position the plunger to the engaging lever.
42. Position the return spring to the solenoid inner tube.
43. Insert the solenoid so that the 'STA' terminal is positioned adjacent to the yoke. Fit two nuts and washers.
44. Connect the motor lead to the solenoid 'STA' terminal.

45. Adjust pinion movement as follows:
Provide a six volt test circuit as shown. Slacken the locknut. Screw the eccentric pin fully in. Energise the circuit to cause the solenoid to move the starter drive to the engage position. Position a feeler gauge between the pinion and the thrust collar as shown. Press the pinion lightly towards the motor to take up any lost motion in the linkage. Rotate the eccentric pin within the indicated 180 degree arc to adjust the gap to 0·005 to 0·015 in. Tighten the locknut. Check that the correct gap has been maintained.

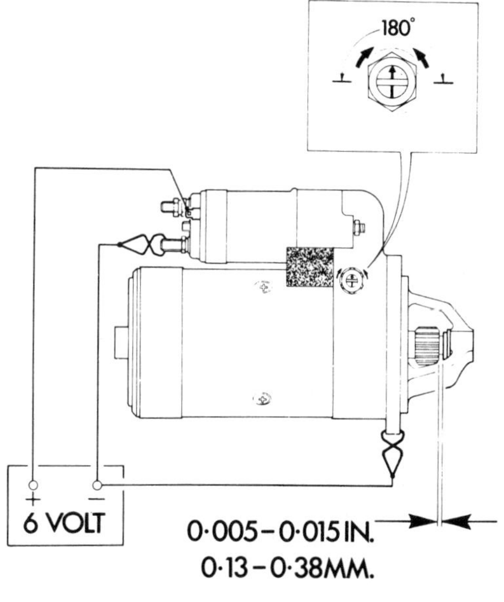

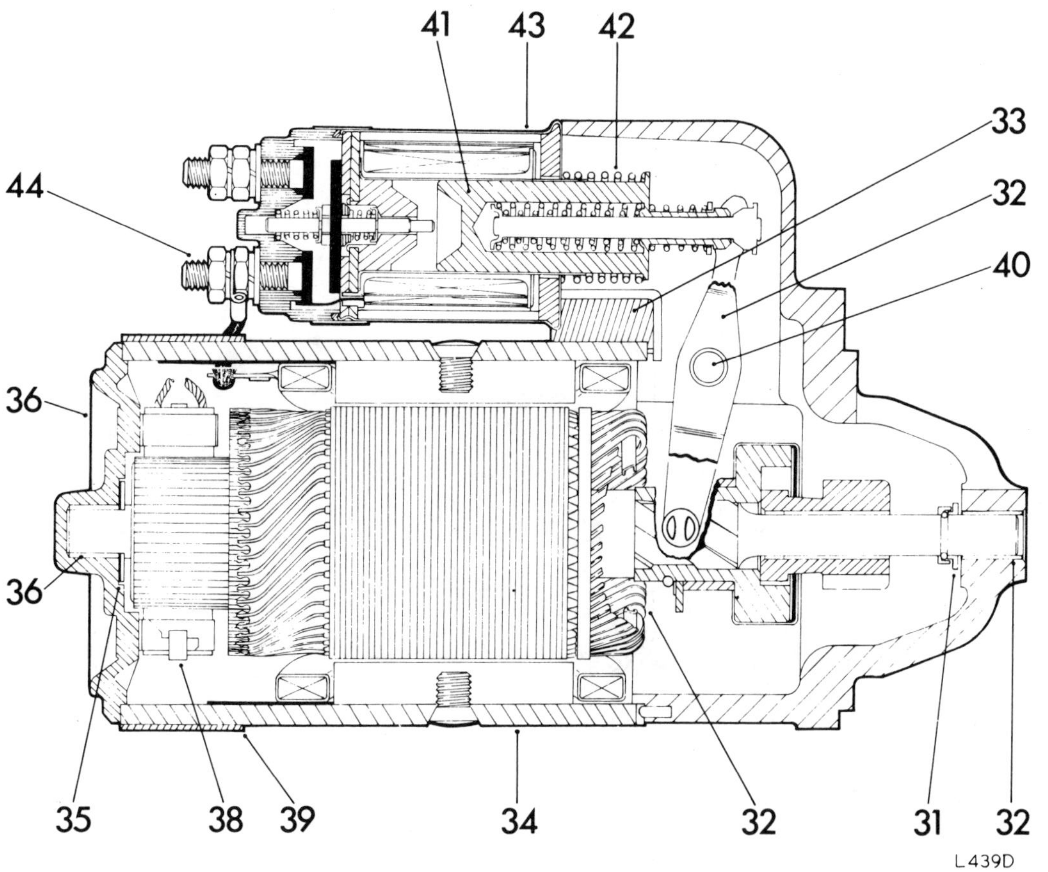

STARTER MOTOR – TYPE 2M100 PE

Overhaul **86.60.13**

Note that two starter motors have been fitted to the TR6 model range. Ensure that information obtained from this manual refers to the appropriate starter motor for the specific vehicle. A Lucas type M418G PE unit was fitted up to engine numbers CP 53636 and CC 63894. A Lucas type 2M100 PE unit was fitted from engine numbers CP 53637 and CC 63895.

Dismantling

NOTE: Dismantling of the starter motor will necessitate the destruction of two Spire retaining rings. Ensure that a new Spire retaining ring for the armature shaft and a new Spire retaining ring for the pivot pin are available before proceeding further. Both these items are included in the Sundry Parts Kit, Lucas Part No. 54246438 or Stanpart No. 520466.

1. Remove the nut, spring washer and washer to free the connector link from the solenoid.
2. Remove the rubber end cap.
3. Use a small chisel to cut a number of claws and remove the Spire retaining ring. Do not prise off the Spire retaining ring without cutting a number of claws as such action may damage the bearing end face, armature shaft and bearing surface when the shaft is withdrawn.
4. Remove two through bolts.
5. Withdraw the yoke and commutator end cover assembly.
6. Remove the thrust washer.
7. Remove the rubber seal block.
8. Employ a second operator to support the yoke by hand. Use a length of wood of approximately 0·75 in (20 mm) diameter to tap the commutator end cover from the yoke.
9. Lift out two field winding brushes from the brush box to separate the commutator end cover from the yoke.
10. Prise off the Spire retaining ring and tap out the pivot pin.
11. Remove two bolts and spring washers. Withdraw the solenoid leaving the plunger attached to the engaging lever.
12. Remove the return spring.
13. Withdraw the armature, roller clutch drive and plunger assembly from the drive end bracket.
14. Unhook the plunger from the engaging lever.

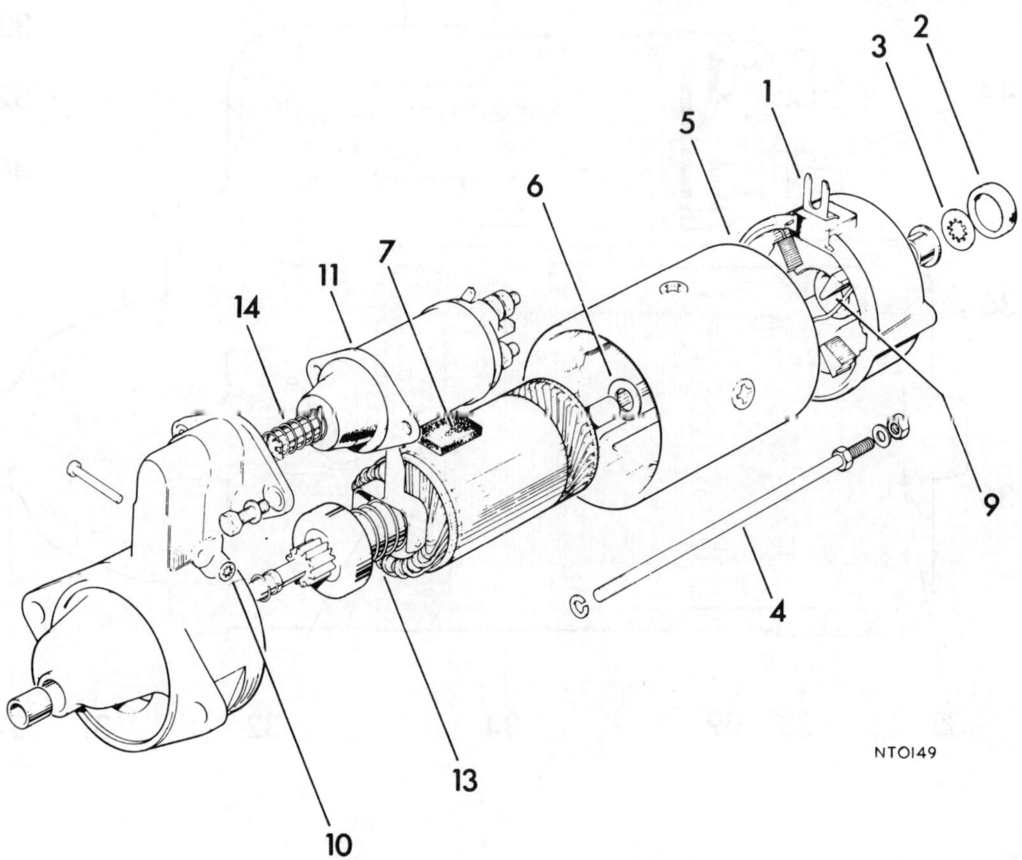

Bearings

15. Inspect the porous bronze bearing bushes for wear.
16. If necessary, renew either bush as follows:
    Extract the bush, using a suitable press and mandrel. Prepare the porous bronze bush by immersing it in thin engine oil for 24 hours or thin engine oil heated to 100°C for two hours. Fit the bush, using a suitable press and a highly polished, shouldered mandrel of the appropriate dimension given in Data. Do not ream the bush after fitting or its porosity may be impaired.

Brushes

17. Clean the brushes and brush box with a petrol-moistened cloth.
18. Check that the brushes move freely in the brush box.
19. Check the brush spring pressure as shown. Position a new brush so that the top protrudes 0·060 in (1·50 mm) above the brush box. Brush spring pressure should be as given in Data. Repeat for the remaining three springs. If the pressure is low, renew the commutator end bracket assembly.
20. Check the brush length. Renew the brushes if less than the length given in Data.
21. If necessary, renew the commutator end cover brushes. Brushes are supplied attached to a new connector link. Withdraw two brushes from the brush box. Withdraw the connector link. Position new brushes as shown. Retain the longer flexible under the flap.
22. If necessary, renew the field winding brushes. Brushes are supplied attached to a common flexible. Cut the old flexibles 0·250 in (6 mm) from the joint. Solder the new flexible to the ends of the old flexible. Do not attempt to solder direct to the field winding strip as the strip may be produced from aluminimum.

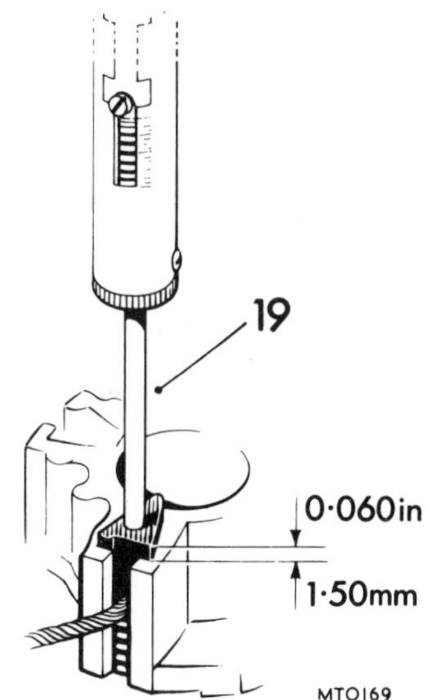

Commutator

23. Clean the commutator with a petrol-moistened cloth. If the commutator is in good condition it will be smooth and free from pits or burned spots.
24. If necessary, polish the commutator with fine glass-paper.
25. If necessary, skim the commutator. Separate the armature from the roller clutch drive by performing 86.60.07. Mount the armature in a lathe and rotate at high speed. Using a very sharp tool, take a light cut. Polish with fine glass-paper. Do not cut below the minimum skimming thickness given in Data. Do not undercut insulators between segments.

Roller clutch drive

26. Do not wash the roller clutch in petrol as such action would remove lubricant from the sealed unit. It may be cleaned by wiping with a petrol-moistened cloth.
27. Check that the clutch locks in one direction and rotates smoothly in the other. The unit should move freely round and along the armature shaft splines.
28. The roller clutch is a sealed unit. If the above conditions are not met, repair by replacement of the roller clutch unit.

Solenoid

29. Assembly of the starter solenoid involves soldering and sealing complications. It is therefore not advisable to attempt to service this unit. If the solenoid operation is suspect, repair by replacement of the solenoid unit.
30. The plunger is matched with the solenoid body. The spares unit of purchase is a matched solenoid and plunger and the box also contains a return spring. All three items should be fitted as a set.

Reassembling

31. Ensure that the bearing surfaces on the armature shaft are burr-free.
32. Hook the plunger onto the engaging lever.
33. Insert the armature, roller clutch drive and plunger assembly into the drive end bracket.
34. Fit the return spring.
35. Fit the solenoid so the 'STA' terminal is adjacent to the yoke. Secure with two bolts and spring washers. Ensure that the plunger does not unhook during this operation.
36. Lightly grease the pivot pin. Align the holes and insert the pivot pin. Secure with a new Spire retaining ring. Ensure that the plunger does not unhook during this operation.
37. Insert two field winding brushes into the brush box with flexibles positioned as shown.
38. Position the commutator end cover to the yoke.
39. Position the rubber seal block.
40. Fit the thrust washer.
41. Holding the commutator end cover firmly to the yoke, insert the assembly.
42. Fit two through bolts.
43. If necessary, adjust the position of the rubber seal block.
44. Fit a new Spire retaining ring to the armature shaft.
45. Fit the rubber end cap.
46. Fit washer, spring washer and nut to secure the connector link to the solenoid.

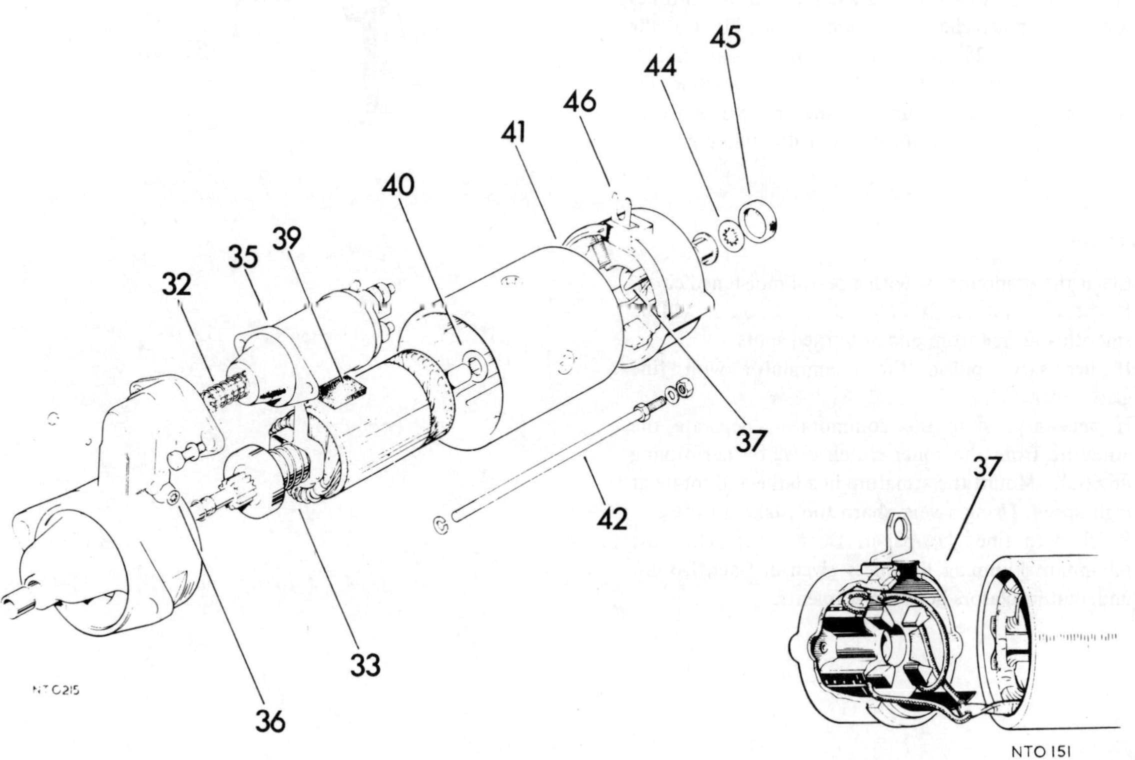

SWITCHES

Data **86.65.00**

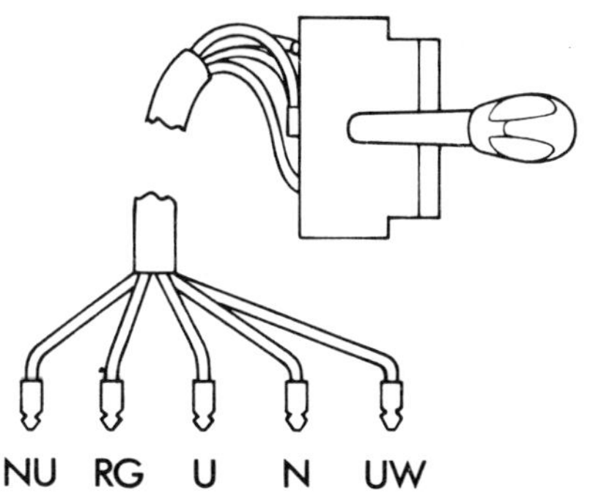

Column light switch

Position	Off	No connections
	Side	NU to RG
	Head	NU to U
	Head flash	N to UW

Note that the switch harness wire colours and the vehicle harness wire colours do not totally match . See appropriate wiring diagram.

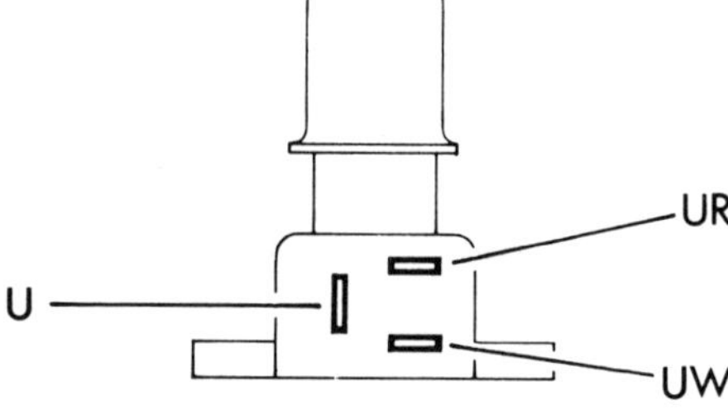

Dip switch

Position	Dip	U to UR
Position	Main	U to UW

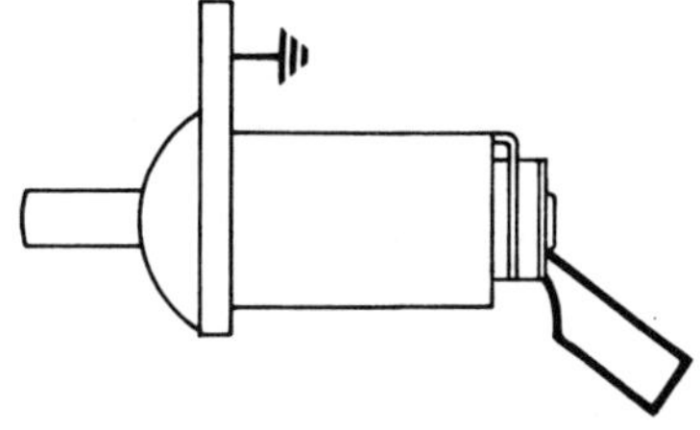

Door switch

Passengers door always and drivers door when key warning system is not fitted to vehicle.

Position	Door closed	No connections
Position	Door open	Terminal to earth

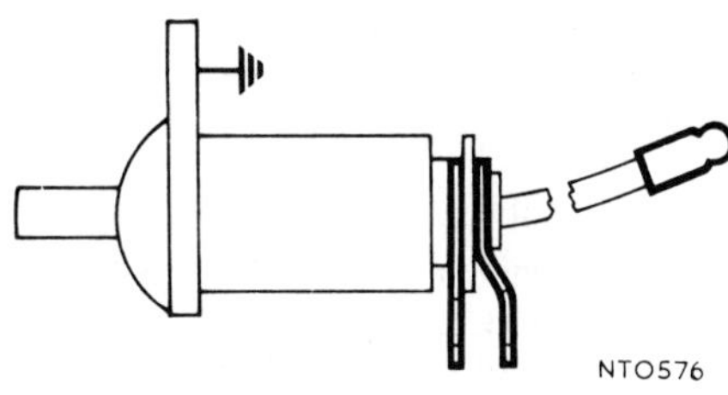

Door switch

Drivers door when key warning system is fitted to vehicle.

Position	Door closed	No connections
Position	Door open	Snap connector bullet on attached wire to earth and Two Lucar blades connected

Hazard switch

Early left hand steer vehicles with hazard circuit using relay.

Position	Off	3 to 4
Position	Hazard	1 to 2

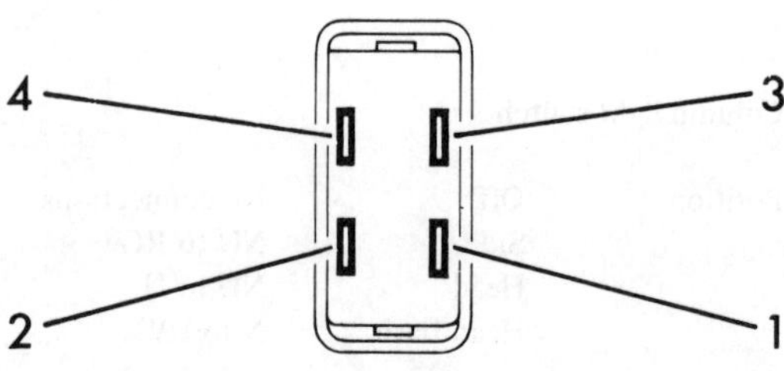

Hazard switch

Later left hand steer vehicles with hazard circuit not using relay.

Position	Off	8 to 7
Position	Hazard	3 to 1 to 2 to 4

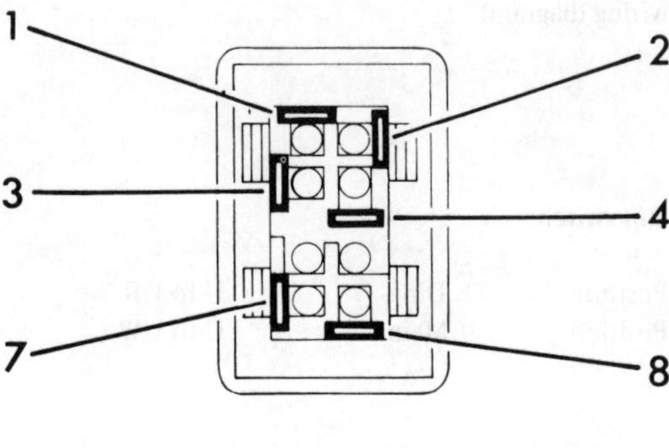

Heater switch

Position in	Off	1 to 6 to 7
Position first pull	Low speed	1 to 4 to 6 to 7
Position second pull	High speed	1 to 4 to 7 to 8

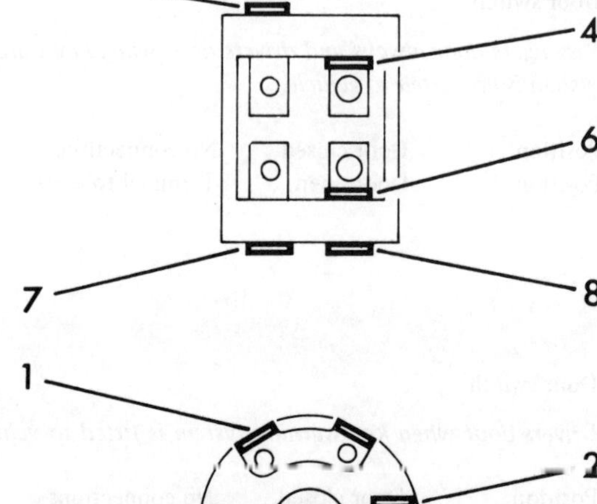

Ignition/starter switch

Early vehicles with ignition/starter switch fitted to central control cowl.

Position	Off	No connections
Position	Ignition	1 to 2 to 4
Position	Start	1 to 2 to 3
Position	Auxiliary	1 to 4

1
2
4
3

NT0577

Ignition/starter switch

Later vehicles with ignition/starter switch fitted to steering column lock assembly.

Position 0	Off	No connections
Position 1	Auxiliary	2 to 5
Position 2	Ignition	2 to 5 to 3
Position 3	Start	2 to 3 to 1

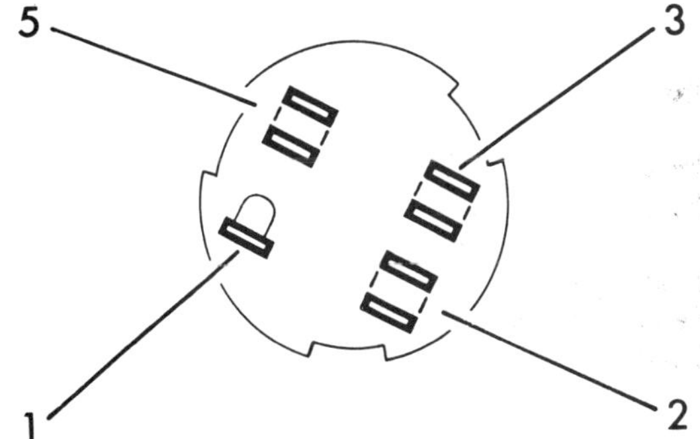

Turn signal switch

Position	Central	No connections
Position	L.H. turn signal	LG/N to GR
Position	R.H. turn signal	LG/N to GW

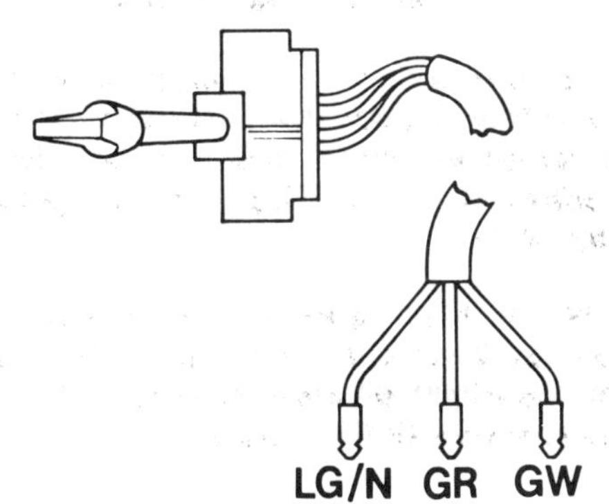

Windscreen wiper switch

Position	Park	4 to 3
Position	Normal speed	2 to 3
Position	High speed	2 to 1

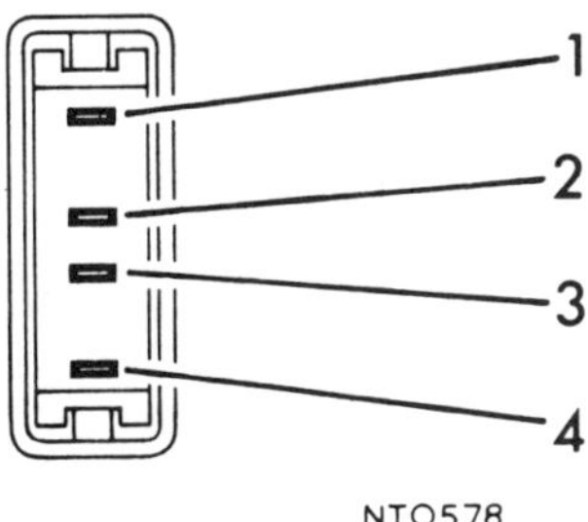

NTO578

Fuel pump inertia cut out switch

Petrol injection vehicles only

Data

Manufacturer	Inertia Switch Limited
Stanpart No.	153052
Operating force	4·5 to 5·5 g
Current capacity	10 amp
Mounting	Switch axis vertical with reset button uppermost

Description

This switch is electrically positioned in the supply line to the Lucas high pressure petrol pump.

The function of the unit is to cut out the electrical supply to the pump after a crash or severe stop. If the crash severs the fuel line the fuel tank contents should not be pumped into the roadway. The possibility of a petrol fire is thereby reduced.

With the button depressed the switch is in its normal operating condition with contacts closed. A shock force over the stated value will cause the switch to trip extending the button and opening the contacts.

After actuation the switch has to be manually reset as detailed, 86.65.59.

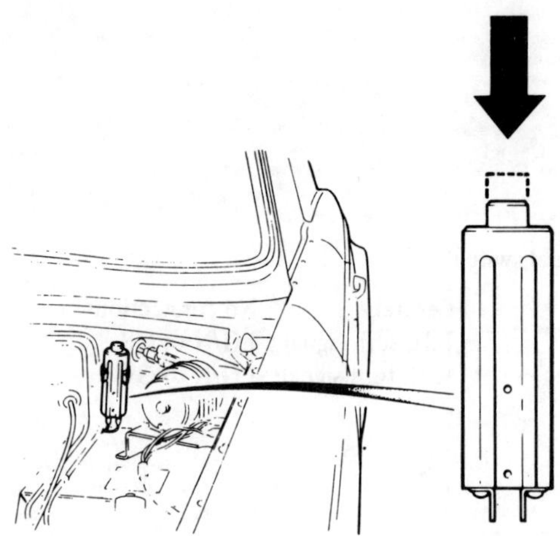

SWITCHES

Ignition/starter switch – remove and refit 86.65.02

Early vehicles with ignition/starter switch fitted to central control cowl.

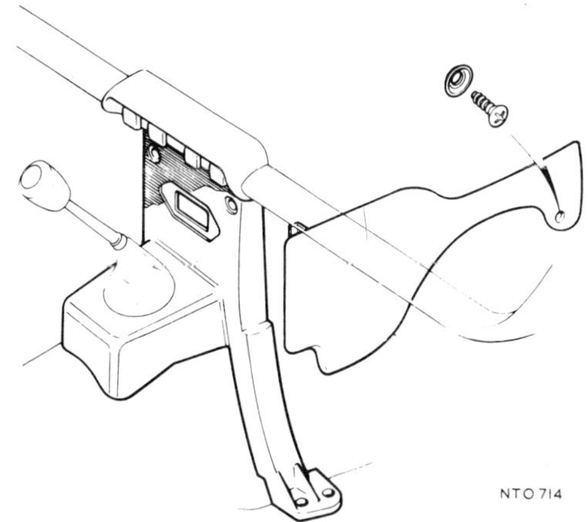

Removing

1. Isolate the battery.
2. Remove single screw and washer and withdraw the gearbox cover side trim panel on the right hand side of the vehicle.
3. Disconnect five Lucar connectors.
4. Unscrew the bezel. Withdraw the switch from the control cowl.

Refitting

5. Reverse instructions 1 to 4. Connect five Lucar connectors as shown on fascia connections 88.00.02.

SWITCHES

Ignition/starter switch – remove and refit 86.65.02

Later vehicles with ignition/starter switch fitted to steering column lock assembly.

Removing

1. Isolate the battery.
2. Carefully pull the plastic cover from the steering column lock assembly and manoeuvre along the harness.
3. Withdraw the ignition/starter switch from the steering column lock assembly.
4. Disconnect five Lucar connectors.

Refitting

5. Ensure that the plastic cover is fitted onto the harness.
6. Connect five Lucar connectors as shown.
7. Insert the switch into the steering column lock assembly. Note the keyway and ensure that the lock shaft and switch shaft align correctly.
8. Carefully fit the plastic cover to secure the switch in position.
9. Connect the battery.

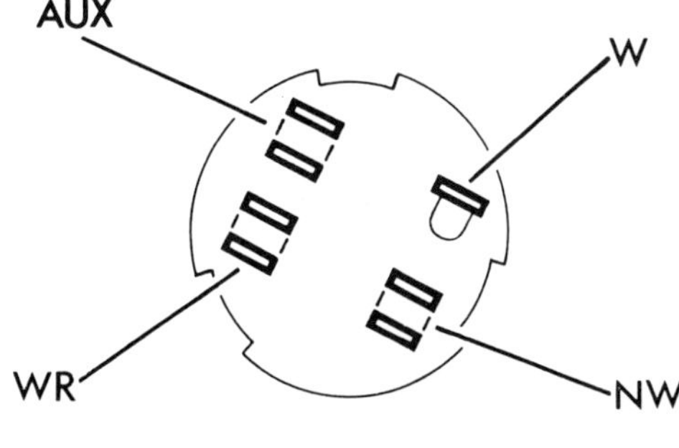

NTO 728

W White wire
NW Brown/white wire
WR White/red wire
AUX Any auxiliary wire

SWITCHES

– Dip switch – remove and refit 86.65.11

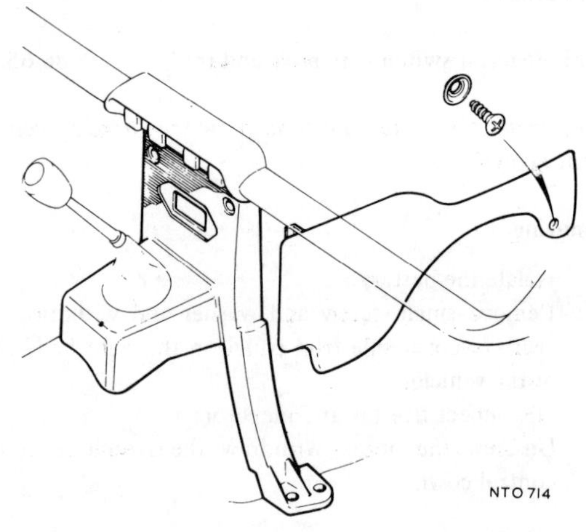

Removing

1. Isolate the battery.
2. Right hand steer vehicles only:–
   Remove single screw and washer and withdraw the gearbox cover side trim panel on the drivers side of the vehicle to release the harness.
3. Remove two screws and spring washers.
4. Disconnect three Lucar connectors.

Refitting

5. Reverse instructions 1 to 4. Connect the three Lucar connectors as shown in data 86.65.00.

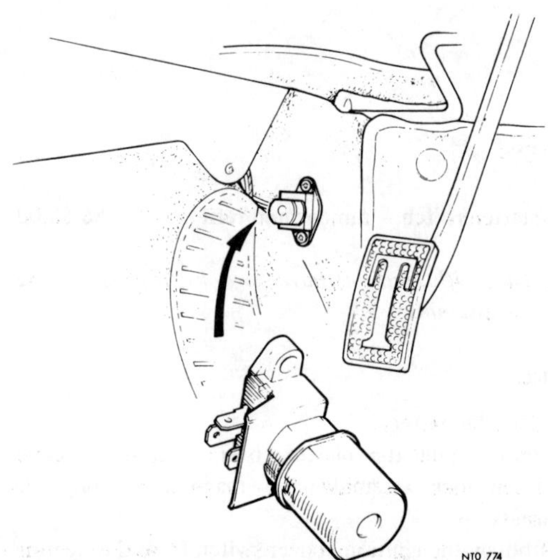

SWITCHES

– Panel rheostat – remove and refit 86.65.12

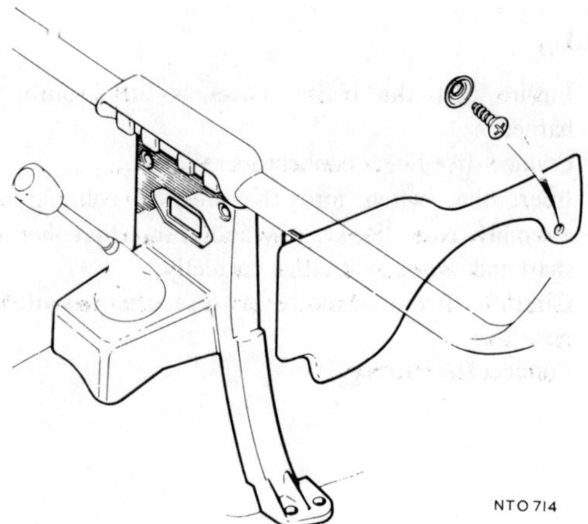

Removing

1. Isolate the battery.
2. Pull off the panel rheostat knob.
3. Remove single screw and washer and withdraw the gearbox cover side trim panel on the passenger side of the vehicle.
4. Note the wire positions by colour code.
5. Disconnect two Lucar connectors.
6. Using a suitable tool unscrew the bezel. Withdraw the switch from the bracket.

Refitting

7. Reverse instructions 1 to 6.

SWITCHES

Door switch – remove and refit **86.65.14**

Passengers door always and drivers door when key warning system is not fitted to vehicle.

Removing

1. Open the appropriate door.
2. Remove the single screw.
3. Withdraw the switch.
4. Disconnect the terminal end.

Refitting

5. Reverse instructions 1 to 4.

SWITCHES

Door switch – remove and refit **86.65.14**

Drivers door when key warning system is fitted to vehicle.

Removing

1. Open the appropriate door.
2. Remove five screws and turn back the dash side trim panel to obtain access to the switch connections.
3. Disconnect two Lucar connectors.
4. Disconnect one snap connector.
5. Remove the single screw.
6. Withdraw the switch.

Refitting

7. Reverse insturctions 1 to 6. Connect the two Lucar connectors either way round.

SWITCHES

– Column light switch – remove and refit **86.65.17**

Removing

1. Isolate the battery.
2. Later vehicles fitted with steering column lock only:–
   Inspect the steering column clamp bolts and note the location of two nuts which are fitted with 'anti-theft' caps. To gain access to any cap fitted uppermost remove the adjacent speedometer 88.30.01 or tachometer 88.30.21. Using a wide bladed screwdriver lever off two caps.
3. Remove two steering column clamp nuts, washers and bolts.
4. Remove the upper half of the steering column clamp.
5. Push the harness cover down the column slightly to release the top clip. Pull the harness cover up the column to release from the steering column clamp.
6. Disconnect five snap connectors.
7. Remove two screws. Withdraw two escutcheons.
8. Remove two screws and anti-vibration washers. Remove the switch with its harness.

Refitting

9. Thread the switch harness through the appropriate steering column apertures, fascia panel aperture and steering column clamp aperture. Do not disturb the position of the felt strip located below the wires in the lower half of the steering column clamp. This operation may be facilitated by taping the ends of the wires together. Position the switch and secure with two screws and anti-vibration washers.
10. Operate the switch into the 'headlamp flash' position. Ensure that no short is possible between the switch contact and the steering column.
11. Position two escutcheons. Secure with two screws.
12. Ensure that the felt strip is correctly located and rectify if necessary.
13. Connect five snap connectors as follows:

    Brown/blue switch wire to brown/white with a small blue indent main harness wire.
    Red/green switch wire to red/green main harness wire.
    Blue switch wire to blue main harness wire.
    Brown switch wire to purple with a small brown indent main harness wire.
    Blue/white switch wire to blue/white main harness wire.

14. Push the harness cover down the column to engage into the steering column clamp. Do not disturb the position of the felt strip. Pull the harness cover up the column slightly to engage the top clip.
15. Position the upper half of the steering column clamp.
16. Fit two steering column clamp bolts, washers and nuts. Ensure that the nuts are positioned uppermost or lowermost as noted at operation 2 above.
17. Later vehicles fitted with steering column lock only:–
    Tap on two 'anti-theft' caps. Fit the speedometer 88.30.01 or the tachometer 88.30.21 as required.
18. Connect the battery.

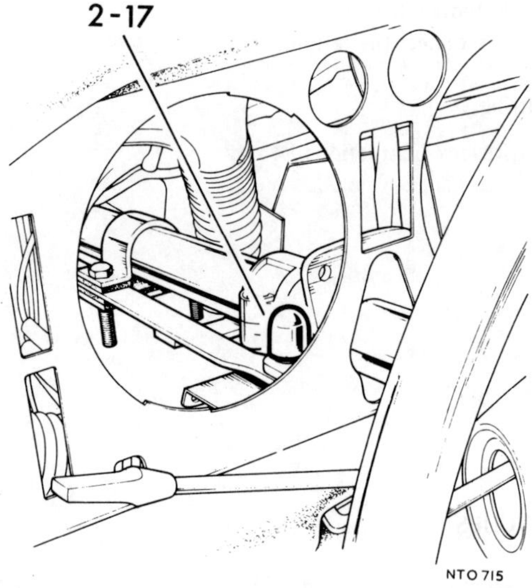

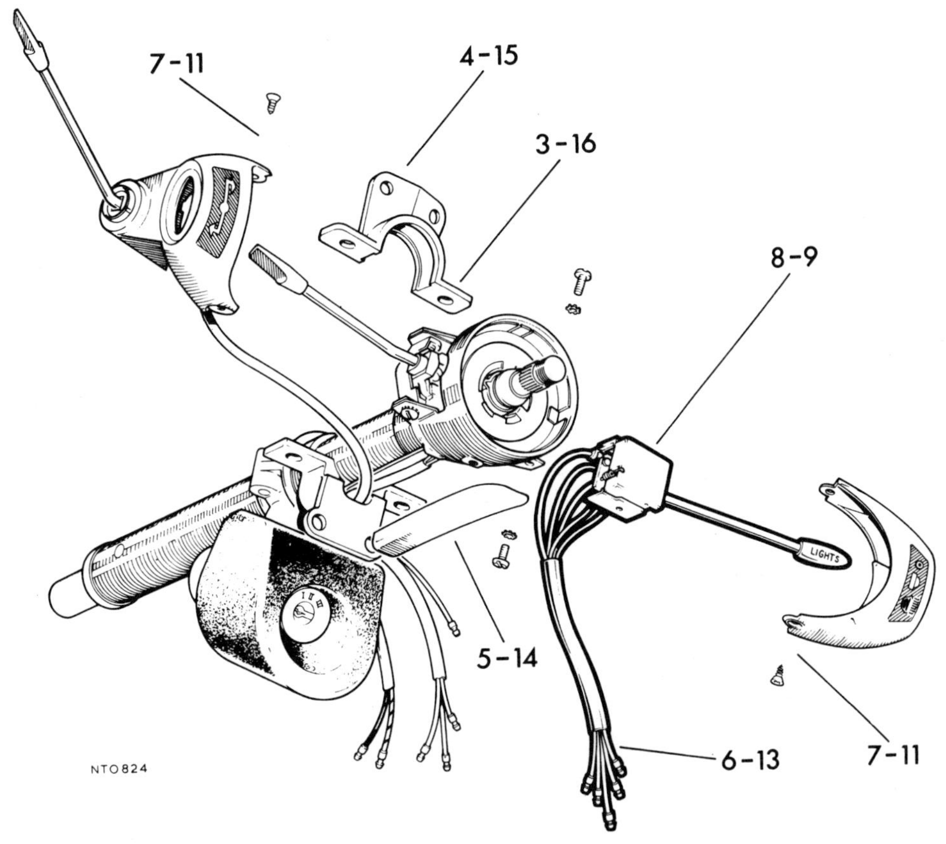
7-11
4-15
3-16
8-9
LIGHTS
5-14
6-13
7-11
NTO824

SWITCHES

– Horn push – remove and refit 86.65.18

Removing

1. Carefully pull the horn push surround pad from its retaining flange.
2. Using a wide blade screwdriver carefully prise the horn push unit from the steering wheel boss as shown.
3. Collect up the small side claw clip (if fitted).
4. Withdraw the connection brush.

Refitting

5. Apply petroleum jelly (vaseline) to the sliding contact end of the connection brush.
6. Insert the connection brush so that the sliding contact end sweeps the slip ring.
7. Ensure that the small side claw clip is fitted (if fitted at operation 3 above).
8. Align the horn push contact strip to the connection brush. Ensure good electrical contact for the side earth clip to the steering wheel boss. Push the horn push unit into the steering wheel boss.
9. Align the six recesses in the horn push surround pad to the six steering wheel bolt heads. Carefully fit the pad to its retaining flange.

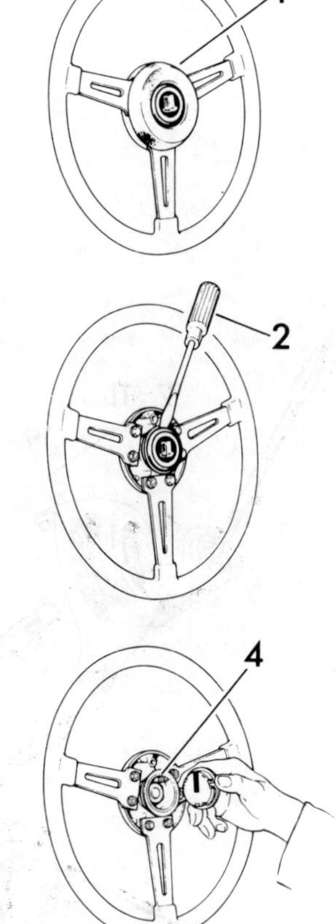

SWITCHES

– Reverse lamp switch – remove and refit 86.65.20

Removing

1. Remove the gearbox tunnel cover 76.25.07.
2. Locate the required switch.
3. Disconnect two Lucar connectors.
4. Using a spanner on the hexagon, unscrew the switch.
5. Collect up the fibre washer/washers if fitted.

Refitting

6. Assemble with the same number of fibre washers as originally fitted. Use new fibre washer/washers if available.
7. Fit the switch and fibre washer/washers to the gearbox.
8. Connect two Lucar connectors. The connectors may be fitted either way round.
9. Perform a functional check of the reverse lamp circuit.
10. Refit the gearbox tunnel cover 76.25.07.

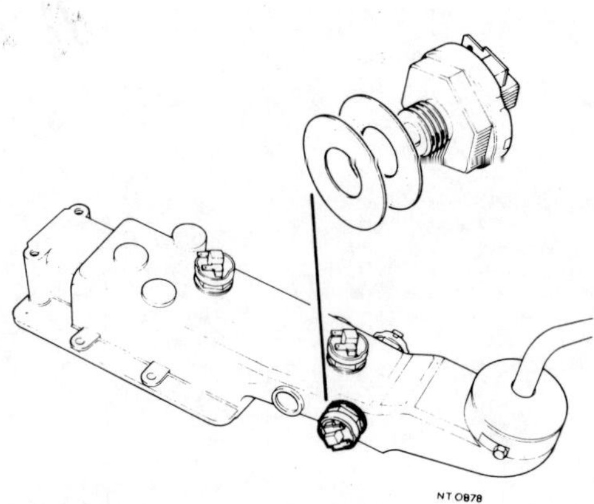

SWITCHES

– Luggage boot lamp switch – remove and refit 86.65.22

Removing

1. Open the luggage boot lid
2. Remove the floor carpet.
3. Remove the spare wheel cover panel.
4. Remove two screws securing the luggage boot lamp.
5. Withdraw the lamp assembly from the petrol tank trim panel.
6. Disconnect two Lucar connectors.
7. Remove eight screws and withdraw the petrol tank trim panel.
8. Locate the switch adjacent to the right hand hinge.
9. Remove two screws.
10. Withdraw the switch.
11. Pull the wire through the bracket hole and disconnect the terminal end.

Refitting

12. Reverse instructions 1 to 11. Connect the lamp assembly Lucar connectors either way round.

SWITCHES

– Cubby box illumination switch – remove and refit 86.65.24

Removing

1. Open the cubby box lid.
2. Remove the rubber buffer from the switch plunger.
3. Ease the switch outwards to release the spring claws from the bracket.
4. Pull the wire through the bracket hole and disconnect the terminal end.

Refitting

5. Reverse instructions 1 to 4.

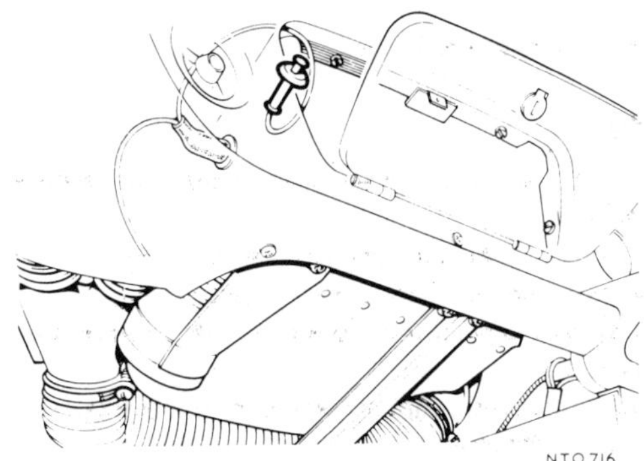

SWITCHES

– Seat belt – gearbox switch – remove and refit **86.65.28**

Later U.S.A. market vehicles only.

Removing

1. Remove the gearbox tunnel cover 76.25.07.
2. Locate the required switch.
3. Disconnect two Lucar connectors.
4. Using a spanner on the hexagon, unscrew the switch.
5. Collect up the fibre washer/washers if fitted.

Refitting

6. Assemble with the same number of fibre washers as originally fitted. Use new fibre washer/washers if available.
7. Fit the switch and fibre washer/washers to the gearbox.
8. Connect two Lucar connectors. The connectors may be fitted either way round.
9. Perform a functional check of the seat belt warning circuit.
10. Refit the gearbox tunnel cover 76.25.07.

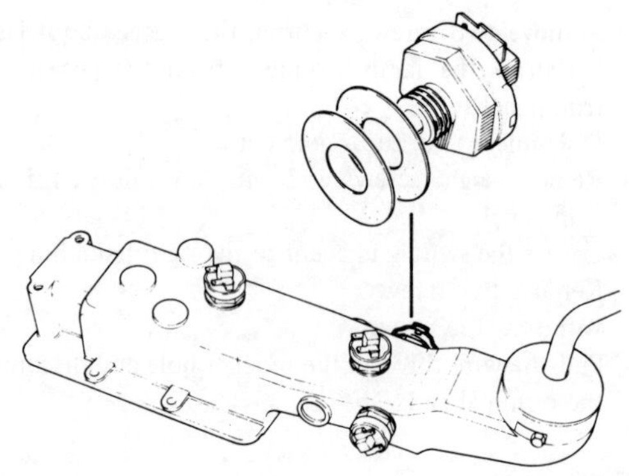
NTO 879

SWITCHES

– Seat belt – passengers seat switch – remove and refit **86.65.29**

Later U.S.A. market vehicles only.

Removing

1. Remove the passengers seat from the vehicle 76.70.05.
2. Unhook two rear diaphragm attachment clips.
3. Unhook two side diaphragm attachment clips.
4. Bend four small clips upwards and remove two washers.
5. To assist refitting, note the wire run through the seat.
6. Withdraw the wires.
7. Remove the switch.

Refitting

8. Reverse instructions 1 to 7.

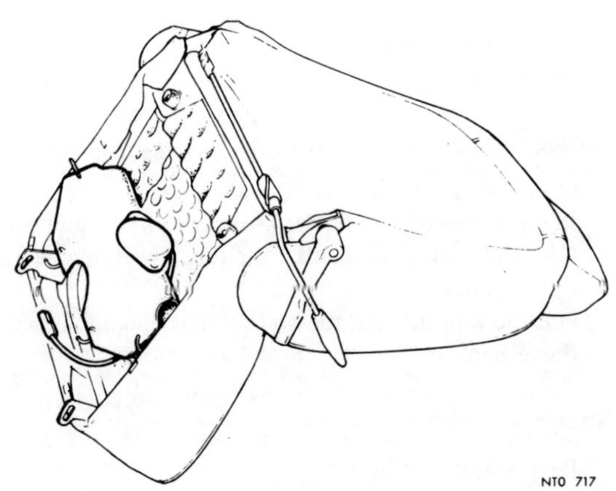
NTO 717

SWITCHES

– Oil pressure switch – remove and refit **86.65.30**

Removing

1. Locate the switch on the left hand side of the engine below the ignition distributor.
2. Disconnect the Lucar connector.
3. Using a spanner, unscrew the switch from the block.

Refitting

4. Screw the switch into the block. The thread is tapered so do not attempt to seat the switch shoulder.
5. Connect the Lucar connector.

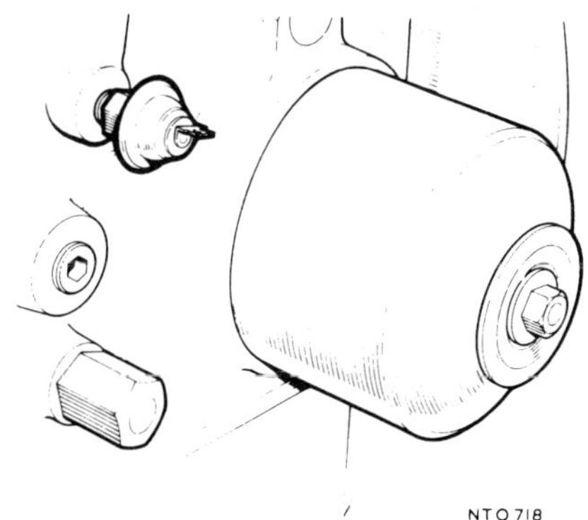
NTO 718

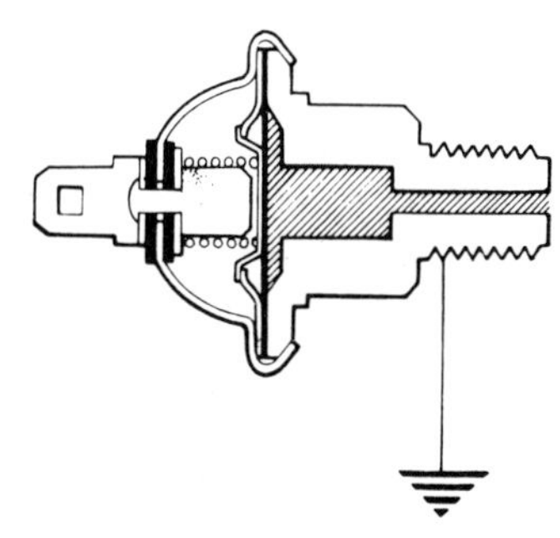
NTO 159

SWITCHES

Seat belt – drivers belt switch – remove and refit **86.65.31**

Seat belt – passengers belt switch – remove and refit **86.65.32**

Later U.S.A. market vehicles only.

Removing

1. Remove the drivers or passengers seat 76.70.04 or 76.70.05.
2. Disconnect the electrical harness plug.
3. Remove single bolt and spring washer. Lift out the buckle and switch unit.

Refitting

4. Reverse instructions 1 to 3. Seal the large plain washer to the floor panel with an approved sealer to ensure a waterproof joint.

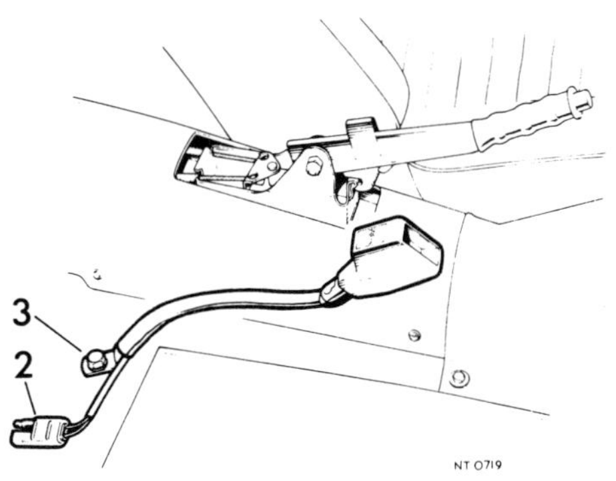

NT 0719

SWITCHES

– Overdrive gearbox switches – remove and refit **86.65.33**

Overdrive vehicles only up to the end of the 1972 model year.

Two overdrive gearbox switches are fitted. One performs the '2nd gear on' function while the other performs the '3rd and 4th gear on' function.

Removing

1. Remove the gearbox tunnel cover 76.25.07
2. Locate the required switch.
3. Disconnect two Lucar connectors.
4. Using a spanner on the hexagon, unscrew the switch.
5. Collect up the fibre washer/washers if fitted.

Refitting

6. Assemble with the same number of fibre washers as originally fitted.. Use new fibre washer/washers if available.
7. Fit the switch and fibre washer/washers to the gearbox.
8. Connect two Lucar connectors. The connectors may be fitted either way round.
9. Perform a functional check of the overdrive circuit.
10. Refit the gearbox tunnel cover 76.25.07.

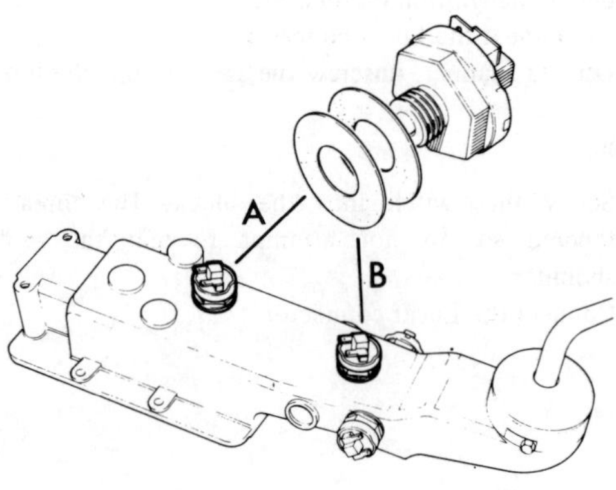

A '2nd gear on' switch
B '3rd and 4th gear on' switch

SWITCHES

– Overdrive manual switch
– remove and refit **86.65.35**

Overdrive vehicles only.

Removing

1. Perform 86.65.17 operations 1 to 5.
2. Disconnect two snap connectors.
3. Remove two screws. Withdraw two escutcheons.
4. Unscrew the bezel. Remove the switch with its harness.

Refitting

5. Thread the switch harness through the appropriate steering column apertures, fascia panel aperture and steering column clamp aperture. Do not disturb the position of the felt strip located below the wires in the lower half of the steering column clamp. This operation may be facilitated by taping the ends of the wires together. Position the switch and secure with the bezel.
6. Position two escutcheons. Secure with two screws.
7. Ensure that the felt strip is correctly located and rectify if necessary.
8. Connect two snap connectors as follows:
   Yellow/green switch wire to yellow/green main harness wire.
   Black switch wire to yellow main harness wire.
9. Perform 86.65.17 operations 14 to 18.

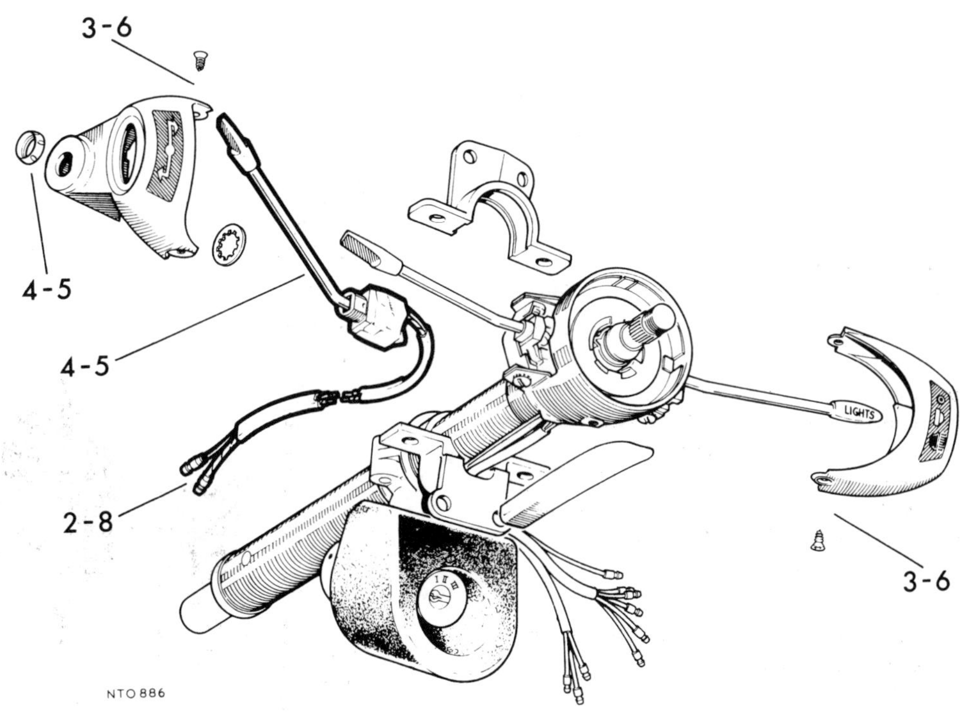

SWITCHES

– Windscreen wiper switch – remove and refit **86.65.38**

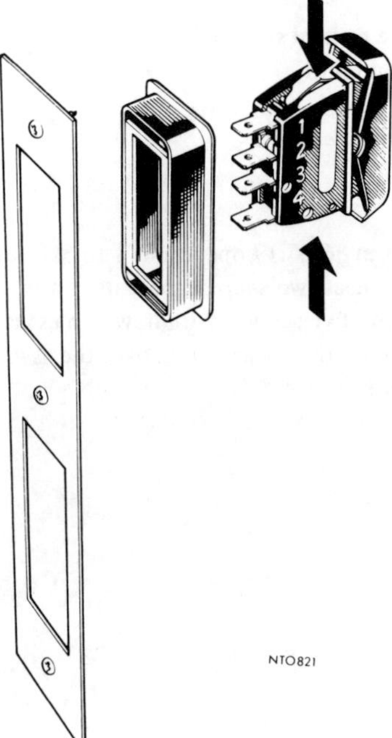

Removing

1. Isolate the battery.
2. Reach up under the fascia and push the switch and escutcheon assembly from the panel.
3. Disconnect four Lucar connectors.
4. Push inwards two spring clips on the switch and withdraw the switch from the escutcheon.

Refitting

5. Reverse instructions 1 to 4. Connect four Lucar connectors as shown on fascia connections 88.00.02 or 88.00.04.

SWITCHES

– Windscreen washer switch – remove and refit **86.65.40**

Removing

1. Isolate the battery.
2. Reach up under the fascia and push the switch and escutcheon assembly from the panel.
3. Disconnect two Lucar connectors.
4. Push inwards two spring clips on the switch and withdraw the switch from the escutcheon.

Refitting

5. Reverse instructions 1 to 4. Connect the Lucar connectors either way round.

SWITCHES

Heater switch – remove and refit 86.65.44

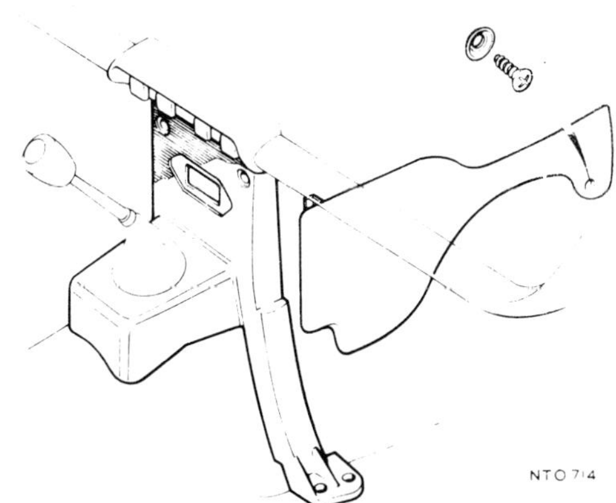

Removing

1. Insert a suitable probe into the hole in the knob and depress the spring plunger while pulling the knob from the shaft.
2. Remove single screw and washer and withdraw the gearbox cover side trim panel on the passenger side of the vehicle.
3. Disconnect three Lucar connectors.
4. Unscrew the bezel. Withdraw the switch from the control cowl.

Refitting

5. Reverse instructions 1 to 4. Connect three Lucar connectors as shown on fascia connections 88.00.02 or 88.00.04.

SWITCHES

– Brake line failure switch
– remove and refit 86.65.47

Left hand steer vehicles only.

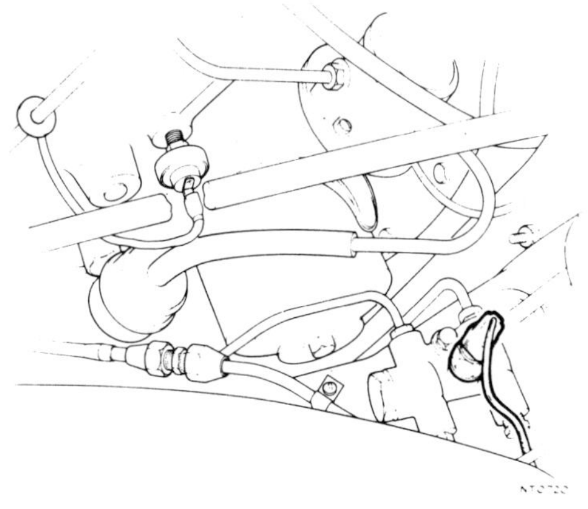

Removing

1. Open the bonnet.
2. Locate the pressure differential warning actuator mounted on the left hand front wheelarch to bulkhead panel.
3. Pull the harness plug from the switch.
4. Using a spanner on the nylon switch body carefully unscrew the switch.

Refitting

5. Carefully screw the switch to the actuator body. Do not overtighten. Torque load to only 12 to 15 in lbf (0·14 to 0·17 kgf m).
6. Fit the harness plug to the switch. Ensure that the plug claws are correctly located. Note that the single wire, but twin socket, harness plug may be fitted either way round as the twin switch pins are electrically common.

SWITCHES

– Hazard switch – remove and refit 86.65.50

Left hand steer vehicles only.

Removing

1. Isolate the battery.
2. To gain access remove either the speedometer 88.30.01 or the tachometer 88.30.21. The choice depends entirely on which operation is preferred by the individual fitter.
3. Push inwards two plastic clips on the switch and withdraw the switch from the panel.
4. Disconnect the Lucar connectors.

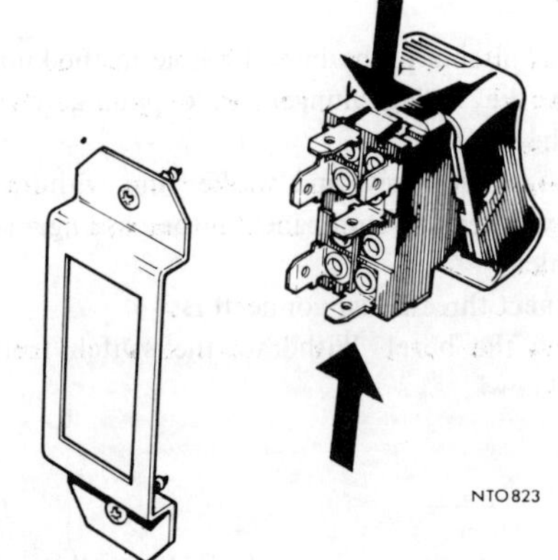

Refitting

5. Early left hand steer vehicles with hazard circuit using relay –
   Connect the Lucar connectors as shown on fascia connections 88.00.02.
6. Later left hand steer vehicles with hazard circuit not using relay –
   Connect the Lucar connectors as shown on fascia connections 88.00.04.
7. Reverse instructions 1 to 3.

SWITCHES

– Stop lamp switch – remove and refit 86.65.51

Removing

1. Locate the switch adjacent to the brake pedal arm.
2. Disconnect two Lucar connectors.
3. Slacken the large hexagon nut.
4. Unscrew the switch from the nut.
5. Collect up the nut and two shakeproof washers.

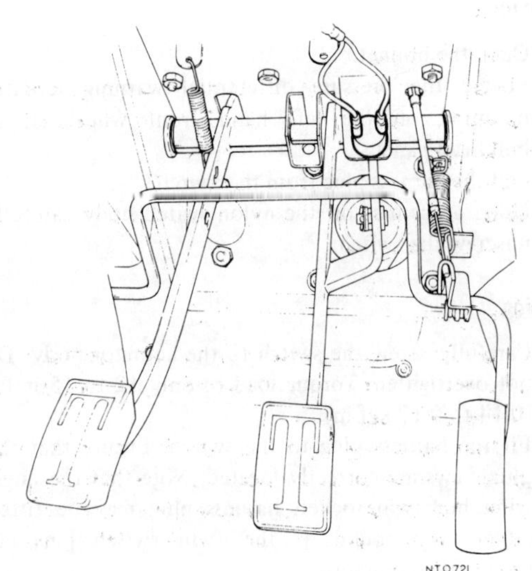

Refitting

6. Assemble the switch, two shakeproof washers and the nut to the bracket. A shakeproof washer should be positioned either side of the bracket. Do not overtighten the nut on the plastic threads or the switch may be damaged.
7. Connect two Lucar connectors either way round.
8. Switch on the ignition and perform a functional check of the stop lamp circuit.

SWITCHES

– Turn signal switch – remove and refit **86.65.54**

Removing

1. Perform 86.65.17 operations 1 to 5.
2. Disconnect three snap connectors.
3. Remove two screws. Withdraw two escutcheons.
4. Remove two screws and anti-vibration washers Remove the switch with its harness.

Refitting

5. Thread the switch harness through the appropriate steering column apertures, fascia panel aperture and steering column clamp aperture. Do not disturb the position of the felt strip located below the wire in the lower half of the steering column clamp. This operation may be facilitated by taping the ends of the wires together. Position the switch and secure with two screws and anti-vibration washers.
6. Position two escutcheons. Secure with two screws.
7. Ensure that the felt strip is correctly located and rectify if necessary.
8. Connect three snap connectors as follows:

   Light green/brown switch wire to light green/brown main harness wire.
   Green/red switch wire to green/red main harness wire.
   Green/white switch wire to green/white main harness wire.

9. Perform 86.65.17 operations 14 to 18.

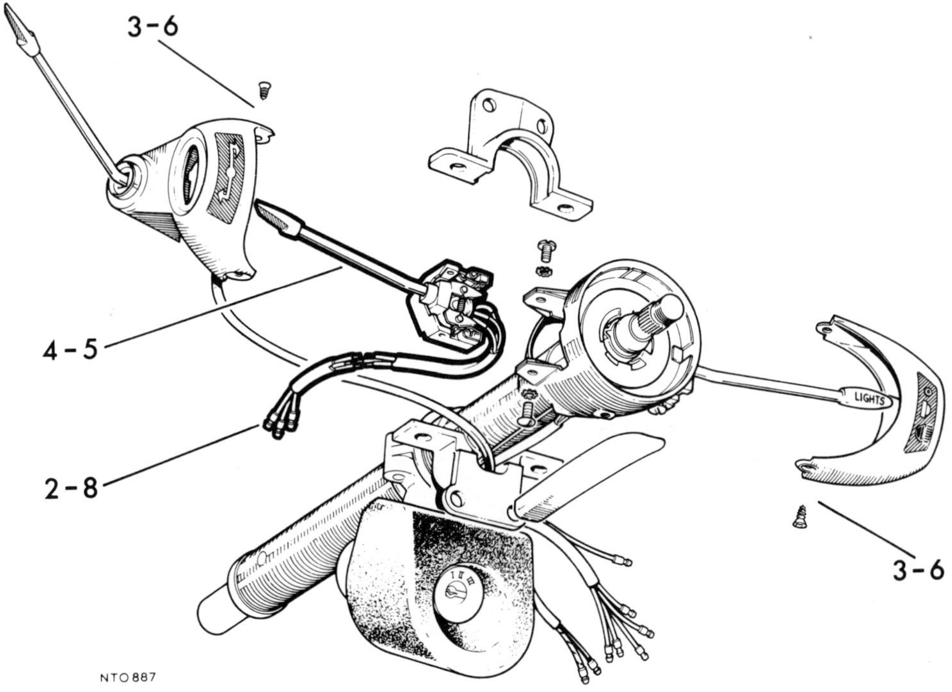

SWITCHES

– Fuel pump inertia cut out switch – remove and refit 86.65.58

Petrol injection vehicles only.

Removing

1. Open the bonnet.
2. Locate the switch mounted in a clip attached to the bulkhead.
3. Pull the switch from the clip.
4. Disconnect two Lucar connectors.

Refitting

5. Connect two Lucar connectors either way round.
6. Fit the switch to the clip.
7. Reset 86.65.59.

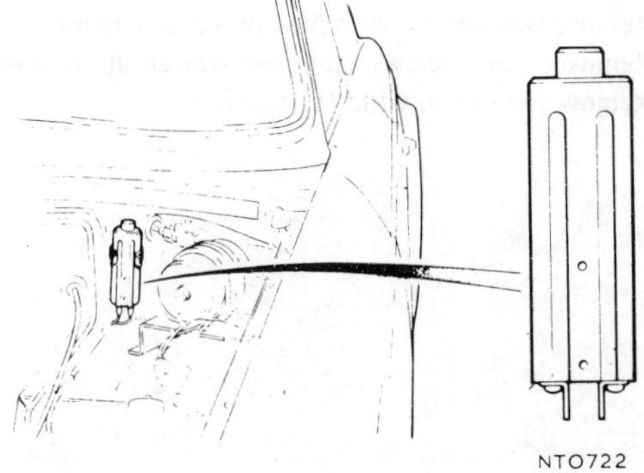

SWITCHES

– Fuel pump inertia cut out switch – reset 86.65.59

Petrol injection vehicles only.

1. Open the bonnet.
2. Locate the switch mounted in a clip attached to the bulkhead.
3. Depress the button so that the switch is in its normal operating condition with the contacts closed.

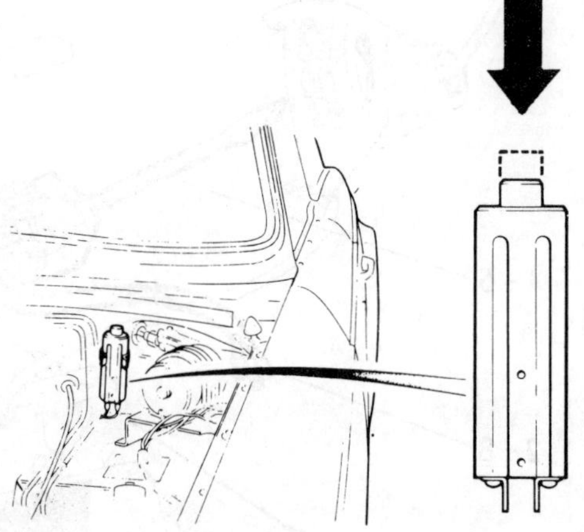

FUSE CHART

Fuse	Circuits	Amps	Colour code	Lucas Part No.	Stanpart No.
BATTERY CONTROL	Cubby box illumination Hazard (when fitted) Headlamp flasher Horn Key light (when fitted) Key warning (when fitted) Luggage boot lamp Transmission tunnel lamp	35	White	188218	58465
COLUMN LIGHT SWITCH CONTROL	Front marker lamp (when fitted) Front parking lamp Instrument illumination Plate illumination lamp Rear marker lamp (when fitted) Tail lamp	35	White	188218	58465
IGNITION CONTROL	Fuel indication Heater Reverse lamp Seat belt warning (when fitted) Stop lamp Temperature indication Turn signal Windscreen washer Windscreen wiper	35	White	188218	58465

FUSE

Remove and refit **86.70.02**

Removing

1. Lift the bonnet and locate the fusebox on the left hand front wheelarch closing panel.
2. Pull off the plastic cover.
3. Identify the defective fuse.
4. Carefully lever the fuse from the contacts.

Refitting

5. Reverse instructions 1 to 4.

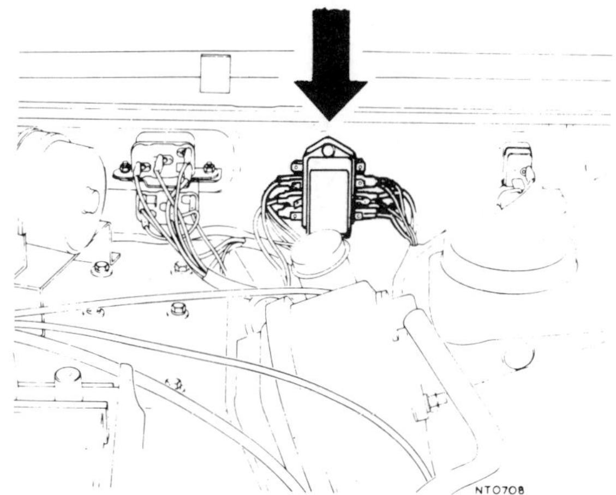

INSTRUMENT OPERATIONS

FASCIA CONNECTIONS

Due to the number of permutations possible, a fascia connections diagram for each market cannot be included in the manual.

To provide full information, two fascia connections diagrams are featured. One shows the 'Early minimum equipment condition' while the other indicates the 'Later maximum equipment condition'.

By referring to both diagrams, service personnel may easily obtain the required information for any specific vehicle.

A summary of the variations involved is given below:

EARLY MINIMUM EQUIPMENT CONDITION – DIAGRAM 1	LATER MAXIMUM EQUIPMENT CONDITION – DIAGRAM 2
Ignition/starter switch fitted to central control cowl.	Ignition/starter switch fitted to steering column lock assembly.
Hazard warning circuit with relay.	Hazard warning circuit without relay.
No key warning system.	Key warning system.
No seat belt warning system.	Seat belt warning system.

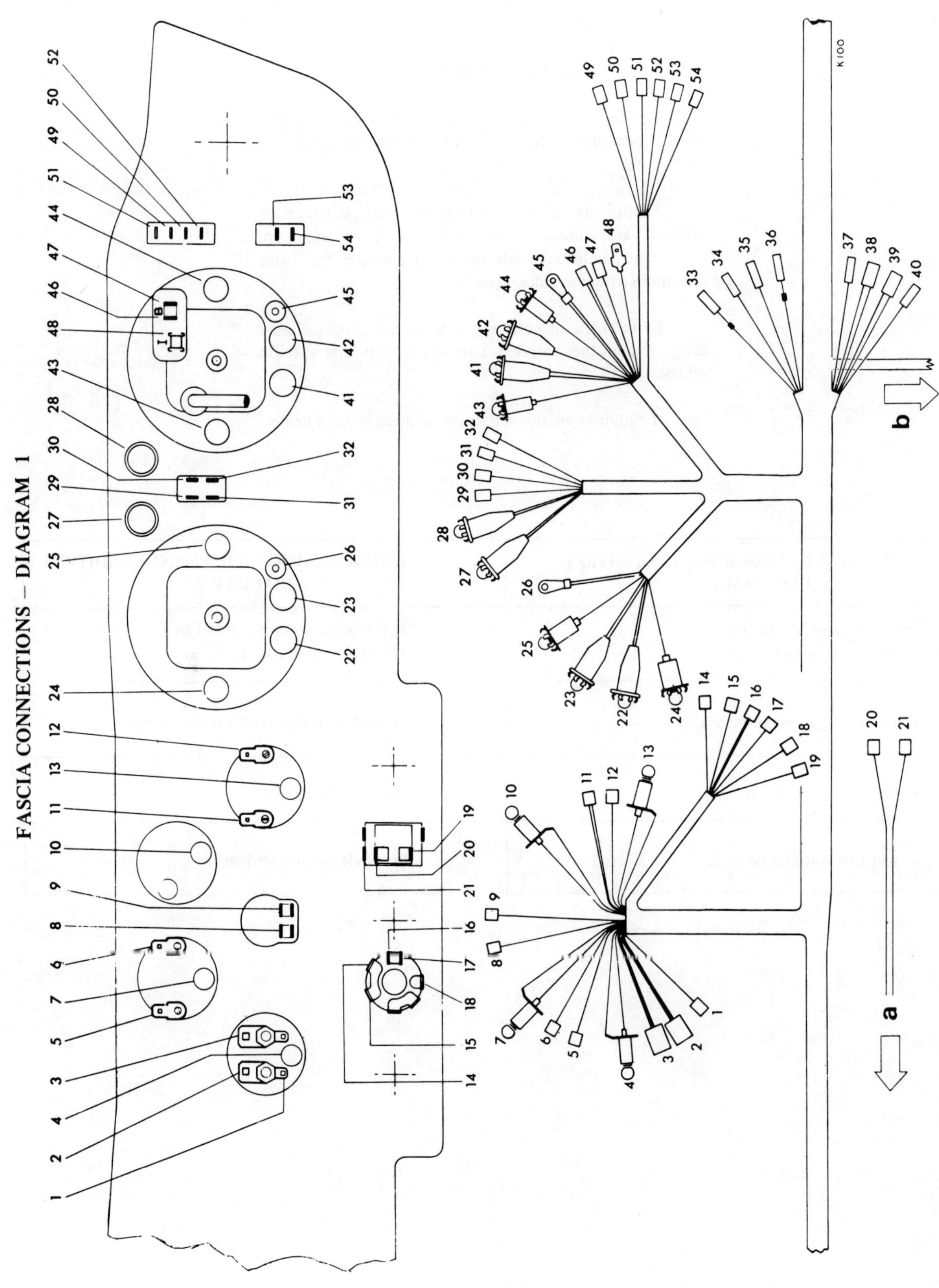

FASCIA CONNECTIONS – DIAGRAM 1

FASCIA CONNECTIONS – DIAGRAM 1

Left hand steer shown – Right hand steer – similar

No.	Colour Code	Connection	Components
1	NW	Lucar	Ammeter
2	NW	Lucar	Ammeter
3	N	Lucar	Ammeter
4	RW and B	Bulb holder	Ammeter
5	LG/G	Lucar	Fuel indicator
6	GB	Lucar	Fuel indicator
7	RW and B	Bulb holder	Fuel indicator
8	R	Lucar	Panel rheostat
9	RW	Lucar	Panel rheostat
10	RW and B	Bulb holder	Oil pressure indicator
11	LG/G	Lucar – 2 wire	Temperature indicator
12	GU	Lucar	Temperature indicator
13	RW and B	Bulb holder	Temperature indicator
14	NW	Lucar	Ignition/starter switch
15	NW	Lucar	Ignition/starter switch
16	W	Lucar – 2 wire	Ignition/starter switch
17	W	Lucar	Ignition/starter switch
18	WR	Lucar	Ignition/starter switch
19	G	Lucar	Heater switch
20	GN	Lucar	Heater switch
21	GY	Lucar	Heater switch
22	W and NY	Bulb holder	Tachometer-ignition warning light
23	WB and WN	Bulb holder	Tachometer-oil pressure warning light
24	RW	Bulb holder	Tachometer
25	RW	Bulb holder	Tachometer
26	B	Eyelet – 2 wire	Tachometer
27	W and WB	Bulb holder	Brake line failure warning light – left hand steer only
28	LG/P and B	Bulb holder	Hazard warning light – left hand steer only
29	LG/N	Lucar	Hazard switch – left hand steer only
30	LG/N	Lucar	Hazard switch – left hand steer only
31	P	Lucar	Hazard switch – left hand steer only
32	PR	Lucar	Hazard switch – left hand
33	NW with blue indent	Snap connector	Column light switch
34	RG	Snap connector	Column light switch
35	U	Snap connector	Column light switch
36	P with brown indent	Snap connector	Column light switch
37	LG/N	Snap connector	Turn signal switch
38	GR	Double snap connector – 2 wire	Turn signal switch
39	GW	Double snap connector – 2 wire	Turn signal switch
40	PB	Snap connector	Horn push
41	GR and GW	Bulb holder	Speedometer-turn signal warning light
42	UW	Bulb holder	Speedometer-main beam warning light
43	RW	Bulb holder	Speedometer
44	RW	Bulb holder	Speedometer
45	B	Eyelet – 2 wire	Speedometer
46	G	Lucar – 2 wire	Voltage stabilizer
47	G	Lucar	Voltage stabilizer
48	LG/G	Lucar blade	Voltage stabilizer
49	G	Lucar	Windscreen wiper switch
50	R/LG	Lucar	Windscreen wiper switch
51	U/LG	Lucar	Windscreen wiper switch
52	N/LG	Lucar	Windscreen wiper switch
53	G	Lucar	Windscreen wiper switch
54	LG/B	Lucar	Windscreen wiper switch

a GN and GY – to heater motor b G and GP – to stop lamp switch

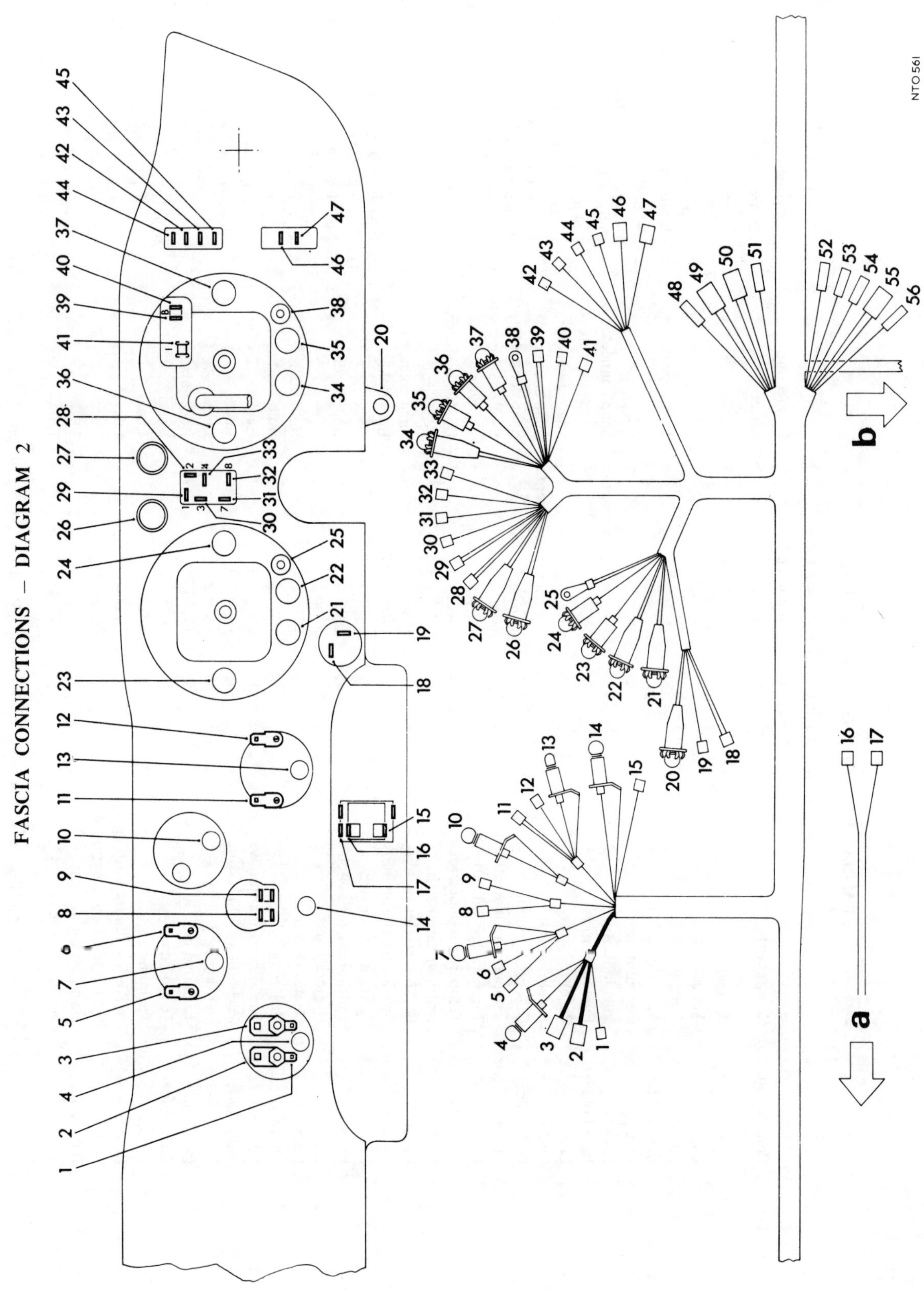
FASCIA CONNECTIONS – DIAGRAM 2
NTO 561
a
b

FASCIA CONNECTIONS – DIAGRAM 2

Left hand steer shown – Right hand steer – similar

No	Colour code	Connection	Component
1	NW	Lucar	Ammeter
2	NW	Lucar	Ammeter
3	N	Lucar	Ammeter
4	RW and B	Bulb holder	Ammeter
5	LG	Lucar	Fuel indicator
6	GB	Lucar	Fuel indicator
7	RW and B	Bulb holder	Fuel indicator
8	R	Lucar	Panel rheostat
9	RW	Lucar	Panel rheostat
10	RW and B	Bulb holder	Oil pressure indicator
11	LG	Lucar – 2 wire	Temperature indicator
12	GU	Lucar	Temperature indicator
13	RW and B	Bulb holder	Temperature indicator
14	LG/O and B	Bulb holder	Seat belt warning light
15	G	Lucar	Heater switch
16	GW	Lucar	Heater switch
17	GY	Lucar	Heater switch
18	PO	Lucar – 2 wire	Buzzer
19	BG	Lucar	Buzzer
20	PO and B	Bulb holder	Key light
21	W and NY	Bulb holder	Tachometer – ignition warning light
22	BP and WN	Bulb holder	Tachometer – oil pressure warning light
23.	RW	Bulb holder	Tachometer
24.	RW	Bulb holder	Tachometer
25.	B	Eyelet – 2 wire	Tachometer
26.	W and BP	Bulb holder	Brake line failure warning light – left hand steer only
27.	LG/G and B	Bulb holder	Hazard warning light – left hand steer only
28.	GW	Lucar – 2 wire	Hazard switch – left hand steer only
29.	GR	Lucar – 2 wire	Hazard switch – left hand steer only

No.	Colour code	Connection	Components
30.	LG/K	Lucar	Hazard switch – left hand steer only
31.	LG/G	Lucar	Hazard switch – left hand steer only
32	LG/S	Lucar	Hazard switch – left hand steer only
33	G	Lucar	Hazard switch – left hand steer only
34	GR and GW	Bulb holder	Speedometer – turn signal warning light
35	UW	Bulb holder	Speedometer – main beam warning light
36	RW	Bulb holder	Speedometer
37	RW	Bulb holder	Speedometer
38	B	Eyelet – 2 wire	Speedometer
39	G	Lucar – 2 wire	Voltage stabilizer
40	G	Lucar	Voltage stabilizer
41	LG	Lucar blade	Voltage stabilizer
42	LG/B	Lucar	Windscreen wiper switch
43	R/LG	Lucar	Windscreen wiper switch
44	U/LG	Lucar	Windscreen wiper switch
45	N/LG	Lucar	Windscreen wiper switch
46	G	Lucar	Windscreen washer switch
47	LG/B	Lucar	Windscreen washer switch
48	PB	Snap connector	Horn push
49	GW	Double snap connector – 2 wire	Turn signal switch
50	GR	Double snap connector – 2 wire	Turn signal swtch
51	LG/N	Snap connector	Turn signal switch
52	P	Snap connector	Column light switch
53	U	Snap connector	Column light switch
54	RG	Snap connector	Column light switch
55	UW	Lucar – 2 wire	Column light switch
56	NW	Snap connector	Column light switch

a. GN and GY To heater motor b. G and GP To stop lamp switch

AMMETER

– Remove and refit **88.10.01**

Removing

1. Obtain access to the rear of the ammeter by reaching over the gearbox cover side trim panel.
2. Pull out the panel light bulb holder.
3. Disconnect the three Lucar connectors.
4. Remove the two knurled nuts, spring washers, and clamp bracket.
5. Withdraw the ammeter from the fascia.

Refitting

6. Reverse instructions 1 to 5.

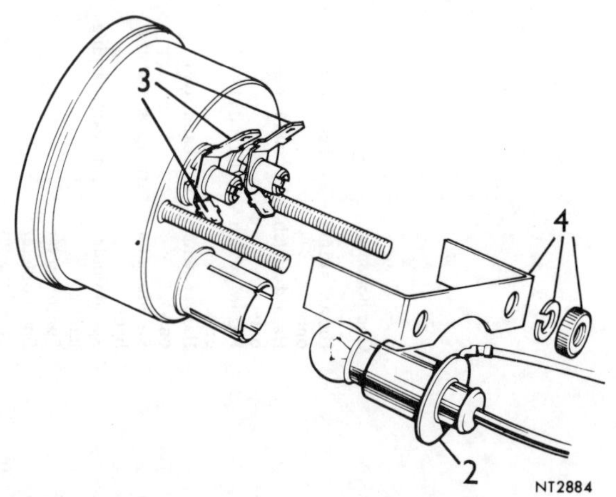

VOLTAGE STABILISER

– Remove and refit **88.20.26**

Removing

1. Remove the speedometer 88.30.01.
2. Remove one screw and lift off the voltage stabiliser.

Refitting

3. Reverse instructions 1 and 2.

OIL PRESSURE GAUGE

– Remove and refit **88.25.01**

Removing

1. Lower the veneered fascia to the service position. Operation 76.46.01 instructions 1 to 6.
2. Pull out the bulb holder.
3. Unscrew the nut securing the oil pipe to the gauge.
4. Remove the two knurled nuts, spring washers and clamp bracket.
5. Withdraw the gauge from the fascia.

Refitting

6. Reverse instructions 1 to 5.

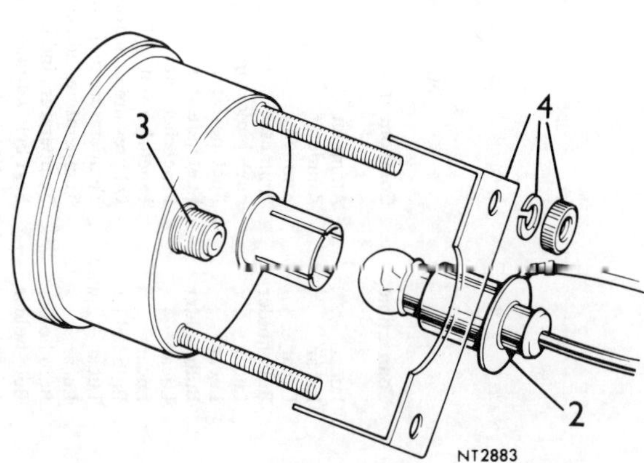

TEMPERATURE INDICATOR

– Remove and refit **88.25.14**

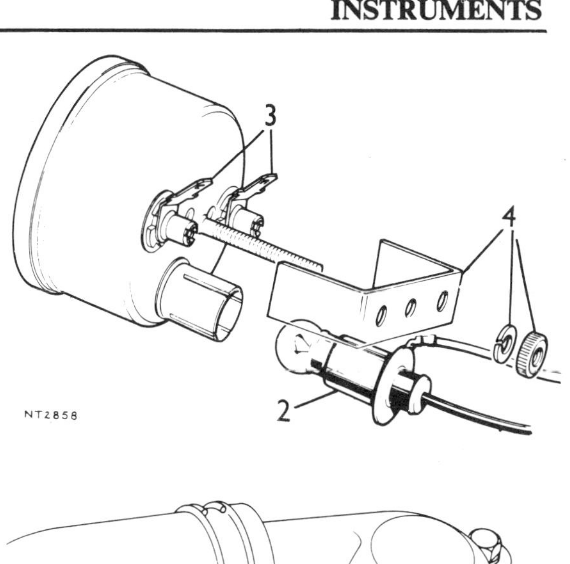

Removing

1. Obtain access to the rear of the indicator by reaching over the gearbox cover side trim panel.
2. Pull out the bulb holder.
3. Disconnect the two Lucar connectors.
4. Remove the knurled nut, spring washer and clamp bracket.
5. Withdraw the indicator from the fascia.

Refitting

6. Reverse instructions 1 to 5.

TEMPERATURE TRANSMITTER

– Remove and refit **88.25.20**

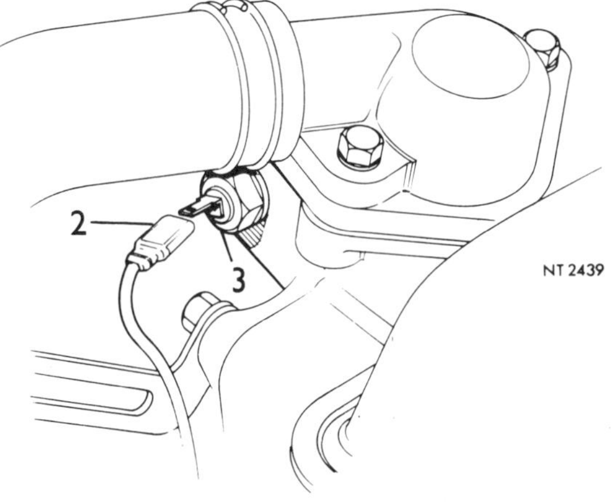

Removing

1. Drain part of the coolant 26.10.01.
2. Disconnect the Lucar connector.
3. Unscrew the transmitter.

Refitting

4. Reverse instructions 1 to 3.

FUEL INDICATOR

– Remove and refit **88.25.26**

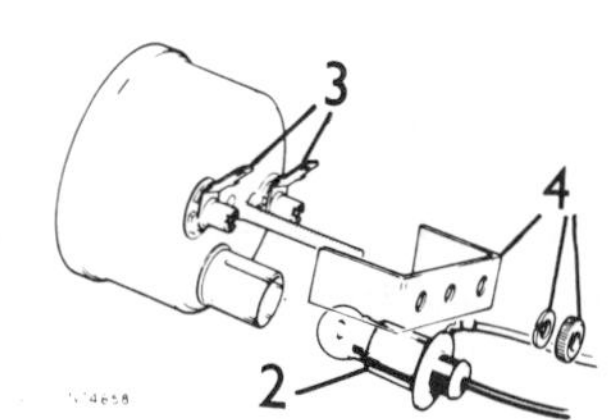

Removing

1. Lower the veneered fascia to the service position. Operation 76.46.01 instructions 1 to 6.
2. Pull out the bulb holder.
3. Disconnect the two Lucar connectors.
4. Remove the knurled nut, spring washer and clamp bracket.
5. Withdraw the indicator from the fascia.

Refitting

6. Reverse instructions 1 to 5.

FUEL TANK UNIT

– Remove and refit **88.25.32**

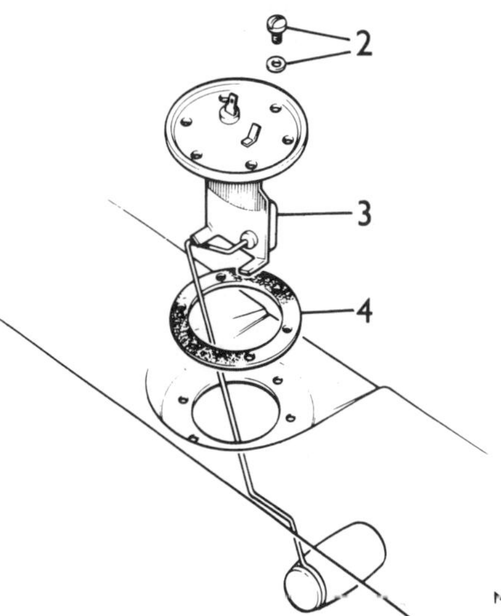

Removing

1. Remove the fuel tank 19.55.01.
2. Remove the six screws and fibre washers.
3. Carefully withdraw the tank unit.
4. Remove the sealing washer.

Refitting

5. Reverse instructions 1 to 4.

SPEEDOMETER

– Remove and refit 88.30.01

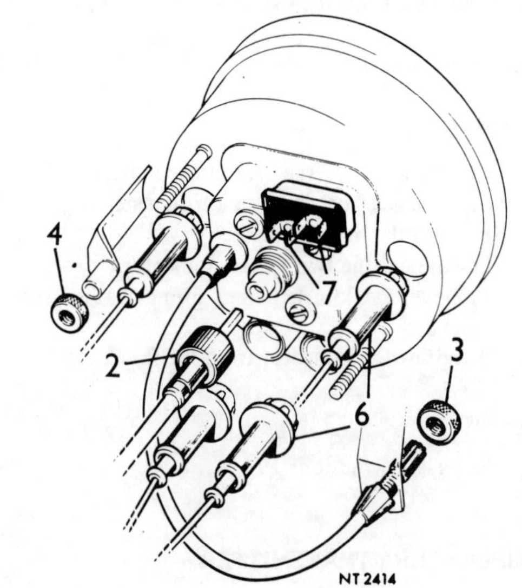

Removing

1. Isolate the battery.
2. Unscrew the knurled nut securing the cable to the speedometer.
3. Unscrew the trip reset knurled nut.
4. Unscrew the two knurled nuts securing the clamp legs and earth lead.
5. Withdraw the speedometer.
6. Pull out the four bulb holders.
7. Disconnect the two Lucar connectors from the voltage stabiliser.

Refitting

8. Reverse instructions 1 to 7.

SPEEDOMETER CABLE – COMPLETE

(Non overdrive models)

– Remove and refit 88.30.06

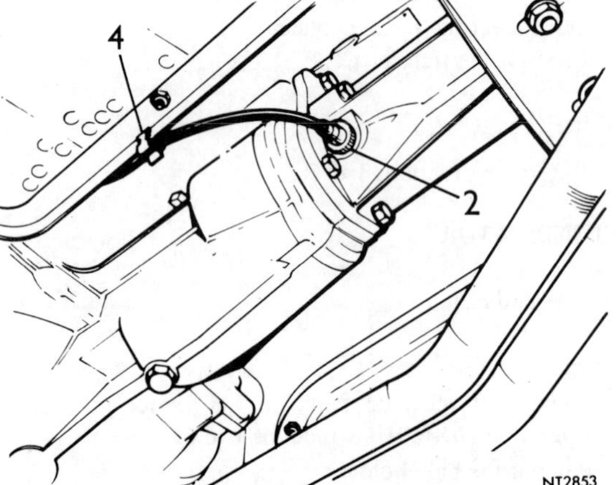

Removing

1. Unscrew the knurled nut securing the cable to the speedometer.
2. Working from below the vehicle, unscrew the knurled nut securing the cable to the gearbox extension.
3. To assist refitting, carefully note the cable position relative to other components.
4. Detach the cable from the clip securing it to the body.
5. Manoeuvre the cable downwards through the grommet aperture and detach it from the vehicle.

Refitting

6. Reverse instructions 1 to 5. Seal the grommet to the bulkhead with Seelastik SR51.

SPEEDOMETER CABLE – COMPLETE

(Overdrive models)

– Remove and refit **88.30.06**

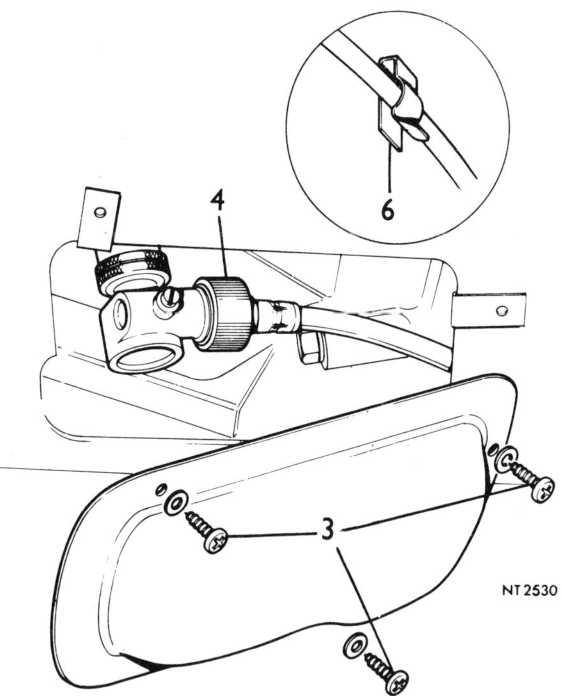

Removing

1. Unscrew the knurled retainer securing the cable to the speedometer.
2. Raise the right hand side of the rear gearbox cover carpet.
3. Remove the three screws and washers. Pull the access plate away from the gearbox cover.
4. Unscrew the knurled retainer securing the cable to the angle drive.
5. To assist refitting, carefully note the cable positions relative to other components.
6. Working from below the vehicle, detach the cable from the clip securing it to the body.
7. Manoeuvre the cable through the grommet aperture and detach it from the vehicle.

Refitting

8. Reverse instructions 1 to 7. Seal the grommet to the bulkhead with Seelastik SR51.

SPEEDOMETER CABLE – INNER

– Remove and refit **88.30.07**

Removing

1. Unscrew the knurled retainer securing the cable to the speedometer.
2. Using long nosed pliers, withdraw the inner cable. Take care not to contaminate the upholstery or fittings with grease.

Refitting

3. Sparingly grease the inner cable. Do not use oil.
4. Feed the inner cable into the outer cable rotating it slightly to assist operation.
5. Withdraw the inner cable about 8 ins (200 mm) and wipe off surplus grease. Re-insert the inner cable, rotating it slightly to assist engagement of the squared end to the drive gear.
6. Engage the inner cable to the speedometer.
7. Refit the knurled retainer.

TACHOMETER

– Remove and refit **88.30.21**

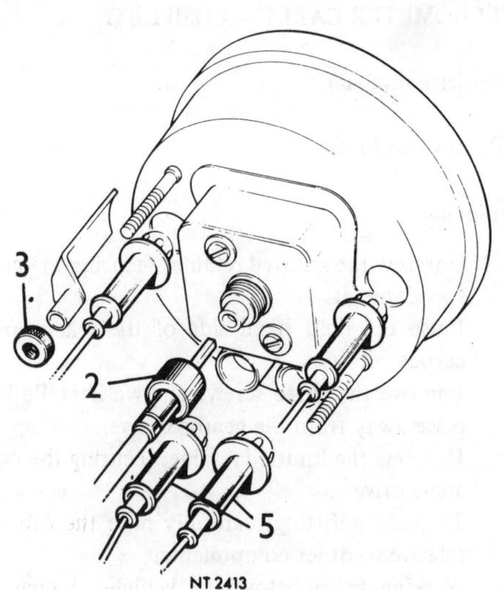

Removing

1. Isolate the battery.
2. Unscrew the knurled retainer securing the cable to the tachometer.
3. Unscrew the two knurled nuts securing the clamp legs and earth lead.
4. Withdraw the tachometer.
5. Pull out the four bulb holders.

Refitting

6. Reverse instructions 1 to 5.

TACHOMETER CABLE – COMPLETE

– Remove and refit **88.30.23**

Removing

1. Unscrew the knurled retainer securing the cable to the distributor.
2. Unscrew the knurled retainer securing the cable to the tachometer.
3. Pull the cable through the grommet aperture and detach it from the vehicle.

Refitting

4. Reverse instructions 1 to 3. Seal the grommet to the bulkhead with Seelastik SR51.

TACHOMETER CABLE – INNER

– Remove and refit **88.30.24**

Removing

1. Unscrew the knurled retainer securing the cable to the tachometer.
2. Using long-nosed pliers, withdraw the inner cable. Take care not to contaminate the upholstery or fittings with grease.

Refitting

3. Sparingly grease the inner cable. Do not use oil.
4. Feed the inner cable into the outer cable, rotating it slightly to assist operation.
5. Withdraw the inner cable about 8 ins (200 mm) and wipe off surplus grease. Re- insert the inner cable, rotating it slightly to assist engagement of the squared end to the drive gear.
6. Engage the inner cable to the tachometer.
7. Refit the knurled retainer.

SERVICE TOOLS

Tool No.	Description
18G.106	Valve spring compressor
47	Multi-purpose hand press
MS51	Trim fastener clamp
60A	Valve guide remover/replacer
S.60A-2A	Valve guide remover/replacer adaptor set
S.60A-7	Valve guide replacer adaptor
S.69B	Gearbox mainshaft circlip remover
M.84B	Pinion bearing setting gauge
M.84B-1	Pinion and dummy bearing set
M.86C	Rear hub remover
S.98A	Pre-load gauge
S.101	Differential case spreader
S.101-1	Differential case spreader adaptor
S.123A	Pinion bearing outer cup remover
S.144	Gearbox mainshaft circlip remover
S.167A	Circlip installer
S.306	Brake adjusting tool
S.314	Mainshaft ball bearing replacer
316X	Valve seat cutter handle
S.317	Rear hub adjusting nut wrench
S.318	Halfshaft assembly holding jig
335	Con rod aligning jig
S.336-4	Con rod arbor adaptor
S.341	Rack mounting compressor
S.351	Petrol Injection pressure test adaptor
RG.421	Coupling flange holding wrench
550	Driver handle
642	Electronic tachometer
S.4221A-5	I.F.S. Coil spring remover and replacer adaptor
S.4221A-10	Differential bearing remover/replacer
S.4221A-11	Pinion bearing cone remover/replacer adaptor
S.4221A-15A	Gearbox ball race remover/replacer adaptor
S.4221A-16	Outer taper bearing remover/replacer adaptor
4235A	Impact remover
S.4235A-2	Constant pinion remover adaptor
7066	Circlip pliers

Tool No.	Description
**** OVERDRIVE TOOLS – 'A' Type ****	
L.178	Freewheel assembly ring
L.182	Accumulator piston housing remover
L.183A	Pump barrel remover
L.183-1	Adaptor
L.184	Oil pump body replacer
L.185A	Dummy drive shaft
L.187	Tailshaft bearing remover/replacer
L.188A	Hydraulic test equipment
L.188-4	Pressure test hose
**** OVERDRIVE TOOLS – 'J' Type**	
L.178A	Freewheel assembly ring
L.188A	Hydraulic test equipment
L.188A–2	Pressure take-off adaptor
L.354A	Oil pump plug spanner
L.401A	Relief valve body and dashpot sleeve remover/replacer
L.402	Pressure adaptor spline release **

All Service Tools mentioned in this Manual must be obtained direct from the manufacturers:

Messrs V.L. Churchill & Co. Ltd.
P.O. Box No. 3
London Road,
Daventry, Northants.

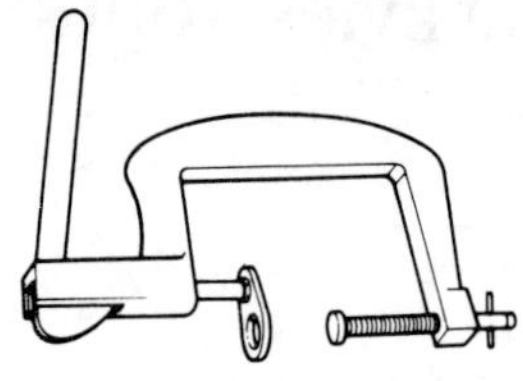

18G.106

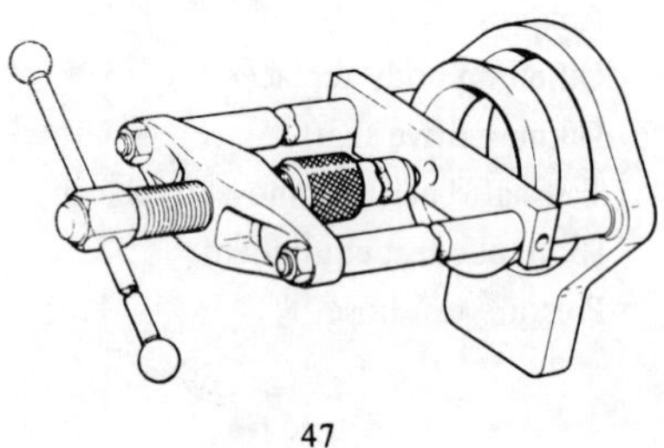

47

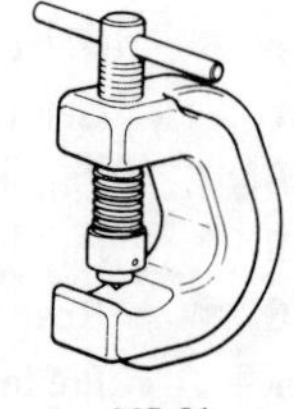

MS.51

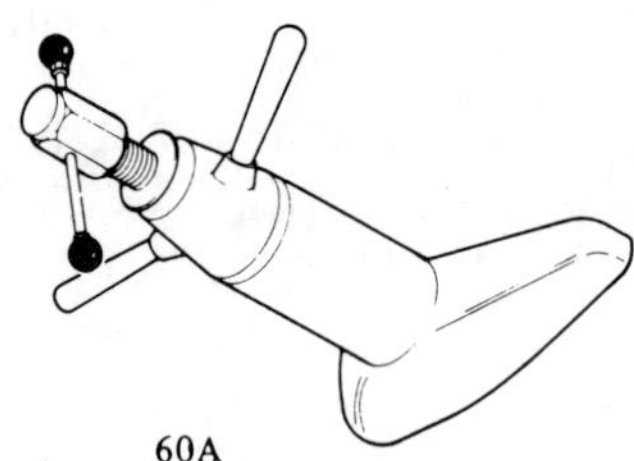

60A

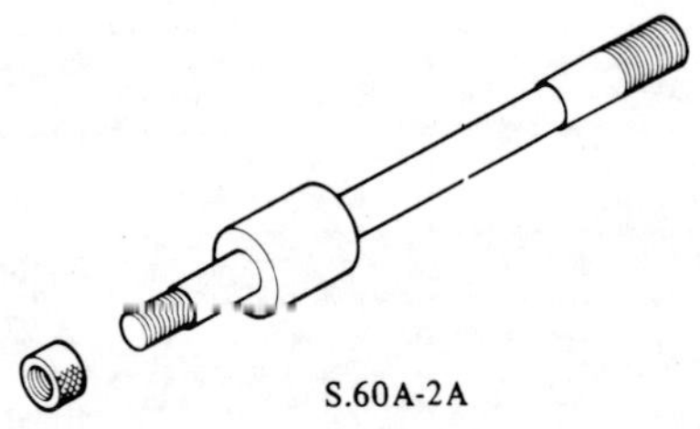

S.60A-2A

S.60A-7

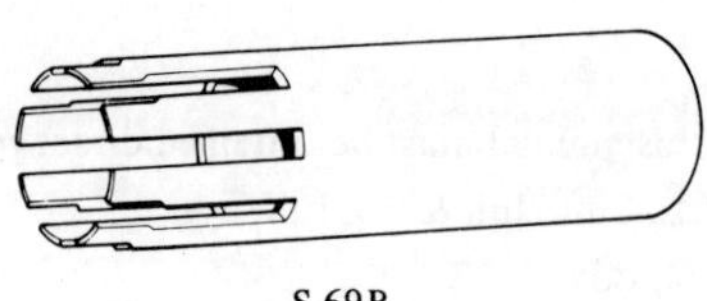

S.69B

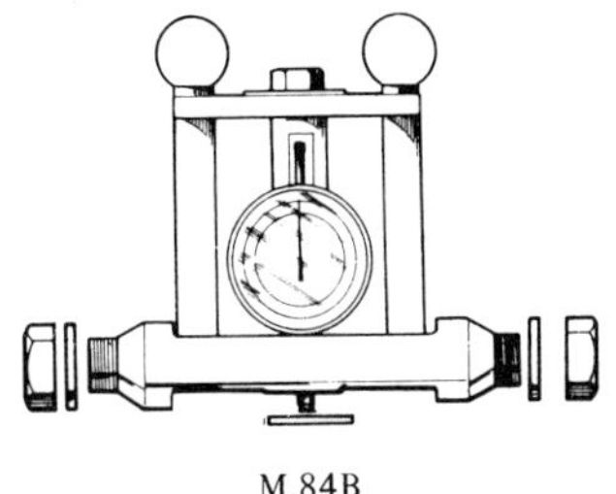
M.84B

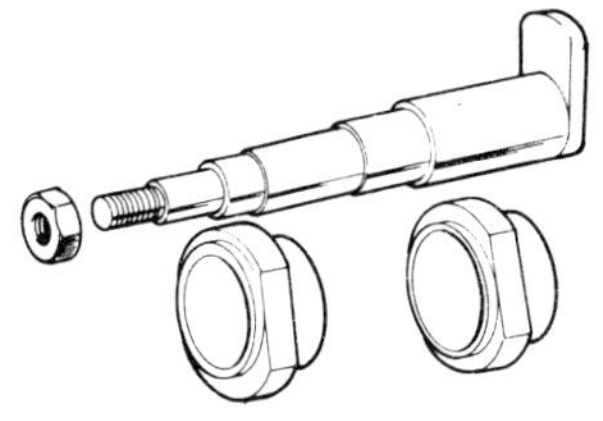
M.84B-1

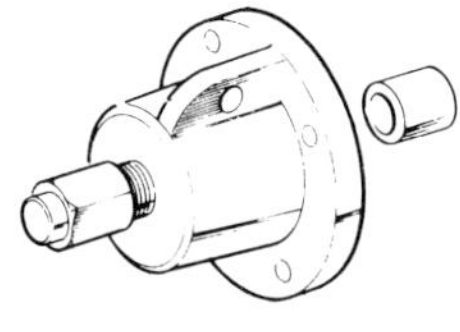
M.86C

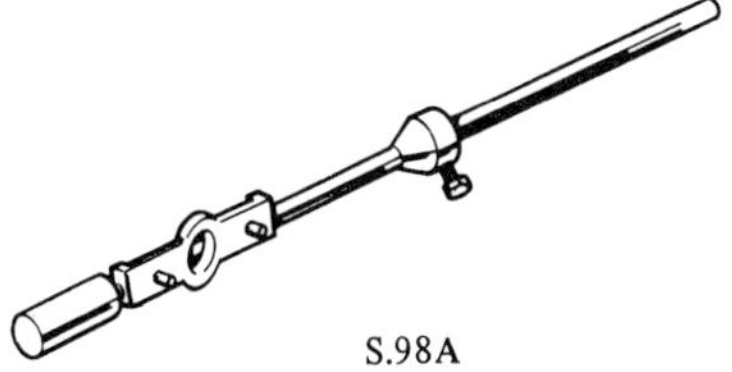
S.98A

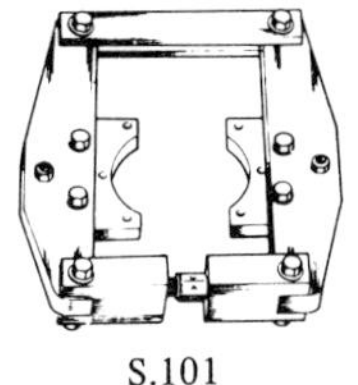
S.101

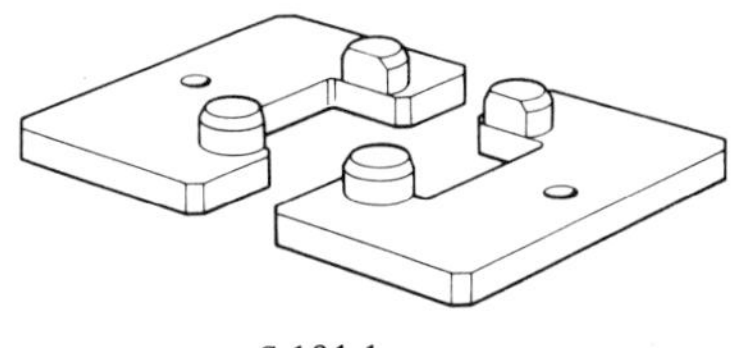
S.101-1

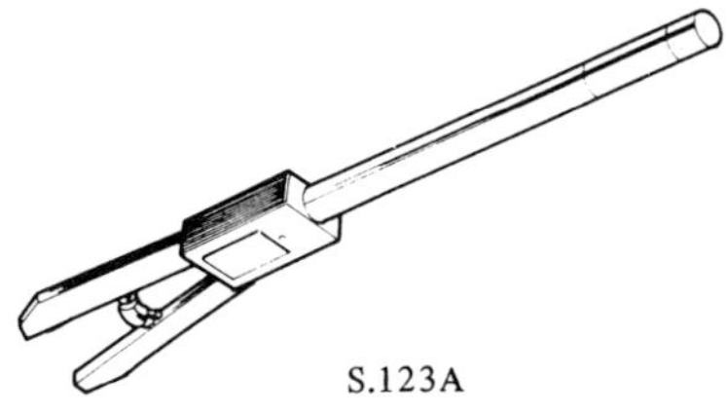
S.123A

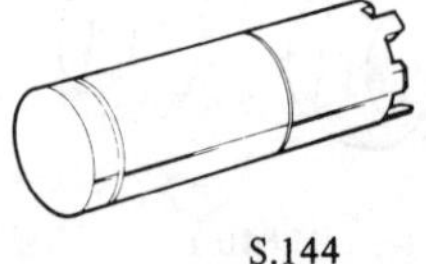
S.144

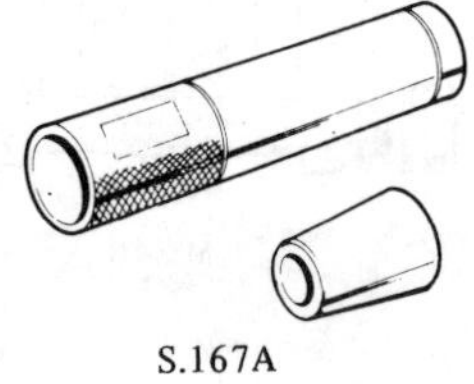
S.167A

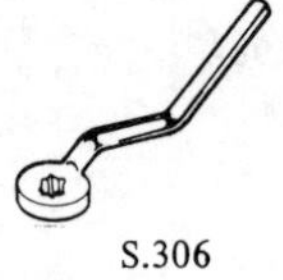
S.306

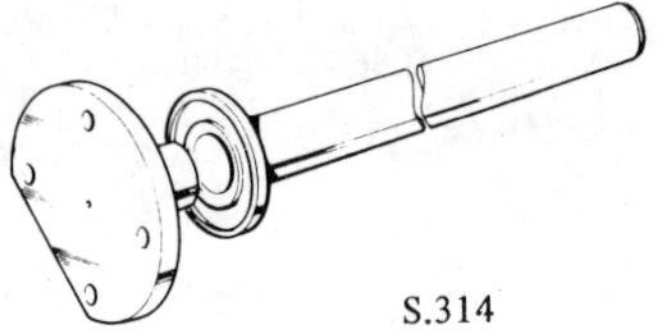
S.314

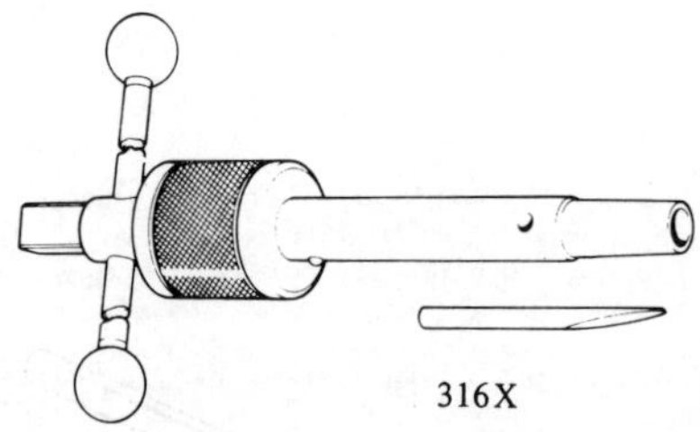
316X

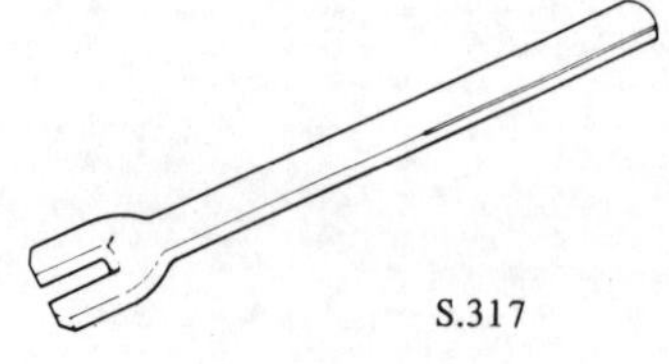
S.317

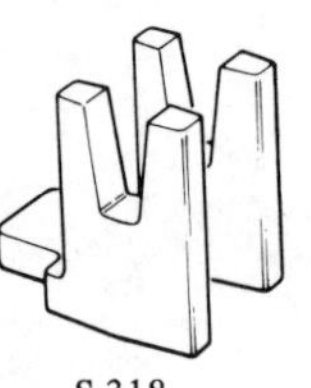
S.318

S.335

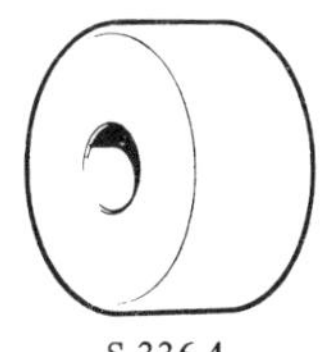
S.336-4

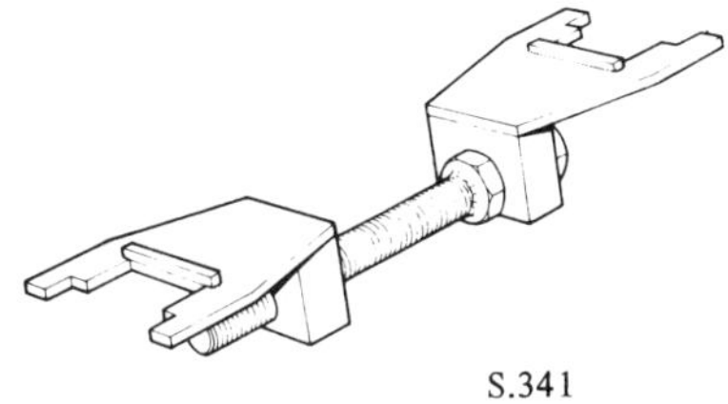
S.341

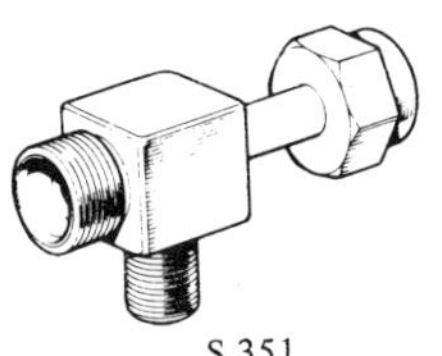
S.351

RG.421

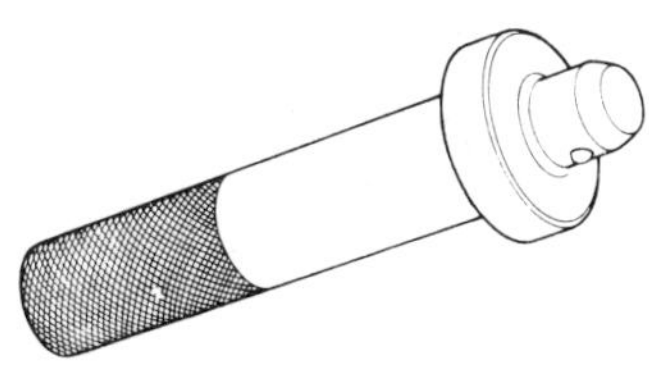
550

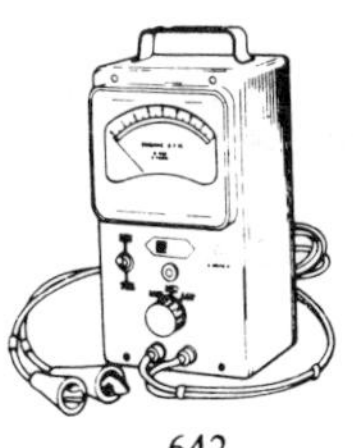
642

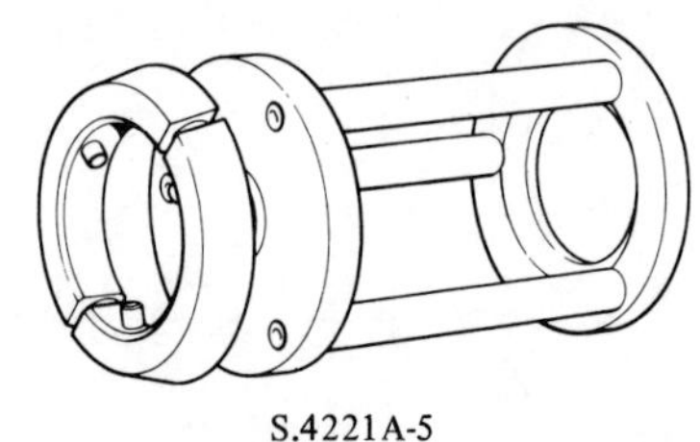

S.4221A-5

S.4221A-10

S.4221A-11

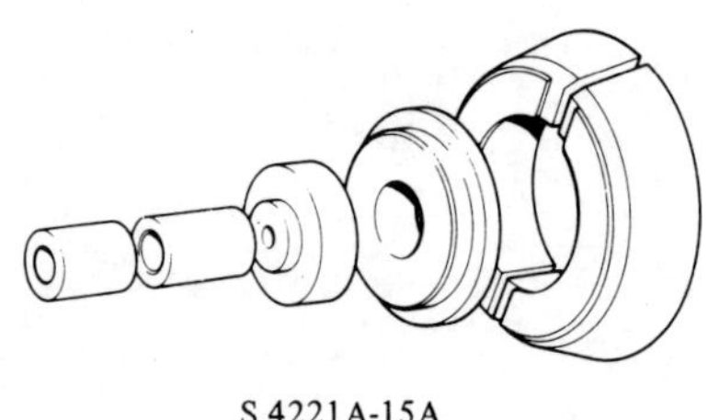

S.4221A-15A

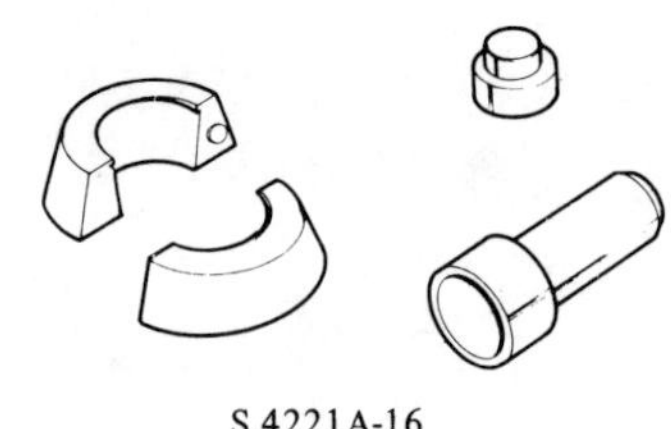

S.4221A-16

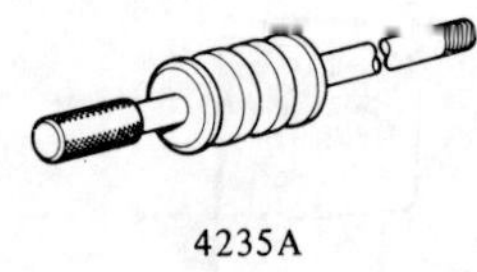

4235A

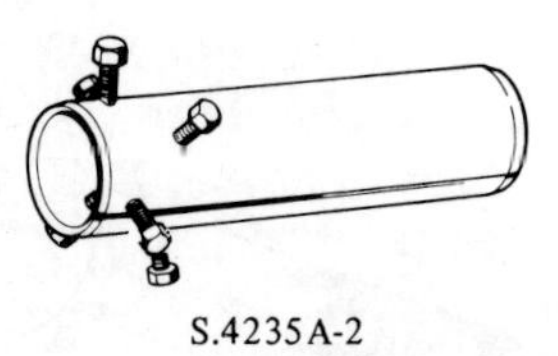

S.4235A-2

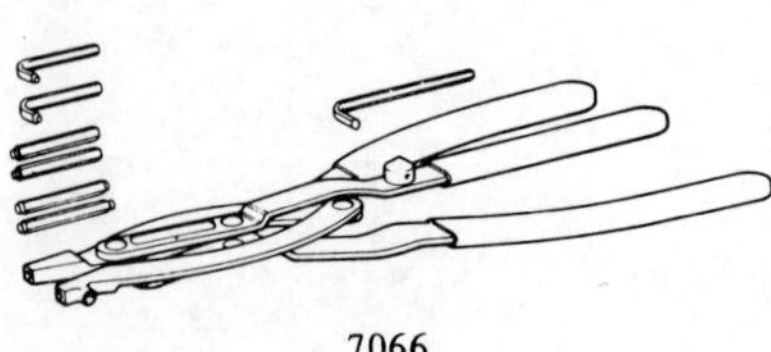

7066

** OVERDRIVE – 'A' TYPE **

L.178

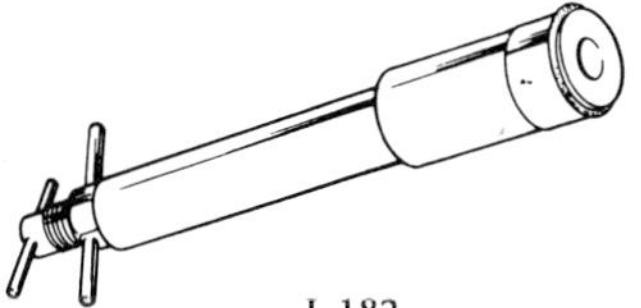
L.182

L.183A

L.183-1

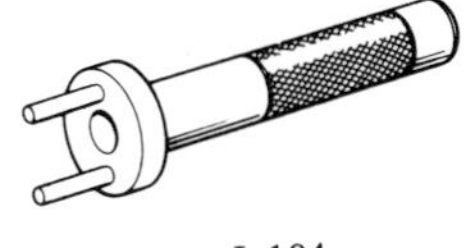
L.184

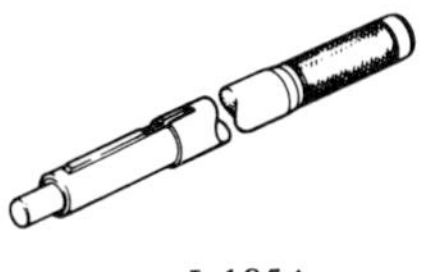
L.185A

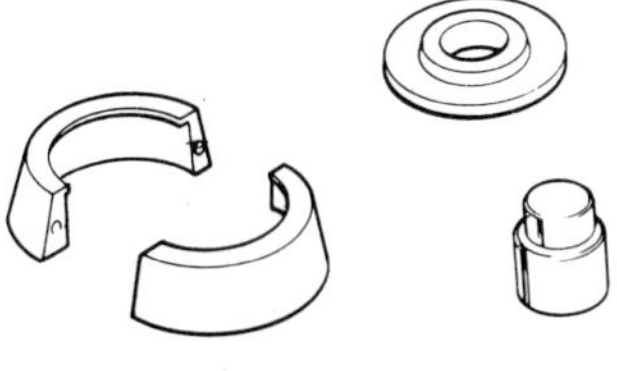
L.187

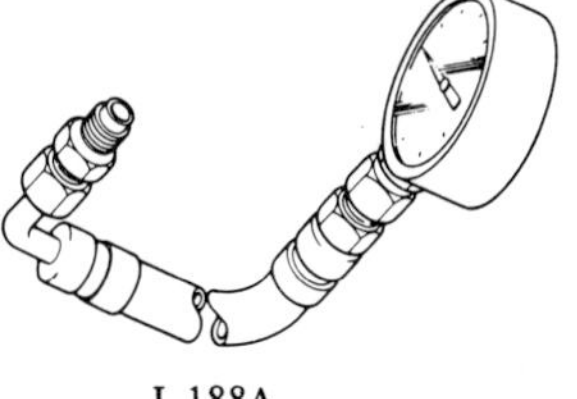
L.188A

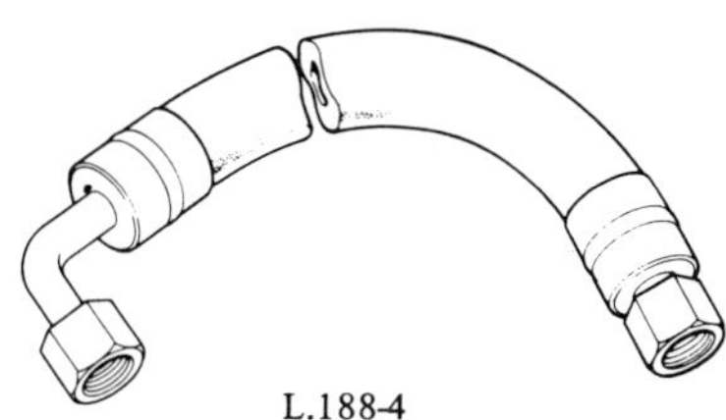
L.188-4

OVERDRIVE – 'J' TYPE

L.178A

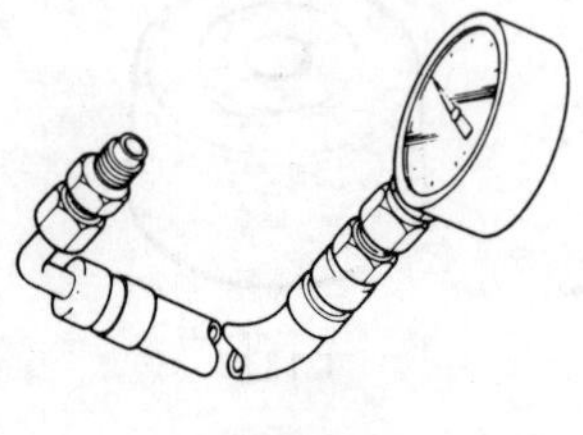

L.188A

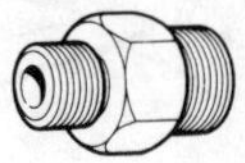

L.188A–2

L.354A

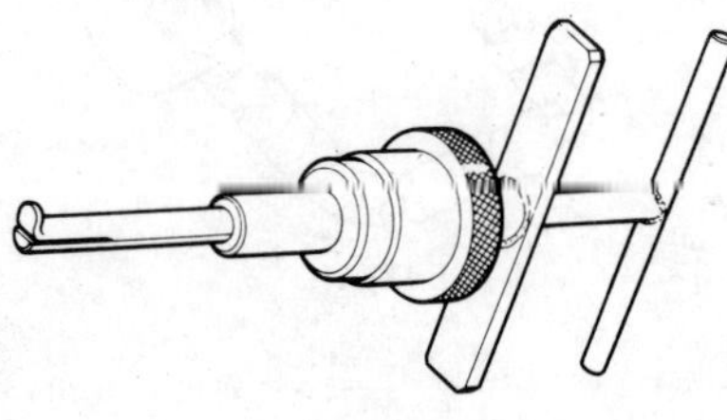

L.401A

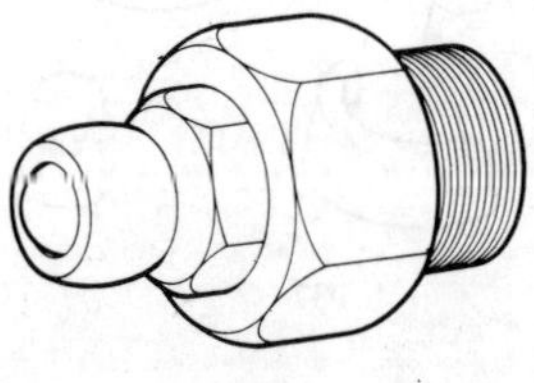

L.402

B-T162WH

ISBN 1 869826 132
Printed and Distributed by:
Brooklands Books Ltd.
PO Box 146, Cobham, Surrey, KT11 1LG
England
Phone: 01932 865051 Fax: 01932 868803